WOMEN'S RELIGIONS
in the GRECO-ROMAN WORLD

WOMEN'S RELIGIONS
in the GRECO-ROMAN WORLD

A Sourcebook

Edited by

ROSS SHEPARD KRAEMER

UNIVERSITY PRESS

2004

OXFORD
UNIVERSITY PRESS

Oxford   New York
Auckland   Bangkok   Buenos Aires   Cape Town   Chennai
Dar es Salaam   Delhi   Hong Kong   Istanbul   Karachi   Kolkata
Kuala Lumpur   Madrid   Melbourne   Mexico City   Mumbai   Nairobi
São Paulo   Shanghai   Taipei   Tokyo   Toronto

Copyright © 2004 by Ross Shepard Kraemer

Published by Oxford University Press, Inc.
198 Madison Avenue, New York, New York 10016

www.oup.com

Oxford is a registered trademark of Oxford University Press

Library of Congress Cataloging-in-Publication Data is available.
ISBN 978-0-19-514278-5 (pbk.)

3 5 7 9 8 6 4 2

Printed in the United States of America

For Michael

Acknowledgments

Many people contributed to the production of this new edition, which was originally published by Fortress Press in 1988 as *Maenads, Martyrs, Matrons, Monastics: A Sourcebook on Women's Religions in the Greco-Roman World*. Carolyn Osiek and Janet Timbie gave me permission again to include their respective translations of selections from Epiphanius and Shenoute's Letter to Tachom. Leigh Gibson, Lynn LiDonnici, and others suggested formatting changes based on their classroom experiences with the original edition. Deb Bucher provided invaluable bibliographic assistance. Mary Rose D'Angelo and Susan Ashbrook Harvey critiqued the revised introductions. Jesse Goodman, Luke Meier, and Heidi Wendt checked references, read proofs, and prepared the index of female names. Kathleen Pappas and Gail Tetreault provided crucial support with correspondence and other time-consuming clerical tasks. Cynthia Read and Theo Calderera at Oxford provided encouragement, advice, and assistance from the inception of this project on.

The introductions to the sections and selections throughout this book are studded with insights and ideas gained through my work with the graduate students at Penn, especially Deb Bucher, Lynn Cohick, Maxine Grossman, Shira Lander, Susan Marks, Jacqueline Pastis, Beth Pollard, and Sarah Schwarz. They are my "spiritual children," and I trust they know it.

One more time, I want to thank my colleagues in the Department of Religious Studies at the University of Pennsylvania for their extraordinary support and collegiality over twenty-five years. Equally, I want to thank my colleagues and students at Brown University, for affording me an opportunity at this stage of my career beyond anything I might have imagined or wished for.

Finally, as always, I want to thank my family: my husband, Michael, my daughter, Jordan, and my wonderful parents-in-law, Honey and Jerry Kraemer, for their unfailing love and support.

National Council of Churches of Christ in the U.S.A., and are used by permission. All rights reserved.

Selections from Tal Ilan, "Matrona and Rabbi Jose," *JSJ* 25 (1994) 18–51, are reprinted with permission of Brill Academic Publishers.

Selection from David Noy, ed., *Jewish Inscriptions of Western Europe, Vol. 2: The City of Rome* (copyright © 1995), is reprinted by permission of Cambridge University Press.

Selections from Paul Harkin, *John Chrysostom, "Against Judaizing Christians,"* (FC 68, copyright © 1977), and Ronald Heine, *Montanist Oracles and Testimonia* (NAPS Vol. #14, copyright © 1989, The North American Patristics Society), are reprinted by permission of the Catholic University Press of America.

Selections from A. Veilleux, *Pachomian Koinonia*, vol. 2, *Pachomian Chronicles and Rules* (copyright © 1981), and R. M. Price, *Theodoret of Cyrrhus, "A History of the Monks of Syria"* (copyright © 1985), are used by permission of Cistercian Publications.

Selections from James Robinson, *The Nag Hammadi Library in English* (copyright © 1978, 1988, E. J. Brill), are used by permission of HarperCollins Publishers, Inc.

Selections from *Corpus Papyrorum Judaicarum*, eds. Victor A. Tcherikover, Alexander Fuks and Menahem Stern (Cambridge, Mass.: Harvard University Press, Copyright © 1957, 1960, 1964, by the Magnes Press, the Hebrew University), are reprinted by permission of the publishers.

Selections from the Loeb Classical Library are reprinted by permission of Harvard University Press and the Trustees of the Loeb Classical Library. The Loeb Classical Library is a registered trademark of the President and Fellows of Harvard College.

Selections from Naphtali Lewis, *The Documents from the Bar Kochba Period in the Cave of the Letters: Greek Papyri* (copyright © 1989), are used by permission of the Israel Exploration Society.

Selections from Mary R. Lefkowitz and Maureen B. Fant, eds., *Women's Life in Greece and Rome* (copyright © 1992), are used by permission of the Johns Hopkins University Press.

The selection from Ute Eisen, *Women Officeholders in Early Christianity* (copyright © 2000), is used by permission of the Liturgical Press.

Selections from *New Documents Illustrating Early Christianity* are used permission of MacQuarie University.

"The Life of Olympias," from Elizabeth A. Clark, *Jerome, Chrysostom and Friends* (copyright © 1979), is used by permission of Edwin Mellen Press.

Selections from Scott Bradbury, *Severus of Minorca, "Letter on the Conversion of the Jews"* (copyright © 1996); Hannah M. Cotton and Ada Yardeni, *Aramaic, Hebrew and Greek Documentary Texts from Nahal Hever and Other Sites* (Discoveries in the Judean Desert 27, copyright © 1997); J. K. Elliott, *Apocryphal New Testament* (copyright © 1993); John Gager, *Curse Tablets and Binding Spells from the Ancient World* (copyright © 1992); Ross S. Kraemer and Mary Rose D'Angelo, *Women and Christian Origins* (copyright © 1999); Herbert Musurillo, *Acts of the Christian Martyrs* (copyright © 1971); Niall Rudd, *Juvenal, "The Satires,"* (OWC, copyright © 1991); Joan Taylor, *Jewish Women Philosophers of First-Century Alexandria* (copyright © 2003); and P. G. Walsh, *Apuleius, "Metamorphoses"* (OWC, copyright © 1994), are used by permission of Oxford University Press.

Selections from George E. Gingras, *Egeria: Diary of a Pilgrimage* (ACW 38, copyright © 1970), and Leslie William Barnard, *Justin Martyr, "The First and Second Apologies"* (ACW 56, copyright © 1997), are used with permission of Paulist Press.

Selections from *Ovid, "Fasti,"* trans. Anthony J. Boyle and Roger D. Woodward (copyright © 2000), are used by permission of Penguin Books.

Selections from James Charlesworth, *The Odes of Solomon* (copyright © 1973); David G. Rice and John E. Stambaugh, *Sources for the Study of Greek Religion* (copyright © 1979); and Robert A. Kraft and Janet Timbie, *The Testament of Job* (copyright © 1974), are used by permission of the Society of Biblical Literature.

Selections from B. P. Reardon, ed., *Collected Ancient Greek Novels* (copyright © 1989, The Regents of the University of California), and Sebastian P. Brock and Susan Ashbrook Harvey, *Holy Women of the Syrian Orient* (copyright © 1987, The Regents of the University of California), are used by permission of the University of California Press.

Selections from Hans Dieter Betz, ed., *The Greek Magical Papyri in Translation* (2nd ed., copyright © 1992), and *Euripides, "Bacchae,"* trans. William Arrowsmith (copyright © 1959), are used by permission of University of Chicago Press.

Selections from Jacob Neusner, *The Mishnah, A New Translation* (copyright © Yale University Press, 1988), are used by permission.

Contents

Abbreviations   xxv

Introduction   3

ONE *Observances, Rituals, and Festivals*

1. Why Women Are Compelled to Worship Dionysos   12
   EURIPIDES *Bacchae* 23–42

2. The Rites of the First Bacchic Worshipers   13
   EURIPIDES *Bacchae* 677–768

3. Women Worshipers of a Dionysian Deity, Sabos   16
   DEMOSTHENES *On the Crown* 259–60

4. Rituals for Brides and Pregnant Women in the Worship of   17
   Artemis   *LSCG Suppl.* 115

5. Objects Dedicated to Artemis Brauronia   *IG II² 1514*   18

6. Women Participants at a Festival of Adonis   18
   THEOCRITUS *Idyll* 15, 95–149

7. Ritual Regulations in a Dionysiac *Thiasos*   *LSAM* 48   20

8. Epitaph of Alcmeonis, a Priestess of Dionysos   21
   Henrichs *HSCP* 82 (1978): 148

9. The Establishment of Dionysiac Rites in Magnesia   21
   I. Magn. 215a.24–40

10. Ritual Equipment for a Women's Festival in Hellenistic Egypt   22
    P. Hib. 54

11. Three Excerpts from Ovid on the Rites of Roman Women   22

    11A.   Roman Matrons Who Celebrate the Matralia (A Festival to   23
    the Goddess, Mother Matuta)   OVID *Fasti* 6.473–568

11B. Roman Matrons Who Wash the Statue of Venus on April 1   25
      OVID *Fasti* 4.133–62

11C. The Ritual Practices of an Old Woman   25
      OVID *Fasti* 2.571–82

12. Women's Rites of Dionysos in Greek Cities   27
    DIODORUS OF SICILY *Library* 4.3.2–5

13. Women Members of a Monastic Jewish Community Outside   28
    Alexandria   PHILO *On the Contemplative Life* 2, 32–33,
    65–69, 83–85, 87–89

14. (Jewish?) Women in Alexandrian Public Life   32
    PHILO *The Special Laws* 3.169–75

15. The Women's Court of the Jerusalem Temple   33
    JOSEPHUS *The Jewish War* 5.198–200, *Against Apion* 2.102–4

16. Excerpts from Plutarch on Greek and Roman Women's Religions   35

    16A. Devotees of Dionysos Protected by Women from the Town   35
          of Amphissa   *On the Bravery of Women* 13 (*Moralia* 249)

    16B. The Dionysiac Proclivities of Olympias, Mother of   36
          Alexander the Great   *Life of Alexander* 2.1–5

    16C. How Women's Bacchic Frenzy Explains an Epithet of the   36
          God (Bacchus)   *Roman Questions* 104 (*Moralia* 288–89)

    16D. Why Roman Matrons Founded a Temple to the Goddess   37
          Carmenta   *Roman Questions* 56 (*Moralia* 278)

    16E. Why Women Use Milk but Not Wine in Offerings to   37
          Rumina   *Roman Questions* 57 (*Moralia* 278)

    16F. Gender Distinctions in Sacrifices to Hercules   38
          Roman Questions 60 (*Moralia* 278)

    16G. Why Seduced Vestal Virgins Are Buried Alive   38
          Roman Questions 96 (*Moralia* 286–87)

    16H. Why Roman Women Wash Their Heads on the Ides of   38
          August   *Roman Questions* 100 (*Moralia* 287)

17. Excerpts from the Travel Writer Pausanias on Greek Women's   39
    Religions

    17A. The Public and Secret Rites to Demeter Performed by   39
          Elder Women in Corinth
          Description of Greece 2 (Corinth) 35.6–8

    17B. The Athletic Contests for Women in Honor of Hera at Elis   40
          Description of Greece 5 (Elis 1) 16.2–8

Contents

17C. Women's Worship of Eileithyia and Sosipolis at Elis   41
Description of Greece 5 (Elis 1) 20.2–3

17D. Women's Rites to Demeter at Achaia   41
Description of Greece 7 (Achaia) 27.9–10

17E. The Festival Laphria, in Honor of Artemis   42
Description of Greece 7 (Achaia) 18.11–12

17F. Women Attacked during a Festival to Demeter, Who   42
Defend Themselves with Sacrificial Implements
Description of Greece 4 (Messenia) 17

18. The Religious Activities of Roman Women as Viewed by a   43
Skeptical Satirist   JUVENAL *Satire* 6

19. Women (and Men) in a Procession to Isis   45
APULEIUS *Metamorphoses* 11.9–10

20. The Deeds of the *Saga* Meroe   47
APULEIUS *Metamorphoses* 1.7–10

21. Photis Reveals the Nefarious Deeds of Her Mistress, Pamphile   49
APULEIUS *Metamorphoses* 3.15–18

22. A Grieving Mother Resurrects and Interrogates the Corpse of Her   51
Son Using "Magic Arts"
HELIODORUS *An Ethiopian Story* 6.13–15

23. Callirhoe Entreats Aphrodite at Her Shrines and Temple   54
CHARITON *Chareas and Callirhoe* 2.2, 7.5, 8.8

24. Festivals and Sacrifices at the Birth of Callirhoe's Son   56
CHARITON *Chareas and Callirhoe* 3.7–9

25. Prospective Brides and Grooms at a Festival of Artemis of   58
Ephesos   XENOPHON OF EPHESOS *Ephesian Tale of Anthia and
Habrocomes* 1.2

26. Anthia Entreats Isis and Apis   59
XENOPHON OF EPHESOS *Ephesian Tale of Anthia and
Habrocomes* 4.3, 5.4

27. Offerings and Festivals for Helios at Rhodes   60
XENOPHON OF EPHESOS *Ephesian Tale of Anthia and
Habrocomes* 5.10–13

28. Anthia and Habrocomes, Reunited, at the Temple of Artemis in   63
Ephesos   XENOPHON OF EPHESOS *Ephesian Tale of Anthia and
Habrocomes* 5.15

29. Leucippe Takes Refuge in a Sanctuary of Artemis   63
ACHILLES TATIUS *Leucippe and Clitophon* 7.13

30. Chloe and Daphnis Worship the Nymphs   64
    LONGUS *Daphnis and Chloe* 2.2, 4.39

31. Devotions at a Private Feast in a Temple of Hermes   65

    31A.   HELIODORUS *An Ethiopian Story* 5.15, 5.34   65

    31B.   Charikleia at the Statue's Feet 5.34   65

32. A Woman Whose Acceptance of Ascetic Christianity Causes Her   65
    Husband to Bring Charges Against Her and Her Christian
    Teachers   JUSTIN MARTYR *Second Apology* 2

33. A Tour of Hellish Torments Related by a Murdered Christian   67
    Woman Raised from the Dead by the Apostle Thomas
    Acts of Thomas 6

34. Admonitions against the Participation of Menstruating Christian   72
    Women (and of Men Who Have Had a Nocturnal Emission) in
    the Eucharist   DIONYSIUS OF ALEXANDRIA *Epistle to the
    Bishop Basilides*, canons II, IV

35. Rabbinic Purity Regulations Concerning Menstruation and Other   74
    Blood Flow   MISHNAH *Niddah* 1.1–2.4

36. Rabbinic Arguments Against a Misogynist Tradition   78
    BABYLONIAN TALMUD *Sotah* 22b

37. Discussions between Matrona and Rabbi Jose ben Halafta   80

    37A.   *Genesis Rabbah* 4.6; 17.7; 25.1; 63.8; 68.4; 84.21; 87.6   81

    37B.   *Leviticus Rabbah* 8.1   83

    37C.   *Exodus Rabbah* 3.12.2   83

    37D.   *Leviticus Rabbah* 28.6   84

    37E.   *Numbers Rabbah* 3.2   84

    37F.   *Ecclesiastes Rabbah* 3.21.1   85

38. Arabian Christian Women of Thracian Descent Who Bake Cakes   85
    to the Virgin Mary and Function as Priests
    EPIPHANIUS *Medicine Box* 78.23

39. A Heresiologist's Attempts to Refute the Teachings of Christian   86
    Women with Regard to Mary and to Disparage the Rituals and
    Religious Offices of Women   EPIPHANIUS *Medicine Box* 79

40. Why Christian Women May Not Write Books in Their Own   93
    Names   *The Debate between a Montanist and an Orthodox*

41. Christian Women in Antioch Participating in Jewish Festivals and   94
    Attending Synagogue   JOHN CHRYSOSTOM *Against Judaizing
    Christians* 2.3.3–6, 4.7.3

Contents

42. A Christian Matron from Rome Visiting the Hermitic Abbot   96
    Arsenius   *Sayings of the Desert Fathers* 2.7

43. Women Monastics and Women Visitors at a Pachomian Women's   98
    Monastery in Fourth-Century C.E. Egypt
    PALLADIUS *Lausiac History* 33, 52, 143

44. Women Blowing the Shofar on Rosh Hashanah (the New Year)   100
    BABYLONIAN TALMUD *Rosh Hashanah* 32b

45. Exempting Women from the Obligation to Eat in the *Sukkah*   100
    during the Jewish Festival of Sukkoth
    BABYLONIAN TALMUD *Sukkah* 28a–b

46. Rabbinic Discussions on the Differences in Rabbinic Law between   103
    a Man and a Woman   BABYLONIAN TALMUD *Kiddushin* 29a–b,
    34a–36a

47. Jewish Women Forcibly Converted to Christianity (and a   110
    Christian Woman Visionary) on the Island of Minorca
    SEVERUS OF MINORCA *Letter on the Conversion of the Jews*
    (selections)

          TWO *Researching Real Women:*
          Documents to, from, and by Women

48. Epitaphs of Women from Leontopolis, Site of an Alternative   121
    Jewish Temple

    48A. Epitaph of a Jewish/Judean Woman Who Died on Her   121
          Wedding Day   *CPJ/CIJ* 1508; *JIGRE* 31

    48B. Epitaph of a Woman, Her Husband, and Daughter   121
          CPJ/CIJ 1509; *JIGRE* 32

    48C. Epitaph of a Woman Who Died in Childbirth   122
          CPJ/CIJ 1510; *JIGRE* 33

    48D. Epitaph of a Thirty-Year-Old Woman   122
          CPJ/CIJ 1513; *JIGRE* 36

    48E. A Dialogue Epitaph of a Young Married Woman   122
          CPJ/CIJ 1530; *JIGRE* 38

49. Disposition of a Lawsuit between a Woman and a Man Living in   123
    Egypt, Both Called "Jews/Judeans"
    CPJ 19; *P. Petr.* 3.21 (g); *P. Gurob* 2, Sp 256

50. A Jewish/Judean Woman's Attacks on a Pregnant Neighbor   124
    CPJ 133; *P. Tebt.* 800

51. The Contract of a Wet Nurse, Possibly Jewish/Judean   125
    CPJ 146; *BGU* 1106

52. A Divorce Agreement from Egypt, Perhaps Jewish/Judean   126
    CPJ 144; *BGU* 1102

53. A Woman, Possibly Jewish/Judean, Settling Her Share of a Debt   127
    CPJ 148; *BGU* 1155

54. Sale of a House between Two Women, the Buyer Perhaps Jewish/   127
    Judean   *CPJ* 483; *BGU* 854

55. Jewish Women Enumerated in a Tax Document from Egypt   128
    CPJ 421

56. Manumission of a Jewish/Judean Female Slave   130
    CPJ 473; *P. Oxy.* 1205

57. Epitaph of a Woman Cursed by Spells   131
    CIL 8.2756

58. A Woman Seeking to Attract the Love of Another Woman with a   131
    Spell   *PGM* 32.1–19

59. A Woman Imploring Oserapis to Avenge Her Against Her   132
    Daughter's Father   *PGM* 40.1–18

60. Royal Women of Judea   133

     60A.   Herodias   133
    JOSEPHUS *Antiquities of the Jews* 18.109–19, 240–55

     60B.   The Daughters and Other Descendants of Herod the Great   136
    JOSEPHUS *Antiquities of the Jews* 18.130–42

     60C.   Drusilla   137
    JOSEPHUS *Antiquities of the Jews* 20.137–43

61. Historians' Reports about the Herodian Princess Berenice,   138
    Coruler with Her Brother, King Agrippa II, and Lover of the
    Roman Emperor Titus

     61A.   Josephus on Berenice   138
    Antiquities of the Jews 19.277, 20.145–46;
    Jewish War 2.309–14

     61B.   Tacitus on Berenice   140
    Histories 2.1.1, 2.2.1, 2.79, 2.81.1–3

     61C.   Suetonius on Berenice   141
    The Divine Titus 7.1–2

     61D.   Cassius Dio on Berenice   142
    Roman History 66.15.3–5

61E.   A Late Epitome on Berenice   142
       Epitome of the Emperors 10.4–7

62. Personal Papers of Babatha of Maoza   143

62A.   Babatha's Marriage Contract   144
       P. Yadin 10

62B.   Babatha Summons the Guardian of Her Son to Court in   145
       Petra   *P. Yadin* 14

62C.   Babatha's Deposition, Including a Statement of Her   146
       Illiteracy   *P. Yadin* 15

62D.   Babatha's Registration of Land, Sworn by the *Genius* of the   147
       Emperor   *P. Yadin* 16

62E.   Babatha's Loan to Her Second Husband, Judah   149
       P. Yadin 17

62F.   The Marriage Contract of Babatha's Stepdaughter,   150
       Shelamzion   *P. Yadin* 18

62G.   A Deed of Gift from Babatha's Husband, Judah, to His   151
       Daughter, Shelamzion   *P. Yadin* 19

62H.   Disputes between Babatha and Her Co-widow, Miriam   152
       P. Yadin 26

63. The Personal Papers of Salome, Also Called Komaïse   152

63A.   Deed of Gift from Salome Gropte to Her Daughter,   153
       Salome Komaïse   *P. XḤev/Se* gr 64

63B.   Marriage Contract of Salome Komaïse and Her Second   154
       Husband   *P. XḤev/Se* gr 65 (= *P. Yadin* 37)

63C.   Canceled Marriage Contract, Where the Bride's Mother   155
       Gives the Bride   *P. XḤev/Se* gr 69

64. A Divorce Bill, Possibly Given by a (Jewish) Woman, Shelamzion,   156
     to Her Husband, Eleazar   *P. Şe'elim* 13

65. Women Associated with the Famous Christian Teacher Origen   157
     (ca. 185 to ca. 254 C.E.)

65A.   Origen Teaches Women and Men   157
       EUSEBIUS *History of the Church* 6.8.1–3

65B.   Origen's Unnamed Female Patron   158
       EUSEBIUS *History of the Church* 6.2.12–14

65C.   Juliana's Copies of the Works of Symmachus   158
       EUSEBIUS *History of the Church* 6.17.1

65D. Origen's Female Scribes   159
       EUSEBIUS *History of the Church* 6.23.1–2

66. Burial Inscriptions, Vows, and Donations of and by Women in   159
     Asia Minor

     66A. A Family Tomb Erected by a Woman under the Protection   160
            of the Mother of the Gods   *I. Smyr.* 232

     66B. Sarcophagus Inscription of a Jewish/Judean Woman, Her   160
            Husband, and Their Children   *CIJ* 775

     66C. Burial Inscription for a Woman and Her Mother   161
            MAMA 6.231

     66D. A Father's Inscription on the Funerary Urn of His Jewish/   161
            Judean Daughter   *TAM* 3 (1941): 448

     66E. A Christian Woman Establishes a Family Tomb   161
            Gibson *Christians for Christians*, 32

     66F. A Burial Monument Funded by a Woman from Her   162
            Dowry   *CIJ* 763

     66G. Epitaphs by Three Christian Women, Possibly Montanist,   162
            Set Up for Their Families
            Gibson *Christians for Christians*, 8, 12, 13

     66H. The Epitaph of a Married Couple, Probably Christian, with   162
            the Husband's Bequests
            Gibson *Christians for Christians*, 15

     66I. A Woman in Ionia Honored by the Jewish Community for   163
            Her Substantial Donations   *CIJ* 738; Lifshitz, *Donateurs*, 13

     66J. A Woman Fulfilling a Vow   163
            CIG 2924; Lifshitz *Donateurs* 30

67. Tablet in Greek to Reunite a Woman and a Man Using Language   163
     Reminiscent of Jewish Scriptures in Greek
     Antike Fluchtafeln, no. 5

68. Ten Inscriptions from a Synagogue Commemorating   165
     Contributions from Women for the Paving of a Mosaic Floor
     Lifshitz *Donateurs* 41–46, 48, 51, 54–55 (*I. Syrie* 1322–27, 1329, 1332,
     1335–36)

69. A Letter from the Abbot Shenoute to Tachom, Head of a   165
     Convent in Egypt   CSCO 42.21–22

70. Instruction for Rearing a Virgin Christian Daughter   167
     Letter 107, Jerome to Laeta

71. The Life of Paula, Leader in Women's Early Monasticism   177
    Letter 108, Jerome to Eustochium

72. Discord between an Ascetic Mother and Daughter, Each of   204
    Whom Was Living with a Monk
    Letter 117, Jerome to the two unnamed women

73. The Life of Marcella, a Founder of Women's Ascetic Enclaves   212
    Letter 127, Jerome to Principia

74. A Consoling Letter from the Exiled John Chrysostom to His   220
    Friend Olympias, Seeking Her Political Support
    Letter 9, John Chrysostom to Olympias

75. The Life of Olympias, Ascetic and Supporter of John Chrysostom   227
    Life of Olympias

76. The Pilgrim Egeria Visits the Shrine of St. Thecla and the   236
    Deaconess Marthana   EGERIA *Diary of a Pilgrimage* 22–23

77. Epitaph of a Gnostic Woman, Flavia Sophē   238
    Ferrua *Rivista di Archeologia Cristiana* 21 (1944/45): 185–93

78. Epitaph of Euterpe, a Christian Woman Called Companion of the   239
    Muses   Guarducci *Epigrafia*, 4:525

79. Donation by a Christian Shipowner and Her Daughter   239
    Guarducci *Epigrafia*, 4:373

        THREE *Religious Office*

80. Honors and Privileges Bestowed on a Priestess of Athena after a 245
    Procession to Pythian Apollo   *IG* II² 1136

81. The Institution of the Vestal Virgins   245
    PLUTARCH *Life of Numa Pompilius* 10

82. How Vestal Virgins Are Chosen   247
    AULUS GELLIUS *Attic Nights* 1.12

83. Honors for Priestesses   248

    83A.   The Titles, Honors, and Offices of Tata of Aphrodisias   249
           MAMA 7.492b

    83B.   Honors for the Priestess Berenice   249
           IG 12, 5, 655

    83C.   A Priestess Honored by the Senate   250
           IG 11, 8, 389

84. Juliane, the First High Priestess of Asia   250
    IvMag 158

85. Three Women Heads of Synagogues   251

   85A.   Epitaph Set Up by Rufina, Head of the Synagogue   251
       CIJ 741

   85B.   Epitaph of Sophia of Gortyn, Head of the Synagogue   251
       CIJ 1.²731c

   85C.   Inscription of Theopempte, Head of the Synagogue   252
       CIJ 756

86. An Unnamed Woman Head of a Synagogue in Ancient   252
Cappadocia   *Unpublished inscription*

87. Epitaph of a Jewish Woman "Leader"   253
CIJ 1.²696b

88. Seven Epitaphs of Jewish Women Elders   253

   88A.   *CIJ* 400; *JIWE* 2: no. 24   253

   88B.   *CIJ* 581; *JIWE* 1: no. 59   253

   88C.   *CIJ* 590; *JIWE* 1: no. 62   254

   88D.   *CIJ* 597; *JIWE* 1: no. 71   254

   88E.   *CIJ* 692   254

   88F.   *SEG* 27 (1977), 1201   254

   88G.   Kraemer *HTR* 78, nos. 3–4 (1985): 431–38   254

89. Three Epitaphs of Jewish Women Possibly Called "Priestesses"   254

   89A.   Epitaph of a Jewish Woman from Egypt   255
       CPJ/CIJ 1514; *JIGRE* 84

   89B.   Epitaph of a Jewish Woman from Rome   255
       CIJ 315; *JIWE* 2: no. 11

   89C.   Epitaph of the Mother of a Jewish Woman   255
       CIJ 1007

90. Two Epitaphs of Christian Women Elders   256

   90A.   Epitaph of Kale   256
       Piraino *Inscrizioni*, 36–37, no. 13

   90B.   Epitaph of Ammion, Perhaps Montanist   256
       Körte *Inscriptiones Bureschianae*, 31, no. 55

91. Six Inscriptions of (Christian) Women Deacons   257

   91A.   Epitaph of Sophia the Deacon, the Second Phoebe   257
       Alt *Griechischen Inschriften*, no. 17

   91B.   Epitaph of the Deaconess Athanasia   258
       Guarducci *Epigrafia*, 4:345, no. 4

Contents

91C.   Epitaph of the Deacon Maria   258
Jacopi *Esplorazioni:* 33–36

91D.   Monument Erected by Domna, the Deacon   259
MAMA 7.471

91E.   A Vow Fulfilled by the Deacon Agrippiane   259
Petsas *Arch. Delt.* 26 (1971): 161–63

91F.   A Vow Fulfilled by a Deaconess   259
NewDocs 2 (1982 [1977]): 194

92.   Opposition to Teaching and Baptizing by Women   259

92A.   TERTULLIAN *On Baptism* 17   260

92B.   TERTULLIAN *On the Veiling of Virgins* 9   261

92C.   TERTULLIAN *On the Prescription against Heretics* 41   261

93.   A Montanist Visionary Who Submits Her Revelation to Careful   262
Scrutiny   TERTULLIAN *On the Soul* 9

94.   Hippolytus on the Montanist Prophets Maximilla and Priscilla   263
HIPPOLYTUS *Refutation of All Heresies* 8.12

95.   Women Bishops, Presbyters, and Prophets among the Followers   264
of Quintilla and Priscilla   EPIPHANIUS *Medicine Box* 49

96.   Fourth-Century Writers on the Montanist Prophets Maximilla   265
and Priscilla

96A.   Eusebius on Maximilla   265
EUSEBIUS *History of the Church* 5.16

96B.   A Saying of Priscilla   266
EPIPHANIUS *Medicine Box* 49.1.3

96C.   Sayings of Maximilla   266
EPIPHANIUS *Medicine Box* 48

97.   The Epitaph of the Female Prophet Nanas   267
Haspels *Highlands of Phrygia*, no. 107

98.   A Woman Philosopher(?), Probably Christian   268
NewDocs 4 (1987 [1979]): 257, no. 126

99.   Regulations for Deaconesses   268
Constitutions of the Holy Apostles 2.26

100.   Regulations for Christian Widows   270
Constitutions of the Holy Apostles 3.3–9, 13–15

101.   Regulations for Deaconesses, Virgins, Widows, and Other   277
Christians during the Worship Service
Constitutions of the Holy Apostles 2.57

FOUR *New Religious Affiliation and Conversion*

102. The Spread of the Bacchic Rites to Rome in 186 B.C.E.,   283
     Attracting Women and Men to Their Frenzied Observance
     LIVY *Annals of Rome* 39.8–18

103. Helena, Queen of Adiabene, Converts to Judaism   292
     JOSEPHUS *Antiquities of the Jews* 20.17–53, 92–96

104. The Jewish Proclivities of Some Non-Jewish Women   296

     104A. Women of Damascus   296
            JOSEPHUS *Jewish War* 2.559–61

     104B. Poppaea Sabina, Wife of the Emperor Nero   296
            JOSEPHUS *Antiquities of the Jews* 20.189–98

105. Thecla of Iconium, an Ascetic Christian and the Prototypical   297
     Convert   *The Acts of Thecla*

106. How the Egyptian Virgin Aseneth Becomes a Devotee of the   308
     God of Israel and Marries the Patriarch Joseph   *Aseneth* 1–21

107. Two Roman Women Proselytes   327

     107A.   *CIJ* 462; *JIWE* 2, no. 62   327

     107B.   *CIJ* 523; *JIWE* 2, no. 577   327

108. Two Women Called "God-fearers"   328

     108A.   *IG* 12.1, 593; *CIJ* 1.²731e   328

     108B.   *CIJ* 642; *JIWE* 1, no. 9   328

FIVE *Holy, Pious, and Exemplary Women*

109. The Exemplary Self-Control and Piety of a Jewish Mother   332
     Forced to Watch the Martyrdom of Her Seven Sons
     2 Maccabees 7; 4 Maccabees 14.11–18.24

110. The Spiritual Inheritance of the Daughters of Job   340
     The Testament of Job 46–52

111. Two Juxtaposed Narratives of the Gullibility of Pious Women   343
     JOSEPHUS *Antiquities of the Jews* 18.65–80, 81–84

112. The Trial Account of Carthaginian Christian Women and Men   346
     The Acts of the Martyrs of Scilli

113. The Martyrdom of the Christian Blandina and Three Male   348
     Companions in 177 C.E.   *Letter of the Churches of Lyons and
     Vienne*, in Eusebius *History of the Church* 5.1.3–63

114. A First-Person Account of a Christian Woman's Persecution   356
The Martyrdom of Saints Perpetua and Felicitas

115. The Martyrdom of Potamiena in the Early Third Century C.E.   368
EUSEBIUS *History of the Church* 6.5.1–7

116. Women Martyred at Antioch under Diocletian in the Early   369
Fourth Century C.E.   EUSEBIUS *History of the Church* 8.12.3–5

117. Three Epitaphs from Fourth-Century Rome   370

     117A.   Praises for the Traditional Roman Piety of Aconia Fabia   370
         Paulina   *ILS* 1259–61

     117B.   Epitaph of Regina, Extolled for Her Piety and Observance   371
         of (Jewish) Law   *CIJ* 476; *JIWE* 2, no. 103

     117C.   Epitaph of Theodora, Teacher of the Faith   371
         ICUR 1.317 / *ILCV* 1.316

118. Charikleia, Condemned as a Poisoner, Rescued by Divine   374
Intervention   HELIODORUS *An Ethiopian Story* 8.9

119. A Letter Written in the Name of a Woman to "Ignatius of   375
Antioch"   PSEUDO-IGNATIUS *The Letter of Maria the Proselyte
to Ignatius*

120. A Former Prostitute Becomes a Christian Ascetic, Taking on   377
Male Disguise   *The Life of Saint Pelagia the Harlot*

121. An Orphaned Prostitute Returns to the Christian Asceticism of   395
Her Youth   *The Life of Saint Mary the Harlot*

122. The Endurance of Two Syrian Christian Monastic Women   404
THEODORET OF CYRRHUS *A History of the Monks of Syria* 29

123. A Syrian Monastic Woman Living in a Hut in Her Mother's   405
Garden   THEODORET OF CYRRHUS *A History of the Monks of
Syria* 30

124. Sayings Attributed to Ascetic Desert Monastic Women   408
Sayings of the Desert Fathers

     124A.   Sayings Attributed to Amma Sarah   408

     124B.   Sayings Attributed to Amma Syncletica   409

     124C.   Sayings Attributed to Amma Theodora   413

SIX   *The Feminine Divine*

125. The Principal Version of the Myth of Demeter   418
The Homeric Hymn to Demeter

126. Two Accounts of the Origins of the Worship of the Great   427
Mother at Rome

     126A.   OVID *Fasti* 4.247–348   427

     126B.   LIVY *Annals of Rome* 29.14   430

127. Imagery of Lactation and Childbearing in a Christian Ode   431
The Odes of Solomon 19

128. The Female Spirit of the Lord   432
The Odes of Solomon 36

129. A Version of the Myth of Isis   433
PLUTARCH *On Isis and Osiris* 12–19 (*Moralia* 355–58)

130. The Experiences of a Male Initiate of Isis   438
APULEIUS *Metamorphoses* bk. 11

131. The Titles of the Goddess Isis   454

     131A.   *P. Oxy.* 11.1380   454

     131B.   *The Kyme Aretalogy*   456

132. Aspects of Female Divinity in Three Gnostic Texts   458

     132A.   *Thunder, Perfect Mind*   459

     132B.   *The Thought of Norea*   465

     132C.   *The Hypostatis of the Archons; or, The Reality of the Rulers*   465

133. The Fall and Deliverance of the Soul, Which Is Feminine   472
The Exegesis on the Soul

Index of Names   479

Index of Ancient Sources   484

Abbreviations

ACW   Ancient Christian Writers
AM   Mittelungen des deutschen archäologischen Instituts
Alt, *Griechische Inschriften*
                A. Alt. *Die griechischen inschriften der Palaestina Tertia westlich der 'Araba*. Berlin: De Gruyter, 1921.
ANF   Ante-Nicene Fathers
ANT   J. K. Elliott, ed. *The Apocryphal New Testament: A Collection of Apocryphal Christian Literature in an English Translation*. Oxford: Oxford University Press, 1993.
AOT   H. F. D. Sparks, ed. *The Apocryphal Old Testament*. Oxford: Oxford University Press, 1984.
Arch. Delt.   *Archaiologikon deltion*
BGU   *Berliner Griechische Urkunden*
BHO   *Bibliotheca Hagiographica Orientalis*
BJS   Brown Judaic Studies
Blessings   Ross Shepard Kraemer. *Her Share of the Blessings: Women's Religions Among Pagans, Jews and Christians in the Greco-Roman World*. Oxford: Oxford University Press, 1992.
Brooten, *Women Leaders*
                Bernadette J. Brooten. *Women Leaders in the Ancient Synagogues*. Brown Judaic Studies 36. Chico, Calif.: Scholars Press, 1982.
Budé   Collection des universités de France, publiée sur le patronage de l'Association Guillaume Budé
CCSL   Corpus Christianorum Series Latina
CIG   *Corpus Inscriptionum Graecarum*
CIJ   *Corpus Inscriptionum Judaicarum*
CIL   *Corpus Inscriptionum Latinarum*
CPJ   *Corpus Papyrorum Judaicarum*
CSCO   Corpus Scriptorum Christianorum Orientalium

CSEL	Corpus Scriptorum Ecclesiasticorum Latinorum
CTS	Cambridge Texts and Studies
EPRO	Etudes préliminaires aux religions orientales dans l'empire Romain
FC	Fathers of the Church
FENHC	Facsimile Edition of the Nag Hammadi Codices

Gager, *Curse Tablets*
> John G. Gager, ed. *Curse Tablets and Binding Spells from the Ancient World.* Oxford: Oxford University Press, 1992.

Gibson, *Christians for Christians*
> Elsa Gibson, ed. *The "Christians for Christians" Inscriptions of Phyrgia.* Missoula, Mont.: Scholars Press, 1978.

GCS	Die griechische christliche Schriftsteller der ersten [drei] Jahrhunderte
GLAJJ	M. Stern, ed. *Greek and Latin Authors on Jews and Judaism.* 3 vols. Jerusalem: Israel Academy of Sciences and Humanities, 1974–84.
GRBS	*Greek, Roman and Byzantine Studies*

Guarducci, *Epigrafia*
> M. Guarducci, ed. *Epigrafia Graeca.* 4 vols. Rome: Istituto poligrafico dello Stato, 1967–78.

Haspels, *Highlands*
> C. H. Emilie Haspels. *The Highlands of Phrygia: Sites and Monuments.* Princeton: Princeton University Press, 1971.

HSCP	*Harvard Studies in Classical Philology*
HTR	*Harvard Theological Review*
ICUR	*Inscriptiones Christianae Urbis Romae*
IEJ	*Israel Exploration Journal*
IG	*Inscriptiones Graecae*
ILCV	*Inscriptiones Latinae Christianae Veteris*
ILS	*Inscriptiones Latinae Selectae*
IvMag.	*Die Inschriften von Magnesia am Meander*
I.Smyr.	*Die Inschriften von Smyrna*
I.Syrie	*Inscriptiones grecques et latines de la Syrie*

Jacopi, *Esplorazioni*
> Giulio Jacopi. *Esplorazioni e studi in Paflagonia e Cappadocia. Relazione sulla seconda Campagna Explorativa Agosto–Ottobre 1936.* Rome: R. Istituto d'Archeologia e Storia dell'Arte, 1937.

JBL	*Journal of Biblical Literature*
JECS	*Journal of Early Christian Studies*
JIGRE	*Jewish Inscriptions of Graeco-Roman Egypt*
JIWE	*Jewish Inscriptions of Western Europe*
JRS	*Journal of Roman Studies*

JSJ	*Journal for the Study of Judaism in the Persian, Hellenistic, and Roman Period*
Körte, *Inscriptiones Bureschlange*	
	Alfred Körte. *Inscriptiones Bureschlange*. Griefswald: Druck von J. Abel, 1902.
Lefkowitz and Fant	
	Mary Lefkowitz and Maureen B. Fant, eds. *Women's Lives in Greece and Rome*. Baltimore, Md.: Johns Hopkins University Press, 1982; 2nd ed. 1992.
Lifshitz, *Donateurs*	
	B. Lifshitz, ed. *Donateurs et fondateurs dans les synagogues juives*. Paris: J. Gabalda et cie. 1967.
LCC	Library of Christian Classics
LCL	Loeb Classical Library
LSAM	*Lois sacrées de l'Asie Mineure*
LSCG suppl.	*Lois sacrées des Cités grecques, supplement*
MAMA	*Monumenta Asiae Minoris Antiqua*
Modrejewski	Joseph Melèze Modrejewski. *The Jews of Egypt: from Rameses II to Emperor Hadrian*. Transl. Robert Cornman. Philadelphia: Jewish Publication Society, 1995.
NewDocs	*New Documents Illustrating Early Christianity*
NHS	Nag Hammadi Studies
NPNFC	Nicene and Post-Nicene Fathers of the Church
NTA	W. Schneemelcher, ed. *New Testament Apocrypha*. Rev. ed. Transl. R. McL. Wilson. 2 vols. Louisville, KY: Westminster/John Knox, 1992.
OCT	Oxford Classical Texts
OTP	James H. Charlesworth, ed. *The Old Testament Apocrypha*. 2 vols. Garden City: Doubleday, 1983–85.
OWC	Oxford's World Classics
Piraino, *Iscrizioni*	
	Maria Teresa Manni Piraino, *Iscrizioni greche lapidarie del Museo di Palermo*. ΣΙΚΕΛΙΚΑ VI. Palermo: S. F. Flaccovio, 1971.
P. Gurob	*Greek Papyri from Gurob*
P. Hib.	*The Hibeh Papyri*
P. Oxy.	*The Oxyrhychus Papyri*
P. Petr.	*The Flinders Petrie Papyri*
P. Se'elim	*Papyrus Se'elim*
P. Tebt.	*The Tebtunis Papyri*
P. Yadin	*Papyrus Yadin*
P. XhevSe gr	*Papyrus Nahal Hever, the Seiyâl Collection II (Greek)*
PG	*Patraegia Graeca*

Pleket, *Epigraphica*

        Henri W. Pleket, ed. *Epigraphica. Vol. II. Texts on the Social History of the Greek World.* Leiden: E. J. Brill, 1969.

PVTG   Pseudepigraphia Veteris Testamenti Graece

RGRW   Religions of the Greco-Roman World

Ritti, *Iscrizioni*

        Tullia Ritti, ed. *Iscrizioni e rilievi greci nel Museo Maffeiano di Verona.* Rome: G. Bretschneider, 1981.

Searching the Scriptures

        Elisabeth Schüssler Fiorenza, ed. *Searching the Scriptures: A Feminist Commentary.* 2 vols. New York: Crossroad, 1993–94.

SC   Sources Chrétiennes

SBLSBS   Society of Biblical Literature Sources for Biblical Study

SBLSP   *Society of Biblical Literature Seminar Papers*

SBLTT   Society of Biblical Literature Texts and Translations

SEG   Supplementum Epigraphicum Graecum

SPCK   Society for Promoting Christian Knowledge

SWR   Studies in Women and Religion

Teubner   Bibliotheca Scriptorum Graecorum et Romanorum Teubneriana

TAM   *Tituli Asiae Minoris*

Women and Christian Origins

        Ross Shepard Kraemer and Mary Rose D'Angelo, eds. *Women and Christian Origins.* Oxford: Oxford University Press, 1999.

ZPE   *Zeitschrift für Papyrologie und Epigraphik*

WOMEN'S RELIGIONS
in the GRECO-ROMAN WORLD

Introduction

When I published the first edition of this sourcebook in 1988, I wanted to assemble in one place, in English translation, major texts and documents pertaining to the study of women's religious activities in the various religions of Greco-Roman antiquity, including Judaism and Christianity. As I pointed out at the time, there were then numerous sourcebooks on the religions of Greco-Roman antiquity (many designed to aid the study of the New Testament and early Christianity), an anthology of texts on women's lives in Greek and Roman society, and several on women in Christian sources. A handful of studies surveyed what were then couched as "attitudes" toward women in Judaism and Christianity, and one Christian feminist theologian had assembled a collection of resources for feminist (Christian) theology. No one, however, had assembled the texts relevant to women's religions in Western antiquity. *Maenads, Martyrs, Matrons, Monastics: A Sourcebook of Women's Religions in the Greco-Roman World* marshaled an array of materials into 135 entries, ranging from Euripides' description of the first ecstatic worshipers of the Greek god Dionysos in his late-fifth-century B.C.E. prize-winning play *The Bacchae* to Philo of Alexandria's report on monastic Jewish women philosophers in the first century C.E. to epitaphs attesting women deacons and elders in numerous Christian communities, and women leaders in late antique Jewish synagogues.

In 1988, feminist scholarship on women's religions, both in the ancient world and elsewhere, was still very much in its infancy. Only five years earlier, I had published a review article on women's religions in the Greco-Roman world, including Christianity and Judaism, in which I was able to offer a reasonably comprehensive survey of twentieth-century scholarship whose bibliography contained about 250 entries. Much of that scholarship was pursued within the context of contemporary theological debates. The evidence for women as leaders in ancient Christian churches was studied for the relevance it might have for debates about the contemporary ordination of women; and the views of ancient male Christian writers from Paul to Tertullian to Jerome and John Chrysostom regarding women

3

were scrutinized with particular regard for their effects on mainstream Christian ideas and ideals. Texts outside the Jewish and Christian canons, including sometimes polytheist goddess traditions, were proffered as potential resources for contemporary women and men seeking alternatives to ancient male-centered theologies and liturgies.

My own questions were somewhat different, rooted in my self-understanding as a feminist historian trained in the study of a wide range of religions in the Greco-Roman period. I was interested in the recovery and accurate description of what women themselves did and thought within contexts that could be labeled "religious" and in theoretical models that might enable me to analyze and explain whatever differences I might find when I concentrated my research on women rather than, as had almost universally been the case previously, on men.[1] The materials I selected, and the categories in which I chose to group them, were very much related to the first set of questions. The first two sections of *Maenads* accounted for half the number of entries in the book. "Observances, Rituals, and Festivals" consisted of ancient descriptions of women's rites, the vast majority from the writings of known male authors, with a few selections from anonymous sources that nevertheless can confidently be assigned to male composition, such as the Mishnah and the Babylonian Talmud. "Researching Real Women: Documents to, from, and by Women" compiled personal and public documents preserved on papyrus or inscribed on stone and other hard surfaces that attested to the practices and occasionally the beliefs of diverse ancient women. It represented my understanding that while ancient male writers might, in fact, provide useful testimony in this regard, what they had to say was a different kind of evidence that required particular standards of scrutiny.

Section 3, "Religious Office," was drawn both from the writings of male authors and from surviving inscriptions and assembled evidence for women's roles as officiants in religious rites and as officials in religious organizations. Section 4, "New Religious Affiliation and Conversion," collected narratives, some of known authorship, some anonymous, relating women's adoption of new religious practices and beliefs, supplemented with a handful of inscriptions attesting women's affiliation with Judaism. Section 5, "Holy, Pious, and Exemplary Women," again assembled narratives of women whose piety was perceived as exemplary in some fashion, together with a few telling epitaphs. The last section was, as I acknowledged at the time, the most anomalous. Titled "The Feminine Divine," it gathered

---

[1] The complexity of the terms "religion," "religious," and so forth is helpfully explored by Jonathan Z. Smith, "Religion, Religions, Religious," in Mark C. Taylor, ed., *Critical Terms for Religious Studies* (Chicago: University of Chicago Press, 1998), 269–84; see also Brian C. Wilson, "From the Lexical to the Polythetic: A Brief History of the Definition of Religion," in T. A. Idinopulos and Brian C. Wilson, eds., *What Is Religion? Origins, Definitions, and Explanations* (Leiden: E. J. Brill, 1998), 141–62.

ancient sources that envisioned the divine as feminine, without regard for any correlation with the sex of those who held such understandings.

The present anthology continues to use the categories of the original sourcebook. Fifteen years later, however, I am much less sanguine about the assumptions that undergirded their initial formulation. I continue to be deeply interested in the project of historical recovery and reconstruction, but I have become much more skeptical about how much the kinds of literary materials that comprise the bulk of sections 1, 4, and 5 can ever tell us about what women in the ancient world did and thought, whether regarding what is usually classed as religion or anything else. When I first began my work on women's religions in the Greco-Roman world as a graduate student at Princeton University in the 1970s, the major problems associated with historical reconstruction seemed to be the relative absence of sources either by or about women and the difficulty of assessing the reliability of those that are available. If only we had enough sources by women themselves and/or enough sources by trustworthy male authors, we would be able to reconstruct a reasonable portrait of women's lives and self understandings in the ancient world.

At the turn of the twenty-first century, things have become more complicated. It has become increasingly apparent to many of those who work in this and related fields that additional impediments hamper our ability to answer historical questions. We have begun to understand that socially constructed and variable ideas about gender—about what it means to be female and male—permeate ancient thought, culture, and experience so extensively that sources that appear to be about women may often instead be devices by which ancient writers, male and perhaps also female, wrote about all sorts of other concerns. Sources written by women might indeed provide important controls for those written by men, but they would not alter this fundamental dilemma that stories about women might really only incidentally correspond to social and historical realities.

Scholarly discussions about a work known as *The Martyrdom* of *Saints Perpetua and Felicitas* (entry 114) provide an instructive illustration. On its face, this work recounts the arrest, detention, and ultimate martyrdom of a young Roman matron named Vibia Perpetua and several of her companions, all recent converts to Christianity, in the North African city of Carthage in the early third century c.e. Although the beginning and the end of the text are told in the third person, the central portion of the text is said to be Perpetua's own account, written while she was detained and awaiting martyrdom. In the 1970s and subsequently, numerous feminist scholars, eager to reclaim the voice of an actual Christian woman, hailed this work as the oldest known writing by a Christian woman and confidently analyzed the narrative as permitting access to Perpetua's experiences and thoughts.[2]

[2] See, e.g., Rosemary Rader, "Perpetua," in Patricia Wilson-Kastner et al., eds., *A Lost Tradition: Women Writers of the Early Church* (Lanham, Md.: University Press of America,

I, too, in my earlier work, considered it highly possible that the so-called diary portion stemmed from Perpetua.[3] More recently, though, I have come to the conclusion that this "diary" material is more likely to be a literary production on the part of the work's author and represents the concerns and interests of the author rather than the relatively spontaneous jottings of an imprisoned Christian proselyte awaiting probable death. Although the nature of the evidence is such that we cannot resolve this question with absolute certainty, I am now convinced it is unwise to presume that this narrative represents anything more than a deliberate construction of an exemplary female martyr.[4] How much, then, we can extract from the story of Perpetua and Felicitas that pertains to the experiences of early Christian women becomes much more difficult to determine.

Conversely, if the sources in section 1 ("Observances, Rituals, and Festivals") were initially problematic primarily because of their male authorship, those in section 2 ("Researching Real Women: Documents to, from, and by Women") seemed immune, or far less tainted. To some degree, this might still be the case, but it is also true that ancient epitaphs and honorific inscriptions closely adhered to ancient and gendered conventions of propriety, so that, for instance, attestations of piety, whether filial, marital, or otherwise, may be more about gendered expectations than about the practices and mental states of individual ancient persons.

These issues have major implications for the way we read and utilize the extant sources, including those collected in this anthology, and major implications for scholarly projects like mine. I have begun to address them in some recent work and hope to pursue them in future studies as well. I have concluded, though, that it is still feasible to organize the sources as I did originally, provided that one approaches these texts with sufficient sophistication and subtlety.

While following the same divisions as the original sourcebook, this one has some significant differences. Originally, I relegated all contextual information and secondary bibliography to a section at the end of the book entitled "About the Authors and Sources." Prompted in part by colleagues concerned to make the collection as user-friendly for students as possible, I have now provided all this information at the beginning of each entry or, in the case of an entry from an author or work previously covered, at the initial entry for that author or work (with an appropriate cross-reference). Most entries contain brief descriptions of

1981), 1–32; Maureen Tilley, "The Passion of Perpetua and Felicity," in Searching the Scriptures, 2:829–58; Brent Shaw, "The Passion of Perpetua," Past and Present 139 (1993): 3–45; Judith Perkins, The Suffering Self: Pain and Narrative Representation in the Early Christian Era (London and New York: Routledge, 1995), although after I shared my latest views with her, Perkins told me in conversation that she agrees that Perpetua did not write the material attributed to her. See also the Introduction to section 5 and entry 114.

   [3] Kraemer, Blessings, 159–63.

   [4] Ross S. Kraemer and Shira L. Lander, "Perpetua and Felicitas," in Philip Esler, ed., The Early Christian World (London: Routledge, 2000), 2:1048–68.

the author or source (the latter for texts of unknown authorship or nonliterary materials), date (or probable date) of composition, original language, and provenance if known. This is followed by an indication of the translation used, critical editions of the text, additional texts and translations. My own translations are identified by my initials, RSK. When using the translations of others, I have generally retained their conventions for identifying missing or illegible letters, missing letters of unknown length, editorial reconstructions of gaps, and words supplied to make better sense in translation. In general, in my own translations, I have adhered to standard practices: three dots in square brackets [. . .] indicates missing or illegible text of known or approximate length; three dashes in square brackets [— — —] indicates missing text of indeterminate length; words supplied in square brackets indicates reconstruction of missing text and words supplied in parenthesis are supplied for English sense.

Most entries also contain a select bibliography of recent relevant scholarship, largely confined to relatively accessible works in English. These begin, where appropriate, with a reference to my own 1992 study, *Her Share of the Blessings: Women's Religions Among Pagans, Jews and Christians in the Greco-Roman World* (abbreviated as *Blessings*), and/or to the anthology I edited with Mary Rose D'Angelo, *Women and Christian Origins* (abbreviated as *Women and Christian Origins*). Subsequent references are alphabetical by author. I have both knowingly and unknowingly omitted studies that serious students will want to pursue.

The revised sourcebook contains approximately forty new selections, spread throughout four of the six sections. For "Observances, Rituals, and Festivals," these include selections from Plutarch's *Roman Questions* on various aspects of women's observances; numerous passages from Greek novels on the practices of women; Justin Martyr's report of an unnamed woman whose acceptance of ascetic Christianity provokes her husband to legal action; a "tour of hell" ascribed to a resurrected murdered Christian woman in the *Acts of Thomas*; rabbinic traditions of conversations between Rabbi Jose ben Halafta and a woman known as Matrona (or, perhaps, "the matron"); an excerpt from *The Debate between a Montanist and an Orthodox* on why Christian women may not write books in their own names; and additional passages from Palladius's *Lausiac History* on a Pachomian women's monastery in Egypt. "Researching Real Women" now includes reports about the Herodian princess Berenice and other royal women of Judea; some of the personal papers of Jewish women from the Judean desert region in the early second century C.E.; extracts from Eusebius on women associated with the third-century Christian teacher Origen; passages from the pilgrimage diary of Egeria in the late fourth century C.E.; additional material from the Pachomian monastery; and the epitaph of a "gnostic" woman named Flavia Sophē. "Religious Office" includes the inscription for the first woman to hold the office of high priestess of Asia and an unpublished inscription from ancient Cappadocia (modern Turkey) providing further documentation of women heads of synagogues. "Holy, Pious, and Exemplary Women" now includes two narratives from Josephus about the gullibility of pious women; accounts in Eusebius of the martyrdom of Potamiaena in the early third century and of women martyred under Diocletian in the early fourth century C.E.; the inscription of a Christian teacher named Theodora; a selection from Heliodorus's *Ethiopian Story* on the piety of the heroine, Charikleia; pseudepigraphic correspondence between "Mary of Cassabola" and "Ignatius of Antioch"; and several narratives of Syrian Christian women monastics. "New Religious Affiliation and Conversion" contains one additional narrative from Josephus, on the apparent sympathy of Poppaea Sabina, wife of the Emperor Nero, for Jews and Judaism. "The Feminine Divine" contains no new entries.

Although this edition has extensive new material, it has about the same number of entries as the original. This is because I have frequently grouped related smaller entries into one larger entry, such as brief excerpts from writers like Ovid and Plutarch or short inscriptions for women heads of synagogues, women elders, priestesses, and so forth. Were all these to be individual entries, there would be about a third more entries.

Astute readers may notice that while some entries in the book refer simply to "Jews," other entries refer to "Jews/Judeans" or to a particular person as "Jew/Judean." When I have used the translations of others, I have retained whatever translations they have chosen for the Greek (or occasionally Latin) terms. When I have used my own translations, however, I have now often used the more ambiguous "Jew/Judean." This reflects a current scholarly debate over whether these terms signify an ethnic classification (Judeans, analogous to Egyptians, or Persians), or something more analogous to what we might call a "religious" classification. It is important to keep in mind that in antiquity, ethnic classification would also have included the religious practices (and beliefs) particular to that ethnic group.[5]

Revising the original sourcebook has been an engaging task, primarily for the opportunity to revisit many of the materials gathered here, to update the bibliography, to rethink and revise the brief section introductions, and to integrate additional materials I have been collecting in files, folders, and notes in the last dozen years. It has also been a little humbling. A little less than twenty years ago, I could write something approximating a comprehensive survey of the scholarly studies on women's religions in the Greco-Roman period, but the field has burgeoned to such an extent in the intervening years that I cannot imagine attempting to write the same survey now with any pretense of thoroughness, let alone comprehensiveness.[6] I would like to think that the first edition of *Maenads* played some role in facilitating and stimulating this scholarship, and very much hope that this new edition will continue to play a role in acquainting new readers with the riches of these materials and in encouraging other scholars to pursue these sources and the issues they enable us to engage.

---

[5] For some discussion of the complex issues here, see Shaye J. D. Cohen, *The Beginnings of Jewishness* (Berkeley: University of California Press, 2000).

[6] Ross S. Kraemer, "Women in the Religions of the Greco-Roman World," *Religious Studies Review* 9 (1983) 2: 127–39.

ONE

Observances, Rituals, and Festivals

This section assembles ancient descriptions of women's engagement in various religious practices. How accurate these descriptions are continues to be an unresolved issue.

At a fairly basic level, how shall we evaluate accounts by men who claim to know the details of women's rites from which men are supposedly excluded? The classical Athenian playwright Euripides, obviously needing to explain his source even within the confines of drama, solves the problem with hidden male observers. In his *Bacchae*, excerpted in this section (entries 1 and 2), a herdsman concealed behind the trees reports back to King Pentheus, who himself then spies on the women worshippers of Dionysos to his ultimate detriment. What sources Euridipes actually had and whether these sources were accurate, or even intended to be, remains uncertain.

The fourth-century orator Demosthenes, on the other hand, was apparently able to describe women's activities for two reasons: at least one male, his opponent Aeschines, is said to have participated in them and at least some of the activities took place in public, where any observer could have seen them (entry 3). This, of course, is no guarantor of the accuracy of his account, but it does address one fundamental difficulty.

With many of these texts, the question of historical reliability extends further. In the case of some Christian texts in particular, the authors report activities they wish to discredit, whether it is Epiphanius's description of women functioning as priests and baking cakes for the Virgin Mary (entry 38) or John Chrysostom's disapproval of the attendance of Christian women at synagogue festivals (entry 41). By a historical principle known sometimes as the criterion of embarrassment (or sometimes of dissimilarity), we might consider such narratives probable. According to this principle, writers are presumed to omit embarrassing or undesirable reports unless they themselves consider them true. Reports of victory by the victorious are to be scrutinized carefully, while reports of defeat by the defeated are more likely to be trustworthy.

Yet authors such as Epiphanius may not have had access to reliable sources or any means of verifying their sources, if the thought of verification even occurred to them. They may have believed their sources to be accurate, but we must be more suspicious. When Origen of Alexandria quotes the accusation of the critic Celsus that Christian missionaries seek only "the foolish, dishonourable and stupid, and only slaves, women and little children,"[1] it is difficult for us to tell whether this is a standard rhetorical calumny (characterizing one's opponents as ignorant, lower class, and female), with little historical utility, or whether it represents a reasonable description of the social composition of most second-century Christian communities, which provided Celsus further grist for his anti-Christian mill.[2] And someone like John Chrysostom, who undeniably had strong views about what was and was not appropriate behavior for Christian women and men, may still be a more accurate reporter when he describes the activities of women in his own community rather than those in some faraway land.

Most of the sources for women's practices, and thus, most of the entries in this section, come from Greek, Roman, and Hellenistic religions other than Judaism and Christianity. Perhaps this results from the fact that such traditions differentiated practices more closely on the basis of gender, particularly public rites and festivals. We know, for example, that certain celebrations and devotions were primarily, if not exclusively, the domain of one sex or the other, although certainly other religious practices involved the participation of both women and men. New to this edition are selections from Plutarch's *Roman Questions* on various Hellenistic and Roman practices (entries 16C–H), as well as numerous representations of women's devotions, processions, and engagement in "magical arts" from Hellenistic Greek novels.

Within extant Jewish sources, it is difficult to discern much evidence for practices peculiar to women. Although we know that Jewish women participated in

---

[1] Origen *Against Celsus* 3.49, translation from Henry Chadwick, *Origen contra Celsum* (Cambridge: Cambridge University Press, 1986).

[2] On the ancient categorization of one's opponents as female, see Ross S. Kraemer, "The Other as Woman: Aspects of Polemic between Pagans, Jews, and Christians in Greco-Roman Antiquity," in Laurence J. Silberstein, and Robert L. Cohn eds., *The Other in Jewish Thought and History: Constructions of Jewish Culture and Identity* (New York: New York University Press, 1994), 121–44. On the actual social composition of early Christian communities, sociologist Rodney Stark has offered a provocative assessment in *The Rise of Christianity: A Sociologist Reconsiders History* (Princeton: Princeton University Press, 1996), which should be read together with "Rodney Stark's The Rise of Christianity: A Discussion," three essays by Todd E. Klutz, Keith Hopkins, and Elizabeth Castelli, and a rejoinder by Stark, in *JECS* 6, no. 2 (1998): 161–267; see also Margaret Y. MacDonald, *Early Christian Women and Pagan Opinion: The Power of the Hysterical Woman* (Cambridge: Cambridge University Press, 1996). On the likely social composition of Jewish communities in the Hellenistic and Roman periods, see Seth Schwartz, *Imperialism and Jewish Society, 200 B.C.E. to 640 C.E.* (Princeton: Princeton University Press, 2001).

some of the same religious activities as Jewish men, we cannot easily say for certain which these were. Some Jewish activities were restricted to certain men (e.g., priestly sacrifices in the Jerusalem temple), and the rabbis considered women exempt from certain obligations binding on men (entry 45). The use of rabbinic texts as evidence for the actual practices of Jewish women is problematic for a number of reasons, not the least of which is the fact that we lack a firm grasp on the extent to which rabbinic regulations (reported in literary sources dating from the early third century c.e. on) describe the social reality of ancient Jewish communities.[3] This section includes several selections from rabbinic sources, with that caveat in mind. New to this edition are rabbinic traditions about conversations between a Rabbi Jose and a woman called either Matrona (a proper name) or perhaps "the Matrona" (an unnamed Roman matron) (entry 37).

Similarly for Christian sources, we possess little in the way of evidence that allows us to see whether men and women shared all ritual activity or whether gender distinctions affected Christian practice (apart from debates over priestly office and the administration of certain rites to others, such as baptism or the Eucharist). Several new entries from Christian sources are included here: Justin Martyr's report of an ascetic woman whose husband brings charges against her and her male Christian teachers (entry 32) and a tour of hellish torments attributed to a murdered woman raised from the dead by the apostle Thomas (entry 33).

[3] For a sweeping indictment of the utility of rabbinic sources for ancient Jewish history, see Schwartz, *Imperialism*; for some discussion of the problems inherent in the use of rabbinic sources, particularly for women's history, see *Blessings*, 93–105; Kraemer, "Jewish Women and Christian Origins: Some Caveats," in *Women and Christian Origins*, 35–49. Additional references may be found in the various entries.

1

Why Women Are Compelled to Worship Dionysos

EURIPIDES *Bacchae* 23–42   405 B.C.E.

AUTHOR: Euripides (ca. 485–406 B.C.E.), one of the most famous of the Athenian playwrights, wrote a number of plays that feature Greek women: *Medea, Andromache, Hecuba, Helen, Electra, Iphigenia at Aulis,* and *Iphigenia in Tauris.* He devoted one of the last of his plays, *The Bacchae* (which posthumously brought him victory at the festival known as the Dionysia in 406 B.C.E.), to the origins and character of women's worship of the Thracian god Dionysos. Modern scholars have continued to wrestle with the correspondence between Euripides' representation of Bacchic worship, set in ancient Thebes, and practices current in the late fifth to early fourth centuries B.C.E. (including Athens and elsewhere). Much of Euripides' description is not significantly at odds with other ancient sources.

TRANSLATION: W. Arrowsmith, *The Bacchae,* in David Grene and Richmond Lattimore, eds., *Greek Tragedies,* vol. 3 (Chicago: University of Chicago Press, 1960).

TEXT: OCT (G. Murray, 1901–13); E. R. Dodds, *Euripides' "Bacchae,"* 2d ed. (Oxford: Clarendon Press, 1970).

ADDITIONAL TEXT AND TRANSLATION: LCL (Arthur S. Way, 1912, vol. 3; David Kovacs, 2002).

ADDITIONAL TRANSLATIONS: There are many English translations of *The Bacchae.* Recent ones include David Franklin, *Euripides' "Bacchae": A New Translation and Commentary* (Cambridge: Cambridge University Press, 2000); Reginald Gibbons and Charles Segal, *Euripides' "Bakhai"* (New York: Oxford University Press, 2001); and C. K. Williams, *"The Bacchae" of Euripides: A New Version* (New York: Farrar, Straus, Giroux, 1990). Also of interest is G. S. Kirk, *The Bacchae* (Englewood Cliffs, N.J.: Prentice-Hall, 1970).

BIBLIOGRAPHY: *Blessings,* 36–49; Susan Guettel Cole, "New Evidence for the Mysteries of Dionysos," *GRBS* 21 (1980): 223–38; Synnove Des Bouvrie, "Euripides' *Bakkhai* and Maenadism," *Classica et Mediaevalia* 48 (1997): 75–114; A. Henrichs, "Greek Maenadism from Olympias to Messalina," *HSCP* 82 (1978): 121–60; Eva Keuls, *The Reign of the Phallus* (New York: Harper and Row, 1985); Valdis Leinieks, *The City of Dionysos: A Study of Euripides' "Bakchai"* (Stuttgart: Teubner, 1996); Deborah Lyons, *Gender and Immortality: Heroines in Ancient Greek Myth and Cult* (Princeton: Princeton University Press, 1997); Nancy Sorkin Rabinowitz, *Anxiety Veiled: Euripides and the Traffic in Women* (Ithaca, N.Y.: Cornell University Press, 1993).

Here in Thebes

I bound the fawn-skin to the women's flesh and armed
their hands with shafts of ivy. For I have come   25
to refute that slander spoken by my mother's sisters—

those who least had right to slander her.
They said that Dionysus was no son of Zeus,
but Semele had slept beside a man in love
and fathered off her shame on Zeus—a fraud, they sneered,   30
contrived by Cadmus to protect his daughter's name.
They said she lied, and Zeus in anger at that lie
blasted her with lightning.
                                              Because of that offense
I have stung them with frenzy, hounded them from home
up to the mountains where they wander, crazed of mind,
and compelled to wear my orgies' livery.
Every woman in Thebes—but the women only—   35
I drove from home, mad. There they sit,
rich and poor alike, even the daughters of Cadmus,
beneath the silver firs on the roofless rocks.
Like it or not, this city must learn its lesson:
it lacks initiation in my mysteries;   40
that I shall vindicate my mother Semele
and stand revealed to mortal eyes as the god
she bore to Zeus

2

The Rites of the First Bacchic Worshipers

EURIPIDES *Bacchae* 677–768   405 B.C.E.

NOTE: See entry 1.

MESSENGER   About that hour
when the sun lets loose its light to warm the earth,
our grazing herds of cows had just begun to climb
the path along the mountain ridge. Suddenly
I saw three companies of dancing women,   680
one led by Autonoë, the second captained
by your mother Agave, while Ino led the third.
There they lay in the deep sleep of exhaustion,
some resting on boughs of fir, others sleeping
where they fell, here and there among the oak leaves—   685
but all modestly and soberly, not, as you think,
drunk with wine, nor wandering, led astray
by the music of the flute, to hunt their Aphrodite
through the woods.
                          But your mother heard the lowing

of our hornèd herds, and springing to her feet,   690
gave a great cry to waken them from sleep.
And they too, rubbing the bloom of soft sleep
from their eyes, rose up lightly and straight—
a lovely sight to see: all as one,
the old women and the young and the unmarried girls.
First they let their hair fall loose, down   695
over their shoulders, and those whose straps had slipped
fastened their skins of fawn with writhing snakes
that licked their cheeks. Breasts swollen with milk,
new mothers who had left their babies behind at home
nestled gazelles and young wolves in their arms,   700
suckling them. Then they crowned their hair with leaves,
ivy and oak and flowering bryony. One woman
struck her thyrsus against a rock and a fountain
of cool water came bubbling up. Another drove   705
her fennel in the ground, and where it struck the earth,
at the touch of god, a spring of wine poured out.
Those who wanted milk scratched at the soil
with bare fingers and the white milk came welling up.   710
Pure honey spurted, streaming, from their wands.
If you had been there and seen these wonders for yourself,
you would have gone down on your knees and prayed
to the god you now deny.
                    We cowherds and shepherds
gathered in small groups, wondering and arguing   715
among ourselves at these fantastic things,
the awful miracles those women did.
But then a city fellow with the knack of words
rose to his feet and said: "All you who live
upon the pastures of the mountain, what do you say?
Shall we earn a little favor with King Pentheus   720
by hunting his mother Agave out of the revels?"
Falling in with his suggestion, we withdrew
and set ourselves in ambush, hidden by the leaves
among the undergrowth. Then at a signal
all the Bacchae whirled their wands for the revels
to begin. With one voice they cried aloud:
"O Iacchus! Son of Zeus!" "O Bromius!" they cried   725
until the beasts and all the mountain seemed
wild with divinity. And when they ran,
everything ran with them.
                    It happened, however,

that Agave ran near the ambush where I lay
concealed. Leaping up, I tried to seize her,   730
but she gave a cry: "Hounds who run with me,
men are hunting us down! Follow, follow me!
Use your wands for weapons."
                          At this we fled
and barely missed being torn to pieces by the women.
Unarmed, they swooped down upon the herds of cattle   735
grazing there on the green of the meadow. And then
you could have seen a single woman with bare hands
tear a fat calf, still bellowing with fright,
in two, while others clawed the heifers to pieces.
There were ribs and cloven hooves scattered everywhere,   740
and scraps smeared with blood hung from the fir trees.
And bulls, their raging fury gathered in their horns,
lowered their heads to charge, then fell, stumbling
to the earth, pulled down by hordes of women   745
and stripped of flesh and skin more quickly, sire,
than you could blink your royal eyes. Then,
carried up by their own speed, they flew like birds
across the spreading fields along Asopus' stream
where most of all the ground is good for harvesting.   750
Like invaders they swooped on Hysiae
and on Erythrae in the foothills of Cithaeron.
Everything in sight they pillaged and destroyed.
They snatched the children from their homes. And when
they piled their plunder on their backs, it stayed in place,   755
untied. Nothing, neither bronze nor iron,
fell to the dark earth. Flames flickered
in their curls and did not burn them. Then the villagers,
furious at what the women did, took to arms.
And *there*, sire, was something terrible to see.   760
For the men's spears were pointed and sharp, and yet
drew no blood, whereas the wands the women threw
inflicted wounds. And then the men *ran*,
routed by women! Some god, I say, was with them.
The Bacchae then returned where they had started,   765
by the springs the god had made, and washed their hands
while the snakes licked away the drops of blood
that dabbled their cheeks.

Observances, Rituals, and Festivals

15

3

Women Worshipers of a Dionysian Deity, Sabos

DEMOSTHENES *On the Crown* 259–60   4th century B.C.E.

AUTHOR: Thought by many to be the greatest of the Athenian orators, Demosthenes (384–322 B.C.E.) is the author of *On the Crown*, which is considered by some to be his greatest oration. It was written as a defense against the accusations of his long-standing opponent Aeschines and concerned Demosthenes' actions during the wars with Philip of Macedon. Although most of Demosthenes' orations similarly address the military-political situation, he did argue some private cases. One oration attributed to him, *Against Neaera*, has received considerable attention from feminist classicists. As is often the case with passages that may shed light on women's practices, the excerpt from *On the Crown* is only incidentally concerned with women themselves. Demosthenes' intent is to impugn Aeschines by accusing him of participating in his mother's religious activities. These accusations feminize Aeschines and impugn his masculinity. Demosthenes' point is ultimately not simply that these activities are questionable (which they may or may not be) but that they are the rites of women.

TRANSLATION: RSK.

TEXT: OCT (S. H. Butcher, [1903] 1966, 1:221–332).

ADDITIONAL TEXTS AND TRANSLATIONS: LCL (C. A. Vince and J. H. Vince, 1926); S. Usher, *Demosthenes' "On the Crown," Translated with Introduction and Commentary* (Warminster, U.K.: Aris and Phillips, 1993).

BIBLIOGRAPHY: *Blessings*, 39–41; Ross S. Kraemer, " '*Euoi Saboi*' in Demosthenes' *De Corona*: In Whose Honor Were the Women's Rites?" *SBLSP* 20 (1981): 229–36.

NOTE: A *thiasos* is a cultic association; a *liknon* is a type of basket used to carry devotional objects.

> On attaining manhood, you abetted your mother in her initiations and the other rituals, and read aloud from the cultic writings. At night, you mixed the libations, purified the initiates, and dressed them in fawnskins. You cleansed them off with clay and cornhusks, and raising them up from the purification, you led the chant, "The evil I flee, the better I find." . . . In the daylight, you led the fine *thiasos* through the streets, wearing their garlands of fennel and white poplar. You rubbed the fat-cheeked snakes and swung them above your head crying, "Euoi Saboi," and dancing to the tune of *"hues attes, attes hues."* Old women hailed you "Leader," "mysteries instructor," "ivy bearer," "*liknon* carrier," and the like.

◉ 4
Rituals for Brides and Pregnant Women in the Worship of Artemis

LSCG Suppl. 115   4th century B.C.E.

WORK: This inscription found at Cyrene prescribes rites for brides and pregnant women in the temple and festivals of the Greek goddess Artemis (the virgin twin sister of Apollo), who was associated with both virginity and fertility. In the Roman period, Artemis was the patron deity of the city of Ephesos, a major metropolis on the western coast of Asia Minor (modern Turkey). For an overview of the use of inscriptions in the study of women's religions, see the Introduction to section 2.

TRANSLATION: Lefkowitz and Fant, p. 120, no. 125.

TEXT: *LSCG Suppl.* 115 = *SEG* 9.72.13–16.

BIBLIOGRAPHY: *Blessings*, 22–29; Susan Guettel Cole, "Domesticating Artemis," in Sue Blundell and Margaret Williamson, eds., *The Sacred and the Feminine in Ancient Greece* (New York: Routledge, 1998), 27–43; Helen King, "Bound to Bleed: Artemis and Greek Women," in Averil Cameron, ed., *Images of Women in Antiquity*, rev. ed. (Detroit: Wayne State University Press, 1993), 109–27; Jennifer Larson, "Handmaidens of Artemis?" *Classical Journal* 92, no. 3 (1997): 249–57.

> 13 [If a bride comes to the dormi]tory, she must sacrifice as a penalty to Artemis. She must not share a roof with her husband and must not be polluted; she must purify the temple of Artemis and as penalty sacrifice a full-grown victim, and then she should go to the dormitory. If she pollutes involuntarily, she must purify the temple.
>
> 14 A bride must make a ceremonial visit to the bride-room at the temple of Artemis at the festival of Artemis, whenever she wishes, but the sooner the better. If she does not make her ceremonial visit, she must make the regular sacrifice to Artemis at the festival of Artemis as one who has made no visit, and she must purify the temple and sacrifice a victim as penalty.
>
> 15 [A pregnant woman] shall make a ceremonial visit [before birth] to the bride-room in the precinct of Artemis and give the Bear priestess feet and head and skin of the sacrifice. If she does not make a ceremonial visit before giving birth she must make a visit afterwards with a full-grown victim. If she makes a ceremonial visit to the temple she must observe ritual purity on the seventh, eighth, and ninth day, and if she does not make a visit, she must perform the rites on these days. If she is polluted, she must purify herself and the temple and sacrifice a full-grown victim as penalty.
>
> 16 If a woman miscarries, if the foetus is fully formed, they are polluted as if by a death; if it is not fully formed, the household is polluted as if from childbirth.

● 5
Objects Dedicated to Artemis Brauronia

IG II² 1514   4th century B.C.E.

WORK: This inscription found at Brauron, Greece, lists the gifts brought by various women worshipers to the temple of Artemis at Brauron, where a festival called the Arkteia (the Bear Festival) was celebrated. For an overview of the use of inscriptions in the study of women's religions, see the Introduction to section 2.

TRANSLATION: Lefkowitz and Fant, p. 120, no. 123.

TEXT: *IG* II² 1514.

BIBLIOGRAPHY: *Blessings*, 22–29; Liliane Bodsen, "L'initiation artemisiaque," in Ries Julien, ed., *Les Rites d'Initiation: Actes du Colloque de Liege et de Louvain-la-Neuve, 20–21 Novembre 1984* (Louvain-la-Neuve: Le Centre, 1986), 299–315; Susan Guettel Cole, "The Social Function of Rituals of Maturation: The Koureion and the Arkteia," *ZPE* 55 (1984): 233–44; Robert Louis Fowler, "Greek Magic, Greek Religion," *Illinois Classical Studies* 20 (1995): 1–22; Lilly Kahil, "L'Artémis de Brauron: Rites et Mystère," *Antike Kunst* 20 (1977): 86–98; Lilly Kahil, "Le sanctuaire de Brauron et la religion grecque," *Comptes rendus de l'Académie des Inscriptions et Belles-Lettres* (November 1988): 799–813; M. B. Walbank, "Artemis Bear-Leader," *Classical Quarterly* 31 (1981): 276–81.

> Archipe [dedicated] a dotted, sleeved tunic in a box during the year Callima-
> chus was archon. Callippe a short tunic, scalloped and embroidered; it has
> letters woven in. Chaerippe and Eucoline, a dotted tunic in a box. Philumene
> a silken tunic, in the year Theophilus was archon. Pythias a dotted robe in
> the year Themistocles was archon. There is an embroidered purple tunic;
> Thyaene and Malthace dedicated it. Phile [dedicated] a woman's girdle; Phei-
> dylla a white woman's cloak in a box. Mneso a frog-green garment. Nausis a
> woman's cloak, with a broad purple border in a wave design.

● 6
Women Participants at a Festival of Adonis

THEOCRITUS *Idyll* 15, 95–149   3d century B.C.E.

AUTHOR: Theocritus (ca. 300-260 B.C.E.) was a bucolic poet from Syracuse, Sicily, who eventually won the admiration of Ptolemy Philadelphus, the king of Egypt. Theocritus is not a major source for women's religions, except for his *Idyll*, excerpted here. The poem, on the worshipers of Adonis, is set in the city of Alexandria in Egypt, where Theocritus lived for some time. The festival of Adonis (originally a Phoenician deity), was celebrated in late July and mourned the death of this beautiful young god, the consort of Aphrodite. Many of Theocritus's other poems concern the vicissitudes of romantic love.

TRANSLATION: Anthony Verity, Theocritus "Idylls," with an Introduction and Explanatory Notes by Richard Hunter (New York: Oxford University Press, 2002).

TEXT AND TRANSLATION: A. S. F. Gow, Theocritus (Cambridge: Cambridge University Press, 1950), vol. 1, 108–21.

ADDITIONAL TRANSLATIONS: LCL (J. M. Edmonds, 1977); Thelma Sargent, The Idylls of Theocritus: A Verse Translation (New York: Norton, 1982).

BIBLIOGRAPHY: Blessings, 30–35; Joan B. Burton, Theocritus's Urban Mimes: Mobility, Gender, and Patronage (Berkeley: University of California Press, 1995); Marcel Detienne, The Gardens of Adonis: Spices in Greek Mythology, trans. Janet Lloyd (Atlantic Highlands, N.J.: Humanities Press, 1977); Frederick T. Griffiths, "Home before Lunch: The Emancipated Woman in Theocritus," in Helene P. Foley, ed., Reflections of Women in Antiquity (New York: Gordon and Breach, 1981), 247–73; Marilyn B. Skinner, "Ladies' Day at the Art Institute: Theocritus, Herodas, and the Gendered Gaze," in André Lardinois and Laura McClure, eds., Making Silence Speak: Women's Voices in Greek Literature and Society (Princeton: Princeton University Press, 2001), 201–22; John J. Winkler, "The Laughter of the Oppressed: Demeter and the Gardens of Adonis," in The Constraints of Desire: The Anthropology of Sex and Gender in Ancient Greece (New York and London: Routledge, 1990), 188–209.

GORGO Hush, Praxinoa, she's going to sing the *Song of Adonis*— 95
   The Argive woman's daughter, that brilliant singer, the one
   Who won the prize last year in the lament. She'll put on
   A good performance, I'm sure. Listen, she's clearing her throat.

THE SINGER Mistress, you who love Golgi, sheer Eryx and Idalium, 100
   Aphrodite, whose sport is golden. See how after a year
   The soft-footed Hours have brought you back Adonis from
   Ever-flowing Acheron—the dear Hours, slowest of the gods,
   Yet all men long for them, for they always bring some gift.
   Cypris, Dione's child, you made mortal Berenice an immortal,
   So men say, sprinkling ambrosia on to her woman's breast.
   And so in your honour, many-shrined and many-named goddess,
   Arsinoa, daughter of Berenice, who resembles Helen, 110
   Now pampers Adonis with delights of every kind.
   Before him are laid in season the burden of fruit trees,
   And delicate plants preserved in baskets of silver,
   And Syrian perfume in jars of gold. Cakes, too, such as
   Women knead, by mixing all manner of colours with
   White wheat flour; and others of sweet honey and moist oil.
   All creatures that inhabit the air and the earth attend him.

Beside him there are fashioned fresh green bowers, heavy with
Soft dill. Boy Loves fly above, like fledgling nightingales   120
Swooping from branch to branch as they try out their wings.
O gold, O ebony, O eagles of white ivory that carry off
To Zeus the son of Cronos a boy to pour his wine.
And the couch's red coverlets, softer than sleep! Milesian women
And shepherds of Samos will say, 'We made the coverlets
For beautiful Adonis' couch.' Cypris embraces him
In her arms, and Adonis' rosy arms hold her. The groom
Is eighteen, nineteen; his kisses do not prick her,
For his lip is covered with nothing but reddish down.   130

Now farewell to Cypris, who holds her lover in her arms.
At dawn, with the dew, we shall bear him in a group
Down to where the waves splash on the shore. Then, with
Our hair flowing free, breasts bare, and our dresses sweeping
Our ankles, we shall strike up the clear and piercing song.

Dear Adonis, you alone of all other demigods, men say, haunt
Both this world and Acheron. Fate would not grant Agamemnon
This gift, nor great Ajax, that hero heavy in anger, nor Hector,
Eldest of Hecuba's twenty sons; not Patroclus, nor Pyrrhus
Returned from Troy, nor even the Lapiths of old, nor Deucalion   141
And his people; nor the descendants of Pelops, nor the
Pelasgian kings of Argos. Be gracious to us, dear Adonis,
Again next year. This year's visitation made us joyful,
And when you come again you will find a welcome.

GORGO She is such a clever creature, that woman, Praxinoa:
Lucky to know so much, and luckier still to have
Such a lovely voice. But it's time to go home—Diocleidas
Has not had his lunch, and he has a sharp temper; it's best to
Leave him alone when he's hungry. Be happy, beloved Adonis,
And may you find *us* happy when you come back here again.

● 7

Ritual Regulations in a Dionysiac *Thiasos*

LSAM 48   276/275 B.C.E.

WORK: This inscription from Miletus, in western Turkey, regulates the practices
of priestesses and women worshipers of Dionysos. For an overview of the use of
inscriptions in the study of women's religions, see the Introduction to section 2.

TRANSLATION: A. Henrichs in Lefkowitz and Fant, p. 113, no. 113.

TEXT: *LSAM* 48.

BIBLIOGRAPHY: See entry 1.

> Whenever the priestess performs the holy rites on behalf of the city . . . , it is not permitted for anyone to throw pieces of raw meat [anywhere], before the priestess has thrown them on behalf of the city, nor is it permitted for anyone to assemble a band of maenads [*thiasos*] before the public *thiasos* [has been assembled]. . . .
>
> . . . to provide [for the women] the implements for initiation in all the orgies . . .
>
> And whenever a woman wishes to perform an initiation for Dionysus Bacchius in the city, in the countryside, or on the islands, she must pay a piece of gold to the priestess at each biennial celebration.

● 8

Epitaph of Alcmeonis, a Priestess of Dionysos

Henrichs *HSCP* 82 (1978): 148   3d or 2d century B.C.E.

WORK: This inscription from Miletus, in western Turkey, commemorates a priestess of Dionysos. For an overview of the use of inscriptions in the study of women's religions, see the Introduction to section 2.

TEXT AND TRANSLATION: Albert Henrichs, "Greek Maenadism from Olympias to Messalina," *HSCP* 82 (1978): 148.

BIBLIOGRAPHY: See entry 1.

> Bacchae of the City, say "Farewell you holy priestess." This is what a good woman deserves. She led you to the mountain and carried all the sacred objects and implements, marching in procession before the whole city. Should some stranger ask for her name: Alcmeonis, daughter of Rhodius, who knew her share of the blessings.

● 9

The Establishment of Dionysiac Rites in Magnesia

I. Magn. 215a: 24–40   3d century B.C.E.

WORK: This inscription from Delphi authorizes the establishment of maenadic rites to Dionysos in the city of Magnesia in ancient Asia Minor (modern Turkey). For an overview of the use of inscriptions in the study of women's religions, see the Introduction to section 2.

TRANSLATION: A. Henrichs in Lefkowitz and Fant, pp. 113–14, no. 115.

Observances, Rituals, and Festivals

TEXT: *I. Magn.* 215a: 24–40.

BIBLIOGRAPHY: See entry 1.

Go to the holy plain of Thebes to fetch maenads from the race of Cadmean Ino. They will bring you maenadic rites and noble customs and will establish troops of Bacchus in your city.

In accordance with the oracle, and through the agency of the envoys, three maenads were brought from Thebes: Cosco, Baubo and Thettale. And Cosco organised the thiasus named after the plane tree, Baubo the thiasus outside the city, and Thettale the thiasus named after Cataebates. After their death they were buried by the Magnesians, and Cosco lies buried in the area called Hillock of Cosco, Baubo in the area called Tabarnis, and Thettale near the theatre.

● **10**

Ritual Equipment for a Women's Festival in Hellenistic Egypt

P. Hibeh 54   3d century B.C.E.

WORK: This letter on papyrus from Egypt requests the recipient to send musicians to play at a women's festival. For an overview of the use of papyri in the study of women's religions, see the Introduction to section 2.

TRANSLATION: M. Lefkowitz in Lefkowitz and Fant, p. 116, no. 114.

TEXT: *P. Hibeh* 54.

Demophon to Ptolemaeus, greetings. Send us at your earliest opportunity the flautist Petoun with the Phrygian flutes, plus the other flutes. If it's necessary to pay him, do so, and we will reimburse you. Also send us the eunuch Zenobius with a drum, cymbals and castanets. The women need them for their festival. Be sure he is wearing his most elegant clothing. Get the special goat from Aristion and send it to us. ... Send us also as many cheeses as you can, a new jug, and vegetables of all kinds, and fish if you have it. Your health! Throw in some policemen at the same time to accompany the boat.

● **11**

Three Excerpts from Ovid on the Rites of Roman Women

OVID *Fasti*   1st century B.C.E. or 1st century C.E.

AUTHOR: A prolific writer, Ovid (43 B.C.E.–17 C.E.) abandoned public service to take up poetry, eventually becoming the leading Roman poet of his time. For reasons still undetermined, he fell out of favor with the emperor Augustus and was banished to Tomis, on the Black Sea. He is probably best known for his *Metamorphoses* and his love poems, collected in *Amores* and *Ars amatoria* (*The Art of Love*). The latter contains three books on the arts of seduction, two written for men and a third added for women. His *Fasti*, or *Festival Calendar*, which covers January through June, is the work of most interest to scholars of religion and contains a number of references to women's religious activities.

TEXT: Teubner (D. E. W. Wormell and E. Courtney, 1978).

BIBLIOGRAPHY: *Blessings*, 50–70; Ariadne Staples, *From Good Goddess to Vestal Virgins: Sex and Category in Roman Religion* (London: Routledge, 1998).

● 11A

Roman Matrons Who Celebrate the Matralia (A Festival to the Goddess, Mother Matuta)

OVID *Fasti* 6.473–568

TRANSLATION: A. J. Boyle and R. D. Woodard, *Ovid, "Fasti"* (London: Penguin Books, 2000).

ADDITIONAL TRANSLATION: Betty Rose Nagle, *"Ovid's Fasti": Roman Holidays* (Bloomington: Indiana University Press, 1995).

> JUNE 11, *MATRALIA NEFASTUS (PUBLICUS)*
>
> Phrygian Tithonus, you complain your bride departs,
>   And watchful Lucifer leaves the eastern waves.
> Go, good mothers (the *Matralia* is your feast)   475
>   And give the Theban goddess golden cakes.
> By the bridges and the great Circus is a busy square
>   Named after its statue of an ox.
> There on this day, it is said, Servius' sceptred hands
>   Gave Mother Matuta a holy shrine.   480
> Who is the goddess? Why does she bar slave girls (she does!)
>   From her temple door and request hot cakes?
> Bacchus of the ivy-clad, berried hair, if this house
>   Belongs to you, direct the poet's work.
>
> Jove's compliance had burned Semele. Ino takes you,   485
>   Child, and suckles you with utmost care.
> Juno ballooned at her rearing a whore-snatched son;
>   But his blood was that of Ino's sister.
> Furies and false visions hound Athamas: you fall,
>   Little Learchus, by your father's hand.   490
> The grieving mother entombed Learchus' shade
>   And performed all rites due to piteous pyres.

After clawing her deathly hair, she, too, runs wild
   And rips you, Melicertes, from your cot.
Confined to a small space, rebuffing twin straits,   495
   Is a single land pounded by two seas.
She comes here frenzied, clutching her son, and hurls him
   With her in the deep from a soaring crag.
Panope and her hundred sisters receive them
   Unharmed, and glide them gently through their realm.   500
(Not yet) Leucothea, (not yet) the boy Palaemon
   Reach the thick whirlpools at the Tiber's mouth.
There was a grove (of Semele or Stimula—who knows?);
   They say Ausonian Maenads lived there.
Ino asks them what race they are. She hears they are   505
   Arcadians and Evander rules the place.
Saturnia, cloaking her godhead, pricks the Bacchantes
   Of Latium with false, insidious words:
"O so naïve, o so blind in all your hearts,
   This stranger comes as no friend to our group.   510
She is a spy and aims to learn our sacred rites.
   There is a sure way of punishing her."
She had hardly finished; the Thyiads fill the breezes
   With howling, as hair streams down their necks.
They lay hands on the boy and fight to wrench him away.   515
   Ino invokes deities yet unknown:
"Gods and men of the place, help a pitiful mother."
   Her cry hits the Aventine's nearby rocks.
The Oetaean had herded his Hiberian cows
   To the stream; he hears and runs to the voice.   520
Hercules' arrival nudged the women's threats
   Of violence into base, female flight.
"What do you want here," (he recognized her) "Bacchus' aunt?
   Or does the same god plague you and me?"
She tells some things. Her son's presence stops her in part;   525
   She is ashamed that madness made her sin.
Rumour, rapid as it is, flies on beating wings,
   And your name, Ino, is on many lips.
It is said you entered Carmenta's faithful house
   As a guest, and ended your long famine.   530
Tradition claims Tegea's priestess offered cakes
   Rushed by hand and cooked on a hasty hearth.
Today, too, the goddess loves cakes at the *Matralia*;
   Rustic kindness delights her more than art.

"Now," she says, "o seer, unseal the coming fates,   535
    If it's allowed. Crown my welcome with this."
There is a small delay. The seer absorbs heaven's power
    And her whole breast bulges with her god.
At once you would hardly know her; she was so much
    Holier and mightier than just now.   540
"I'll sing pure joy. Rejoice at your toil's end, Ino,"
    She said, "and always favour this people.
You'll be a sea goddess; ocean, too, will take your son.
    Assume different names in your waters.
The Greeks will call you Leucothea, we Matuta.   545
    Your son will have complete control of ports:
*Port*unus to us, Palaemon in his own tongue.
    Go, and, I ask you both, smile on this place."
She nodded, a promise was made. They ended their toil
    And renamed. He is a god, she a goddess.   550

You ask why she bars slave girls from entry? She hates them.
    I'll sing the source of that hate, if she lets me.
One of your female attendants, Cadmeïs,
    Often enjoyed your husband's embraces.
Evil Athamas loved her in secret. She revealed   555
    That you gave the farmers roasted seeds.
You deny it of course, but it is locked in rumour.
    This is why you hate a slave girl's service.
No pious mother should pray to her for her child;
    She seemed not the happiest of parents.   560
You will do better to give her another's child;
    She aided Bacchus more than her children.

"Why rush?" they say she asked you, Rutilius. "Consul,
    When my day dawns, you'll fall to Marsian foe."
Results followed words, and the Tolenus river   565
    Purpled, as the water mingled with blood.
The next year came. At the same rising of Pallantis,
    Butchered Didius doubled the foe's force.

● 11B

Roman Matrons Who Wash the Statue of Venus on April 1

OVID *Fasti* 4.133–62

TRANSLATION: A. J. Boyle and R. D. Woodard, *Ovid, "Fasti"* (London and New York: Penguin Books, 2000).

Yours are the goddess' rites, Latin mothers and brides,
    You, too, without the headband and long gown.
Remove the golden necklace from her marble neck,   135
    Remove the jewels: bathe the goddess whole.
Dry her neck and return the golden necklace to it;
    Then dress her with flowers and new roses.
She tells you, too, to bathe beneath the green myrtle,
    And the cause of this (learn it!) is certain.   140
She was naked on a beach, drying her dripping hair,
    When a randy band of satyrs saw her.
She noticed them and screened her body with myrtle.
    This saved her; and she tells you to repeat it.
Now learn why you give incense to Fortuna Virilis   145
    In a place sodden with cooling water.
That place welcomes all women stripped of their clothing
    And views every flaw of naked bodies.
Fortuna Virilis vows to screen these flaws from men,
    And answers prayers after a little incense.   150
Do not flinch at the poppy crushed in snowy milk
    And the liquid honey squeezed from the comb.
When Venus was first led to her lusting husband,
    She drank this. She was a wife thereafter.
Appease her with suppliant words. Her power secures   155
    Beauty and character and noble fame.

Rome fell from chastity in our ancestors' time.
    You ancients consulted Cumae's crone.
She orders a shrine to Venus. It was duly built,
    And Venus henceforth named "Heart-Changer."   160
Fairest, always view the Aeneadae with kindness,
    and protect, goddess, your many daughters.

● 11C

The Ritual Practices of an Old Woman

OVID *Fasti* 2.571–82

TRANSLATION AND BIBLIOGRAPHY: Gager, *Curse Tablets,* 252.

An old woman sits among girls and performs rites in honor of Tacita ("Silent
One"), though she herself does not remain silent. With three fingers she puts
three lumps of incense under the threshold where the little mouse has made
a secret path for her. Then she binds enchanted threads together with dark

lead and mutters with seven black beans in her mouth. She roasts in the fire
the head of a small fish which she has sewn up, sealed with pitch and pierced
with a bronze needle. She also drops wine on it. . . . Then, as she leaves, she
says, "We have bound up hostile tongues and unfriendly mouths."

● 12
Women's Rites of Dionysos in Greek Cities

DIODORUS OF SICILY *Library* 4.3.2–5   1st century B.C.E.

AUTHOR: Originally from Agyrium, in Sicily, Diodorus remains an enigmatic figure. The exact dates of his life are not known, but his works are thought to date
from 60 to 30 B.C.E. His forty-volume history of the world drew extensively on
the works of various earlier historians and annalists. Although his work has been
considered undistinguished by modern scholars, it contains some intriguing references to the religious activities of women, including the one excerpted here.
Regrettably, because he depended so heavily on other authors, it is particularly
difficult to assess the reliability of his information.

TRANSLATION: LCL (C. H. Oldfather, C. L. Sherman, R. M. Geer, and F. R. Wal-
ton, 1933–67, 12 vols.).

TEXT: Teubner (F. Vogel, C. T. Fisher, and L. Dindorf [1887] 1970–85, 6 vols.).

ADDITIONAL TRANSLATION: F. M. Salter and H. L. R. Edwards, eds., *The "Bibliotheca Historica" of Diodorus Siculus*, trans. John Skelton, 2 vols. (New York:
Oxford University Press, 1968–71).

BIBLIOGRAPHY: See entry 1.

And the Boetians and other Greeks and the Thracians, in memory of the
campaign in India, have established sacrifices every other year to Dionysus,
and believe that at that time the god reveals himself to human beings. Consequently in many Greek cities every other year Bacchic bands of women
gather, and it is lawful for the maidens to carry the thyrsus and to join in the
frenzied revelry, crying out "Euai!" and honouring the god; while the matrons, forming in groups, offer sacrifices to the god and celebrate his mysteries and, in general, extol with hymns the presence of Dionysus, in this manner acting the part of the Maenads who, as history records, were of old the
companions of the god. He also punished here and there throughout all the
inhabited world many men who were thought to be impious, the most renowned among the number being Pentheus and Lycurgus. And since the discovery of wine and the gift of it to human beings were the source of such
great satisfaction to them, both because of the pleasure which derives from
the drinking of it and because of the greater vigour which comes to the bodies of those who partake of it, it is the custom, they say, when unmixed wine

is served during a meal to greet it with the words, "To the Good Deity!" but when the cup is passed around after the meal diluted with water, to cry out "To Zeus Saviour!" For the drinking of unmixed wine results in a state of madness, but when it is mixed with the rain from Zeus the delight and pleasure continue, but the ill effect of madness and stupor is avoided. And, in general, the myths relate that the gods who receive the greatest approval at the hands of human beings are those who excelled in their benefactions by reason of their discovery of good things, namely, Dionysus and Demeter, the former because he was the discoverer of the most pleasing drink, the latter because she gave to the race of men the most excellent of the dry foods.

● 13
Women Members of a Monastic Jewish Community Outside Alexandria

PHILO *On the Contemplative Life* 2, 32–33, 65–69, 83–85, 87–89   1st century C.E.

AUTHOR: The best known of ancient Jewish philosophers, Philo of Alexandria came from a prominent family with extensive ties to the ruling Roman elite in the first century C.E. His brother, Alexander, was the alabarch of Egypt, and his nephew Tiberius Julius Alexander was procurator of Judea, prefect of Egypt, and a staff general for Titus during the siege of Jerusalem. Another nephew, Marcus Julius Alexander, appears to have been briefly married to Berenice, a member of the Herodian royal family in Judea (who herself was later the lover of the Roman emperor Titus). Philo's prolific writings include lengthy allegorical interpretations of Jewish Scriptures (which he read in his native Greek) and a small number of apologetic treatises with significant historical content. His *Embassy to Gaius* describes an embassy he undertook with other Jewish leaders to plead the cause of Alexandrian Jews before the emperor Gaius Caligula (37–41 C.E.), and several of his writings offer descriptions of contemporaneous ascetic communities, including the Essenes and a monastic group of philosophers usually known as the Therapeutae. Philo's allegorical method was extremely attractive to later generations of Alexandrian Christian biblical exegetes, and his writings were ultimately preserved, not by Jews, but by Christians.

Although Philo provides relatively little concrete information about either Jewish women or Jewish men in first-century Alexandria, occasional observations and hints are interspersed throughout his writings, which also make extensive use of gender as a category of analysis and interpretation. His description of the women philosophers whom he calls Therapeutrides is fascinating, although scholars continue to puzzle over whether such a community actually existed or was a product of Philo's utopian imagination. Also of interest is Philo's interpretation of female figures in the Jewish Scriptures, such as Sarah, Rachael, and Rebecca, and his occasional use of feminine language for aspects of the divine.

TRANSLATION: Joan E. Taylor, *Jewish Women Philosophers of First-Century Alexandria: Philo's "Therapeutae" Reconsidered* (Oxford: Oxford University Press, 2003).

TEXT: Leopold Cohn and Paul Wendlandt, *Philonis Operae Quae Supersunt*, 7 vols. in 8 (Berlin: George Reimer, 1896–1930).

ADDITIONAL TEXT AND TRANSLATION: LCL (F. H. Colson, G. H. Whitaker, W. Earp, and R. Marcus, 1929–62, 12 vols.).

ADDITIONAL TRANSLATIONS: Gail Paterson Corrington, "Philo, *On the Contemplative Life:* or, *The Suppliants* (The Fourth Book on the Virtues)," in Vincent L. Wimbush, ed., *Ascetic Behavior in Greco-Roman Antiquity: A Sourcebook*, Studies in Antiquity and Christianity (Minneapolis: Fortress Press, 1990), 134–55; D. Winston, *Philo of Alexandria: The "Contemplative Life," the "Giants," and Selections*, Classics of Western Spirituality (New York: Paulist Press, 1981)

BIBLIOGRAPHY: *Blessings*, 113–17; Richard Baer, *Philo's Use of the Categories Male and Female* (Leiden: E. J. Brill, 1970); Troels Engberg-Pedersen, "Philo's De Vita Contemplativa as a Philosopher's Dream," *JSJ* 30 (1999): 40–64; David Hay, "Things Philo Did and Did Not Say about the Therapeutae," *SBLSP* 31 (1992): 673–83; Ross S. Kraemer, "Monastic Jewish Women in Greco-Roman Egypt: Philo Judaeus on the Therapeutrides," *Signs: Journal of Women in Culture and Society* 14, no. 2 (1989): 342–70; Peter G. Richardson and Valerie Heuchan, "Jewish Voluntary Associations in Egypt and the Roles of Women," in John S. Kloppenborg and Stephen G. Wilson, eds., *Voluntary Associations in the Graeco-Roman World* (London and New York: Routledge, 1996), 226–51; Dorothy Sly, *Philo's Perception of Women*, BJS 209 (Atlanta: Scholars Press, 1990); Holger Szesnat, " 'Mostly Aged Virgins': Philo and the Presence of the Therapeutrides at Lake Mareotis," *Neotestamentica* 32 (1998): 191–201; Taylor, *Jewish Women Philosophers in First-Century Alexandria*; Joan E. Taylor, "Virgin Mothers: Philo on the Women Therapeutae," *Journal for the Study of the Pseudepigrapha* 12 (2001): 37–63; Joan E. Taylor and Philip R. Davies, "The So-Called Therapeutae of *De Vita Contemplativa*: Identity and Character," *HTR* 91, no. 1 (1998): 3–24.

2 The intention of the philosophers is immediately apparent by the name (given to them), for they are called "(devoted) attendants," male and female, (Greek: *therapeutai* and *therapeutrides*, either because they profess medical skill (to attend/treat the sick) better than that in the cities—for that attends bodies alone, while theirs (attends) souls which have been conquered by terrible and nearly incurable diseases, which are inflicted by pleasures and desires and griefs and fears, by covetous acts and follies and unrighteousness, and the countless multitude of other passions and evils—or else because they have been instructed by Nature and the sacred laws to attend (as cultic servants)

the Being who is better than a Good, purer than a One, and older than a Monad.

32 And this common reverence-place into which they come together on seventh days is a double enclosure: one part (is set apart) for men, and the other is set apart for women. For indeed also women customarily participate in listening (like the men), having the same zeal and purpose.

33 The wall between the areas rises upwards from the ground up to three or four cubits in the form of breastwork, but the upper section going up to the roof is wide open. (This arrangement is) for two reasons: so that the modesty which is becoming to the female nature be preserved, and so that, by their sitting in earshot, everything is easily audible, for nothing obstructs the voice of the speaker.

65 First of all, these people assemble on (every) seventh seventh-day, holding in awe not only the simple number of seven, but also the square (of it). For they know its purity and eternal virginity. And it is also the eve of the great special day which the number fifty has been assigned; fifty being the most holy and natural of numbers, since it is the square of the right handed triangle which is the origin of the composition of the whole universe.

66 So then they come together clothed in white, radiant with the utmost seriousness, when a certain person from the "dailies"—as it is the custom to call those performing these services—gives a sign. Before they recline, they duly stand in order in a row, with their eyes and hands lifted up to heaven. The eyes have been trained to see things worth looking at, and the hands are clean of income, and are not defiled by any gain. They pray to God that they might meet according to His mind and that their feast will be pleasing (to Him).

67 After the prayers the seniors recline following the order of (their) admission. They do not consider as seniors the ones who are old in years and aged, but still they may be regarded entirely as "children" if they have come to love the practice only recently. They are those who from early youth have matured and grown up in the contemplative part of philosophy, which indeed is the most beautiful and godly.

68 Women eat together (here) also. They are mostly elderly virgins. They strongly maintain the purity, not out of necessity, as some of the priestesses of the Greeks (do), but out of their own free will, because of a zeal and yearning for Wisdom, which they are eager to live with. They take no heed of the pleasures of the body, and desire not a mortal offspring, but an immortal one, which only a soul which is loved by God is able to give birth to, by itself, because the Father has sown in it lights of intelligence which enable her to see the doctrines of Wisdom.

69 The (order of) reclining is divided, with men by themselves on the right, and women by themselves on the left. Surely no one by chance supposes that (they have) mattresses, which are not in fact expensive but still softer for people of good birth and erudite (conversation) who are trained in philosophy? (No indeed), for (the couches) are rough beds of cheap wood, upon which are altogether frugal strewings of local papyrus, slightly raised at the bend of the arm (so that) they can lean on them. For while they modify the Laconian harsh way of life a little, always and everywhere they practise noble contentment, and they hate with all their might the charms of pleasure.

83 After the dinner they celebrate the sacred (eve) all night. And the night festival is celebrated in this way. They all stand up together and, firstly, place themselves in the middle of the dining room in two choirs, one of men and the other of women. The leader and chief is selected for each one as being the most honoured and also most musical.

84 Then they sing hymns to God composed of many metres and melodies, singing all together, then again antiphonically and harmonically, tapping time with hands and feet, engaging in procession, then continuous song, and in the turns and counter-turns of choral dancing.

85 When each of the choirs has sated itself by itself—as in the Bacchic rites they drink the liquor of the god's love—they blend together and become one choir from out of two, a memory of the one established of old by the Red Sea, by reason of the wonderful works there.

87 Seeing and experiencing this (salvation), which is a work greater than in word, thought and hope, both men and women were filled with inspiration and became a choir singing hymns of thanksgiving to God the Saviour. The men were led by Moses the prophet, and the women by Miriam the prophetess.

88 On this (model) most of all the choir of the (devoted) attendants—male and female—is based. They sing with (canonic) echoes and re-echoes, with men having the bass parts and women the treble, combined together, and resulting in a really musical harmonious concord. The thoughts are lovely, the words are lovely, the choral singers are majestic, and the purpose of the thoughts and the words and the choral singers is piety.

89 So they are drunk (in this way) until dawn, with this beautiful drunkenness, with no heavy head or dosing, but (rather) they are roused more awake than when they came into the dining room. Then they stand with eyes and their whole bodies (turned) to the east, and when they see the rising sun, they stretch out their hands up to heaven, and pray for a "bright day" and truth and clearness of reasoning. And after the prayers they go back into each their own reverence-place, again to ply their trade and cultivate the use of philosophy.

(Jewish?) Women in Alexandrian Public Life

PHILO *The Special Laws* 3.169–75   1st century C.E.

TRANSLATION, TEXT, AND BIBLIOGRAPHY: See entry 13.

169 Market-places and council-halls and law-courts and gatherings and meet-ings where a large number of people are assembled, and open-air life with full scope for discussion and action—all these are suitable to men both in war and peace. The women are best suited to the indoor life which never strays from the house, within which the middle door is taken by the maidens as their boundary, and the outer door by those who have reached full wom-anhood.

170 Organized communities are of two sorts, the greater which we call cities and the smaller which we call households. Both of these have their governors; the government of the greater is assigned to men under the name of states-manship, that of the lesser, known as household management, to women.

171 A woman, then, should not be a busybody, meddling with matters out-side her household concerns, but should seek a life of seclusion. She should not shew herself off like a vagrant in the streets before the eyes of other men, except when she has to go to the temple, and even then she should take pains to go, not when the market is full, but when most people have gone home, and so like a free-born lady worthy of the name, with everything quiet around her, make her oblations and offer her prayers to avert the evil and gain the good.

172 The audacity of women who when men are exchanging angry words or blows hasten to join in, under the pretext of assisting their husbands in the fray, is reprehensible and shameless in a high degree. And so in wars and campaigns and emergencies which threaten the whole country they are not allowed to take their place according to the judgement of the law, having in view the fitness of things, which it was resolved to keep unshaken always and everywhere and considered to be in itself more valuable than victory or lib-erty or success of any kind.

173 If indeed a woman learning that her husband is being outraged is over-come by the wifely feeling inspired by her love for him and forced by the stress of the emotion to hasten to his assistance, she must not unsex herself by a boldness beyond what nature permits but limit herself to the ways in which a woman can help. For it would be an awful catastrophe if any woman in her wish to rescue her husband from outrage should outrage herself by befouling her own life with the disgrace and heavy reproaches which boldness carried to an extreme entails.

174 What, is a woman to wrangle in the market-place and utter some or other of the words which decency forbids? Should she not when she hears bad language stop her ears and run away? As it is, some of them go to such a length that, not only do we hear amid a crowd of men a woman's bitter tongue venting abuse and contumelious words, but see her hands also used to assault—hands which were trained to weave and spin and not to inflict blows and injuries like pancratiasts and boxers.

175 And while all else might be tolerable, it is a shocking thing, if a woman is so lost to a sense of modesty, as to catch hold of the genital parts of her opponent. The fact that she does so with the evident intention of helping her husband must not absolve her. To restrain her over-boldness she must pay a penalty which will incapacitate herself, if she wishes to repeat the offence, and frighten the more reckless members of her sex into proper behaviour. And the penalty shall be this—that the hand shall be cut off which has touched what decency forbids it to touch.

● 15

The Women's Court of the Jerusalem Temple

JOSEPHUS *The Jewish War* 5.198–200,
Against Apion 2.102–104   1st century C.E.

AUTHOR: The writings of the historian Flavius Josephus constitute our major source for Jewish history in the first century C.E. During the Jewish revolt against Rome (66–73 C.E.), he reluctantly led Jewish forces in Galilee. Ultimately, he surrendered to the Roman general Vespasian, whose favor he claims to have won by predicting Vespasian's elevation to Emperor (which in fact took place shortly thereafter). Vespasian initially enslaved Josephus, but later freed him, giving him the rank of freedperson (and Vespasian's family name, Flavius). After the war, Josephus settled in Rome, where under the patronage of the Flavian emperors, he wrote an account of the War, a history of the Jews, and apologia for Judaism, and a defense of his behavior during the war. It is interesting and significant that although Josephus spent many years living in Rome, he tells us virtually nothing about the Jewish community (or communities) there.

As we might expect, Josephus shows no particular concern for the history of Jewish women per se. Nevertheless, his writings contain significant evidence for aristocratic Jewish women, including the Hellenistic queen, Salome Alexandra; Helena of Adiabene, whose conversion to Judaism he recounts at length [entry 103]; and many women of the royal Hasmonean and Herodian families [entries 60–61]. In addition, his writings contain many occasional references that shed light on Jewish women in the first century C.E.

TRANSLATION (AND TEXT): LCL (H. St. J. Thackeray, R. Marcus, A. Wikgren, and L. H. Feldman, 9 vols., 1926–65).

TEXT: B. Niese, *Flavii Josephii Opera* (Berlin: Wiedmann, [1887–89] 1955); S. A. Naber, *Flavius Josephus, Opera Omnia* (Leipzig: B. G. Teubner, 1888–96).

BIBLIOGRAPHY: Betsey Halperin Amaru, "Portraits of Biblical Women in Josephus' *Antiquities*" *JJS* 39 (1988): 143–70; Cheryl Anne Brown, *No Longer Be Silent: First-Century Jewish Portraits of Biblical Women, Gender and the Biblical Tradition* (Louisville: Westminster/John Knox Press, 1992); Shelly Matthews, "Ladies' Aid: Gentile Noblewomen as Saviors and Benefactors in the *Antiquities*," *HTR* 92 (1999): 199–218; see also entry 60.

JOSEPHUS *The Jewish War* 5.198–200   1st century C.E.

From this again other flights of five steps led up to the gates. Of these there were eight on the north and south, four on either side, and two on the east—necessarily; since in this quarter a special place of worship was walled off for the women, rendering a second gate requisite; this approach opened opposite to the first. On the other sides there was one gate on the south and one on the north giving access to the women's court; for women were not permitted to enter by the others nor yet to pass by way of their own gate beyond the partition wall. This court was, however, thrown open for worship to all Jewish women alike, whether natives of the country or visitors from abroad. The west end of the building had no gate, the wall there being unbroken. The porticoes between the gates, on the inner side of the wall in front of the treasury chambers, were supported by exceedingly beautiful and lofty columns; these porticoes were single, but, except in point of size, in no way inferior to those in the lower court.

JOSEPHUS *Against Apion* 2.102–4   1st century C.E.

All who ever saw our temple are aware of the general design of the building, and the inviolable barriers which preserved its sanctity. It had four surrounding courts, each with its special statutory restrictions. The outer court was open to all, foreigners included; women during their impurity were alone refused admission. To the second court all Jews were admitted and, when uncontaminated by any defilement, their wives; to the third male Jews, if clean and purified; to the fourth the priests robed in their priestly vestments. The sanctuary was entered only by the high-priests, clad in the raiment peculiar to themselves.

Excerpts from Plutarch on Greek and Roman Women's Religions

AUTHOR: A noted philosopher and biographer, Plutarch of Chaeronea (ca. 50–120 C.E.) was particularly interested in religious matters, to which many of his treatises are devoted. His works are now generally divided into two categories, the *Moralia* (essays of varying length on a wide range of topics) and the *Lives*. Plutarch's writings are unusual for their relatively sympathetic and sometimes laudatory representation of women's actions, such as his work *On the Bravery of Women*.

Plutarch was apparently close friends with a priestess named Clea at Delphi (the center of devotion to Apollo where he himself may have served as a priest). Both *On the Bravery of Women*, excerpted in this entry, and his well-known *On Isis and Osiris*, excerpted in entry 129, are dedicated to her. References to women's religions are also scattered throughout his other writings, as in the passage from his *Life of Alexander* and numerous passages from his *Roman Questions*, excerpted here.

BIBLIOGRAPHY: Peter Walcot, "Plutarch on Women," *Symbolae Osloenses* 74 (1999): 163–83; see also entry 11.

● 16A

Devotees of Dionysos Protected by Women from the Town of Amphissa

On the Bravery of Women 13 (*Moralia* 249)   1st or 2d century C.E.

TRANSLATION (AND TEXT): LCL (F. C. Babbitt, 1931, vol. 3).

TEXT: Teubner (W. Nachstädt, W. Sieveking, J. B. Titchener, 1971, vol. 2, fasc. 1).

BIBLIOGRAPHY: See entry 1.

> When the despots in Phocis had seized Delphi, and the Thebans were waging war against them in what has been called the Sacred War, the women devotees of Dionysus, to whom they give the name of Thyads, in Bacchic frenzy wandering at night unwittingly arrived at Amphissa. As they were tired out, and sober reason had not yet returned to them, they flung themselves down in the market-place, and were lying asleep, some here, some there. The wives of the men of Amphissa, fearing, because their city had become allied with the Phocians, and numerous soldiers of the despots were present there, that the Thyads might be treated with indignity, all ran out into the market-place, and, taking their stand round about in silence, did not go up to them while they were sleeping, but when they arose from their slumber, one devoted herself to one of the strangers and another to another, bestowing attentions on them and offering them food. Finally, the women of Amphissa, after winning

the consent of their husbands, accompanied the strangers, who were safely escorted as far as the frontier.

● 16B

The Dionysiac Proclivities of Olympias, Mother of Alexander the Great

Life of Alexander 2.1–5   1st or 2d century C.E.

TRANSLATION (AND TEXT): LCL (B. Perrin, 1919, vol. 7).

TEXT: Budé (R. Flacelière and E. Chambry, 1975, vol. 9); Teubner (K. Ziegler, 1935, vol. 2, fasc. 2, 175–289).

BIBLIOGRAPHY: France LeCorsu, *Plutarque et les femmes dans les Vies Parallèles* (Paris: Les Belles Lettres, 1981).

But concerning these matters there is another story to this effect: all the women of these parts were addicted to the Orphic rites and the orgies of Dionysus from very ancient times (being called Klodones and Mimallones), and imitated in many ways the practices of the Edonian women and the Thracian women about Mount Haemus, from whom, as it would seem, the word "threskeuein" came to be applied to the celebration of extravagant and superstitious ceremonies. Now Olympias, who affected these divine possessions more zealously than other women, and carried out these divine inspirations in wilder fashion, used to provide the revelling companies with great tame serpents, which would often lift their heads from out the ivy and the mystic winnowing-baskets, or coil themselves about the wands and garlands of the women, thus terrifying the men.

● 16C

How Women's Bacchic Frenzy Explains an Epithet of the God (Bacchus)

Roman Questions 104 (*Moralia* 288–89)   1st or 2d century C.E.

TRANSLATION (AND TEXT): LCL (F. C. Babbitt, 1936, vol. 4).

TEXT: See entry 16A.

104 Why do they call Bacchus *Liber Pater* ("Free Father")?

Or was this also a symbolic prohibition of Bacchic revels and orgies? For women possessed by Bacchic frenzies rush straightway for ivy and tear it to pieces, clutching it in their hands and biting it with their teeth; so that not altogether without plausibility are they who assert that ivy, possessing as it does an exciting and distracting breath of madness, deranges persons and agitates them, and in general brings on a wineless drunkenness and joyousness in those that are precariously disposed towards spiritual exaltation.

Why Roman Matrons Founded a Temple to the Goddess Carmenta

Roman Questions 56 (*Moralia* 278)   1st or 2d century C.E.

TRANSLATION (AND TEXT): LCL (F. C. Babbitt, 1936, vol. 4).

TEXT: See entry 16A.

56 Why are the matrons supposed to have founded the temple of Carmenta originally, and why do they reverence it now above all others?

There is a certain tale repeated that the women were prevented by the senate from using horse-drawn vehicles; they therefore made an agreement with one another not to conceive nor to bear children, and they kept their husbands at a distance, until the husbands changed their minds and made the concession to them. When children were born to them, they, as mothers of a fair and numerous progeny, founded the temple of Carmenta.

Some assert that Carmenta was the mother of Evander and that she came to Italy; that her name was Themis, or, as others say, Nicostratê; and that because she chanted oracles in verse, she was named Carmenta by the Latins, for they call verses *carmina*.

But others think that Carmenta is a Fate, and that this is the reason why the matrons sacrifice to her. The true meaning of the name is "deprived of sense," by reason of her divine transports. Wherefore Carmenta was not so named from *carmina*, but rather *carmina* from her, because, in her divine frenzy, she chanted oracles in verse and metre.

● 16E

Why Women Use Milk but Not Wine in Offerings to Rumina

Roman Questions 57 (*Moralia* 278)   1st or 2d century C.E.

TRANSLATION (AND TEXT): LCL (F. C. Babbitt, 1936, vol. 4).

TEXT: See entry 16A.

57 Why do the women that sacrifice to Rumina pour milk over the offerings, but make no oblation of wine in the ceremony?

Is it because the Latins call the teat *ruma*, and assert that Ruminalis acquired its name inasmuch as the she-wolf offered its teat to Romulus? Therefore, as we call wet-nurses *thelonai* from *thele* (teat), even so Rumina is she that gives suck, the nurse and nurturer of children; she does not, therefore, welcome pure wine, since it is harmful for babes.

Gender Distinctions in Sacrifices to Hercules

Roman Questions 60 (*Moralia* 278)   1st or 2d century C.E.

TRANSLATION (AND TEXT): LCL (F. C. Babbitt, 1936, vol. 4).

TEXT: See entry 16A.

> 60 Why, when there are two altars of Hercules, do women receive no share
> nor taste of the sacrifices offered on the larger altar?
>
> Is it because the friends of Carmenta came late for the rites, as did also the
> clan of the Pinarii? Wherefore, as they were excluded from the banquet while
> the rest were feasting, they acquired the name *Pinarii* (Starvelings). Or is it
> because of the fable of Deianeira and the shirt?

● 16G

Why Seduced Vestal Virgins Are Buried Alive

Roman Questions 96 (*Moralia* 286–87)

TRANSLATION (AND TEXT): LCL (F. C. Babbitt, 1936, vol. 4).

TEXT: See entry 16A.

BIBLIOGRAPHY: For bibliography on Vestal Virgins, see entry 81.

> 96 Why do they inflict no other punishment on those of the Holy Maidens
> who have been seduced, but bury them alive?
>
> Is it because they cremate their dead, and to use fire in the burial of a
> woman who had not guarded the holy fire in purity was not right?
>
> Or did they believe it to be against divine ordinance to annihilate a body that
> had been consecrated by the greatest of lustral ceremonies, or to lay hands
> upon a holy woman? Accordingly they devised that she should die of herself;
> they conducted her underground into a chamber built there, in which had
> been placed a lighted lamp, a loaf of bread, and some milk and water.
> Thereafter they covered over the top of the chamber with earth. And yet not
> even by this manner of avoiding the guilt have they escaped their supersti-
> tious fear, but even to this day the priests proceed to this place and make
> offerings to the dead.

● 16H

Why Roman Women Wash Their Heads on the Ides of August

Roman Questions 100 (*Moralia* 287)

TRANSLATION (AND TEXT): LCL (F. C. Babbitt, 1936, vol. 4).

TEXT: See entry 16A.

100 Why is that on the Ides of August, formerly called Sextilis, all the slaves, female and male, keep holiday, and the Roman women make a particular practice of washing and cleansing their heads?

Do the servants have release from work because on this day King Servius was born from a captive maid-servant? And did the washing of their heads begin with the slave-women, because of their holiday, and extend itself to free-born women?

● 17

Excerpts from the Travel Writer Pausanias on Greek Women's Religions

PAUSANIAS *Description of Greece*   mid–2d century C.E.

AUTHOR: We have little biographic information on Pausanias (ca. mid–second century C.E.), the author of the ten-volume *Description of Greece*, an extensive travelogue. Pausanias was particularly fascinated by religious monuments—temples, statues, shrines, and the like—and by religious beliefs and rites. His work is filled with reports of local mythologies and worship, including many accounts of the activities of women.

TRANSLATION (AND TEXT): LCL (W. H. S. Jones, 1918–35, 5 vols.).

TEXT: Teubner (M. H. R. Pereira, 1973–81, 3 vols.).

● 17A

The Public and Secret Rites to Demeter Performed by Elder Women in Corinth

Description of Greece 2 (Corinth) 35.6–8   mid–2d century C.E.

Those who form the procession are followed by men leading from the herd a full-grown cow, fastened with ropes, and still untamed and frisky. Having driven the cow to the temple, some loose her from the ropes that she may rush into the sanctuary, others, who hitherto have been holding the doors open, when they see the cow within the temple, close to the doors. Four old women, left behind inside, are they who dispatch the cow. Whichever gets the chance cuts the throat of the cow with a sickle. Afterwards the doors are opened, and those who are appointed drive up a second cow, and a third after that, and yet a fourth. All are dispatched in the same way by the old women, and the sacrifice has yet another strange feature. On whichever of her sides the first cow falls, all the others must fall on the same. Such is the manner in which the sacrifice is performed by the Hermionians. Before the temple stand a few statues of the women who have served Demeter as her priestess, and on passing inside you see seats on which the old women wait for the cows to be driven in one by one, and images, of no great age, of Athena and Demeter. But the thing itself that they worship more than all else, I never saw, nor yet has any other man, whether stranger or Hermionian. The old women may keep their knowledge of its nature to themselves.

● 17B

The Athletic Contests for Women in Honor of Hera at Elis

Description of Greece 5 (Elis 1) 16.2–8   mid–2d century C.E.

Every fourth year there is woven for Hera a robe by the Sixteen women, and the same also hold games called Heraea. The games consist of foot-races for maidens. These are not all of the same age. The first to run are the youngest; after them come the next in age, and the last to run are the oldest of the maidens. They run in the following way: their hair hangs down, a tunic reaches to a little above the knee, and they bare the right shoulder as far as the breast. These too have the Olympic stadium reserved for their games, but the course of the stadium is shortened for them by about one-sixth of its length. To the winning maidens they give crowns of olive and a portion of the cow sacrificed to Hera. They may also dedicate statues with their names inscribed upon them. Those who administer to the Sixteen are, like the presidents of the games, married women. The games of the maidens too are traced back to ancient times; they say that, out of gratitude to Hera for her marriage with Pelops, Hippodameia assembled the Sixteen Women, and with them inaugurated the Heraea. They relate too that a victory was won by Chloris, the only surviving daughter of the house of Amphion, though with her they say survived one of her brothers. As to the children of Niobe, what I myself chanced to learn about them I have set forth in my account of Argos. Besides the account already given they tell another story about the Sixteen Women as follows. Damophon, it is said, when tyrant of Pisa did much grievous harm to the Eleans. But when he died, since the people of Pisa refused to participate as a people in their tyrant's sins, and the Eleans too became quite ready to lay aside their grievances, they chose a woman from each of the sixteen cities of Elis still inhabited at that time to settle their differences, this woman to be the oldest, the most noble, and the most esteemed of all the women. The cities from which they chose the women were Elis, . . . The women from these cities made peace between Pisa and Elis. Later on they were entrusted with the management of the Heraean games, and with the weaving of the robe for Hera. The Sixteen Women also arrange two choral dances, one called that of Physcoa and the other that of Hippodameia. This Physcoa they say came from Elis in the Hollow, and the name of the parish where she lived was Orthia. She mated they say with Dionysus, and bore him a son called Narcaeus. When he grew up he made war against the neighbouring folk, and rose to great power, setting up moreover a sanctuary of Athena surnamed Narcaea. They say too that Narcaeus and Physcoa were the first to pay worship to Dionysus. So various honours are paid to Physcoa, especially that of the choral dance, named after her and managed by the Sixteen Women. The Eleans still adhere to the other ancient customs, even though some of the cities have been destroyed. For they are now divided into eight tribes, and they choose two women from each. Whatever ritual it is the duty of either the Sixteen Women or the Elean umpires to perform, they do not perform before they have purified themselves with a pig meet for purification and with water. Their purification takes place at the spring Piera. You reach this spring as you go along the flat road from Olympia to Elis.

● 17C

Women's Worship of Eileithyia and Sosipolis at Elis

Description of Greece 5 (Elis 1) 20.2–3   mid–2d century C.E.

At the foot of Mount Cronius, on the north . . . , between the treasuries and the mountain, is a sanctuary of Eileithyia, and in it Sosipolis, a native Elean deity, is worshipped. Now they surname Eileithyia Olympian, and choose a priestess for the goddess every year. The old woman who tends Sosipolis herself too by an Elean custom lives in chastity, bringing water for the god's bath and setting before him barley cakes kneaded with honey. In the front part of the temple, for it is built in two parts, is an altar of Eileithyia and an entrance for the public; in the inner part Sosipolis is worshipped, and no one may enter it except the woman who tends the god, and she must wrap her head and face in a white veil. Maidens and matrons wait in the sanctuary of Eileithyia chanting a hymn; they burn all manner of incense to the god, but it is not the custom to pour libations of wine.

● 17D

Women's Rites to Demeter at Achaia

Description of Greece 7 (Achaia) 27.9–10   mid–2d century C.E.

About sixty stades distant from Pellene is the Mysaeum, a sanctuary of the Mysian Demeter. It is said that it was founded by Mysius, a man of Argos, who according to Argive tradition gave Demeter a welcome in his home. There is a grove in the Mysaeum, containing trees of every kind, and in it rises a copious supply of water from springs. Here they also celebrate a seven days' festival in honour of Demeter. On the third day of the festival the men withdraw from the sanctuary, and the women are left to perform on that night the ritual that custom demands. Not only men are excluded, but even male dogs. On the following day the men come to the sanctuary, and the men and the women laugh and jeer at one another in turn.

● 17E

The Festival Laphria, in Honor of Artemis

Description of Greece 7 (Achaia) 18.11–12   mid–2d century C.E.

Every year too the people of Patrae celebrate the festival Laphria in honour of their Artemis, and at it they employ a method of sacrifice peculiar to the place. Round the altar in a circle they set up logs of wood still green, each of them sixteen cubits long. On the altar within the circle is placed the driest of their wood. Just before the time of the festival they construct a smooth ascent to the altar, piling earth upon the altar steps. The festival begins with a most splendid procession in honour of Artemis, and the maiden officiating as priestess rides last in the procession upon a car yoked to deer. It is, however, not till the next day that the sacrifice is offered, and the festival is not only a state function but also quite a popular general holiday. For the people throw alive upon the altar edible birds and every kind of victim as well; there are wild boars, deer and gazelles; some bring wolf-cubs or bear-cubs, others the full-grown beasts. They also place upon the altar fruit.

● 17F

Women Attacked during a Festival to Demeter, Who Defend Themselves with Sacrificial Implements

Description of Greece 4 (Messenia) 17   mid–2d century C.E.

There is a place Aegila in Laconia, where is a sanctuary sacred to Demeter. Aristomenes and his men knowing that the women were keeping festival there . . . the women were inspired by the goddess to defend themselves, and most of the Messenians were wounded with the knives with which the women sacrificed the victims and the spits on which they pierced and roasted the meat. Aristomenes was struck with the torches and taken alive. Nevertheless he escaped to Messenia during the same night. Archidameia, the priestess of Demeter, was charged with having released him, not for a bribe but because she had been in love with him before; but she maintained that Aristomenes had escaped by burning through his bonds.

The Religious Activities of Roman Women as Viewed by a Skeptical Satirist

JUVENAL *Satire 6*   1st to 2d century C.E.

AUTHOR: Little is known of the life of the Roman satirist Juvenal, including the dates of his birth and death. His earliest extant satire dates to ca. 100–110 C.E., and he was still writing ca. 127. He was not well known during his lifetime, and his works did not acquire any popularity until the late fourth century. His sixteen extant satires present an acerbic critique of Roman society. The excerpts here are taken from his *Sixth Satire*, a vicious indictment of Roman women as potential wives and the only one that substantially concerns women. Note also his representation of a Jewish woman as prophetic medium at the conclusion of this selection.

TRANSLATION: Niall Rudd, trans., *Juvenal, "The Satires,"* with introduction and notes by William Barr (New York: Oxford University Press, 1999).

TEXTS: OCT (W. V. Clausen, *Persius and Juvenal, "Satires,"* 1959); John Ferguson, *Juvenal, "The Satires"* (New York: St. Martins Press, 1979).

ADDITIONAL TEXT AND TRANSLATION: LCL (C. G. Ramsay, 1918).

BIBLIOGRAPHY: Susanna H. Braund, "Juvenal—Misogynist or Misogamist?" *JRS* 82 (1992): 71–86; Barbara K. Gold, " 'The House I Live in Is Not My Own': Women's Bodies in Juvenal's *Satires*," *Arethusa* 31, no. 3 (1998): 368–86.

> The secrets of the Good Goddess are scarcely a secret. The pelvis
> is stirred by the pipe, and Priápus' maenads are swept along,
> frenzied by horn and wine alike, swinging their hair
> in a circle, and howling. Then what a yearning for sex erupts
> in their hearts; what cries are emitted as their lust pulsates; what rivers
> of vintage liquor come coursing down their drunken legs!
> Tossing her garland in, Saufeia challenges harlots   320
> trained in a brothel, and takes the award for undulant hips;
>
> she in turn admires Medullina's rippling buttocks.
> The prize is between the ladies; their birth is matched by their valour.
> Nothing is done by way of illusion; in every performance
> the real thing is enacted—a sight that would warm the blood
> of old king Priam himself, or the ancient organ of Nestor.
> Then, as their itch can't wait any longer, every disguise
> is stripped from the women. The chorus is heard throughout the grotto:
> 'The time is here! Let in the men!' If her lover's asleep,
> his son must don a cloak and hood and hurry to join her.   330
> If that's no good, the slaves are assaulted; what if there isn't

a slave at hand? They'll hire the man who delivers the water.
If *he* is sought in vain, and no human aid is forthcoming,
then she'll dispose her rump to take the weight of a donkey.
Would that the ancient rites, or at least the public observances,
might take place without such foul desecration! But every
Moor and Indian knows which 'lady lutanist' carried
a penis longer than both the *Anticatos* of Caesar
to a place which even a mouse, aware that his testes will witness
against him, leaves in a hurry, where every picture portraying   340
the form of the other sex must be decently covered.
Look at what's coming—   510
the troupe of frenzied Bellona and the Mother of the Gods, including
a giant eunuch (revered by his smaller degenerate friend).
He snatched up a sherd and severed his genitals long ago,
foregoing his sex. Now he drowns the shrieking mob and their timbrels,
his common cheeks enclosed in the flaps of a Phrygian bonnet.
In portentous tones he warns her to fear September, and with it
the wind from the south, unless she has offered a hundred eggs
and presented him with the plum-coloured dress she's no longer
    wearing.
(Thus any sudden or serious threats will enter the clothes,   520
and she, with a single act, will have made her peace for a year.)
On a winter's morning she will break the ice and enter the Tiber,
plunging into the water thrice and dipping her fearful
head right into the eddies. Emerging, half-dressed and shaking,
she will crawl across the entire field of Tarquin the Proud
on her bleeding knees; if milk-white Io tells her to do so,
she will make her way to sweltering Meroe, beyond the border
of Egypt, in order to fetch some water that she may sprinkle
in Isis' temple, which stands right next to the ancient sheepfold.

She believes she received her orders direct from the voice of the
    goddess—   530
a likely soul and mind for the gods to talk to at night-time!
Hence the highest, most special, honour is paid to the one
who, followed by creatures in linen robes with shaven heads,
trots along as Anubis, and mocks at the wailing crowd.
He intercedes whenever a woman has failed to refrain
from sex with her husband on days which ought to be honoured as holy,
when a heavy penalty is due to be paid for polluting the mattress,
and when Isis' silver serpent is seen to nod its head.
Anubis' tears ensure, along with his ritual murmurs,

that Osiris will not refuse to forgive the sin—provided,
of course, he is bribed with a big fat goose and a little cake.

When he has moved on, a palsied Jewess puts down her hay-box
and comes a-begging, whispering secretly into her ear.
She interprets the laws of Jerusalem, *she* is the priestess
of the tree, who truly conveys the will of highest heaven.
She too gets something, but less, for the Jews will sell you
whatever view of a dream you like for a couple of coppers.

● **19**

Women (and Men) in a Procession to Isis

APULEIUS *Metamorphoses* 11.9–10   2d century C.E.

AUTHOR: Born in North Africa, in 123 C.E., perhaps in Madaura, Apuleius is probably best known for his Latin *Metamorphoses*, also known as *The Golden Ass*. This tale recounts the adventures of one unfortunate Lucius, who turns into an ass through the misuse of magical arts, and is ultimately restored to his proper form by the goddess Isis. Apuleius' depiction of Lucius' initiations into the worship of the Egyptian goddess and her consort, Osiris, in Book 11, may be autobiographical. Apuleius himself was accused and acquitted of using magical arts to induce his wealthy older wife to marry him, and set forth his defense in his *Apology*. Of particular interest is Apuleius' representation of women's practice of these arts, almost always for nefarious purposes [entries 20 and 21]. Most of his other works are not extant.

TRANSLATION: P. G. Walsh, *Apuleius, The Golden Ass* (Oxford: Oxford University Press, 1994).

TEXT: Teubner (R. Helm, 1955); Budé (D. S. Robertson, 3 vols. 1940–45).

ADDITIONAL TRANSLATION (AND TEXT): LCL (J. Arthur Hanson, 2 vols., 1989).

ADDITIONAL TRANSLATION: J. Gwyn Griffiths, *The Isis-Book (Metamorphoses XI: Apuleius of Madaura*, EPRO 39 (Leiden: E. J. Brill, 1975); E. J. Kenney, *Apuleius, The Golden Ass* (Harmondsworth: Penguin, 1998).

BIBLIOGRAPHY: James Timothy Golnick, *The Religious Dreamworld of Apuleius' Metamorphoses: Recovering a Forgotten Hermeneutic* (Waterloo, Ont.: Wilfred Laurier University Press, 1999); C. C. Schlam, *The Metamorphoses of Apuleius: On Making an Ass of Oneself* (Chapel Hill: University of North Carolina Press, 1992); Nancy C. Shumate, *Crisis and Conversion in Apuleius, Metamorphoses* (Ann Arbor: University of Michigan Press, 1996); John Winkler, *Auctor and Actor: A Narratological Reading of Apuleius' Golden Ass* (Berkeley: University of California Press, 1985); see also bibliography for entry 130.

9 While the participants in these comic diversions for the townsfolk were prancing about here and there, the special procession in honour of the saviour goddess was being set in motion. Some women, sparkling in white dresses, delighting in their diverse adornments and garlanded with spring flowers, were strewing the ground with blossoms stored in their dresses along the route on which the sacred company was to pass. Others had gleaming mirrors attached to their backs to render homage to the goddess as she drew near them, and others with ivory combs gestured with their arms and twirled their fingers as if adorning and combing their queen's tresses. Others again sprinkled the streets with all manner of perfumes, including the pleasing balsam-scent which they shook out in drops. Besides these there was a numerous crowd of both sexes who sought the favour of the creator of the celestial stars by carrying lamps, torches, tapers and other kinds of artificial light. Behind them came musical instruments, pipes and flutes which sounded forth the sweetest melodies. There followed a delightful choir of specially chosen youths clad in expensive white tunics, who kept hymning a charming song composed to music by a talented poet with the aid of the Muses; the theme incorporated chants leading up to the greater votive prayers to follow. In the procession too were flautists dedicated to the great god Sarapis; the pipes in their hands extended sideways to their right ears, and on them they repeatedly played the tune regularly associated with their temple and its god. There were also several officials loudly insisting that a path be cleared for the sacred procession.

10 Next, crowds of those initiated into the divine rites came surging along, men and women of every rank and age, gleaming with linen garments spotlessly white. The women had sprayed their hair with perfume, and covered it with diaphanous veils; the men had shaved their heads completely, so that their bald pates shone. With their rattles of bronze, silver, and even gold, they made a shrill, tinkling sound. Accompanying them were the stars of the great world-religion, the priests of the cult who were drawn from the ranks of famed nobility; they wore white linen garments which fitted tightly across their chests and extended to their feet, and they carried striking attributes of most powerful deities. Their leader held out a lamp gleaming with brilliant light; it did not much resemble those lanterns of ours which illumine our banquets at night, but it was a golden, boat-shaped vessel feeding quite a large flame from an opening at its centre. The second priest was similarly garbed; he carried in both hands the altar which they call the "altar of help," a name specifically bestowed on it by the providential help of the highest goddess. A third priest advanced, bearing a palm-branch, its leaves finely worked in gold; he carried also the staff of Mercury. A fourth priest exhibited a deformed left hand with palm outstretched, symbolizing justice; since it was impaired by nature and endowed with no guile or cunning, it was thought

more suited to represent justice than the right hand. He also carried a small golden vessel rounded like a woman's breast, from which he poured libations of milk. A fifth priest bore a winnowing-fan of gold, fashioned from laurel-twigs, and a sixth carried an amphora.

● 20

The Deeds of the *Saga* Meroe

APULEIUS *Metamorphoses* 1.7–10   2d century c.e.

AUTHOR, TRANSLATION, AND TEXT: See entry 19.

BIBLIOGRAPHY: Christopher Faraone, *Ancient Greek Love Magic* (Cambridge: Harvard University Press, 1999).

7 "But he would not budge, and kept his head covered. 'Leave me, let me be!' he cried, 'Let Fortune feast her eyes longer on me as the token of her victory!' But I induced him to accompany me, and at the same time I slipped off one of my two shirts, and hastily clothed him, or rather covered him up. There and then I hauled him off to the baths, coughed up for the oil and towels, and vigorously scrubbed off a huge deposit of filth. Once he was well cleaned up, I took him to an inn, supporting his exhausted body with great difficulty, for I too was tired out. I made him lie down to recover, gave him a good meal and a relieving drink, and chatted with him to enable him to relax. In no time he showed an eager desire to talk; he joked, even indulging in some clever repartee and unassuming wit. But then he heaved a tortured sigh from the depths of his heart, and beat his forehead repeatedly and savagely with his hand.

" 'What a mess I'm in!' he began. 'I have fallen into this misfortune through seeking a diversion at a celebrated gladiatorial show. You will remember that I made for Macedonia on a business-trip. I was busy there for nine months and more, and was making my way home with a good bit of money in my pocket. Shortly before reaching Larissa, where I intended to take in the show as I was passing through, I was making my way along a trackless, pitted valley when I was held up by some brigands of massive physique who robbed me of all my money. When I finally got away I stopped at an inn, because I was badly shaken up. It was run by a woman called Meroë, who was getting on in years, but was still quite attractive. I explained to her the circumstances of my long period away from home, my eagerness to get back, and the robbery that I had suffered. Her reaction was to treat me with extraordinary sympathy. She set me down without payment in front of a welcome supper, and then as she was feeling sexy she took me to her bed. From the moment I slept with her my misery began. The scourge of a long and baneful association sprang from that one act of sexual intercourse. Even the shabby clothes which those generous brigands had left me to cover my body I surrendered to her, and every penny I earned as a porter, as long as I still had my strength. So the combination of such a kind wife as this and malevolent Fortune has brought me to the condition which you have just witnessed.'

8 " 'Good Lord!' I exclaimed. 'You certainly deserve to suffer the worst possible fate, if there is anything worse than your recent experiences, because you put the pleasures of sex and a leather-skinned whore before your home and children.' Socrates put his index-finger to his lips, registering shocked alarm. 'Hush!' he said, looking round to see if it was safe to speak. 'Don't mention the prophetess in case your loose tongue brings you harm.'

" 'Really?' I replied. 'What sort of woman is this mighty queen of inn-keepers?'

" 'She's a witch [saga],' he said, 'with supernatural powers. She can bring down the sky, raise the earth, freeze running waters, melt mountains, raise ghosts, dispatch gods to the world below, black out the stars, and light up hell itself!'

" 'Come, come,' I said, 'ring down the tragic curtain, fold up the backcloth, and do please use the language of every day.'

" 'Would you care to hear one or two of her magic feats, or still better, a whole string of them? She makes not only the locals fall madly in love with her, but also Indians, both lots of Ethiopians, and even Antipodeans, but such things as these are trivial aspects of her art, mere play. Just hear what she brought about with dozens of people watching.

9 " 'A lover of hers went after another woman. With one word the witch transformed him into a beaver. Why a beaver? Because that animal in fear of captivity escapes its pursuers by biting off its own genitals, and she wanted the same fate to befall him likewise for having made love to this other woman. Then there was a neighbouring innkeeper competing for custom with her; she changed him into a frog, and now the old man swims in a barrel of his own wine, and as he squats in the lees he greets his former customers with dutiful croaks. Another man she changed into a ram because he was a barrister who prosecuted her, and now it's as a ram that he pleads his cases. Then there was the wife of a lover of hers who was heavy with child. Because she made witty and disparaging remarks about the witch, Meroë has condemned her to an indefinite pregnancy by sealing up her womb and postponing the birth. The general estimate is that the poor woman has now been carrying her burden for eight years, and is so misshapen it's as though she were giving birth to an elephant.

10 " 'Because of these periodic outrages that brought harm to many there was a general swell of indignation, and the community decreed that on the

following day she should suffer the extreme punishment of stoning. But she anticipated this plan by the potency of her spells. You remember the case of Medea, who won a respite of a single short day from Creon, and ignited his whole house and daughter and the old man himself with flames which burst out from the bridal crown? Well, Meroë confided to me recently, when she was drunk, that she dug a trench and performed rites of black magic in it by invoking the spirits of the dead. By this means she locked the entire community in their houses by the silent powers of supernatural spirits, so that for two whole days they could not break the bars, force open the doors, or even tunnel through the walls. Eventually the citizens bolstered each other and made a united appeal to her, swearing by all that was holy that they would not lay a finger on her, and that if anyone had ideas to the contrary, they would rescue her. Once they had appeased her in this way, she set the whole town free. As for the man who had summoned the public gathering, she shifted him and his entire barred dwelling—walls, floor and foundations—to another community at dead of night. This town was a hundred miles away, perched on the tip of a rugged mountain, and waterless owing to its position. But the houses of the residents there were so closely packed that they allowed no room for a new arrival, so the witch just dumped the house in front of the town gate, and made off.' "

21

Photis Reveals the Nefarious Deeds of Her Mistress, Pamphile

APULEIUS *Metamorphoses* 3.15–18   2d century C.E.

AUTHOR, TRANSLATION, AND TEXT: See entry 19.

15 Her high spirits now restored, "Please wait a moment," she said, "until I carefully close the bedroom door. I don't wish to commit a grievous error by carelessly and sacrilegiously letting my tongue run free." As she spoke, she thrust home the bolts and fastened the hook securely. Then she came back to me, and took my neck in both her hands. In a low and quite restrained voice, she said: "I am fearful and mortally terrified of revealing the secrets of this house, and of exposing the hidden mysteries wrought by my mistress. But I have considerable trust in you and your learning. In addition to the noble distinction of your birth and your outstanding intellect, you have been initiated into several sacred cults, and you are certainly aware of the need for the sacred confidentiality of silence. So all that I entrust to the sanctuary of your pious heart you must for ever enclose and guard within its confines, and thus repay the ingenuous trust of my revelations with the steadfast security of your silence. The love which holds me fast to you compels me to reveal to you things which I alone know. You are now to gain acquaintance

with the entire nature of our household, with the wondrous and secret spells of my mistress. To these the spirits hearken and the elements are enslaved, and by them the stars are dislocated and the divine powers harnessed. But for no purpose does my mistress have recourse to the power of this art so much as when she eyes with pleasure some young man of elegant appearance, and indeed this is a frequent practice of hers.

16 "At the moment she is passionately obsessed with a young and extremely handsome Boeotian, and she eagerly deploys every device and every technique of her art. Only this evening I heard her with my own ears threatening the sun itself with cloud cover and unbroken darkness because it had not retired from the sky quickly enough, and had yielded to nightfall too late for her to practise the enticements of magic. Yesterday, when she was on her way back from the baths, she happened to catch sight of the young man sitting in the barber's, and she ordered me to remove secretly his hair which had been snipped off by the scissors and was lying on the floor. As I was carefully and unobtrusively gathering it, the barber caught me at it. Now we in this city have a bad name for practising the art of sorcery, so he grabbed me brusquely and rebuked me. 'You brazen hussy, is there no end to your repeatedly stealing the hair of eligible young men? If you don't finally stop this criminal practice, I'll have you up at once before the magistrates.' He followed up his words with action; he thrust his hands between my breasts, felt around, and angrily extracted some hair which I had already hidden there. I was extremely concerned at this turn of events, remembering my mistress's usual temper. She often gets quite annoyed if she is frustrated in this way, and she takes it out on me most savagely. I actually thought of running away from her, but the thought of you at once caused me to reject the idea.

17 "I was just returning dispirited and afraid to go back empty-handed from the barber's, when I saw a man paring some goatskins with scissors. Once I watched the skins inflated, tightly tied, and hanging up, and the hair from them lying on the ground and of the same blonde colour as that of the young Boeotian, I abstracted a quantity of it and passed it to my mistress, concealing its true provenance. So it was that in the first hours of darkness, before you returned from your dinner, my mistress Pamphile in a fit of ecstatic madness climbed up towards the overlapping roof. On the far side of the house there is an area which is uncovered and exposed to the elements. It commands every view on the eastern side, as well as those in other directions. So it is especially convenient for those magical arts of hers, and she practises them there in secret. First of all she fitted out her infernal laboratory with the usual supplies, including every kind of aromatic plant, metal strips inscribed with unintelligible letters, the surviving remains of ill-omened birds, and a fairly large collection of corpses' limbs, earlier mourned over by relatives and in some cases even buried. Noses and fingers were in a heap in

one place, and in another, nails from the gibbet to which there still clung flesh from the men hanged there. In yet another place the blood of slaughtered men was kept, and also gnawed skulls, torn from the fangs of wild beasts.

18 "Then, after chanting spells over quivering entrails, she poured propitiating offerings of various liquids—now springwater, now cow's milk, now mountain-honey; she also poured out mead. She twisted and entwined the locks of hair with each other, and placed them on live coals to be burnt with a variety of fragrant plants. Immediately, through this combination of the irresistible power of her magic lore and the hidden energy of the harnessed deities, the bodies from which the hair was crackling and smoking acquired human breath, and were able to feel and walk. They headed for the place to which the stench from the hair they had shed led them, and thus they took the place of the Boeotian youth in barging at the doors, in their attempt to gain entrance. At that moment you appeared on the scene, drunk with wine and deceived by the darkness of the sightless night. You drew your short sword, and armed yourself for the role of the mad Ajax. But whereas he inflicted violence on living cattle and lacerated whole herds, you much more courageously dealt the death-blow to three inflated goatskins. Thus you laid low the enemy without shedding a drop of blood, so that I can embrace not a homicide but an utricide."

● 22

A Grieving Mother Resurrects and Interrogates the Corpse of Her Son Using "Magic Arts"

HELIODORUS *An Ethiopian Story* 6.13–15   3d or 4th century C.E.?

AUTHOR: Nothing is known about the author, nor can this Greek novel be reliably dated. Most scholars place it around the third century C.E., although some argue for a mid-fourth-century date.

TRANSLATION: J. R. Morgan, in B. P. Reardon, ed., *Collected Ancient Greek Novels* (Berkeley: University of California Press, 1989).

TEXT: Budé (R. M. Rattenbury and T. W. Lumb, 3 vols., 1935–43); A. Colonna, ed., *Heliodorus, "Aethiopica"* (Rome, 1938).

ADDITIONAL TRANSLATION: Moses Hadas, *Heliodorus, "An Ethiopian Romance"* (Ann Arbor: University of Michigan Press, 1957; repr., Philadelphia: University of Pennsylvania Press, 1999).

... "I have certain rites for the dead to perform that can be performed only at night. But if you care to wait—though in fact you have no choice in the matter—move off a little way, find some spot not too far away clear of dead bodies, and wait there. At daybreak I shall accompany you to the village, and my protection will ensure your safety."

14 Kalasiris repeated to Charikleia all that the old woman had said, and together they moved away. After stepping over the corpses for a short distance, they found a little hillock, and there Kalasiris stretched himself out, pillowing his head on the quiver, while Charikleia sat, using her pouch as a seat. The moon had just risen and was bathing the whole scene in bright light, for it was the second night after full moon. Kalasiris, naturally enough for an old man, especially one fatigued by his travels, lay fast asleep, but the anxieties that beset Charikleia kept her awake; and thus she found herself witnessing a performance which, abominable as it may be, is common practice among the women of Egypt.

Supposing herself now secure against any intrusion or observation, the old woman began by digging a pit, to one side of which she lit a fire. After positioning her son's body between the two, she took an earthenware bowl from a tripod that stood beside her and poured a libation of honey into the pit, likewise of milk from a second bowl, and lastly of wine from a third. Then she took a cake made out of fine wheat flour and shaped into the effigy of a man, crowned it with bay and fennel, and flung it into the pit. Finally she picked up a sword and, in an access of feverish ecstasy, invoked the moon by a series of grotesque and outlandish names, then drew the blade across her arm. She wiped the blood onto a sprig of bay and flicked it into the fire. There followed a number of other bizarre actions, after which she knelt over the dead body of her son and whispered certain incantations into his ear, until she woke the dead man and compelled him by her magic arts to stand upright.

Even before this Charikleia had been somewhat alarmed by the scene she was observing, but now her horror at this appalling ritual became so great that she began to tremble with fear. She shook Kalasiris awake so that he was able to see with his own eyes what was taking place. Positioned as they were in the darkness, they were invisible but could observe with little difficulty all that took place in the light cast by the fire, and were also close enough to hear distinctly what was being said, particularly as the old woman had now begun to question the corpse in a somewhat louder voice. What she wanted to know was whether the corpse's brother, her one surviving son, would live to return home.

The dead man made no reply, merely nodded his head in a way that left some doubt as to whether his mother could expect her wishes to be fulfilled or not. Then he suddenly collapsed and fell flat on his face. The old woman rolled the body over onto its back and persisted with her questions. Employing apparently more powerful spells of compulsion this time, she repeated her string of incantations into his ears, and, leaping, sword in hand, from fire to pit, from pit to fire, she succeeded in waking the dead man a second time and, once he was on his feet, began to put the same questions to him as before, forcing him to use speech as well as nods of the head to make his prophecy unambiguous.

While the old woman was engaged in this, Charikleia desperately sought Kalasiris's permission to draw closer and put a question themselves concerning Theagenes. But he refused, saying that the mere sight of such things was unclean and that he could only tolerate it because he had no alternative; it was not proper for a priest either to take part in or to be present at such rites; the prophetic powers of priests proceeded from legitimate sacrifices and pure prayer, whereas those of the profane were obtained literally by crawling upon the ground and skulking among corpses, as the accidents of circumstances had permitted them to see this Egyptian woman doing.

15 Before Kalasiris could finish, the corpse spoke, its voice a hoarse whisper, sinister and cavernous, as if rising from some infernal abyss.

"Till now I have been merciful to you, Mother," it said. "I tolerated your transgression of the laws of man's nature, your affront to the ordinances of destiny, your use of the black arts to move the immovable, for even in the afterlife we continue to respect our parents so far as we may. But the respect I had for you is now forfeit by your own actions: not content with the first sin of compelling a dead body to stand upright and nod its head, you are taking your sinfulness to the extreme of extorting speech from me as well. With no thought for anything but your own concerns, you neglect the rites that are my due in death and keep me from the company of the other souls. Learn now what I have hitherto kept from telling you! Your son shall not return alive, nor shall you escape death by the sword. The whole of your life you have spent in sinful practices such as this, but soon you will meet the violent end that awaits all such as you. These are forbidden mysteries, cloaked in secrecy and darkness, but you have had the audacity to perform them, not in solitary privacy but in the presence of others, and you even parade the secrets of the dead before witnesses such as these: one is a high priest—and in his case the offense is of lesser importance, for he is wise enough to lock such secrets away in the silence of his heart and never divulge them; besides, the gods love him: his sons are armed; they are facing one another ready to fight to the death, but if he makes haste, his arrival will stay their hands on the very point of joining single combat. What is worse is that a young girl is also witness to your necromancy and can hear every word that is spoken, a young lady distraught with love and wandering over virtually the whole face of the earth in search of some loved one; but after hardships and dangers beyond counting, at earth's farthest boundaries, she will pass her life at his side in glorious and royal estate."

With these words the corpse fell limp to the ground. The old woman realized that it was the strangers that had been spying on her, and there and then she launched herself after them, sword in her hand and madness in her heart. She scoured the battlefield, suspecting that they were hiding among the dead bodies and meaning to kill them if she discovered them, for she presumed that they had spied on her necromancy from malicious and hostile motives. But her fury was so great that she did not look where she was going as she hunted through the corpses, and ended by accidentally impaling herself through the groin on a broken spear that stood upright in the ground. So she died, bringing instant and fitting fulfilment to the prophecy that her son had given her.

● 23
Callirhoe Entreats Aphrodite at Her Shrines and Temple

CHARITON *Chareas and Callirhoe* 2.2, 7.5, 8.8   1st to 2d century C.E.?

AUTHOR: According to the text itself, Chariton lived in Aphrodisias, a city in southwestern Turkey. Famed in antiquity for the beauty of its buildings and its location, Aphrodisias was excavated extensively in the late twentieth century. Apart from this, though, nothing is known of the author or the date of the novel. To some scholars, its style seems consistent with a date in the late first to mid–second century C.E. Although set in the fictional past, the text also seems consistent with social life and practices in Greek Asia Minor in this same period. Although the work is traditionally known as *Chareas and Callirhoe*, the final line suggests that its initial title may have been just *Callirhoe*.

The plot of the novel conforms to the basic ancient Greek romance in which two young lovers, usually of aristocratic class, sometimes seeking to marry and sometimes already married, are separated against their will and endure numerous trials and attacks on their chastity or marital fidelity before they are ultimately reunited. Religious themes and devotions figure prominently.

TRANSLATION: B. P. Reardon, in B. P. Reardon, ed., *Collected Ancient Greek Novels* (Berkeley: University of California Press, 1989).

TEXT: Budé (G. Molinié, 1979); W. E. Blake, *Charitonis Aphrodisiensis de Chaerea et Callirhoe Amatoriarum Narrationum Libri Octo* (Oxford, 1938).

ADDITIONAL TEXT AND TRANSLATION: LCL (G. P. Goold, 1995).

BIBLIOGRAPHY: Graham Anderson, *Ancient Fiction: The Novel in the Graeco-Roman World* (Totowa, N.J.: Barnes and Noble, 1984); Margaret Anne Doody, *The True Story of the Novel* (New Brunswick, N.J.: Rutgers University Press, 1996); Brigitte Egger, "Women and Marriage in the Greek Novels: The Boundaries of Romance," in James Tatum, ed., *The Search for the Ancient Novel* (Baltimore: Johns

Hopkins University Press, 1994), 260–80; Christopher Gill and T. P. Wiseman, eds., *Lies and Fiction in the Ancient World* (Austin: University of Texas Press, 1993); Judith Evans Grubb, "Pagan and Christian Marriage: The State of the Question," *JECS* 2, no. 4 (1994): 361–412; David Konstan, *Sexual Symmetry: Love in the Ancient Novel and Related Genres* (Princeton: Princeton University Press, 1994); Mary R. Lefkowitz, "Did Ancient Women Write Novels," in Amy-Jill Levine, ed., *"Women Like This": New Perspectives on Jewish Women in the Greco-Roman Period*, Septuagint and Cognate Studies (Atlanta: Scholars Press, 1991), 199–219; John Morgan and Richard Stoneman, eds., *Greek Fiction: The Greek Novel in Context* (New York: Routledge, 1994); Judith Perkins, *The Suffering Self: Pain and Narrative Representation in the Early Christian Era* (New York: Routledge, 1995); Gareth Schmeling, ed., *The Novel in the Ancient World*, Mnemosyne, Bibliotheca Classica Batava Supplement 159 (Leiden: E. J. Brill, 1996).

2.2 The shrine was near Dionysius's house, just by the main road. Callirhoe kneeled in front of Aphrodite and embraced her feet. "You were the first to show Chaereas to me," she said. "You made a handsome couple of us, but you have not watched over us—and yet we paid you honor! But since that was your will, I ask one thing of you: grant that I attract no man after Chaereas." Aphrodite refused her prayer. After all, she is the mother of Eros, and she was now planning another marriage—which she did not intend to preserve either.

7.5 Aradus is an island three or four miles from the mainland. It contains an old shrine of Aphrodite; the women lived there as in a house, feeling completely secure. Callirhoe stood in front of Aphrodite, looking at her. At first she said nothing but wept; her tears reproached the goddess. Then she managed to find her voice. "So now it is Aradus; a small island instead of great Sicily—and there is no one here of my own people. My lady, that is enough. How long are you going to be at war with me? I may really have given you offense; but you have punished me for it. Perhaps my ill-starred beauty evoked your indignation; but it has been my ruin. Now I have experienced the one misfortune I had never known—war. Compared to my present situation, even Babylon was charitable to me. There Chaereas was near at hand. Now he is assuredly dead; he would not have stayed alive when I left the city. But I do not know from whom I can find out what has happened to him. All are strangers to me, all are foreigners; they envy me, they hate me—and worse than those who hate me are those who love me! My lady, reveal to me whether Chaereas is alive!" With these words on her lips she went away.

8.8 While the crowd was in the theater, Callirhoe went to Aphrodite's temple before entering her house. She put her hands on the goddess's feet, placed her face on them, let down her hair, and kissed them. "Thank you, Aphrodite!" she said. "You have shown Chaereas to me once more in Syracuse, where I saw him as a maiden at your desire. I do not blame you, my lady, for what I have suffered; it was my fate. Do not separate me from Chaereas again, I beg of you; grant us a happy life together, and let us die together!"

That is my story about Callirhoe.

● 24
Festivals and Sacrifices at the Birth of Callirhoe's Son

CHARITON *Chareas and Callirhoe* 3.7–9   1st to 2d century C.E.?

AUTHOR, TRANSLATION, AND TEXT: See entry 23.

. . . Seven months after the wedding she gave birth to a son, ostensibly Dionysius's child, but in reality that of Chaereas. The town mounted a great festival, and delegations came from all over as people shared in Miletus's happiness at the addition to Dionysius's family. The master, in his joy, yielded to his wife in everything and made her mistress of his house. He filled the temples with votive gifts and invited the whole town to sacrificial banquets.

8 Callirhoe was worried that her secret would be betrayed, so she asked for Plangon to be freed. Plangon was the only person besides herself who knew she was pregnant when she came to Dionysius, and Callirhoe wanted to make sure of having her loyalty, not just as a matter of sentiment but on the basis of her material position. "I will gladly recognize the help Plangon has given us in our courtship," said Dionysius, "but we are acting wrongly if, when we have rewarded the servant, we are not to show gratitude to Aphrodite, in whose temple we first saw each other." "I want to more than you do," said Callirhoe, "since my debt to her is greater than yours. For the moment I am still recovering from the birth; it will be safer if we wait a few days before we go to the country."

She quickly recovered from the birth and grew stronger and bigger, no longer a girl, but now a mature woman. When they reached the estate, Phocas arranged magnificent sacrifices—a large crowd had followed them from town. As he began the public offering, Dionysius said: "Lady Aphrodite, you are the source of all my blessings; it is you who gave me Callirhoe, you who gave me my son; you have made me a husband and a father. I was satisfied to have Callirhoe—she is sweeter to me than country or parents—but I love my child, for making his mother more surely mine; I have a guarantee of her goodwill. I beg you, my lady, keep Callirhoe safe for my sake and keep my son safe for her sake." The crowd of people standing round said amen to his prayer and pelted them with roses or violets or whole garlands, so that the temple grounds were filled with flowers. Well, Dionysius had voiced his prayer in the hearing of everyone, but Callirhoe wanted to speak to Aphrodite alone. First she took her son in her own arms; that formed a beautiful sight, such as no painter has ever yet painted nor sculptor sculpted nor poet recounted, since none of them has represented Artemis or Athena holding a baby in her arms. Dionysius wept for joy when he saw it and quietly addressed a propitiatory prayer to Nemesis. Callirhoe told Plangon alone to stay with her and sent everyone else ahead to the house. When they had left, she stood near to Aphrodite and held up her child. "On his behalf I am grateful to you, mistress," she said. "On my own behalf I am not sure. I should be grateful to you for myself as well if you had watched over Chaereas for me. But you have given me an image of my dear husband; you have not taken Chaereas from me altogether. Grant, I pray you, that my son be more fortunate than his parents, and like his grandfather. May he too sail on a flagship— and when he is in action, may people say, 'Hermocrates' grandson is greater than he was!' His grandfather too will be happy to see his courage inherited; and we shall be happy, his parents, even if we are dead. I beg you, mistress, be at peace with me now; I have had enough misfortune! I have died and come to life again. I have been taken by pirates and made an exile; I have been sold and been a slave; and I reckon my second marriage a greater burden yet than all this. I beg one favor of you, and of the other gods through you, to requite all: preserve my fatherless child!" She would have said more but could not for her tears.

9 After a short time she called the priestess. The old woman came when called. "Why are you crying, child," she asked, "when you have such good fortune? Why, foreigners are actually worshiping you as a goddess now. The other day two handsome young men sailed by here, and one of them almost fainted when he saw your image—that is how famous Aphrodite has made you." These words struck at Callirhoe's heart; she stared as though she had gone out of her mind and cried: "Who were the foreigners? Where had their ship come from? What story did they tell you?" The old woman was frightened and at first stood there speechless; then she managed to speak. "I only saw them," she said. "I didn't hear anything." "What did they look like? Try to recall their appearance." The old woman told her, not in detail, but Callirhoe suspected the truth all the same—people always believe what they want to be the case. She looked at Plangon. "Perhaps poor Chaereas has wandered to these parts and is here now," she said. "What then has happened to him? Let us look for him—but say nothing about it."

Now when she joined Dionysius she told him only what the priestess had told her; she knew that love is naturally inquisitive, and that Dionysius would try of his own accord to find out what had happened. That was just how it turned out.

Prospective Brides and Grooms at a Festival of Artemis of Ephesos

XENOPHON OF EPHESOS *Ephesian Tale of Anthia and*
Habrocomes 1.2   date uncertain

AUTHOR: Nothing is known about the author. The text is known only from one
thirteenth-century manuscript that also contains the only complete text of Chariton's *Chareas and Callirhoe.* As with several other ancient novels in Greek, it is
often thought to date from about the second century C.E., but without any reliable
basis.

The plot of the novel conforms to the basic ancient Greek romance (see comments at entry 23).

TRANSLATION: Graham Anderson, in B. P. Reardon, ed., *Collected Ancient Greek
Novels* (Berkeley: University of California Press, 1989).

TEXT: Budé (G. Dalmeyda, 1924).

BIBLIOGRAPHY: See entry 23.

... The local festival of Artemis was in progress, with its procession from the
city to the temple nearly a mile away. All the local girls had to march in procession, richly dressed, as well as all the young men of Habrocomes' age—he
was around sixteen, already a member of the Ephebes, and took first place in
the procession. There was a great crowd of Ephesians and visitors alike to see
the festival, for it was the custom at this festival to find husbands for the girls
and wives for the young men. So the procession filed past—first the sacred
objects, the torches, the baskets, and the incense; then horses, dogs, hunting
equipment ... some for war, most for peace. And each of the girls was
dressed as if to receive a lover. Anthia led the line of girls; she was the
daughter of Megamedes and Euippe, both of Ephesus. Anthia's beauty was an
object of wonder, far surpassing the other girls'. She was fourteen; her beauty
was burgeoning, still more enhanced by the adornment of her dress. Her hair
was golden—a little of it plaited, but most hanging loose and blowing in the
wind. Her eyes were quick; she had the bright glance of a young girl, and yet
the austere look of a virgin. She wore a purple tunic down to the knee, fastened with a girdle and falling loose over her arms, with a fawnskin over it, a
quiver attached, and arrows for weapons; she carried javelins and was followed by dogs. Often as they saw her in the sacred enclosure the Ephesians
would worship her as Artemis. And so on this occasion too the crowd gave a
cheer when they saw her, and there was a whole clamor of exclamations from
the spectators: some were amazed and said it was the goddess in person;
some that it was someone else made by the goddess in her own image. But
all prayed and prostrated themselves and congratulated her parents. "The
beautiful Anthia!" was the cry on all the spectators' lips. When the crowd of

girls came past, no one said anything but "Anthia!" But when Habrocomes came in turn with the Ephebes, then, although the spectacle of the women had been a lovely sight, everyone forgot about them and transferred their gaze to him and were smitten at the sight. "Handsome Habrocomes!" they exclaimed. "Incomparable image of a handsome god!" Already some added, "What a match Habrocomes and Anthia would make!"

● 26

Anthia Entreats Isis and Apis

XENOPHON OF EPHESOS *Ephesian Tale of Anthia and Habrocomes* 4.3, 5.4   date uncertain

AUTHOR, TRANSLATION, AND TEXT: See entry 25.

4.3 ... When she had left Alexandria and arrived in Memphis, she stood before the temple and prayed to Isis. "Greatest of goddesses," she pleaded, "until now I have remained chaste, since I was regarded as sacred to you, and I preserve my marriage to Habrocomes undefiled. But from this point I go to India, far from the land of Ephesus, far from the remains of Habrocomes. So either deliver this poor woman from here and give me back to Habrocomes if he is still alive, or if it is absolutely fated that we should die apart, bring it about that I remain faithful to his corpse."

5.4 Meanwhile Polyidus, who had a wife in Alexandria, fell passionately in love with Anthia. In his passion he at first tried to persuade her with great promises; but at length when they reached Memphis on their way down to Alexandria, Polyidus tried to use force on Anthia. She was able to escape, went to the temple of Isis, and took refuge as a suppliant. "Mistress of Egypt," she exclaimed, "who have helped me often, save me yet again. Let Polyidus spare me as well, since I am keeping myself chaste for Habrocomes, thanks to you." Polyidus revered the goddess, but he also loved Anthia and pitied her fate. He came to the temple alone and promised never to use force on her or commit any insult against her, but to respect her chastity as long as she wished, for in his infatuation he would be content only to look at her and talk to her.

Anthia was persuaded by his oaths and left the temple. And when they decided to rest in Memphis for three days, she went to the temple of Apis. This is the most illustrious shrine in Egypt, and the god gives oracles to those who wish them. For whenever a person comes and prays and makes an enquiry to the god, he comes out, and the Egyptian children in front of the temple foretell the future, sometimes in prose, sometimes in verse. So Anthia too came and prostrated herself before Apis. "Kindest of gods," she prayed, "who have pity on all strangers, have pity on me too in my misery and make me a true prophecy about Habrocomes. For if I am to see him again and have him as my husband, I will remain alive. But if he is dead, it is well that I too should depart this unhappy life." With this prayer she wept and left the temple. But meanwhile the children playing in front of the precinct shouted out in chorus,

Anthia will soon recover her own husband, Habrocomes.

When she heard this she took heart and prayed to the gods. And at once they left for Alexandria.

● 27
Offerings and Festivals for Helios at Rhodes

XENOPHON OF EPHESOS *Ephesian Tale of Anthia and Habrocomes* 5.10–13   date uncertain

AUTHOR, TRANSLATION, AND TEXT: See entry 25.

Meanwhile Leucon and Rhode, who were staying in Rhodes, had made an offering to the temple of Helius beside the gold panoply that Anthia and Habrocomes had dedicated. They put up a pillar inscribed in gold to commemorate Habrocomes and Anthia, with their own names, Leucon and Rhode, inscribed as donors. Habrocomes had come to pray to the god and noticed the pillar. He read the inscription, recognized the donors, and realized how thoughtful his servants had been. And when he saw the panoply nearby, he sat down beside the pillar and moaned loudly: "I am unlucky in everything! I come to the end of my life and remember my own misfortunes. Here before me is the very panoply I set up with Anthia; I sailed away with her, and now I come back without her. And if this is the offering set up by our companions for both of us, what is to become of me now that I am alone; where will I find those dearest to me?"

So he lamented, and meanwhile Leucon and Rhode suddenly appeared; they prayed as usual to the gods, and saw Habrocomes sitting beside the pillar and looking at the panoply. They did not recognize him, but wondered who would stay beside someone else's offerings. And so Leucon spoke to him. "Why are you sitting weeping, young man, and lamenting beside offerings that have nothing to do with you? What concern of yours are these? And what do you have in common with the people named here?" Habrocomes replied, "I am the very person the offerings of Leucon and Rhode are for, and after Anthia it is them I am praying to see; I am the unfortunate Habrocomes!" When Leucon and Rhode heard this they were immediately dumbfounded, but gradually recovered and recognized him by his appearance and voice, from what he said, and from his mention of Anthia; and they fell at his feet and told their own story—their journey to Syria from Tyre, Manto's anger, the sale of Lycia, their master's death, their wealth, their arrival in Rhodes. And so they took him with them and brought him to their lodgings, made over their possessions to him, took care of him, looked after him, and tried to console him. But to him there was nothing more precious than Anthia, and time after time he mourned for her.

11 And so he lived in Rhodes with his companions, thinking over what to do. Meanwhile Hippothous decided to take Anthia from Italy to Ephesus, to restore her to her parents; he also hoped to find out something about Habrocomes there. And so he put everything he had into a large Ephesian ship and set sail with Anthia; they put in during the night in Rhodes after a few days' welcome voyage, and there took lodgings with an old woman called Althaea, near the sea; he brought Anthia to his hostess and himself rested that night. The next day they were already getting ready to sail, but a magnificent public festival was being celebrated by the whole population of Rhodes in honor of Helius with a procession and sacrifice, and a great crowd of citizens was taking part in the revels. Leucon and Rhode were there, not so much to take part in the festival as in an attempt to find out something about Anthia. Now Hippothous came to the temple with Anthia. And she looked at the offerings and remembered the past. "O Helius," she exclaimed, "who look over the affairs of all men and pass over only me in my misery, when I was in Rhodes before I worshiped you in happiness and made sacrifices with Habrocomes, and at the time people thought I was happy; but now I am a slave instead of a free woman, a captive wretch instead of that happy girl, and I am going to Ephesus alone and will appear before my family without Habrocomes."

She said this and shed many tears and asked Hippothous to let her cut off a lock of her hair, as an offering to Helius, and put up a prayer about Habrocomes. Hippothous agreed; cutting off what she could of her hair and choosing a suitable opportunity, when everyone had gone away, she offered it with the inscription

> ON BEHALF OF HER HUSBAND HABROCOMES
> ANTHIA DEDICATED HER HAIR TO THE GOD.

When she had done this and prayed, she went away with Hippothous.

12 But Leucon and Rhode, who had been at the procession up to this point, stopped at the temple, looked at the offerings, and recognizing the names of their masters, first kissed the hair and lamented as much as if they were looking at Anthia, but finally went round to see if they could find her anywhere (the names were already familiar to the Rhodian crowd from their previous visit). That day they could find nothing and went away and told Habrocomes

what was in the temple. His heart was disturbed at this unexpected event, but he had high hopes of finding Anthia.

The next day Anthia again arrived at the temple with Hippothous, since they were unable to sail. She sat by the offerings and wept and wailed. Meanwhile Leucon and Rhode came too, leaving Habrocomes at home, since he was depressed for the same reasons as before. They came and saw Anthia but as yet did not recognize her; but they reflected on everything: the girl's love, her tears, the offerings, the names, and her appearance; and in this way they gradually recognized her. Falling to their knees, they lay dumbfounded. But she wondered who they were and what they wanted, for she never expected to see Leucon and Rhode. But when they recovered, they said: "Mistress Anthia, we are your slaves, Leucon and Rhode, who shared your voyage and the pirate lair. But what chance brings you here? Have courage, mistress; Habrocomes is safe; and he is here, always mourning for you." When Anthia heard this she was amazed at the news: she came to herself with difficulty, recognized them, embraced them and greeted them, and learned in the greatest detail all about Habrocomes.

13 When the Rhodians heard that Anthia and Habrocomes had been found, they all surged together. Hippothous too was among them; he was recognized by Leucon and Rhode, and learned in turn who they were. And now they had everything they wanted, except that Habrocomes still did not know the news. They ran to the house just as they were. And when he heard from one of the Rhodians that Anthia had been found, Habrocomes ran through the middle of the city like a madman, shouting, "Anthia!" And so he met Anthia near the temple of Isis, followed by a great crowd of Rhodians. When they saw each other, they recognized each other at once, for that was their fervent desire. They embraced each other and fell to the ground. A host of different emotions took hold of them at once—joy, grief, fear, memory of past events, and anxiety for the future. The Rhodians cheered and shouted in their excitement, hailing Isis as a great goddess and exclaiming, "Now once again we see Habrocomes and Anthia, the beautiful pair!" They recovered, sprang up, and came into the temple of Isis, saying, "To you, greatest goddess, we owe thanks for our safety; it is you, the goddess we honor most of all, who have restored us." Paying homage before the precinct they fell down before the altar. Then they betook themselves to Leucon's house, Hippothous transferred his belongings there, and they were ready for the voyage to Ephesus.

● 28

Anthia and Habrocomes, Reunited, at the Temple of Artemis in Ephesos

XENOPHON OF EPHESOS *Ephesian Tale of Anthia and Habrocomes* 5.15   date uncertain

AUTHOR, TRANSLATION, AND TEXT: See entry 25.

> ... And after a few days' voyage they put in to Ephesus. The news had already reached the whole city that they were safe. And when they disembarked, they immediately went just as they were to the temple of Artemis, offered many prayers, and made their sacrifice, and among their offerings they set up an inscription in honor of the goddess, commemorating all their sufferings and all their adventures. When they had done this, they went up into the city and built large tombs for their parents (for they had already died from old age and despair), and they themselves lived happily ever after; the rest of their life together was one long festival.

● 29

Leucippe Takes Refuge in a Sanctuary of Artemis

ACHILLES TATIUS *Leucippe and Clitophon* 7.13   2d century C.E.

AUTHOR: Virtually nothing is known about the author. The text itself can be dated, on the basis of several ancient papyrus fragments, to the second century C.E. The plot of the novel conforms to the basic ancient Greek romance (see comments at entry 23).

TRANSLATION: John J. Winkler, in B. P. Reardon, ed., *Collected Ancient Greek Novels* (Berkeley: University of California Press, 1989).

TEXT: LCL (S. Gaselee, 1917; rev. ed., 1969); E. Vilborg, ed., *Achilles Tatius: "Leucippe and Clitophon,"* 2 vols. (Stockholm: Almqvist and Wiksell 1955–62).

BIBLIOGRAPHY: See entry 23.

> And so, since the sanctuary of Artemis was close to the estate, she ran to it and took refuge in the temple.
>
> From ancient days this temple had been forbidden to free women who were not virgins. Only men and virgins were permitted here. If a nonvirgin woman passed inside, the penalty was death, unless she was a slave accusing her master, in which case she was allowed to beseech the goddess, and the magistrates would hear the case between her and her master. If the master had in fact done no wrong, he recovered his maidservant, swearing that he would not bear a grudge for her flight. If it was decided that the serving girl had a just case, she remained there as a slave to the goddess.

Observances, Rituals, and Festivals

63

Chloe and Daphnis Worship the Nymphs

LONGUS *Daphnis and Chloe* 2.2, 4.39 date uncertain

AUTHOR: Virtually nothing is known about the author, although he locates himself on the Greek island of Lesbos. The plot of the novel conforms to the basic ancient Greek romance (see comments at entry 23). Although in most of these novels, the lovers are members of the elite classes, Daphnis and Chloe are simple shepherds living an idealized pastoral life.

TRANSLATION: Christopher Gill, in B. P. Reardon, ed., *Collected Ancient Greek Novels* (Berkeley: University of California Press, 1989).

TEXT: Budé (G. Dalmeyda, 1934); Teubner (M. D. Reeve, 1982).

ADDITIONAL TRANSLATION: Ronald McCail, *Longus, "Daphnis and Chloe,"* OWC (New York: Oxford University Press, 2002).

ADDITIONAL TEXT AND TRANSLATIONS: LCL (J. M. Edmond, 1916; rev. trans. by George Thornley); O. Schönberger, *Longos, "Daphnis und Chloe"* (Berlin, 1960; 2d ed., 1973).

BIBLIOGRAPHY: See entry 23.

2.2 A few days later, the vines were harvested, the sweet new wine was in jars, and there was no longer any need for many hands. Daphnis and Chloe drove their flocks down to the plain and, in a happy mood, worshiped the Nymphs, bringing them bunches of grapes still on the shoots as firstfruits of the grape harvest. Not that they ever went past them and neglected them before; they always visited them when they went to pasture and worshiped them when they left the pasture and without fail brought them some kind of offering, a flower or a fruit or some green leaves or a libation of milk. For this, they received a reward from the goddesses later on.

4.39 Not only then but for as long as they lived, Daphnis and Chloe spent most of their time living the pastoral life. They worshiped as their gods the Nymphs, Pan, and Love, owned numerous flocks of sheep and goats, and thought that fruit and milk were the sweetest kind of food. When they had a baby boy, they put him under a she-goat for nursing, and when their second child was born to them, a little girl, they had her suck the teat of a ewe. They called the boy Philopoemen, and the girl Agele. They also decorated the cave and set up images in it and established an altar to Love the Shepherd, and gave Pan a temple to live in instead of the pine, calling him Pan the Soldier.

Devotions at a Private Feast in a Temple of Hermes

● 31A

HELIODORUS *An Ethiopian Story* 5.15   3d or 4th century C.E.?

AUTHOR, TRANSLATION, AND TEXT: See entry 22.

> 5.15 Acting on these words, he led the way to the feast. The inside of the
> temple had been set aside specially for the ladies, while tables had been laid
> for the men in the temple forecourt. When their appetites for the pleasures
> of the table were satisfied, the tables were removed to make way for wine
> bowls, and the men sang and poured a libation of departure to Dionysos,
> while the women danced a hymn of thanksgiving to Demeter. But Charikleia
> found a private place to perform her own rites, and there she prayed to the
> gods to preserve her life for Theagenes' sake, and his for hers.

● 31B

Charikleia at the Statue's Feet

HELIODORUS *An Ethiopian Story* 5.34   3d or 4th century C.E.?

AUTHOR, TRANSLATION, AND TEXT: See entry 22.

> 5.34 Thereupon the libation was passed around the table, and the guests dis-
> persed. Kalasiris was looking out for Charikleia; he watched the people go
> past but could not see her in the throng. Eventually a woman told him where
> she was, and he went through into the shrine, where he found her clinging
> fast to the feet of the holy statue. Exhausted by her protracted prayers and by
> the ravages of sorrow, she had slipped into a deep sleep. Kalasiris shed a tear
> or two and implored the god to let her life take a happier turn. Then, gently,
> he woke her and led her back to their lodgings. She blushed, apparently at
> having allowed sleep to get the better of her without realizing. Then she with-
> drew into the privacy of the women's room, but, lying in bed beside Nausi-
> kles' daughter, she was unable to sleep for all the fears and anxieties preying
> on her mind.

● 32

A Woman Whose Acceptance of Ascetic Christianity Causes Her Husband to Bring Charges Against Her and Her Christian Teachers

JUSTIN MARTYR *Second Apology* 2   mid–2d century C.E.

AUTHOR: Born in Flavia Neapolis (the biblical Shechem) around 100 C.E., Justin
apparently studied philosophy extensively before becoming a Christian, sometime

before about 135 C.E. In addition to two defenses of Christianity (the *First Apology* and *Second Apology*), he also wrote a lengthy *Dialogue with Trypho,* supposedly a record of his public debate with a Jewish man named Trypho. Justin was martyred in Rome in 165 C.E.

TRANSLATION: Leslie William Barnard, *The First and Second Apologies: St. Justin Martyr,* ACW 56 (New York: Paulist Press, 1997).

TEXT: André Wartelle, *St. Justin, "Apologies": Introduction, texte critique, traduction, commentaire et index* (Paris: Études Augustiniennes, 1987).

BIBLIOGRAPHY: Robert M. Grant, "A Woman of Rome: The Matron in Justin, *Apology* 2.1–9," *Church History* 54 (1985): 461–72.

A certain woman lived with an intemperate husband, she herself also having once been intemperate. But when she came to the knowledge of the teachings of Christ she became sober-minded and tried to persuade her husband in like manner to be temperate, bringing forward the teachings, and assuring him that there will be punishment in eternal fire inflicted on those who do not live temperately and in conformity to right reason. But he, continuing in the same extravagances, alienated his wife from him by his deeds. For she, considering it wicked to live any longer as a wife with a husband who sought in every way means of pleasure contrary to the law of nature and in violation of what is right, wished to be divorced from him.

And when she was entreated earnestly by her friends, who advised her still to continue with him, with the thought that some time or other her husband might show hope of amendment, she did violence to her own inclinations and remained with him. But since her husband had gone to Alexandria, and was reported as to be conducting himself worse than ever—that by continuing in matrimonial connection with him, and by sharing his table and bed, she might not become a sharer also in his evils and impieties—she gave him what is called a bill of divorce, and was separated from him. But this noble husband of hers—while he should have been rejoicing that those deeds which before she committed without hesitation with the servants and hirelings, when she delighted that he too should give up the same—when she had separated from him since he refused to alter his ways, brought an accusation against her, saying that she was a Christian. And she presented a paper to the emperor requesting that first she should be allowed to arrange her affairs, and afterward make her defense against the accusation, when her affairs were set in order; and this was granted. And her erstwhile husband, since he was now no longer able to prosecute her, directed his assaults against a certain Ptolemaeus, whom Urbicus punished, who had been her teacher of Christian doctrines—and this he did in the following manner. He persuaded a centurion who had cast Ptolemaeus into prison, and who was friendly to himself, to seize Ptolemaeus and interrogate him on this point alone—is he a Christian? And Ptolemaeus, being a lover of truth and not of a deceitful nor false nature, when he confessed that he was a Christian, was put in bonds by the centurion, and for a long period was punished in the prison. And at last when the man came to Urbicus, he was asked only this question—whether he was a Christian. And again, conscious of the good which he owed to the teaching which proceeded from Christ, he confessed the doctrine of divine virtue. For he who denies anything, either denies it because he has condemned it, or shrinks from confessing it, because he knows himself to be unworthy of and alien to it; neither of which is that of the true Christian. And when Urbicus ordered him to be led away to punishment, a certain Lucius, who was also himself a Christian, seeing the unreasonable judgment which had thus been given, said to Urbicus: "What is the basis of this judgment? Why have you punished this man, not as an adulterer, nor fornicator, nor murderer, nor thief, nor robber, nor convicted of any crime at all, but as one who has only confessed that he is called by the name of Christian? This judgment of yours, O Urbicus, does not become the Emperor Pius, nor the philosopher-son of Caesar nor the Sacred Senate." And he said nothing else in answer to Lucius than this: "You also seem to me to be such a one." And when Lucius answered, "Most certainly I am," he again ordered him to be led away. And he gave thanks, knowing that he was delivered from such wicked rulers, and was going to the Father and King of the heavens. And also a third having come forward was sentenced to be punished.

● 33

A Tour of Hellish Torments Related by a Murdered Christian Woman Raised from the Dead by the Apostle Thomas

Acts of Thomas 6   probably 3d century C.E.

WORK: Probably composed in Syriac in the third century C.E., in Syria, the *Acts of Thomas* narrates the travels of the apostle Thomas in India. The longest and most cohesive of the so-called *Apocryphal Acts of the Apostles*, the *Acts of Thomas* contains numerous tales about Thomas's conversion of aristocratic women to an ascetic form of Christianity, tales that have their counterparts in numerous other apocryphal Acts (including the *Acts of [Paul and] Thecla*; see entry 105). Tours of the rewards and punishments awaiting the dead were a popular genre in Jewish and Christian literature of this period.

TRANSLATION: *ANT*, from the Greek.

TEXTS: M. Bonnet, *Acta Apostolorum Apocrypha*, vol. 2.2 (1903; repr., Darmstadt: Wissenschaftliche Buchgesellschaft, 1959), 99–288, Greek; A. F. J. Klijn, *The Acts of Thomas: Introduction, Text, Commentary*, Supplement to Novum Testamentum 5

(Leiden: E. J. Brill, 1962), Syriac. The existing Syriac version dates to the fourth century C.E. or later.

ADDITIONAL TRANSLATION: *NTA.*

BIBLIOGRAPHY: Martha Himmelfarb, *Ascent to Heaven in Jewish and Christian Apocalypses* (Oxford: Oxford University Press, 1993); Martha Himmelfarb, *Tours of Hell: An Apocalyptic Form in Jewish and Christian Literature* (Philadelphia: University of Pennsylvania Press, 1983); Ross S. Kraemer, "The Conversion of Women to Ascetic Forms of Christianity," *Signs: Journal of Women in Culture and Society* 6 (1980): 298–307, reprinted in Judith M. Bennet, Elizabeth A. Clark, Jean O'Barr, B. Anne Vilen, and Sarah Westphal-Wihl, eds., *Sisters and Workers in the Middle Ages* (Chicago: University of Chicago Press, 1989), 198–207. See also entry 105.

CONCERNING THE YOUNG MAN WHO KILLED THE MAIDEN

51 Now there was a certain young man, who had committed a nefarious deed. He came and partook of the eucharist. And his two hands withered, so that he could no longer put them to his mouth. When those present saw him, they told the apostle what had happened. And the apostle called him and said, "Tell me, my son, and be not afraid of what you have done before you came here. For the eucharist of the Lord has convicted you. For this gift, by entering many, brings healing, especially to those who come in faith and love; but you it has withered away, and what has happened has happened not without some justification." And the young man convicted by the eucharist of the Lord came up, fell at the apostle's feet, and besought him and said, "An evil deed has been done by me, whilst I thought to do something good. I loved a woman who lived in an inn outside the city, and she loved me also. And when I heard about you, believing that you proclaim the living God, I came and received the seal from you along with the others. And you said, 'Whoever shall indulge in impure intercourse, especially in adultery, shall not have life with the God whom I preach.' As I loved her very much, I entreated her and tried to persuade her to live with me in chaste and pure conduct, as you teach. And she would not. Since she would not, I took a sword and killed her. For I could not see her commit adultery with another."

52 When the apostle heard this he said, "O insane intercourse, how you lead to shamelessness! O unrestrained lust, how have you excited this man to do this! O work of the serpent, how you rage in your own!" And the apostle ordered some water to be brought in a dish. And when the water had been brought he said, "Come, waters from the living waters; everlasting, sent to us from the everlasting; rest, sent to us from the one who gives rest; power of salvation, proceeding from that power which overcomes all and subjects it to its will—come and dwell in these waters, that the gift of the Holy Spirit may be completely fulfilled in them!" And to the young man he said, "Go, wash

your hands in these waters." And when he had washed them they were restored. And the apostle said to him, "Do you believe in our Lord Jesus Christ, that he can do all things?" And he said, "Though I am the least, yet I believe. But I did this in the hope of doing something good. For I entreated her, as I told you already, but she would not be persuaded by me to keep herself chaste."

53 And the apostle said to him, "Come, let us go to the inn where you committed the deed, and let us see what happened." And the young man went before the apostle on the road. When they had come to the inn they found her lying there. And when the apostle saw her he was sad, for she was a beautiful girl. And he ordered her to be brought into the middle of the inn. And putting her on a couch they carried it out and set it in the midst of the courtyard of the inn. And the apostle laid his hand on her and began to say, "Jesus, who appear to us at all times—for this is your will, that we should always seek you, and you have given us the right to ask and to receive, and have not only permitted us this, but have also taught us how to pray—who are not seen by us with the bodily eyes, but who are never hidden from those of our soul, and who are hidden in form, but manifested to us by your works; by your many deeds we have recognized you as much as we are able, and you have given us your gifts without measure saying, 'Ask, and it shall be given you; seek, and you shall find; knock, and it shall be opened unto you.' We pray, therefore, being afraid of our sins. And we ask you not for riches or gold or silver or possessions or any of those things that come from earth and go into the earth again; but we beg of you and entreat that in your holy name you raise this woman lying here by your power, to your glory and to an awakening of faith in those who stand by."

54 And he said to the young man, after sealing him, "Go and take her hand and say to her, 'With iron I killed you with my hands, and with my hands I raise you because of faith in Jesus.' " And the young man went and stood by her, saying, "I have believed in you, O Christ Jesus." And looking upon Judas Thomas the apostle, he said to him, "Pray for me, that my Lord, upon whom I call, may come to my help." And laying his hand on her hand he said, "Come, Lord Jesus Christ, give her life and me the reality of your faith." And he drew her by the hand, and she sprang up and sat looking at the great multitude standing around. And she also saw the apostle standing opposite her, and leaving her couch she sprang up and fell at his feet and took hold of his garments, saying, "I pray, Lord, where is your companion who has not left me to remain in that fearful and grievous place, but has given me up to you, saying, 'Take this one, that she may be made perfect, and thereafter be brought into her own place'?"

55 And the apostle said to her, "Tell us where you have been." And she answered, "Do you, who were with me, to whom also I was entrusted, wish to

hear?" And she commenced thus: "An ugly-looking man, entirely black, received me; and his clothing was exceedingly filthy. And he took me to a place where there were many chasms, and a great stench and most hateful vapour were given forth thence. And he made me look into each chasm, and in the first I saw blazing fire, and fiery wheels running, and souls were hung upon these wheels, dashing against each other. And there was crying and great lamentation and no Saviour was there. And that man said to me, 'These souls are akin to you, and in the days of reckoning they were delivered to punishment and destruction. And then others are brought in their stead; in like manner all these are again succeeded by others. These are they who perverted the intercourse of man and wife.' And again I looked down, and saw infants heaped upon each other, struggling and lying upon each other. And he said to me, 'These are their children, and for this they are placed here for a testimony against them.'

56 "And he brought me to another chasm, and as I looked into it I saw mud and worms spouting forth, and souls wallowing there; and I heard a great gnashing of teeth come from them. And that man said to me, 'These are the souls of women who left their husbands and committed adultery with others, and they have been brought to this torment.' And he showed me another chasm, and looking into it I saw souls hung up, some by the tongue, some by the hair, some by the hands, others by the feet, head downward, and reeking with smoke and sulphur. Concerning these the man who accompanied me said the following: 'The souls hung up by the tongue are slanderers and such as have spoken false and disgraceful words and are not ashamed. Those hung up by their hair are the shameless, who are not ashamed at all and go about with uncovered heads in the world. Those hung up by the hands are they who took that which did not belong to them and have stolen, and who never gave anything to the poor, nor helped the afflicted; but they did so because they wished to get everything, and cared neither for law nor right. And these hung up by the feet are those who lightly and eagerly walked in wicked ways and disorderly paths, not visiting the sick nor escorting those who depart this life. On this account each soul receives what it has done.'

57 "And again he led me forth and showed me a very dark cavern, exhaling a very bad stench. Many souls were peeping out thence, wishing to get some share of the air. And their keepers would not let them look out. And my companion said to me, 'This is the prison of those souls which you saw. For when they have fully received their punishment for that which each has done, others succeed them. Some are fully consumed, others are given up to other punishments.' And the keepers of the souls in the dark cavern said to the man that had charge of me, 'Give her to us, that we may bring her to the others till the time comes when she is handed over to punishment.' But he said to them, 'I will not give her to you, because I am afraid of him who

delivered her to me. For I was not told to leave her here; I shall take her back with me, till I get an injunction about her.' And he took me and brought me to another place, where there were men who were cruelly tortured. He who is like you took me and gave me up to you, saying to you, 'Take her, for she is one of the sheep which have wandered away.' And received by you, I now stand before you; I beg, therefore, and supplicate you that I may not come to those places of punishment which I have seen."

58 And the apostle said, "You have heard what this woman has recounted. And these are not the only punishments, but there are others worse than these. And you too, unless you turn to the God whom I preach, and abstain from your former works and from the deeds which you did in ignorance, shall find your end in these punishments. Believe, therefore, in Christ Jesus, and he will forgive you the former sins and will cleanse you from all your bodily desires that remain on the earth, and will heal you from the faults that follow after you and go along with you and are found before you. Let every one of you put off the old man and put on the new, and leave your former course of conduct and behaviour. Those who steal, let them steal no more, but let them live, labouring and working. The adulterers are no more to commit adultery, lest they give themselves up to everlasting punishment. For with God adultery is an evil exceedingly wicked above all other evils. Put away also covetousness and lying and drunkenness and slandering, and do not return evil for evil! For all these are alien and strange to the God whom I preach. But walk rather in faith and meekness and holiness and hope, in which God rejoices, that you may become his kinsmen, expecting from him those gifts which only a few receive."

59 The whole people therefore believed and presented obedient souls to the living God and Christ Jesus, rejoicing in the blessed works of the Most High and in his holy service. And they brought money for the service of the widows. For he had them gathered together in the cities, and he sent to all of them by his deacons what was necessary, both clothing as well as food. He himself did not cease to preach and to speak to them and to show that this Jesus is the Messiah of whom the Scriptures have spoken that he should be crucified and be raised after three days from the dead. He also showed to them and explained, beginning from the prophets, what was said concerning the Messiah, that it was necessary for him to come, and that everything had to be accomplished which had been prophesied of him. And the fame of him spread over all the cities and villages, and all who had sick persons or such as were troubled by unclean spirits brought them to him; and some they laid on the road by which he was to pass, and he healed all by the power of the Lord. And those who were healed by him said with one accord and one voice, "Glory to you, Jesus, who in like manner has given healing to all through your servant and apostle Thomas! And being in good health and re-

joicing, we pray that we may become members of your flock and be counted among your sheep. Receive us, therefore, O Lord, and consider not our trespasses and our former transgressions, which we did while we were in ignorance!"

60 And the apostle said, "Glory be to the only-begotten of the Father, glory to the first-born of many brethren; glory to you, the helper and defender of those who come to your refuge. You are the sleepless one who awaken those who sleep, and who live and bring to life those lying in death; O God Jesus Christ, Son of the living God, redeemer and helper, refuge and rest of all those that labour in your work, who heal those who for your name's sake bear the burden and heat of the day, we give thanks for the gifts given to us by you, and for the help from you bestowed upon us, and your providential care that has come upon us from you.

61 "Perfect these things upon us to the end, that we may have confidence in you. Look upon us because for your sake we have left our houses and our patrimony, and for your sake we have gladly and willingly become strangers. Look upon us, O Lord, because for your sake we have given up our own possessions, that we might obtain you for a possession that shall not be taken away. Look upon us, O Lord, because we have left those related to us by ties of kindred, in order that we may be united in relationship to you. Look upon us, O Lord, who have left our fathers and mothers and guardians, that we may behold your father and be satisfied with his divine nourishment. Look upon us, O Lord, because for your sake we have left our bodily consorts and our earthly fruit, in order that we may share in that true and lasting communion and bring forth true fruits, whose nature is from above, which no one can take from us, in which we abide and they abide with us."

● 34

Admonitions against the Participation of Menstruating Christian Women (and of Men Who Have Had a Nocturnal Emission) in the Eucharist

DIONYSIUS OF ALEXANDRIA *Epistle to the Bishop Basilides*   3d century C.E.

AUTHOR: The child of wealthy non-Christian parents, Dionysius studied with Origen of Alexandria and ultimately became bishop of that city in 247 C.E. During the persecutions by the emperor Decius he went into hiding rather than suffer. Although Dionysius was hardly alone in his response to the persecutions, fleeing torture and martyrdom was highly controversial among Christians in North Africa in the mid–third century, and Dionysius's actions may explain, in part, why his writings were preserved only in fragments, mostly in Eusebius. His *Epistle to the*

Bishop Basilides was preserved in a larger collection of epistles of the Greek church that served as one of the sources of that church's canon law.

TRANSLATION: *ANF* 6:94–96.

TEXTS: C. L. Feltoe, *Dionusiou Leipsana: The Letters and Other Remains of Dionysius of Alexandria* (Cambridge: Cambridge University Press, 1904), 91–105; PG 10, 1272–77.

CANON II

The question touching women in the time of their separation, whether it is proper for them when in such a condition to enter the house of God, I consider a superfluous inquiry. For I do not think that, if they are believing and pious women, they will themselves be rash enough in such a condition either to approach the holy table or to touch the body and blood of the Lord. Certainly the woman who had the issue of blood of twelve years' standing did not touch (the Lord) Himself, but only the hem of His garment, with a view to her cure. For to pray, however a person may be situated, and to remember the Lord, in whatever condition a person may be, and to offer up petitions for the obtaining of help, are exercises altogether blameless. But the individual who is not perfectly pure both in soul and in body, shall be interdicted from approaching the holy of holies.

CANON IV

As to those who are overtaken by an involuntary flux in the nighttime, let such follow the testimony of their own conscience, and consider themselves as to whether they are doubtfully minded in this matter or not. And he that doubteth in the matter of meats, the apostle tells us, "is damned if he eat." In these things, therefore, let every one who approaches God be of a good conscience, and of a proper confidence, so far as his own judgment is concerned. And, indeed, it is in order to show your regard for us (for you are not ignorant, beloved) that you have proposed these questions to us, making us of one mind, as indeed we are, and of one spirit with yourself. And I, for my part, have thus set forth my opinions in public, not as a teacher, but only as it becomes us with all simplicity to confer with each other. And when you have examined this opinion of mine, my most intelligent son, you will write back to me your notion of these matters, and let me know whatever may seem to you to be just and preferable, and whether you approve of my judgment in these things. That it may fare well with you, my beloved son, as you minister to the Lord in peace, is my prayer.

● 35
Rabbinic Purity Regulations Concerning Menstruation and Other Blood Flow

MISHNAH *Niddah* 1.1–2.4   3d century C.E.

WORK: The many texts generally grouped under the label "ancient rabbinic sources," including the Mishnah, the Tosefta, the Babylonian and Jerusalem Talmuds, Midrash Rabbah, and others, were compiled between the third and seventh centuries C.E. There is much debate about how accurately they depict the practices and beliefs of Jewish women (and most Jewish men) in antiquity. Increasingly, many scholars recognize that these texts envision a world that corresponds loosely at best to the actual social experiences of most Jews in the Roman period. In many cases, the stories and legal discussions in these texts may tell us more about what some Jewish rabbis thought about women, or imagined about women, than they do about what women did and thought themselves. Nevertheless, these sources constitute the largest body of literary evidence for Jews and Judaism in late antiquity, and the difficulties of extracting reliable historical information from them do not excuse us from closely examining their commentary on women.

The selections in this entry are taken from the Mishnah: subsequent selections are taken from the Babylonian Talmud and from commentaries on various biblical books known collectively as Midrash Rabbah. Comparable in some ways to a combination of case law and theoretical legal discussions, the Mishnah (meaning "teaching" or "oral instruction") is a collection of Jewish traditions, particularly concerned with legal matters, that attains foundational status in subsequent mainstream Judaism. It contains sixty-three tractates grouped into six divisions (Seeds [on agriculture], Set Feasts, Women, Damages, Holy Things, and Purities). Tradition assigns its compilation to Rabbi Judah the Prince around the beginning of the third century C.E., a date that most scholars accept.

There are presently no critical editions of rabbinic texts comparable to those generally available for ancient writings in Greek and Latin (including Christian authors).

TRANSLATION: Jacob Neusner, *The Mishnah: A New Translation* (New Haven: Yale University Press, 1988).

TEXT: Hanokh Albeck, *Shishah Sidre Mishnah* (Jerusalem: Mosad Bialik, 1952–58); P. Blackman, *Mishnayoth* (London: Mishna Press, 1951–56).

TEXT AND TRANSLATION: Philip Blackman, *Mishnayoth: Pointed Hebrew Text, English Translation, Introductions, Notes, Supplement, Appendix, Indexes, Addenda, Corrigenda* (Gateshead, UK: Judaica Press, 1963, repr. 1983).

ADDITIONAL TRANSLATION: H. Danby, *The Mishnah* (London: Oxford University Press, 1933).

BIBLIOGRAPHY: *Women and Christian Origins*, 35–49; Judith R. Baskin, *Midrashic Women: Formations of the Feminine in Rabbinic Literature* (Hanover, N.H.: University Press of New England for Brandeis University Press, 2002; Daniel Boyarin, *Carnal Israel: Reading Sex in Talmudic Culture* (Berkeley: University of California Press, 1993); Charlotte Fonrobert, *Menstrual Purity: Rabbinic and Christian Constructions of Biblical Gender* (Stanford, Calif.: Stanford University Press, 2000); Judith Hauptman, *Rereading the Rabbis: A Woman's Voice* (Boulder, Colo.: Westview Press, 1997); Tal Ilan, *Jewish Women in Greco-Roman Palestine: An Inquiry into Image and Status*, Texte und Studien zum Antiken Judentum 44 (Tübingen: J. C. B. Mohr [Siebeck], 1995); Tal Ilan, *Integrating Women into Second Temple History*, Texte und Studien zum Antiken Judentum 76 (Tübingen: J. C. B. Mohr [Siebeck], 1999); Tal Ilan, *Mine and Yours Are Hers: Retrieving Women's History from Rabbinic Literature* (Leiden: E. J. Brill, 1997); Miriam Peskowitz, *Spinning Fantasies: Rabbis, Gender, and History* (Los Angeles: University of California Press, 1997); Jacob Neusner, *A History of the Mishnaic Law of Women*, Studies in Judaism in Late Antiquity (Leiden: E. J. Brill, 1980); Judith Romney Wegner, *Chattel or Person? The Status of Women in the Mishnah* (Oxford: Oxford University Press, 1988); Judith Romney Wegner, "The Image and Status of Women in Classical Rabbinic Judaism," in Judith Baskin, ed., *Jewish Women in Historical Perspective*, 2d ed. (Detroit: Wayne State University Press, 1998), 73–100.

1:1

A Shammai says, "[For] all women [it is] sufficient for them [to reckon uncleanness from] their time [of discovering a flow]."

B Hillel says, "[They are deemed unclean retroactively] from the [time of examination, at which the flow of blood was discovered] to the [last] examination [she made beforehand].

C "And even for many days."

D And sages say not in accord with the opinion of this one nor in accord with the opinion of that one, but:

E [the woman is held to have been unclean only] during [the preceding] twenty-four hours [when] this lessens the period from the examination to the [last] examination,

F [and she is held to have been unclean only] during the period from examination to examination [when] this lessens the period of twenty-four hours.

G Every woman who has a fixed period—sufficient for her is her time.

H She who makes use of test-rags, lo, this is equivalent to an examination,

I which lessens either the period of the twenty-four hours or the period from examination to examination.

Observances, Rituals, and Festivals

1:2

A How [is the case in which] her time suffices for her?

B [If] she was sitting on the bed and engaged in things requiring cleanness and arose and saw [a drop of blood],

C she is unclean,

D but all of those [things requiring cleanness] are clean.

E Even though they have said, "She renders unclean [whatever she touched during the preceding] twenty-four hour period," she takes count [of the days prescribed in the Torah] only from the time that she saw a drop of blood.

1:3

A R. Eliezer says, "Four women [fall into the category of those for whom the] time [of first seeing blood] suffices:

B "(1) the virgin, (2) the pregnant woman, (3) the nursing mother, and (4) the old lady."

C Said R. Joshua, "I heard only [that this rule applies to] the virgin."

D But the law is in accord with the opinion of R. Eliezer.

1:4

E Who is (1) the virgin?

F Any girl who never in her life saw a drop of blood, even though she is married.

G (2) A pregnant woman?

H Once it is known that the foetus is present.

I (3) A nursing mother?

J Until she will wean her son.

K [If] she gave her son to a wet-nurse, weaned him, or he died—

L R. Meir says, "She conveys uncleanness [to everything she touched] during the preceding twenty-four hours."

M And sages say, "Sufficient for her is her time."

1:5

N (4) Who is an old woman?

O Any woman for whom three periods have gone by without a flow near to the time of her old age.

P R. Eliezer says, "Any woman for whom three periods have passed without her suffering a flow—sufficient for her is her time."

Q R. Yosé says, "A pregnant woman and a nursing mother for whom three periods have passed—sufficient for them is their time."

1:6

A And of what case did they speak when they said, "Sufficient for her is her time"?

B In the case of the first appearance of a drop of blood.

C But in the case of the second appearance of such a drop of blood, she conveys uncleanness to whatever she touched during the preceding twenty-four hours.

D But if she saw the first flow by reason of constraint [through abnormal causes], even in the case of the second drop of blood, sufficient for her is her time.

1:7

A Even though they have said, "Sufficient for her is her time," (1) she must nonetheless examine herself,

B except for (a) the menstruating woman,

C and (b) the woman who is sitting in the blood of her purifying [after having given birth].

D And (2) she makes use of test rags,

E except for (a) the one who is sitting in the blood of her purifying,

F and (b) a virgin, whose drops of blood are clean.

G And (3) twice must she [who has a fixed period] examine herself:

H (a) in the morning and (b) at twilight,

I and (c) when she prepares for sexual relations.

J Beyond these examinations, women of the priestly caste [must examine themselves] when they eat heave-offering.

K R. Judah says, "Also: when they finish eating heave-offering."

2:1

A Any hand which makes many examinations—in the case of women is to be praised and in the case of men is to be cut off.

B The deaf-mute, and the imbecile, and the blind, and the unconscious woman—

C if there are women of sound sense, they care for them, and they eat heave-offering.

D It is the way of Israelite women to make use of two test-rags, one for him and one for her.

E The pious prepare yet a third, to take care of the house.

2:2

A If it [a drop of blood] is found on his, they are unclean and liable for a sacrifice.

B If it is found on hers at the time itself, they are unclean [for seven days] and liable for a sacrifice.

C If it is found on hers after a while, their uncleanness remains in doubt, and they are exempt from an offering.

2:3

D What is meant by "after a while"?

E Sufficient time that the woman may descend from the bed and wash her face [sexual organs].

F And afterward [if a drop of blood appears], she imparts uncleanness [to objects she touched] during the preceding twenty-four-hour period but does not impart uncleanness [as a menstruant for seven days] to him who has had sexual relations with her.

G R. 'Aqiva says, "Also: she imparts uncleanness to him who has sexual relations with her."

H And sages agree with R. 'Aqiva in the case of one who sees a bloodstain, that she imparts uncleanness to him who has sexual relations with her.

2:4

A All women are assumed to be clean for their husbands.

B Those that come home from a trip—their wives are assumed to be clean for them.

C The House of Shammai say, "She requires two test-rags for each act of sexual relations.

D "Or she should have intercourse in the light of a lamp."

E And the House of Hillel say, "It suffices for her [to make use of] two test-rags for the entire night."

● 36

Rabbinic Arguments Against a Misogynist Tradition

BABYLONIAN TALMUD *Sotah* 22b   6th century C.E.?

WORK: The selection here (and in entries 44–46) is taken from the Talmud (meaning "study," "learning," or "instruction"), the classic compilation of Jewish law. The Talmud contains both the Mishnah (see entry 35) and commentary (known as Gemara), in Aramaic, on many, although not all, tractates of the Mishnah. The

Babylonian Talmud, usually referred to as *the* Talmud, contains traditions attributed to rabbis living in Sassanid Babylonia (modern-day Iraq), while the less well known Jerusalem Talmud (or Talmud of the Land of Israel) contains traditions attributed to rabbis living in the land of Israel (essentially, the Galilee). Given the complex nature of both Talmudim, dating them is quite difficult. The Jerusalem Talmud is generally thought to have been redacted in the early fifth century C.E., while the Babylonian Talmud appears to be somewhat later, perhaps sixth century. As with the Mishnah (see previous entry), there are no critical editions of the Talmud.

TRANSLATION (AND TEXT): I. Epstein, ed., *The Babylonian Talmud*, 35 vols. (London: Soncino, 1935–52).

TEXT: *Talmud Babli* (Wilna, 1880–86); *Talmud Jerushalmi* (Wilna, 1922).

ADDITIONAL TRANSLATIONS: Jacob Neusner, *The Talmud of Babylonia: An American Translation*, 68 vols. BJS (Chico, Calif.: Scholars Press; Atlanta, Ga.: Scholars Press, 1984–93); Jacob Neusner, *The Talmud of the Land of Israel: A Preliminary Translation and Explanation*, 35 vols. (Chicago: University of Chicago Press, 1982–94). The tractate *Sotah* appears in vol. 27 of *Talmud of the Land of Israel* (1984).

BIBLIOGRAPHY: See entry 35.

MISHNAH:

A She hardly sufficed to drink it before her face turns yellow, her eyes bulge out, and her veins swell.

B And they say, "Take her away! Take her away!"

C so that the Temple-court will not be made unclean [by her corpse].

D [But if nothing happened], if she had merit, she would attribute [her good fortune] to it.

E There is the possibility that merit suspends the curse for one year, and there is the possibility that merit suspends the curse for two years, and there is the possibility that merit suspends the curse for three years.

F On this basis Ben Azzai says, "A man is required to teach Torah to his daughter.

G "For if she should drink the water, she should know that [if nothing happens to her], merit is what suspends [the curse from taking effect]."

H R. Eliezer says, "Whoever teaches Torah to his daughter teaches her sexual satisfaction."

I R. Joshua says, "A woman wants a qab [of food] with sexual satisfaction more than nine qabs with abstinence."

J He would say, "A foolish saint, a smart knave, an abstemious woman,

K "and the blows of abstainers (perushim)—

L "lo, these wear out the world."

GEMARA:

A An abstemious woman [M. 3:4J]:

B Our rabbis have taught on Tannaite authority:

C A virgin who prays a great deal, a widow who runs hither and yon, and a minor whose months are not complete—lo, these destroy the world.

D Is that so? And has not R. Yohanan stated, "We learn fear of heaven from a virgin, [certainty of] receiving a reward from a widow.

E "Fear of sin from a virgin": For R. Yohanan heard a virgin fall on her face [in prayer] and say, "Lord of the world, you have created the Garden of Eden and you have created Gehenna, you have created righteous men and you have created wicked men. May it be pleasing to you that no men should stumble through me."

F "[Certainty of] receiving a reward from a widow": A widow has a synagogue in her neighborhood, but she used every day to come and pray in the study house of R. Yohanan. He said to her, "My daughter, isn't there a synagogue in your neighborhood?"

G She said to him, "My lord, is there no reward accruing for the steps that I take [in walking a great distance to pray with you]?"

H When it is stated [that the virgin and the widow destroy the world], it is, for example, such as Yohani, daughter of Retibi [a widow who by witchcraft made childbirth difficult for a woman and then offered prayer for her].

● 37

Discussions between Matrona and Rabbi Jose ben Halafta

WORKS: The various works known as *Midrash Rabbah* are, for the most part, a kind of scriptural commentary, arranged at least nominally in the order of the individual biblical books. They appear to have undergone considerable accretion, if not also revision, and are notoriously difficult to date. One of the earliest appears to be *Genesis Rabbah* (the "great" Genesis), which may date mostly from about the fourth century C.E. Others may be dated considerably later, some well into the early medieval period.

Matrona is both a personal name attested for Jewish (and non-Jewish) women in the Roman period and the Latin term for a respectable married woman. Some scholars see these discussions as traditions about one or more anonymous Roman *matronae*, while others consider them stories about a particular Jewish woman named Matrona. Rabbi Jose is traditionally thought to have lived in Sepphoris, in the Galilee, in the second half of the second century C.E. Additional traditions about Matrona and Rabbi Jose may be found in a range of rabbinic sources summarized and/or translated in the articles by Gershenzon and Slomovic and by Ilan, cited below.

TRANSLATIONS: Entries 37A and 37B are from Tal Ilan, "Matrona and Rabbi Jose: An Alternative Interpretation," *JSJ* 25 (1994): 18–51, who herself used the translation from H. Freedman and Maurice Simon, eds., *Midrash Rabbah*, 3d ed. (London and New York: Soncino Press, 1983) which she modified at numerous points. Except where noted, the portions in italics represent Ilan's divergence from Freedman's translation. The other entries are from Freedman and Simon. When I have used their translation, however, I have substituted the more ambiguous "Matrona" where the translators have preferred the generic "a matron."

TEXT: See references in Ilan, "Matrona and Rabbi Jose," 18–19 n. 2.

ADDITIONAL TRANSLATIONS: In their articles, Gershenzon and Slomovic, and Ilan, provide their own translations, sometimes based on different textual readings from those used by Freedman and Simon.

BIBLIOGRAPHY: R. Gershenzon and E. Slomovic, "A Second Century Jewish-Gnostic Debate: Rabbi Jose ben Halafta and the Matrona," *JSJ* 16 (1985): 1–41; Ilan, "Matrona and Rabbi Jose."

37A
Selections from *Genesis Rabbah*   4th century C.E.?

4.6

Matrona asked Rabbi Jose: Why is "for it was good" not written in connection with the second day? *He said to her: Nevertheless, in the end, he* . . . included them all . . . for it is said: "And God saw *everything* that he had made, and behold, it was very good" (Gen. 1:31). Said she to him: Supposing six men came to you and you gave a *maneh* to all but one, and then you gave a second *maneh* to all of them: would not each now have a maneh and a sixth, while the one would only have a sixth? *I wonder.* Then he explained it a second time in the same way as Rabbi Samuel bar Nahman viz.: because the making of the water was not finished. Hence "for it was good" (Gen. 1:10; 12) is written twice in connection with the third day. Once on account of the making of the water and once on account of the work done that day.

17.7

Matrona asked Rabbi Jose: Why [was woman created] by theft? *He replied*: Imagine. . . . a man depositing an ounce of silver with you in secret and you returning him a *pound* of silver openly; is that theft(?)! *She pursued*: Yet why in secret? *He answered*: At first he created her for him and he saw her full of *slime* and blood; thereupon he [*Adam*] removed her from himself and [*God*] created her a second time.

(An alternative translation, from Freedman: At first He created her for him and he saw her full of discharge and blood; thereupon He removed her from him and created her a second time.)

She retorted: I can corroborate your words. . . . it had been arranged that I should be married to my mother's brother, but because I was brought up with him in the same home, I became plain in his eyes and he went and married another woman, who is not as beautiful as I.

25.1

Matrona asked Rabbi Jose: We do not find death [stated] of Enoch. Said he to her: If it stated "And Enoch walked with God" and no more, I would agree with you. Since, however, it *adds* "And he was not, for God took him" (Gen. 5:24), it means that he was no more in the world . . . "for God took him."

63.8

Matrona asked Rabbi Jose ben Halafta: Why *was* Esau issued first? *He answered her*: Because the first drop was *that which formed* Jacob. For consider: if you place two *pearls* in a tube, does not the one put in first come out last? So also, the first drop was that which formed Jacob.

68.4

Matrona asked Rabbi Jose ben Halafta. *She said to him*: In how many days did the Holy One blessed be He create His world? *He answered*: In six days. She said to him: And what has He been doing since then? He answered: He sits and makes matches, *man to woman and woman to man*. *She said*: If that is *difficult*, I . . . can *match a hundred male slaves and a hundred female slaves in one night*. She went and matched *a hundred male slaves and a hundred female slaves in one night. Forthwith they* beat one another, *and injured one another, he saying: I will not take her, she saying: I will not take him*. . . . Said he to her: If it is easy in your eyes, it is difficult before the Holy One blessed be He as the dividing of the Red Sea. *That is what is written: "God sets the solitary in families, he brings out those who are bound into prosperity"* (Ps. 68:7).

84.21

"But he refused to be comforted" (Gen. 31:35). *Matrona* asked R. Jose. *She said to him*: It is written "For Judah prevailed *among* his brethren" (I Chron. 5:2), and we read, "And Judah was comforted" (Gen. 38:12) *and* this *one* [Jacob] *who* is the father of them all. . . . "He refused to be comforted"? *He answered*: You can be comforted *over* the dead. . . . but not *over* the living.

87.6

Matrona asked Rabbi Jose: Is it possible that Joseph, at seventeen years of age, *in all his heat*, could act thus? Thereupon, he produced the Book of Genesis *before her* and *began reading* the stories of Reuben and Judah. *He said to her:* If Scripture did not suppress aught in the case of these, who were older, and in their father's home, how much more in the case of Joseph, who was younger and his own master.

37B

An Alternative Version of the Story in *Genesis Rabbah* 68.4

Leviticus Rabbah 8.1   date uncertain

NOTE: In Ilan's translation, used here, the portions in italics indicate divergences from the version in *Genesis Rabbah*. Portions underlined in italics represent Aramaic additions.

Matrona asked Rabbi Jose ben Halaftah: In how many days did the Holy One blessed be He create his world? He answered: In six days, *as it is written: "for in six days the Lord made the heavens and the earth (Ex. 31:17).* She said to him, And what has he been *sitting and* doing since that time? He answered: He is joining couples, *proclaiming: A's wife is allotted to A; A's daughter is allotted to B, so and so's wealth is to so and so.* She said: *How many male slaves and how many female slaves I have: I can match them one with the other in no time. He said to her: If it is easy in your eyes, it is in His eyes as hard a task as the dividing of the Red Sea, since it is written: "God sets the solitary in families"* (Ps. 68:7). Rabbi Jose ben Halafta went home. *What did she do? She sent for a thousand male slaves and a thousand female slaves, placed them in rows and said to them: Male A shall marry female B, C shall marry D. Next morning they came to her. One had a head wounded, another had an eye taken out, one a broken arm and another a broken leg. He saying: I don't want her, she saying: I don't want him. She sent for him and said: Your Torah is true, fine and excellent.* Said he to her: *Have I not told you that* if in your eyes it is an easy task, it is difficult for the Holy One blessed be He as the dividing of the Red Sea, *since it is written:* "God sets the solitary in families, he brings out those who are bound into prosperity" (Ps. 68:7).

37C

Exodus Rabbah 3.12.2   date uncertain

AND MOSES FLED FROM BEFORE IT. [Matrona] once boasted to R. Jose: "My God is greater than yours." "In which way?" he asked. She replied: "For when your God revealed Himself unto Moses at the thorn-bush, he merely hid his face, but when he beheld the serpent, who is my god, immediately he fled from before it." To which he replied: "Woe to her. When our God revealed Himself at the thorn-bush, there was no room for him to flee anywhere. Where could he flee? To the heavens? Or to the sea, or dry land? See what it says in reference to our God: *Do not I fill heaven and earth? saith the Lord* (Jer. XXIII. 24). Whereas, your god, the serpent, a man can escape from merely by running away a few paces; for this reason does it say, AND MOSES FLED FROM BEFORE IT." Another reason of his flight is because he had sinned by his words. Had he not sinned, he would not have fled, for not the serpent brings death, but sin, as it is written in the story of R. Ḥanina b. Dosa. AND THE LORD SAID UNTO MOSES: PUT FORTH THY HAND, AND TAKE IT BY THE TAIL (IV, 4). We have already explained what the serpent implied for Moses; but what did this sign signify for Israel? R. Eleazar opined that the rod was converted into a serpent as symbolic of Pharaoh who was called a serpent, as it says: *Behold, I am against thee, Pharaoh King of Egypt, the great-dragon* (Ezek. XXIX, 3). He is also referred to as *the leviathan the slant serpent* (Isa. XXVII, 1), because he bit Israel. God said to him [Moses]: "Dost thou see Pharaoh who is like a serpent? Well, thou wilt smite him with the rod and in the end he will become like wood; and just as the rod cannot bite, so he will no longer bite"; hence: PUT FORTH THY HAND AND TAKE IT BY THE TAIL. THAT THEY MAY BELIEVE THAT THE LORD, THE GOD OF THEIR FATHERS ... HATH APPEARED UNTO THEE (IV, 5). Go and perform before them this miracle that they should believe that I appeared unto thee.

● 37D
Leviticus Rabbah 28.6   date uncertain

... [Matrona] addressed a question to R. Jose. She said to him: "How grieved that righteous man [Ezekiel] must have been! How many menservants and maidservants he had, yet they rejected his food and his drink!" He answered her: "Why all this? To inform you that as long as Israel are in sorrow the righteous also suffer sorrow with them."

● 37E
Numbers Rabbah 3.2   date uncertain

[Matrona] addressed a query to R. Jose. She said to him: "Your God brings near to Himself indiscriminately whomsoever He pleases." He brought her a basket of figs and she scrutinised them well, picking the best and eating. Said he to her: "You, apparently, know how to select, but the Holy One, blessed be He, does not know how to select! The one whose actions He perceives to be good, him He chooses and brings near to Himself."

● 37F

Ecclesiastes Rabbah 3.21.1   date uncertain

[Matrona] asked R. Jose b. Ḥalafta, "What is the meaning of the text, WHO KNOWETH THE SPIRIT OF MAN WHETHER IT GOETH UPWARD?" He replied, "It refers to the souls of the righteous which are placed in the Divine treasury. For so spake Abigail to David by the Holy Spirit, *'The soul of my lord shall be bound in the bundle of life.'* It might be thought that this will also happen to the souls of the wicked; therefore it is stated, *'And the souls of thine enemies, them shall He sling out as from the hollow of a sling.'* " She asked him, "What, then, is the meaning of the text, AND THE SPIRIT OF THE BEAST WHETHER IT GOETH DOWNWARD TO THE EARTH?" He replied, "It refers to the souls of the wicked which descend to Gehinnom below, as it is stated, *In the day when he went down to the netherworld I caused the deep to mourn and cover itself for him"* (Ezek. XXXI, 15).

● 38

Arabian Christian Women of Thracian Descent Who Bake Cakes to the Virgin Mary and Function as Priests

EPIPHANIUS *Medicine Box* 78.23   4th century C.E.

AUTHOR: Epiphanius was born in Eleutheropolis in Roman Palestine in the early fourth century C.E. He founded one of the early Christian monasteries there in ca. 335 and eventually became bishop of Salamis in Cyprus. He is best known for his lengthy *Panarion*, or the *Medicine Box* (sometimes also called the *Refutation of All Heresies*). This work describes eighty Christian heresies as illnesses and prescribes antidotes for the afflicted and preventives for potential victims. A significant number of the heresies concern the activities of women.

TRANSLATION: Carolyn Osiek (for the 1988 edition of this sourcebook).

TEXT: GCS 37 (1985).

ADDITIONAL TRANSLATIONS: Philip R. Amidon, S.J., ed., *The Panarion of St. Epiphanius, Bishop of Salamis, Selected Passages* (Oxford: Oxford University Press, 1990); Frank Williams, *The Panarion of Epiphanius of Salamis, Books I–III, Sects 1–80*, 2 vols. (Leiden: E. J. Brill, 1987–94).

BIBLIOGRAPHY: *Blessings*, 157–73; Stephen J. Benko, *The Virgin Goddess: Studies in the Pagan and Christian Roots of Mariology* (Leiden: E. J. Brill, 1993); Virginia Burrus, "The Heretical Woman as Symbol in Alexander, Athanasius, Epiphanius and Jerome," *HTR* 84 (1991): 229–48; Gail Corrington Streete, "Women as Sources of Redemption and Knowledge," in *Women and Christian Origins*, 330–54.

For it is related that some women in Arabia, who come from the region of Thrace, put forward this silly idea: they prepare a kind of cake in the name of the ever-Virgin, assemble together, and in the name of the holy Virgin they attempt to undertake a deed that is irreverent and blasphemous beyond measure—in her name they function as priests for women. Now all this is godless and irreverent, a degeneration from the proclamation of the Holy Spirit, all of it a diabolic device and the teaching of an unclean spirit. In their regard the saying is fulfilled: "Some will separate themselves from the sound teaching, clinging to myths and demonic teachings" [1 Tim. 4:1]. They will be worshipers of the dead, even as they (the dead) were worshiped in Israel. But the glory given to God by the Saints each in his proper time has become as good as error to those who do not see the truth.

● 39

A Heresiologist's Attempts to Refute the Teachings of Christian Women with Regard to Mary and to Disparage the Rituals and Religious Offices of Women

EPIPHANIUS *Medicine Box 79*   4th century C.E.

AUTHOR, TRANSLATION, TEXT, AND BIBLIOGRAPHY: See entry 38.

1 Next a heresy has appeared, about which I made mention just above, because of the letter written to Arabia, namely, the one about Mary. This heresy was once more taken up in Arabia from Thrace and the upper parts of Scythia, and has come to our attention. It is quite a ridiculous joke to those who know better. Let us begin to search out and describe what is connected with it. For it will be thought of as silly rather than intelligent, just like others similar to it. For just as those mentioned above, because of an insulting attitude regarding Mary, sow harmful fantasies in human minds by many conjectures, so too these who incline to the opposite extreme are seized by such consummate foolhardiness. Thus what is sung about by some outside (i.e., pagan) philosophers is fulfilled in them, namely, opposite extremes are the same. The harm is equal in both these heresies, of those who disparage the holy Virgin, and again of those who glorify her beyond what is necessary. Are not those who teach this merely women? The female sex is easily mistaken, fallible, and poor in intelligence. It is apparent that through women the devil has vomited this forth. As previously the teaching associated with Quintilla, Maximilla, and Priscilla was utterly ridiculous, so also is this one. For some women prepare a certain kind of little cake with four indentations, cover it with a fine linen veil on a solemn day of the year, and on certain days they set forth bread and offer it in the name of Mary. They all partake of the bread; this is part of what we refuted in the letter written to Arabia.

But now we shall clearly set forth everything about it and the refutations against it, and beseeching God, we will give an explanation to the best of our ability, so that by cutting off the roots of this idol-making heresy we may be able, in God, to destroy such madness.

2 Come now, servants of God, let us put on a manly mind and disperse the mania of these women. The whole of this deception is female; the disease comes from Eve who was long ago deceived. Rather it is from the serpent, that seductive beast who spoke to her in the deceptive promise, bringing nothing out into the open and not accomplishing what was promised, but rather bringing about only death by calling real what was unreal, and through the appearance of the tree causing disobedience and turning away from the truth to many diversions. Consider what kind of seed the deceiver sowed by saying, "You will be like gods." Even so the lightheadedness of these women fits well the nature of this beast, by which nature death was produced a long time ago, as I have often said. By looking quickly through the ages until now to whom is it not obvious that this teaching and the form it takes is of the devil and that the undertaking is perverted? Never in any way did a woman function as priest to God, not even Eve herself who had indeed fallen into transgression. But she did not dare to perform such an irreverent thing, nor did one of her daughters, even though Abel was a priest to God, and Cain offered sacrifices before the Lord though they were not acceptable, and Enoch was found pleasing and was taken away, and Noah presented offerings of thanksgiving to the Lord from the surplus of the ark, thus giving a sure sign of a willing disposition and giving thanks to his savior. Abraham the just one performed priestly service to God, and Melchisedech was the priest of the most high God; Isaac was found pleasing to God, and Jacob offered what he could upon the rock, by pouring oil upon the stone of his sons; Levi received the priesthood next in succession; from his descendants are those who received the priestly order, such as Moses, the prophet and revealer of sacred things; Aaron and his sons, Eleazer and Phineas; and Ithamar, his offspring. But why must I tell of the multitude of the priests of God in the Old Covenant? Achitob was a priest; the Korites, the Gersonites, the Memaritai were entrusted with the levitical order, the house of Eli, those after him who were his relatives in the house of Abimelech, Abiathar, Chelkias, and Bouzei, all the way up to Jesus the great priest, Esdras the priest, and the others. And never did a woman exercise priesthood.

3 I go now to the New Testament. If women were assigned to be priests to God or to do anything official in the church, it would certainly have been fitting for Mary herself to exercise priesthood in the New Testament, she who was considered worthy to take to her breasts the heavenly King of all, Son of God, she whose womb became a temple and was prepared as a dwelling place for the incarnate activity of the Lord according to God's love for humanity

and the amazing mystery. But it did not please him to do so, nor was she entrusted with the administering of baptism, since Christ could have been baptized by her instead of by John. But John son of Zachary was commissioned to perform a baptism of repentance of sins in the desert, and his father was a priest of God who had a vision at the hour when he offered incense. Peter and Andrew, James and John, Philip and Bartholomew, Thomas, Thaddeus, James the son of Alpheus, Judas son of James, Simon the Canaanite, and Matthias, who was chosen to complete the Twelve—all these were chosen as apostles, who perform the priesthood of the gospel throughout the earth together with Paul and Barnabas and others, as leaders of the mysteries with James the brother of the Lord and first bishop of Jerusalem. From this bishop and the above-mentioned apostles a succession of bishops and presbyters was established in the house of God. There was no woman established among them. There were four daughters of Philip the evangelist who prophesied, but they were not priests. There was Anna the prophetess, daughter of Phanuel, but she was not entrusted with priesthood. It was fitting that the prophecy be fulfilled, that "your sons shall prophesy and your daughters shall dream dreams, and your young men shall see visions." Now there is an order of deaconesses in the church, but not to perform priestly functions nor to be allowed any official work but because of the modesty of the female sex, whether at the time of washing (i.e., baptism), medical examination, or labor, and whenever a woman's body must be undressed. Thus the body need be seen not by a male officiant but by a deaconess who is directed as needed by the priest to care for a woman in need when her body is undressed; in this way the good order and ecclesiastical harmony have been well and sensibly safeguarded according to good measure. Thus neither does the divine word allow a woman to speak in church, nor to have authority over men. There is much to say about this.

4 It is to be observed that only the ecclesiastical rank of deaconesses was required, though he (Paul) named widows, yet as the most elderly and revered, not as presbyteresses or priestesses. Neither are deacons in the ecclesiastical order entrusted with performing any of the sacraments, but only with assisting at services. Whence comes this new myth to us? Whence this female conceit and womanish madness? Whence this evil nourished again by the female element pouring out upon us who know better the effeminacy of deceit, working its own way of luxury, setting upon wretched human nature to drive it out of itself? But let us take on the solid thinking of Job, the skilled fighter, let us arm ourselves by putting the right answer upon our lips, let them say, "You have spoken like one of the silly women." Why will such a thing not appear totally stupid to anyone who has some sense and who has laid hold of God? How is this business not the making of idols and a diabolic undertaking? Under the guise of righteousness the devil always sneaks into the human

mind, divinizes mortal nature in human estimation, and skillfully delineates idols after human fashion. Those who worship them have died, but they bring in their idols to be worshiped—though they were never alive (nor can they die which were never alive)—by minds that are adulterous toward the one and only God, like the promiscuous prostitute who is aroused to indiscriminate intercourse while casting off the sobriety of being ruled by a single man.

Now certainly the body of Mary was holy, but she was not God. Indeed she was a virgin and is reverenced as such, but is not given to us to be worshiped; rather she worships him who was born of her flesh, he who came from heaven from the paternal bosom. Because of this we are safeguarded by the gospel saying spoken by the Lord himself, namely, "What is it to me and to you, woman? My hour has not yet come." Or the saying, "Woman, what is it to me and to you?" Lest some think that the holy Virgin is something special, he called her woman, as if prophesying that there would in the future be schisms on earth and heresies, lest any be too much in awe of the holy Virgin and therefore fall prey to this ridiculous heresy.

5 The whole narrative of this heresy is, as I have said, utter nonsense, an old wives' tale. What part of Scripture speaks of it? Which of the prophets allowed a human being to be worshiped, to say nothing of a woman? The vessel is select (even though a woman), in no way corrupted in nature, and is to be held in respect regarding judgment and feeling just like the bodies of the saints—and if I might say anything in excessive praise, like Elias who was a virgin from the womb, who remained so permanently, was taken up, and did not see death; like John who reclined on the breast of the Lord and whom Jesus loved; like holy Thecla; and Mary is to be more honored than the last-named because of the divine plan of which she was found worthy. But neither is Elias to be worshiped, even though he is among the living; nor is John to be worshiped although through his own prayers he achieved a wondrous passing, or rather obtained it as a gift of God. Neither Thecla nor any of the saints is worshiped. The ancient error will not rule over us, that error of abandoning the Living One and adoring what was made by him. "For they adored and reverenced the creature above the creator," and acted like fools. If he does not wish angels to be worshiped, how much more her who was born of Anna, bestowed on Anna through Joachim, given to her father and mother according to a promise because of their prayer and full devotion, not born any differently from the usual human way but like everyone else from the seed of a man and the womb of a woman? If the account of and traditions about Mary have it that it was said to her father Joachim in the desert, "Your wife has conceived," it did not happen without sexual union, nor without male seed, but the angel was sent to foretell what was to come, lest anyone

doubt that she was truly born to that just man and already appointed by God.

6 Let us look at what the Scriptures have to say. Isaiah foretold what was to be fulfilled in the Son of God, saying, "Behold the virgin will conceive and bear a son and they will name him Emmanuel." Now she who conceived was a virgin and he whose name means "God with us" was conceived in a woman. Lest the true event be in doubt in the mind of the prophet, he sees (it) in a vision under the impulse of the Holy Spirit and speaks thus: "And he went in to the prophetess," speaking of the gospel account of the entrance of Gabriel, who was sent from God to tell of the arrival of the only begotten Son of God into the world and his birth from Mary. "And she conceived," he says, "and bore a son. And the Lord said to me, call him 'Take the spoils quickly, despoliate brutally.' Before the child knows how to call father or mother, he will receive the power of Damascus, the spoils of Samaria," etc. All this was not yet completed. It was to happen in the Son of God and be fulfilled after about sixteen hundred years. The prophet saw what was to come many generations after that as already happening. Was it then false? Far from it. But what is arranged by God is trustworthy. It is proclaimed, as if already completed, so that the truth might not be disbelieved, so that the amazing and wondrous mystery to come might not fall in doubt in the mind of the prophet. Do you not see how what was proclaimed does indeed follow, as the holy Isaiah himself says, "He was led as a sheep to the slaughter, like a lamb speechless before his shearer, so did he not open his mouth; who will tell of his generation? For his life is taken up from the earth," and, "I will give (him) evil men for his grave," and the rest? See how the first things are recounted later, and the later things he interprets as having happened, saying, "He was led as a sheep to the slaughter." It is said as if completed. He did not say, "He *is* led," though the one mentioned by Isaiah had not yet been led. It was said by the prophet as if the event had already been accomplished. The mysterious way of God is unchangeable. As he went on, he no longer spoke as if what he said had already happened, lest he give rise to error. "But," he says, "his life is taken up from the earth." From the two prophecies together he shows the truth because "he was led" is already accomplished and "he is taken up" is still to be fulfilled, so that from what has happened you might know the truthfulness and reliability of God's promise, while from what is still to come you will be able to recognize the mysteries as they are revealed.

7 Thus the angel foretold about Mary what her father was to receive from God when he entered into his own house: that which had been requested through the prayers and supplications of father and mother, namely, "Behold, your wife has conceived," so that the mind of the faithful man might be strongly confirmed in the promise. But this seemed foolish to some. Such a

birth was considered impossible on earth according to human nature. It was fitting for him alone; nature yielded for him alone. Thus as sculptor and director of the enterprise he fashioned himself from a virgin as from the earth, God who came from heaven, the Word who clothed himself with flesh from the holy Virgin. But this did not happen so that women should be appointed priests after so many generations. God did not wish that in the case of Salome, nor even for Mary herself. He did not permit her to baptize or bless disciples. He did not assign her authority over the earth, but only to be holy, and to be worthy of his kingdom. Neither to the woman called the mother of Rufus, nor to those who followed him from Galilee, nor to Martha the sister of Lazarus and Mary, nor to any of the holy women found worthy to be saved by his coming, who ministered to him out of their own goods, nor to the Canaanite woman, nor to the woman with the hemorrhage even though she was saved, not to any woman on earth did he give the privilege of doing this.

Whence are the twisted designs renewed? Let Mary be held in reverence, but let the Father, Son, and Holy Spirit be worshiped—let no one worship Mary. I say that not to a woman, nor to a man, but to God is the holy mystery directed; not even angels can receive this kind of glorification. May what was written deceitfully in the heart of the deceived be blotted out; let the lust of the tree be dimmed in our eyes; let the creature turn back again to the master; let Eve along with Adam reverence God alone; may she not be led by the voice of the serpent but may she remain obedient to the command of God: "Do not eat of the tree." The tree itself was not error, but through the tree came erroneous disobedience. Let no one eat of the error related to holy Mary. Even if the tree was blossoming, it was not meant for food, and even if Mary is beautiful and holy and to be honored, she is not to be worshiped.

8 These women revive the old mixed cup of Fortuna and prepare their table for the devil, not for God, as it is written, "The food of ungodliness was eaten," as the divine word says, and, "The women threshed flour and the children collected firewood to make cakes to the heavenly army." Such women were silenced by Jeremiah so that they might not disturb the world—lest they say, "Let us honor the queen of heaven." Taphnas knew that these would be punished; the regions of the Magdulians knew that they would receive the bodies of these women to have them rot there. Do not listen to a woman, O Israel. Raise your head above the evil designs of a woman, for a woman hunts for the noble souls of men. But her feet lead to hell those who consort with death. Do not associate with a common woman. "Honey drips from the lips of a promiscuous woman, which for a short time is smooth in your throat but later you will find it more bitter than bile and sharper than a two-edged sword." Do not believe such a vulgar woman. For every heresy is a vulgar woman, but this female heresy is more—it is that of the one who

deceived the first woman. Our mother Eve is to be honored as having been formed by God, but let her not be heeded, lest she persuade her children to eat from the tree and transgress the commandment. Let her repent from useless talk, let her turn back in shame covered with a fig leaf. Let Adam observe her well and no longer obey her. For the persuasion of error and the contrary counsel of a woman bring death to her own husband—not only to him but also to her children. Eve subverted creation through her transgression when she was aroused by the speech and promise of the serpent, and she pulled away from God's teaching and wandered into a strange way of thinking.

9 That is why the Master and Savior of all, wanting to heal the suffering, rebuild what had been razed, and rectify what had been altered, since death had come into the world through a woman, was himself born of a virginal woman so that he might lock up death, restore what was lacking, and perfect what had been altered. Evil returns again to us, so that what is inferior might enter the world. But neither young nor old men listen to the woman because of the good sense given from above. The Egyptian woman did not succeed in her game with the sensible Joseph nor corrupt him even though she pursued her wicked intentions toward the young man through many machinations. Neither can the man who receives his counsel from the Holy Spirit be manipulated, nor does he hide his discretion, so that he might not disgrace his nobility. He abandons his garments and does not destroy the body. He flees the place so as not to fall into the snare. He is afflicted for a time but reigns forever. He is thrown into prison, but it is preferable to remain in prison or in "the corner of a roof" than with a contentious and loquacious woman. Now what is all this saying? Either these idle women offer the cake to Mary as if worshiping her or they undertake to offer on her behalf the above-mentioned rotten fruit. The whole thing is silly and strange, from diabolic activity, all arrogance and deceit.

So as not to prolong these remarks, let what has been said suffice for us. Let Mary be honored and the Lord worshiped. The just ones contrive error for no one. God has no experience of evil and does not tempt anyone to error, nor do the servants of God. Everyone is tempted by being drawn away and baited by his own lusts. Then "lust brings forth sin and sin acted upon gives birth to death."

We have considered all this sufficiently, beloved, so let us proceed, as I have said, crushing with the word of truth the beetle that is golden to the sight but really feathered and winged, having a poisonous sting within itself; let us proceed against this one that still remains, beseeching God to stand by us as we search out the way of truth and to be a perfect defender against the opposition.

Why Christian Women May Not Write Books in Their Own Names

The Debate between a Montanist and an Orthodox   4th century C.E.?

WORK: Little is known about this text, which is extant in Greek. It is conventionally dated to the fourth century, or perhaps a little later.

TRANSLATION AND TEXT: Ronald Heine, *Montanist Oracles and Testimonia* (Macon: Ga.: Mercer University Press, 1989), 124–26.

ADDITIONAL TEXT: G. Ficker, "Widerlegung eines Montanisten," *Zeitschrift für Kirchengeschichte* 26 (1905): 447–63.

BIBLIOGRAPHY: Ross S. Kraemer, "Women's Authorship of Jewish and Christian Literature in the Greco-Roman Period," in Amy-Jill Levine, ed., *"Women Like This": New Perspectives on Jewish Women in the Greco-Roman Period*, Early Judaism and Its Literature 1 (Atlanta: Scholars Press, 1991), 221–42. See also entry 93.

—M: And why do you also repudiate the saints Maximilla and Priscilla, and say that it is not permissible for a woman to prophesy? Did not Philip have four daughters who prophesied, and was not Deborah a prophetess (cf. Acts 21:9; Judg 4:4)? And does not the apostle say: "Every woman who prays or prophesies with uncovered head . . ." (1 Cor 11:5)? If it is not possible for a woman to prophesy, neither can she pray. But if they can pray, let them also prophesy.

—O: We do not repudiate the prophecies of women. Even the holy Mary prophesied and said: "Henceforth all generations will call me blessed" (Luke 1:48). And as even you yourself said, the holy Philip had four daughters who prophesied, and Mary the sister of Aaron prophesied (cf. Exod 15:20f). But we do not permit them to speak in Churches nor to have authority over men (cf. 1 Tim 2:12), with the result that books too are written under their names. For this is what it means for women to pray and prophesy without a veil, and this, then, has brought shame on her head (cf. 1 Cor 11:5), that is her husband, For could not the holy Mary, mother of God, have written books under her own name? But she did not, so that she might not bring shame on her head by exercising authority over men.

—M: Is not writing books the meaning of the statement about praying or prophesying with uncovered head?

—O: It certainly is.

—M: Then if the holy Mary says, "Henceforth all generations will call me blessed" (Luke 1:48), is she being outspoken and speaking in an unveiled manner or not?

—O: She has the evangelist as her veil. For the Gospel has not been written under her name.

Observances, Rituals, and Festivals

—M: Don't take allegories as though they were doctrines with me.

—O: Saint Paul especially, then, also took allegories for the confirmation of dogmas when he said: "Abraham had two wives" (cf. Gal 4:22), "which things are allegories. For they are two covenants" (Gal 4:24). But let us grant that the covering of the head does not have reference to an allegory. Put a stop to the allegorical meaning for me in the presence of everyone: Suppose there is a poor woman and she does not have the means to veil herself. Must she neither pray nor prophesy?

—M: Is it possible for a woman to be so poor that she does not have the means to cover herself?

—O: We have frequently seen women so poor that they did not have the means to cover themselves. But since you yourself are not willing to admit that there are women so poor that they do not have the means to cover themselves, what do you do in the case of those who are baptized? Is it not necessary that the women themselves pray when they are baptized? And what do you say also in the case of men who often cover their head on account of distress? Do you also prevent them from praying or prophesying?

—M: He uncovers himself at the time he prays or prophesies.

—O: It is not necessary, then, for him to pray without ceasing, but he must disregard the teaching of the apostle who says: "Pray without ceasing" (1 Thess 5:17). And you also counsel a woman not to pray when she is baptized.

—M: Is it because Priscilla and Maximilla composed books that you do not receive them?

—O: It is not only for this, but also because they were false prophetesses with their leader Montanus.

—M: Why do you say they were false prophetesses?

—O: Did they not say the same things as Montanus?

—M: Yes.

—O: Montanus has been refuted as having said things contrary to the divine Scriptures. Therefore, these women too will be cast out along with him.

● 41

Christian Women in Antioch Participating in Jewish Festivals and Attending Synagogue

JOHN CHRYSOSTOM *Against Judaizing Christians* 2.3.3–6,
4.7.3   late 4th century C.E.

AUTHOR: John Chrysostom (ca. 354(?)–407 C.E.) was a prolific preacher who had earned the epithet Chrysostom (golden-mouthed) by the sixth century. He is a particularly important source for the life of Olympias, his devoted friend and benefactor (entries 74–75). Seventeen of his letters to her are still extant, although none of hers to him have survived.

Like many Christians of his time, John was not born to Christian parents. He converted at age eighteen. His father died while he was an infant, and his mother, to whom he was apparently greatly attached, provided his early education. He spent six years in monastic seclusion, during which he became seriously ill. Returning to Syrian Antioch in 381, he became a deacon and then a priest in 386. Eleven years later, he was abducted to Constantinople by the emperor's order and elected bishop, a post he held from 397 until 404. His criticisms of the powerful empress Eudoxia ultimately led to his banishment: he was exiled to Cucusus in Armenia and died at Comana of the stresses of an enforced march in 407.

Among his many surviving sermons are those entitled *Against Judaizing Christians*, many of whom seem to have been women. He also wrote several treatises advocating asceticism and virginity.

TRANSLATION: *FC* (Paul Harkins, 1977).

TEXT: PG 48, 843–942.

BIBLIOGRAPHY: *Blessings*, 102–3, 108; David Ford, *Women and Men in the Early Church: The Full Views of St. John Chrysostom* (South Canaan, Penn.: St. Tikhon's Seminary Press; 1996); Pieter W. van der Horst, "Jews and Christians in Antioch at the End of the Fourth Century," in Stanley E. Porter and Brook W. R. Pearson, eds., *Christian-Jewish Relations through the Centuries* (Sheffield, U.K.: Sheffield Academic Press, 2000), 228–38.

2.3.3 If God, then, showed us such honor, will we not deem him deserving of equal honor? Will we let him be outraged by our wives? Will we permit this even though we realize that the greatest punishment and vengeance will be stored up for us when we neglect the salvation of our wives?

2.3.4 This is why he made you to be head of the wife. This is why Paul gave the order: "If wives wish to learn anything, let them ask their own husbands at home," so that you, like a teacher, a guardian, a patron, might urge her to godliness. Yet when the hour set for the services summons you to the church, you fail to rouse your wives from their sluggish indifference. But now that the devil summons your wives to the feast of Trumpets and they turn a ready ear to his call, you do not restrain them. You let them entangle themselves in accusations of ungodliness, you let them be dragged off into licentious ways. For, as a rule, it is the harlots, the effeminates, and the whole chorus from the theater who rush to that festival.

2.3.5 And why do I speak of the immorality that goes on there? Are you not afraid that your wife may not come back from there after a demon has possessed her soul? Did you not hear in my previous discourse the argument which clearly proved to us that demons dwell in the very souls of the Jews and in the places in which they gather? Tell me, then. How do you Judaizers have the boldness, after dancing with demons, to come back to the assembly of the apostles? After you have gone off and shared with those who shed the blood of Christ, how is it that you do not shudder to come back and share in the sacred banquet, to partake of his precious blood? Do you not shiver, are you not afraid when you commit such outrages? Have you so little respect for that very banquet?

2.3.6 I have spoken these words to you. You will speak them to those Judaizers, and they to their wives. "Fortify one another." If a catechumen is sick with this disease, let him be kept outside the church doors. If the sick one be a believer and already initiated, let him be driven from the holy table. For not all sins need exhortation and counsel; some sins, of their very nature, demand cure by a quick and sharp excision. The wounds we can tolerate respond to more gentle cures; those which have festered and cannot be cured, those which are feeding on the rest of the body, need cauterization with a point of steel. So is it with sins. Some need long exhortation; others need sharp rebuke.

4.7.3 Whenever your brother needs correction, even if you must lay down your life, do not refuse him. Follow the example of your Master. If you have a servant or if you have a wife, be very careful to keep them at home. If you refuse to let them go to the theater, you must refuse all the more to let them go to the synagogue. To go to the synagogue is a greater crime than going to the theater. What goes on in the theater is, to be sure, sinful; what goes on in the synagogue is godlessness. When I say this I do not mean that you let them go to the theater, for the theater is wicked; I say it so that you will be all the more careful to keep them away from the synagogue.

● 42

A Christian Matron from Rome Visiting the Hermitic Abbot Arsenius

Sayings of the Desert Fathers 2.7   5th century C.E.

WORK: Sayings attributed to the ascetics who lived in the Egyptian desert in the fourth and fifth centuries C.E. have come down to us in several forms, interspersed with anecdotes about the monastic life. Extant in Latin and in Greek, and arranged sometimes by subject and sometimes alphabetically by the hermit's name, the vast majority of sayings are attributed to men. A handful, however, are given in the names of women, and a few stories are told about pious ascetic women, although the collections also contain many misogynist remarks and warnings about the dangers women pose to monastic males.

TRANSLATION: Benedicta Ward, *The Desert Christian: Sayings of the Desert Fathers: The Alphabetical Collection* (New York: Macmillan, 1980).

TEXT: *PG* 65: 71–440; J. B. Cotelier, *Ecclesiae Graecae Monumenta* 1.338–712 (1677), supplemented by F. Nau, "Histoires des solitaires Égyptiens," *Revue de l'orient chrétien* (Paris, 1907–); *PL* 73, 855–1022.

ADDITIONAL TRANSLATIONS: Helen Waddell, *The Desert Fathers* (London: Constable and Co, 1936); Owen Chadwick, ed., *Western Asceticism*, Library of Christian Classics (Philadelphia: Westminster Press, 1958).

BIBLIOGRAPHY: See entry 124.

At one time when the abbot Arsenius was living in Canopus, there came from Rome in hope to see him a lady, a virgin, of great wealth, and one that feared God: and Theophilus the archbishop received her. And she prayed him to use his good offices with the old man, that she might see him. And the archbishop came to him and asked him, saying, "A certain lady hath come from Rome, and would see thee." But the old man would not consent to have her come to him. So when this was told the lady, she commanded her beasts to be saddled, saying, "I trust in God, that I shall see him. For in my own city there are men to spare: but I am come to see the prophets." And when she came to the old man's cell, by the ordering of God it chanced that he was found outside his cell. And when the lady saw him, she cast herself at his feet. But with indignation did he raise her up; and gazing upon her, said, "If thou dost desire to look upon my face, here am I: look." But she for shame did not lift her eyes to his face. And the old man said to her, "Hast thou not heard what I do? To see the work is enough. How didst thou dare to take upon thee so great a voyage? Dost thou not know that thou art a woman, and ought not to go anywhere? And wilt thou now go to Rome and say to the other women, 'I have seen Arsenius,' and turn the sea into a high road of women coming to me?" But she said, "If God will that I return to Rome, I shall let no woman come hither: But pray for me, and always remember me." He answered and said, "I pray God that He will wipe the memory of thee from my heart." And hearing this, she went away troubled. And when she had come back into the city, she fell into a fever for sorrow. And it was told the archbishop that she was sick: and he came to comfort her, and asked her what ailed her. And she said to him, "Would that I had not come hither! For I said to the old man, 'Remember me.' And he said to me, 'I pray God that He will wipe the memory of thee from my heart,' and behold I am dying of that sorrow." And the archbishop said to her, "Knowest thou not that thou art a woman, and through women doth the Enemy lay siege to holy men? For this reason did the old man say it, but he doth ever pray for thy soul." And so her mind was healed. And she departed with joy to her own place.

Women Monastics and Women Visitors at a Pachomian Women's Monastery in Fourth-Century C.E. Egypt

PALLADIUS *Lausiac History* 33, 52, 143   5th century C.E.

AUTHOR: Born in Galatia in ca. 363, Palladius took up the monastic life in his midtwenties but modified his ascetic rigor because of poor health. His *Lausiac History* was dedicated to Lausus, chamberlain in the court of Theodosius II. Originally written in Greek in 419–20 and subsequently translated into Latin, it represents a major source for early monasticism in Egypt, Palestine, Syria, and Asia Minor. Though the bulk of the work describes male monastics and their communities, the work also contains important references to early women's monasteries and anecdotes about female ascetics.

TRANSLATION: A. Veilleux, *Pachomian Koinonia*, vol. 2, *Pachomian Chronicles and Rules*, Cistercian Studies 45 (Kalamazoo, Mich.: Cistercian Pubs., 1981).

TEXT: PG 34, 991–1262; CTS 6 (C. Butler, 1904); CSCO (R. Draguet, 1978, 389–90, 398–99). Draguet also provides corrections to Butler's text in various articles, for which see M. Geerard, *Clavis Patrum Graecorum* 3:169.

ADDITIONAL TRANSLATION: W. K. L. Clarke, *The Lausiac History of Palladius* (London: SPCK, 1918).

BIBLIOGRAPHY: Alanna Emmett, "Female Ascetics in the Greek Papyri," *Jahrbuch der österreichischen Byzantinistik* 32/2 (1982): 507–15; Alanna Emmett, "An Early Fourth-Century Female Monastic Community in Egypt?" in A. Moffatt, ed., *Maistor: Classical, Byzantine, and Renaissance Studies for Robert Browning*, Byzantina Australiensia 5 (Canberra: Australian Association for Byzantine Studies, 1984), 77–83; Rebecca Krawiec, *Shenoute and the Women of the White Monastery: Egyptian Monasticism in Late Antiquity* (Oxford: Oxford University Press, 2002). See also entry 124.

33 They also have a monastery of about four hundred women, with the same constitution and the same way of life, except for the goat skin. The women are across the river and the men opposite them. When a virgin dies, the other virgins prepare her body for the burial; they carry it and place it on the bank of the river. The brothers cross over on a ferry, with palm leaves and olive branches and carry the body across with psalmody. Then they bury it in their own tombs.

No one goes over to the women's monastery. A tailor from the world crossed over through ignorance, looking for work. A young [sister] who had come out—for the place is deserted—met him involuntarily and gave him this answer, "We have our own tailors."

Another [sister] saw them talking. Some time later, on the occasion of a quarrel, she accused falsely that [sister] before the community, by a diabolical insinuation [and moved by] great wickedness and boiling temper. A few others joined her in this nasty act. The other was so grieved at undergoing such an accusation, of a thing that had not even come to her mind, that not being able to bear it, she threw herself secretly into the river and died.

Then the slanderer realized that she had slandered out of wickedness and committed that crime. She also could stand it no longer; she went and hanged herself.

When the priest came, the other sisters told him what had happened. Then he ordered that the Eucharist should not be offered for either of them. Those who had not effected a reconciliation between the two, he excommunicated and deprived them from the Eucharist for a period of seven years for their complicity with the slanderer and for having believed what was said.

52 If seculars, or infirm people or *weaker vessels*—that is, women—come to the door, they shall be received in different places according to their calling and their sex. Above all, women shall be cared for with greater honor and diligence. They shall be given a place separate from all areas frequented by men, so there may be no occasion for slander. If they come in the evening, it would be wicked to drive them away; but, as we have said, they shall be lodged in a separate and enclosed place with every discipline and caution, so that the flock of the brothers may freely tend to its duty and no occasion for detraction be given to anybody.

143 Let us speak also about the monastery of virgins: No one shall go to visit them unless he has there a mother, sister, or daughter, some relatives or cousins, or the mother of his own children.

And if it is necessary to see them for any evident reason, and if some paternal inheritance is due them from the time before their renunciation of the world and their entry into the monastery, or if there is some obvious reason, they shall be accompanied by a man of proven age and life; they shall see them and return together. No one shall go to visit them except those we have just mentioned.

When they want to see them, they shall first inform the father of the monastery, and he shall inform the elders appointed to the virgins' ministry. These shall meet [the virgins] and with them see those whom they need with all discipline and fear of God. When they see the virgins, they shall not speak to them about worldly matters.

● 44

Women Blowing the Shofar on Rosh Hashanah (the New Year)

BABYLONIAN TALMUD *Rosh Hashanah* 32b   6th century C.E.?

WORK, TRANSLATION, TEXT, AND BIBLIOGRAPHY: See entry 36.

MISHNAH: [For the sake of] the shofar of New Year it is not allowed to disregard the distance limit nor to remove debris nor to climb a tree nor to ride on an animal nor to swim on the water. It must not be shaped either with an implement the use of which is forbidden on account of Shebuth or with one the use of which is forbidden by express prohibition. If one, however, desires to pour wine or water into it he may do so. Children need not be stopped from blowing; on the contrary, they may be helped till they learn how to blow. One who blows merely to practise does not thereby fulfill his religious obligation, nor does one who hears the blast made by another when practising.

GEMARA: Children need not be stopped from blowing. This would imply that women are stopped. [But how can this be], seeing that it has been taught: "Neither children nor women need be stopped from blowing the *shofar* on the Festival"?—Abaye replied: There is no discrepancy; the one statement follows R. Judah, the other R. Jose and R. Simeon, as it has been taught: "*Speak unto the children* [bene] *of Israel*: [this indicates that] the 'sons' [bene] of Israel lay on hands but not the 'daughters' of Israel. So R. Judah, R. Jose and R. Simeon say that women also have the option of laying on hands."

● 45

Exempting Women from the Obligation to Eat in the *Sukkah* during the Jewish Festival of Sukkoth

BABYLONIAN TALMUD *Sukkah* 28a–b   6th century C.E.?

TRANSLATION: Jacob Neusner, *The Talmud of Babylonia: An American Translation*, BJS (Chico, Calif.: Scholars Press, 1984–94).

WORK, TEXT, AND BIBLIOGRAPHY: See entry 36.

A Women, slaves, and minors are exempt from the religious requirement of dwelling in a sukkah.

B A Minor who can take care of himself is liable to the religious requirement of dwelling in a sukkah.

C M'SH W: Shammai the Elder's daughter-in-law gave birth, and he broke away some of the plaster and covered the hole with sukkah-roofing over her bed, on account of the infant. (Mishnah 2:8)

A How do we know on that basis of Scripture [the rule at M. 2:8A]?

B It is in accord with that which our rabbis have taught:

C "Homeborn" (Lev. 23:42) by itself [without "the" and "every"] would have included every homeborn [encompassing women and minors].

D [Since it says,] "The homeborn," it means to exclude women, and "Every..." serves to encompass minors. [That explains M. 2:8A, B.]

E A master has said, " 'The homeborn' (Lev. 23:42) serves to exclude women."

F Does this then imply that the word, "homeborn" [without the] applies both to women and to men?

G And has it not been taught, "The homeborn" (Lev. 16:29) [in regard to observance of the Day of Atonement] serves to encompass homeborn women, indicating that they are liable to undertake the distress [of the fast]?

H Therefore when the word "homeborn" is used [without the "the"] it means to refer only to males.

I Said Rabbah, "[In fact] these are matters of received law, and the purpose of rabbis was simply to find scriptural support for the received law."

J Which [of the two laws, the one referring to the *sukkah* or the one about the fasting on the Day of Atonement then] is based on Scripture and which is a received law?

K And further, what need do I have to make reference either to a received law or to Scripture? In the case of the requirement to dwell in a *sukkah*, that is a religious duty calling for an act of commission and based upon a particular time, and any religious duty calling for an act of commission and based upon a particular time leaves women exempt. [They do not have to keep a law which requires them to do something at a particular time, since they have prior obligations to their families.]

L As to the Day of Atonement, it derives from a teaching in accord with that which R. Judah said R. Rab said.

M For R. Judah said Rab said, and so too did a Tannaite authority of the house of R. Ishmael state, "Scripture has said, 'Man or woman' (Num. 5:6), so treating men and women as equal in regard to all those acts subject to penalty that are listed in the Torah." [Accordingly, both matters—*sukkah*, Day of Atonement, derive from secondary exegesis of the law. In no way do they depend upon either a received tradition or a primary exegesis or proof text.]

N Said Abayye, "Under all circumstances, the *sukkah* [rule concerning women] is a received law, and it is necessary [to make the matter explicit as a received law].

O "[Why so?] I might have thought to argue as follows: 'You shall dwell' (Lev. 23:42) in the manner in which you ordinarily dwell. Just as, in the case of an ordinary dwelling, a man and his wife [live together], so in the case of a *sukkah*, a man and his wife must live together. [Thus I might have reached the conclusion that a woman is liable to dwell in the *sukkah*.] So we are informed [that that is not the case.]"

P Said Raba, "It indeed was necessary to provide such a proof [but it is different from Abayye's argument in the same regard]. For I might have said that we shall derive the rule governing the fifteenth [of Tishri, that is, *Sukkot*] from the fifteenth [of Nisan,] that is the festival of the unleavened bread.

Q "Just as, in the latter case, women are liable [to eat unleavened bread], so in the present case, women are liable [to dwell in a *sukkah*]. So we are informed [that that is not the case]."

R Now that you have maintained that the rule about women's exemption from the *sukkah* is a received law, what need do I have for a Scriptural proof-text?

S It is to encompass proselytes [within the requirement to dwell in a *sukkah*].

T You might have said, "The homeborn in Israel" (Lev. 23:34) is what the All-Merciful has said, thus excluding proselytes.

U So we are informed that that is not the case, [and proselytes come under the obligation].

V As to the Day of Atonement, since what R. Judah said what Rab said has provided an adequate proof, [that women must fast on the Day of Atonement, what need do we have for further proof]?

W The proof-text encompasses additional affliction [on the eve of the Day of Atonement, prior to nightfall. The fast begins even before sunset. That additional time is added to the fast, and it applies to women as much as to men.]

X You might have thought that since the All-Merciful has excluded the additional affliction from the penalties of punishment and admonition [so that, if one does not observe that additional period of fasting, he is not punished on that account], women are not obligated to observe that additional period at all.

Y Accordingly, we are informed [that that is not the case, and women are obligated as much as are men].

Rabbinic Discussion on the Differences in Rabbinic Law between a Man and a Woman

Babylonian Talmud *Kiddushin*   6th century C.E.?

NOTE: See entry 36.

MISHNAH: What [differences are there in law] between a man and a woman? A man rends his clothes and loosens his hair, but a woman does not rend her clothes and loosen her hair. A man may vow that his son will become a Nazirite, but a woman may not vow that her son will become a Nazirite. A man may be shaved on account of the Naziriteship of his father, but a woman cannot be shaved on account of the Naziriteship of her father. A man may sell his daughter, but a woman may not sell her daughter. A man may give his daughter in betrothal, but a woman may not give her daughter in betrothal. A man is stoned naked, but a woman is not stoned naked. A man is hanged, but a woman is not hanged. A man is sold for his theft, but a woman is not sold for her theft.

29A–B

MISHNAH: All obligations of the son upon the father, men are bound, but women are exempt. But all obligations of the father upon the son, both men and women are bound. All affirmative precepts limited to time, men are liable and women are exempt. But all affirmative precepts not limited to time are binding upon both men and women. And all negative precepts, whether limited to time or not limited to time, are binding upon both men and women; excepting, Ye shall not round [the corners of your heads], neither shalt thou mar [the corner of thy beard], and, He shall not defile himself to the dead.

GEMARA: What is the meaning of all obligations of the son upon the father? Shall we say, all obligations which the son is bound to perform for his father? Are then women [i.e., daughters] exempt? But it was taught: [*Every man, his mother and his father ye shall fear:*] *"every man"*: I know this only of a man; whence do I know it of a woman? When it is said, *"Every man, his mother and father ye shall fear"*—behold, two are [mentioned] here.—Said Rab Judah: This is the meaning: all obligations of the son, [which lie] upon the father to do to his son, men are bound, but women [mothers] are exempt. We thus learnt [here] what our Rabbis taught: The father is bound in respect of his son, to circumcise, redeem, teach him Torah, take a wife for him, and teach him a craft. Some say, to teach him to swim too. R. Judah said: He who does not teach his son a craft, teaches him brigandage, "Brigandage"! can you really think so!—But it is as though he taught him brigandage.

"To circumcise him." How do we know it?—Because it is written, *And Abraham circumcised his son Isaac.* And if his father did not circumcise him, Beth din is bound to circumcise him, for it is written, *Every male among you shall be circumcised.* And if Beth din did not circumcise him, he is bound to circumcise himself, for it is written, *And the uncircumcised male who will not circumcise the flesh of his foreskin, that soul shall be cut off.*

How do we know that she [the mother] has no such obligation?—Because it is written, [*"And Abraham circumcised his son . . .*] *as God had commanded him"*: *"him,"* but not *"her"* [the mother]. Now, we find this so at that time; how do we know it for all times?—The School of R. Ishmael taught: whenever *"command"* is stated, its only purpose is to denote exhortation for then and all time. Exhortation, as it is written. *But charge Joshua, and encourage him, and strengthen him.* Then and for all time, as it is written, *from the day that the Lord gave commandment, and onward throughout your generations.*

"To redeem him." How do we know it?—Because it is written, *and all the firstborn of man among thy sons shalt thou redeem.* And if his father did not redeem him, he is bound to redeem himself, for it is written, [*nevertheless the firstborn of man*] *thou shalt surely redeem.* And how do we know that she [his mother] is not obliged [to redeem him]?—Because it is written, *thou shalt redeem* [*tifdeh*] [which may also be read] *thou shalt redeem thyself* [*tippadeh*]: one who is charged with redeeming oneself is charged to redeem others; whereas one who is not charged to redeem oneself is not charged to redeem others. And how do we know that she is not bound to redeem herself?— Because it is written, *thou shalt redeem* [*tifdeh*], [which may be read] *thou shalt redeem thyself*: the one whom others are commanded to redeem, is commanded to redeem oneself: the one whom others are not commanded to redeem is not commanded to redeem oneself. And how do we know that others are not commanded to redeem her?—Because the Writ saith, *"and all the firstborn of man among thy sons shalt thou redeem"*: *"thy sons,"* but not thy daughters.

"To teach him Torah." How do we know it?—Because it is written, *And ye shall teach them your sons.* And if his father did not teach him, he must teach himself, for it is written, *and ye shall study.* How do we know that she [the mother] has no duty [to teach her children]?—Because it is written, *welimaddetem* [*and ye shall teach*], [which also reads] *u-lemadetem* [*and ye shall study*]: [hence] whoever is commanded to study, is commanded to teach; whoever is not commanded to study, is not commanded to teach. And how do we know that she is not bound to teach herself?—Because it is written, *welimaddetem* [*and ye shall teach*]—*u-lemadetem* [*and ye shall learn*]: the one whom others are commanded to teach is commanded to teach oneself; and the one whom others are not commanded to teach, is not commanded to teach oneself. How then do we know that others are not commanded to teach her?—Because it is written, *"And ye shall teach them your sons"*—but not your daughters.

All affirmative precepts limited to time etc. Our Rabbis taught: Which are affirmative precepts limited to time? *Sukkah, lulab, shofar,* fringes, and phylacteries. And what are affirmative precepts not limited to time? *Mezuzah,* "battlement," [returning] lost property, and the "*dismissal of the nest.*"

Now, is this a general principle? But unleavened bread, rejoicing [on Festivals], and "assembling," are affirmative precepts limited to time, and yet incumbent upon women. Furthermore, study of the Torah, procreation, and the redemption of the son, are not affirmative precepts limited to time, and yet women are exempt [therefrom]?—R. Johanan answered: We cannot learn from general principles, even where exceptions are stated. For we learnt: An "*erub*" and a partnership, may be made with all comestibles, excepting water and salt. Are there no more [exceptions]: lo, there are mushrooms and truffles! But [we must answer that] we cannot learn from general principles, even where exceptions are stated.

And affirmative precepts limited to time, women are exempt. Whence do we know it?—It is learned from phylacteries: just as women are exempt from phylacteries, so are they exempt from all affirmative precepts limited to time. Phylacteries [themselves] are derived from the study of the Torah: just as women are exempt from the study of the Torah, so are they exempt from phylacteries. But let us [rather] compare phylacteries to *mezuzah?*—Phylacteries are assimilated to the study of the Torah in both the first section and the second; whereas they are not assimilated to *mezuzah* in the second section. Then let *mezuzah* be assimilated to the study of the Torah?—You cannot think so, because it is written, [*And thou shalt write them upon the* mezuzah *of thine house. . . .*] *That your days may be multiplied*: do then men only need life, and not women!

But what of *sukkah*, which is an affirmative precept limited to time, as it is written, *ye shall dwell in booths seven days,* yet the reason [of woman's exemption] is that Scripture wrote *ha-ezrah,* to exclude women, but otherwise women would be liable?—Said Abaye, It is necessary: I would have thought, since it is written, *ye shall dwell in booths seven days,*" "*ye* shall dwell" [meaning] even as ye [normally] dwell [in a house]: just as [normal] dwelling [implies] a husband and wife [together], so must the *sukkah* be [inhabited by] husband and wife!—But Raba said, It is necessary [for another reason]: I might have thought, we derive [identity of law from the employment of] "*fifteen*" here and in connection with the Feast of unleavened bread: just as there, women are liable, so here too. Hence it is necessary.

But what of pilgrimage, which is an affirmative command limited to time, yet the reason [of woman's exemption] is that Scripture wrote, [*Three times in the year all*] *thy males* [*shall appear before the Lord thy God*], thus excluding women; but otherwise women would be liable?—It is necessary: I would have thought, we learn the meaning of "appearance" from "assembling."

Now, instead of deriving an exemption from phylacteries, let us deduce an obligation from [the precept of] rejoicing?—Said Abaye: As for a woman, her husband must make her rejoice. Then what can be said of a widow?—It refers to her host.

Now, let us learn [liability] from [the precept of] "assembling"?—Because unleavened bread and "assembling" are two verses [i.e., precepts] with the same purpose, and wherever two verses have the same purpose, they cannot throw light [upon other precepts]. If so, phylacteries and pilgrimage are also two verses with one purpose, and cannot illumine [other precepts]?—They are both necessary: for had the Divine Law stated phylacteries but not pilgrimage, I would have thought, let us deduce the meaning of "appearance" from "assembling." While had the Divine Law written pilgrimage but not phylacteries, I would have reasoned, Let phylacteries be assimilated to *mezuzah*. Thus both are necessary. If so, unleavened bread and "assembling" are also necessary?—For what are they necessary? Now, if the Divine Law stated "assembling" but not unleavened bread, it were well: for I would argue, let us deduce "fifteen," "fifteen," from the feast of Tabernacles. But let the Divine Law write unleavened bread, and "assembling" is unnecessary, for I can reason, If it is incumbent upon children, how much more so upon women! Hence it is a case of two verses with the same purpose, and they cannot throw light [upon other precepts].

Now, that is well on the view that they do not illumine [other cases]. But on the view that they do, what may be said? Furthermore, [that] affirmative precepts not limited to time are binding upon women; how do we know it? Because we learn from fear: just as fear is binding upon women, so are all affirmative precepts not limited to time incumbent upon women. But let us [rather] learn from the study of the Torah?—Because the study of the Torah and procreation are two verses which teach the same thing, and wherever two verses teach the same thing, they do not illumine [others]. But according to R. Joḥanan b. Beroka, who maintained, Concerning *both* [Adam and Eve] it is said, *And God blessed them: and God said unto them, Be fruitful and multiply*, what can be said?—Because the study of the Torah and redemption of the first born are two verses with one purpose, and such do not illumine [others]. But according to R. Joḥanan b. Beroka too, let procreation and fear be regarded as two verses with one purpose, which do not illumine [other cases]?—Both are necessary. For if the Divine Law wrote fear and not procreation, I would argue, The Divine Law stated, [*Be fruitful, and multiply, and replenish the earth,*] *and conquer it*: only a man, whose nature it is to conquer, but not a woman, as it is not her nature to conquer. And if Scripture wrote procreation and not fear, I would reason: A man, who has the means to do this [*sc.* to shew fear to his parents] is referred to, but not a woman, seeing that she lacks the means to fulfil this; and that being so, she has no obligation at all. Thus both are necessary. Now, that is well on the view that two verses with the same teaching do not illumine [others]: but on the view that they do, what can be said?—Said Raba, The Papunians know the reason of this thing, and who is it? R. Aḥa b. Jacob. Scripture saith, *And it shall be for a sign unto thee upon thine hand, and for a memorial between thine eyes, that the Torah of the Lord may be in thy mouth*: hence the whole Torah is compared to phylacteries: just as phylacteries are an affirmative command limited to time, and women are exempt, so are they exempt from all positive commands limited to time. And since women are exempt from affirmative precepts limited to time, it follows that they are subject to those not limited to time. Now, that is well on the view that phylacteries are a positive command limited to time; but what can be said on the view that they are not?— Whom do you know to maintain that phylacteries are an affirmative precept not limited to time? R. Meir. But he holds that there are two verses with the same teaching, and such do not illumine [others]. But according to R. Judah, who maintains that two verses with the same teaching illumine [others], and [also] that phylacteries are a positive command limited to time, what can be said?—Because unleavened bread, rejoicing [on Festivals], and "assembling" are three verses with the same teaching, and such do not illumine [others].

And all negative precepts etc. Whence do we know it?—Said Rab Judah in Rab's name, and the School of R. Ishmael taught likewise, Scripture saith, *When a man or a woman shall commit any sin that men commit [... then that soul shall be guilty]*: thus the Writ equalised woman and man in respect of all penalties [decreed] in the Torah. The School of R. Eliezer taught, Scripture saith, *[Now these are the judgments] which thou shalt set before them*: The Writ equalised woman and man in respect of all civil laws in Scripture. The School of Hezekiah taught, Scripture saith, *[but if the ox were wont to gore ...] and he kill a man or woman [the ox shall be stoned, and his owner also shall be put to death]*; the Writ placed woman on a par with man in respect of all death sentences [decreed] in Scripture. Now, it is necessary [that all three should be intimated]. For if the first [only] were stated, [I would say] that the All-Merciful had compassion upon her [woman], for the sake of atonement; but as for civil law, I might argue that it applies only to man, who engages in commerce, but not to woman, who does not. While if the second [alone] were intimated, that is because one's livelihood depends thereon; but as for ransom, I might argue, it applies only to man, who is subject to precepts, but not to woman, who is not subject to them. And if the last [alone] were intimated,—since there is loss of life, the All-Merciful had compassion upon her; but in the first two I might say that it is not so. Thus they are [all] necessary.

Excepting, ye shall not round [the corner of your heads] neither shalt thou mar, etc. As for defiling oneself to the dead, that is well, because it is written, *Speak unto the priests the sons of Aaron*: [*There shall none defile himself for the dead among his people*]: [hence], the sons of Aaron, but not the daughters of Aaron. But how do we know [that she is exempt from] the injunction against rounding [etc.] and marring [etc.]?—Because it is written, *ye shall not round the corner of your heads, neither shalt thou mar the corners of thy beard*: whoever is included in [the prohibition of] marring is included in [that of] rounding; but women, since they are not subject to [the prohibition of] marring, are not subject to [that of] rounding. And how do we know that they are not subject to [the injunction against] marring?—Either by common sense, for they have no beard. Or, alternatively, [from] Scripture. For Scripture saith, *ye shall not round the corner of your heads, neither shalt thou mar the corner of thy* beard; since Scripture varies its speech, for otherwise the Divine Law should write, "*the corner of your* beards"; why, "*thy beard*"? [To intimate], "thy beard," but not thy wife's beard. Is it then not? But it was taught: The beard of a woman and that of a *saris* who grew hair, are like a [man's] beard in all matters. Surely that means in respect to marring?—Said Abaye: You cannot say that it is in respect to marring, for we learn "*corner*" "*corner*" from the sons of Aaron: just as there, women are exempt; so here too, women are exempt. But if we hold that "*the* sons *of Aaron*" is written with reference to the whole section, let the Writ refrain from it, and it follows *a fortiori*. For I can argue, If [of] priests, upon whom Scripture imposes additional precepts, [we say] "*the* sons *of Aaron*" but not the daughters of Aaron, how much more so of Israelites!—But for the *gezerah shawah* I would reason that the connection is broken. Then now too let us say that the connection is broken; and as for the *gezerah shawah*,—that is required for what was taught: "*They shall not shave*": I might think that if he shaves it with scissors, he is liable [for violating the injunction]: therefore it is stated, *thou shalt not mar*. I might think that if he plucks it [his hair] out with pincers or a remover, he is liable: therefore it is stated, "*they shall not shave*." How then is it meant? Shaving which involves marring, viz., with a razor. If so, let Scripture write, [*"ye shall not round the corner of your heads, neither shalt thou mar*] that of thy beard"? why [repeat] "*the* corner *of thy beard*"? Hence both are inferred.

Then when it was taught, "The beard of a woman and that of a *saris* who grew hair, are like a [man's] beard in all respects": to what law [does it refer]?—Said Mar Zuṭra: To the uncleanliness of leprosy. "The uncleanliness of leprosy!" But that is explicitly stated, *If a man or a woman have a plague upon the head or the beard*?—But, said Mar Zuṭra, [it is] in respect of purification from leprosy. But purification from leprosy too is obvious; since she is liable to uncleanliness [through her beard], she needs [the same] purification! —It is necessary: I might have assumed, it is written with separate subjects:

[thus:] *"If a man or a woman have a plague upon the head"*: while *"or the beard"* reverts to the man [alone]; therefore we are informed [otherwise].

Issi taught: Women are exempt from the injunction against baldness too. What is Issi's reason?—Because he interprets thus: *Ye are sons of the Lord your God: ye shall not cut yourselves, nor make any baldness between your eyes for the dead. For thou art an holy people unto the Lord thy God*; [the implied limitation] *"sons"* but not daughters [is] in respect of baldness. You say, in respect of baldness; yet perhaps it is not so, but rather in respect of cutting? When it is said, *"For thou art an holy people unto the Lord thy God,"* cutting is referred to; hence, how can I interpret [the implication] *"sons"* but not daughters? In respect to baldness. And why do you prefer to include cutting and exclude baldness? I include cutting which is possible both where there is hair and where there is no hair, and I exclude baldness which is possible only in the place of hair. Yet perhaps *"sons"* but not daughters applies to both baldness and cutting, while *"For thou art an holy people unto the Lord thy God"* relates to incision!—Issi holds that incision [*seritah*] and cutting [*gedidah*] are identical.

Abaye said: This is Issi's reason, viz., he learns *"baldness,"* *"baldness,"* from the sons of Aaron: just as there, women are exempt, so here too, women are exempt. But if we hold that the phrase [*"the sons of Aaron"*] relates to the whole section, let Scripture refrain from it, and it [woman's exemption] follows *a fortiori.* For I may argue, If [of] priests, upon whom the Writ imposes additional precepts, [we say] *"the sons of Aaron"* but not the daughters of Aaron, how much more so of Israelites! —But for the *gezerah shawah* I would think the connection is broken. Then now too, let us say that the connection is broken; and as for the *gezerah shawah,* that is required for what was taught, *They shall not make a baldness*: I might think that even if one makes four or five bald patches he is liable for only one [transgression]; therefore it is stated, *karhah* [a baldness], intimating liability for each separate act. What is taught by, *"upon their head"*? Because it is said, *"Ye shall not cut yourselves, nor make any baldness between your eyes for the dead"*: I might think that one is liable only for between the eyes. Whence do I know to include the whole head? Therefore it is stated, *"upon their head,"* to teach liability for the [whole] head as for between the eyes. Now, I know this only of priests, upon whom Scripture imposes additional precepts; whence do we know it of Israelites?—*Karhah* [baldness] is stated here, and *karhah* is also stated below; just as there, one is liable for every act of making baldness, and for the [whole] head as for between the eyes, so here too, one is liable for every act of baldness and in respect of the whole head as for between the eyes. And just as below, [baldness] for the dead [is meant], so here too it is for the dead! If so, let Scripture write *kerah* [baldness]: why *karhah*? That both may be inferred.

Raba said: This is Issi's reason, viz., he learns [the applicability of] *"between your eyes"* from phylacteries: just as there, women are exempt, so here too, women are exempt.

Now, why does Raba not say as Abaye?—[The distinction between] *ḳeraḥ* and *ḳarḥah* is not acceptable to him. And why does Abaye reject Raba's reason?— He can tell you. Phylacteries themselves are learnt from this: just as there, [*"between the eyes"* means] the place where a baldness can be made [viz.,] on the upper part of the head, so here too, the place for wearing [phylacteries] is the upper part of the head.

Now, according to both Abaye and Raba, how do they interpret this [verse], *"Ye are sons* [etc."]?—That is wanted for what was taught: *"Ye are sons of the Lord your God"*; when you behave as sons you are designated sons; if you do not behave as sons, you are not designated sons: this is R. Judah's view. R. Meir said: In both cases you are called sons, for it is said, *they are sottish children,* and it is also said, *They are children in whom is no faith,* and it is also said, *a seed of evil-doers, sons that deal corruptly,* and it is said, *and it shall come to pass that, in the place where it was said unto them, Ye are not my people, it shall be said unto them, Ye are the sons of the living God.* Why give these additional quotations?—For should you reply, only when foolish are they designated sons, but not when they lack faith—then come and hear: And it is said, *"They are sons in whom is no faith."* And should you say, when they have no faith they are called sons, but when they serve idols they are not called sons—then come and hear: And it is said, *"a seed of evil-doers, sons that deal corruptly."* And should you say, they are indeed called sons that act corruptly, but not good sons—then come and hear: And it is said, *and it shall come to pass that, in the place where it was said unto them, Ye are not my people, it shall be said unto them, Ye are the sons of the living God.*

MISHNAH: The [rites of] laying hands, waving, bringing near [the meal-offering], taking the handful, burning [the fat], wringing [the neck of bird sacrifices], receiving and sprinkling [the blood], are performed by men but not by women, excepting the meal-offering of a sotah and a nezirah, where they [themselves] do perform waving.

● 47

Jewish Women Forcibly Converted to Christianity (and a Christian Woman Visionary) on the Island of Minorca

SEVERUS OF MINORCA *Letter on the Conversion of the Jews*   early 5th century B.C.E.

AUTHOR: Severus was bishop of Minorca in the early fifth century C.E. Apart from what this letter itself suggests, little is known of its author. The letter narrates the forcible conversion to Christianity of the Jewish community on the island of Minorca in February 418. According to Severus, the arrival on the island of relics of the Christian "protomartyr" (first martyr), Stephen (Acts 6.8–8.1), inflamed the missionary fervor of local Christians, disrupting the previously cordial relations between Jewish and Christian communities on the island. Ultimately, Severus relates, a Christian mob burnt the local Jewish synagogue, and the entire Jewish community, 540 persons, accepted Christianity.

Severus's account is unique in its detailed description of a diaspora Jewish community in this period, with numerous references to women and a fascinating account of the temporary resistance of three elite Jewish women. This account raises intriguing questions about history and ideology: were these women, in fact, the final holdouts against Christian pressures, whom Severus then fashions into an example of Christ's power over Jewish "hardheartedness"? If so, we might read this text as a distorted but still useful mirror of the experiences of some Jewish women in fifth-century Minorca. Alternatively, perhaps Severus has intentionally cast women as the ultimate exemplars of such Jewish unbelief, in which case the text may tell us little if anything about these particular women and the constraints under which they became Christians, and more about the uses of gender in this particular narrative.

The *Letter* is also noteworthy for its description of the Christian visionary Theodora. Symbolizing both church and synagogue as women was common in Christian literature of this period.

TRANSLATION, TEXT, AND BIBLIOGRAPHY: Scott Bradbury, *Severus of Minorca, "Letter on the Conversion of the Jews," Edited with an Introduction, Translation and Notes,* Oxford Early Christian Texts (Oxford: Clarendon Press, 1996). Portions in italics are my paraphrases.

> 4.2 Doubtless at the inspiration of the martyr himself [a certain priest] placed in the church of Magona some relics of St Stephen the martyr, which had recently come to light and which he had intended to transport to Spain. . . .
> 4.4. Immediately, our complacency heated up. . . . At one moment, zeal for the faith would fire our hearts; at another moment, the hope of saving a multitude would spur us on.

> 5.1 In the end, even the obligation of greeting one another was suddenly broken off. . . . 5.2 In every public place, battles were waged against the Jews over the Law, in every house struggles over the faith.

> 6.1 The Jewish people relied particularly on the influence and knowledge of a certain Theodorus, who was pre-eminent in both wealth and worldly honour not only among the Jews but also among the Christians of that town [Magona]. 6.2 Among the Jews he was a teacher of the Law and, if I may use their own phrase, the Father of Fathers. 6.3 In the town, on the other hand,

he had already fulfilled all the duties of the town council and had served as
defensor, and even now he is considered the *patronus* of his fellow citizens. . . .

*After Theodorus, who had been on Majorca on business, returns to Magona, the
Christians apparently temporarily backed off from their missionary zeal. The Jews,
however, appealing to the example of the Maccabean martyrs, stockpiled weapons in
the synagogue against a possible Christian attack.*

10.1 There was among us a certain devout and very religious woman with the
name of Theodora, who, because of her virginity, her religious way of life,
and even the significance of her name ["gift of God"], could rightfully serve
as a symbol of the church. 10.2 She saw in a night vision a certain very noble widow sending a request to me in the form of a letter, in which she
humbly offered me all her fields to sow, although I occupy the priesthood
not from merit, but from the bounty of divine favor. 10.3 By a similar
dream, Christ also deigned to summon me as well, the last among all sinners,
in order that I prepare myself for the sowing: 10.4 for another very noble
widow, who without any doubt symbolized the synagogue, begged me [in the
dream] to take over her untilled fields and to cultivate them carefully, since
the season for sowing was close at hand. 10.5 Who then is the noble widow
but that widow who, by impiously killing Christ, cruelly widowed herself?. . . .

11.2 Theodorus, the high priest of that faithless people, recounted a dream
vision that he had seen not only to Jews, but in particular to a certain kinswoman, a distinguished matriarch of that town, and to many Christians as
well.

*Theodorus dreams that twelve men bar his way into the synagogue, warning him of
a lion within. Peering into the synagogue, Theodorus sees monks singing sweetly and
flees, terrified, to the side of a female relative, who soothes his fears.*

11.8 . . . who is the lion, but that "Lion of the tribe of Judah, the Root of
David [Rev. 5:5]? Who is that kinswoman, if not that one of whom it is written, "My kinswoman is but one"?

*A group of Christians from the neighboring town of Jamona, also seized with mis-
sionary fervor, now travel to Magona with the author, apparently to conduct a dis-
putation with the Jews. When Severus invites the Jews to debate in the church, they
decline, claiming that it would be inappropriate for them to enter a church on the
Sabbath. Instead, they eventually appear at the house where Severus is staying, where
he accuses them of stockpiling weapons at the synagogue. When the Jews attempt to
swear an oath that they have not done so, Severus counters that they should all just
go to the synagogue and see for themselves.*

13.3 . . . But before we reached the synagogue, certain Jewish women (by
God's arrangement, I suppose) acted recklessly, and doubtless to rouse our

people from their gentleness, began to throw huge stones down on us from a higher spot. 13.4 Although the stones, marvellous to relate, fell like hail over a closely packed crowd, not only was none of our people harmed by a direct hit, but no one was even touched. 13.5 At this point, that terrible Lion took away for a short while the mildness from his lambs. 13.6 While I protested in vain, they all snatched up stones. . . . 13.9 . . . the slave of a certain Christian. . . . 13.10 alone was greedy to steal something from the synagogue, and he was struck by a stone for his offence. In fact, someone from our group threw the stone, though he was aiming at a Jew, but it struck the slave on the head. . . . 13.11 Although the wound was not dangerous, it both forced him to confess his greedy desire for theft, and, by its obvious retribution, it put fear in everyone else lest they lapse in a similar way. 13.12 Therefore, after the Jews had retreated and we had gained control of the synagogue, no one, I won't say, "stole" anything, but no one even considered "looting" anything! 13.13 Fire consumed the synagogue itself and all of its decorations, with the exception of the books and silver. We removed the sacred books so that they wouldn't suffer harm among the Jews, but the silver we returned to them so that there would be no complaining either about us taking spoils or about them suffering losses.

14.1 And so, while all the Jews stood stupefied at the destruction of the synagogue, we set out for the church to the accompaniment of hymns. . . .

The next day, Severus relates, the first Jew, a man named Reuben, converted. Three days later, when no other Jews had done so, Theodorus himself came to the site of the despoiled synagogue.

16.3 There Theodorus debated boldly about the Law, and after he had mocked and twisted all our objections, the Christian throng, seeing that he could not be vanquished by human arguments, prayed for assistance from heaven. 16.4 They all shouted together and cried in thunderous unison, "Theodorus, believe in Christ." . . . 16.7 . . . the Jewish bystanders misinterpreted the phrase spoken by our people, for they all thought they had heard, "Theodorus has believed in Christ." . . .

Shortly thereafter, seeing elements of his earlier dream fulfilled when he finds monks singing in the synagogue, Theodorus does, in fact, agree to convert and to endeavor to convert other Jews as well. Severus then relates the conversion of numerous other Jewish men, frequently accompanied by miracles of one sort or another, including the dusting of the island with a sweet-smelling fine hail, which Severus interprets as a divine deed comparable to the manna God sent the Israelites in the desert.

21.1 Accordingly, on the following day, everyone reminded Theodorus with great anticipation that he should make good his pledge. 21.2 He believed, for what seemed to him justifiable reasons, that the vows of all the Jews should be postponed, saying that first he wanted to bring his wife here, whom he had left on the island of Majorca. His concern was that she might, if she learned that her husband had converted without her agreement, remain firm in her faithlessness, as usually happens. Further, she might become confused in her judgment and, at the instigation of her mother in particular, who was still alive, abandon both the marriage and her husband's religion. 21.3 When Theodorus had made these pleas, the Christians were amenable, but the Jews who had converted persisted in a bitter disturbance. The delay was cut short and Theodorus himself flew swiftly to the bosom of his kinswoman, as he had seen [in the dream]. 21.4 After him, the whole synagogue, as if a stumbling block had been removed, flowed together to the church. 21.5 Marvellous to relate, aged teachers of the Law began to believe, without any verbal wrangling, without any dispute over the Scriptures. 21.6 After debating for so long whether they were willing to accept faith in Christ, they professed that they believed in Christ and desired to be made Christians without delay.

24.1 . . . only three women, although very noble women among the Jews, did Christ permit to hold out a little longer, in order to extend the glory of his power amidst the hardheartedness of their unbelief. 24.2 Artemisia, the daughter of Litorius, who recently governed this province and who is now said to be a Count, was distraught at the conversion of her husband Meletius. Without any thought for feminine frailty and with just one friend, a nurse, and a few servant girls, she deserted her husband's house and escaped to a cave, which, though located in a vineyard, was none the less in quite a remote spot. 24.3 In the vineyard, there was a small, new winepress, and a newly-made vat, which seemed somehow to serve as a symbol of the faithful people. 24.4 For we either believe or can see that the Jews have received the "must" of the New Testament not like "old wineskins," but like "new wine-vats" [Luke 5: 37]. 24.5 This woman had passed two days in that spot, implacable and angry with her husband. As soon as the third day dawned, she ordered a maidservant to draw water for her so that she could wash her face in her usual way. The water came from the winevat, which was full from a rainshower. When she realized that the water resembled honey in the sweetness of its taste and smell, at first she began to grow angry with the servant and asked indignantly why she had put honey in the pitcher. 24.6 Afterwards, however, as if to disprove the servant's denials, she went to the vat, drew forth a little water with cupped hands, and found that the water she had been using for two days was changed into the sweetest, most delightful honey. 24.7 Then she called over all the women present and told them to taste the water, lest by chance a falsely sweet taste was deceiving her throat alone. 24.8 All of them tasted it and were stirred with such marvellous delight they decided it was not water infused with honey, but the purest honey with only a resemblance to water. 24.9 Struck with wonder, they investigated more carefully while they were preparing to return to town and discovered that the dew, which was on much of the grass, also had a similar taste. 24.10 Accordingly, the previously mentioned lady set out for the town, reported these things to her husband, and immediately, without resistance, she assented to faith in Christ. 24.11 However, on the same day when Meletius' wife was compelled by the honey to cast away the bitterness of her unbelief. . . . the entire church grew fragrant with such a marvellous and truly heavenly odour that nearly all the brethren sensed the presence of the Holy Spirit. . . .

26.1 There still remained two women who refused to race to the fragrance of Christ's unguents: the wife of that Innocentius, whom we mentioned above, along with her sister, a widow of excellent reputation. 26.2 Yet the moment she learned that her sister's husband, Innocentius, had been converted, she boarded ship. We not only permitted her to do this, we even encouraged her, because she could not be turned to faith in Christ by either words or miracles.

27.1 Moreover, Innocentius' wife for nearly four days rejected with deaf ears the word of salvation that we were administering. 27.2 Since she was overwhelmed by the incurable sickness of her unbelief and refused all our medicine, 27.3 and could not be swayed by Innocentius' threats nor his prayers nor his tears, the whole crowd of the brethren, at Innocentius' request, gathered together at the house where he lived, feeling great pain in their spirits because so great an abundance of happiness was being opposed by a single woman (since her sister was thought already to have set sail). 27.4 After we had forced vain words on deaf ears for a long time and had accomplished nothing, we hastened to the known assistance of prayer and turned toward heavenly mercy the prayers which mortal impiety rejected. 27.6 . . . Stretched out on the floor, we wept for a long time. 27.7 And when the people had exclaimed "Amen" at the end of the prayer, that woman added that she believed and that she wanted to be made a Christian. . . .

28.1 On the following day. . . . 28.3 . . . that widowed kinswoman of Innocentius was carried back from the open sea. 28.4 Suddenly, she wrapped herself about my knees and begged with tears for the assistance of our faith. 28.5 "Why, woman," I asked, "did you wish to desert your brothers in such foolhardiness?" To which she replied, "Even the prophet Jonah wished to flee from the countenance of God, and yet he fulfilled, although unwillingly, the will of God [Jonah 1: 1–4]. 28.6 Therefore, receive not just myself, but these orphans too, and nourish them in Christ." 28.7 While she was making this pitiful plea, she led her two little daughters to me. 28.8 Who did not weep for joy? From whom did this abundance of happiness not wring tears? 28.9 To be sure, I accepted the sheep (the only one from the whole flock we knew to have wandered off) and I recalled her with her twin offspring to the fold of Christ.

The letter concludes with Severus's report that 540 Jews were "added to the church" and that not only did the Jews bear the expense for leveling the old synagogue and constructing the foundations of a new Christian basilica, but they also bore the stones on their very shoulders.

TWO

Researching Real Women:
Documents to, from, and by Women

If the evidence for the religious activities of women in the Greco-Roman world is limited, the evidence for the religious activities of specific historical women, those for whom we have some concrete personal data, is even more limited. We possess no ancient literary religious texts known to have been written by women before the fourth century c.e.[1] A significant proportion of Jewish and Christian texts from the Greco-Roman period have come down to us either with author unknown (anonymous) or with an ascription we consider patently impossible (pseudonymous). Scholars routinely used to assume male authorship for all these texts, but a heightened sensitivity due to feminist scholarship has led many scholars to re-think those assumptions and to question whether women authors are hidden beyond the labels of anonymous and pseudonymous. Candidates for possible female authorship include some portions of the various apocryphal Acts of the Apostles, *(Joseph and) Aseneth*, the *Testament of Job*, Pseudo-Philo's *Biblical Antiquities*, and several texts found in Egypt near Nag Hammadi such as the *Hypostatis of the Archons* (or *The Reality of the Rulers*).[2]

---

[1] The few writings by Christian women have been collected in English translation in Patricia Wilson-Kastner et al., *A Lost Tradition: Women Writers of the Early Church* (Washington, D.C.: University Press of America, 1981). As discussed below, however, I now disagree with the inclusion of *The Martyrdom of Saints Perpetua and Felicitas* in this category.

[2] The suggestion that women may have composed or written one or more of the stories in the apocryphal Acts has been argued by Stevan L. Davies, *The Revolt of the Widows: The Social World of the Apocryphal Acts* (Carbondale: Southern Illinois University Press, 1980). See also Dennis R. MacDonald, *The Legend and the Apostle: The Battle for Paul in Story and Canon* (Philadelphia: Westminster Press, 1983); and Dennis R. MacDonald, "The Role of Women in the Production of the Apocryphal Acts of the Apostles," *Iliff Review* 41 (1984): 21–28. This view has been challenged, with good reasons, by Jean Daniel Kaestli, "Fiction litteraire et réalité sociale: Que peut-on savoir de la place des femmes dans le milieu du production des Actes apocryphes des apôtres?" in *La fable apocryphe* 1 (1990): 279–302; see also my own critique in

In the previous edition of this anthology, I considered that the evidence to substantiate female authorship of any of these texts was insufficient to warrant their inclusion in this section. I did, however, include an excerpt from *The Martyrdom of Saints Perpetua and Felicitas*, on the strength of the view of many scholars that the first-person portion of that account was composed by Perpetua herself while she was imprisoned awaiting her death in the arena, as the narrative frame of the *Martyrdom* itself claims. In the intervening years, though, I have considered this question further, and have concluded that Perpetua is unlikely to be the author of this section.[3] I have consequently moved that selection to section 5, "Holy, Pious, and Exemplary Women," together with other martyrdom narratives. Along a similar vein, I have relocated to that same section the collections of sayings attributed to the Desert Mothers Sarah, Syncletica, and Theodora, on the grounds that they represent exemplary desert ascetics whose historicity cannot be independently verified.

In the absence of writings by women themselves, some of the most important evidence for women's lives in antiquity, including evidence for religious practices and beliefs, comes from nonliterary sources, everything from burial epitaphs to private letters to tax registers. Although the preservation of this material is subject to the vagaries of time and weather, among other things, it is somewhat less susceptible to the gender bias that affects literary sources, which are written, transmitted, and translated principally by men. The factors determining which women were commemorated, either in life or in death, or which women commissioned inscriptions of various sorts are complex and very much related to ancient social practices generally, but once engraved on stone or marble, these inscriptions were considerably less dependent on copying to survive to modern times. Similarly, the special combination of the climate in Egypt and in comparable areas such as the Judean desert together with the characteristics of writing material made from the papyrus plant have enabled ordinary correspondence and documents to survive

"Women's Authorship of Jewish and Christian Literature in the Greco-Roman Period," in Amy-Jill Levine, ed., *"Women Like This": New Perspectives on Jewish Women in the Greco-Roman Period*, Early Judaism and Its Literature 1 (Atlanta: Scholars Press, 1991), 221–42. In the same article, I discuss the possibilities for female authorship of *Aseneth* and the *Testament of Job*. Periodically, there has also been discussion of women's authorship of the Gospels according to Mark and to John, as well as of the Letter to the Hebrews (see Mary Rose D'Angelo, "Hebrews," in *WBC*, 364–65; Cynthia Briggs Kittredge, "Hebrews," in *Searching the Scriptures*, 2:428–52, esp. 431–34). Recently, female authorship has been proposed for Ps.-Philo, *Biblical Antiquities*; see Mary Therese Descamp, "Why Are These Women Here? An Examination of the Sociological Setting of Pseudo-Philo through Comparative Reading," *Journal for the Study of Pseudepigrapha* 16 (1997): 53–80.

[3] Ross S. Kraemer and Shira L. Lander, "Perpetua and Felicitas," in Philip Esler, ed., *The Early Christian World* (London: Routledge, 2000), 2:1048–68.

two thousand years and to emerge from archaeological discoveries in the last century or so. Inscriptions and papyrus documents have often been neglected by scholars of early Judaism and early Christianity in favor of literary texts, although this has changed somewhat in recent years, and the disciplines of epigraphy and papyrology are highly intimidating to the uninitiated.[4] Many inscriptions and papyrus documents are available only in esoteric collections, and not necessarily in English translation. Nevertheless, they are well worth the effort for those who study women in antiquity.

Some of the selections in this section, particularly those on Jewish women and a few on Christian women, do not bear explicitly on activities of these women that might reasonably be considered religious.[5] I have included them anyway for two reasons: we know so little about specific Jewish women that it seemed helpful to include some of the relevant inscriptions and documents here. Second, and perhaps more important, these sources may shed indirect light on the religious lives of Jewish women. For example, texts that help us assess the degree to which Jewish women were or were not relatively secluded may enable us to reevaluate our perceptions of what women did in synagogues: if we have evidence that Jewish women were active participants in the economic and social lives of their com-

---

[4] When the first edition of this anthology was published in 1988, many Jewish inscriptions were unavailable in English translation, with the notable exception of inscriptions (and papyri) from Egypt in *CPJ* and an appendix of Jewish inscriptions from Rome in Harry J. Leon, *The Jews of Ancient Rome* (Philadelphia: Jewish Publication Society, 1960). In recent years, three important volumes of Jewish inscriptions have been published with original transcriptions, English translations, notes, and bibliography: *JIGRE* (2 vols.)and *JIWE*. A short, although fairly technical, introduction to Jewish funerary inscriptions is Pieter W. van der Horst, *Ancient Jewish Epigraphs: An Introductory Survey of a Millennium of Jewish Funeral Epigraphy (300 B.C.E.–700 C.E.)* (Kampen, the Netherlands: Kok Pharos, 1991). Most identifiable Christian funeral epitaphs are third century C.E. and later, and there is no comparable introduction to the topic, although see now Ute Eisen, *Women Office Holders in Early Christianity: Epigraphical and Literary Studies*, trans. Linda M. Maloney (Collegeville, Minn.: Michael Glazier, Liturgical Press, 2000). An excellent primer on papyrology is Roger Bagnall, *Reading Papyri, Writing Ancient History* (London and New York: Routledge, 1995).

[5] The classification of inscriptions and papyrus documents as "Jewish" or as referring to Jewish persons can be fairly complicated. Many inscriptions come from ancient catacombs and burial sites that are identified as Jewish on the basis of numerous factors, while others come from ancient sites that have been reasonably securely identified as synagogues. The classification of papyri as Jewish is often based more on references within the documents themselves, including names, ethnic indicators, and the like, than on the location of discovery (which is not always securely known). Nevertheless, for various reasons, these identifications are often tenuous: see Ross S. Kraemer, "Jewish Tuna and Christian Fish: Identifying Religious Affiliation in Epigraphic Sources," *HTR* 84, no. 2 (1991): 141–62. On the term "religious," see the main introduction, note 1.

munities, playing various public roles, we must take that evidence seriously when we try to assess what roles women might have played in synagogues.[6] Evidence for social relationships between Jewish and non-Jewish women may require us to reconsider our understanding of the nature of Jewish-gentile relationships generally in the Greco-Roman period and may offer insight into the extent to which individual Jewish women observed regulations concerning food (*kashrut*) or menstrual purity (*niddah*) and so forth. In short, although much of the evidence for actual Jewish women sheds little light on their religious lives (the same, though, is true for actual Jewish men, at least in the papyri and inscriptions), what we learn from these sources may enable us to rethink some of the assumptions we hold when we ask questions about Jewish practice and thinking in the Greco-Roman period.

In the initial version of this anthology, I lamented the inability to include selections from the personal papers of Babatha of Maoza, discovered in 1959–60 by Israeli archaeologists in caves associated with the Bar Kokhba rebellion of ca. 132–35 C.E. In the intervening years, most of these papyri have now been published, together with the personal papers of several other women from the same period, and a generous sampling of these are excerpted here, including several marriage documents, litigation over guardianship, and documents witnessing the tensions in Babatha's polygynous second marriage.

Also included in this section are letters written by men to women, notably by Jerome and John Chrysostom. We know from Jerome and others that correspondence such as this was not one-sided: women also wrote to men. It is significant and ironic that the letters by women have by and large not been preserved. We should also keep in mind that correspondence by men and women need not imply the actual ability on the part of either correspondent to write. Professional scribes were available in antiquity to any who could pay for their services and were employed both by those who could write and by those who could not. In most of the letters included here, it is clear that the recipients as well as the writers were highly literate.

6. The stimulus for all recent discussions of this topic is Brooten, *Women Leaders*. Brooten's work has prompted extensive response: for recent presentation of the question, see Lee I. Levine, "Women in the Synagogue," in *The Ancient Synagogue: The First Thousand Years* (New Haven: Yale University Press, 2000), 471–90; see also Hannah Safrai, "Women and the Ancient Synagogue," in S. Grossman and R. Haut, eds., *Daughters of the King: Women and the Synagogue: A Survey of History, Halakhah, and Contemporary Realities* (Philadelphia: Jewish Publication Society, 1992), 39–49.

● 48

Epitaphs of Women From Leontopolis, Site of an Alternative Jewish Temple

WORKS: A series of burial inscriptions in Greek from Tell el-Yahoudieh (ancient Leontopolis, in Egypt) were found at or near a Jewish cemetery excavated in the late nineteenth century. Under the auspices of Ptolemy VI, Philomotor, a Jewish high priest, Onias IV, built an alternative temple at Leontopolis in the first half of the second century B.C.E. that was closed by the Romans at the end of the first Jewish revolt (73/74 C.E.).

TRANSLATION: All except 48B: David Lewis, *CPJ* 3; 48B: *JIGRE*.

TEXT AND TRANSLATION: *JIGRE*, *CPJ* 3

ADDITIONAL TEXT (WITH FRENCH TRANSLATION): *CIJ* 2.

BIBLIOGRAPHY: *JIGRE*; Modrejewski, *Jews of Egypt*.

● 48A

Epitaph of a Jewish/Judean Woman Who Died On Her Wedding Day

CPJ/CIJ 1508; *JIGRE* 31   mid–2d century B.C.E. to early 2d century C.E.?

Weep for me, stranger, a maiden ripe for marriage, who formerly shone in a great house. For, decked in fair bridal garments, I, untimely, have received this hateful tomb as my bridal chamber. For when a noise of revellers already at my doors told that I was leaving my father's house, like a rose in a garden nurtured by fresh rain, suddenly Hades came and snatched me away. And I, stranger, who had accomplished twenty revolving years (?) . . .

● 48B

Epitaph of a Woman, Her Husband, and Daughter

CPJ/CIJ 1509; *JIGRE* 32   2d century B.C.E.–2d century C.E.?

This is the tomb of Horaia, wayfarer. Shed a tear. . . . . Daughter of. . . . laos, she was unfortunate in all things, and fulfilled three decades of years. Three of us are here, husband, daughter and I whom they inflamed with grief. . . . . . . on the third, then on the fifth my daughter Eirene, to whom marriage was not granted, and I then with no portion of joy was laid here after them under the earth on the seventh of Choiak. But stranger, you have clearly all there is to know of us; tell all men of the swiftness of death. In the 10th year, Choiak 7.

● 48C

Epitaph of a Woman Who Died in Childbirth

CPJ/CIJ 1510; *JIGRE* 33   mid–2d century–1st century B.C.E.?

This is the grave of Arsinoe, wayfarer. Stand by and weep for her, unfortunate in all things, whose lot was hard and terrible. For I was bereaved of my mother when I was a little girl, and when the flower of my youth made me ready for a bridegroom, my father married me to Phabeis, and Fate brought me to the end of my life in bearing my firstborn child. I had a small span of years, but great grace flowered in the beauty of my spirit. This grave hides in its bosom my chaste body, but my soul has flown to the holy ones. Lament for Arsinoe. In the 25th year, Mechir 2.

● 48D

Epitaph of a Thirty-Year-Old Woman

CPJ/CIJ 1513; *JIGRE* 36   mid–2d century B.C.E.–2d century C.E.?

Citizens and strangers, all weep for Rachelis, chaste, friend of all, about thirty years old. Do not weep vainly empty (tears?) for me. If I did live but a short allotted span, nevertheless I await a good hope of mercy. And Agathokles, about 38 years old.

● 48E

A Dialogue Epitaph of a Young Married Woman

CPJ/CIJ 1530; *JIGRE* 38   2d century B.C.E.–2d century C.E.?

The speaking stele.
"Who are you who lie in the dark tomb? Tell me your country and birth."
"Arsinoe, daughter of Aline, and Theodosios. The famous land of Onias reared me."
"How old were you when you slipped down the dark slope of Lethe?"
"At twenty I went to the sad place of the dead."
"Were you married?"
"I was."
"Did you leave him a child?"
"Childless I went to the house of Hades."
"May earth, the guardian of the dead, be light on you."
"And for you, stranger, may she bear fruitful crops."
In the 16th year, Payni 21.

Disposition of a Lawsuit between a Woman and a Man Living in Egypt, Both Called "Jews/Judeans"

CPJ 19; P. Petrie 3.21 (g); P. Gurob 2, SP 256   226 B.C.E.

WORK: Two papyrus copies exist of this disposition, internally dated to 226 B.C.E., from Krokodilopolis, in the Fayûm, Egypt. On the translation "Jew/Judean," see the main introduction, p. 8.

TRANSLATION AND TEXT: David Lewis, *CPJ* 1, 151–56.

BIBLIOGRAPHY: Modrejewski, *Jews of Egypt*.

> In the 22nd year of the reign of Ptolemy, son of Ptolemy and Arsinoe, gods Adelphoi, the priest of Alexander and the gods Adelphoi and the gods Euergetai and the kanephoros of Arsinoe Philadelphos being those officiating in Alexandria, the 22nd of the month Dystros, at Krokodilopolis in the Arsinoite nome, under the presidency of Zenothemis, the judges being Diomedes, Polykles, Andron, Theophanes, Maiandrios, Sonikos, Diotrephes. Polydeukes, the clerk of the court, having constituted us in accordance with the order sent to him by Aristomachos, appointed strategos of the Arsinoite nome, of which this is a copy:
>
> "To Polydeukes greeting. Herakleia has requested the king in her petition to form and swear in a court for her of all the judges except such as either party may challenge in accordance with the regulations. Year 21, Dystros 16, Pachon 19."
>
> We have given judgment as below in the action brought by Dositheos against Herakleia according to the following indictment:
>
> "Dositheos son of . . . , Jew of the Epigone, to Herakleia daughter of Diosdotos, Jewess, as you in your . . . of yourself declared(?), (I state) that on Peritios 22 of year 21, as I with other persons was entering the . . . of Apion . . . from the so-called house of Pasytis which is in Krokodilopolis in the Arsinoite nome opposite the so-called house of Pasytis the . . . , you came to that place with Kallippos the . . . and abused me saying that I had told certain persons that (you are a . . .) woman, and on my abusing you in return you not only spat on me but seizing the loop of my mantle . . . me and . . . until . . . and the said Kallippos . . . as the people present rebuked you and Kallippos . . . you ceased your insults . . . to which I have borne witness. Wherefore I bring an action of assault against you for 200 drachmai, the assessment of damages being . . . drachmai. And as the assaulted party I by this indictment . . . The 21st year, the priest of Alexander and the gods Adelphoi and the gods Euergetai being Galestes son of Philistion, the kanephoros of Arsinoe Philadelphos being Berenike daughter of Sosipolis, the 26th of the month Peritios. The case will be presented against you in the court sitting in the Arsinoite nome, of

which Polydeukes is the clerk, on Peritios ... of the 21st year, and you have received the indictment and have been personally summoned, the witnesses of the summons being ... phanes son of Nikias, Thracian, official employee, Zopyros son of Symmachos, Persian of the Epigone."

Whereas this was the indictment, and Dositheos neither appeared in person nor put in a written statement nor was willing to plead his case; and whereas Herakleia appeared with her guardian Aristides son of Proteas, Athenian of the Epigone, and put in both a written statement and justificatory documents, and was also willing to defend her case; and whereas the code of regulations which was handed in by Herakleia among the justificatory documents directs us to give judgment in a ... manner on all points which any person knows or shows us to have been dealt with in the regulations of king Ptolemy, in accordance with the regulations, and on all points which are not dealt with in the regulations, but in the civic laws, in accordance with the laws, and on all other points to follow the most equitable view; but when both parties have been summoned before the court and one of them is unwilling to put in a written statement or plead his case or acknowledge defeat(?) ... he shall be judged guilty of injustice; we have dismissed the case.

● 50
A Jewish/Judean Woman's Attacks on a Pregnant Neighbor

CPJ 133; *P. Tebt.* 800   mid–2d century B.C.E.

WORK: This papyrus letter was found in the region in Egypt known as the Fayûm. The identification of Johanna as a Jew or Judean (see main introduction, p. 8) relies on the explicit designation of the sender of the letter as *Ioudaios* (Jew/Judean) and the names of the sender and recipient, both of which are attested elsewhere for Jews/Judeans.

TRANSLATION AND TEXT: *CPJ* 1, 246–47.

BIBLIOGRAPHY: Modrejewski, *Jews of Egypt.*

To ..., scribe of the village of ..., from Sabbataios son of ..., a Jew, one of the hired labourers of the same village. On Payni 20 in the 28th year, when I was ...

In consequence of the blows and fall she is suffering severely; she has had to take to her bed and her child is in danger of miscarriage and death. I present you this petition in order that, when you have visited the spot and observed her (?) condition, Johanna may be secured until the result is apparent and that it may not happen that Johanna in case of any untoward event go scot-free. The 28th year, Payni 21.

Registered Payni 25.

❂ 51
The Contract of a Wet Nurse, Possibly Jewish/Judean

CPJ 146; BGU 1106   13 B.C.E.

WORK: This is one of several papyri found in the late nineteenth century at Bousiris (Abusir el-Meleq), in the ancient Herakleopolite nome (administrative district) of Egypt, that appear, largely by virtue of the persons named, to refer to Jews/Judeans. The names of the wet nurse, her father, and her husband are all consistent with names used by Jews/Judeans in this period. The details are fairly standard for ancient wet nurse contracts.

TEXT AND TRANSLATION: A. Fuks, *CPJ* 2, 15–19.

BIBLIOGRAPHY: Keith R. Hopkins, "Wet-Nursing at Rome: A Study in Social Relations," in Beryl Rawson, ed., *The Family in Ancient Rome: New Perspectives* (Ithaca, N.Y.: Cornell University Press, 1986), 201–29.

(1st hand) To Protarchos in charge of the court. (2d hand) From Marcus Aemilius son of Marcus of the Claudian tribe and from Theodote daughter of Dositheos, a Persian, acting with her guardian and guarantor of the terms of this agreement, her husband, Sophron the son of . . . archos, a Persian of the Epigone. With regard to this matter, Theodote agrees that she will for 18 months from Phamenoth of the present 17th year of Caesar (Augustus) bring up and suckle in her own house in the city with her own milk pure and uncontaminated the foundling slave baby child Tyche which Marcus has entrusted to her, receiving from him each month as payment for her milk and care 8 drachmai of silver besides olive-oil, and Theodote has duly received from Marcus by her guarantor Sophron for the agreed 18 months wages for 9 months adding up to 72 drachmai; and if the child chances to die within this time, Theodote will take up another child and nurse it and suckle it and restore it to Marcus for the same 9 months, receiving no wages, since she has undertaken to nurse continually, providing her monthly care honestly and taking fitting thought for the child, not damaging her milk, not lying with a man, not conceiving, not taking another child to suckle. Whatever she takes or is entrusted with, she will keep safe and restore when it is asked or will pay the value of each thing, except in the case of a manifest loss, which will release her if it is proved. She will not give up her nursing before the time. If she defaults, she and Sophron may be seized and held until they pay back her wages and whatever else she receives and half as much again and the damages and the costs and another 300 drachmai of silver. The distraint may be made on either or both of them, since they guarantee each other, and on their property as if a judgement had been made against them, and whatever guarantees they give and all resort to protection shall be invalid. But if she duly performs everything, Marcus Aemilius will give her the monthly wages for the remaining 9 months and will not take the child away within the time or will himself pay the same penalty. Theodote shall bring the child to Marcus for inspection each month. Surety . . .

Theodote daughter of Dositheos and her husband Sophron for a slave child Tyche for 18 months, for which they have received 8 drachmai for 9 months, in the city.

● **52**

A Divorce Agreement from Egypt, Perhaps Jewish/Judean

CPJ 144; *BGU* 1102   13 B.C.E.

WORK: Another papyrus from Bousiris, this one is considered Jewish on the basis of the names of the wife's parents, which are attested for Jews/Judeans in Egypt in this period. Apart from this, the agreement contains nothing explicitly or distinctively Jewish and much that is common in non-Jewish documents of this period. The editors of *CPJ* note that the papyrus might point to a marriage between a Jewish woman and a non-Jewish man.

TEXT AND TRANSLATION: A. Fuks, *CPJ* 2, 10–12.

BIBLIOGRAPHY: *Women and Christian Origins*, 59–60; Bernadette J. Brooten, "Mark 10.2–12, Divorced Wife," in *WIS*, 428–30; Tal Ilan, "Notes and Observations on a Newly Published Divorce Bill from the Judean Desert," *HTR* 89 (1996): 195–202; A. Schremer, "Divorce in Papyrus Ṣeʿelim 13 Once Again: A Reply to Tal Ilan," *HTR* 91 (1998): 193–204 (with response by Ilan).

> To Protarchos, from Apollonia daughter of Sambathion with her guardian, her mother's brother, Herakleides son of Herakleides, and from Hermogenes son of Hermogenes an Archistrateian. Apollonia and Hermogenes agree that they have dissolved their marriage by an agreement made through the same court in the 13th year of Caesar (Augustus) in the month Pharmouthi. Apollonia agrees that she has duly received back from Hermogenes the dowry of 60 drachmai which he had on her account from her parents Sambathion and Eirene according to the marriage-agreement. They agree therefore that the marriage-agreement is void, and that neither Apollonia nor anyone proceeding on her behalf will proceed against Hermogenes to recover the dowry, and that neither of them will proceed against the other on any matter arising from the marriage or from any other matter arising up to the present day, and that from this day it shall be lawful for Apollonia to marry another man and Hermogenes to marry another woman without penalty, and that whosoever transgresses this agreement shall be liable to the appointed penalty. The 17th year of Caesar (Augustus), Phamenoth 14.

⊛ 53

A Woman, Possibly Jewish/Judean, Settling Her Share of a Debt

CPJ 148; *BGU* 1155   10 B.C.E.

WORK: Another papyrus from Bousiris, this one is considered Jewish on the basis of the name Martha.

TRANSLATION AND TEXT: A. Fuks, *CPJ* 2, 20–22.

> To Protarchos, from Apollonios the son of Theon and from Martha (the freedwoman) of Protarchos, acting with her guardian, Herakleides the son of Herakleides. Whereas Apollonios presented to the archidikastes Artemidoros in the present 20th year of Caesar (Augustus) in the month Hathyr a petition demanding from Martha and also from Protarchos son of Protarchos 200 drachmai of silver with interest which he submitted to be owing to him from the deceased Protarchos son of Polemon, the patron of Martha and the father of Protarchos, on the evidence of the promissory note he produced and of the agreements made by Protarchos; now, since he has been satisfied by Martha in respect of her half share and has duly received from her her half share, Apollonios agrees that neither he himself nor anyone acting on his behalf will proceed in any way against the property left by her deceased patron Protarchos with respect to Martha's half share of the principal and the interest . . . , nor with respect to the . . . nor to any other loan or demand whatsoever, written or unwritten, arising from that time to the present day. . . . (And whosoever transgresses) this agreement, shall be liable to damages and the fine legally established. This shall not prejudice Apollonios' right to proceed against Protarchos for the remaining half of the principal, 100 drachmai and the interest on them. . . .

⊛ 54

Sale of a House between Two Women, the Buyer Perhaps Jewish/Judean

CPJ 483; *BGU* 854   45 C.E.

WORK: This papyrus is from Soknopaiou Nesos, a village in the Fayûm. The name (Sambathion) of the father of the buyer is attested for Jews/Judeans, although not all persons with this or related names, such as Sabbatios (thought to designate persons born on the Sabbath), are known to have been Jews/Judeans. Herieus, the buyer, was illiterate (as was the seller, and as were most persons in antiquity), and the young man who signs for her has a name (Leontas) that may well be Jewish/Judean, as does his father (Eirenaios). It is possible that Leontas was in some way related to Herieus, which would strengthen the suggestion that she, too, was Jewish/Judean.

(I, Thases daughter of Panephremmis . . . acknowledge that I have sold) to Herieus daughter of Sambathiôn, mother Thases, the two-storied house and all its appurtenances which I own at . . . , where the neighbours of the entire house are: south and west, a public street; north, house . . . of Tesenuphis . . . ; east, house of Herieus daughter of Sambathiôn. And I have forthwith received, in cash on the spot, the whole agreed price in full, and I will guarantee (the transaction) with every form of guarantee from the present day for all time, and I will carry out the other provisions stated above, and I have ordered . . . the clerk at the record-office to endorse (this deed) and to . . . Papais son of Pa . . ses wrote for her because she is illiterate.

(2d hand) I, Herieus daughter of Sambathiôn, mother Thases, have bought it as stated above. Leontas son of Eirenaios wrote for her because she is illiterate.

(1st hand?) Sale and cession of house and all its appurtenances at Soknopaiou Nesos in the division of Herakleides, where the neighbours of the entire house are: south and west, public street; north, house . . . of Tesenuphis in the possession of his children; east, house of Herieus daughter of Sambathiôn; and she has received the price and guarantees (the sale): which sale is made by Thases daughter of Panephremmis . . . with a mole on her forehead to the left, and Herieus daughter of Sambathiôn, mother Thases, about 38 years old, likewise with a mole on her forehead to the left. Signatory for the seller, Papais son of Pa . . ses . . . ; for the other party, Leontas son of Eirenaios, about 20 years old, without markings. Fifth year of Tiberius Claudius Caesar Augustus Germanicus Imperator, Pachon 20. Registered through the record-office at Soknopaiou Nesos.

● **55**

Jewish Women Enumerated in a Tax Document from Egypt

CPJ 421   73 C.E.

WORK: This papyrus from Arsinoë, a village in the Fayûm, is dated just to the end of the first Jewish revolt. It lists the persons liable for the Jewish tax, which was instituted by the Roman emperor Vespasian as punishment and reparation (to the Romans) for the revolt, which was exceedingly costly to quell. All Jewish persons over the age of three were liable for the tax. This detailed list provides important and interesting demographic data.

TRANSLATION AND TEXT: V. Tcherikover and A. Fuks, *CPJ* 2, 204–8.

The report of Herakleides *amphodarches* of the quarter of "Apollonios' Camp." The liability for the Jewish tax for the fifth year of the Emperor Caesar Vespasian Augustus being an abstract according to the statement of the fourth year. The number of Jews taken up by previous accounts are 5 adult males, 6 adult females, of whom one is over age and was adjudged as such being 59 years of age in the fourth year, one minor, being four years of age in the fourth year, total of names 12. And those taken up through a transcript of the preceding *epikrisis* shown to be three years of age in the fourth year, being one year old in the second year. Males: Philiskos, son of Ptollas, grandson of Philiskos, mother Erotion. Females: Protous, daughter of Simon, son of Ptolemaios, mother Dosarion, total 2, 14 in all, of these adult males 5, minor male 1, who in the fifth year was four years old, adult females 6, minor female 1, who in the fifth year was five years old, likewise 1 minor female four years old . . . total of names 14. In addition there is enrolled in the Jewish tax in the fifth year of the Emperor Caesar Vespasian Augustus, of minors who in the third year were one year old and so in the fifth year three years old, of males taken up, Seuthes, son of Theodoros, grandson of Ptolemaios, mother Philous found to be two years old in the fourth year, in the *epikrisis* of the fourth year; total of names 15; of which adult males 5, 1 minor male who in the fifth year is five years old, adult females 6, 1 female minor who in the fifth year is five years old, likewise 1 four years old, total 15. Of these 5 adult males being of those in the list as liable to the maximum rate of the *laographia*, 5 names, and the remaining names 10. These individually are: adult females: Tryphaina, daughter of . . . spas, granddaughter of Kales, mother Dosarion, of those who are over age, having been adjudged in the fourth year to be 59 years old, now 61 years old. Dosarion, daughter of Jakoubos, son of Jakoubos, mother Sambous, the wife of Simon, 22 years old, Philous (daughter of) . . . , mother Ptollous, wife of Theodoros, 20 years old. Sambathion, daughter of Sabinos, mother Herais, wife of Thegenes, 18 years old. S . . . daughter of . . . mother Theudous, wife of Sambathion . . . years old. Erotion, daughter of . . . on, mother Euterpe, wife of Ptollas, 22 years old, total 6. Minor males, four years old in the fifth year: Philiskos, son of Ptollas, grandson of Philiskos, mother Erotion, 1 name, likewise those three years old in the fifth year: Seuthes, son of Theodoros, grandson of Ptolemaios, mother Philous, 1. Females five years old in the fifth year. Protous, daughter of Theodoros, mother Philous, 1. Likewise those four years old in the fifth year: Protous, daughter of Simon, son of Ptolemaios, mother Dosarion, 1. Total of names 10. Together with the 5 names of those liable to the maximum rate of the *laographia*, total as above 15 names, at 8 drachmai and 2 oboloi each, 125 drachmai, for the *aparchai* 15 drachmai, total 140 drachmai. A similar copy has been deposited with the royal scribe through Amoutio . . . the scribe, in the fifth year of Vespasian on the 20th of Germanikios.

● 56

Manumission of a Jewish/Judean Female Slave

CPJ 473; P. Oxy. 1205   291 C.E.

WORK: The largest corpus of ancient papyri from Egypt was found in the village of Oxyrhynchus in the late nineteenth century. That the slave in this document was a Jewish/Judean woman seems certain from the fact that her freedom was purchased by representatives of the "community of the Jews" (or, perhaps, Judeans). A significant number of manumission documents survive, often in the form of inscriptions on the walls of temples, a handful of which demonstrably concern Jews either as slaves or slave owners.

TRANSLATION AND TEXT: Tcherikover, *CPJ* 3, 33–36, trans. V. Tcherikover.

BIBLIOGRAPHY: Leigh Gibson, *The Jewish Manumission Inscriptions of the Bosporus Kingdom,* Texts and Studies in Ancient Judaism 75 (Tübingen: Mohr Siebeck, 1999).

> Translation of manumission. We, Aurelius . . . of the illustrious and most illustrious city of Oxyrhynchos, and his sister by the same mother Aurelia . . . daughter of . . . the former *exegetes* and senator of the same city, with her guardian . . . the admirable . . . , have manumitted and discharged *inter amicos* our house-born slave Paramone, aged 40 years, and her children . . . with a scar on the neck, aged 10 years, and Jakob, aged 4 years, . . . from all the rights and powers of the owner: fourteen talents of silver having been paid to us for the manumission and discharge by the community of the Jews through Aurelius Dioskoros . . . and Aurelius Justus, senator of Ono in Syrian Palestine, father of the community. . . . And, the question being put, we have acknowledged that we have manumitted and discharged them, and that for the said manumission and discharge of them we have paid the above-mentioned sum, and that we have no rights at all and no powers over them from the present day, because we have been paid and have received for them the above-mentioned money, once and for all, through Aurelius Dioskoros and Aurelius Justus. Transacted in the illustrious and most illustrious city of Oxyrhynchos . . . , in the second consulship of Tiberianus and the first of Dion, year 7 of Imperator Caesar Gaius Aurelius Valerius Diocletianus and year 6 of Imperator Caesar Marcus Aurelius Valerius Maximianus, Germanici, Maximi, Pii, Felices, Augusti: Pharmouthi . . . nineteenth day.
>
> (2d hand) . . . Paramone and her children . . . and Jakob . . . (I witness) the agreement as stated above. I, Aurelius . . . (wrote for him) as he is illiterate.
>
> (3d hand) Aurelius Theon also called . . . of the money . . . piety (Eusebia?) . . . rights . . . of Dioskoros . . . Justus . . . the (talents) of silver . . . manumit . . . illiterate.

● 57
Epitaph of a Woman Cursed by Spells

CIL 8.2756   after 212 C.E.?

WORK: This epitaph from Lambaesis, Numidia (modern Tunisia), is for the wife of a Roman soldier. Her death at about age twenty-eight is here attributed to spells. Gager et al. propose a date after 212 C.E., when it became licit for Roman soldiers to marry.

TRANSLATION AND BIBLIOGRAPHY: Gager, *Curse Tablets*, p. 246.

TEXT: *CIL 8.2756*.

> . . . Here lies Ennia Fructuosa, most beloved wife, of unmistakable modesty, a matron to be praised for her unusual loyalty. She took the name of wife at age fifteen, but was unable to live with it for more than thirteen years. She did not receive the kind of death she deserved—cursed by spells, she long lay mute so that her life was rather torn from her by violence than given back to nature. Either the infernal gods or the heavenly deities will punish this wicked crime which has been perpetrated. Aelius Proculinus, her husband, a tribune in the great Third Legion, the Augusta, erected this monument.

● 58
A Woman Seeking to Attract the Love of Another Woman with a Spell

PGM 32.1–19   date uncertain

WORK: "Greek Magical Papyri" is a contemporary label for an assortment of ancient spells, incantations, hymns, ritual prescriptions, and other materials preserved on papyrus in Egypt. The papyri themselves date primarily from the third and fourth centuries C.E., although the material they preserve may be of various dates. For a fascinating introduction to the modern discovery of these papyri, see Betz, below. Erotic spells are common in the papyri, although this is a rare example of a homoerotic spell.

TRANSLATION: E. N. O'Neil, in Hans Dieter Betz, ed., *The Greek Magical Papyri in Translation, Including the Demotic Spells*, 2d ed. (Chicago: Chicago University Press, 1992), 266.

TEXT: *PGM 32.1–19*.

BIBLIOGRAPHY: Bernadette J. Brooten, " 'Inflame Her Liver with Love': Greek Erotic Spells from Egypt," in *Love between Women: Early Christian Responses to Female Homoeroticism* (Chicago: University of Chicago Press, 1996), 73–113.

I adjure you, Evangelos, by Anubis and Hermes and all the rest down below; attract and bind Sarapias whom Helen bore, to this Herais, whom Thermoutharin bore, now, now; quickly, quickly. By her soul and heart attract Sarapias herself, whom [Helen] bore from her own womb. MAEI OTE ELBŌSATOK ALAOUBĒTO ŌEIO ... AĒN. Attract and [bind the soul and heart of Sarapias], whom [Helen bore, to this] Herais, [whom] Thermoutharin [bore] from her womb [now, now; quickly, quickly].

● 59

A Woman Imploring Oserapis to Avenge Her Against Her Daughter's Father

PGM 40.1–18   4th century B.C.E.

WORK: Found at the temple of Oserapis at Memphis, Egypt, this appeal for justice has generally been construed as a woman's complaint against her husband for robbing the grave of their daughter. Pollard proposes that the central concern is rather improper burial.

TRANSLATION: R. F. Hock in Hans Dieter Betz, ed., *The Greek Magical Papyri in Translation*, 2d ed. (Chicago: University of Chicago Press, 1992), 280 (with incorrect date of fourth century C.E.).

TEXT: *PGM* 40.1–18.

BIBLIOGRAPHY: Elizabeth A. Pollard, "Magic Accusations against Women in the Greco-Roman World from the First through the Fifth Centuries C.E." (Ph.D. diss., University of Pennsylvania, 2002), 296–300.

O master Oserapis and the gods who sit with Oserapis, I [pray] to you, I Artemisie, daughter of Amasis, against my daughter's father, [who] robbed [her] of the funeral gifts and tomb. So if he has not acted justly toward me and his own children—as indeed he has acted unjustly toward me and his own children—let Oserapis and the gods grant that he not approach the grave of his children, nor that he bury his own parents. As long as my cry for help is deposited here, he and what belongs to him should be utterly destroyed badly, both on earth and on sea, by Oserapis and the gods who sit together with Oserapis, nor should he attain propitiation from Oserapis nor from the gods who sit with Oserapis.

Artemisie has deposited this supplication, supplicating Oserapis and the gods who sit with Oserapis to punish justly. As long as my supplication [is deposited] here, the father of this girl should not by any means attain propitiation from the gods.

Royal Women of Judea

JOSEPHUS *Antiquities of the Jews*   late 1st century C.E.

NOTE: This entry, together with the following entry, is neither by, from, or to women, but because it is about actual historical women, whose identities are attested in numerous sources, including inscriptions, it seemed most appropriate here. For other information, see entry 15.

BIBLIOGRAPHY: Tal Ilan, *Jewish Women in Greco-Roman Palestine: An Inquiry into Image and Status*, Texte und Studien zum Antiken Judentum 44 (Tübingen: J. C. B. Mohr [Siebeck], 1995); Tal Ilan, "Josephus and Nicolaus on Women," in Peter Schäfer, ed., *Geschichte—Tradition—Reflexion: Festschrift für Martin Hengel zum 70. Geburtstag*, vol. 1, *Judentum* (Tübingen: J. C. B. Mohr [Siebeck], 1996), 221–62; Tal Ilan, *Integrating Women into Second Temple History*, Texte und Studien zum Antiken Judentum 76 (Tübingen: J. C. B. Mohr [Siebeck], 1999); Nikos Kokkinos, *The Herodian Dynasty: Origins, Role in Society and Eclipse*, JSOPseud Suppl. 30 (Sheffield, U.K.: Sheffield Academic Press, 1998); Ross S. Kraemer, "Jewish Women and Women's Judaism(s) at the Beginning of Christianity," in *Women and Christian Origins*, 50–79; Ross S. Kraemer, "Herodias 1," "Herodias 2," "Salome 2," in *WIS*, 92–95, 148–49; Grace H. Macurdy, "Royal Women in Judaea," in *Vassal Queens and Some Contemporary Women in the Roman Empire*, Johns Hopkins University Studies in Archaeology 22 (Baltimore: Johns Hopkins University Press; London: Humphrey Milford, Oxford University Press, 1937; repr., in *Two Studies on Women in Antiquity*, Chicago: Ares Press, 1993), 63–91; Peter Richardson, *Herod: King of the Jews and Friend of the Romans* (Columbia: University of South Carolina Press, 1996).

● 60A

Herodias

JOSEPHUS *Antiquities of the Jews* 18.109–19, 240–55   late 1st century C.E.

(109) In the meantime, a quarrel, whose origin I shall relate, arose between Aretas, king of Petra, and Herod. The tetrarch Herod had taken the daughter of Aretas as his wife and had now been married to her for a long time. When starting out for Rome, he lodged with his half-brother Herod, who was born of a different mother, namely, the daughter of Simon the high priest. (110) Falling in love with Herodias, the wife of this half-brother—she was a daughter of their brother Aristobulus and sister to Agrippa the Great—, he brazenly broached to her the subject of marriage. She accepted and pledged herself to make the transfer to him as soon as he returned from Rome. It was stipulated that he must oust the daughter of Aretas. (111) The agreement made, he set sail for Rome. On his return after transacting his business in Rome, his wife who had got wind of his compact with Herodias, before any

information reached him that she had discovered everything, asked him to send her away to Machaerus [a fortress], which was on the boundary between the territory of Aretas and that of Herod. She gave no hint, however, of her real purpose. (112) Herod let her go, since he had no notion that the poor woman saw what was afoot. Some time earlier she herself had dispatched messengers to Machaerus, which was at that time subject to her father, so that when she arrived all preparations for her journey had been made by the governor. She was thus able to start for Arabia as soon as she arrived, being passed from one governor to the next as they provided transport. So she speedily reached her father and told him what Herod planned to do. (113) Aretas made this the start of a quarrel. There was also a dispute about boundaries in the district of Gabalis. Troops were mustered on each side and they were now at war, but they dispatched others as commanders instead of going themselves. (114) In the ensuing battle, the whole army of Herod was destroyed when some refugees, who had come from the tetrarchy of Philip and had joined Herod's army, played him false. (115) Herod sent an account of these events to Tiberius. The latter was incensed to think that Aretas had begun hostilities and wrote Vitellius to declare war and either bring Aretas to him in chains, if he should be captured alive, or, if he should be slain, to send him his head. Such were the instructions of Tiberius to his governor in Syria.

(116) But to some of the Jews the destruction of Herod's army seemed to be divine vengeance, and certainly a just vengeance, for his treatment of John, surnamed the Baptist. (117) For Herod had put him to death, though he was a good man and had exhorted the Jews to lead righteous lives, to practise justice towards their fellows and piety towards God, and so doing to join in baptism. In his view this was a necessary preliminary if baptism was to be acceptable to God. They must not employ it to gain pardon for whatever sins they committed, but as a consecration of the body implying that the soul was already thoroughly cleansed by right behaviour. (118) When others too joined the crowds about him, because they were aroused to the highest degree by his sermons, Herod became alarmed. Eloquence that had so great an effect on mankind might lead to some form of sedition, for it looked as if they would be guided by John in everything that they did. Herod decided therefore that it would be much better to strike first and be rid of him before his work led to an uprising, than to wait for an upheaval, get involved in a difficult situation and see his mistake. (119) Though John, because of Herod's suspicions, was brought in chains to Machaerus, the stronghold that we have previously mentioned, and there put to death, yet the verdict of the Jews was that the destruction visited upon Herod's army was a vindication of John, since God saw fit to inflict such a blow on Herod.

(240) Herodias, the sister of Agrippa and wife of Herod, tetrarch of Galilee

and Peraea, begrudged her brother his rise to power far above the state that her husband enjoyed. Agrippa had had to flee for lack of money to pay his debts, but now he had returned in grandeur and with such great prosperity. It was consequently painful and depressing for her to see so great a reversal in his fortunes. (241) The spectacle of his royal visits in the customary regalia before the multitudes made her especially helpless to keep this unfortunate envy to herself. Instead she instigated her husband, urging him to embark for Rome and sue for equal status. (242) For their life was unbearable, she said, if Agrippa, who was the son of that Aristobulus who had been condemned to death by his father, who had himself known such helpless poverty that the necessities of daily life had entirely failed him, and who had set out on his voyage to escape from his creditors, should have returned as a king, while Herod himself, the son of a king, who was called by his royal birth to claim equal treatment, should rest content to live as a commoner to the end of his life. (243) "Even if, O Herod," she said, "you were not distressed in the past to be lower in rank than the father from whom you sprang, now at least I beg of you to move in quest of the high position that you were born to. Do not patiently admit defeat by a man outranking you, who has bent the knee to your affluence. Do not inform the world that his poverty can make better use of manly qualities than our riches. Never regard it as anything but a disgrace to play second fiddle to those who were but yesterday dependent on your bounty for survival. (244) Come, let us go to Rome; let us spare neither pains nor expense of silver and gold, since there is no better use for which we might hoard them than to expend them on the acquisition of a kingdom."

(245) For a while he resisted and tried to change her mind, for he was content with his tranquillity and was wary of the Roman bustle. The more, however, she saw him shying away, the more urgently she insisted, bidding him not to be remiss in seeking a throne at any cost. (246) The upshot was that she never flagged till she carried the day and made him her unwilling partisan, for there was no way of escape once she had cast her vote on this matter. And so, supplied as lavishly as possible and sparing no expense, he set sail for Rome, accompanied by Herodias. (247) But Agrippa, when he learned of their plan and their preparations, made his own preparations. And when he heard that they had set sail, he himself also dispatched Fortunatus, one of his freedmen, to Rome, charged with presents for the emperor and letters against Herod, and ready to tell his story to Gaius himself as the opportunity presented itself. (248) Fortunatus, putting out to sea in pursuit of Herod's party, had a favourable voyage and was so little behind Herod that while the latter had obtained an audience with Gaius, he landed and delivered his letters. Both of them had made port at Dicaearchia and had found Gaius at Baiae. (249) This is a little city in Campania situated at a distance of about five furlongs from Dicaearchia. There are royal residences there lavishly furnished, for each of the emperors was ambitious to outdo his prede-

cessors. The locality also affords hot baths, which spring naturally from the ground and have a curative value for those who use them, not to mention their contribution to easy living in other ways. (250) At the very time that he was greeting Herod, whom he interviewed first, Gaius was perusing the letters of Agrippa which were composed as an indictment of him. The letters accused Herod of conspiring with Sejanus against the government of Tiberius and of being now in league with Artabanus the Parthian against the government of Gaius. (251) As proof of this charge the letters stated that equipment sufficient for 70,000 heavy-armed foot-soldiers was stored in Herod's armouries. Spurred by these words, Gaius asked Herod whether the report about the arms was true. (252) When Herod replied that the arms were there—for it was impossible for him to deny it in face of the truth—Gaius, regarding the accusations of revolt as confirmed, relieved him of his tetrarchy and added it to the kingdom of Agrippa. He likewise gave Herod's property to Agrippa and condemned Herod to perpetual exile, assigning him as his residence Lyons, a city in Gaul. (253) When Gaius learned that Herodias was a sister of Agrippa, he offered to allow her to keep all her personal property and told her to regard her brother as the bulwark who had protected her from sharing her husband's fate. (254) She, however, replied: "Indeed, O emperor, these are generous words and such as befit your high office, but my loyalty to my husband is a bar to my enjoyment of your kind gift, for it is not right when I have shared in his prosperity that I should abandon him when he has been brought to this pass." (255) Gaius, angered at her proud mood, exiled her also, together with Herod, and presented her possessions to Agrippa. And so God visited this punishment on Herodias for her envy of her brother and on Herod for listening to a woman's frivolous chatter.

● 60B

The Daughters and Other Descendants of Herod the Great

JOSEPHUS *Antiquities of the Jews* 18.130-42   late 1st century C.E.

(130) Herod the Great had two daughters by Mariamme the daughter of Hyreanus. One of them, Salampsio, was given in marriage by her father to Phasael, her cousin, the son of Herod's brother Phasael; the other, Cypros, also married a cousin, Antipater, the son of Herod's sister Salome. (131) By Salampsio Phasael had three sons—Antipater, Alexander, and Herod—and two daughters—Alexandra and Cypros. Cypros' husband was Agrippa, the son of Aristobulus; Alexandra's was Timius of Cyprus, a man of some importance, in union with whom she died childless. (132) By Agrippa Cypros had two sons, named Agrippa and Drusus, and three daughters, Berenice, Mariamme, and Drusilla. Of these children Drusus died before reaching adolescence. (133) Agrippa, together with his brothers Herod and Aristobulus, was raised by

their father. Berenice, the daughter of Costobar and of Herod's sister Salome, and these sons of Aristobulus, Herod the Great's son, were raised together. (134) These were left as infants by Aristobulus when, as I have previously related, he, together with his brother Alexander, was put to death by his father. When they had reached adolescence, Herod, the brother of Agrippa, married Mariamme, the daughter of Olympias—who was herself the daughter of King Herod—and of Joseph—who was the son of Joseph, the brother of King Herod. By her he had a son Aristobulus. (135) The other brother of Agrippa, Aristobulus, married Jotape, the daughter of Sampsigeramus king of Emesa. They had a daughter also named Jotape, who was a deaf-mute. Such were the children of the sons. (136) Their sister Herodias was married to Herod, the son of Herod the Great by Mariamme, daughter of Simon the high priest. They had a daughter Salome, after whose birth Herodias, taking it into her head to flout the way of our fathers, married Herod, her husband's brother by the same father, who was tetrarch of Galilee; to do this she parted from a living husband. (137) Her daughter Salome was married to Philip, Herod's son and tetrarch of Trachonitis. When he died childless, Aristobulus, the son of Agrippa's brother Herod, married her. Three sons were born to them—Herod, Agrippa, and Aristobulus. (138) Such then was the line of Phasael and Salampsio. As to Cypros, a daughter named Cypros was born to her of Antipater; Alexas, who was surnamed Helcias and was the son of Alexas, married this daughter, and she in turn had a daughter named Cypros. Herod and Alexander, who, as I have said, were the brothers of Antipater, died childless. (139) Alexander, King Herod's son, who had been put to death by his father, had two sons, Alexander and Tigranes, by the daughter of Archelaus king of Cappadocia. Tigranes, who was king of Armenia, died childless after charges were brought against him at Rome. (140) Alexander had a son who had the same name as his brother Tigranes and who was sent forth by Nero to be king of Armenia. This Tigranes had a son Alexander, who married Jotape, the daughter of Antiochus, king of Commagene; Vespasian appointed him king of Cetis in Cilicia. (141) The offspring of Alexander abandoned from birth the observance of the ways of the Jewish land and ranged themselves with the Greek tradition. (142) The other daughters of King Herod, it turned out, died childless. Of the descendants of Herod, those whom I have enumerated were still alive at the time when Agrippa the Great received his royal office.

● 60C

Drusilla

JOSEPHUS *Antiquities of the Jews* 20.137–43   late 1st century C.E.

(137) Claudius now sent Felix, the brother of Pallas, to take charge of matters in Judaea. (138) When he had completed the twelfth year of his reign, he

granted to Agrippa the tetrarchy of Philip together with Batanaea, adding thereto Trachonitis and Lysanias' former tetrarchy of Abila; but he deprived him of Chalçis, after he had ruled it for four years. (139) After receiving this gift from the emperor, Agrippa gave his sister Drusilla in marriage to Azizus king of Emesa, who had consented to be circumcised. Epiphanes, son of King Antiochus, had rejected the marriage since he was not willing to convert to the Jewish religion, although he had previously contracted with her father to do so. (140) Agrippa also gave his daughter Mariamme in marriage to Archelaus, the son of Helcias, to whom he had previously betrothed her. Of this marriage there was born a daughter named Berenice.

(141) Not long afterwards Drusilla's marriage to Azizus was dissolved under the impact of the following circumstances. (142) At the time when Felix was procurator of Judaea, he beheld her; and, inasmuch as she surpassed all other women in beauty, he conceived a passion for the lady. He sent to her one of his friends, a Cyprian Jew named Atomus, who pretended to be a magician, in an effort to persuade her to leave her husband and to marry Felix. Felix promised to make her supremely happy if she did not disdain him. (143) She, being unhappy and wishing to escape the malice of her sister Berenice— for Drusilla was exceedingly abused by her because of her beauty—, was persuaded to transgress the ancestral laws and to marry Felix. By him she gave birth to a son whom she named Agrippa.

● 61

Historians' Reports about the Herodian Princess Berenice, Coruler with Her Brother, King Agrippa II, and Lover of the Roman Emperor Titus

BIBLIOGRAPHY: Ross S. Kraemer, "Typical and Atypical Jewish Family Dynamics: The Cases of Babatha and Berenice," in Carolyn Osiek and David Balch, eds., *Early Christian Families in Context* (Grand Rapids, Mich.: Eerdmans, 2002), 114–39; Ross S. Kraemer, "Berenice," in *Women in Scripture*, 59–61; Klaus-Stefan Krieger, "Berenike, die Schwester König Agrippas II; bei Flavius Josephus," *JSJ* 18 (1997): 1–11. Grace H. Macurdy, "Julia Berenice," *American Journal of Philology* 56 (1935): 246–53; see also entry 60.

● 61A

Josephus on Berenice

JOSEPHUS *Antiquities of the Jews* 19.277　　　　　late 1st century C.E.

AUTHOR, TEXT, AND ADDITIONAL BIBLIOGRAPHY: See entry 15.

NOTE: The first marriage reported here made Berenice the niece of Philo of Alexander (who was the brother of Alexander the Alabarch) and the sister-in-law of

Tiberius Julius Alexander, an extremely prominent Roman official who was, among other things, an advisor to the imperial family during the first Jewish revolt.

TRANSLATION: RSK.

> ... and [Marcus Julius Alexander, son of Alexander, the alabarch of Egypt,] married Berenice, the daughter of Agrippa. Agrippa then gave her to his brother, Herod, for Marcus, the son of Alexander, who had taken Berenice as a virgin, died. ...

JOSEPHUS *Antiquities of the Jews* 20.145–46   late 1st century C.E.

TRANSLATION: LCL (L. H. Feldman, 1965, vol. 9).

> 145 After the death of Herod, who had been her uncle and husband, *Berenice* lived for a long time as a widow. But when a report gained currency that she had a liaison with her brother, she induced Polemo, king of Cilicia, to be circumcised and to take her in marriage; for she thought that she would demonstrate in this way that the reports were false.
>
> 146 Polemo was prevailed upon chiefly on account of her wealth. The marriage did not, however, last long, for Berenice, out of licentiousness, according to report, deserted Polemo. And he was relieved simultaneously of his marriage and of further adherence to the Jewish way of life.

JOSEPHUS *The Jewish War* 2.309–14

TRANSLATION: LCL (H. St. J. Thackeray, 1927, vol. 3).

> 308 The calamity was aggravated by the unprecedented character of the Romans' cruelty. For Florus ventured that day to do what none had ever done before, namely, to scourge before his tribunal and nail to the cross men of equestrian rank, men who, if Jews by birth, were at least invested with that Roman dignity.
>
> 309 King Agrippa, at this moment, was absent, having gone to Alexandria to offer his congratulations to Alexander, recently sent to take over the government of Egypt, with which he had been entrusted by Nero. 310 Agrippa's sister Berenice, however, who was at Jerusalem, witnessed with the liveliest emotion the outrages of the soldiers, and constantly sent her cavalry-commanders and life-guards to Florus to implore him to put a stop to the carnage. 311 But he, regarding neither the number of the slain nor the exalted rank of his suppliant, but only the profit accruing from the plunder, turned a deaf ear to her prayers. 312 The mad rage of the soldiers even vented itself upon the queen. Not only did they torture and put their captives to death under her eyes, but they would have killed her also, had she not hastened to seek refuge in the palace, where she passed the night surrounded

by guards, dreading an attack of the troops. 313 She was visiting Jerusalem to discharge a vow to God; for it is customary for those suffering from illness or other affliction to make a vow to abstain from wine and to shave their heads during the thirty days preceding that on which they must offer sacrifices. 314 These rites Berenice was then undergoing, and she would come barefoot before the tribunal and make supplication to Florus, without any respect being shown to her, and even at the peril of her life.

● 61B

Tacitus on Berenice

TACITUS *Histories* 2.1.1, 2.2.1, 2.79, 2.81.1–3   early 2d century C.E.

AUTHOR: Tacitus was a high-ranking Roman official in the late first/early second centuries C.E. He wrote two major historical works on the history of the first century, the *Histories* and the *Annals*, of which only parts of each survive.

TRANSLATION AND TEXT: LCL (C. H. Moore, 1925, repr. 1962).

ADDITIONAL TEXT: OCT (C. D. Fisher, H. Furneaux, 1907); Teubner (S. Borzsak and K. Wellesley, 1986).

BIBLIOGRAPHY: Ronald Syme, "Titus and Berenice: a Tacitean Fragment," *Roman Papers* VII, ed. Anthony R. Birley (Oxford: Clarendon Press, 1991), 647–62.

2.1.1 Titus Vespasianus had been dispatched by his father from Judaea while Galba was still alive. The reason given out for his journey was a desire to pay his respects to the emperor, and the fact that Titus was now old enough to begin his political career. But the common people, who are always ready to invent, had spread the report that he had been summoned to Rome to be adopted. . . . 2.2.1 These considerations and others like them made him waver between hope and fear; but hope finally won. Some believed that he turned back because of his passionate longing to see again Queen Berenice; and the young man's heart was not insensible to Berenice, but his feelings towards her proved no obstacle to action. He spent his youth in the delights of self-indulgence, but he showed more self-restraint in his own reign than in that of his father.

2.79 The transfer of the imperial power to Vespasian began at Alexandria, where Tiberius Alexander acted quickly, administering to his troops the oath of allegiance on the first of July. This day has been celebrated in later times as the first of Vespasian's reign, although it was on the third of July that the army in Judaea took the oath before Vespasian himself, and did it with such enthusiasm that they did not wait even for his son Titus, who was on his way back from Syria and was the medium of communication between Mucianus and his father.... 2.81.1 Before the fifteenth of July all Syria had sworn the same allegiance. Vespasian's cause was now joined also by Sohaemus with his entire kingdom, whose strength was not to be despised, and by Antiochus who had enormous ancestral wealth, and was in fact the richest of the subject princes. Presently Agrippa, summoned from Rome by private messages from his friends, while Vitellius was still unaware of his action, quickly crossed the sea and joined the cause. 2.81.2 Queen Berenice showed equal spirit in helping Vespasian's party: she had great youthful beauty, and commended herself to Vespasian for all his years by the splendid gifts she made him. All the provinces on the coast to the frontiers of Achaia and Asia, as well as all the inland provinces as far as Pontus and Armenia, took the oath of allegiance; but their governors had no armed forces, since Cappadocia had as yet no legions. 2.81.3 A grand council was held at Berytus. Mucianus came there with all his lieutenants and tribunes, as well as his most distinguished centurions and soldiers; the army in Judaea also sent its best representatives. This great concourse of foot and horse, with princes who rivalled one another in splendid display, made a gathering that befitted the high fortune of an emperor....

61C

Suetonius on Berenice

SUETONIUS *The Divine Titus* 7.1–2   early 2d century C.E.

AUTHOR: Writer of numerous lives of famous Roman men, Suetonius was born ca. 69 C.E. His works date to the first quarter of the second century.

TRANSLATION AND TEXT: LCL (J. C. Rolfe, 1914; rev. ed. 1997–98)

ADDITIONAL TEXT: Teubner (M. Ihn, 1967).

1 Besides cruelty, [Titus] was also suspected of riotous living, since he protracted his revels until the middle of the night with the most prodigal of his friends; likewise of unchastity because of his troops of catamites and eunuchs, and his notorious passion for queen Berenice, to whom it was even said that he promised marriage. He was suspected of greed as well; for it was well known that in cases which came before his father he put a price on his influence and accepted bribes. In short, people not only thought, but openly declared, that he would be a second Nero. But this reputation turned out to his advantage, and gave place to the highest praise, when no fault was discovered in him, but on the contrary the highest virtues. (2) His banquets were pleasant rather than extravagant. He chose as his friends men whom succeeding emperors also retained as indispensable alike to themselves and to the State, and of whose services they made special use. Berenice he sent from Rome at once, against her will and his own.

Cassius Dio on Berenice

CASSIUS DIO *Roman History* 66.15.3–5   early 3d century C.E.

AUTHOR: Born to a senatorial family in Nicaea (Asia Minor/modern Turkey) in the later second century C.E., Cassius Dio wrote a history of Rome from its beginnings through 229 C.E. Portions of this work survive in their entirety, but other sections, including the excerpt below, are known only through an epitome made by Xiphilinus in the eleventh century.

TRANSLATION AND TEXT: LCL (E. Cary, 1961–84).

ADDITIONAL TEXT: U. P. Boissevain, *Cassii Dionis Cocceiani Historiarum Romanarum Quae Supersunt* (Berlin: Weidmann, 1895–1931); Teubner (L. Dindorf and I. Melber, 1890–1928).

> 3 Berenice was at the very height of her power and consequently came to Rome along with her brother Agrippa. 4 The latter was given the rank of praetor, while she dwelt in the palace, cohabiting with Titus. She expected to marry him and was already behaving in every respect as if she were his wife; but when he perceived that the Romans were displeased with the situation, he sent her away. 5 For, in addition to all the other talk that there was, certain sophists of the Cynic school managed somehow to slip into the city at this time, too; and first Diogenes, entering the theatre when it was full, denounced the pair in a long, abusive speech; for which he was flogged; and after him Heras, expecting no harsher punishment, gave vent to many senseless yelpings in true Cynic fashion, and for this was beheaded.

● 61E

A Late Epitome on Berenice

Epitome of the Emperors 10.4–7   early 5th century C.E.

WORK: Taken from a late, problematic abbreviation of earlier sources, this entry contains traditions about Titus and Berenice that are not found in the more contemporaneous sources excerpted above. These traditions, including the designation of Berenice as Titus's wife, are not necessarily reliable.

TRANSLATION AND TEXT: *GLAJJ* 2:645–46.

> 4 For after Titus in his father's reign had attained to the post of prefect of the *praetoriani* he sent to the theatres and camps people who raised invidious charges against everybody who was suspected in his eyes and in opposition to him, and demanded their punishment. All these he executed as if already convicted of a crime. Among those executed was Caecina, an ex-consul, who was invited by him to dinner. He [scil. Titus] ordered him to be strangled as

soon as he left the dining-room, because he suspected him of committing adultery with his wife Berenice. 5 The judicial cases which had been put to sale by him during the life of his father [proved] him eager for plunder; hence all people who thought him and called him a Nero felt vexed when he obtained supreme power. 6 However, this expectation changed for the better to bring him immortal glory, so that he was called the darling and delight of the human race. 7 At last when he obtained royal power he enjoined Berenice, who hoped to be married to him, to return to her country. He also ordered the droves of effeminates to leave.

● 62
Personal Papers of Babatha of Maoza

WORK: In the late 1950s, Israeli archaeologists excavating a cave associated with Simeon bar Kokhba, leader of the second Jewish revolt against Rome (ca. 132–35 C.E.), found a set of papyrus documents rolled up in a leather bag. These turned out to contain the personal papers of a Jewish woman named Babatha, who was probably born around the year 100 C.E., and who may have died in the revolt. Although the find was described quickly in preliminary publications, the first volume of the papyri was not published until 1989, and a second volume is still awaited. Named for the lead archaeologist, Yigael Yadin, these papyri include marriage contracts, loan documents, guardianship papers, land registrations, and more. Written in Greek, Aramaic, and the regional language of Nabatean, transacted in diverse legal jurisdictions, and involving Jews, Roman citizens (who may or may not have been Jews), and Nabateans, these papyri throw into sharp relief the diverse cultural and legal environments in which Babatha and those around her lived their lives. They offer us the most detailed portrait yet of an actual Jewish woman from Greco-Roman antiquity (although it should be noted that a few scholars have raised questions about Babatha's ethnicity/"religion"). Frustratingly, though, these papyri speak indirectly at best to questions of religious practice.

TRANSLATION AND TEXT: Naphtali Lewis, Yigael Yadin and Jonas C. Greenfield, eds., *The Documents from the Bar Kokhba Period in the Cave of Letters*, Judean Desert Studies 2 (Jerusalem: Israel Exploration Society; Hebrew University: Shrine of the Book, 1989); Yigael Yadin, [posthumously], Jonas C. Greenfield, and Ada Yardeni, "Babatha's Ketubbah," *IEJ* 44, nos. 1–2 (1994): 75–101 (for 62A).

BIBLIOGRAPHY: Hannah M. Cotton and J. C. Greenfield, "Babatha's Property and the Law of Succession in the Babatha Archive," *ZPE* 104 (1994): 211–24; Hannah M. Cotton and Ada Yardeni, *Aramaic, Hebrew and Greek Documentary Texts from Nahal Hever and Other Sites, with an Appendix Containing Alleged Qumran Texts*, (the Seiyâl Collection II), Discoveries in the Judean Desert 27 (Oxford: Clarendon Press, 1997); Mordechai A. Friedman, "Babatha's Ketubba: Some Preliminary Observations," *IEJ* 46, nos. 1–2 (1996): 55–76; Martin Goodman, "Babatha's Story," *JRS* 81 (1991): 169–76; Ross S. Kraemer, "Typical and Atypical Jewish Family Dynamics: The Cases of Babatha and Berenice," in Carolyn Osiek and David Balch, eds., *Early Christian Families in Context* (Grand Rapids, Mich.: Eerdmans, 2002), 114–39; Ross S. Kraemer, "Jewish Women and Women's Judaism(s) at the Beginning of Christianity," in *Women and Christian Origins*, 50–79; Michael Satlow, *Jewish Marriage in Antiquity* (Princeton: Princeton University Press, 2001); Yigael Yadin, *Bar Kokhba: The Rediscovery of the Legendary Hero of the Second Jewish Revolt against Rome* (New York: Random House, 1971).

● 62A

Babatha's Marriage Contract

P. Yadin 10   exact date uncertain: probably before 125 C.E.

1   On the [thi]rd of Adar in the consulship of

2

3

4   ... [that you will be]

5   my wife [according to the la]w of Moses and the "Judaeans" and I will [feed you] and [clothe] you and I will bring you (into my house) by means of your *ketubba*

6   and I owe you the sum of four hundred denarii (*zūzīn*) which equal one hundred tetradrachms (*șōrīn*) whichever

7   you wish "to take and to .[.] ..." from ... together with the due amount of your food, and your clothes, and your bed(?),

8   provision fitting for a free woman ... the sum of four hundred denarii (*zūzīn*) which equal one hundred tetradrachms (*sil'īn*)

9   whichever you wish "to take and to .[. ... " from] ... together with the due amount of your food, and your bed(?),

10   and your clothes, as a free woman. And if you are taken captive, I will redeem you, from my house and from my estate,

11   and I will take you back as my wife, and I owe you your *ketubba* money ...

12–13 [and if I go to my eternal home before you, male children which you will have by me will inherit your *ketubba* money, beyond their share with their brothers,]

14   female [child]ren shall dwell and be provided for from my house and [from my estate un]til the time when they will be [mar]ried. And if

15 >and if< I go to my eternal h[ome] before you, you w[il]l [d]well in
my house and be provided for from my house and from my estate

16 [until] the time that my heirs wish to give you your *ketubba* money.
And when ever you tell me

17 [I will exchange this document as is proper]. **lacunae and fragments of
letters containing the warranty clause**

18 [And I Yehudah son of El'azar Khthousion], I [acce]pt [all that] is written [above]

Verso

| ... for Babatha daughter of Sim'on due from Yehudah son of El'azar

Signatures

1 [Yehudah son of El'azar for himse]lf wrote it

2 Baba[ta daughter of] Shim['on] for herself

3 **fragment of name** witness

4 Toma son of Shim'on wi[tn]ess

5 [   ]n   wi[tness]

6 [   ]r[   ]

7 [?]

● **62B**

Babatha Summons the Guardian of Her Son to Court in Petra

P. Yadin 14   October 11 or 12, 125 C.E.

Outer text

In the ninth year of Imperator Traianus Hadrianus Caesar Augustus, in the
consulship of Marcus Valerius Asiaticus for the 2nd time and Titius Aquilinus
four days before the ides of October, and according to the compute of the
province of Arabia year twentieth on the twenty-fourth of month Hyperberetaios called Thesrei, in Maoza, Zoara district, before the attending witnesses
Babatha daughter of Simon son of Menahem—through her guardian for this
matter, Judah son of Khthousion—summoned John son of Joseph Eglas, one
of the guardians appointed by the council of Petra for her son Jesus the orphan of Jesus, saying: On account of your not having given . . . to my son,
the said orphan . . . just as 'Abdoöbdas son of Ellouthas, your colleague, has
given by receipt, therefore I summon you to attend at the court of the gover-

nor Julius Julianus in Petra the metropolis of Arabia until we are heard in the tribunal in Petra[1] on the second day of the month Dios(?) or at his next sitting in Petra . . .

The attending witnesses: John son of Makhouthas, Sammouos son of Menahem, Thaddeus son of Thaddeus, Joseph son of Ananias, Jesus(?) son of Libanos(?).

On the back, individual signatures

Yohana son of Makhoutha, witness
Shammu'a son of Menahem, witness
Thaddeus son of Thaddeus, witness
Yehosef son of Hananiah, witness
          ?

[1] *The inner text adds:* before Julianus, governor.

● 62C

Babatha's Deposition, Including a Statement of Her Illiteracy

P. Yadin 15   October 11 or 12, 125 C.E.

Outer text

In the ninth year of Imperator Traianus Hadrianus Caesar Augustus, in the consulship of Marcus Valerius Asiaticus for the 2nd time and Titius Aquilinus four days before the ides of October, and according to the compute of the province of Arabia year twentieth on the twenty-fourth of the month Hyperberetaios called Thesrei, in Maoza, Zoara district, before the attending witnesses Babatha daughter of Simon son of Menahem deposed against John son of Joseph Eglas and 'Abdoöbdas son of Ellouthas, guardians of her orphan son Jesus son of Jesus, appointed guardians for the said orphan by the council of Petra, in the presence of the said guardians, saying:

On account of your not having given my orphan son generous(?) maintenance money commensurate with the income from the interest on his money and the rest of his property, and commensurate in particular with a style of life which befits(?) him, and you contribute for him as interest on the money only one half-denarius per hundred denarii [per month], as I have property equivalent in value to this money of the orphan's that you have, therefore I previously deposed in order that you might decide to give me the money on security involving a hypothec of my property, with me contributing interest on the money at the rate of a denarius and a half per hundred denarii, wherewith my son may be raised in splendid style, rendering thanks to the[se] most blessed times of the governorship of Julius Julianus, our governor, before whom I, Babatha, summoned the aforesaid John, one of the guardians of the orphan, for his refusal of disbursement of the [appropriate] maintenance money. Otherwise this deposition will serve as documentary evidence of [your] profiteering from the money of the orphan by giving . . .

Babatha deposed as aforestated through her guardian for this matter, Judah son of Khthousion, who was present and subscribed. [2nd hand] I, Babatha daughter of Simon, have deposed through my guardian Judah son of Khthousion against John son of Eglas and ʿAbdoöbdas son of Ellouthas, guardians of my orphan son Jesus, according to the aforestated conditions. I, Eleazar son of Eleazar, wrote for her by request, because of her being illiterate.

[1st hand] And there were at hand seven witnesses.

[3rd hand, Aramaic] Yehudah son of Khthousion "lord" of Babatha: In my presence Babatha confirmed all that is written above. Yehudah wrote it.

[4th hand, Nabatean] ʿAbdʿobdath son of Elloutha: In my presence and in the presence of Yoḥana, my colleague, son of ʿEgla, this testimony is written according to what is written above. ʿAbdʿobdath wrote it.

[5th hand, Aramaic] Yehoḥanan son of Aleks, by the hand of Yehoseph his son.

[1st hand] The writer of this [is] Theënas son of Simon, *librarius*.

On the back, individual signatures

[   ]
[   ]
. . . son of . . . , witness
Thaddeus son of Thaddeus, witness
Yehosef son of Ḥananiah
Tomah son of Shimʿon, witness
Yeshuʿa son of Yeshuʿa, witness

● **62D**

Babatha's Registration of Land, Sworn by the *Genius* of the Emperor

P. Yadin 16   December 2 and 4, 127 C.E.

Inner text

Verified exact copy of a document of registration which is displayed in the basilica here, and it is as appended below.

Outer text

Verified exact copy of a document of registration which is displayed in the basilica here, and it is as appended below.

In the reign of Imperator Caesar divi Traiani Parthici filius divi Nervae nepos Traianus Hadrianus Augustus pontifex maximus tribuniciae potestatis XII consul III, in the consulship of Marcus Gavius Gallicanus and Titus Rufus Titianus four days before the nones of December, and according to the compute of the new province of Arabia year twenty-second month Appellaios the sixteenth, in the city of Rabbath-Moab. As a census of Arabia is being conducted by Titus Aninius Sextius Florentinus, legatus Augusti pro praetore, I, Babtha daughter of Simon, of Maoza in the Zoarene [district] of the Petra administrative region, domiciled in my own private property in the said Maoza, register what I possess (present with me as my guardian being Judanes son of Elazar, of the village of En-gedi in the district of Jericho in Judaea, domiciled in his own private property in the said Maoza), viz. within the boundaries of Maoza a date orchard called Algiphiamma, the area of sowing one saton three kaboi of barley, paying as tax, in dates, Syrian and mixed fifteen sata, "splits" ten sata, and for crown tax one "black" and thirty sixtieths, abutters a road and the Sea; within the boundaries of Maoza a date orchard called Algiphiamma, the area of sowing one kabos of barley, paying as tax a half share of the crops produced each year, abutters *moschantic* estate of our lord Caesar and the Sea; within the boundaries of Maoza a date orchard called Bagalgala, the area of sowing three sata of barley, paying as tax, in dates, Syrian and Noaran(?) one koros, "splits" one koros, and for crown tax three "blacks" and thirty sixtieths, abutters heirs of Thesaios son of Sabakas and Iamit son(?) of Manthanthes; within the boundaries of Maoza a date orchard called Bethphaaraia, the area of sowing twenty sata of barley, paying as tax, in dates, Syrian and Noaran(?) three kaboi, "splits" two koroi, and for crown tax eight "blacks" and forty-five sixtieths, abutters Tamar daughter of Thamous and a road.

Translation of subscription: I, Babtha daughter of Simon, swear by the *genius* of our lord Caesar that I have in good faith registered as has been written above. I, Judanes son of Elazar, acted as guardian and wrote for her. [2nd hand] Translation of subscription of the prefect: I, Priscus, prefect of cavalry, received [this] on the day before the nones of December in the consulship of Gallicanus and Titianus.

On the back, individual signatures   *right edge*

'Abdu son of Muqimu, witness   Babatha
Manthanta son of Amru, witness
'Awd'el son of_____, witness
Yoḥana son of 'Abd'obdat Makhoutha, witness
Shahru son of_____, witness.

Babatha's Loan to Her Second Husband, Judah

P. Yadin 17   February 21, 128 C.E.

Outer text

In the consulship of Publius Metilius Nepos for the 2nd time and Marcus
Annius Libo ten days before the kalends of March, and by the compute of
the new province of Arabia year twenty-second on the sixth of the month
Dystros, in Maoza, Zoara district, of his own free will and consent Judah son
of Eleazar also known as Khthousion, En-gedian, acknowledged to Babatha
daughter of Simon, his own wife, present with her as her guardian for the
purpose of this matter being Jacob son of Jesus, all of them residing here, to
the effect that Judah has received from her on account of a deposit three
hundred denarii of silver in coin of genuine legal tender, on condition that
he have and owe them [as a debt] on deposit until such time as it may please
Babatha, or anyone acting through her or for her, to request the aforesaid
denarii of the deposit from the said Judah. And if Judah when so requested
does not promptly repay, in accordance with the law of deposit he shall be
liable to repay the deposit to her twofold in addition to damages, and he
shall also be answerable to a charge of illegality in such matters, the said Babatha or anyone producing this contract on her behalf having the right of
execution upon Judah and all his possessions everywhere—both those which
he possesses and those which he may validly acquire in addition—in whatever manner the executor may choose to carry out the execution. In good
faith the formal question was asked and it was agreed in reply that this is
thus rightly done.

[2nd hand, Aramaic] Yehudah son of Elazar: I acknowledge that I have received from Babatha my wife, with the knowledge of Jacob her "lord" son of
Yeshu'a, on account of deposit, three hundred silver denarii, and I will return
them to her at any time that she will wish, as is written above, with nothing
withheld(?) according to the law of deposit. Yehudah son of Elazar wrote it.

[1st hand] I, Theënas son of Simon, *librarius*, wrote [this].

On the back, individual signatures

[*illegible*   ]
[*illegible*   ]
[*illegible*   ]
Tomah son of Shim'on, witness
   ?   son of Yehudah, witness
Yohsef son of Hananiah, witness
Elazar son of   ?   , witness

The Marriage Contract of Babatha's Stepdaughter, Shelamzion

P. Yadin 18   April 5, 128 c.e.

In the consulship of Publius Metilius Nepos for the 2nd time and Marcus
Annius Libo on the nones of April, and by the compute of the new province
of Arabia year twenty-third on the fifteenth of month Xandikos, in Maoza,
Zoara district, Judah son of Eleazar also known as Khthusion, gave over Shelamzion, his very own daughter, a virgin, to Judah surnamed Cimber son of
Ananias son of Somalas, both of the village of En-gedi in Judaea residing
here, for Shelamzion to be a wedded wife to Judah Cimber for the partnership of marriage according to the laws, she bringing to him on account of
bridal gift feminine adornment in silver and gold and clothing appraised by
mutual agreement, as they both say, to be worth two hundred denarii of silver, which appraised value the bridegroom Judah called Cimber acknowledged that he has received from her[1] by hand forthwith from Judah her father and that he owes to the said Shelamzion his wife together with another
three hundred denarii which he promised to give to her in addition to the
sum of her aforesaid bridal gift, all accounted toward her dowry, pursuant to
his undertaking of feeding and clothing both her and the children to come in
accordance with Greek custom upon the said Judah Cimber's good faith and
peril and [the security of] all his possessions, both those which he now possesses in his said home village and here and all those which he may in addition validly acquire everywhere, in whatever manner his wife Shelamzion may
choose, or whoever acts through her or for her may choose, to carry out the
execution. Judah called Cimber shall redeem this contract for his wife Shelamzion, whenever she may demand it of him, in silver secured in due form, at
his own expense interposing no objection. If not, he shall pay to her all the
aforestated denarii twofold, she having the right of execution, both from Judah Cimber her husband and upon the possessions validly his, in whatever
manner Shelamzion or whoever acts through her or for her may choose to
carry out the execution. In good faith the formal question was asked and it
was acknowledged in reply that this is thus rightly done.

[2nd hand, Aramaic] Yehudah son of Elazar Khthousion: I have given my
daughter Shelamzion, a virgin, in marriage to Yehudah Cimber son of Hananiah son of Somala, according to what is written above. Yehudah wrote it.

[3rd hand, Aramaic] Yehudah Cimber son of Hananiah son of Somala: I acknowledge the debt of silver denarii five hundred, the dowry of Shelamzion
my wife, according to what they wrote above. Yehudah wrote it.

[1st hand] I, Theënas son of Simon, *librarius*, wrote [this].

On the back, individual signatures

Yehudah son of Elazar wrote it.
Yehudah son of Ḥananiah [wrote it.]
Of_____ son of_____, the hand?
Shimʿon son of_____, witness
Eliezer son of Ḥilqiah, witness
Yohsef son of Ḥananiah, witness
Wanah son of_____, for himself.

¹ *Inner text*: from the said Shelamzious his wife.

● 62G

A Deed of Gift from Babatha's Husband, Judah, to His Daughter, Shelamzion

P. Yadin 19   April 16, 128 C.E.

In the consulship of Publius Metilius Nepos for the second time and Marcus Annius Libo sixteen days before the kalends of May, according to the compute of the new province year twenty-third on the twenty-sixth of Xandikos, in Maoza of Zoara district, Judah son of Elazar Khthousion, an En-gedian domiciled in Maoza, willed to Shelamzious, his daughter, all his possessions in En-gedi, viz. half of the courtyard across from(?) the synagogue(?) . . . including(?) half of the rooms and the upper-storey rooms therein, but excluding the small old court near the said courtyard, and the other half of the courtyard and rooms Judah willed to the said Shelamzious [to have] after his death; of which courtyard and rooms the abutters [are], on the east [property] of Jesus son of Maddaronas and and [*sic*] empty lot, on the west the testator, on the south a market, on the north a street (and Shelamzious shall not be responsible for any error [in this statement] of boundaries), together with entrances and exits, bricks, roof, doors, windows and existing appurtenances of every kind, so that the aforesaid Shelamzious shall have the half of the aforesaid courtyard and rooms from today, and the other half after the death of the said Judah, validly and securely for all time, to build, raise up, raise higher, excavate, deepen, possess, use, sell and manage in whatever manner she may choose, all valid and secure. And whenever Shelamzious summons the said Judah he will register it with the public authorities.

[2nd hand, Aramaic] Yehudah son of Elazar Khthousion: I have given the courtyard and the house therein to Shelamzion my daughter according to what is written above. . . . Yehudah wrote it.

[1st hand], I, _____ as son of Simon, wrote [this].

On the back, individual signatures

Elazar son of Ḥilqiyah, witness
_____ son of _____, witness
Yeshu'a son of _____, witness
S]oumaios son of Ka.abaios, witness
   ?
Yehudah son of Yehudah, witness
_____ son of _____, witness

● 62H

Disputes between Babatha and Her Co-widow, Miriam

P. Yadin 26   July 9, 131 C.E.

Before the attending witnesses who also affixed their signatures, Babathas [*sic*], a Maozene woman, daughter of Simon, summoned Miriam, an Engedian woman, daughter of Beianos, to accompany her in person before Haterius Nepos, legatus Augusti pro praetore, wherever his venue may be, [to answer] why you seized everything in the house of Judah son of Eleazar Khthousion my and your late husband . . . and, equally important, to attend before the said Nepos until judgment. Miriam replied, saying: Before this I summoned you not to go near the possessions of my and your late husband [and according to?] the . . . and prescriptions(?) of Judah my husband you have no claim against the said Judah regarding his estate and . . . Done in Maoza in the district of Zoöra, in the consulship of Laenas Pontianus and Rufinus seven days before the ides of July. Two copies were written.

It was written by Germanos son of Judah.

On the back, individual signatures

Elazar son of Ḥilqiyah, witness
Mattat son of Shim'on, witness
Yehosef son of Mattat, witness
Yehudah son of _____, witness
Elazar son of Mattat, witness

● 63

The Personal Papers of Salome, Also Called Komaïse

WORK: In addition to the Babatha archive (see entry 62) and papyri associated with the second Jewish revolt under Bar Kokhba, papyri found in the Judean desert also testify to the lives of Jewish women and men in the same period. The following selections pertain to a woman named Salome, also called Komaïse.

TRANSLATION, TEXT, AND BIBLIOGRAPHY: Hannah M. Cotton and Ada Yardeni, *Aramaic, Hebrew and Greek Documentary Texts from Naḥal Ḥever and Other Sites, with an Appendix Containing Alleged Qumran Texts* (the Seiyâl Collection II), Discoveries in the Judean Desert 27 (Oxford: Clarendon Press, 1997).

ADDITIONAL BIBLIOGRAPHY: Tal Ilan, "Premarital Cohabitation in Ancient Judea: The Evidence of the Babatha Archive and the Mishnah (*Ketubbot* 1:4)," *HTR* 86 (1993): 247–64; Michael Satlow, *Jewish Marriage in Antiquity* (Princeton: Princeton University Press, 2001).

● 63A

Deed of Gift from Salome Gropte to her Daughter, Salome Komaïse

P. XḤev/Se gr 64   November 9, 129 C.E.

(The inner text is written in Roman font; the outer text is written in italics; when the texts coincide, it is written in bold.)

Recto

In the second consulship of Publius Iuventius Celsus and Lucius Neratius Marcellus, the ninth [of November, according to the computation of the new province of Arabia] year twenty-four, on the twentieth (twenty-third?) of Dios in Mahoza in the district of Zo'ar, Salome, who is also Gropte, daughter of Menahem, present with her as a guardian for the purpose of this matter, Yosef son of Shim'on, **her husband, to Salome who is also Komaïse, daughter of Levi, her daughter, all of them living in Mahoza,** greetings. I acknowledge that I have given you as a gift from this day and for ever my (*her*) **property in Mahoza, which items are listed as follows: a date orchard called the Garden of Asadaia with its** [*the*] **water** [**allowance**] (*of that orchard*), **once a week on the fourth day, for one half-hour** *which will pay every year to the account of the fiscus of our Lord ten sata of "splits," and six sata of the Syrian and the na'aran dates.* **The abutters on the east the orchard of our Lord** [**the Emperor**] **called the Garden of 'Abbaidaia, on the west the heirs of Aretas, on the south a road and on the north the heirs of Yosef son of Baba.** Together with entrances and exits and all the existing appurtenances of every kind so that the above mentioned Salome Komaïse will hold [the gift written above]. **Similarly also half a courtyard which opens to the south with** (*half*) **two rooms and the upper storey room(s) therein. The abutters on the east Sammouos son of Shim'on, on the west Menahem son of Iohannes, on the south the heirs** of Jacob . . . **on the north Yosef** . . . *possession . . . that the above-mentioned Komaïse will hold the gift written above* **validly and securely** *for all* [*time*] . . . to manage in whatever manner she chooses to. Everything valid . . .

42	[Shalom daughter of Menaḥem in person]
43	Yose[f son of Shim'on wrote for her]
44	Reisha son of Yehudah wr[ote ?]
45	Malik son of A . . . [, witness]
46	Yeshu'a son of Yoḥanan, wit[ness]
47	Timadushra son of 'Abdḥare[tat, witness]
48	Yehosaf son of Shullai, witness
49	Y[ohe]saf son of Ḥana[n]iah, wit[ness]

● 63B

Marriage Contract of Salome Komaïse and Her Second Husband

P. XḤev/Se gr 65 (= P. Yadin 37)   August 7, 131 C.E.

In the consul[ship] of Sergius Octavius Laenas Pontia[nus and Marcus Anton]ius Rufinus, the seve[nth] of August, and according to the computation of the ne[w] province of Arabia year [twenty-six] on the nineteenth of month Loos, [in Maḥoza in the district of Z]o'ar [of the administrative region of] Petra, metropolis of Arabia, Yeshu'a son of Menaḥem, from [the village] of Soffathe . . . in the district of the city of Livias of the administrative region of P[eraea . . . agreed with Sal]ome also called K[omaïse, daughter of Levi], his wife, who is from Maḥoza, [that they continue] life together . . . as also before this time . . . , [and that he owes?] the above-mentioned Komaïse, as her dowry, ninety-six denarii of silver, [which the bridegroom], the above-mentioned Yeshu'a, [acknowledged] to have received from her on the present day, as the written evaluation of feminine adornment in sil[ver and gold and clo]thing and other feminine articles equivalent to the above-mentioned amount of money, (combined) with his undertaking to feed [and clothe both her] and her children to come in accordance with Greek custom and Greek manner upon [the above-mentioned Yeshu'a's good faith] and on peril of all his [posses]sions, as both those which he possesses in his home village of Soffathe . . . [and those which he has here(?) as well as those which he may in addition] acquire. [She has the right of execution both upon] the above-mentioned Yeshu'a and [upon all(?)] his [validly] held possessions [everywhere], in whatever manner the above-mentioned Komaïse, or whoever [acts] through her or [for her, may choose to carry out the execution,] regarding this being thus rightly done, the formal question having in good faith been as[ked and acknowledged, in reply. X] son of Menaḥem, guardian of the above-mentioned Komaïse was present with her. Ad[dendum . . .].

Canceled Marriage Contract, Where the Bride's Mother Gives the Bride

P. XHev/Se gr 69   130 C.E.

Recto, Outer Text, Frg. a

1   In the fourteenth year of the Emperor Tra[jan Hadrian Caesar Augus-
    tus, in the consul-]

2   ship of Marcus Flavius Aper and Quintus Fabius [Catullinus . . .]

3   in Aristoboulias of the Zeiphênê. Sela.e[   ] gave in marriage[her
    daughter (?) Selampious . . .]

4   through Bork . . . Agla, her guardian for this matter[. . .]

5   to Aqabas son of Meir from the village of Iaqim [of the Zephene . . . she
    bringing]

6   to him on account of bridal gift of the dowry(?) in sil[ver and gold . . .
    all appraised in money value as five]

7   hundred *denarii* which are the equivalent of [one hundred and twenty-
    fi]ve staters, [and the groom acknowledges]

8   to have received and to ho[ld from her . . .]

9   five hundred *denarii* forthwith by hand [. . .]

10 wedded (wife) so that Selampious is nourished and cloth[ed . . . upon
    the security of all his posse-]

11 ssions, both those which he has now and those which he will acquire.
    And in the event of the death of [. . .]

12 [   ] the male children or if heirs [. . .]

13 [   ] the daughters will be nourished and clothed [. . .]

14 [   ] and if he who is mentioned before [. . .]

15 [   ] five hundred *denarii* [. . .]

16 [   ]

Verso, Frg. a

1   Joseph son of S..demon, witness.

2   Sou[lai]os son of Eleazar, witness.

3   Maro.es . . . witness.

4   [

5   [

● 64

A Divorce Bill, Possibly Given by a (Jewish) Woman, Shelamzion, to Her Husband, Eleazar

P. Şe'elim 13   ca. 2d century c.e.

WORK: One of many papyri found in the Judean desert pertaining to Jewish life around the second century c.e., this particular document has provoked extensive controversy. While some scholars, including Yardeni, consider it the receipt for a divorce document (Hebrew, *get*), others take it to be a *get* issued by a woman to her former husband (Milik, Ilan).

TRANSLATION, TEXT, AND BIBLIOGRAPHY: Tal Ilan, "Notes and Observations on a Newly Published Divorce Bill from the Judaean Desert," *HTR* 89, no. 2 (1996): 195–202.

ADDITIONAL TRANSLATION, TEXT, AND BIBLIOGRAPHY: Ada Yardeni, *Naḥal Şe'elim Documents* (Jerusalem: Israel Exploration Society and Ben Gurion University in the Negev Press, 1995).

ADDITIONAL BIBLIOGRAPHY: David Instone Brewer, "Jewish Women Divorcing Their Husbands in Early Judaism: The Background to Papyrus Şe'elim 13," *HTR* 92, no. 3 (1999): 349–57; J. T. Milik, "Le travail d'édition des manuscrits du désert de Juda," *Volume du congres Strasbourg 1956*, Supplements to *Vetus Testamentum* 4 (Leiden: E. J. Brill, 1956), 17–26; Michael Satlow, *Jewish Marriage in Antiquity* (Princeton: Princeton University Press, 2001); A. Schremer, "Divorce in Papyrus Şe'elim Once Again: A Reply to Tal Ilan," *HTR* 91, no. 2 (1998): 193–204 (with response from Ilan).

1 On the twentieth of Sivan, year three of Israel's freedom

2 In the name of Simon bar Kosibah, the Nasi of Israel

3 . . . . I do not have. . . .

4 I, Shelamzion, daughter of Joseph Qebshan

5 Of Ein Gedi, with you, Eleazar son of Hananiah

6 Who had been the husband before this time, that

8 this is from me to you a bill of divorce and release

9 ? I do not have with you . . .

10 Eleazar anything (I wish for?), as is my duty and remains upon me.

11 I Shelamzion (accept) all that is written (in this document)

28 Shelamzion present, lent her hand writing (?)

29 Mattat son of Simon by her order

30 . . . son of Simon, witness

31 Masbala, son of Simon, witness

● 65

Women Associated with the Famous Christian Teacher Origen
(ca. 185 to ca. 254 C.E.)

AUTHOR: Eusebius (ca. 260–340 C.E.) was bishop of Caesarea and is best known as the major ancient historian of the early churches in the eastern portion of the Roman Empire. His extensive *History of the Church* is often our only source for certain ancient texts, which Eusebius often quoted uncritically and at great length. As with most ancient authors, Eusebius did not have a particular interest in women's history and religious life, but now and again he preserves significant evidence for women in early Christianity.

TRANSLATION AND TEXT: LCL (K. Lake, 1926; J. E. L. Oulton and H. J. Lawlor, 1932).

ADDITIONAL TRANSLATIONS: FC 19, 29 (R. J. Deferrari, 1953–55); G. A. Williamson, *The History of the Church from Christ to Constantine [by] Eusebius* (Baltimore: Penguin Books, 1965).

ADDITIONAL TEXT: GCS 9 (E. Schwartz and T. Mommsen, 1903–9).

BIBLIOGRAPHY: Elizabeth A. Clark, "Eusebius on Women in Early Church History," in Harold W. Attridge and Gohei Hata, eds., *Eusebius, Christianity and Judaism* (Detroit: Wayne State University Press, 1992), 256–69.

● 65A

Origen Teaches Women and Men

EUSEBIUS *History of the Church* 6.8.1–3   4th century C.E.

1 At that time, while Origen was performing the work of instruction at Alexandria, he did a thing which gave abundant proof of an immature and youthful mind, yet withal of faith and self-control. 2 For he took the saying, "There are eunuchs which made themselves eunuchs for the kingdom of heaven's sake," in too literal and extreme a sense, and thinking both to fulfil the Saviour's saying, and also that he might prevent all suspicion of shameful slander on the part of unbelievers (for, young as he was, he used to discourse on divine things with women as well as men), he hastened to put into effect the Saviour's saying, taking care to escape the notice of the greater number of his pupils. 3 But, wishful though he might be, it was not possible to hide a deed of this nature. In fact Demetrius got to know of it later, since he was

presiding over the community at that place; and while he marvelled exceedingly at him for his rash act, he approved the zeal and the sincerity of his faith, bade him be of good cheer, and urged him to attach himself now all the more to the work of instruction.

● 65B

Origen's Unnamed Female Patron

EUSEBIUS *History of the Church* 6.2.12–14   4th century C.E.

12 But when his father had been perfected by martyrdom, he was left destitute with his mother and six smaller brothers, when he was not quite seventeen. 13 His father's property was confiscated for the imperial treasury, and he found himself, along with his relatives, in want of the necessaries of life. Yet he was deemed worthy of divine aid, and met with both welcome and refreshment from a certain lady, very rich in this world's goods, and otherwise distinguished, who nevertheless was treating with honour a well-known person, one of the heretics at Alexandria at that time. He was an Antiochene by race, but the lady we have mentioned kept him at her house as her adopted son, and treated him with especial honour. 14 But although Origen of necessity had to consort with him, he used to give clear proofs of his orthodoxy, at that age, in the faith.

● 65C

Juliana's Copies of the Works of Symmachus

EUSEBIUS *History of the Church* 6.17.1   4th century C.E.

Now as regards these same translators it is to be noted that Symmachus was an Ebionite. Those who belong to the heresy of the Ebionites, as it is called, affirm that the Christ was born of Joseph and Mary, and suppose Him to be a mere man, and strongly maintain that the law ought to be kept in a more strictly Jewish fashion, as also we saw somewhere from the foregoing history. And memoirs too of Symmachus are still extant, in which, by his opposition to the Gospel according to Matthew, he seems to hold the above-mentioned heresy. These, along with other interpretations of the Scriptures by Symmachus, Origen indicates that he had received from a certain Juliana, who, he says, inherited in her turn the books from Symmachus himself.

● 65D

Origen's Female Scribes

EUSEBIUS *History of the Church* 6.23.1–2   4th century C.E.

1 Starting from that time also Origen's commentaries on the divine Scriptures had their beginning, at the instigation of Ambrose, who not only plied him with innumerable verbal exhortations and encouragements, but also provided him unstintingly with what was necessary. 2 For as he dictated there were ready at hand more than seven shorthand-writers, who relieved each other at fixed times, and as many copyists, as well as girls skilled in penmanship; for all of whom Ambrose supplied without stint the necessary means.

● 66

Burial Inscriptions, Vows, and Donations of and by Women in Asia Minor

WORKS: Presented here are various inscriptions from ancient Asia Minor (modern Turkey), most of which are dated to the second or third century C.E. The curses and fines prescribed for persons who violate these tombs, seen in several of these examples, are widespread in this area in this period. Many tombs from Asia Minor were aboveground sarcophagi, each able to hold a limited number of bodies, although this may not entirely explain the concerns of these inscriptions. I have left untranslated some of the Greek terminology for the burial receptacles and the burial sites. In Asia Minor, a wide range of terminology was employed for the vessel into which the body was placed, the burial monuments, and the burial site, and it is no longer always clear why particular terms were preferred or what distinctions they implied.

All of these are my own translations, except for those from Elsa Gibbons's collections, cited below. The phrase I have rendered "anyone who dares [to open or disturb, etc., the tomb or grave] shall pay" more literally reads, "if anyone [m.] dares . . . he shall pay. . . ." I have chosen this translation to avoid more awkward English constructions and to convey my perception that the burial prohibitions are not intended to be read as gender-specific. If, as these inscriptions amply demonstrate, women as well as men could set up tombs, presumably they were also thought capable of violating them as well, and thus legally liable.

BIBLIOGRAPHY: Ross S. Kraemer, "Jewish Women in the Diaspora World of Late Antiquity," in Judith Baskin, ed., *Jewish Women in Historical Perspective,* 2d ed. (Detroit: Wayne State University Press, 1998), 46–72; Elena Miranda, "La Comunità giudaica di Hierapolis di Frigia," *Epigraphica Anatolica: Zeitschrift für Epigraphik und historische Geographie Anatoliens* 31 (1999): 109–56, Riet van Bremen, *The Limits of Participation: Women and Civic Life in the Greek East in the Hellenistic* and *Roman Periods*, Dutch Monographs on Ancient History and Archaeology 15 (Amsterdam: J. C. Gieben, 1996).

● 66A

A Family Tomb Erected by a Woman under the Protection of the Mother of the Gods

I. Smyr. 232   Smyrna (modern Izmir), late 2d or early 3d century c.e.

NOTE: The goddess invoked here derives her epithet, Sipylenes, from Mount Sipylos; a *heröon* is a term for "tomb" derived from the practice of venerating certain humans as "heroes" as divine after death.

TRANSLATION: RSK.

TEXT: *I. Smyr.* 232; Ritti, *Inscriptiones* 38.

> Aurelia Tryphaina, daughter of Alexandros, erected the ancestral *heröon* for herself and for her heirs and freedpersons, and for Antonios Melitinos with his wife, Homoia, and their children, and Pamphilos only, having purchased the new sarcophagus of Prokkonnesian marble by the sundial. No one has the authority to put another into the new sarcophagus, except Tryphaina only— similarly neither to [put her] into another ancestral sarcophagus nor to give the *heröon* over to strangers. Anyone who shall dare to do this shall give twenty-five hundred denaria to the Mother of the Gods Sipylenes. A copy of this inscription has been placed in the archive, Ailios Bionos being *stephanephoros*, in the third month.

● 66B

Sarcophagus Inscription of a Jewish/Judean Woman, Her Husband, and Their Children

CIJ 775   Hierapolis (modern Pammukkale), 2d or 3d century c.e.

NOTE: On the translation "Jew/Judean," see the main introduction, p. 8.

> This *soros* and the area surrounding it belong to Aurelia Augusta, daughter of Zotikos, in which she is to be buried, and her husband Glukonianos, also called Apros, and their children. Anyone else who buries [someone] in it shall give . . . denaria to the community of Jews/Judeans resident in Hierapolis as reparation, and 2000 denaria to the plaintiff. A copy [of this inscription] has been deposited in the archive of the Jews/Judeans.

● 66C

Burial Inscription for a Woman and Her Mother

MAMA 6.231   Apameia (modern Dinar) 3d century C.E.

I, Aurelios Zosimos, erected the *heröon* to Aurelia Syncletica, also called Tatia, my wife, in which I am also to be buried; and to Aurelia Flavia, daughter of Skymnos, my mother-in-law, a gift in gratitude. No one has the right to put another in. Anyone who dares (to do so) shall give 2000 [denaria] to the most holy treasury and shall have to reckon with the hand of God.

● 66D

A Father's Inscription on the Funerary Urn of His Jewish/Judean Daughter

TAM 3 (1941): 448   Termessus (modern Güllük) 3d century C.E.

NOTE: The designation of the daughter (but not the father) as *Ioudaia* in Greek raises questions about whether only the daughter was Jewish/Judean: see Ross S. Kraemer, "On the Meaning of the Term 'Jew' in Greco-Roman Inscriptions," *HTR* 82, no. 1 (1989): 35–53, repr. in Andrew Overman and R. S. Maclennan, eds., *Diaspora Judaism: Essays in Honor of and in Dialogue with A. Thomas Kraabel,* South Florida Studies in Judaism (Atlanta: Scholars Press, 1992), 311–29; see also the main introduction, p. 8.

Marcus Aurelios Ermaios, son of Keues the son of Keues [set up] a funerary urn for his daughter, Aurelia Artemeis, a Jew/Judean, only. No one has the right to bury anyone else. Anyone who attempts to will pay 1000 denaria to the most sacred treasury and will be liable for breaking into graves.

● 66E

A Christian Woman Establishes a Family Tomb

GIBSON *Christians for Christians*, 32   296/97 C.E.

TRANSLATION, TEXT, AND BIBLIOGRAPHY: Gibson, *Christians for Christians.*

ADDITIONAL BIBLIOGRAPHY: William Tabbernee, *Montanist Inscriptions and Testimonia: Epigraphic Sources Illustrating the History of Montanism*, North American Patristic Society Patristic Monograph Series 16 (Macon, Ga.: Mercer University Press, 1997).

Aurelia Julia for her father . . . and her mother, Beroneikiane and for my sweetest child Severus and Moundane (my) daughter-in-law, in memory. Christians.

● 66F

A Burial Monument Funded by a Woman from Her Dowry

CIJ 763   Akmonia, 3d or 4th century c.e.?

Ammai, daughter of Eutyches, prepared a monument for her husband, Sali-machos, and herself, from her own dowry. Let there be a curse unto the children's children lest anyone entomb anyone except my son Eutyches and his wife.

● 66G

Epitaphs by Three Christian Women, Possibly Montanist, Set Up for Their Families

GIBSON *Christians for Christians*, 8, 12, 13   Akça, ca. 305 c.e.

8 Aurelia Domna for her husband, Meles, and for herself (while still) alive; and their children Kyrillos and Alexandros and Istratonikes and Eythychei-anes and Tationos and Alexandria and Auxanon and Kyriakes and Eusebis and Domnos for their father and mother, who is (still) alive, Christians for Christians.

12 Aurelia Appes for her sweetest husband, Trophimos, called also Krasos, and their children Trophimos and Nikomachos and Domna and Appes for their father and their mother, who is (still) alive, Christians for Christians.

13 Aurelia Tation, daughter of Philomelos, for her child Mikos, and Hermi-ones for her husband, Mikos, and Mikalos for his father, Christians for Christians in memory.

● 66H

The Epitaph of a Married Couple, Probably Christian, with the Husband's Bequests to His Wife and Others

GIBSON *Christians for Christians*, 15   Akça, ca. 305 c.e.

Aurelios Onesimos and Stratonikos and Trophimas took possession of the portions (of land) which were bequeathed to them; and let no one ever make any claim, either himself or through another.

Aurelios Papylos son of Onesimos, and Appes, for their children Eugenious and Amias; and for their grandchild Epiktetos and Eugenia; and for them-selves (while still) alive; and their children Papylos and Amianos for their father and mother; and Ardemas and Amias and Trophimos for their sweetest parents-in-law and their sweetest brother-in-law, in memory. I, Aurelios Papylos, leave my (tool) chest and tools and the portions (of land) which were bequeathed to me, to Papylos and Amianos. Then I leave to Euthychiane and Appe(s) 30 measures of barley mixed with wheat and to my wife I leave 30 measures and a sheep.

● 661

A Woman in Ionia Honored by the Jewish Community for Her Substantial Donations

CIJ 738; Lifshitz, *Donateurs,* 13   Phocaea, 3d century C.E.?

NOTE: Following Louis Robert, I have here and elsewhere translated the genitive of a man's name, when it follows a woman's name, as "daughter of..." rather than as "wife of..." Although either translation is possible, Robert presents cogent evidence that "daughter of..." is the far more likely reading in the majority of cases. In this inscription, I have translated *hē synagogē tōn Ioudaiōn* as "the synagogue of the Jews," but it might equally be translated as "the community of the Jews [or: Judeans]," which is the meaning it bears in a number of our other inscriptions.

> Tation, daughter of Straton, son of Empedon, having erected the assembly hall and the enclosure of the open courtyard with her own funds, gave them as a gift to the Jews. The synagogue of the Jews honored Tation, daughter of Straton, son of Empedon, with a golden crown and the privilege of sitting in the seat of honor.

● 66J

A Woman Fulfilling a Vow for Herself, her Children and her Grandchildren

CIG 2924; Lifshitz, *Donateurs* 30   Tralles (Caria), 3d century C.E.

> I, Capitolina, the [most?] noteworthy and [most?] God-revering one, having made the entire dais, made the revetment of the stairs, in fulfillment of a vow for myself, and (my) children and (my) grandchildren. Blessings.

● 67

Tablet in Greek to Reunite a Woman and a Man Using Language Reminiscent of Jewish Scriptures in Greek

Antike Fluchtafeln, no. 5   Hadrumentum, North Africa, 3d century C.E.?

TEXT: R. Wünsch, *Antike Fluchtafeln* (Bonn: Weidmann, 1912).

TRANSLATION AND BIBLIOGRAPHY: Gager, *Curse Tablets,* 112–15.

> I invoke you *daimonion* spirit who lies here, by the holy name ΑΟΘ ΑΒΑΟΘ, the god of Abraham and *ΙΑΟ, the god of Jacob, ΙΑΟ ΑΟΘ ΑΒΑΟΘ, god of Israma, hear the honored, dreadful and great name, go away to Urbanus, to

whom Urbana gave birth, and bring him to Domitiana, to whom Candida
gave birth, (so that) loving, frantic, and sleepless with love and desire for her,
he may beg her to return to his house and become his wife. I invoke you, the
great god, eternal[1] and more than eternal, almighty and exalted above the exalted ones. I invoke you, who created the heaven and the sea.[2] I invoke you,
who set aside the righteous.[3] I invoke you, who divided the staff in the sea, to
bring Urbanus, to whom Urbana gave birth, and unite him with Domitiana,
to whom Candida gave birth, loving, tormented, and sleepless with desire and
love for her, so that he may take her into his house as his wife. I invoke you,
who made the mule unable to bear offspring. I invoke you, who separated
light from darkness.[4] I invoke you, who crushes rocks.[5] I invoke you, who
breaks apart mountains. I invoke you, who hardened the earth on its foundations.[6] I invoke you, by the holy name which is not spoken. . . . I will mention it by a word with the same numerical equivalent and the *daimones* will
be awakened, startled, terrified, to bring Urbanus, to whom Urbana gave
birth, and unite him with Domitiana, to whom Candida gave birth, loving
and begging for her. Now! Quickly! I invoke you, who made the heavenly
lights and stars[7] by the command of your voice, so that they should shine on
all men. I invoke you, who shook the entire world, who breaks the back of
mountains and casts them up out of the water, who causes the whole earth
to tremble and then renews all its inhabitants.[8] I invoke you, who made signs
in the heaven, on earth and on sea, to bring Urbanus, to whom Urbana gave
birth, and unite him as husband with Domitiana, to whom Candida gave
birth, loving her, sleepless with desire for her, begging for her, and asking
that she return to his house and become his wife. I invoke you, great, everlasting and almighty god, whom the heavens and the valleys fear throughout
the whole earth,[9] through whom the lion gives up its spoil and the mountains tremble with earth and sea, and (through whom) each becomes wise
who possesses fear of the Lord[10] who is eternal, immortal, vigilant, hater of
evil, who knows all things that have happened, good and evil, in the sea and
rivers, on earth and mountain, ΑΟΘΗ, ΑΒΑΟΘΗ, the god of Abraham and ΙΑΟ
of Jacob, ΙΑΟ ΑΟΘΗ, ΑΒΑΟΘΗ, god of Israma, bring Urbanus, to whom Urbana gave birth, and unite him with Domitiana, to whom Candida gave
birth, loving, frantic, tormented with love, passion, and desire for Domitiana,
whom Candida bore; unite them in marriage and as spouses in love for all
the time of their lives. Make him as her obedient slave, so that he will desire
no other woman or maiden apart from Domitiana alone, to whom Candida
gave birth, and will keep her as his spouse for all the time of their lives. Now,
now! Quickly, quickly!

---

[1] Isaiah 26.4.   [2] Genesis 1.1; 14.19, 22.   [3] Sirach 33.11ff.   [4] Genesis 1.4.
[5] 1 Kings 19.11.   [6] Proverbs 8.29.   [7] Genesis 1.16ff.   [8] Psalm 33.14.   [9] Psalm 33.8.
[10] Proverbs 1.7.

⊛ 68

Ten Inscriptions from a Synagogue Commemorating Contributions from Women for the Paving of a Mosaic Floor

Lifshitz *Donateurs*, 41–46, 48, 51, 54–55;
I. Syrie 1322–27, 1329, 1332, 1335–36   Apamea, Syria, ca. 391 C.E.

TRANSLATION: RSK.

ADDITIONAL TRANSLATION AND TEXT: Bernadette J. Brooten, "Appendix: Women as Donors in the Ancient Synagogue," in *Women Leaders*, 157–65.

ADDITIONAL TEXT: *CIJ* 2.806–811, 816.

> 41 Alexandra, in fulfillment of a vow, gave 100 feet for the welfare of (her) whole household.
>
> 42 Ambrosia, in fulfillment of a vow, gave 50 feet for the welfare of (her) whole household.
>
> 43 Domnina, in fulfillment of a vow, gave 100 feet for the welfare of all (her) household.
>
> 44 Eupithis, in fulfillment of a vow, gave 100 feet for the welfare of all (her) household.
>
> 45 Diogenis, in fulfillment of a vow, gave 100 feet for the welfare of all (her) household.
>
> 46 Saprikia, in fulfillment of a vow, gave 150 feet for the welfare of all (her) household.
>
> 48 Thaumasis, together with Hesychion, (his) wife, and children and Eustathis, (his) mother-in-law, gave 100 feet.
>
> 51 Colonis, in fulfillment of a vow, gave 75 feet for her welfare and that of her children.
>
> 54 So-and-so, for her welfare and that of [her children] and of (her) grandchildren, gave . . .
>
> 55 Eupithis, in fulfillment of a vow, for the welfare of herself and that of (her) husband and of (her) children and all her household gave this place.

⊛ 69

A Letter from the Abbot Shenoute to Tachom, Head of a Convent in Egypt

CSCO 42.21–22   5th century C.E.

AUTHOR: Shenoute of Atripe was born in the latter part of the fourth century and entered the Pachomian White Monastery in Egypt as a young boy. After the death of his uncle Pgol, he assumed the leadership of the monastery, ruling it until his death in 466. According to his pupil Besa he lived 118 years. The White Monastery was a large complex of buildings and land extending about twenty square miles. The Arabic *Life of Shenoute* states that twenty-two hundred monks and eighteen hundred nuns were under Shenoute's authority in this complex. The *Letter to Tachom* implies that there was a separate community of women having some kind of connection with the White Monastery. In the Pachomian system, separate communities of men and women in the area around Egyptian Thebes were all supervised by the abbot at the chief monastery, Pbow. Shenoute writes as though he occupied a similar position of authority relative to Tachom's community.

Nothing is known about Tachom herself except her name (which is the feminine form of Pachom/Pachomius) and her leadership of the women's community.

TRANSLATION: Janet Timbie.

TEXT: CSCO 41.21–22 (J. Leipoldt and W. E. Crum, 1906).

BIBLIOGRAPHY: Heike Behlmer, "Visitors to Shenoute's Monastery," in David Frankfurter, ed., *Pilgrimage and Holy Space in Late Antique Egypt*, RGRW 134 (Leiden: E. J. Brill, 1998), 341–71; Alanna Emmett, "Female Ascetics in the Greek Papyri," *Jahrbuch der österreichischen Byzantinistik* 32, no. 2 (1982): 507–15; Alanna Emmett, "An Early Fourth-Century Female Monastic Community in Egypt?" in A. Moffatt, ed., *Maistor: Classical, Byzantine, and Renaissance Studies for Robert Browning*, Byzantina Australiensia 5 (Canberra: Australian Association for Byzantine Studies, 1984), 77–83; Rebecca Krawiec, *Shenoute and the Women of the White Monastery* (New York: Oxford University Press, 2002).

> Shenoute writes to Tachom as one barbarian to another, not as a father to a mother, nor as a brother to a sister.
>
> Though you did not know me until today, I knew you. I did not learn about you recently; I have known about you from the first. If I say, "If I have changed (toward you), what would you have done?" it must mean that if I did not change, you would not have begun to "build the tower."
>
> When did I come to you vengefully since the sound of your folly fills the village where you are, not because I am lord over you, but for the love of God? When the Lord God confused their language, we didn't hear or find it written that they returned and built that tower (again), did we? And I am amazed, for many times God has confused the speech between you and me. I am talking about our false knowledge and our selfish doctrine and our evil thoughts that deceive us. And we turn around and build the tower (again).
>
> At that time, those people made bricks from earth. They had their reward, in

accordance with their desires, in the forbearance of God, who is exalted, the one who gave it to them in accordance with their desires. Those, on the other hand, who build the tower now—though I do not speak of everyone—their whole plan comes from the wickedness of Satan. Then, they said senselessly, "We will build it so that the top (of the tower) reaches up to heaven" (Gen. 11:4). Now, those who build this in every place think that they are wise, that their heart reaches the throne and judgment seat of God.

I said, "If you do not know what (message) is proper to send us—namely, 'Forgive me'—even if we sinned against you by not again sending you the one whom you did deem worthy to meet, then you do not understand anything." And if your "father" is not the one we sent in accordance with order and the rules of God, then you yourself are not a "mother." If you say of the one whom we sent, "We are not his," though he is your brother in the flesh, then you have separated yourself from us. If you say, "We are his," then the one who is writing to you is the one you would not meet, nor deem worthy of it. Or perhaps you have a case at law with him? If you are not a wise mother, what will those who call you "mother" do to become wise without you? If some are wise, even one hundred are not enough to take counsel with you. . . .

⦾ 70

Instruction for Rearing a Virgin Christian Daughter

JEROME *Letter* 107, to Laeta   403 C.E.

AUTHOR: A prominent biblical scholar in his time, Jerome (ca. 342–420 C.E.) is best known for his translation of most of the Bible into Latin, in an edition known as the Vulgate. Adopting the ascetic life by his early thirties, he spent a number of years in the Syrian desert as a hermit and there learned Hebrew. He arrived in Rome in 382 C.E. an ordained priest and developed such close ties with a small circle of ascetic and aristocratic Christian women that he was forced to leave Rome three years later under suspicion of having had inappropriate relationships with them. Relocating in Bethlehem, he founded a monastery for men while his Roman friend and pupil Paula, together with her daughter Eustochium, ran a nearby monastery for women. His letter to Eustochium on the death of her mother is one of his most famous and is an important source for the study of Roman Christian ascetic women in the fourth century. Jerome wrote many letters to women both known and unknown to him, urging them to adopt and maintain an ascetic life. Not surprisingly, many of his letters have survived, while none of theirs to him remain.

TRANSLATION: NPNFC ser. 2 vol. 6.

TEXT: PL 22–30; SC (Jerome Labourt, 1949–63, 8 vols.).

ADDITIONAL TRANSLATIONS: ACW (C. C. Mierow and T. C. Lawler, 1963–); selected letters in LCL (F. A. Wright, 1933).

BIBLIOGRAPHY: Virginia Burrus, *Begotten, Not Made: Conceiving Manhood in Late Antiquity* (Stanford, Calif.: Stanford University Press, 2000); Virginia Burrus, "The Heretical Woman as Symbol in Alexander, Athanasius, Epiphanius, and Jerome," *HTR* 84, no. 3 (1991): 229–48; Elizabeth A. Clark, *Jerome, Chrysostom, and Friends: Essays and Translations*, 2d ed. (New York: Edwin Mellen Press, 1982); Elizabeth A. Clark, "Theory and Practice in Late Ancient Asceticism: Jerome, Chrysostom, and Augustine," *Journal of Feminist Studies in Religion*, 5, no. 1 (1989): 25–46; Gillian Clark, *Women in Late Antiquity: Pagan and Christian Lifestyles* (Oxford: Clarendon Press; New York: Oxford University Press, 1993); Gillian Cloke, *This Female Man of God: Women and Spiritual Power in the Patristic Age, 350–450* (London and New York: Routledge, 1995); Margaret Y. MacDonald, *Early Christian Women and Pagan Opinion: The Power of the Hysterical Woman* (Cambridge: Cambridge University Press, 1996).

1 The apostle Paul writing to the Corinthians and instructing in sacred discipline a church still untaught in Christ has among other commandments laid down also this: "The woman which hath an husband that believeth not, and if he be pleased to dwell with her, let her not leave him. For the unbelieving husband is sanctified by the believing wife, and the unbelieving wife is sanctified by the believing husband; else were your children unclean but now are they holy." Should any person have supposed hitherto that the bonds of discipline are too far relaxed and that too great indulgence is conceded by the teacher, let him look at the house of your father, a man of the highest distinction and learning, but one still walking in darkness; and he will perceive as the result of the apostle's counsel sweet fruit growing from a bitter stock and precious balsams exhaled from common canes. You yourself are the offspring of a mixed marriage; but the parents of Paula—you and my friend Toxotius—are both Christians. Who could have believed that to the heathen pontiff Albinus should be born—in answer to a mother's vows—a Christian granddaughter; that a delighted grandfather should hear from the little one's faltering lips Christ's Alleluia, and that in his old age he should nurse in his bosom one of God's own virgins? Our expectations have been fully gratified. The one unbeliever is sanctified by his holy and believing family. For, when a man is surrounded by a believing crowd of children and grandchildren, he is as good as a candidate for the faith. I for my part think that, had he possessed so many Christian kinsfolk when he was a young man, he might then have been brought to believe in Christ. For though he may spit upon my letter and laugh at it, and though he may call me a fool or a madman, his son-in-law did the same before he came to believe. Christians are not born but made. For all its gilding the Capitol is beginning to look dingy. Every temple in Rome is covered with soot and cobwebs. The city is stirred to its

depths and the people pour past their half-ruined shrines to visit the tombs of the martyrs. The belief which has not been accorded to conviction may come to be extorted by very shame.

2 I speak thus to you, Laeta my most devout daughter in Christ, to teach you not to despair of your father's salvation. My hope is that the same faith which has gained you your daughter may win your father too, and that so you may be able to rejoice over blessings bestowed upon your entire family. You know the Lord's promise: "The things which are impossible with men are possible with God." It is never too late to mend. The robber passed even from the cross to paradise. Nebuchadnezzar also, the king of Babylon, recovered his reason, even after he had been made like the beasts in body and in heart and had been compelled to live with the brutes in the wilderness. And to pass over such old stories which to unbelievers may well seem incredible, did not your own kinsman Gracchus whose name betokens his patrician origin, when a few years back he held the prefecture of the City, overthrow, break in pieces, and shake to pieces the grotto of Mithras and all the dreadful images therein? Those I mean by which the worshippers were initiated as Raven, Bridegroom, Soldier, Lion, Perseus, Sun, Crab, and Father? Did he not, I repeat, destroy these and then, sending them before him as hostages, obtain for himself Christian baptism?

Even in Rome itself paganism is left in solitude. They who once were the gods of the nations remain under their lonely roofs with horned-owls and birds of night. The standards of the military are emblazoned with the sign of the Cross. The emperor's robes of purple and his diadem sparkling with jewels are ornamented with representations of the shameful yet saving gibbet. Already the Egyptian Serapis has been made a Christian; while at Gaza Marnas mourns in confinement and every moment expects to see his temple overturned. From India, from Persia, from Ethiopia we daily welcome monks in crowds. The Armenian bowman has laid aside his quiver, the Huns learn the psalter, the chilly Scythians are warmed with the glow of the faith. The Getæ, ruddy and yellow-haired, carry tent-churches about with their armies: and perhaps their success in fighting against us may be due to the fact that they believe in the same religion.

3 I have nearly wandered into a new subject, and while I have kept my wheel going, my hands have been moulding a flagon when it has been my object to frame an ewer. For, in answer to your prayers and those of the saintly Marcella, I wish to address you as a mother and to instruct you how to bring up our dear Paula, who has been consecrated to Christ before her birth and vowed to His service before her conception. Thus in our own day we have seen repeated the story told us in the Prophets, of Hannah, who though at first barren afterwards became fruitful. You have exchanged a fertility bound up with sorrow for offspring which shall never die. For I am confident that

having given to the Lord your first-born you will be the mother of sons. It is the first-born that is offered under the Law. Samuel and Samson are both instances of this, as is also John the Baptist who when Mary came in leaped for joy. For he heard the Lord speaking by the mouth of the Virgin and desired to break from his mother's womb to meet Him. As then Paula has been born in answer to a promise, her parents should give her a training suitable to her birth. Samuel, as you know, was nurtured in the Temple, and John was trained in the wilderness. The first as a Nazarite wore his hair long, drank neither wine nor strong drink, and even in his childhood talked with God. The second shunned cities, wore a leathern girdle, and had for his meat locusts and wild honey. Moreover, to typify that penitence which he was to preach, he was clothed in the spoils of the hump-backed camel.

4 Thus must a soul be educated which is to be a temple of God. It must learn to hear nothing and to say nothing but what belongs to the fear of God. It must have no understanding of unclean words, and no knowledge of the world's songs. Its tongue must be steeped while still tender in the sweetness of the psalms. Boys with their wanton thoughts must be kept from Paula: even her maids and female attendants must be separated from worldly associates. For if they have learned some mischief they may teach more. Get for her a set of letters made of boxwood or of ivory and called each by its proper name. Let her play with these, so that even her play may teach her something. And not only make her grasp the right order of the letters and see that she forms their names into a rhyme, but constantly disarrange their order and put the last letters in the middle and the middle ones at the beginning that she may know them all by sight as well as by sound. Moreover, so soon as she begins to use the style upon the wax, and her hand is still faltering, either guide her soft fingers by laying your hand upon hers, or else have simple copies cut upon a tablet; so that her efforts confined within these limits may keep to the lines traced out for her and not stray outside of these. Offer prizes for good spelling and draw her onwards with little gifts such as children of her age delight in. And let her have companions in her lessons to excite emulation in her, that she may be stimulated when she sees them praised. You must not scold her if she is slow to learn but must employ praise to excite her mind, so that she may be glad when she excels others and sorry when she is excelled by them. Above all you must take care not to make her lessons distasteful to her lest a dislike for them conceived in childhood may continue into her maturer years. The very words which she tries bit by bit to put together and to pronounce ought not to be chance ones, but names specially fixed upon and heaped together for the purpose, those for example of the prophets or the apostles or the list of patriarchs from Adam downwards as it is given by Matthew and Luke. In this way while her tongue will be well-trained, her memory will be likewise developed. Again, you must

choose for her a master of approved years, life, and learning. A man of culture will not, I think, blush to do for a kinswoman or a highborn virgin what Aristotle did for Philip's son when, descending to the level of an usher, he consented to teach him his letters. Things must not be despised as of small account in the absence of which great results cannot be achieved. The very rudiments and first beginnings of knowledge sound differently in the mouth of an educated man and of an uneducated. Accordingly you must see that the child is not led away by the silly coaxing of women to form a habit of shortening long words or of decking herself with gold and purple. Of these habits one will spoil her conversation and the other her character. She must not therefore learn as a child what afterwards she will have to unlearn. The eloquence of the Gracchi is said to have been largely due to the way in which from their earliest years their mother spoke to them. Hortensius became an orator while still on his father's lap. Early impressions are hard to eradicate from the mind. When once wool has been dyed purple who can restore it to its previous whiteness? An unused jar long retains the taste and smell of that with which it is first filled. Grecian history tells us that the imperious Alexander who was lord of the whole world could not rid himself of the tricks of manner and gait which in his childhood he had caught from his governor Leonides. We are always ready to imitate what is evil; and faults are quickly copied where virtues appear inattainable. Paula's nurse must not be intemperate, or loose, or given to gossip. Her bearer must be respectable, and her fosterfather of grave demeanour. When she sees her grandfather, she must leap upon his breast, put her arms round his neck, and, whether he likes it or not, sing Alleluia in his ears. She may be fondled by her grandmother, may smile at her father to shew that she recognizes him, and may so endear herself to everyone, as to make the whole family rejoice in the possession of such a rosebud. She should be told at once whom she has for her other grandmother and whom for her aunt; and she ought also to learn in what army it is that she is enrolled as a recruit, and what Captain it is under whose banner she is called to serve. Let her long to be with the absent ones and encourage her to make playful threats of leaving you for them.

5 Let her very dress and garb remind her to Whom she is promised. Do not pierce her ears or paint her face consecrated to Christ with white lead or rouge. Do not hang gold or pearls about her neck or load her head with jewels, or by reddening her hair make it suggest the fires of gehenna. Let her pearls be of another kind and such that she may sell them hereafter and buy in their place the pearl that is "of great price." In days gone by a lady of rank, Praetextata by name, at the bidding of her husband Hymettius, the uncle of Eustochium, altered that virgin's dress and appearance and arranged her neglected hair after the manner of the world, desiring to overcome the resolution of the virgin herself and the expressed wishes of her mother. But

lo in the same night it befell her that an angel came to her in her dreams. With terrible looks he menaced punishment and broke silence with these words, "Have you presumed to put your husband's commands before those of Christ? Have you presumed to lay sacrilegious hands upon the head of one who is God's virgin? Those hands shall forthwith wither that you may know by torment what you have done, and at the end of five months you shall be carried off to hell. And farther, if you persist still in your wickedness, you shall be bereaved both of your husband and of your children." All of which came to pass in due time, a speedy death marking the penitence too long delayed of the unhappy woman. So terribly does Christ punish those who violate His temple, and so jealously does He defend His precious jewels. I have related this story here not from any desire to exult over the misfortunes of the unhappy, but to warn you that you must with much fear and carefulness keep the vow which you have made to God.

6 We read of Eli the priest that he became displeasing to God on account of the sins of his children; and we are told that a man may not be made a bishop if his sons are loose and disorderly. On the other hand it is written of the woman that "she shall be saved in childbearing, if they continue in faith and charity and holiness with chastity." If then parents are responsible for their children when these are of ripe age and independent; how much more must they be responsible for them when, still unweaned and weak, they cannot, in the Lord's words, "discern between their right hand and their left:"— when, that is to say, they cannot yet distinguish good from evil? If you take precautions to save your daughter from the bite of a viper, why are you not equally careful to shield her from "the hammer of the whole earth"? to prevent her from drinking of the golden cup of Babylon? to keep her from going out with Dinah to see the daughters of a strange land? to save her from the tripping dance and from the trailing robe? No one administers drugs till he has rubbed the rim of the cup with honey; so, the better to deceive us, vice puts on the mien and the semblance of virtue. Why then, you will say, do we read:—"the son shall not bear the iniquity of the father, neither shall the father bear the iniquity of the son," but "the soul that sinneth it shall die"? The passage, I answer, refers to those who have discretion, such as he of whom his parents said in the gospel:—"he is of age . . . he shall speak for himself." While the son is a child and thinks as a child and until he comes to years of discretion to choose between the two roads to which the letter of Pythagoras points, his parents are responsible for his actions whether these be good or bad. But perhaps you imagine that, if they are not baptized, the children of Christians are liable for their own sins; and that no guilt attaches to parents who withhold from baptism those who by reason of their tender age can offer no objection to it. The truth is that, as baptism ensures the salvation of the child, this in turn brings advantage to the parents. Whether you

would offer your child or not lay within your choice, but now that you have offered her, you neglect her at your peril. I speak generally for in your case you have no discretion, having offered your child even before her conception. He who offers a victim that is lame or maimed or marked with any blemish is held guilty of sacrilege. How much more then shall she be punished who makes ready for the embraces of the king a portion of her own body and the purity of a stainless soul, and then proves negligent of this her offering?

7 When Paula comes to be a little older and to increase like her Spouse in wisdom and stature and in favour with God and man, let her go with her parents to the temple of her true Father but let her not come out of the temple with them. Let them seek her upon the world's highway amid the crowds and the throng of their kinsfolk, and let them find her nowhere but in the shrine of the scriptures, questioning the prophets and the apostles on the meaning of that spiritual marriage to which she is vowed. Let her imitate the retirement of Mary whom Gabriel found alone in her chamber and who was frightened, it would appear, by seeing a man there. Let the child emulate her of whom it is written that "the king's daughter is all glorious within." Wounded with love's arrow let her say to her beloved, "the king hath brought me into his chambers." At no time let her go abroad, lest the watchmen find her that go about the city, and lest they smite and wound her and take away from her the veil of her chastity, and leave her naked in her blood. Nay rather when one knocketh at her door let her say: "I am a wall and my breasts like towers. I have washed my feet; how shall I defile them?"

8 Let her not take her food with others, that is, at her parents' table; lest she see dishes she may long for. Some, I know, hold it a greater virtue to disdain a pleasure which is actually before them, but I think it a safer self-restraint to shun what must needs attract you. Once as a boy at school I met the words: "It is ill blaming what you allow to become a habit." Let her learn even now not to drink wine "wherein is excess." But as, before children come to a robust age, abstinence is dangerous and trying to their tender frames, let her have baths if she require them, and let her take a little wine for her stomach's sake. Let her also be supported on a flesh diet, lest her feet fail her before they commence to run their course. But I say this by way of concession not by way of command; because I fear to weaken her, not because I wish to teach her self-indulgence. Besides why should not a Christian virgin do wholly what others do in part? The superstitious Jews reject certain animals and products as articles of food, while among the Indians the Brahmans and among the Egyptians the Gymnosophists subsist altogether on porridge, rice, and apples. If mere glass repays so much labour, must not a pearl be worth more labour still? Paula has been born in response to a vow. Let her life be as the lives of those who were born under the same conditions. If the grace accorded is in both cases the same, the pains bestowed ought to be so too.

Let her be deaf to the sound of the organ, and not know even the uses of the pipe, the lyre, and the cithern.

9 And let it be her task daily to bring to you the flowers which she has culled from scripture. Let her learn by heart so many verses in the Greek, but let her be instructed in the Latin also. For, if the tender lips are not from the first shaped to this, the tongue is spoiled by a foreign accent and its native speech debased by alien elements. You must yourself be her mistress, a model on which she may form her childish conduct. Never either in you nor in her father let her see what she cannot imitate without sin. Remember both of you that you are the parents of a consecrated virgin, and that your example will teach her more than your precepts. Flowers are quick to fade and a baleful wind soon withers the violet, the lily, and the crocus. Let her never appear in public unless accompanied by you. Let her never visit a church or a martyr's shrine unless with her mother. Let no young man greet her with smiles; no dandy with curled hair pay compliments to her. If our little virgin goes to keep solemn eves and all-night vigils, let her not stir a hair's breadth from her mother's side. She must not single out one of her maids to make her a special favourite or a confidante. What she says to one all ought to know. Let her choose for a companion not a handsome well-dressed girl, able to warble a song with liquid notes but one pale and serious, sombrely attired and with the hue of melancholy. Let her take as her model some aged virgin of approved faith, character, and chastity, apt to instruct her by word and by example. She ought to rise at night to recite prayers and psalms; to sing hymns in the morning; at the third, sixth, and ninth hours to take her place in the line to do battle for Christ; and, lastly, to kindle her lamp and to offer her evening sacrifice. In these occupations let her pass the day, and when night comes let it find her still engaged in them. Let reading follow prayer with her, and prayer again succeed to reading. Time will seem short when employed on tasks so many and so varied.

10 Let her learn too how to spin wool, to hold the distaff, to put the basket in her lap, to turn the spinning wheel and to shape the yarn with her thumb. Let her put away with disdain silken fabrics, Chinese fleeces, and gold brocades: the clothing which she makes for herself should keep out the cold and not expose the body which it professes to cover. Let her food be herbs and wheaten bread with now and then one or two small fishes. And that I may not waste more time in giving precepts for the regulation of appetite (a subject I have treated more at length elsewhere) let her meals always leave her hungry and able on the moment to begin reading or chanting. I strongly disapprove—especially for those of tender years—of long and immoderate fasts in which week is added to week and even oil and apples are forbidden as food. I have learned by experience that the ass toiling along the high way makes for an inn when it is weary. Our abstinence may turn to glutting, like

that of the worshippers of Isis and of Cybele who gobble up pheasants and turtle-doves piping hot that their teeth may not violate the gifts of Ceres. If perpetual fasting is allowed, it must be so regulated that those who have a long journey before them may hold out all through; and we must take care that we do not, after starting well, fall halfway. However in Lent, as I have written before now, those who practise self-denial should spread every stitch of canvas, and the charioteer should for once slacken the reins and increase the speed of his horses. Yet there will be one rule for those who live in the world and another for virgins and monks. The layman in Lent consumes the coats of his stomach, and living like a snail on his own juices makes ready a paunch for rich foods and feasting to come. But with the virgin and the monk the case is different; for, when these give the rein to their steeds, they have to remember that for them the race knows of no intermission. An effort made only for a limited time may well be severe, but one that has no such limit must be more moderate. For whereas in the first case we can recover our breath when the race is over, in the last we have to go on continually and without stopping.

11 When you go a short way into the country, do not leave your daughter behind you. Leave her no power or capacity of living without you, and let her feel frightened when she is left to herself. Let her not converse with people of the world or associate with virgins indifferent to their vows. Let her not be present at the weddings of your slaves and let her take no part in the noisy games of the household. As regards the use of the bath, I know that some are content with saying that a Christian virgin should not bathe along with eunuchs or with married women, with the former because they are still men at all events in mind, and with the latter because women with child offer a revolting spectacle. For myself, however, I wholly disapprove of baths for a virgin of full age. Such an one should blush and feel overcome at the idea of seeing herself undressed. By vigils and fasts she mortifies her body and brings it into subjection. By a cold chastity she seeks to put out the flame of lust and to quench the hot desires of youth. And by a deliberate squalor she makes haste to spoil her natural good looks. Why, then, should she add fuel to a sleeping fire by taking baths?

12 Let her treasures be not silks or gems but manuscripts of the holy scriptures; and in these let her think less of gilding, and Babylonian parchment, and arabesque patterns, than of correctness and accurate punctuation. Let her begin by learning the psalter, and then let her gather rules of life out of the proverbs of Solomon. From the Preacher let her gain the habit of despising the world and its vanities. Let her follow the example set in Job of virtue and of patience. Then let her pass on to the gospels never to be laid aside when once they have been taken in hand. Let her also drink in with a willing heart the Acts of the Apostles and the Epistles. As soon as she has enriched the

storehouse of her mind with these treasures, let her commit to memory the prophets, the heptateuch, the books of Kings and of Chronicles, the rolls also on Ezra and Esther. When she has done all these she may safely read the Song of Songs but not before: for, were she to read it at the beginning, she would fail to perceive that, though it is written in fleshly words, it is a marriage song of a spiritual bridal. And not understanding this she would suffer hurt from it. Let her avoid all apocryphal writings, and if she is led to read such not by the truth of the doctrines which they contain but out of respect for the miracles contained in them; let her understand that they are not really written by those to whom they are ascribed, that many faulty elements have been introduced into them, and that it requires infinite discretion to look for gold in the midst of dirt. Cyprian's writings let her have always in her hands. The letters of Athanasius and the treatises of Hilary she may go through without fear of stumbling. Let her take pleasure in the works and wits of all in whose books a due regard for the faith is not neglected. But if she reads the works of others let it be rather to judge them than to follow them.

13 You will answer, 'How shall I, a woman of the world, living at Rome, surrounded by a crowd, be able to observe all these injunctions?' In that case do not undertake a burthen to which you are not equal. When you have weaned Paula as Isaac was weaned and when you have clothed her as Samuel was clothed, send her to her grandmother and aunt; give up this most precious of gems, to be placed in Mary's chamber and to rest in the cradle where the infant Jesus cried. Let her be brought up in a monastery, let her be one amid companies of virgins, let her learn to avoid swearing, let her regard lying as sacrilege, let her be ignorant of the world, let her live the angelic life, while in the flesh let her be without the flesh, and let her suppose that all human beings are like herself. To say nothing of its other advantages this course will free you from the difficult task of minding her, and from the responsibility of guardianship. It is better to regret her absence than to be for ever trembling for her. For you cannot but tremble as you watch what she says and to whom she says it, to whom she bows and whom she likes best to see. Hand her over to Eustochium while she is still but an infant and her every cry is a prayer for you. She will thus become her companion in holiness now as well as her successor hereafter. Let her gaze upon and love, let her "from her earliest years admire" one whose language and gait and dress are an education in virtue. Let her sit in the lap of her grandmother, and let this latter repeat to her granddaughter the lessons that she once bestowed upon her own child. Long experience has shewn Paula how to rear, to preserve, and to instruct virgins; and daily inwoven in her crown is the mystic century which betokens the highest chastity. O happy virgin! happy Paula, daughter of Toxotius, who through the virtues of her grandmother and aunt is nobler in holiness than she is in lineage! Yes, Laeta: were it possible for you with your own eyes to

see your mother-in-law and your sister, and to realize the mighty souls which animate their small bodies; such is your innate thirst for chastity that I cannot doubt but that you would go to them even before your daughter, and would emancipate yourself from God's first decree of the Law to put yourself under His second dispensation of the Gospel. You would count as nothing your desire for other offspring and would offer up yourself to the service of God. But because "there is a time to embrace, and a time to refrain from embracing," and because "the wife hath not power of her own body," and because the apostle says "Let every man abide in the same calling wherein he was called" in the Lord, and because he that is under the yoke ought so to run as not to leave his companion in the mire, I counsel you to pay back to the full in your offspring what meantime you defer paying in your own person. When Hannah had once offered in the tabernacle the son whom she had vowed to God she never took him back; for she thought it unbecoming that one who was to be a prophet should grow up in the same house with her who still desired to have other children. Accordingly after she had conceived him and given him birth, she did not venture to come to the temple alone or to appear before the Lord empty, but first paid to Him what she owed; and then, when she had offered up that great sacrifice, she returned home and because she had borne her firstborn for God, she was given five children for herself. Do you marvel at the happiness of that holy woman? Imitate her faith. Moreover, if you will only send Paula, I promise to be myself both a tutor and a fosterfather to her. Old as I am I will carry her on my shoulders and train her stammering lips; and my charge will be a far grander one than that of the worldly philosopher; for while he only taught a King of Macedon who was one day to die of Babylonian poison, I shall instruct the handmaid and spouse of Christ who must one day be offered to her Lord in heaven.

● 71

The Life of Paula, Leader in Women's Early Monasticism

JEROME *Letter* 108, to Eustochium   404 C.E.

NOTE: This "life" of Paula, composed by Jerome (see entry 70) as his funerary consolation to her daughter, Eustochium, could also have been included in section 5, "Holy, Pious, and Exemplary Women." Although Paula was unquestionably a historical person, Jerome's representation of her here owes much to ancient conventions and constructions of gender and exemplifies many of the methodological and theoretical questions posed in the various introductory sections to this anthology.

1 If all the members of my body were to be converted into tongues, and if each of my limbs were to be gifted with a human voice, I could still do no

justice to the virtues of the holy and venerable Paula. Noble in family, she was nobler still in holiness; rich formerly in this world's goods, she is now more distinguished by the poverty that she has embraced for Christ. Of the stock of the Gracchi and descended from the Scipios, the heir and representative of that Paulus whose name she bore, the true and legitimate daughter of that Martia Papyria who was mother to Africanus, she yet preferred Bethlehem to Rome, and left her palace glittering with gold to dwell in a mud cabin. We do not grieve that we have lost this perfect woman; rather we thank God that we have had her, nay that we have her still. For "all live unto" God, and they who return unto the Lord are still to be reckoned members of his family. We have lost her, it is true, but the heavenly mansions have gained her; for as long as she was in the body she was absent from the Lord and would constantly complain with tears:—"Woe is me that I sojourn in Mesech, that I dwell in the tents of Kedar; my soul hath been this long time a pilgrim." It was no wonder that she sobbed out that even she was in darkness (for this is the meaning of the word Kedar) seeing that, according to the apostle, "the world lieth in the evil one;" and that, "as its darkness is, so is its light"; and that "the light shineth in darkness and the darkness comprehended it not." She would frequently exclaim: "I am a stranger with thee and a sojourner as all my fathers were," and again, I desire "to depart and to be with Christ." As often too as she was troubled with bodily weakness (brought on by incredible abstinence and by redoubled fastings), she would be heard to say: "I keep under my body and bring it into subjection; lest that by any means, when I have preached to others, I myself should be a castaway"; and "It is good neither to eat flesh nor to drink wine"; and "I humbled my soul with fasting"; and "thou wilt make all" my "bed in" my "sickness"; and "Thy hand was heavy upon me: my moisture is turned into the drought of summer." And when the pain which she bore with such wonderful patience darted through her, as if she saw the heavens opened she would say: "Oh that I had wings like a dove! for then would I fly away and be at rest."

2 I call Jesus and his saints, yes and the particular angel who was the guardian and the companion of this admirable woman to bear witness that these are no words of adulation and flattery but sworn testimony every one of them borne to her character. They are, indeed, inadequate to the virtues of one whose praises are sung by the whole world, who is admired by bishops, regretted by bands of virgins, and wept for by crowds of monks and poor. Would you know all her virtues, reader, in short? She has left those dependent on her poor, but not so poor as she was herself. In dealing thus with her relatives and the men and women of her small household—her brothers and sisters rather than her servants—she has done nothing strange: for she has left her daughter Eustochium—a virgin consecrated to Christ for whose

comfort this sketch is made—far from her noble family and rich only in faith and grace.

3 Let me then begin my narrative. Others may go back a long way even to Paula's cradle and, if I may say so, to her swaddling-clothes, and may speak of her mother Blaesilla and her father Rogatus. Of these the former was a descendant of the Scipios and the Gracchi; whilst the latter came of a line distinguished in Greece down to the present day. He was said, indeed, to have in his veins the blood of Agamemnon who destroyed Troy after a ten years' siege. But I shall praise only what belongs to herself, what wells forth from the pure spring of her holy mind. When in the gospel the apostles ask their Lord and Saviour what He will give to those who have left all for His sake, He tells them that they shall receive an hundredfold now in this time and in the world to come eternal life. From which we see that it is not the possession of riches that is praiseworthy but the rejection of them for Christ's sake; that, instead of glorying in our privileges, we should make them of small account as compared with God's faith. Truly the Saviour has now in this present time made good His promise to His servants and handmaidens. For one who despised the glory of a single city is to-day famous throughout the world; and one who while she lived at Rome was known by no one outside it has by hiding herself at Bethlehem become the admiration of all lands Roman and barbarian. For what race of men is there which does not send pilgrims to the holy places? And who could there find a greater marvel than Paula? As among many jewels the most precious shines most brightly, and as the sun with its beams obscures and puts out the paler fires of the stars; so by her lowliness she surpassed all others in virtue and influence and, while she was least among all, was greater than all. The more she cast herself down, the more she was lifted up by Christ. She was hidden and yet she was not hidden. By shunning glory she earned glory; for glory follows virtue as its shadow; and deserting those who seek it, it seeks those who despise it. But I must not neglect to proceed with my narrative or dwell too long on a single point forgetful of the rules of writing.

4 Being then of such parentage, Paula married Toxotius in whose veins ran the noble blood of Aeneas and the Julii. Accordingly his daughter, Christ's virgin Eustochium, is called Julia, as he Julius.

A name from great Iulus handed down.

I speak of these things not as of importance to those who have them, but as worthy of remark in those who despise them. Men of the world look up to persons who are rich in such privileges. We on the other hand praise those who for the Saviour's sake despise them; and strangely depreciating all who keep them, we eulogize those who are unwilling to do so. Thus nobly born, Paula through her fruitfulness and her chastity won approval from all, from her husband first, then from her relatives, and lastly from the whole city. She bore five children; Blaesilla, for whose death I consoled her while at Rome; Paulina, who has left the reverend and admirable Pammachius to inherit both her vows and property, to whom also I addressed a little book on her death; Eustochium, who is now in the holy places, a precious necklace of virginity and of the church; Rufina, whose untimely end overcame the affectionate heart of her mother; and Toxotius, after whom she had no more children. You can thus see that it was not her wish to fulfil a wife's duty, but that she only complied with her husband's longing to have male offspring.

5 When he died, her grief was so great that she nearly died herself: yet so completely did she then give herself to the service of the Lord, that it might have seemed that she had desired his death.

In what terms shall I speak of her distinguished, and noble, and formerly wealthy house; all the riches of which she spent upon the poor? How can I describe the great consideration she shewed to all and her far reaching kindness even to those whom she had never seen? What poor man, as he lay dying, was not wrapped in blankets given by her? What bedridden person was not supported with money from her purse? She would seek out such with the greatest diligence throughout the city, and would think it a misfortune were any hungry or sick person to be supported by another's food. So lavish was her charity that she robbed her children; and, when her relatives remonstrated with her for doing so, she declared that she was leaving to them a better inheritance in the mercy of Christ.

6 Nor was she long able to endure the visits and crowded receptions, which her high position in the world and her exalted family entailed upon her. She received the homage paid to her sadly, and made all the speed she could to shun and to escape those who wished to pay her compliments. It so happened that at that time the bishops of the East and West had been summoned to Rome by letter from the emperors to deal with certain dissensions between the churches, and in this way she saw two most admirable men and Christian prelates, Paulinus bishop of Antioch and Epiphanius, bishop of Salamis or, as it is now called, Constantia, in Cyprus. Epiphanius, indeed, she received as her guest; and, although Paulinus was staying in another person's house, in the warmth of her heart she treated him as if he too were lodged with her. Inflamed by their virtues she thought more and more each moment of forsaking her home. Disregarding her house, her children, her servants, her property, and in a word everything connected with the world, she was eager— alone and unaccompanied (if ever it could be said that she was so)—to go to the desert made famous by its Pauls and by its Antonies. And at last when the winter was over and the sea was open, and when the bishops were returning to their churches, she also sailed with them in her prayers and desires. Not to prolong the story, she went down to Portus accompanied by her

brother, her kinsfolk and above all her own children eager by their demonstrations of affection to overcome their loving mother. At last the sails were set and the strokes of the rowers carried the vessel into the deep. On the shore the little Toxotius stretched forth his hands in entreaty, while Rufina, now grown up, with silent sobs besought her mother to wait till she should be married. But still Paula's eyes were dry as she turned them heavenwards; and she overcame her love for her children by her love for God. She knew herself no more as a mother, that she might approve herself a handmaid of Christ. Yet her heart was rent within her, and she wrestled with her grief, as though she were being forcibly separated from parts of herself. The greatness of the affection she had to overcome made all admire her victory the more. Among the cruel hardships which attend prisoners of war in the hands of their enemies, there is none severer than the separation of parents from their children. Though it is against the laws of nature, she endured this trial with unabated faith; nay more she sought it with a joyful heart: and overcoming her love for her children by her greater love for God, she concentrated herself quietly upon Eustochium alone, the partner alike of her vows and of her voyage. Meantime the vessel ploughed onwards and all her fellow-passengers looked back to the shore. But she turned away her eyes that she might not see what she could not behold without agony. No mother, it must be confessed, ever loved her children so dearly. Before setting out she gave them all that she had, disinheriting herself upon earth that she might find an inheritance in heaven.

7 The vessel touched at the island of Pontia ennobled long since as the place of exile of the illustrious lady Flavia Domitilla who under the Emperor Domitian was banished because she confessed herself a Christian; and Paula, when she saw the cells in which this lady passed the period of her long martyrdom, taking to herself the wings of faith, more than ever desired to see Jerusalem and the holy places. The strongest winds seemed weak and the greatest speed slow. After passing between Scylla and Charybdis she committed herself to the Adriatic sea and had a calm passage to Methone. Stopping here for a short time to recruit her wearied frame

> She stretched her dripping limbs upon the shore:
> Then sailed past Malea and Cythera's isle,
> The scattered Cyclades, and all the lands
> That narrow in the seas on every side.

Then leaving Rhodes and Lycia behind her, she at last came in sight of Cyprus, where falling at the feet of the holy and venerable Epiphanius, she was by him detained ten days; though this was not, as he supposed, to restore her strength but, as the facts prove, that she might do God's work. For she visited all the monasteries in the island, and left, so far as her means allowed, substantial relief for the brothers in them whom love of the holy man had brought thither from all parts of the world. Then crossing the narrow sea she landed at Seleucia, and going up thence to Antioch allowed herself to be detained for a little time by the affection of the reverend confessor Paulinus. Then, such was the ardour of her faith that she, a noble lady who had always previously been carried by eunuchs, went her way—and that in midwinter—riding upon an ass.

8 I say nothing to her journey through Coele-Syria and Phoenicia (for it is not my purpose to give you a complete itinerary of her wanderings); I shall only name such places as are mentioned in the sacred books. After leaving the Roman colony of Berytus and the ancient city of Zidon she entered Elijah's town on the shore at Zarephath and therein adored her Lord and Saviour. Next passing over the sands of Tyre on which Paul had once knelt she came to Acco or, as it is now called, Ptolemais, rode over the plains of Megiddo which had once witnessed the slaying of Josiah, and entered the land of the Philistines. Here she could not fail to admire the ruins of Dor, once a most powerful city; and Strato's Tower, which though at one time insignificant was rebuilt by Herod king of Judaea and named Caesarea in honour of Caesar Augustus. Here she saw the house of Cornelius now turned into a Christian church; and the humble abode of Philip; and the chambers of his daughters the four virgins "which did prophesy." She arrived next at Antipatris, a small town half in ruins, named by Herod after his father Antipater, and at Lydda, now become Diospolis, a place made famous by the raising again of Dorcas and the restoration to health of Aeneas. Not far from this are Arimathaea, the village of Joseph who buried the Lord, and Nob, once a city of priests but now the tomb in which their slain bodies rest. Joppa too is hard by, the port of Jonah's flight: which also—if I may introduce a poetic fable—saw Andromeda bound to the rock. Again resuming her journey, she came to Nicopolis, once called Emmaus, where the Lord became known in the breaking of bread; an action by which He dedicated the house of Cleopas as a church. Starting thence she made her way up lower and higher Bethhoron, cities founded by Solomon but subsequently destroyed by several devastating wars; seeing on her right Ajalon and Gibeon where Joshua the son of Nun when fighting against the five kings gave commandments to the sun and moon, where also he condemned the Gibeonites (who by a crafty stratagem had obtained a treaty) to be hewers of wood and drawers of water. At Gibeah also, now a complete ruin, she stopped for a little while remembering its sin, and the cutting of the concubine into pieces, and how in spite of all this three hundred men of the tribe of Benjamin were saved that in after days Paul might be called a Benjamite.

9 To make a long story short, leaving on her left the mausoleum of Helena queen of Abiabene who in time of famine had sent corn to the Jewish people, Paula entered Jerusalem, Jebus, or Salem, that city of three names which

after it had sunk to ashes and decay was by Aelius Hadrianus restored once more as Aelia. And although the proconsul of Palestine, who was an intimate friend of her house, sent forward his apparitors and gave orders to have his official residence placed at her disposal, she chose a humble cell in preference to it. Moreover, in visiting the holy places so great was the passion and the enthusiasm she exhibited for each, that she could never have torn herself away from one had she not been eager to visit the rest. Before the Cross she threw herself down in adoration as though she beheld the Lord hanging upon it: and when she entered the tomb which was the scene of the Resurrection she kissed the stone which the angel had rolled away from the door of the sepulchre. Indeed so ardent was her faith that she even licked with her mouth the very spot on which the Lord's body had lain, like one athirst for the river which he has longed for. What tears she shed there, what groans she uttered, and what grief she poured forth, all Jerusalem knows; the Lord also to whom she prayed knows. Going out thence she made the ascent of Zion; a name which signifies either "citadel" or "watch-tower." This formed the city which David formerly stormed and afterwards rebuilt. Of its storming it is written, "Woe to Ariel, to Ariel"—that is, God's lion (and indeed in those days it was extremely strong)—"the city which David stormed:" and of its rebuilding it is said, "His foundation is in the holy mountains: the Lord loveth the gates of Zion more than all the dwellings of Jacob." He does not mean the gates which we see to-day in dust and ashes; the gates he means are those against which hell prevails not and through which the multitude of those who believe in Christ enter in. There was shewn to her upholding the portico of a church the bloodstained column to which our Lord is said to have been bound when He suffered His scourging. There was shewn to her also the spot where the Holy Spirit came down upon the souls of the one hundred and twenty believers, thus fulfilling the prophecy of Joel.

10 Then, after distributing money to the poor and her fellow-servants so far as her means allowed, she proceeded to Bethlehem stopping only on the right side of the road to visit Rachel's tomb. (Here it was that she gave birth to her son destined to be not what his dying mother called him, Benoni, that is the "Son of my pangs" but as his father in the spirit prophetically named him Benjamin, that is "the Son of the right hand.") After this she came to Bethlehem and entered into the cave where the Saviour was born. Here, when she looked upon the inn made sacred by the virgin and the stall where the ox knew his owner and the ass his master's crib, and where the words of the same prophet had been fulfilled "Blessed is he that soweth beside the waters where the ox and the ass trample the seed under their feet:" when she looked upon these things I say, she protested in my hearing that she could behold with the eyes of faith the infant Lord wrapped in swaddling clothes and crying in the manger, the wise men worshipping Him, the star shining overhead,

the virgin mother, the attentive foster-father, the shepherds coming by night to see "the word that was come to pass" and thus even then to consecrate those opening phrases of the evangelist John "In the beginning was the word" and "the word was made flesh." She declared that she could see the slaughtered innocents, the raging Herod, Joseph and Mary fleeing into Egypt; and with a mixture of tears and joy she cried: "Hail Bethlehem, house of bread, wherein was born that Bread that came down from heaven. Hail Ephratah, land of fruitfulness and of fertility, whose fruit is the Lord Himself. Concerning thee has Micah prophesied of old, 'Thou Bethlehem Ephratah art not the least among the thousands of Judah, for out of thee shall he come forth unto me that is to be ruler in Israel; whose goings forth have been from of old, from everlasting. Therefore wilt thou give them up, until the time that she which travaileth hath brought forth: then the remnant of his brethren shall return unto the children of Israel.' For in thee was born the prince begotten before Lucifer. Whose birth from the Father is before all time: and the cradle of David's race continued in thee, until the virgin brought forth her son and the remnant of the people that believed in Christ returned unto the children of Israel and preached freely to them in words like these: 'It was necessary that the word of God should first have been spoken to you; but seeing ye put it from you and judge yourselves unworthy of everlasting life, lo, we turn to the Gentiles.' For the Lord hath said: 'I am not sent but unto the lost sheep of the house of Israel.' At that time also the words of Jacob were fulfilled concerning Him, 'A prince shall not depart from Judah nor a lawgiver from between his feet, until He come for whom it is laid up, and He shall be for the expectation of the nations.' Well did David swear, well did he make a vow saying: 'Surely I will not come into the tabernacle of my house nor go up into my bed: I will not give sleep to mine eyes, or slumber to my eyelids, or rest to the temples of my head, until I find out a place for the Lord, an habitation for the . . . God of Jacob.' And immediately he explained the object of his desire, seeing with prophetic eyes that He would come whom we now believe to have come. 'Lo we heard of Him at Ephratah: we found Him in the fields of the wood.' The Hebrew word *Zo* as I have learned from your lessons means not *her*, that is Mary the Lord's mother, but *him* that is the Lord Himself. Therefore he says boldly: 'We will go into His tabernacle: we will worship to His footstool.' I too, miserable sinner though I am, have been accounted worthy to kiss the manger in which the Lord cried as a babe, and to pray in the cave in which the travailing virgin gave birth to the infant Lord. 'This is my rest' for it is my Lord's native place; 'here will I dwell' for this spot has my Saviour chosen. 'I have prepared a lamp for my Christ' 'My soul shall live unto Him and my seed shall serve him.'"

After this Paula went a short distance down the hill to the tower of Edar, that is "of the flock," near which Jacob fed his flocks, and where the shepherds keeping watch by night were privileged to hear the words: "Glory to God in the highest and on earth peace, good-will toward men." While they were keeping their sheep they found the Lamb of God; whose fleece bright and clean was made wet with the dew of heaven when it was dry upon all the earth beside, and whose blood when sprinkled on the doorposts drove off the destroyer of Egypt and took away the sins of the world.

11 Then immediately quickening her pace she began to move along the old road which leads to Gaza, that is to the "power" or "wealth" of God, silently meditating on that type of the Gentiles, the Ethiopian eunuch, who in spite of the prophet changed his skin and whilst he read the old testament found the fountain of the gospel. Next turning to the right she passed from Bethzur to Eshcol which means "a cluster of grapes." It was hence that the spies brought back that marvellous cluster which was the proof of the fertility of the land and a type of Him who says of Himself: "I have trodden the wine press alone; and of the people there was none with me." Shortly afterwards she entered the home of Sarah and beheld the birthplace of Isaac and the traces of Abraham's oak under which he saw Christ's day and was glad. And rising up from thence she went up to Hebron, that is Kirjath-Arba, or the City of the Four Men. These are Abraham, Isaac, Jacob, and the great Adam whom the Hebrews suppose (from the book of Joshua the son of Nun) to be buried there. But many are of opinion that Caleb is the fourth and a monument at one side is pointed out as his. After seeing these places she did not care to go on to Kirjath-sepher, that is "the village of letters;" because despising the letter that killeth she had found the spirit that giveth life. She admired more the upper springs and the nether springs which Othniel the son of Kenaz the son of Jephunneh received in place of a south land and a waterless possession, and by the conducting of which he watered the dry fields of the old covenant. For thus did he typify the redemption which the sinner finds for his old sins in the waters of baptism. On the next day soon after sunrise she stood upon the brow of Capharbarucha, that is, "the house of blessing," the point to which Abraham pursued the Lord when he made intercession with Him. And here, as she looked down upon the wide solitude and upon the country once belonging to Sodom and Gomorrah, to Admah and Zeboim, she beheld the balsam vines of Engedi and Zoar. By Zoar I mean that "heifer of three years old" which was formerly called Bela and in Syriac is rendered Zoar that is "little." She called to mind the cave in which Lot found refuge, and with tears in her eyes warned the virgins her companions to beware of "wine wherein is excess"; for it was to this that the Moabites and Ammonites owe their origin.

12 I linger long in the land of the midday sun for it was there and then that the spouse found her bridegroom at rest and Joseph drank wine with his brothers once more. I will return to Jerusalem and, passing through Tekoa

the home of Amos, I will look upon the glistening cross of Mount Olivet from which the Saviour made His ascension to the Father. Here year by year a red heifer was burned as a holocaust to the Lord and its ashes were used to purify the children of Israel. Here also according to Ezekiel the Cherubim after leaving the temple founded the church of the Lord.

After this Paula visited the tomb of Lazarus and beheld the hospitable roof of Mary and Martha, as well as Bethphage, "the town of the priestly jaws." Here it was that a restive foal typical of the Gentiles received the bridle of God, and covered with the garments of the apostles offered its lowly back for Him to sit on. From this she went straight on down the hill to Jericho thinking of the wounded man in the gospel, of the savagery of the priests and Levites who passed him by, and of the kindness of the Samaritan, that is, the guardian, who placed the half-dead man upon his own beast and brought him down to the inn of the church. She noticed the place called Adomim or the Place of Blood, so-called because much blood was shed there in the frequent incursions of marauders. She beheld also the sycamore tree of Zacchaeus, by which is signified the good works of repentance whereby he trod under foot his former sins of bloodshed and rapine, and from which he saw the Most High as from a pinnacle of virtue. She was shewn too the spot by the wayside where the blind men sat who, receiving their sight from the Lord, became types of the two peoples who should believe upon Him. Then entering Jericho she saw the city which Hiel founded in Abiram his firstborn and of which he set up the gates in his youngest son Segub. She looked upon the camp of Gilgal and the hill of the foreskins suggestive of the mystery of the second circumcision; and she gazed at the twelve stones brought thither out of the bed of Jordan to be symbols of those twelve foundations on which are written the names of the twelve apostles. She saw also that fountain of the Law most bitter and barren which the true Elisha healed by his wisdom changing it into a well sweet and fertilising. Scarcely had the night passed away when burning with eagerness she hastened to the Jordan, stood by the brink of the river, and as the sun rose recalled to mind the rising of the sun of righteousness; how the priest's feet stood firm in the middle of the riverbed; how afterwards at the command of Elijah and Elisha the waters were divided hither and thither and made way for them to pass; and again how the Lord had cleansed by His baptism waters which the deluge had polluted and the destruction of mankind had defiled.

13 It would be tedious were I to tell of the valley of Achor, that is, of "trouble and crowds," where theft and covetousness were condemned; and of Bethel, "the house of God," where Jacob poor and destitute slept upon the bare ground. Here it was that, having set beneath his head a stone which in Zechariah is described as having seven eyes and in Isaiah is spoken of as a corner-stone, he beheld a ladder reaching up to heaven; yes, and the Lord

standing high above it holding out His hand to such as were ascending and hurling from on high such as were careless. Also when she was in Mount Ephraim she made pilgrimages to the tombs of Joshua the son of Nun and of Eleazar the son of Aaron the priest, exactly opposite the one to the other; that of Joshua being built at Timnath-serah "on the north side of the hill of Gaash," and that of Eleazar "in a hill that pertained to Phinehas his son." She was somewhat surprised to find that he who had had the distribution of the land in his own hands had selected for himself portions uneven and rocky. What shall I say about Shiloh where a ruined altar is still shewn to-day, and where the tribe of Benjamin anticipated Romulus in the rape of the Sabine women? Passing by Shechem (not Sychar as many wrongly read) or as it is now called Neapolis, she entered the church built upon the side of Mount Gerizim around Jacob's well; that well where the Lord was sitting when hungry and thirsty He was refreshed by the faith of the woman of Samaria. Forsaking her five husbands by whom are intended the five books of Moses, and that sixth not a husband of whom she boasted, to wit the false teacher Dositheus, she found the true Messiah and the true Saviour. Turning away thence Paula saw the tombs of the twelve patriarchs, and Samaria which in honour of Augustus Herod renamed Augusta or in Greek Sebaste. There lie the prophets Elisha and Obadiah and John the Baptist than whom there is not a greater among those that are born of women. And here she was filled with terror by the marvels she beheld; for she saw demons screaming under different tortures before the tombs of the saints, and men howling like wolves, baying like dogs, roaring like lions, hissing like serpents and bellowing like bulls. They twisted their heads and bent them backwards until they touched the ground; women too were suspended head downward and their clothes did not fall off. Paula pitied them all, and shedding tears over them prayed Christ to have mercy on them. And weak as she was she climbed the mountain on foot; for in two of its caves Obadiah in a time of persecution and famine had fed a hundred prophets with bread and water. Then she passed quickly through Nazareth the nursery of the Lord; Cana and Capernaum familiar with the signs wrought by Him; the lake of Tiberias sanctified by His voyages upon it; the wilderness where countless Gentiles were satisfied with a few loaves while the twelve baskets of the tribes of Israel were filled with the fragments left by them that had eaten. She made the ascent of mount Tabor whereon the Lord was transfigured. In the distance she beheld the range of Hermon; and the wide stretching plains of Galilee where Sisera and all his host had once been overcome by Barak; and the torrent Kishon separating the level ground into two parts. Hard by also the town of Nain was pointed out to her, where the widow's son was raised. Time would fail me sooner than speech were I to recount all the places to which the revered Paula was carried by her incredible faith.

14 I will now pass on to Egypt, pausing for a while on the way at Socoh, and at Samson's well which he clave in the hollow place that was in the jaw. Here I will lave my parched lips and refresh myself before visiting Moresbeth; in old days famed for the tomb of the prophet Micah, and now for its church. Then skirting the country of the Horites and Gittites, Mareshah, Edom, and Lachish, and traversing the lonely wastes of the desert where the tracks of the traveller are lost in the yielding sand, I will come to the river of Egypt called Sihor, that is "the muddy river," and go through the five cities of Egypt which speak the language of Canaan, and through the land of Goshen and the plains of Zoan on which God wrought his marvellous works. And I will visit the city of No, which has since become Alexandria; and Nitria, the town of the Lord, where day by day the filth of multitudes is washed away with the pure nitre of virtue. No sooner did Paula come in sight of it than there came to meet her the reverend and estimable bishop, the confessor Isidore, accompanied by countless multitudes of monks many of whom were of priestly or of Levitical rank. On seeing these Paula rejoiced to behold the Lord's glory manifested in them; but protested that she had no claim to be received with such honour. Need I speak of the Macarii, Arsenius, Serapion, or other pillars of Christ! Was there any cell that she did not enter? Or any man at whose feet she did not throw herself? In each of His saints she believed that she saw Christ Himself; and whatever she bestowed upon them she rejoiced to feel that she had bestowed it upon the Lord. Her enthusiasm was wonderful and her endurance scarcely credible in a woman. Forgetful of her sex and of her weakness she even desired to make her abode, together with the girls who accompanied her, among these thousands of monks. And, as they were all willing to welcome her, she might perhaps have sought and obtained permission to do so; had she not been drawn away by still greater passion for the holy places. Coming by sea from Pelusium to Maioma on account of the great heat, she returned so rapidly that you would have thought her a bird. Not long afterwards, making up her mind to dwell permanently in holy Bethlehem, she took up her abode for three years in a miserable hostelry; till she could build the requisite cells and monastic buildings, to say nothing of a guest house for passing travellers where they might find the welcome which Mary and Joseph had missed. At this point I conclude my narrative of the journeys that she made accompanied by Eustochium and many other virgins.

15 I am now free to describe at greater length the virtue which was her peculiar charm; and in setting forth this I call God to witness that I am no flatterer. I add nothing. I exaggerate nothing. On the contrary I tone down much that I may not appear to relate incredibilities. My carping critics must not insinuate that I am drawing on my imagination or decking Paula, like Aesop's crow, with the fine feathers of other birds. Humility is the first of Christian graces, and hers was so pronounced that one who had never seen

her, and who on account of her celebrity had desired to see her, would have believed that he saw not her but the lowest of her maids. When she was surrounded by companies of virgins she was always the least remarkable in dress, in speech, in gesture, and in gait. From the time that her husband died until she fell asleep herself she never sat at meat with a man, even though she might know him to stand upon the pinnacle of the episcopate. She never entered a bath except when dangerously ill. Even in the severest fever she rested not on an ordinary bed but on the hard ground covered only with a mat of goat's hair; if that can be called rest which made day and night alike a time of almost unbroken prayer. Well did she fulfil the words of the psalter: "All the night make I my bed to swim; I water my couch with my tears"! Her tears welled forth as it were from fountains, and she lamented her slightest faults as if they were sins of the deepest dye. Constantly did I warn her to spare her eyes and to keep them for the reading of the gospel; but she only said: "I must disfigure that face which contrary to God's commandment I have painted with rouge, white lead, and antimony. I must mortify that body which has been given up to many pleasures. I must make up for my long laughter by constant weeping. I must exchange my soft linen and costly silks for rough goat's hair. I who have pleased my husband and the world in the past, desire now to please Christ." Were I among her great and signal virtues to select her chastity as a subject of praise, my words would seem superfluous; for, even when she was still in the world, she set an example to all the matrons of Rome, and bore herself so admirably that the most slanderous never ventured to couple scandal with her name. No mind could be more considerate than hers, or none kinder towards the lowly. She did not court the powerful; at the same time, if the proud and the vainglorious sought her, she did not turn from them with disdain. If she saw a poor man, she supported him: and if she saw a rich one, she urged him to do good. Her liberality alone knew no bounds. Indeed, so anxious was she to turn no needy person away that she borrowed money at interest and often contracted new loans to pay off old ones. I was wrong, I admit; but when I saw her so profuse in giving, I reproved her alleging the apostle's words: "I mean not that other men be eased and ye burthened; but by an equality that now at this time your abundance may be a supply for their want, that their abundance also may be a supply for your want." I quoted from the gospel the Saviour's words: "he that hath two coats, let him impart one of them to him that hath none"; and I warned her that she might not always have means to do as she would wish. Other arguments I adduced to the same purpose; but with admirable modesty and brevity she overruled them all. "God is my witness," she said, "that what I do I do for His sake. My prayer is that I may die a beggar not leaving a penny to my daughter and indebted to strangers for my winding sheet." She then concluded with these words: "I, if I beg, shall find many to give to me; but if this beggar does not obtain help from me who by borrowing can give it to him, he will die; and if he dies, of whom will his soul be required?" I wished her to be more careful in managing her concerns, but she with a faith more glowing than mine clave to the Saviour with her whole heart and poor in spirit followed the Lord in His poverty, giving back to Him what she had received and becoming poor for His sake. She obtained her wish at last and died leaving her daughter overwhelmed with a mass of debt. This Eustochium still owes and indeed cannot hope to pay off by her own exertions; only the mercy of Christ can free her from it.

16 Many married ladies make it a habit to confer gifts upon their own trumpeters, and while they are extremely profuse to a few, withhold all help from the many. From this fault Paula was altogether free. She gave her money to each according as each had need, not ministering to self-indulgence but relieving want. No poor person went away from her empty handed. And all this she was enabled to do not by the greatness of her wealth but by her careful management of it. She constantly had on her lips such phrases as these: "Blessed are the merciful for they shall obtain mercy"; and "water will quench a flaming fire; and alms maketh an atonement for sins"; and "make to yourselves friends of the mammon of unrighteousness that . . . they may receive you into everlasting habitations"; and "give alms . . . and behold all things are clean unto you"; and Daniel's words to King Nebuchadnezzar in which he admonished him to redeem his sins by almsgiving. She wished to spend her money not upon these stones, that shall pass away with the earth and the world, but upon those living stones, which roll over the earth; of which in the apocalypse of John the city of the great king is built; of which also the scripture tells us that they shall be changed into sapphire and emerald and jasper and other gems.

17 But these qualities she may well share with a few others and the devil knows that it is not in these that the highest virtue consists. For, when Job has lost his substance and when his house and children have been destroyed, Satan says to the Lord: "Skin for skin, yea all that a man hath, will he give for his life. But put forth thine hand now and touch his bone and his flesh, and he will curse thee to thy face." We know that many persons while they have given alms have yet given nothing which touches their bodily comfort; and while they have held out a helping hand to those in need are themselves overcome with sensual indulgences; they whitewash the outside but within they are "full of dead men's bones." Paula was not one of these. Her self-restraint was so great as to be almost immoderate; and her fasts and labours were so severe as almost to weaken her constitution. Except on feast days she would scarcely ever take oil with her food; a fact from which may be judged what she thought of wine, sauce, fish, honey, milk, eggs, and other things agreeable to the palate. Some persons believe that in taking these they are

extremely frugal; and, even if they surfeit themselves with them, they still fancy their chastity safe.

18 Envy always follows in the track of virtue: as Horace says, it is ever the mountain top that is smitten by the lightning. It is not surprising that I declare this of men and women, when the jealousy of the Pharisees succeeded in crucifying our Lord Himself. All the saints have had illwishers, and even Paradise was not free from the serpent through whose malice death came into the world. So the Lord stirred up against Paula Hadad the Edomite to buffet her that she might not be exalted, and warned her frequently by the thorn in her flesh not to be elated by the greatness of her own virtues or to fancy that, compared with other women, she had attained the summit of perfection. For my part I used to say that it was best to give in to rancour and to retire before passion. So Jacob dealt with his brother Esau; so David met the unrelenting persecution of Saul. I reminded her how the first of these fled into Mesopotamia; and how the second surrendered himself to the Philistines, and chose to submit to foreign foes rather than to enemies at home. She however replied as follows: "Your suggestion would be a wise one if the devil did not everywhere fight against God's servants and handmaidens, and did he not always precede the fugitives to their chosen refuges. Moreover, I am deterred from accepting it by my love for the holy places; and I cannot find another Bethlehem elsewhere. Why may I not by my patience conquer this ill will? Why may I not by my humility break down this pride, and when I am smitten on the one cheek offer to the smiter the other? Surely the apostle Paul says 'Overcome evil with good.' Did not the apostles glory when they suffered reproach for the Lord's sake? Did not even the Saviour humble Himself, taking the form of a servant and being made obedient to the Father unto death, even the death of the cross, that He might save us by His passion? If Job had not fought the battle and won the victory, he would never have received the crown of righteousness, or have heard the Lord say: 'Thinkest thou that I have spoken unto thee for aught else than this, that thou mightest appear righteous.' In the gospel those only are said to be blessed who suffer persecution for righteousness' sake. My conscience is at rest, and I know that it is not from any fault of mine that I am suffering; moreover affliction in this world is a ground for expecting a reward hereafter." When the enemy was more than usually forward and ventured to reproach her to her face, she used to chant the words of the psalter: "While the wicked was before me, I was dumb with silence; I held my peace even from good:" and again, "I as a deaf man heard not; and I was as a dumb man that openeth not his mouth:" and "I was as a man that heareth not, and in whose mouth are no reproofs." When she felt herself tempted, she dwelt upon the words in Deuteronomy: "The Lord your God proveth you, to know whether ye love the Lord your God with all your heart and with all your soul." In tribulations and afflictions

she turned to the splendid language of Isaiah: "Ye that are weaned from the milk and drawn from the breasts, look for tribulation upon tribulation, for hope also upon hope: yet a little while must these things be by reason of the malice of the lips and by reason of a spiteful tongue." This passage of scripture she explained for her own consolation as meaning that the weaned, that is, those who have come to full age, must endure tribulation upon tribulation that they may be accounted worthy to receive hope upon hope. She recalled to mind also the words of the apostle, "we glory in tribulations also: knowing that tribulation worketh patience, and patience experience, and experience hope: and hope maketh not ashamed" and "though our outward man perish, yet the inward man is renewed day by day": and "our light affliction which is but for a moment worketh in us an eternal weight of glory; while we look not at the things which are seen but at the things which are not seen: for the things which are seen are temporal but the things which are not seen are eternal." She used to say that, although to human impatience the time might seem slow in coming, yet that it would not be long but that presently help would come from God who says: "In an acceptable time have I heard thee, and in a day of salvation have I helped thee." We ought not, she declared, to dread the deceitful lips and tongues of the wicked, for we rejoice in the aid of the Lord who warns us by His prophet: "fear ye not the reproach of men, neither be ye afraid of their revilings; for the moth shall eat them up like a garment, and the worm shall eat them like wool": and she quoted His own words, "In your patience ye shall win your souls": as well as those of the apostle, "the sufferings of this present time are not worthy to be compared with the glory which shall be revealed in us": and in another place, "we are to suffer affliction" that we may be patient in all things that befall us, for "he that is slow to wrath is of great understanding: but he that is hasty of spirit exalteth folly."

19 In her frequent sicknesses and infirmities she used to say, "when I am weak, then am I strong:" "we have our treasure in earthen vessels" until "this corruptible shall have put on incorruption and this mortal shall have put on immortality" and again "as the sufferings of Christ abound in us, so our consolation also aboundeth by Christ:" and then "as ye are partakers of the sufferings, so shall ye be also of the consolation." In sorrow she used to sing: "Why art thou cast down, O my soul? and why art thou disquieted within me? hope thou in God for I shall yet praise him who is the health of my countenance and my God." In the hour of danger she used to say: "If any man will come after me, let him deny himself and take up his cross and follow me:" and again "whosoever will save his life shall lose it," and "whosoever will lose his life for my sake the same shall save it." When the exhaustion of her substance and the ruin of her property were announced to her she only said: "What is a man profited, if he shall gain the whole world and

lose his own soul? or what shall a man give in exchange for his soul:" and "naked came I out of my mother's womb, and naked shall I return thither. The Lord gave, and the Lord hath taken away: blessed be the name of the Lord:" and Saint John's words, "Love not the world neither the things that are in the world. For all that is in the world, the lust of the flesh, and the lust of the eyes and the pride of life, is not of the Father but is of the world. And the world passeth away and the lust thereof." I know that when word was sent to her of the serious illnesses of her children and particularly of Toxotius whom she dearly loved, she first by her self-control fulfilled the saying: "I was troubled and I did not speak," and then cried out in the words of scripture, "He that loveth son or daughter more than me is not worthy of me." And she prayed to the Lord and said: Lord "preserve thou the children of those that are appointed to die," that is, of those who for thy sake every day die bodily. I am aware that a talebearer—a class of persons who do a great deal of harm—once told her as a kindness that owing to her great fervour in virtue some people thought her mad and declared that something should be done for her head. She replied in the words of the apostle, "we are made a spectacle unto the world and to angels and to men," and "we are fools for Christ's sake" but "the foolishness of God is wiser than men." It is for this reason she said that even the Saviour says to the Father, "Thou knowest my foolishness," and again "I am as a wonder unto many, but thou are my strong refuge." "I was as a beast before thee; nevertheless I am continually with thee." In the gospel we read that even His kinsfolk desired to bind Him as one of weak mind. His opponents also reviled him saying "thou art a Samaritan and hast a devil," and another time "he casteth out devils through Beelzebub the chief of the devils." But let us, she continued, listen to the exhortation of the apostle, "Our rejoicing is this, the testimony of our conscience that in simplicity and sincerity . . . by the grace of God we have had our conversation in the world." And let us hear the Lord when He says to His apostles, "If ye were of the world the world would love his own; but because ye are not of the world . . . therefore the world hateth you." And then she turned to the Lord Himself, saying, "Thou knowest the secrets of the heart," and "all this is come upon us; yet have we not forgotten thee, neither have we dealt falsely in thy covenant; our heart is not turned back." "Yea for thy sake are we killed all the day long; we are counted as sheep for the slaughter." But "the Lord is on my side: I will not fear what man doeth unto me." She had read the words of Solomon, "My son, honour the Lord and thou shalt be made strong; and beside the Lord fear thou no man." These passages and others like them she used as God's armour against the assaults of wickedness, and particularly to defend herself against the furious onslaughts of envy; and thus by patiently enduring wrongs she soothed the violence of the most savage breasts. Down to the very day of her death two things were conspicuous in her life, one her great patience and the other the jealousy which was manifested towards her. Now jealousy gnaws the heart of him who harbours it: and while it strives to injure its rival raves with all the force of its fury against itself.

20 I shall now describe the order of her monastery and the method by which she turned the continence of saintly souls to her own profit. She sowed carnal things that she might reap spiritual things; she gave earthly things that she might receive heavenly things; she forewent things temporal that she might in their stead obtain things eternal. Besides establishing a monastery for men, the charge of which she left to men, she divided into three companies and monasteries the numerous virgins whom she had gathered out of different provinces, some of whom are of noble birth while others belonged to the middle or lower classes. But, although they worked and had their meals separately from each other, these three companies met together for psalm-singing and prayer. After the chanting of the Alleluia—the signal by which they were summoned to the Collect—no one was permitted to remain behind. But either first or among the first Paula used to await the arrival of the rest, urging them to diligence rather by her own modest example than by motives of fear. At dawn, at the third, sixth, and ninth hours, at evening, and at midnight they recited the psalter each in turn. No sister was allowed to be ignorant of the psalms, and all had every day to learn a certain portion of the holy scriptures. On the Lord's day only they proceeded to the church beside which they lived, each company following its own mother-superior. Returning home in the same order, they then devoted themselves to their allotted tasks, and made garments either for themselves or else for others. If a virgin was of noble birth, she was not allowed to have an attendant belonging to her own household lest her maid having her mind full of the doings of the old days and of the license of childhood might by constant converse open old wounds and renew former errors. All the sisters were clothed alike. Linen was not used except for drying the hands. So strictly did Paula separate them from men that she would not allow even eunuchs to approach them; lest she should give occasion to slanderous tongues (always ready to cavil at the religious) to console themselves for their own misdoing. When a sister was backward in coming to the recitation of the psalms or shewed herself remiss in her work, Paula used to approach her in different ways. Was she quick-tempered? Paula coaxed her. Was she phlegmatic? Paula chid her, copying the example of the apostle who said: "What will ye? Shall I come to you with a rod or in love and in the spirit of meekness?" Apart from food and raiment she allowed no one to have anything she could call her own, for Paula had said, "Having food and raiment let us be therewith content." She was afraid lest the custom of having more should breed covetousness in them; an appetite which no wealth can satisfy, for the more it has the more it requires, and neither opulence nor indigence is able to diminish it. When the sisters quar-

relled one with another she reconciled them with soothing words. If the younger ones were troubled with fleshly desires, she broke their force by imposing redoubled fasts; for she wished her virgins to be ill in body rather than to suffer in soul. If she chanced to notice any sister too attentive to her dress, she reproved her for her error with knitted brows and severe looks, saying; "a clean body and a clean dress mean an unclean soul. A virgin's lips should never utter an improper or an impure word, for such indicate a lascivious mind and by the outward man the faults of the inward are made manifest." When she saw a sister verbose and talkative or forward and taking pleasure in quarrels, and when she found after frequent admonitions that the offender shewed no signs of improvement; she placed her among the lowest of the sisters and outside their society, ordering her to pray at the door of the refectory instead of with the rest, and commanding her to take her food by herself, in the hope that where rebuke had failed shame might bring about a reformation. The sin of theft she loathed as if it were sacrilege; and that which among men of the world is counted little or nothing she declared to be in a monastery a crime of the deepest dye. How shall I describe her kindness and attention towards the sick or the wonderful care and devotion with which she nursed them? Yet, although when others were sick she freely gave them every indulgence, and even allowed them to eat meat; when she fell ill herself, she made no concessions to her own weakness, and seemed unfairly to change in her own case to harshness the kindness which she was always ready to shew to others.

21 No young girl of sound and vigorous constitution could have delivered herself up to a regimen so rigid as that imposed upon herself by Paula whose physical powers age had impaired and enfeebled. I admit that in this she was too determined, refusing to spare herself or to listen to advice. I will relate what I know to be a fact. In the extreme heat of the month of July she was once attacked by a violent fever and we despaired of her life. However by God's mercy she rallied, and the doctors urged upon her the necessity of taking a little light wine to accelerate her recovery; saying that if she continued to drink water they feared that she might become dropsical. I on my side secretly appealed to the blessed pope Epiphanius to admonish, nay even to compel her, to take the wine. But she with her usual sagacity and quickness at once perceived the stratagem, and with a smile let him see that the advice he was giving her was after all not his but mine. Not to waste more words, the blessed prelate after many exhortations left her chamber; and, when I asked him what he had accomplished, replied, "Only this that old as I am I have been almost persuaded to drink no more wine." I relate this story not because I approve of persons rashly taking upon themselves burthens beyond their strength (for does not the scripture say: "Burden not thyself above thy power"?) but because I wish from this quality of perseverance in her to shew

the passion of her mind and the yearning of her believing soul; both of which made her sing in David's words, "My soul thirsteth for thee, my flesh longeth after thee." Difficult as it is always to avoid extremes, the philosophers are quite right in their opinion that virtue is a mean and vice an excess, or as we may express it in one short sentence "In nothing too much." While thus unyielding in her contempt for food Paula was easily moved to sorrow and felt crushed by the deaths of her kinsfolk, especially those of her children. When one after another her husband and her daughters fell asleep, on each occasion the shock of their loss endangered her life. And although she signed her mouth and her breast with the sign of the cross, and endeavoured thus to alleviate a mother's grief; her feelings overpowered her and her maternal instincts were too much for her confiding mind. Thus while her intellect retained its mastery she was overcome by sheer physical weakness. On one occasion a sickness seized her and clung to her so long that it brought anxiety to us and danger to herself. Yet even then she was full of joy and repeated every moment the apostle's words: "O wretched man that I am! who shall deliver me from the body of this death?" The careful reader may say that my words are an invective rather than an eulogy. I call that Jesus whom she served and whom I desire to serve to be my witness that so far from unduly eulogizing her or depreciating her I tell the truth about her as one Christian writing of another; that I am writing a memoir and not a panegyric, and that what were faults in her might well be virtues in others less saintly. I speak thus of her faults to satisfy my own feelings and the passionate regret of us her brothers and sisters, who all of us love her still and all of us deplore her loss.

22 However, she has finished her course, she has kept the faith, and now she enjoys the crown of righteousness. She follows the Lamb whithersoever he goes. She is filled now because once she was hungry. With joy does she sing: "as we have heard, so have we seen in the city of the Lord of hosts, in the city of our God." O blessed change! Once she wept but now laughs for evermore. Once she despised the broken cisterns of which the prophet speaks; but now she has found in the Lord a fountain of life. Once she wore haircloth but now she is clothed in white raiment, and can say: "thou hast put off my sack-cloth, and girded me with gladness." Once she ate ashes like bread and mingled her drink with weeping; saying "my tears have been my meat day and night"; but now for all time she eats the bread of angels and sings: "O taste and see that the Lord is good"; and "my heart is overflowing with a goodly matter; I speak the things which I have made touching the king." She now sees fulfilled Isaiah's words, or rather those of the Lord speaking through Isaiah: "Behold, my servants shall eat but ye shall be hungry: behold, my servants shall drink but ye shall be thirsty: behold, my servants shall rejoice, but ye shall be ashamed: behold, my servants shall sing for

joy of heart, but ye shall cry for sorrow of heart, and shall howl for vexation of spirit." I have said that she always shunned the broken cisterns: she did so that she might find in the Lord a fountain of life, and that she might rejoice and sing: "as the hart panteth after the waterbrooks, so panteth my soul after Thee, O God. When shall I come and appear before God?"

23 I must briefly mention the manner in which she avoided the foul cisterns of the heretics whom she regarded as no better than heathen. A certain cunning knave, in his own estimation both learned and clever, began without my knowledge to put to her such questions as these: What sin has an infant committed that it should be seized by the devil? Shall we be young or old when we rise again? If we die young and rise young, we shall after the resurrection require to have nurses. If however we die young and rise old, the dead will not rise again at all: they will be transformed into new beings. Will there be a distinction of sexes in the next world? Or will there be no such distinction? If the distinction continues, there will be wedlock and sexual intercourse and procreation of children. If however it does not continue, the bodies that rise again will not be the same. For, he argued, "the earthy tabernacle weigheth down the mind that museth upon many things," but the bodies that we shall have in heaven will be subtle and spiritual according to the words of the apostle: "it is sown a natural body: it is raised a spiritual body." From all of which considerations he sought to prove that rational creatures have been for their faults and previous sins subjected to bodily conditions; and that according to the nature and guilt of their transgression they are born in this or that state of life. Some, he said, rejoice in sound bodies and wealthy and noble parents; others have for their portion diseased frames and poverty stricken homes; and by imprisonment in the present world and in bodies pay the penalty of their former sins. Paula listened and reported what she heard to me, at the same time pointing out the man. Thus upon me was laid the task of opposing this most noxious viper and deadly pest. It is of such that the Psalmist speaks when he writes: "deliver not the soul of thy turtle dove unto the wild beast," and "Rebuke the wild beast of the reeds"; creatures who write iniquity and speak lies against the Lord and lift up their mouths against the Most High. As the fellow had tried to deceive Paula, I at her request went to him, and by asking him a few questions involved him in a dilemma. Do you believe, said I, that there will be a resurrection of the dead or do you disbelieve? He replied, I believe. I went on: Will the bodies that rise again be the same or different? He said, The same. Then I asked: What of their sex? Will that remain unaltered or will it be changed? At this question he became silent and swayed his head this way and that as a serpent does to avoid being struck. Accordingly I continued, As you have nothing to say I will answer for you and will draw the conclusion from your premises. If the woman shall not rise again as a woman nor the man as a man, there will

be no resurrection of the dead. For the body is made up of sex and members. But if there shall be no sex and no members what will become of the resurrection of the body, which cannot exist without sex and members? And if there shall be no resurrection of the body, there can be no resurrection of the dead. But as to your objection taken from marriage, that, if the members shall remain the same, marriage must inevitably be allowed; it is disposed of by the Saviour's words: "ye do err not knowing the scriptures nor the power of God. For in the resurrection they neither marry nor are given in marriage but are as the angels." When it is said that they neither marry nor are given in marriage, the distinction of sex is shewn to persist. For no one says of things which have no capacity for marriage such as a stick or a stone that they neither marry nor are given in marriage; but this may well be said of those who while they can marry yet abstain from doing so by their own virtue and by the grace of Christ. But if you cavil at this and say, how shall we in that case be like the angels with whom there is neither male nor female, hear my answer in brief as follows. What the Lord promises to us is not the nature of angels but their mode of life and their bliss. And therefore John the Baptist is called an angel even before he is beheaded, and all God's holy men and virgins manifest in themselves even in this world the life of angels. When it is said "ye shall be like the angels," likeness only is promised and not a change of nature.

24 And now do you in your turn answer me these questions. How do you explain the fact that Thomas felt the hands of the risen Lord and beheld His side pierced by the spear? And the fact that Peter saw the Lord standing on the shore and eating a piece of a roasted fish and a honeycomb. If He stood, He must certainly have had feet. If He pointed to His wounded side He must have also had chest and belly for to these the sides are attached and without them they cannot be. If He spoke, He must have used a tongue and palate and teeth. For as the bow strikes the strings, so to produce vocal sound does the tongue come in contact with the teeth. If His hands were felt, it follows that He must have had arms as well. Since therefore it is admitted that He had all the members which go to make up the body, He must have also had the whole body formed of them, and that not a woman's but a man's; that is to say, He rose again in the sex in which He died. And if you cavil farther and say: We shall eat then, I suppose, after the resurrection; or How can a solid and material body enter in contrary to its nature through closed doors? you shall receive from me this reply. Do not for this matter of food find fault with belief in the resurrection: for our Lord after raising the daughter of the ruler of the synagogue commanded food to be given her. And Lazarus who had been dead four days is described as sitting at meat with Him, the object in both cases being to shew that the resurrection was real and not merely apparent. And if from our Lord's entering in through closed doors you strive

to prove that His body was spiritual and aerial, He must have had this spiritual body even before He suffered; since—contrary to the nature of heavy bodies—He was able to walk upon the sea. The apostle Peter also must be believed to have had a spiritual body for he also walked upon the waters with buoyant step. The true explanation is that when anything is done against nature, it is a manifestation of God's might and power. And to shew plainly that in these great signs our attention is asked not to a change in nature but to the almighty power of God, he who by faith had walked on water began to sink for the want of it and would have done so, had not the Lord lifted him up with the reproving words, "O thou of little faith wherefore didst thou doubt?" I wonder that you can display such effrontery when the Lord Himself said, "reach hither thy finger, and behold my hands; and reach hither thy hand and thrust it into my side: and be not faithless but believing," and in another place, "behold my hands and my feet that it is I myself: handle me and see; for a spirit hath not flesh and bones as ye see me have. And when he had thus spoken he shewed them his hands and his feet." You hear Him speak of bones and flesh, of feet and hands; and yet you want to palm off on me the bubbles and airy nothings of which the stoics rave!

25 Moreover, if you ask how it is that a mere infant which has never sinned is seized by the devil, or at what age we shall rise again seeing that we die at different ages; my only answer—an unwelcome one, I fancy—will be in the words of scripture: "The judgments of God are a great deep," and "O the depth of the riches both of the wisdom and knowledge of God! how unsearchable are his judgments, and his ways past finding out! For who hath known the mind of the Lord? or who hath been his counsellor?" No difference of age can affect the reality of the body. Although our frames are in a perpetual flux and lose or gain daily, these changes do not make us different individuals. I was not one person at ten years old, another at thirty and another at fifty; nor am I another now when all my head is gray. According to the traditions of the church and the teaching of the apostle Paul, the answer must be this; that we shall rise as perfect men in the measure of the stature of the fulness of Christ. At this age the Jews suppose Adam to have been created and at this age we read that the Lord and Saviour rose again. Many other arguments did I adduce from both testaments to stifle the outcry of this heretic.

26 From that day forward so profoundly did Paula commence to loathe the man—and all who agreed with him in his doctrines—that she publicly proclaimed them as enemies of the Lord. I have related this incident less with the design of confuting in a few words a heresy which would require volumes to confute it, than with the object of shewing the great faith of this saintly woman who preferred to subject herself to perpetual hostility from men rather than by friendships hurtful to herself to provoke or to offend God.

27 To revert then to that description of her character which I began a little time ago; no mind was ever more docile than was hers. She was slow to speak and swift to hear, remembering the precept, "Keep silence and hearken, O Israel." The holy scriptures she knew by heart, and said of the history contained in them that it was the foundation of the truth; but, though she loved even this, she still preferred to seek for the underlying spiritual meaning and made this the keystone of the spiritual building raised within her soul. She asked leave that she and her daughter might read over the old and new testaments under my guidance. Out of modesty I at first refused compliance, but as she persisted in her demand and frequently urged me to consent to it, I at last did so and taught her what I had learned not from myself—for self-confidence is the worst of teachers—but from the church's most famous writers. Wherever I stuck fast and honestly confessed myself at fault she would by no means rest content but would force me by fresh questions to point out to her which of many different solutions seemed to me the most probable. I will mention here another fact which to those who are envious may well seem incredible. While I myself beginning as a young man have with much toil and effort partially acquired the Hebrew tongue and study it now unceasingly lest if I leave it, it also may leave me; Paula, on making up her mind that she too would learn it, succeeded so well that she could chant the psalms in Hebrew and could speak the language without a trace of the pronunciation peculiar to Latin. The same accomplishment can be seen to this day in her daughter Eustochium, who always kept close to her mother's side, obeyed all her commands, never slept apart from her, never walked abroad or took a meal without her, never had a penny that she could call her own, rejoiced when her mother gave to the poor her little patrimony, and fully believed that in filial affection she had the best heritage and the truest riches. I must not pass over in silence the joy which Paula felt when she heard her little granddaughter and namesake, the child of Laeta and Toxotius—who was born and I may even say conceived in answer to a vow of her parents dedicating her to virginity—when, I say, she heard the little one in her cradle sing "alleluia" and falter out the words "grandmother" and "aunt." One wish alone made her long to see her native land again; that she might know her son and his wife and child to have renounced the world and to be serving Christ. And it has been granted to her in part. For while her granddaughter is destined to take the veil, her daughter-in-law has vowed herself to perpetual chastity, and by faith and alms emulates the example that her mother has set her. She strives to exhibit at Rome the virtues which Paula set forth in all their fulness at Jerusalem.

28 What ails thee, my soul? Why dost thou shudder to approach her death? I have made my letter longer than it should be already; dreading to come to the end and vainly supposing that by saying nothing of it and by occupying

myself with her praises I could postpone the evil day. Hitherto the wind has been all in my favour and my keel has smoothly ploughed through the heaving waves. But now my speech is running upon the rocks, the billows are mountains high, and imminent shipwreck awaits both you and me. We must needs cry out: "Master, save us, we perish:" and "awake, why sleepest thou, O Lord?" For who could tell the tale of Paula's dying with dry eyes? She fell into a most serious illness and thus gained what she most desired, power to leave us and to be joined more fully to the Lord. Eustochium's affection for her mother, always true and tried, in this time of sickness approved itself still more to all. She sat by Paula's bedside, she fanned her, she supported her head, she arranged her pillows, she chafed her feet, she rubbed her stomach, she smoothed down the bedclothes, she heated hot water, she brought towels. In fact she anticipated the servants in all their duties, and when one of them did anything she regarded it as so much taken away from her own gain. How unceasingly she prayed, how copiously she wept, how constantly she ran to and fro between her prostrate mother and the cave of the Lord! imploring God that she might not be deprived of a companion so dear, that if Paula was to die she might herself no longer live, and that one bier might carry to burial her and her mother. Alas for the frailty and perishableness of human nature! Except that our belief in Christ raises us up to heaven and promises eternity to our souls, the physical conditions of life are the same for us as for the brutes. "There is one event to the righteous and to the wicked; to the good and to the evil; to the clean and to the unclean; to him that sacrificeth and to him that sacrificeth not: as is the good so is the sinner; and he that sweareth as he that feareth an oath." Man and beast alike are dissolved into dust and ashes.

29 Why do I still linger, and prolong my suffering by postponing it? Paula's intelligence shewed her that her death was near. Her body and limbs grew cold and only in her holy breast did the warm beat of the living soul continue. Yet, as though she were leaving strangers to go home to her own people, she whispered the verses of the psalmist: "Lord, I have loved the habitation of thy house and the place where thine honour dwelleth," and "How amiable are thy tabernacles, O Lord of hosts! My soul longeth yea even fainteth for the courts of the Lord," and "I had rather be an outcast in the house of my God than to dwell in the tents of wickedness." When I asked her why she remained silent refusing to answer my call, and whether she was in pain, she replied in Greek that she had no suffering and that all things were to her eyes calm and tranquil. After this she said no more but closed her eyes as though she already despised all mortal things, and kept repeating the verses just quoted down to the moment in which she breathed out her soul, but in a tone so low that we could scarcely hear what she said. Raising her finger also to her mouth she made the sign of the cross upon her lips. Then her

breath failed her and she gasped for death; yet even when her soul was eager to break free, she turned the death-rattle (which comes at last to all) into the praise of the Lord. The bishop of Jerusalem and some from other cities were present, also a great number of the inferior clergy, both priests and levites. The entire monastery was filled with bodies of virgins and monks. As soon as Paula heard the bridegroom saying: "Rise up my love my fair one, my dove, and come away: for, lo, the winter is past, the rain is over and gone," she answered joyfully "the flowers appear on the earth; the time to cut them has come" and "I believe that I shall see the good things of the Lord in the land of the living."

30 No weeping or lamentation followed her death, such as are the custom of the world; but all present united in chanting the psalms in their several tongues. The bishops lifted up the dead woman with their own hands, placed her upon a bier, and carrying her on their shoulders to the church in the cave of the Saviour, laid her down in the centre of it. Other bishops meantime carried torches and tapers in the procession, and yet others led the singing of the choirs. The whole population of the cities of Palestine came to her funeral. Not a single monk lurked in the desert or lingered in his cell. Not a single virgin remained shut up in the seclusion of her chamber. To each and all it would have seemed sacrilege to have withheld the last tokens of respect from a woman so saintly. As in the case of Dorcas, the widows and the poor shewed the garments Paula had given them; while the destitute cried aloud that they had lost in her a mother and a nurse. Strange to say, the paleness of death had not altered her expression; only a certain solemnity and seriousness had overspread her features. You would have thought her not dead but asleep.

One after another they chanted the psalms, now in Greek, now in Latin, now in Syriac; and this not merely for the three days which elapsed before she was buried beneath the church and close to the cave of the Lord, but throughout the remainder of the week. All who were assembled felt that it was their own funeral at which they were assisting, and shed tears as if they themselves had died. Paula's daughter, the revered virgin Eustochium, "as a child that is weaned of his mother," could not be torn away from her parent. She kissed her eyes, pressed her lips upon her brow, embraced her frame, and wished for nothing better than to be buried with her.

31 Jesus is witness that Paula has left not a single penny to her daughter but, as I said before, on the contrary a large mass of debt; and, worse even than this, a crowd of brothers and sisters whom it is hard for her to support but whom it would be undutiful to cast off. Could there be a more splendid instance of self-renunciation than that of this noble lady who in the fervour of her faith gave away so much of her wealth that she reduced herself to the last degree of poverty? Others may boast, if they will, of money spent in charity,

or large sums heaped up in God's treasury, of votive offerings hung up with cords of gold. None of them has given more to the poor than Paula, for Paula has kept nothing for herself. But now she enjoys the true riches and those good things which eye hath not seen nor ear heard, neither have they entered into the heart of man. If we mourn, it is for ourselves and not for her; yet even so, if we persist in weeping for one who reigns with Christ, we shall seem to envy her her glory.

32 Be not fearful, Eustochium: you are endowed with a splendid heritage. The Lord is your portion; and, to increase your joy, your mother has now after a long martyrdom won her crown. It is not only the shedding of blood that is accounted a confession: the spotless service of a devout mind is itself a daily martyrdom. Both alike are crowned; with roses and violets in the one case, with lilies in the other. Thus in the Song of Songs it is written: "my beloved is white and ruddy"; for, whether the victory be won in peace or in war, God gives the same guerdon to those who win it. Like Abraham your mother heard the words: "get thee out of thy country, and from thy kindred, unto a land that I will shew thee"; and not only that but the Lord's command given through Jeremiah: "flee out of the midst of Babylon, and deliver every man his soul." To the day of her death she never returned to Chaldaea, or regretted the fleshpots of Egypt or its strong-smelling meats. Accompanied by her virgin bands she became a fellow-citizen of the Saviour; and now that she has ascended from her little Bethlehem to the heavenly realms she can say to the true Naomi: "thy people shall be my people and thy God my God."

33 I have spent the labour of two nights in dictating for you this treatise; and in doing so I have felt a grief as deep as your own. I say in "dictating" for I have not been able to write it myself. As often as I have taken up my pen and have tried to fulfil my promise; my fingers have stiffened, my hand has fallen, and my power over it has vanished. The rudeness of the diction, devoid as it is of all elegance or charm, bears witness to the feeling of the writer.

34 And now, Paula, farewell, and aid with your prayers the old age of your votary. Your faith and your works unite you to Christ; thus standing in His presence you will the more readily gain what you ask. In this letter "I have built" to your memory "a monument more lasting than bronze," which no lapse of time will be able to destroy. And I have cut an inscription on your tomb, which I here subjoin; that, wherever my narrative may go, the reader may learn that you are buried at Bethlehem and not uncommemorated there.

THE INSCRIPTION OF PAULA'S TOMB

> Within this tomb a child of Scipio lies,
> A daughter of the farfamed Pauline house,

A scion of the Gracchi, of the stock
Of Agamemnon's self, illustrious:
Here rests the lady Paula, well-beloved
Of both her parents, with Eustochium
For daughter; she the first of Roman dames
Who hardship chose and Bethlehem for Christ.

In front of the cavern there is another inscription as follows:

Seest thou here hollowed in the rock a grave,
'Tis Paula's tomb; high heaven has her soul.
Who Rome and friends, riches and home forsook
Here in this lonely spot to find her rest.
For here Christ's manger was, and here the kings
To Him, both God and man, their off'rings made.

35 The holy and blessed Paula fell asleep on the seventh day before the Kalends of February, on the third day of the week, after the sun had set. She was buried on the fifth day before the same Kalends, in the sixth consulship of the Emperor Honorius and the first of Aristaenetus. She lived in the vows of religion five years at Rome and twenty years at Bethlehem. The whole duration of her life was fifty-six years eight months and twenty-one days.

● 72

Discord between an Ascetic Mother and Daughter, Each of Whom Was Living with a Monk

JEROME *Letter* 117, to the two unnamed women   405 C.E.?

AUTHOR, TRANSLATION, TEXT, AND BIBLIOGRAPHY: See entry 70.

INTRODUCTION

1 A certain brother from Gaul has told me that his virgin-sister and widowed mother, though living in the same city, have separate abodes and have taken to themselves clerical protectors either as guests or stewards; and that by thus associating with strangers they have caused more scandal than by living apart. When I groaned and expressed what I felt more by silence than words; "I beseech you," said he, "rebuke them in a letter and recall them to mutual harmony; make them once more mother and daughter." To whom I replied, "a nice task this that you lay upon me, for me a stranger to reconcile two women whom you, a son and brother, have failed to influence. You speak as though I occupied the chair of a bishop instead of being shut up in a monastic cell where, far removed from the world's turmoil, I lament the sins of the past and try to avoid the temptations of the present. Moreover, it is surely inconsistent, while one buries oneself out of sight, to allow one's tongue free

course through the world." "You are too fearful," he replied; "where is that old hardihood of yours which made you 'scour the world with copious salt,' as Horace says of Lucilius?" "It is this," I rejoined, "that makes me shy and forbids me to open my lips. For through accusing crime I have been myself made out a criminal. Men have disputed and denied my assertions until, as the proverb goes, I hardly know whether I have ears or feeling left. The very walls have resounded with curses levelled at me, and 'I was the song of drunkards.' Under the compulsion of an unhappy experience I have learned to be silent, thinking it better to set a watch before my mouth and to keep the door of my lips than to incline my heart to any evil thing, or, while censuring the faults of others, myself to fall into that of detraction." In answer to this he said: "Speaking the truth is not detraction. Nor will you lecture the world by administering a particular rebuke; for there are few persons, if any, open to this special charge. I beg of you, therefore, as I have put myself to the trouble of this long journey, that you will not suffer me to have come for nothing. The Lord knows that, after the sight of the holy places, my principal object in coming has been to heal by a letter from you the division between my sister and my mother." "Well," I replied, "I will do as you wish, for after all the letters will be to persons beyond the sea and words written with reference to definite persons can seldom offend other people. But I must ask you to keep what I say secret. You will take my advice with you to encourage you by the way; if it is listened to, I will rejoice as much as you; while if, as I rather think, it is rejected, I shall have wasted my words and you will have made a long journey for nothing."

THE LETTER

2 In the first place my sister and my daughter, I wish you to know that I am not writing to you because I suspect anything evil of you. On the contrary I implore you to live in harmony, so as to give no ground for any such suspicions. Moreover had I supposed you fast bound in sin—far be this from you— I should never have written, for I should have known that my words would be addressed to deaf ears. Again, if I write to you somewhat sharply, I beg of you to ascribe this not to any harshness on my part but to the nature of the ailment which I attempt to treat. Cautery and the knife are the only remedies when mortification has once set in; poison is the only antidote known for poison; great pain can only be relieved by inflicting greater pain. Lastly I must say this that even if your own consciences acquit you of misdoing, yet the very rumour of such brings disgrace upon you. Mother and daughter are names of affection; they imply natural ties and reciprocal duties; they form the closest of human relations after that which binds the soul to God. If you love each other, your conduct calls for no praise: but if you hate each other, you have committed a crime. The Lord Jesus was subject to His parents. He

reverenced that mother of whom He was Himself the parent; He respected the foster-father whom He had Himself fostered; for He remembered that He had been carried in the womb of the one and in the arms of the other. Wherefore also when He hung upon the cross He commended to His disciple the mother whom He had never before His passion parted from Himself.

3 Well, I shall say no more to the mother, for perhaps age, weakness, and loneliness make sufficient excuses for her, but to you the daughter I say: "Is a mother's house too small for you whose womb was not too small? When you have lived with her for ten months in the one, can you not bear to live with her for one day in the other? or are you unable to meet her gaze? Can it be that one who has borne you and reared you, who has brought you up and knows you, is dreaded by you as a witness of your home-life? If you are a true virgin, why do you fear her careful guardianship; and, if you have fallen, why do you not openly marry? Wedlock is like a plank offered to a ship-wrecked man and by its means you may remedy what previously you have done amiss. I do not mean that you are not to repent of your sin or that you are to continue in evil courses; but, when a tie of the kind has been formed, I despair of breaking it altogether. However, a return to your mother will make it easier for you to bewail the virginity which you have lost through leaving her. Or if you are still unspotted and have not lost your chastity, be careful of it for you may lose it. Why must you live in a house where you must daily struggle for life and death? Can any one sleep soundly with a viper near him? No; for, though it may not attack him it is sure to frighten him. It is better to be where there is no danger, than to be in danger and to escape. In the one case we have a calm; in the other careful steering is necessary. In the one case we are filled with joy; in the other we do but avoid sorrow."

4 But you will perhaps reply: "my mother is not well-behaved, she desires the things of the world, she loves riches, she disregards fasting, she stains her eyes with antimony, she likes to walk abroad in gay attire, she hinders me from the monastic vow, and so I cannot live with her." But first of all, even though she is as you say, you will have the greater reward for refusing to forsake her with all her faults. She has carried you in her womb, she has reared you; with gentle affection she has borne with the troublesome ways of your childhood. She has washed your linen, she has tended you when sick, and the sickness of maternity was not only borne for you but caused by you. She has brought you up to womanhood, she has taught you to love Christ. You ought not to be displeased with the behaviour of a mother who has consecrated you as a virgin to the service of your spouse. Still if you cannot put up with her dainty ways and feel obliged to shun them, and if your mother really is, as people so often say, a woman of the world, you have others, virgins like yourself, the holy company of chastity. Why, when you forsake your

mother, do you choose for companion a man who perhaps has left behind him a sister and mother of his own? You tell me that she is hard to get on with and that he is easy; that she is quarrelsome and that he is amiable. I will ask you one question: Did you go straight from your home to the man or did you fall in with him afterwards? If you went straight to him, the reason why you left your mother is plain. If you fell in with him afterwards, you shew by your choice what you missed under your mother's roof. The pain that I inflict is severe and I feel the knife as much as you. "He that walketh uprightly walketh surely." Only that my conscience would smite me, I should keep silence and be slow to blame others where I am not guiltless myself. Having a beam in my own eye I should be reluctant to see the mote in my neighbour's. But as it is I live far away among Christian brothers; my life with them is honourable as eyewitnesses of it can testify; I rarely see, or am seen by, others. It is most shameless, therefore, in you to refuse to copy me in respect of self-restraint, when you profess to take me as your model. If you say: "my conscience is enough for me too. God is my judge who is witness of my life. I care not what men may say"; let me urge upon you the apostle's words: "provide things honest" not only in the sight of God but also "in the sight of all men." If any one carps at you for being a Christian and a virgin, mind it not; you have left your mother it may be said to live in a monastery among virgins, but censure on this score is your glory. When men blame a maid of God not for self-indulgence but only for insensibility to affection, what they condemn as callous disregard of a parent is really a lively devotion towards God. For you prefer to your mother Him whom you are bidden to prefer to your own soul. And if the day ever comes that she also shall so prefer Him, she will find in you not a daughter only but a sister as well.

5 "What then?" you will say, "is it a crime to have a man of religion in the house with me?" You seize me by the collar and drag me into court either to sanction what I disapprove or else to incur the dislike of many. A man of religion never separates a daughter from her mother. He welcomes both and respects both. A daughter may be as religious as she pleases; still a mother who is a widow is a guaranty for her chastity. If this person whoever he is is of the same age with yourself, he should honour your mother as though she were his own; and, if he is older, he should love you as a daughter and subject you to a mother's discipline. It is not good either for your reputation or for his that he should like you more than your mother: for his affection might appear to be less for you than for your youth. This is what I should say if a monk were not your brother and if you had no relatives able to protect you. But what excuse has a stranger for thrusting himself in where there are both a mother and a brother, the one a widow and the other a monk? It is good for you to feel that you are a daughter and a sister. However, if you

cannot manage both, and if your mother is too hard a morsel to swallow, your brother at any rate should satisfy you. Or, if he is too harsh, she that bore you may prove more gentle. Why do you turn pale? Why do you get excited? Why do you blush, and with trembling lips betray the restlessness of your mind? One thing only can surpass a woman's love for her mother and brother; and that is her passion for her husband.

6 I am told, moreover, that you frequent suburban villas and their pleasant gardens in the company of relatives and intimate friends. I have no doubt that it is some female cousin or connexion who for her own satisfaction carries you about with her as a novel kind of attendant. Far be it from me to suspect that you would desire men's society; even though they should be those of your own family. But pray, maiden, answer me this; do you appear alone in your kinsfolk's society? or do you bring your favourite with you? Shameless as you may be, you will hardly venture to flaunt him in the eyes of the world. If you ever do so, your whole circle will cry out about both you and him; every one's finger will be pointed at you; and your cousins who in your presence to please you call him a monk and a man of religion, will laugh at you behind your back for having such an unnatural husband. If on the other hand you go out alone—which I rather suppose to be the case—you will find yourself clothed in sober garb among slave youths, women married or soon to be so, wanton girls, and dandies with long hair and tight-fitting vests. Some bearded fop will offer you his hand, he will hold you up if you feel tired, and the pressure of his fingers will either be a temptation to you, or will shew that you are a temptation to him. Again when you sit down to table with married men and women, you will have to see kisses in which you have no part, and dishes partaken of which are not for you. Moreover it cannot but do you harm to see other women attired in silk dresses and gold brocades. At table also whether you like it or not, you will be forced to eat flesh and that of different kinds. To make you drink wine they will praise it as a creature of God. To induce you to take baths they will speak of dirt with disgust; and, when on second thoughts you do as you are bid, they will with one voice salute you as spotless and open, a thorough lady. Meantime some singer will give to the company a selection of softly flowing airs; and as he will not venture to look at other men's wives, he will constantly fix his eyes on you who have no protector. He will speak by nods and convey by his tone what he is afraid to put into words. Amid inducements to sensuality so marked as these, even iron wills are apt to be overcome with desire; an appetite which is the more imperious in virgins because they suppose that sweetest of which they have no experience. Heathen legends tell us that sailors actually ran their ships on the rocks that they might listen to the songs of the Sirens; and that the lyre of Orpheus had power to

draw to itself trees and animals and to soften flints. In the banquet-hall chastity is hard to keep. A shining skin shews a sin-stained soul.

7 As a schoolboy I have read of one—and have seen his effigy true to the life in the streets—who continued to cherish an unlawful passion even when his flesh scarcely clung to his bones, and whose malady remained uncured until death cured it. What then will become of you a young girl physically sound, dainty, stout, and ruddy, if you allow yourself free range among flesh-dishes, wines, and baths, not to mention married men and bachelors? Even if when solicited you refuse to consent, you will take the fact of your being asked as evidence that you are considered handsome. A sensual mind pursues dishonourable objects with greater zest than honourable ones; and when a thing is forbidden hankers after it with greater pleasure. Your very dress, cheap and sombre as it is, is an index of your secret feelings. For it has no creases and trails along the ground to make you appear taller than you are. Your vest is purposely ripped asunder to shew what is beneath and while hiding what is repulsive, to reveal what is fair. As you walk, the very creaking of your black and shiny shoes attracts the notice of the young men. You wear stays to keep your breasts in place, and a heaving girdle closely confines your chest. Your hair covers either your forehead or your ears. Sometimes too you let your shawl drop so as to lay bare your white shoulders; and, as if unwilling that they should be seen, you quickly conceal what you have purposely disclosed. And when in public you for modesty's sake cover your face, like a practised harlot you only shew what is likely to please.

8 You will exclaim "How do you know what I am like, or how, when you are so far away, can you see what I am doing?" Your own brother's tears and sobs have told me, his frequent and scarcely endurable bursts of grief. Would that he had lied or that his words had been words of apprehension only and not of accusation. But, believe me, liars do not shed tears. He is indignant that you prefer to himself a young man, not it is true clothed in silk or wearing his hair long but muscular and dainty in the midst of his squalor; and that this fellow holds the purse-strings, looks after the weaving, allots the servants their tasks, rules the household, and buys from the market all that is needed. He is at once steward and master, and as he anticipates the slaves in their duties, he is carped at by all the domestics. Everything that their mistress has not given them they declare that he has stolen from them. Servants as a class are full of complaints; and no matter what you give them, it is always too little. For they do not consider how much you have but only how much you give; and they make up for their chagrin in the only way they can, that is, by grumbling. One calls him a parasite, another an impostor, another a money-seeker, another by some novel appellation that hits his fancy. They noise it abroad that he is constantly at your bed-side, that when you are sick he runs to fetch nurses, that he holds basins, airs sheets, and folds bandages

for you. The world is only too ready to believe scandal, and stories invented at home soon get afloat abroad. Nor need you be surprised if your servant-men and servantmaids get up such tales about you, when even your mother and your brother complain of your conduct.

9 Do, therefore, what I advise you and entreat you to do: if possible, be reconciled with your mother; or, if this may not be, at least come to terms with your brother. Or if you are filled with an implacable hatred of relationships usually so dear, separate at all events from the man, whom you are said to prefer to your own flesh and blood, and, if even this is impossible for you (for, if you could leave him, you would certainly return to your own), pay more regard to appearances in harbouring him as your companion. Live in a separate building and take your meals apart; for if you remain under one roof with him slanderers will say that you share with him your bed. You may thus easily get help from him when you feel you need it, and yet to a considerable degree escape public discredit. Yet you must take care not to contract the stain of which Jeremiah tells us that no nitre or fuller's soap can wash it out. When you wish him to come to see you, always have witnesses present; either friends, or freedmen, or slaves. A good conscience is afraid of no man's eyes. Let him come in unembarrassed and go out at his ease. Let his silent looks, his unspoken words and his whole carriage, though at times they may imply embarrassment, yet indicate peace of mind. Pray, open your ears and listen to the outcry of the whole city. You have already both of you lost your own names and are known each by that of the other. You are spoken of as his, and he is said to be yours. Your mother and your brother have heard this and are ready to take you in between them. They implore you to consent to this arrangement, so that the scandal of your intimacy with this man which is confined to yourself may give place to a glory common to all. You can live with your mother and he with your brother. You can more boldly shew your regard for one who is your brother's comrade; and your mother will more properly esteem one who is the friend of her son and not of her daughter. But if you frown and refuse to accept my advice, this letter will openly expostulate with you. "Why," it will say, "do you beset another man's servant? Why do you make Christ's minister your slave? Look at the people and scan each face as it comes under your view. When he reads in the church all eyes are fixed upon you; and you, using the licence of a wife, glory in your shame. Secret infamy no longer contents you; you call boldness freedom; 'you have a whore's forehead and refuse to be ashamed.' "

10 Once more you exclaim that I am over-suspicious, a thinker of evil, too ready to follow rumours. What? I suspicious? I ill-natured? I, who as I said in the beginning have taken up my pen because I have no suspicions? Or is it you that are careless, loose, disdainful? You who at the age of twenty-five have netted in your embrace a youth whose beard has scarcely grown? An

excellent instructor he must be, able no doubt by his severe looks both to warn and frighten you! No age is safe from lust, yet gray hairs are some security for decent conduct. A day will surely come (for time glides by imperceptibly) when your handsome young favourite will find a wealthier or more youthful mistress. For women soon age and particularly if they live with men. You will be sorry for your decision and regret your obstinacy in a day when your means and reputation shall be alike gone, and when this unhappy intimacy shall be happily broken off. But perhaps you feel sure of your ground and see no reason to fear a breach where affection has had so long a time to develop and grow.

11 To you also, her mother, I must say a word. Your years put you beyond the reach of scandal; do not take advantage of this to indulge in sin. It is more fitting that your daughter should learn from you how to part from a companion than that you should learn from her how to give up a paramour. You have a son, a daughter, and a son-in-law, or at least one who is your daughter's partner. Why then should you seek other society than theirs, or wish to kindle anew expiring flames? It would be more becoming in you to screen your daughter's fault than to make it an excuse for your own misdoing. Your son is a monk, and, if he were to live with you, he would strengthen you in your religious profession and in your vow of widowhood. Why should you take in a complete stranger, especially in a house not large enough to hold a son and a daughter? You are old enough to have grandchildren. Invite the pair home then. Your daughter went away by herself; let her return with this man. I say "man" and not "husband" that none may cavil. The word describes his sex and not his relation to her. Or if she blushes to accept your offer or finds the house in which she was born too narrow for her, then move both of you to her abode. However limited may be its accommodation, it can take in a mother and a brother better than a stranger. In fact, if she lives in the same house and occupies the same room with a man, she cannot long preserve her chastity. It is different when two women and two men live together. If the third person concerned—he, I mean, who fosters your old age—will not make one of the party and causes only dissension and confusion, the pair of you can do without him. But if the three of you remain together, then your brother and son will offer him a sister and a mother. Others may speak of the two strangers as step-father and son-in-law; but your son must speak of them as his foster-father and his brother.

NOTE

12 Working quickly I have completed this letter in a single night anxious alike to gratify a friend and to try my hand on a rhetorical theme. Then early in the morning he has knocked at my door on the point of starting. I wish

also to shew my detractors that like them I too can say the first thing that comes into my head. I have, therefore, introduced few quotations from the scriptures and have not, as in most of my books, interwoven its flowers in my discourse. The letter has been, in fact, dictated off-hand and poured forth by lamp-light so fast that my tongue has outstripped my secretaries' pens and that my volubility has baffled the expedients of shorthand. I have said this much that those who make no allowances for want of ability may make some for want of time.

● 73

The Life of Marcella, a Founder of Women's Ascetic Enclaves

JEROME *Letter* 127, to Principia   412 C.E.

NOTE: This "life" of Marcella, apparently composed by Jerome at the behest of Principia, another Roman Christian ascetic woman, could also have been included in section 5, "Holy, Pious, and Exemplary Women." Although Marcella was unquestionably a historical person, Jerome's representation of her here owes much to ancient conventions (his own protestations to the contrary notwithstanding) and constructions of gender. Like his life of Paula (entry 70), it exemplifies many of the methodological and theoretical questions posed in the various introductory sections to this anthology.

1 You have besought me often and earnestly, Principia, virgin of Christ, to dedicate a letter to the memory of that holy woman Marcella, and to set forth the goodness long enjoyed by us for others to know and to imitate. I am so anxious myself to do justice to her merits that it grieves me that you should spur me on and fancy that your entreaties are needed when I do not yield even to you in love of her. In putting upon record her signal virtues I shall receive far more benefit myself than I can possibly confer upon others. If I have hitherto remained silent and have allowed two years to go over without making any sign, this has not been owing to a wish to ignore her as you wrongly suppose, but to an incredible sorrow which so overcame my mind that I judged it better to remain silent for a while than to praise her virtues in inadequate language. Neither will I now follow the rules of rhetoric in eulogizing one so dear to both of us and to all the saints, Marcella the glory of her native Rome. I will not set forth her illustrious family and lofty lineage, nor will I trace her pedigree through a line of consuls and praetorian prefects. I will praise her for nothing but the virtue which is her own and which is the more noble, because forsaking both wealth and rank she has sought the true nobility of poverty and lowliness.

2 Her father's death left her an orphan, and she had been married less than seven months when her husband was taken from her. Then as she was

young, and highborn, as well as distinguished for her beauty—always an attraction to men—and her self-control, an illustrious consular named Cerealis paid court to her with great assiduity. Being an old man he offered to make over to her his fortune so that she might consider herself less his wife than his daughter. Her mother Albina went out of her way to secure for the young widow so exalted a protector. But Marcella answered: "had I a wish to marry and not rather to dedicate myself to perpetual chastity, I should look for a husband and not for an inheritance;" and when her suitor argued that sometimes old men live long while young men die early, she cleverly retorted: "a young man may indeed die early, but an old man cannot live long." This decided rejection of Cerealis convinced others that they had no hope of winning her hand.

In the gospel according to Luke we read the following passage: "there was one Anna, a prophetess, the daughter of Phanuel, of the tribe of Aser: she was of great age, and had lived with an husband seven years from her virginity; and she was a widow of about fourscore and four years, which departed not from the temple but served God with fastings and prayers night and day." It was no marvel that she won the vision of the Saviour, whom she sought so earnestly. Let us then compare her case with that of Marcella and we shall see that the latter has every way the advantage. Anna lived with her husband seven years; Marcella seven months. Anna only hoped for Christ; Marcella held Him fast. Anna confessed him at His birth; Marcella believed in Him crucified. Anna did not deny the Child; Marcella rejoiced in the Man as king. I do not wish to draw distinctions between holy women on the score of their merits, as some persons have made it a custom to do as regards holy men and leaders of churches; the conclusion at which I aim is that, as both have one task, so both have one reward.

3 In a slander-loving community such as Rome, filled as it formerly was with people from all parts and bearing the palm for wickedness of all kinds, detraction assailed the upright and strove to defile even the pure and the clean. In such an atmosphere it is hard to escape from the breath of calumny. A stainless reputation is difficult nay almost impossible to attain; the prophet yearns for it but hardly hopes to win it: "Blessed," he says, "are the undefiled in the way who walk in the law of the Lord." The undefiled in the way of this world are those whose fair fame no breath of scandal has ever sullied, and who have earned no reproach at the hands of their neighbours. It is this which makes the Saviour say in the gospel: "agree with," or be complaisant to, "thine adversary whilst thou art in the way with him." Who ever heard a slander of Marcella that deserved the least credit? Or who ever credited such without making himself guilty of malice and defamation? No; she put the Gentiles to confusion by shewing them the nature of that Christian widowhood which her conscience and mien alike set forth. For women of the world

are wont to paint their faces with rouge and white-lead, to wear robes of shining silk, to adorn themselves with jewels, to put gold chains round their necks, to pierce their ears and hang in them the costliest pearls of the Red Sea, and to scent themselves with musk. While they mourn for the husbands they have lost they rejoice at their own deliverance and freedom to choose fresh partners—not, as God wills, to obey these but to rule over them.

With this object in view they select for their partners poor men who contented with the mere name of husbands are the more ready to put up with rivals as they know that, if they so much as murmur, they will be cast off at once. Our widow's clothing was meant to keep out the cold and not to shew her figure. Of gold she would not wear so much as a seal-ring, choosing to store her money in the stomachs of the poor rather than to keep it at her own disposal. She went nowhere without her mother, and would never see without witnesses such monks and clergy as the needs of a large house required her to interview. Her train was always composed of virgins and widows, and these women serious and staid; for, as she well knew, the levity of the maids speaks ill for the mistress and a woman's character is shewn by her choice of companions.

4 Her delight in the divine scriptures was incredible. She was for ever singing, "Thy words have I hid in mine heart that I might not sin against thee," as well as the words which describe the perfect man, "his delight is in the law of the Lord; and in his law doth he meditate day and night." This meditation in the law she understood not of a review of the written words as among the Jews the Pharisees think, but of action according to that saying of the apostle, "whether, therefore, ye eat or drink or what soever ye do, do all to the glory of God." She remembered also the prophet's words, "through thy precepts I get understanding," and felt sure that only when she had fulfilled these would she be permitted to understand the scriptures. In this sense we read elsewhere that "Jesus began both to do and teach." For teaching is put to the blush when a man's conscience rebukes him; and it is in vain that his tongue preaches poverty or teaches alms-giving if he is rolling in the riches of Croesus and if, in spite of his threadbare cloak, he has silken robes at home to save from the moth.

Marcella practised fasting, but in moderation. She abstained from eating flesh, and she knew rather the scent of wine than its taste; touching it only for her stomach's sake and for her often infirmities. She seldom appeared in public and took care to avoid the houses of great ladies, that she might not be forced to look upon what she had once for all renounced. She frequented the basilicas of apostles and martyrs that she might escape from the throng and give herself to private prayer. So obedient was she to her mother that for her sake she did things of which she herself disapproved. For example, when her mother, careless of her own offspring, was for transferring all her property from her children and grandchildren to her brother's family, Marcella wished the money to be given to the poor instead, and yet could not bring herself to thwart her parent. Therefore she made over her ornaments and other effects to persons already rich, content to throw away her money rather than to sadden her mother's heart.

5 In those days no highborn lady at Rome had made profession of the monastic life, or had ventured—so strange and ignominious and degrading did it then seem—publicly to call herself a nun. It was from some priests of Alexandria, and from pope Athanasius, and subsequently from Peter, who, to escape the persecution of the Arian heretics, had all fled for refuge to Rome as the safest haven in which they could find communion—it was from these that Marcella heard of the life of the blessed Antony, then still alive, and of the monasteries in the Thebaid founded by Pachomius, and of the discipline laid down for virgins and for widows. Nor was she ashamed to profess a life which she had thus learned to be pleasing to Christ. Many years after her example was followed first by Sophronia and then by others, of whom it may be well said in the words of Ennius:

> Would that ne'er in Pelion's woods
> Had the axe these pinetrees felled.

My revered friend Paula was blessed with Marcella's friendship, and it was in Marcella's cell that Eustochium, that paragon of virgins, was gradually trained. Thus it is easy to see of what type the mistress was who found such pupils.

The unbelieving reader may perhaps laugh at me for dwelling so long on the praises of mere women; yet if he will but remember how holy women followed our Lord and Saviour and ministered to Him of their substance, and how the three Marys stood before the cross and especially how Mary Magdalen—called the tower from the earnestness and glow of her faith—was privileged to see the rising Christ first of all before the very apostles, he will convict himself of pride sooner than me of folly. For we judge of people's virtue not by their sex but by their character, and hold those to be worthy of the highest glory who have renounced both rank and wealth. It was for this reason that Jesus loved the evangelist John more than the other disciples. For John was of noble birth and known to the high priest, yet was so little appalled by the plottings of the Jews that he introduced Peter into his court, and was the only one of the apostles bold enough to take his stand before the cross. For it was he who took the Savior's parent to his own home; it was the virgin son who received the virgin mother as a legacy from the Lord.

6 Marcella then lived the ascetic life for many years, and found herself old before she bethought herself that she had once been young. She often quoted with approval Plato's saying that philosophy consists in meditating on death.

A truth which our own apostle indorses when he says: "for your salvation I die daily." Indeed according to the old copies our Lord himself says: "whosoever doth not bear His cross daily and come after me cannot be my disciple." Ages before, the Holy Spirit had said by the prophet: "for thy sake are we killed all the day long: we are counted as sheep for the slaughter." Many generations afterwards the words were spoken: "remember the end and thou shalt never do amiss," as well as that precept of the eloquent satirist: "live with death in your mind; time flies; this say of mine is so much taken from it." Well then, as I was saying, she passed her days and lived always in the thought that she must die. Her very clothing was such as to remind her of the tomb, and she presented herself as a living sacrifice, reasonable and acceptable, unto God.

7 When the needs of the Church at length brought me to Rome in company with the reverend pontiffs, Paulinus and Epiphanius—the first of whom ruled the church of the Syrian Antioch while the second presided over that of Salamis in Cyprus—I in my modesty was for avoiding the eyes of highborn ladies, yet she pleaded so earnestly, "both in season and out of season" as the apostle says, that at last her perseverance overcame my reluctance. And, as in those days my name was held in some renown as that of a student of the scriptures, she never came to see me that she did not ask me some question concerning them, nor would she at once acquiesce in my explanations but on the contrary would dispute them; not, however, for argument's sake but to learn the answers to those objections which might, as she saw, be made to my statements. How much virtue and ability, how much holiness and purity I found in her I am afraid to say; both lest I may exceed the bounds of men's belief and lest I may increase your sorrow by reminding you of the blessings that you have lost. This much only will I say, that whatever in me was the fruit of long study and as such made by constant meditation a part of my nature, this she tasted, this she learned and made her own. Consequently after my departure from Rome, in case of a dispute arising as to the testimony of scripture on any subject, recourse was had to her to settle it. And so wise was she and so well did she understand what philosophers call *to prepon*, that is, "the becoming," in what she did, that when she answered questions she gave her own opinion not as her own but as from me or some one else, thus admitting that what she taught she had herself learned from others. For she knew that the apostle had said: "I suffer not a woman to teach," and she would not seem to inflict a wrong upon the male sex many of whom (including sometimes priests) questioned her concerning obscure and doubtful points.

8 I am told that my place with her was immediately taken by you, that you attached yourself to her, and that, as the saying goes, you never let even a hair's-breadth come between her and you. You both lived in the same house

and occupied the same room so that every one in the city knew for certain that you had found a mother in her and she a dauhter in you. In the suburbs you found for yourselves a monastic seclusion, and chose the country instead of the town because of its loneliness. For a long time you lived together, and as many ladies shaped their conduct by your examples, I had the joy of seeing Rome transformed into another Jerusalem. Monastic establishments for virgins became numerous, and of hermits there were countless numbers. In fact so many were the servants of God that monasticism which had before been a term of reproach became subsequently one of honour. Meantime we consoled each other for our separation by words of mutual encouragement, and discharged in the spirit the debt which in the flesh we could not pay. We always went to meet each other's letters, tried to outdo each other in attentions, and anticipated each other in courteous inquiries. Not much was lost by a separation thus effectually bridged by a constant correspondence.

9 While Marcella was thus serving the Lord in holy tranquillity, there arose in these provinces a tornado of heresy which threw everything into confusion; indeed so great was the fury into which it lashed itself that it spared neither itself nor anything that was good. And as if it were too little to have disturbed everything here, it introduced a ship freighted with blasphemies into the port of Rome itself. The dish soon found itself a cover; and the muddy feet of heretics fouled the clear waters of the faith of Rome. No wonder that in the streets and in the market places a soothsayer can strike fools on the back or, catching up his cudgel, shatter the teeth of such as carp at him, when such venomous and filthy teaching as this has found at Rome dupes whom it can lead astray. Next came the scandalous version of Origen's book *On First Principles*, and that "fortunate" disciple who would have been indeed fortunate had he never fallen in with such a master. Next followed the confutation set forth by my supporters, which destroyed the case of the Pharisees and threw them into confusion. It was then that the holy Marcella, who had long held back lest she should be thought to act from party motives, threw herself into the breach. Conscious that the faith of Rome—once praised by an apostle—was now in danger, and that this new heresy was drawing to itself not only priests and monks but also many of the laity besides imposing on the bishop who fancied others are guileless as he was himself, she publicly withstood its teachers choosing to please God rather than men.

10 In the gospel the Saviour commends the unjust steward because, although he defrauded his master, he acted wisely for his own interests. The heretics in this instance pursued the same course; for, seeing how great a matter a little fire had kindled, and that the flames applied by them to the foundations had by this time reached the housetops, and that the deception practised on many could no longer be hid, they asked for and obtained letters of commendation

from the church, so that it might appear that till the day of their departure they had continued in full communion with it. Shortly afterwards the distinguished Anastasius succeeded to the pontificate; but he was soon taken away, for it was not fitting that the head of the world should be struck off during the episcopate of one so great. He was removed, no doubt, that he might not seek to turn away by his prayers the sentence of God passed once for all. For the words of the Lord to Jeremiah concerning Israel applied equally to Rome: "pray not for this people for their good. When they fast I will not hear their cry; and when they offer burnt-offering and oblation, I will not accept them; but I will consume them by the sword and by the famine and by the pestilence." You will say, what has this to do with the praises of Marcella? I reply, She it was who originated the condemnation of the heretics. She it was who furnished witnesses first taught by them and then carried away by their heretical teaching. She it was who showed how large a number they had deceived and who brought up against them the impious books *On First Principles*, books which were passing from hand to hand after being "improved" by the hand of the scorpion. She it was lastly who called on the heretics in letter after letter to appear in their own defence. They did not indeed venture to come, for they were so conscience-stricken that they let the case go against them by default rather than face their accusers and be convicted by them. This glorious victory originated with Marcella, she was the source and cause of this great blessing. You who shared the honour with her know that I speak the truth. You know too that out of many incidents I only mention a few, not to tire out the reader by a wearisome recapitulation. Were I to say more, ill natured persons might fancy me, under pretext of commending a woman's virtues, to be giving vent to my own rancour. I will pass now to the remainder of my story.

11 The whirlwind passed from the West into the East and threatened in its passage to shipwreck many a noble craft. Then were the words of Jesus fulfilled: "when the son of man cometh, shall he find faith on the earth?" The love of many waxed cold. Yet the few who still loved the true faith rallied to my side. Men openly sought to take their lives and every expedient was employed against them. So hotly indeed did the persecution rage that "Barnabas also was carried away with their dissimulation"; nay more he committed murder, if not in actual violence at least in will. Then behold God blew and the tempest passed away; so that the prediction of the prophet was fulfilled, "thou takest away their breath, they die, and return to their dust. In that very day his thoughts perish," as also the gospel-saying, "Thou fool, this night thy soul shall be required of thee: then whose shall those things be, which thou hast provided?"

12 Whilst these things were happening in Jebus a dreadful rumour came from the West. Rome had been besieged and its citizens had been forced to

buy their lives with gold. Then thus despoiled they had been besieged again so as to lose not their substance only but their lives. My voice sticks in my throat; and, as I dictate, sobs choke my utterance. The City which had taken the whole world was itself taken; nay more famine was beforehand with the sword and but few citizens were left to be made captives. In their frenzy the starving people had recourse to hideous food; and tore each other limb from limb that they might have flesh to eat. Even the mother did not spare the babe at her breast. In the night was Moab taken, in the night did her wall fall down. "O God, the heathen have come into thine inheritance; thy holy temple have they defiled; they have made Jerusalem an orchard. The dead bodies of thy servants have they given to be meat unto the fowls of the heaven, the flesh of thy saints unto the beasts of the earth. Their blood have they shed like water round about Jerusalem; and there was none to bury them."

> Who can set forth the carnage of that night?
> What tears are equal to its agony?
> Of ancient date a sovran city falls;
> And lifeless in its streets and houses lie
> Unnumbered bodies of its citizens.
> In many a ghastly shape doth death appear.

13 Meantime, as was natural in a scene of such confusion, one of the bloodstained victors found his way into Marcella's house. Now be it mine to say what I have heard, to relate what holy men have seen; for there were some such present and they say that you too were with her in the hour of danger. When the soldiers entered she is said to have received them without any look of alarm; and when they asked her for gold she pointed to her coarse dress to shew them that she had no buried treasure. However they would not believe in her self-chosen poverty, but scourged her and beat her with cudgels. She is said to have felt no pain but to have thrown herself at their feet and to have pleaded with tears for you, that you might not be taken from her, or owing to your youth have to endure what she as an old woman had no occasion to fear. Christ softened their hard hearts and even among bloodstained swords natural affection asserted its rights. The barbarians conveyed both you and her to the basilica of the apostle Paul, that you might find there either a place of safety or, if not that, at least a tomb. Hereupon Marcella is said to have burst into great joy and to have thanked God for having kept you unharmed in answer to her prayer. She said she was thankful too that the taking of the city had found her poor, not made her so, that she was now in want of daily bread, that Christ satisfied her needs so that she no longer felt hunger, that she was able to say in word and in deed: "naked came I out of my mother's womb, and naked shall I return thither: the Lord gave and the Lord hath taken away; blessed be the name of the Lord."

14 After a few days she fell asleep in the Lord; but to the last her powers remained unimpaired. You she made the heir of her poverty, or rather the poor through you. When she closed her eyes, it was in your arms; when she breathed her last breath, your lips received it; you shed tears but she smiled, conscious of having led a good life and hoping for her reward hereafter.

In one short night I have dictated this letter in honour of you, revered Marcella, and of you, my daughter Principia; not to shew off my own eloquence but to express my heartfelt gratitude to you both; my one desire has been to please both God and my readers.

● 74

A Consoling Letter from the Exiled John Chrysostom to His Friend Olympias, Seeking Her Political Support

JOHN CHRYSOSTOM *Letter* 9, John Chrysostom to Olympias   404 C.E.

AUTHOR: See entry 41.

TRANSLATION: NPNFC, ser. 1, vol. 9.

TEXT: SC 13 (A.-M. Malingrey, 2d ed., 1968).

BIBLIOGRAPHY: Elizabeth A. Clark, *Jerome, Chrysostom, and Friends: Essays and Translations*, 2d ed. (New York: Edwin Mellen Press, 1982); Elizabeth A. Clark, "Theory and Practice in Late Ancient Asceticism: Jerome, Chrysostom, and Augustine," *Journal of Feminist Studies in Religion* 5, no. 1 (1989): 25–46; Gillian Clark, *Women in Late Antiquity: Pagan and Christian Life-styles* (Oxford: Clarendon Press; New York: Oxford University Press, 1993); Gillian Cloke, *This Female Man of God: Women and Spiritual Power in the Patristic Age, 350–450* (London and New York: Routledge, 1995); Margaret Y. MacDonald, *Early Christian Women and Pagan Opinion: The Power of the Hysterical Woman* (Cambridge: Cambridge University Press, 1996); Phyllis Rodgerson Pleasants, "The Quest for the Historical Olympias," *Communio Viatorum* 39, nos. 2–3 (1997): 155–179.

1 Why do you lament? why do you belabour yourself, and demand of yourself a punishment which your enemies were not able to demand from you, having thus abandoned your soul to the tyranny of dejection? For the letters which you sent to me by the hands of Patricius have discovered to me the wounds which have been inflicted on your mind. Wherefore also I am very sorrowful and much distressed that when you ought to be using every exertion and making it your business to expel dejection from your soul, you go about collecting distressing thoughts, even inventing things (so you say) which do not exist, and tearing yourself to pieces for no purpose, and to your very great injury. For why are you grieved because you could not remove me from Cucusus? Yet indeed, as far as you were concerned, you did

remove me, having made every exertion and endeavour for this purpose. And even if it has not been actually accomplished you ought not to be vexed on that account. For perhaps it seemed good to God that I should be set to run the longer double course, in order that the garland of victory might be rendered more glorious. Why then are you vexed on account of these things, in consequence of which my fame is spread abroad, when you ought to leap and dance for joy and bind wreaths upon your brow, because I have been deemed worthy of so great an honour which far exceeds my merits? Is it the desolation of this place which grieves you? Yet what can be pleasanter than my sojourn here? I have quietness, and tranquillity, plenty of leisure and good bodily health. For although the town has neither market-place nor market that is nothing to me. For all things are poured abundantly upon me as out of a flowing spring. I find my lord the Bishop here and my lord Dioscorus are constantly employed in providing for my refreshment. And the good Patricius will tell you that as far as my sojourn here is concerned I pass my time cheerfully and gladly, surrounded by attention. But if you lament the events which occurred in Caesarea, here again your conduct is unworthy of yourself. For there also bright garlands of victory were woven for me, inasmuch as all were proclaiming and publishing my praises, and expressing wonder and astonishment at the ill-treatment to which I had been subjected followed by expulsion. Meanwhile however do not let any one know these things, although they are the theme of much gossip. For my lord Poeanius has disclosed to me that the presbyters of Pharetrius himself have arrived on the spot, who declare that they were in communion with me and had no communication or intercourse or partnership with my adversaries. Therefore to avoid upsetting them do not let any one know these things. For certainly the things which befell me were very grievous: and if I had not suffered any other distress the events which happened there would have sufficed to procure innumerable rewards for me: so extreme was the danger which I encountered. Now I beseech you to keep these matters secret, and so I will give you a short account of them, not in order to grieve you but rather to make you glad. For herein consists the material of my gain, herein consists my wealth, herein the means of getting rid of my sins—that my journey is continually encompassed by trials of this kind, and that they are inflicted upon me by persons from whom they were quite unexpected. For when I was about to enter the region of Cappadocia, having escaped from that man of Galatia, who nearly threatened me with death, many persons met me on the way saying "the lord Pharetrius is awaiting you, and going about in all directions for fear of missing the pleasure of meeting you, and making every possible endeavour to see you, and embrace you, and show you all manner of affectionate regard; and he has set the monasteries of men and women in motion for this purpose." Now when I heard these things I did not expect that any of them would really take place, but formed an impression in my own mind precisely the reverse: but of this I said nothing to any of those who brought me this message.

2 Now when I arrived late one evening at Caesarea, in an exhausted and worn-out condition, being in the very height of a burning fever, faint and suffering to the last degree, I lighted upon an inn situated just at the outskirts of the city, and took great pains to find some physicians and allay this fiery fever; for it was now the height of my tertian malady. And in addition to this there was the fatigue of the journey, the toil, the strain, the total absence of attendants, the difficulty of getting supplies, the want of a physician, the wasting effects of toil, and heat and sleeplessness; thus I was well nigh a dead man when I entered the city. Then indeed I was visited by the whole body of the clergy, and the people, monks, nuns, physicians, and I had the benefit of great attention, as all paid me every kind of ministration and assistance. Yet even thus, being oppressed by the lethargy arising from the feverish heat I was in an extremely distressed condition. At length by degrees the malady was coming to an end and abating. Pharetrius however nowhere appeared; but waited for my departure, I know not with what purpose in view. When then I saw that my disorder had slightly abated I began to form plans for my journey so as to reach Cucusus, and enjoy a little repose after the calamities of the way. And whilst I was thus situated it was suddenly announced that the Isaurians in countless multitudes were overrunning the district of Caesarea, and had burnt a large village, and were most violently disposed. The tribune, having heard this, took the soldiers which he had and went out. For they were afraid lest the enemy should make an assault also upon the city, and all were in terror, and in an agony of alarm the very soil of their country being in jeopardy, so that even the old men undertook the defence of the walls. While affairs were in this condition suddenly towards dawn a rabble of monks (for so I must call them, indicating their frenzy by the expression) rushed up to the house where we were, threatening to set fire to it, and to treat us with the utmost violence unless we turned out of it. And neither the fear of the Isaurians, nor my own infirmity which was so grievously afflicting me, nor anything else made them more reasonable, but they pressed on, animated by such fierce rage that even the proconsular soldiers were terrified. For they kept threatening them with blows and boasted that they had shamefully beaten many of the proconsular soldiers. The soldiers having heard these things, sought refuge with me, and entreated and beseeched me, saying "even if we are to fall into the hands of the Isaurians deliver us from these wild beasts." When the governor heard this he hastened down to the house intending to succour me. But the monks would not pay any heed to his exhortations, and in fact he was powerless. Perceiving the great strait in which affairs were placed and not daring to advise me either to go out to certain death, or on the other hand to stay indoors, owing to the excessive fury of

these men, he sent to Pharetrius beseeching him to grant a few days respite on account of my infirmity and the impending danger. But even then nothing was effected, and on the morrow the monks arrived even fiercer than before, and none of the presbyters dared to stand by me and help me, but covered with shame and blushes (for they said that these things were done by the instructions of Pharetrius) they concealed themselves and lay hid, not responding even when I called them. What need to make a long story? Although such great terrors were imminent, and death well nigh a certainty, and the fever was oppressing me (for I had not yet got relief from the troubles arising from that cause) I flung myself at high noon into the litter, and was carried out thence, all the people shrieking and howling, and imprecating curses on the perpetrator of these deeds, whilst every one wailed and lamented. But when I got outside the city, some of the clergy also gradually came out and escorted me, mourning as they went. And having heard some persons say "Where are you leading him away to manifest death?" one of those who was warmly attached to me said to me "Depart I entreat you; fall into the hands of the Isaurians, provided you get clear away from us. For wherever you may fall, you will fall into a place of security, if only you escape our hands." Having heard and seen these things the good Seleucia, the generous wife of my lord Ruffinus (a most attentive friend she was to me), exhorted and entreated me to lodge at her suburban house which was about five miles from the city and she sent some men to escort me, and so I departed thither.

3 But not even there was this plot against me to come to an end. For as soon as Pharetrius knew what she had done, he published, as she said, many threats against her. But when she received me into her suburban villa I knew nothing of these things; for when she came out to meet me she concealed these things from me, but disclosed them to her steward who was there, and ordered him to afford me every possible means of repose, and if any of the monks should make an assault, wishing to insult or maltreat me, he was to collect the labourers from her other farms, and thus marshal a force against them. Moreover she besought me to take refuge in her house, which had a fortress and was impregnable, that I might escape the hands of the bishop and monks. This however I could not be induced to do, but remained in the villa, knowing nothing of the plans which were devised after these things. For even then they were not content to desist from their fury against me but Pharetrius beset the lady as she says, straitly threatening her, constraining and forcing her to expel me even from the suburbs, so that at midnight, I knowing nothing of these things, the lady being unable to endure his annoyance, announced, without my knowledge, that the barbarians were at hand, for she was ashamed to mention the compulsion which she had undergone. So in the middle of the night Evethius the presbyter came to me, and having roused

me from sleep, exclaimed with a loud voice "Get up, I pray you, the barbarians are upon us, they are close at hand." Imagine my condition on hearing this! Then, when I said to him what must we do? we cannot take refuge in the city lest we suffer worse things than what the Isaurians are going to do to us, he compelled me to go out. It was midnight, a dark, murky night without a moon—a circumstance which filled up the measure of our perplexity—we had no companion, no assistant, for all had deserted us. Nevertheless under the pressure of fear and in the expectation of immediate death, I got up, suffering as I was, having ordered torches to be lit. These however the presbyter ordered to be put out, for fear as he said lest the barbarians should be attracted by the light and attack us; so the torches were extinguished. Then the mule which carried my litter fell on its knees, the road being rugged, and steep and stony, and I who was inside was thrown down and narrowly escaped destruction, after which I dismounted, and was dragged along on foot, being held fast by Evethius the presbyter (for he also had alighted from his mule), and so I plodded on, led, or rather hauled by the hand, for to walk was impossible through such a difficult country, and amongst steep mountains in the middle of the night. Imagine what my sufferings must have been, encompassed as I was by such calamities, and oppressed by the fever, ignorant of the plans which had been made, but in terror of the barbarians and trembling with the expectation of falling into their hands. Do you not think that these sufferings alone, even if nothing else besides had befallen me, would avail to blot out many of my sins, and afford ample material for obtaining praise with God? Now the reason of all this, at least as I suppose, was, that as soon as I arrived in Caesarea, those who were in official positions, the learned men who were ex-vicars, and ex-governors, the ex-tribunes and indeed the whole people visited me every day, paid me great attention, and treated me as the apple of their eye; I suppose these things irritated Pharetrius and that the envy which drove me from Constantinople did not refrain from pursuing me even here. This at least is what I suppose, for I do not positively declare it but only suspect it to be the fact.

And what is one to say about the other events which happened on the way, the fears and the perils? As I recall them day by day, and continually bear them in mind, I am elated with pleasure, I leap for joy as one who has a great treasure laid up in store for him; for such is my position and feeling about them. Wherefore also I beseech your honour to rejoice at these things, to be glad, and leap for joy, and to glorify God who has counted me worthy to suffer these things. And I beseech you to keep these matters to yourself, and not to divulge them to any one, although for the most part the proconsular soldiers can fill all the city (with the story) as they themselves have undergone extreme danger.

4 Nevertheless do not let any one know this from your prudence, but rather put down those who talk about it. But if you are distressed lest the consequences of my ill-treatment should remain, know for certain that I have shaken myself entirely free from them, and that I am in better bodily health than when I was sojourning in Caesarea. And why do you dread the cold? for a suitable dwelling has been prepared for me, and my lord Dioscorus does and arranges everything so as to prevent my having the least sensation of cold. And if I may form a conjecture from the outset of my experience, the climate now seems to me oriental in character, no less than that of Antioch. So great is the warmth, so pleasant is the temperature. But you have grieved me much by saying "perhaps you are annoyed with me as having neglected you," yet I despatched a letter many days ago to your honour begging you not to move me from this place. Now I have had occasion to consider that you need a strong defence and much toil and labour to be able to make a satisfactory apology for this expression. But perhaps you have made a partial apology, by saying "I am generally occupied in thinking how to increase my affliction." But I in my turn reckon it as the greatest accusation that you should say "I take a pride in increasing my sorrow by thinking over it": for when you ought to make every possible effort to dispel your affliction you do the devil's will, by increasing your despondency and sorrow. Are you not aware how great an evil despondency is?

As to the Isaurians, dismiss your fears in future concerning them: for they have returned into their own country: and the governor has done everything necessary in this respect; and I am in far greater security here than when I was in Caesarea. For in future I have no one to fear so much as the bishops, with a few exceptions. On the account of the Isaurians then fear nothing: for they have retreated, and when winter has set in they are confined to their own homes, although they may possibly come out after Whitsuntide. And what do you mean by saying that you have not the benefit of letters from me? I have already sent you three long letters, one by the proconsular soldiers, one by Antonius, and the third by Anatolius my servant; two of them were a salutary medicine capable of reviving anyone who was desponding or stumbling, and conducting him into a healthy state of serenity. When you have received these letters then go over them constantly and thoroughly, and you will perceive their force and enjoy experience of their healing power, and benefit, and will inform me that you have derived much advantage therefrom. I have also a third letter ready, similar to these, which I do not choose to send at the present time having been exceedingly vexed at your saying "I accumulate sorrowful thoughts, even inventing things which do not exist," an utterance unworthy of yourself, which makes me hide my head for shame. But read those letters which I have sent, and you will no longer say these things, even if you are infinitely bent on being despondent. I at least have not ceased, and will not cease saying that sin is the only thing which is really distressing, and that all other things are but dust and smoke. For what is there grievous in inhabiting a prison and wearing a chain? or in being ill-treated when it is the occasion of so much gain? or why should exile be grievous or confiscation of goods? These are mere words, destitute of any terrible reality, words void of sorrow. For if you speak of death you only mention that which is the debt of nature: a thing which must in any case be undergone even if no one hastens it: and if you speak of exile you mention that which only involves a change of country and the sight of many cities: or if you speak of confiscation of goods you mention what is only freedom and emancipation from care.

5 Do not cease to pay attention to Maruthas the Bishop, as far as it concerns you, so as to lift him up out of the pit. For I have special need of him on account of the affairs in Persia. And ascertain from him, if you can, what has been accomplished there through his agency, and for what purpose he has come home, and let me know whether you have delivered the two epistles which I sent to him: and if he is willing to write to me, I will write to him again: but if he should not be willing let him at least signify to your prudence whether anything more has taken place there, and whether he is likely to accomplish anything by going thither again. For on this account I was anxious to have an interview with him. Nevertheless let all things which depend on you be done, and take care to fulfill your own part, even if all men are rushing headlong to ruin. For your reward will thus be perfected. By all means therefore make friends with him as far as it is possible. I beseech you not to neglect what I am about to say, but to pay diligent heed to it. The Marsian and Gothic monks where the Bishop Serapion has constantly been concealed have informed me that Moduarius the deacon has come bringing word that Unitas, that excellent bishop whom I lately ordained and sent into Gothia, has been laid to rest, after achieving many great exploits: and the deacon was the bearer of a letter from the king of the Goths begging that a bishop might be sent to them. Since then I see no other means of meeting the threatened catastrophe with a view to its correction save delay and postponement (as it is impossible for them to sail into the Bosporus or into those parts at the present time), take measures to put them off for a time on account of the winter season: and do not by any means neglect this: for it is a matter of the greatest importance. For there are two things which would specially distress me if they were to happen, which God forbid: one is that a bishop should be appointed by these men who have wrought such great wickedness, and who have no right to appoint, and the other is that any one should be made without consideration. For you know yourself that they are not anxious to create some worthy man bishop, and if this should take place, which heaven forbid, you are aware what will follow. Use all diligence

therefore to prevent either of these things happening: but if it were possible for Moduarius quietly and secretly to hasten out to me it would be of the greatest advantage. But if this is not possible let what is practicable under the circumstances be done. For that which takes place in the case of money, and actually occurred in the case of the widow in the gospel, also holds good in the case of practical affairs. For as that poor woman when she had cast two mites into the treasury surpassed all those who had cast in more, because she used up her whole substance: even so they who devote themselves to the work in hand with all their might discharge it completely, so far as they are concerned, even if nothing results from it, and they have their reward perfected.

I am very grateful to Hilarius the bishop: for he wrote to me asking to be allowed to depart to his own country, and to set things in order there, and then to come back again. As his presence therefore is of great service (for he is a devout, inflexible, and zealous man) I have urged him to depart and to return speedily. Take care then that the letter is quickly and safely delivered to him and not cast on one side: for he eagerly and earnestly begged for letters from me, and his presence is a great benefit. By all means therefore have a care of the letters; and if Herodius the presbyter be not on the spot see that they are delivered to my friends by the hands of some discreet man who has a head on his shoulders.

● 75
The Life of Olympias, Ascetic and Supporter of John Chrysostom

Life of Olympias   5th century C.E.

WORK: While virtually nothing is known about the anonymous author of the fifth-century C.E. *Life of Olympias*, numerous ancient texts testify to the person of Olympias. Born to a family recently promoted to nobility under Constantine, she was orphaned at an early age and apparently educated by a woman named Theodosia, who was associated with a group of pious Christian women. After her husband of only a brief time left her a widow, she chose the ascetic life. Well connected in Constantinople, she became the benefactor of the bishop Nectarius, who ordained her a deaconess. When Nectarius died and John Chrysostom came to Constantinople, she became his friend and supporter, in a relationship that endured until his death.

TRANSLATION: Elizabeth A. Clark, *Jerome, Chrysostom, and Friends*, SWR 2 (1979), 127–42.

TEXT: SC 13 (A.-M. Malingrey, 1968).

BIBLIOGRAPHY: See entry 74.

Life or regime and action of the pious, blessed and righteous Olympias, who was deaconess of the very holy cathedral of Constantinople. Bless me, father.

1 The Kingdom of our Savior Jesus Christ, existing before the ages and shining forth to ages without end, confers immortality on those who have served as its shield-bearers, who have completed the race and kept their faith in God spotless and steadfast. There are those who have practiced hospitality, the crown of perfections, such as the holy forefather Abraham and his nephew Lot; others have fought for self-control, as the holy Joseph; others have contended with sufferings to win patience, as the blessed Job; others have delivered their bodies to the fire and to tortures in order to receive the crown of incorruptibility. Not fearing the outrages of tyrants, but as noble combatants they have trampled the devil under foot and have been received as inheritors of the Kingdom of God. Among them was Thecla, a citizen of heaven, a martyr who conquered in many contests, the holy one among women, who despised wealth, hated the sharp and transitory pleasures of this world, refused a pecunious marriage and confessed that she would present herself a chaste virgin to her true Bridegroom. Having followed the teachings of Paul, the blessed apostle, and having taken into her heart the divinely inspired Scriptures, she received the crown of incorruptibility from our Lord and Savior Jesus Christ and to ages without end she rests with all the saints who from eternity have pleased the Lord Jesus Christ. Olympias walked in the footsteps of this saint, Thecla, in every virtue of the divinely-inspired way of life. Olympias, most serious and zealous for the road leading to heaven, followed the intent of the divine Scriptures in everything and was perfected through these things.

2 She was daughter according to the flesh of Seleucus, one of the *comites*, but according to the spirit, she was the true child of God. It is said that she was descended from Ablabius who was governor and she was bride for a few days of Nebridius, the prefect of the city of Constantinople, but in truth she did not grace the bed of anyone. For it is said that she died an undefiled virgin, having become a partner of the divine Word, a consort of every true humility, a companion and servant of the holy, catholic and apostolic church of God. Left an orphan, she was joined in marriage to a husband, but by the goodness of God she was preserved uncorrupted in flesh and in spirit. For God, who watches over everything, who foresees the outcome of humans, did not deem it worthy for the one who was briefly her husband to live with her for a year. The debt of nature was shortly demanded of him and she was preserved a blameless virgin until the end.

3 Again she could have used the apostolic rule which says, "I wish young widows to marry, run a household," but she did not agree to this, although

she had birth, wealth, a very expensive education, a naturally good disposition, and was adorned with the bloom of youth; like a gazelle, she leapt over the insufferable snare of a second marriage. "For the law was not laid down for the righteous man, but for the unruly, the impure, and the insatiable." Through a certain demonic jealousy, it transpired that her untimely widowhood became the subject of mischief. She was falsely accused before the emperor Theodosius of having dispensed her goods in a disorderly fashion. Since indeed she was his relation, he took pains to unite her in marriage with a certain Elpidius, a Spaniard, one of his own relatives. He directed many persistent entreaties to her and when he failed to achieve his goal, he was annoyed. The pious Olympias, however, explained her position to the emperor Theodosius: "If my King, the Lord Jesus Christ, wanted me to be joined with a man, he would not have taken away my first husband immediately. Since he knew that I was unsuited for the conjugal life and was not able to please a man, he freed him, Nebridius, from the bond and delivered me of this very burdensome yoke and servitude to a husband, having placed upon my mind the happy yoke of continence."

4 She clarified these things to the emperor. Theodosius in this manner, before the plot against the most holy John, patriarch of Constantinople. The emperor, when he had heard the testimony against the pious Olympias, commanded the man then prefect of the city, Clementius, to keep her possessions under guard until she reached her thirtieth year, that is, her physical prime. And the prefect, having received the guardianship from the emperor, oppressed her to such a degree at Elpidius' urging (she did not have the right either to meet with the notable bishops nor to come near the church) so that groaning under the strain, she would meekly bear the option of marriage. But she, even more grateful to God, responded to these events by proclaiming, "You have shown toward my humble person, O sovereign master, a goodness befitting a king and suited to a bishop, when you commanded my very heavy burden to be put under careful guard, for the administration of it caused me anxiety. But you will do even better if you order that it be distributed to the poor and to the churches, for I prayed much to avoid the vainglory arising from the apportionment, lest I neglect true riches for those pertaining to material things."

5 The emperor, upon his return from the battle against Maximus, gave the order that she could exercise control over her own possessions, since he had heard of the intensity of her ascetic discipline. But she distributed all of her unlimited and immense wealth and assisted everyone, simply and without distinction. For the sake of many she surpassed that Samaritan of whom an account is given in the holy Gospels. Once upon a time he found on the road down to Jericho a man who was crushed half-dead by robbers; he raised

him onto his own beast, carried him as far as the inn, and having mixed the oil of generosity with strong wine, he healed his wounds.

Then straightway after the distribution and sealing up of all her goods, there was rekindled in her the divine love and she took refuge in the haven of salvation, the great, catholic, and apostolic church of this royal city. She followed to the letter with intelligence the divinely-inspired teachings of the most holy archbishop of this sacred church, John, and gave to him for this holy church (imitating also in this act those ardent lovers and disciples of Christ who in the beginning of salvation's proclamation brought to the feet of the apostles their possessions) ten thousand pounds of gold, twenty thousand of silver and all of her real estate situated in the provinces of Thrace, Galatia, Cappadocia Prima, and Bithynia; and more, the houses belonging to her in the capital city, the one situated near the most holy cathedral, which is called "the house of Olympias"; together with the house of the tribune, complete with baths, and all the buildings near it; a mill; and a house which belonged to her in which she lived near the public baths of Constantinople; and another house of hers which was called the "house of Evander"; as well as all of her suburban properties.

6 Then by the divine will she was ordained deaconess of this holy cathedral of God and she built a monastery at an angle south of it. She owned all the houses lying near the holy church and all the shops which were at the southern angle mentioned. She constructed a path from the monastery up to the narthex of the holy church, and in the first quarter she enclosed her own chambermaids, numbering fifty, all of whom lived in purity and virginity. Next, Elisanthia, her relative who had seen the good work pleasing to God, which God gave to her to carry out, also herself a virgin, emulating the divine zeal, bade farewell to the ephemeral and empty things of life with her sisters Martyria and Palladia, also virgins. Then the three entered with all the others, having made over in advance all of their possessions to the same holy monastery. Likewise, also Olympia, the niece of the aforesaid holy Olympias, with many other women of senatorial families, chose the Kingdom of Heaven and disdained these lowly things below which drag us down, in accordance with the grace and good favor of God who wishes all to be saved and who fosters the divine love in them. They entered also with the rest, so that all those who gathered together according to the grace of God in that holy fold of Christ numbered two hundred and fifty, all adorned with the crown of virginity and practicing the most exalted life which befits the saints.

7 When these events had transpired in this manner by divine assistance, the noble servant of God Olympias again brought to the above-mentioned hallowed church through the most holy patriarch John the entire remainder of all her real estate, situated in all the provinces, and her interest in the public bread supply. And he also ordained as deaconesses of the holy church her

three relatives, Elisanthia, Martyria, and Palladia, so that the four deaconesses would be able to be together without interruption in the most sacred monastery founded by her.

8 One was struck with amazement at seeing certain things in the holy chorus and angelic institution of these holy women: their incessant continence and sleeplessness, the constancy of their praise and thanksgiving to God, their "charity which is the bond of perfection," their stillness. For no one from the outside, neither man nor woman, was permitted to come upon them, the only exception being the most holy patriarch John, who visited continuously and sustained them with his most wise teachings. Thus fortified each day by his divinely-inspired instruction, they kindled in themselves the divine love so that their great and holy love streamed forth to him. The pious and blessed Olympias (who in these matters too imitated the women disciples of Christ who served him from their possessions) prepared for the holy John his daily provisions and sent them to the bishop, for there was not much separation between the episcopal residence and the monastery, only a wall. And she did this not only before the plots against him, but also after he was banished; up to the end of his life she provided for all his expenses as well as for those who were with him in his exile.

9 Then the devil could not bear the great and wondrous way of life of these pious women, the way of life, first of all, consistently made straight by God's grace, and secondly, a way made straight by the uninterrupted teaching of the most holy patriarch. Evil men who were hateful and had enmity to John among the holy men because he was no respecter of persons in his scrutiny of the unrighteous, the devil, the hater of good, suborned and struck with the arrow of calumny and they contrived a diabolical machination against both him, i.e. John, and that holy woman. He was slandered by them not only in respect to her, but also concerning ecclesiastical affairs; according to their whim, they condemned and exiled him. The herald and teacher of truth, however, received the assaults of his antagonists like a noble athlete and carried off the prize of victory, departing the storm of the present life and being transposed to the calm above. And this pious woman after his exile did not give way but made a motion for his recall to every royal and priestly person. The opposition encompassed her with numerous evils; they stitched together slanders and untimely abuse against her until the occasion when they made her appear before the city prefect for interrogation by him.

10 When they saw her openness concerning the truth, they could not bear the nobility and immutability of her love for God. They wished to put a stop to the constant activity in which she was engaged on behalf of the holy John's recall and they sent her as well into exile in Nicomedia, the capital city of the province of Bithynia. But she, strengthened by the divine grace, nobly and courageously, for the sake of love of God, bore the storms of trials and di-

verse tribulations which came upon her. The whole rest of her life she passed in the capital city of Nicomedia, performing every ascetic act and maintaining her rule of life unchanged there. Victorious in the good fight, she crowned herself with the crown of patience, having turned over her flock by the divine allotment to Marina, among the blessed, who was her relative and spiritual daughter, whom she had received from the undefiled and salvatory baptism; she prayed that she receive in turn the souls unto herself and be preserved in tranquillity in all things. And Marina did this for Olympias, not only for the remaining time which the holy Olympias passed in the metropolis of Nicomedia, but also after her death. For when the pious woman was about to join the holy fathers, both to be set free from the present life and to be with Christ, again she decreed in writing that the aforesaid Marina of divine choice exhibit much care and succor, and committed to her, after God, all the sisters and their care. Having done this, she escaped from the storm of human woes and crossed over to the calm haven of our souls, Christ the God.

11 But before her holy body was buried, she appeared in a dream to the metropolitan of the same city of Nicomedia, saying, "Place my remains in a casket, put it on a boat, let the boat go adrift into the stream, and at the place where the boat stops, disembark onto the ground and place me there." The metropolitan did what had been told him in the vision concerning Olympias and put the casketed body in the boat and let the boat loose into the stream. Toward the hour of midnight the boat reached the shore in front of the gallery of the pure house of the holy apostle Thomas which is in Brochthoi and there it rested without advancing further. At the same hour an angel of the Lord appeared in a dream to the superior and to the sacristan of the same august house, saying, "Rise and put the casket which you have found in the boat which has come to anchor on the shore in front of the gallery in the sanctuary." When they heard this, they saw all the church gates open by themselves, but since they were still asleep, they thought that the event was an illusion. Having secured the gates again, there appeared to them once more the previous vision. Still a third time, the angel pressed them with much earnestness and said, "Go out and take the casket of the holy Olympias, for she has suffered much for the sake of God, and put the casket in the sanctuary." Then they arose, again saw the gates of the church open, and no longer remained disbelieving. Taking the holy Gospels, the cross, the candelabra with candles, along with the incense, they went out praying into the gallery and found her holy remains in the boat. They called together all the female and male ascetics, and holding the candles and making great praise and thanksgiving to God, they deposited her holy remains in the sanctuary of the aforementioned venerable house of the holy apostle Thomas in Brochthoi. People could see numerous cures taking place at her holy tomb; impure spir-

its were banished and many diverse illnesses departed from those afflicted with them. And the holy, pious blessed servant of God, Olympias, ended her life in the month of July, on the 25th, in the reign of Arcadius, the most divine and pious emperor. She is numbered in the choir of the pious confessors and reigns together with the immortal King, Christ our God, for ages without end.

12 After her death, the truly noble servant of God, Marina, the friend of Christ, Olympias' relative and spiritual daughter, whom, as has been said, she received from the holy, undefiled, salvatory baptism, made clear to everyone the love which she had for that blessed soul. Performing and fulfilling the deposit from Olympias and everything which she had commanded her, she took in her arms, preserved safe, and governed the whole caravan of her flock which Olympias had placed in her hands, after those of God and our Lady, the completely holy Mother of God, so that none of the sisters experienced any deprivation by their separation from that woman Olympias who is among the saints. And after the death of the pious woman Marina, there was chosen as leader of that holy flock of Christ, the very dear friend of God who was mentioned above, the deaconess Elisanthia, her relative, who preserved unchanged the entire rule which she had received from that pious and blessed soul, and she followed all her virtues.

13 Let these things be said. I have deemed it necessary and entirely useful for the profit of many to run over in the narrative one by one the holy virtues of the noble servant of God, Olympias, who is among the saints. For no place, no country, no desert, no island, no distant setting, remained without a share in the benevolence of this famous woman; rather, she furnished the churches with liturgical offerings and helped the monasteries and convents, the beggars, the prisoners, and those in exile; quite simply, she distributed her alms over the entire inhabited world. And the blessed Olympias herself burst the supreme limit in her almsgiving and her humility, so that nothing can be found greater than what she did. She had a life without vanity, an appearance without pretence, character without affectation, a face without adornment; she kept watch without sleeping, she had an immaterial body, a mind without vainglory, intelligence without conceit, an untroubled heart, an artless spirit, charity without limits, unbounded generosity, contemptible clothing, immeasurable self-control, rectitude of thought, undying hope in God, ineffable almsgiving; she was the ornament of all the humble and was in addition worthily honored by the most holy patriarch John. For she abstained from eating meat and for the most part she went without bathing. And if a need for a bath arose through sickness (for she suffered constantly in her stomach), she came down to the waters with her shift on, out of modesty even for herself, so they said.

14 And she looked after the needs of many fathers, as I have said, and of those of the most blessed John the archbishop, proving herself worthy of his virtue. For when he had been plotted against and exiled, as has already been explained, the pious woman provided without distraction for his need and for those with him. This is no small thing for the workers of Christ who are anxious both night and day for Christ's affairs. As Paul greeted Persis, Tryphaena, and Tryphosa, the pious Olympias, imitator of God, perhaps received the same greeting.

And I know that this completely virtuous and divinely-inspired Olympias provided also for the blessed Nectarius, the archbishop of Constantinople, who was completely persuaded by her even in the affairs of the church, and for Amphilochius, bishop of Iconium, and Optimus, and Peter, and Gregory the brother of the holy Basil, and Epiphanius the archbishop of Constantia in Cyprus, and many others of the saints and inspired fathers who lived in the capital city. Why is it necessary to say that she also bestowed upon them property in the country and money? And when the aforesaid Optimus died in Constantinople at this time, she shut the eyes of the great man with her own hands. In addition, she relieved the piteous without measure in all ways. She sustained Antiochus of Ptolemais, and Acacius, the bishop of Beroea, and the holy Severian, the bishop of Gabala, and in a word, all the priests residing there, in addition to innumerable ascetics and virgins.

15 And due to her sympathy for them, she endured many trials by the actions of a willfully evil and vulgar person; contending eagerly in not a few contests on behalf of the truth of God, she lived faultlessly in unmeasured tears night and day, "submitting to every human being for the sake of the Lord," full of every reverence, bowing before the saints, venerating the bishops, honoring the presbyters, respecting the priests, welcoming the ascetics, being anxious for the virgins, supplying the widows, raising the orphans, shielding the elderly, looking after the weak, having compassion on sinners, guiding the lost, having pity on all, pity without stinting anything on the poor. Engaging in much catechizing of unbelieving women and making provision for all the necessary things of life, she left a reputation for goodness throughout her whole life which is ever to be remembered. Having called from slavery to freedom her myriad household servants, she proclaimed them to be of the same honor as her own nobility. Or rather, if it is necessary to speak truthfully, they appeared more noble in their way of dress than that holy woman. For there could be found nothing cheaper than her clothing; the most ragged items were coverings unworthy of her manly courage. And she cultivated in herself a gentleness so that she surpassed even the simplicity of children themselves. Never any blame, not even from her neighbors, was incurred by that image of Christ, but her whole intolerable life was spent in penitence and in a great flood of tears. One was more likely to see the fount

run dry in the trenches than her eyes, lowered, always gazing on Christ, leave off crying for a while. Why go on? For to whatever extent I might provide leisure for my mind to recount the contests and virtues of this ardent soul, one will find many and poor the descriptions of the deeds. And does anyone not believe that I speak with restraint concerning the steadfast Olympias, who besides was an entirely precious vessel of the Holy Spirit? There was an eyewitness who also viewed the life of this blessed woman, her angelic regime; since he was her true spiritual friend and related to her family, much was distributed by him in accordance with her intent.

16 Accordingly, the divine and divinely-inspired Olympias herself, no longer having any fleshly thought, submitted herself to the authorities, obedient to the powers, bowed before the churches, venerated the bishops and the presbyters, honored all the clergy, was deemed worthy as a confessor on behalf of the truth and received the many storms of unjust slander; her life was judged to be among the confessors by as many pious people as dwelt in Constantinople. For close to death, she took the risk in the contests for God. Having perfected herself in these, she won the blessed glory and is crowned in an endless age. And she is a member of the chorus in the undefiled mansions where she lives with the pious souls like herself and where she openly demands from the Lord God the recompense for good deeds.

17 Let us ask that her prayers importune the benevolent God who pities everybody, that he give up tortures for our sins and quench the Gehenna kindled by our failures, that we may turn in repentance to the good-hearted God and receive from him abundant pity. And the holy and blessed woman exhorts us who read and hear, she teaches us in Christ Jesus by the voice of St. Paul, the chorus leader of the holy apostles, "Preserve the traditions which you have learned beforehand, and watch, how you walk not as the foolish, but as the wise; redeem the time, for the days are evil, for the battle is not against flesh and blood but against the princes, against the powers, against the world-rulers of this dark age, against the spiritual powers of evil in the heavens," that is, not only does he mean against men but against the unclean spirits, who suggest to each person to continue in errors and destructively subvert those who have their heads in the air. Therefore put on the armor of God, that is, purity of body and spirit, humility, gentleness, continence. Return no one evil for evil, but if you see your brother stumbling in some way, or about to be cast down by the devil, do not remain silent, lest he fall, but just as the divine Scriptures teach us, accuse him, censure him, exhort him, looking out for yourself lest you also be tempted. Then let no one deceive you by persuasiveness and the flattery of empty and idle words, but behave in a seemly fashion to everyone, most of all to those in the household of faith. And watch out also for this: for if a woman married to a mortal and perishable man is found to be corrupted by another, she will be subjected to punish-

ments, torments, and exiles, how much more will the one who is promised in marriage to our ruler and Lord Jesus Christ, if she abandon him and cleave to this vain and transitory life, merit a worse punishment? But may the Lord make us pure and blameless before his face in love, in the embassy of our holy, honored Lady, the Mother of God and ever-virgin Mary, and of the holy Olympias, and both the readers and the hearers with their whole souls. May the Lord give grace and pity on the day of judgment and he will deliver us all completely from the devil's deeds, in Christ Jesus our Lord.

18 And I ask you, I the sinner who also has written this, I adjure you according to the benevolent God, the ruler of all, and to our Lord Jesus Christ and to the Holy Spirit, that you who read in peace and listen in true hope pray on behalf of my poor soul for the remission of sins and that a favorable judgment be offered to me and to all readers by our benevolent Savior Jesus Christ, the true and living God, for to him belong glory, honor, and adoration, with the Father and the Holy Spirit, now and forever, throughout the ages. Amen.

● 76

The Pilgrim Egeria Visits the Shrine of St. Thecla and the Deaconess Marthana

EGERIA *Diary of a Pilgrimage* 22–23   late 4th or early 5th century C.E.

AUTHOR: Sometime around the end of the fourth century C.E., a Christian woman whose name was probably Egeria went on a pilgrimage to various shrines and monastic centers in Egypt, Syria, and Asia Minor, as well as numerous sites in the Holy Land and elsewhere mentioned in Scripture. A first-person diary written in Latin chronicles her travels. Virtually nothing is known about the pilgrim (whose identification with the author has not been contested) apart from what may be deduced from the diary itself. Thought by most scholars to have been a consecrated virgin, she appears to have been well connected and of considerable financial means.

TRANSLATION: George E. Gingras, *Egeria: Diary of a Pilgrimage*, ACW 38 (New York and Ramsay, N.J.: Newman Press, 1970).

TEXT: CCSL 175 (E. Franceschini and R. Weber, 1965), 27–90; SC 21 (H. Pétré, 1948); SC 296 (P. Maraval, 1982; repr. with corrections, 1997).

BIBLIOGRAPHY: P. Devos, "La date du voyage d'Egérie," *Analecta Bollandiana* 85 (1967): 105–43; Sivan Hagith, "Holy Land Pilgrimage and Western Audiences; Some Reflections on Egeria and Her Circle," *Catholic Quarterly* 38 (1988): 528–35.

CHAPTER 22

After I had returned to Antioch, I remained there for a whole week, until whatever was necessary for our journey had been prepared. I then set out from Antioch and, after journeying for several days, arrived in the province called Cilicia, the capital city of which is Tarsus, the same Tarsus in which I had already been on my trip down to Jerusalem. Since the shrine of Saint Thecla is located a three-day journey from Tarsus, in Isauria, it was a great pleasure for me to go there, particularly since it was so near at hand.

CHAPTER 23

I set out from Tarsus and I came to a certain city by the sea, still in Cilicia, called Pompeiopolis. From there I crossed over into the regions of Isauria, and I stayed at a city called Corycus. On the third day I arrived at a city called Seleucia of Isauria. On arriving there, I went to the bishop, a very holy man and a former monk. I also saw there in the same city a very beautiful church. Since it is around fifteen hundred feet from the city to the shrine of Saint Thecla, which lies beyond the city on a rather flat hill, I thought it best to go out there to make the overnight stop which I had to make.

At the holy church there is nothing but countless monastic cells for men and women. I met there a very dear friend of mine, and a person to whose way of life everyone in the East bears witness, the holy deaconess Marthana, whom I had met in Jerusalem, where she had come to pray. She governs these monastic cells of *aputactitae*, or virgins. Would I ever be able to describe how great was her joy and mine when she saw me? But to return to the subject: There are many cells all over the hill, and in the middle there is a large wall which encloses the church where the shrine is. It is a very beautiful shrine. The wall is set there to guard the church against the Isaurians, who are evil men, who frequently rob and who might try to do something against the monastery which is established there. Having arrived there in the name of God, a prayer was said at the shrine and the complete Acts of Saint Thecla was read. I then gave unceasing thanks to Christ our God, who granted to me, an unworthy woman and in no way deserving, the fulfillment of my desires in all things. And so, after spending two days there seeing the holy monks and the *aputactitae*, both men and women, who live there, and after praying and receiving Communion, I returned to Tarsus and to my journey.

I made a three-day stop before setting out on my journey from there, in the name of God. On the same day I arrived at the resting station called Mansocrenae, located at the base of Mount Tarsus, and I stopped there. The next day I climbed Mount Tarsus and travelled by a route, already known to me, through several provinces that I had already crossed on my journey down, that is, Cappadocia, Galatia, and Bithynia. Then I arrived at Chalcedon, where I stopped because of the very famous shrine of Saint Euphemia, already known to me from before. On the following day, after crossing the sea, I arrived in Constantinople, giving thanks to Christ our God who deigned to bestow such favor on me, an unworthy and undeserving person. Not only did He deign to fulfill my desire to go there, but He granted also the means of visiting what I desired to see, and of returning again to Constantinople.

After arriving there, I did not cease giving thanks to Jesus our God, who had deigned to bestow His grace upon me, in the various churches, that of the apostles and the numerous shrines that are here. As I send this letter to Your Charity and to you, reverend ladies, it is already my intention to go, in the name of Christ our God, to Asia, that is, to Ephesus, to pray at the shrine of the holy and blessed apostle John. If, after this, I am still living, I will either tell Your Charity in person—if God will deign to grant that—about whatever other places I shall have come to know, or certainly I will write you of it in letters, if there is anything else I have in mind.

You, my sisters, my light, kindly remember me, whether I live or die.

● 77
Epitaph of a Gnostic Woman, Flavia Sophē

Ferrua *Rivista di archeologia cristiana* 21, 185–93   Rome, 3d century c.e.

TRANSLATION AND BIBLIOGRAPHY: Anne McGuire, "Women, Gender and Gnosis in Gnostic Texts and Traditions," in *Women and Christian Origins*, 257–99.

TEXT: A. Ferrua, "Questioni di Epigrafia Eretica Romana," *Rivista di Archeologia Cristiana* 21 (1944/45): 165–221, esp. 185–93; M. Guarducci, "Valentiniani a Roma," *Mitteilungen des Deutsches Archäologisches Institut, Römische Abteilung*, 80 (1973): 169–86.

Flavia Sophē
You, who did yearn for the paternal light
Sister, spouse, my Sophē
Anointed in the baths of Christ with everlasting, holy oil
Hasten to gaze at the divine features of the aeons
The great Angel of the great council
The true Son
You entered into the bridal chamber and deathless ascended
To the bosom of the father

● 78

Epitaph of Euterpe, a Christian Woman Called Companion of the Muses

Guarducci *Epigrafia*, 4:525   Sicily, 5th century C.E.

TEXT: Guarducci, *Epigrafia*, 4:525.

TRANSLATION: RSK.

Here lies Euterpe, the companion of the Muses. She lived chastely and piously and blamelessly for 22 years, 3 months. She died on November 27.

● 79

Donation by a Christian Shipowner and Her Daughter

Guarducci *Epigrafia*, 4:373   Cos, 5th century C.E.

TEXT: Guarducci, *Epigrafia*, 4:373.

TRANSLATION: RSK.

Eustochiane, the most modest shipowner, and Maria, her daughter, adorned the portico with mosaic.

THREE

Religious Office

A significant portion of the evidence we have for women's religious activities in Greco-Roman antiquity relates to their roles as officiants in religious rites and as officeholders in religious communities. This evidence is often quite concrete. Various inscriptions and epitaphs identify specific women as officials and leaders, whether in pagan, Jewish, or Christian contexts. An inscription honoring Tata of Aphrodisias (entry 83A) informs us that she was a priestess of Hera for life and a *stephanephorus* (crown-bearer) in the imperial cult. It also indicates in some detail her responsibilities in those capacities.

Testimony to the leadership roles of women in religious contexts has received a mixed response from scholars. Many classicists have seemed willing to take at face value the evidence for women as priestesses and other cult officials, but until relatively recently, scholars of early Judaism and early Christianity routinely misinterpreted or discounted the sources documenting women as religious leaders in early synagogues and churches. Several generations of scholars insisted that synagogue offices attributed to women in Jewish inscriptions must have been "honorary" in nature, by which they meant that women bore the titles only and played no meaningful and official roles in their communities. The titles were explained as a reward for women's financial contributions, conferring some public recognition but no authority. Alternatively, but without any substantiating evidence, women's titles were dismissed as the titles of their husbands or fathers. In 1982 Bernadette Brooten published her Harvard doctoral dissertation, in which she argued persuasively that there was no basis for such interpretations apart from the unsubstantiated assumptions of scholars that women could not have held legitimate religious office in ancient Jewish synagogues.[1] Although some scholars have

---

[1] Brooten, *Women Leaders*. For support of Brooten, see Ross S. Kraemer, "A New Inscription from Malta and the Question of Women Elders in Diaspora Jewish Communities," *HTR* 78, nos. 3–4 (1985): 431–38. For an overview of current scholarship on women in ancient Jewish

critiqued selected details of Brooten's work, her larger methodological argument has become standard in recent scholarship.[2]

Evidence for women leaders in early Christian churches was similarly received by generations of scholars. At the beginning of the third century C.E., Tertullian railed against those who would interpret the story of Thecla (entry 92) as evidence that women could baptize and teach, and centuries of commentators have not departed significantly from his assumption that the evidence for there being women in strong leadership positions is not to be taken as authoritative. Ironically, Tertullian's motive was not far different from that of modern interpreters: namely, the fear that an account of a woman baptizing and teaching would be used to legitimate the authority of other women to baptize and teach. Twentieth-century discussions of women's leadership in early Judaism and early Christianity were initially undertaken in the context of debates about the legitimacy of women priests, ministers, and rabbis in our own time. Both supporters and antagonists of having women hold modern religious office have looked to ancient practice to substantiate their positions.

Since the publication of the first edition of this sourcebook, considerable work has been done on the exercise of leadership and authority by women in ancient contexts, including those we might label religious.[3] This work has focused on which

synagogues, see Lee I. Levine, "Women in the Synagogue," in *The Ancient Synagogue: The First Thousand Years* (New Haven: Yale University Press, 2000), 471–90.

[2] For some critique of aspects of Brooten's work, see, e.g., G. H. R. Horsley, "An *archisynagogos* of Corinth?" *NewDocs* 4 (1987 [1979]): 213–20, esp. 219–20; Tessa Rajak, "The Jewish Community and Its Boundaries," in Judith Lieu, John North, and Tessa Rajak, eds., *The Jews among Pagans and Christians in the Roman Empire* (London: Routledge, 1995), 22–24; Leonard Rutgers, *The Jews in Late Ancient Rome: Evidence of Cultural Interaction in the Roman Diaspora*, RGRW 126 (Leiden: E. J. Brill, 1995), 131–36.

[3] See *Blessings*, 80–92, 106–27, 174–98 (on "pagan," Jewish, and Christian women, respectively); Steven J. Friesen, "Ephesian Women and Men in Public Office During the Roman Imperial Period," in Herwig Friesinger and Friedrich Krinzinger, eds., *100 Jahre österreichische Forschungen in Ephesos: Akten des Symposions Wien 1995* (Vienna: Austrian Archaeological Institute, 1999), 107–13; Rosalinde A. Kearsley, "Asiarchs, Αρχιερεις, and the Αρχιερειαι of Asia," GRBS 27 (1986): 183–92; Rosalinde A. Kearsley, "Asiarchs, Archiereis and Archiereiai of Asia: New Evidence from Amorium in Phrygia," *Epigraphica Anatolia* 16 (1990): 69–80; Rosalinde A. Kearsley, "The Asiarchs," in David W. J. Gill and Conrad Gempf, eds., *The Book of Acts in Its Graeco-Roman Setting* (Grand Rapids: Eerdmans; Carlisle: Paternoster Press, 1994), 363–76; Riet van Bremen, *The Limits of Participation: Women and Civic Life in the Greek East in the Hellenistic and Roman Periods*, Dutch Monographs on Ancient History and Archaeology 15 (Amsterdam: J. C. Gieben, 1996); Francine Cardman, "Women, Ministry, and Church Order," in *Women and Christian Origins*, 300–329; Ute E. Eisen, *Women Office Holders in Early Christianity: Epigraphical and Literary Studies*, trans. Linda M. Maloney (Collegeville, Minn.: Michael Glazier, Liturgical Press, 2000). Also pertinent is Karen Jo Torjesen, *When Women Were Priests: Women's Leadership in the Early Church and the Scandal of Their Subordination in the Rise of Christianity* (San Francisco: HarperSanFrancisco, 1993).

offices women held and what activities, authority, prestige, honors, and responsibility went with those offices, as well as exploring how one attained religious offices including factors of family connections, financial contributions, and the like. Additional work, however, remains to be done.

Somewhat less has been done exploring the correlations between the gender of the deity and the gender of the deity's officiants. In the extremely popular cult of Isis in the Roman period, which had many women devotees, cult offices were held by both women and men, but the higher offices seem to have been held mostly by men, as Françoise Dunand noted twenty-five years ago.[4] Continued precise, detailed work, modeled by Dunand and pursued more recently by scholars such as Steven Friesen, Rosalinde Kearsley, Riet van Bremen, and others, is needed to explore whether women were more likely to hold religious office in the service of goddesses than in the service of male gods, and if so, why.

For Jewish and Christian communities, such analysis might initially seem pointless, for aside from the theological insistence that God has no gender, God is routinely presented in early Jewish and Christian materials as male. Considerable scholarship of the last several decades, though, has articulated the degree to which significant feminine aspects of divinity are present in an array of ancient Jewish and Christian sources, whether in the figure of Wisdom (which is feminine both in Hebrew and in Greek), in the description of the divine daughter, Metanoia, in a work of uncertain identity (*Aseneth*, entry 106), or the extensive, and now extensively studied, use of feminine imagery for the divine in the various texts found near Nag Hammadi in Egypt (entries 132 and 133,) and often designated "gnostic."[5] Prior to the fifth century C.E., the Holy Spirit is almost invariably feminine in Syriac (the noun for 'spirit,' *ruḥa*, is grammatically feminine).[6] While the question remains complex, there is evidence that at least in some instances, women played greater leadership roles in communities that employed such texts, language, and imagery, evidence that remains to be explored and tested.[7]

Finally, while the careful analysis of these sources may allow us to understand more about women's actual service in ancient religious offices, many of the extant

[4] Françoise Dunand, "Le statut des Hiereiai en Égypte romaine," in M. B. de Boer and T. A. Edridge, eds., *Hommages à Maarten J. Vermaseren*, vol. 1 (Leiden: E. J. Brill, 1978), 352–74.

[5] On Wisdom, see Claudia Camp and Anne McGuire, "Woman Wisdom," in *Women in Scripture*, 548–55; on Aseneth, see Ross Shepard Kraemer, *When Aseneth Met Joseph: A Late Antique Tale of the Biblical Patriarch and His Egyptian Wife, Revisited* (Oxford: Oxford University Press, 1998), 191–224; on the Nag Hammadi and related texts, see Karen I. King, ed., *Images of the Feminine in Gnosticism*, Studies in Antiquity and Christianity (Philadelphia: Fortress Press, 1988); see also numerous contributions in *Searching the Scriptures*.

[6] Susan Ashbrook Harvey, "Feminine Imagery for the Divine: The Holy Spirit, the *Odes of Solomon* and Early Syriac Tradition," *St. Vladimir's Theological Quarterly* 37 (1993): 111–39.

[7] For an overview of this literature and these issues, see Anne McGuire, "Women, Gender, and Gnosis in Gnostic Texts and Traditions," in *Women and Christian Origins*, 257–99.

literary sources that document ancient debates about such service may also suggest that these debates are another instance of the problem laid out in the general introduction. For while these sources seem to be evidence for women's actual practices, they also suggest that ancient debates about women's religious offices are as much about ancient conflicts over gender as anything else. As in the contemporary world, it may well be that what many ancient persons found objectionable about women in leadership roles, religious and otherwise, was the potential to undercut fundamental notions of masculinity as active and superordinate, and femininity as passive and subordinate. When women's official service could be constructed within acceptable notions of femininity (for instance, as motherly care extended to the civic realm), it might be far less controversial than when such service was seen to compromise gender arrangements that were themselves viewed as divinely ordained or inherent in nature or both.

● 80

Honors and Privileges Bestowed on a Priestess of Athena after a Procession to Pythian Apollo

IG II² 1136   Delphi, 2d century B.C.E.

TRANSLATION: Lefkowitz and Fant, no. 121, p. 118.

... Greetings. Whereas the people of Athens led a Pythian procession to
Pythian Apollo in a grand manner worthy of the god and their particular excellence: the priestess of Athena, Chrysis daughter of Nicetes, also was present
with the procession; she made the journey out and the return well, appropri-
ately, and worthily of the people of Athens and of our own city. With good
fortune, it was voted by the city of Delphi to praise Chrysis, daughter of Nicetes, and to crown her with the god's crown that is customary among the
Delphians. It was voted also to give *proxenia* to her and to her descendants
from the city, and the right to consult the oracle, priority of trial, safe conduct, freedom from taxes, and a front seat at all the contests held by the city,
the right to own land and a house and all the other honours customary for
proxenoi and benefactors of the city.

● 81

The Institution of the Vestal Virgins

PLUTARCH *Life of Numa Pompilius* 10   1st century C.E.

AUTHOR, TEXT, AND TRANSLATION: See entry 16.

BIBLIOGRAPHY: *Blessings* 80–92; Mary Beard, "The Sexual Status of the Vestal
Virgins," *JRS* 70 (1980): 12–27, repudiated in her subsequent article, "Re-reading
(Vestal) Virginity," in *Women in Antiquity: New Assessments*, ed. Richard Hawley
and Barbara Levick (London: Routledge, 1995), 166–77; Judith Hallett, *Fathers and
Daughters in Roman Society: Women and the Elite Family* (Princeton: Princeton
University Press, 1984); Ariadne Staples, *From Good Goddess to Vestal Virgins: Sex
and Category in Roman Religion* (London and New York: Routledge, 1998).

1 In the beginning, then, they say that Gegania and Verenia were consecrated
to this office by Numa, who subsequently added to them Canuleia and Tarpeia; that at a later time two others were added by Servius, making the number which has continued to the present time. It was ordained by the king that
the sacred virgins should vow themselves to chastity for thirty years; during
the first decade they are to learn their duties, during the second to perform
the duties they have learned, and during the third to teach others these duties. 2 Then, the thirty years being now passed, any one who wishes has lib-
erty to marry and adopt a different mode of life, after laying down her

sacred office. We are told, however, that few have welcomed the indulgence, and that those who did so were not happy, but were a prey to repentance and dejection for the rest of their lives, thereby inspiring the rest with superstitious fears, so that until old age and death they remained steadfast in their virginity.

3 But Numa bestowed great privileges upon them, such as the right to make a will during the life time of their fathers, and to transact and manage their other affairs without a guardian, like the mothers of three children. When they appear in public, the fasces are carried before them, and if they accidentally meet a criminal on his way to execution, his life is spared; but the virgin must make oath that the meeting was involuntary and fortuitous, and not of design. He who passes under the litter on which they are borne, is put to death. 4 For their minor offences the virgins are punished with stripes, the Pontifex Maximus sometimes scourging the culprit on her bare flesh, in a dark place, with a curtain interposed. But she that has broken her vow of chastity is buried alive near the Colline gate. Here a little ridge of earth extends for some distance along the inside of the city-wall; the Latin word for it is "agger." 5 Under it a small chamber is constructed, with steps leading down from above. In this are placed a couch with its coverings, a lighted lamp, and very small portions of the necessaries of life, such as bread, a bowl of water, milk, and oil, as though they would thereby absolve themselves from the charge of destroying by hunger a life which had been consecrated to the highest services of religion. 6 Then the culprit herself is placed on a litter, over which coverings are thrown and fastened down with cords so that not even a cry can be heard from within, and carried through the forum. All the people there silently make way for the litter, and follow it without uttering a sound, in a terrible depression of soul. No other spectacle is more appalling, nor does any other day bring more gloom to the city than this.

7 When the litter reaches its destination, the attendants unfasten the cords of the coverings. Then the high-priest, after stretching his hands toward heaven and uttering certain mysterious prayers before the fatal act, brings forth the culprit, who is closely veiled, and places her on the steps leading down into the chamber. After this he turns his face, as do the rest of the priests, and when she has gone down, the steps are taken up, and great quantities of earth are thrown into the entrance to the chamber, hiding it away, and making the place level with the rest of the mound. Such is the punishment of those who break their vow of virginity.

● 82
How Vestal Virgins Are Chosen

AULUS GELLIUS *Attic Nights* 1.12   2d century C.E.

AUTHOR: Born ca. 130 C.E., Gellius is the author of *Attic Nights*, a collection of short chapters on philosophy, history, law, grammar, literary criticism, and the like. The collection was explicitly written to entertain and instruct his children. Because he relied so heavily on quotations from earlier Greek and Latin sources, his work is a major source for later writers and historians, both ancient and modern.

TRANSLATION: LCL (J. C. Rolfe, 1927, 3 vols.).

TEXT: Editio maior: (M. Hertz, Berlin, 1883–85), 2 vols.; Budé (R. Marache, books 1–4, 1967; 5–10, 1978); OCT (P. K. Marshall, 1968, 2 vols.); Teubner (C. Hosius, 1903).

1 Those who have written about "taking" a Vestal virgin, of whom the most painstaking is Antistius Labeo, have stated that it is unlawful for a girl to be chosen who is less than six, or more than ten, years old; 2 she must also have both father and mother living; 3 she must be free too from any impediment in her speech, must not have impaired hearing, or be marked by any other bodily defect; 4 she must not herself have been freed from paternal control, nor her father before her, even if her father is still living and she is under the control of her grandfather; 5 neither one nor both of her parents may have been slaves or engaged in mean occupations. 6 But they say that one whose sister has been chosen to that priesthood acquires exemption, as well as one whose father is a flamen or an augur, one of the Fifteen in charge of the Sibylline Books, one of the Seven who oversee the banquets of the gods, or a dancing priest of Mars. 7 Exemption from that priesthood is regularly allowed also to the betrothed of a pontiff and to the daughter of a priest of the tubilustrium. 8 Furthermore the writings of Ateius Capito inform us that the daughter of a man without residence in Italy must not be chosen, and that the daughter of one who has three children must be excused.

9 Now, as soon as the Vestal virgin is chosen, escorted to the House of Vesta and delivered to the pontiffs, she immediately passes from the control of her father without the ceremony of emancipation or loss of civil rights, and acquires the right to make a will.

10 But as to the method and ritual for choosing a Vestal, there are, it is true, no ancient written records, except that the first to be appointed was chosen by Numa. 11 There is, however, a Papian law, which provides that twenty maidens be selected from the people at the discretion of the chief pontiff, that a choice by lot be made from that number in the assembly, and that the girl whose lot is drawn be "taken" by the chief pontiff and become Vesta's. 12 But

that allotment in accordance with the Papian law is usually unnecessary at present. For if any man of respectable birth goes to the chief pontiff and offers his daughter for the priesthood, provided consideration may be given to her candidacy without violating any religious requirement, the senate grants him exemption from the Papian law.

13 Now the Vestal is said to be "taken," it appears, because she is grasped by the hand of the chief pontiff and led away from the parent under whose control she is, as if she had been taken in war. 14 In the first book of Fabius Pictor's *History* the formula is given which the chief pontiff should use in choosing a Vestal. It is this: "I take thee, Amata, as one who has fulfilled all the legal requirements, to be priestess of Vesta, to perform the rites which it is lawful for a Vestal to perform for the Roman people, the Quirites."

15 Now, many think that the term "taken" ought to be used only of a Vestal. But, as a matter of fact, the flamens of Jupiter also, as well as the augurs, were said to be "taken." 16 Lucius Sulla, in the second book of his *Autobiography*, wrote as follows: "Publius Cornelius, the first to receive the surname Sulla, was taken to be flamen of Jupiter." 17 Marcus Cato, in his accusation of Servius Galba, says of the Lusitanians: "Yet they say that they wished to revolt. I myself at the present moment wish a thorough knowledge of the pontifical law; shall I therefore be taken as chief pontiff? If I wish to understand the science of augury thoroughly, shall anyone for that reason take me as augur?"

18 Furthermore, in the *Commentaries on the Twelve Tables* compiled by Labeo we find this passage: "A Vestal virgin is not heir to any intestate person, nor is anyone her heir, should she die without making a will, but her property, they say, reverts to the public treasury. The legal principle involved is an unsettled question."

19 The Vestal is called "Amata" when taken by the chief pontiff, because there is a tradition that the first one who was chosen bore that name.

● 83
Honors for Priestesses

WORKS: The following inscriptions are from various cities and honor women for their service as priestesses and in other cult offices, such as *stephanephorus* (crown-bearer). Such inscriptions were often inscribed on the bases of statues of the honorees, which were set up in highly visible public spaces.

BIBLIOGRAPHY: *Blessings*, 80–92; Riet van Bremen, *The Limits of Participation: Women and Civic Life in the Greek East in the Hellenistic and Roman Periods*, Dutch Monographs on Ancient History and Archaeology 15 (Amsterdam: J. C. Gieben, 1996); see also the Introduction to this section, note 3.

The Titles, Honors, And Offices of Tata of Aphrodisias

MAMA 7.492b   Aphrodisias, Caria (Turkey), 2d century C.E.

TRANSLATION: Lefkowitz and Fant, no. 259, p. 260.

TEXT: Pleket, *Epigraphica*, 18.

> The council and the people and the senate honour with first-rank honours
> Tata, daughter of Diodorus son of Diodorus son of Leon, reverend priestess
> of Hera for life, mother of the city, who became and remained the wife of
> Attalus son of Pytheas the *stephanephorus*, herself a member of an illustrious
> family of the first rank, who, as priestess of the imperial cult a second time,
> twice supplied oil for athletes in hand-bottles, filled most lavishly from basins
> for the better part of the night as well [as in the day], who became a *stepha-*
> *nephorus*, offered sacrifices throughout the year for the health of the imperial
> family, who held banquets for the people many times with couches provided
> for the public, who herself, for dances and plays, imported the foremost per-
> formers in Asia and displayed them in her native city (and the neighbouring
> cities could also come to the display of the performance), a woman who
> spared no expense, who loved honour, glorious in virtue and chastity.

● 83B

Honors for the Priestess Berenice

IG 12, 5, 655   Syros, 2d or 3d century C.E.

TRANSLATION: Lefkowitz and Fant, no. 263, pp. 261–62.

TEXT: Pleket, *Epigraphica*, 25.

> The resolution of the *prytaneis* approved by the council and the people:
> Whereas Berenice, daughter of Nicomachus, wife of Aristocles son of Isido-
> rus, has conducted herself well and appropriately on all occasions, and after
> she was made a magistrate, unsparingly celebrated rites at her own expense
> for gods and men on behalf of her native city, and after she was made priest-
> ess of the heavenly gods and the holy goddesses Demeter and Kore and cele-
> brated their rites in a holy and worthy manner, has given up her life—mean-
> while she had also raised her own children. Voted to commend the span of
> this woman's lifetime, to crown her with the gold wreath which in our fa-
> therland is customarily used to crown good women. Let the man who pro-
> posed this resolution announce at her burial: "The people of Syros crown
> Berenice daughter of Nicomachus with a gold crown in recognition of her
> virtue and her good will towards them."

● 83c

A Priestess Honored by the Senate

IG 11, 8, 389   Thasos, 4th century C.E.?

TRANSLATION: Lefkowitz and Fant, no. 264, p. 262.

TEXT: Pleket, *Epigraphica*, 29

> With good fortune. The senate honours Flavia Vibia Sabina, most noteworthy
> high priestess, and because of her ancestors uniquely mother of the council:
> she is the only woman, first in all time to have honours equal to those of the
> senators.

● 84

Juliane, the First High Priestess of Asia

IvMag 158   Magnesia on the Meander, mid–1st century C.E.

WORK: This is one of many inscriptions found in the ancient city of Magnesia,
on the Meander River in western Asia Minor (modern Turkey). It is particularly
important for reconstructing and dating the roles of elite women in the imperial
cult in Roman Asia Minor. Of particular debate has been the question of whether
women with the title of high priestess of Asia held the title only by virtue of being
married to male high priests (Juliane was the wife of a high priest), or whether
they held the title and the office on their own, as other examples suggest. Unfortunately, the original inscription, on marble, disappeared in the late nineteenth
century, making it difficult to resolve certain questions about the most likely reading. In this translation, I have added square brackets to indicate scholarly reconstruction of gaps in the inscription.

TRANSLATION, TEXT, AND BIBLIOGRAPHY: Translation adapted from Steven J.
Friesen, "Ephesus: Twice Neokoros" (Ph.D. diss., Harvard University, 1990), 113;
also in Steven J. Friesen, *Twice Neokoros: Ephesus, Asia and the Cult of the Flavian
Imperial Family*, RGRW 116 (Leiden: E. J. Brill, 1993).

ADDITIONAL TEXT: Otto Kern, ed., *Die Inschriften von Magnesia am Maeander*
(Berlin: W. Spemann, 1910), no. 158 (repr. Berlin: De Gruyter, 1967).

ADDITIONAL BIBLIOGRAPHY: Bernadette J. Brooten, "Excursus: What Is an Honorific Title?" in her *Women Leaders*, 7–10; Steven J. Friesen, "Asiarchs," *ZPE* 126
(1999): 275–90; see also bibliography in the introduction to this section, note 3.

> The council [and the people honored] Juliane—daughter of [Eus]tra[tos] (?)
> [son of Phan]ostratos (?), wi[fe of Al]kiphranos [the high] priest of A[sia],
> the [f]irst amo[ng women] (to serve as) hi[gh] priestess of Asia, *ste-
> phan[ephor]os, gymn[asiarch]*, pri[est]ess for l[ife] (?) of Aph[rod]ite an[d of

the goddess Agrip]pina the [moth]er, an[d] p[riest]ess for life of De[met]er [in E]phesus—because of a[ll] her [ex]cellence.

● 85
Three Women Heads of Synagogues

WORKS: The following Greek inscriptions explicitly designate a woman as *archisynagogos* (head of the synagogue). Two inscriptions are the work of the women themselves, while the third is an epitaph, probably set up by others. One woman appears to have held two offices: synagogue head and elder. For further discussion and bibliography, see the Introduction to this section.

TRANSLATION: RSK.

ADDITIONAL TRANSLATION, TEXT, AND BIBLIOGRAPHY: Brooten, *Women Leaders*.

● 85A
Epitaph Set Up by Rufina, Head of the Synagogue

CIJ 741   Smyrna (modern Izmir, Turkey), 2d century C.E.?

NOTE: On the translation "Jewish/Judean" see the main introduction, p. 8.

BIBLIOGRAPHY: *Blessings*, 106–27; Ross S. Kraemer, "Jewish Women in the Diaspora World of Late Antiquity," in Judith Baskin, ed., *Jewish Women in Historical Perspective*, 2d ed. (Detroit, Mich.: Wayne State University Press, 1998), 46–72.

Rufina, a Jewish [or "Judean"] woman, head of the synagogue, built this tomb for her freed slaves and the slaves raised in her house. No one else has the right to bury anyone (here). Anyone who dares to do (so) will pay 1500 denaria to the sacred treasury and 1000 denaria to the Jewish people [or "the Judean *ethnos*"]. A copy of this inscription has been placed in the (public) archives.

● 85B
Epitaph of Sophia of Gortyn, Head of the Synagogue

CIJ 1².731c   Kastelli Kissamou, Crete, 4th or 5th century C.E.

BIBLIOGRAPHY: Pieter W. van der Horst, "The Jews of Ancient Crete," *Journal of Jewish Studies* 39 (1988): 183–200, repr. in Pieter W. van der Horst, *Essays on the Jewish World of Early Christianity* (Gottingen: Vandenhoeck and Ruprecht, 1990), 148–65; see also entry 85A.

Sophia of Gortyn, elder and head of the synagogue of Kisamos, (lies) here. The memory of the righteous one forever. Amen.

● 85C

Inscription of Theopempte, Head of the Synagogue

CIJ 756   Myndos (Caria), modern Turkey, 4th to 5th century C.E.

WORK: This inscription was found on a chancel screen post, identifying the donors.

[From Th]eopempte, head of the synagogue, and her son Eusebios.

● 86

An Unnamed Woman Head of a Synagogue in Ancient Cappadocia

Unpublished inscription   Göre, Cappadocia, 3d to 4th centuries C.E.?

WORK: In 1894, a Turkish scholar traveling in Cappadocia saw and transcribed a handful of Greek inscriptions in a small Turkish village now called Göre, outside Nevçehir. When he returned some time later to continue his work, the inscriptions had apparently been effaced. He subsequently published his initial transcriptions in an obscure Turkish almanac written in Karamanli, a form of Turkish written in Greek characters. Serendipitously, these inscriptions, which appear to be Jewish and to date from the third or fourth century C.E., came to the attention of Bernadette Brooten after she had completed her own study of women leaders in ancient Jewish synagogues. Brooten quickly shared them with me and eventually gave them to her student, Christine M. Thomas, to research and publish. Thomas's publication is forthcoming. In the interim, I give here a translation of the one inscription that refers to a female head of a congregation (here *archisynagogisas*). The inscription is unquestionably that of a woman, but her name is no longer extant.

NOTE: On the translation "Jew/Judean," see the main introduction, p. 8.

BIBLIOGRAPHY: Christine M. Thomas, "A Woman as Head of Synagogue in Ancient Cappadocia: Six New Jewish Inscriptions," forthcoming; Brooten, *Women Leaders*.

[tomb of so-and-so], a Jew [f.]/Judean, head of the synagogue. In peace be her sleep.

● 87
Epitaph of a Jewish Woman "Leader"

CIJ 1².696b   Thebes in Phthiotis, Thessaly, date uncertain

TEXT: *CIJ* 1².696b.

TRANSLATION: RSK.

ADDITIONAL TRANSLATION, TEXT, AND BIBLIOGRAPHY: Brooten, *Women Leaders.*

⎮ Tomb of Peristeria, leader.

● 88
Seven Epitaphs of Jewish Women Elders

WORKS: These burial inscriptions come from various places in the ancient Mediterranean, three from Venosa in Italy, and each designates a woman by the term "elder." These inscriptions pose a somewhat unusual problem, for the terms *presbyteros* and *presbytes*, "elder," can designate absolute age (an old person), relative age (perhaps to distinguish two persons of the same name), and a Jewish or Christian religious office. As a result, it is sometimes difficult to know how to read these and related terms whether in masculine or feminine form, and interpreters of these inscriptions differ in their conclusions. For example, while Brooten gives both translations for Sara Ura, from Rome, Noy prefers to consider her an old woman. One of the strongest cases for translating the term as a religious office can be made for 88G.

TRANSLATION: RSK, except 88F: Brooten, *Women Leaders.*

TEXT: *CIJ*, except for 88F and 88G.

ADDITIONAL TRANSLATION, TEXT, AND BIBLIOGRAPHY: Brooten, *Women Leaders* (except 88G); *JIWE* (88A–D).

● 88A
CIJ 400; *JIWE* 2:24   Rome, 3d or 4th century C.E.

⎮ Here lies Sara Ura, elder.

● 88B
CIJ 581; *JIWE* 1:59   Venosa, Italy, 5th century C.E.

⎮ Tomb of Beronike, elder and daughter of Ioses.

● **88c**

CIJ 590; *JIWE* 1:62   Venosa, Italy, 5th century C.E.

NOTE: The term "father" (*pater*) is a title, probably a civic one. A Jewish woman from Venosa called *pateressa* is memorialized in another inscription, *CIJ* 606 (*JIWE* 1:63).

Tomb of Mannine, elder; daughter of Longinus, father; granddaughter of Faustinus, father; 38 years (old).

● **88D**

CIJ 597; *JIWE* 1:71   Venosa, Italy, 5th century C.E.

Tomb of Faustina, elder.

● **88E**

CIJ 692   Bizye, Thrace, 4th or 5th century C.E. (or later?)

Tomb of Rebeka, the elder, who has fallen asleep.

● **88F**

SEG 27 (1977) 1201   Oea, Tripolitania, North Africa, 4th or 5th century C.E. (or later?)

Tomb of Makaria [or "the blessed"] Mazauzala, elder. She lived . . . years. Rest. God is with the holy and the righteous.

● **88G**

Kraemer, *HTR* 78 (1985): 431–38   Malta, 4th or 5th century C.E.

TRANSLATION, TEXT, AND BIBLIOGRAPHY: Ross S. Kraemer, "A New Inscription from Malta and the Question of Women Elders in Diaspora Jewish Communities," *HTR* 78, nos. 3–4 (1985): 431–38.

[So-and-so], head of the council of elders, lover of the commandments, and Eulogia, the elder, his wife.

● **89**

Three Epitaphs of Jewish Women Possibly Called "Priestess"

WORKS: The following burial inscriptions, in Greek, come from diverse places and dates, and in each a woman is designated by the feminine form, *hierissa*, of the Greek word for "priest." The interpretation of these inscriptions is even more vexing than the interpretation of inscriptions designating women as "elders" (see entry 88), since the literary evidence from the Hebrew Bible on seems to suggest that only men were Jewish priests. As a result, most scholars have taken these inscriptions to refer to women who were members of priestly families. Brooten, however, has argued that their interpretation is more complex. Noy and Horbury are somewhat inconsistent in their translations, although not their discussion (compare *JIGRE* 84 with *JIWE* 2.11).

TRANSLATION: RSK.

ADDITIONAL TRANSLATION, TEXT, AND BIBLIOGRAPHY: Brooten, *Women Leaders.*

● 89A

Epitaph of a Jewish Woman from Egypt

CPJ/CIJ 1514; *JIGRE* 84   Leontopolis, Egypt, June 7, 27 B.C.E.

NOTE: On other inscriptions from Leontopolis, see entry 48.

> O Marin, priestess [or "of priestly descent"], worthy, friend to all, and who brought no one grief, and loved her neighbors, farewell. About 50 years old. In the third year of Caesar, Payni 13.

● 89B

Epitaph of a Jewish Woman from Rome

CIJ 315; *JIWE* 2.11   Rome, 3d or 4th century C.E.?

NOTE: The language of this inscription is quite typical of inscriptions from Roman Jewish catacombs, particularly the phrase "in peace (be) her sleep."

> Here lies Gaudentia, 24, priestess [or "of priestly descent"].
> In peace (be) her sleep.

● 89C

Epitaph of the Mother of a Jewish Woman Called "Priestess"

CIJ 1007   Beth She'arim, Israel, 4th century C.E.

ADDITIONAL TRANSLATION, TEXT, AND BIBLIOGRAPHY: Benjamin Mazar, *Beth She'arim: Report on the Excavations During 1936–1940, Volume Two: The Greek Inscriptions* (New Brunswick, N.J.: Rutgers University Press, 1974), 42–43, no. 66.

> Sara, daughter of Naimia, mother of the priestess [or "priestly"] Lady Maria, lies here.

● 90

Two Epitaphs of Christian Women Elders

WORKS: Each of these burial inscriptions from Sicily and Asia Minor designates a Christian woman by the term "elder." See entry 88 for discussion of the problem posed by this term. As with the Jewish inscriptions, interpreters of this type of inscription differ in their readings of individual inscriptions.

TRANSLATIONS: RSK.

ADDITIONAL TRANSLATION, TEXT, AND BIBLIOGRAPHY: Ute E. Eisen, *Women Officeholders in Early Christianity: Epigraphical and Literary Studies*, trans. Linda M. Maloney (Collegeville, Minn.: Michael Glazier, Liturgical Press, 2000).

● 90A

Epitaph of Kale

PIRAINO, *Inscrizioni*, 36–37, no. 13.   Centuripae, Sicily, 4th or 5th century C.E.

TEXT: Maria Teresa Manni Piraino, *Inscrizioni greche lapidare del Museo di Palermo*, ΣΙΚΕΛΙΚΑ 6 (Palermo: S. F. Flaacovio, 1973), 36–37, no. 13.

ADDITIONAL TRANSLATION, TEXT, AND BIBLIOGRAPHY: *NewDocs* 1 (1981): 121, no. 79.

Here lies Kale the elder. She lived fifty years blamelessly.

She completed her life on September 14.

● 90B

Epitaph of Ammion, Perhaps Montanist

KÖRTE, *Inscriptiones Bureschianae*, 31, no. 55.   Uçak, Phrygia (modern Turkey),
3d century C.E.

NOTE: Although many scholars have thought it likely that this is a Montanist inscription (see entries 66G and 66H), Eisen questions this identification, which she sees as based, at least in part, on the tendency to classify evidence for Christian women officeholders as from heretical sects.

TEXT: Alfred Körte, *Inscriptiones Bureschianae* (Greifswald: Druck von J. Abel, 1902), 31 no. 55.

ADDITIONAL TRANSLATION, TEXT, AND BIBLIOGRAPHY: Gibson, *Christians for Christians; NewDocs* 4 (1987): 240; William Tabbernee, *Montanist Inscriptions and Testimonia: Epigraphic Sources Illustrating the History of Montanism*, North American Patristic Society Patristic Monograph Series 16 (Macon, Ga.: Mercer University Press, 1997).

| Diogas, the bishop, for Ammion [f.], the elder, in memory.

⬤ 91
Six Inscriptions of (Christian) Women Deacons

WORKS: Three of the following inscriptions are epitaphs for Christian women called by some form of the Greek term *diakonos*, two are votive inscriptions made by such women, and one epitaph was set up by a woman deacon for her relatives. There is less contention about the general meaning of the term "deacon" but much discussion about how extensive the responsibilities and authority of female deacons might have been. The choice of translations here is intended to reflect distinctions in the Greek terminology of the inscriptions themselves: "deacon" here signifies the use of the feminine article with the masculine form (*hē diakonos*); "deaconess" signifies the use of a feminine article with a feminized form (e.g., *hē diakonissa*). The use of the feminine article with a masculine form occurs in Greek in numerous other instances (including, among others, the term *hē theos* for a female deity). Additional inscriptions are collected in Eisen, *Women Officeholders*.

TRANSLATIONS: RSK.

BIBLIOGRAPHY: *Blessings*, 174–90.

ADDITIONAL TRANSLATION, TEXT, AND BIBLIOGRAPHY: Ute E. Eisen, *Women Officeholders in Early Christianity: Epigraphical and Literary Studies*, trans. Linda M. Maloney (Collegeville, Minn.: Michael Glazier, Liturgical Press, 2000), 158–98 (lacking 91D).

⬤ 91A
Epitaph of Sophia the Deacon, the Second Phoebe

Alt *Griechischen Inschriften* 17   Mount of Olives, Jerusalem, late 4th century C.E.

NOTE: The reference to Phoebe is almost certainly to the woman of that name described by Paul (Rom. 16.1–2) as *diakonos* of the assembly at Cenchreae, the port city of Corinth.

TEXT: Albrecht Alt, *Der griechischen Inschriften der Palaestina tertia westlich der 'Araba* (Berlin and Leipzig: Walter de Gruyter, 1921), 17; Guarducci, *Epigrafia*, 4, 445, no. 3.

ADDITIONAL TRANSLATION, TEXT, AND BIBLIOGRAPHY: *NewDocs* 4 (1987 [1979]): 239, no. 122.

Here lies the servant and bride of Christ
Sophia the deacon, the second Phoebe,
Falling asleep in peace on the 21st of the month of March
In the 11th indiction.
. . . Lord God . . .

● 91B

Epitaph of the Deaconness Athanasia

Guarducci, *Epigrafia*, 4, 345, no. 4   Delphi, Greece, 5th century C.E.

The most pious deaconess Athanasia,
having lived a blameless life modestly,
having been ordained a deaconess by the most holy bishop Pantamianos,
made this monument: in it lie her remains.
Anyone who dares to open this monument,
in which the deaconess has been deposited,
will have the portion of Judas,
the betrayer of our Lord, Jesus Christ. No less so, those clerics who may
    be present at this time
and assent [to the removal of] the aforementioned deaconess . . .

● 91C

Epitaph of the Deacon Maria

Jacobi *Esplorazioni*, 33–36.   Archelais, Cappadocia (Turkey), 6th century C.E.

NOTE: The "speech of the apostle" is a reference to 1 Timothy 4.10, which lays
out obligations for enrolled widows.

TEXT: Giulio Jacopi, *Esplorazioni e studi in Paflagonia e Cappadocia: Relazione sulla
seconda campagna explorativa, agosto–ottobre 1936* (Rome: F. Palumbi, 1937), 33–36;
SEG 27 (1977) 948A.

ADDITIONAL TRANSLATION, TEXT, AND BIBLIOGRAPHY: *NewDocs* 2 (1982
[1977]): 193–94, no. 109.

Here lies Maria the deacon, of pious and blessed memory,
who in accordance with the speech of the apostle reared children,
practiced hospitality, washed the feet of the saints, shared her bread with the
    afflicted.
Remember her, Lord, when you come in (or "into") your kingdom.

91D

Monument erected by Domna, the Deacon

MAMA 7.471   Bulduk (Turkey), date uncertain

| Domna the deacon, daughter of Theophilos the elder, set up (the monument) to her own father-in-law, Miros, and to her husband, Patroklos, in memory.

91E

A Vow Fulfilled by the Deacon Agrippiane

Petsas *Arch. Delt.* 26 (1971): 161–63   Patrae, Greece, date uncertain

TEXT: P. Petsas, *Archaiologikon Deltion* 26 (1971): 161–63.

ADDITIONAL TRANSLATION, TEXT, AND BIBLIOGRAPHY: *NewDocs* 4 (1987 [1979]): 239, no. 122 n.2.

| The deacon Agrippiane, most beloved of God, made the mosaic because of her vow.

91F

A Vow Fulfilled by a Deaconess

NewDocs 2 (1982 [1977]): 194   Stobi, Macedonia, 4th or 5th century C.E.

NOTE: Recent commentators on this inscription read it in different ways.

TEXT AND BIBLIOGRAPHY: *New Docs* 2 (1982 [1977]): 194–95.

| Because of her vow, Mat(rona?) [or "of the vow of the matron"], the most pious deaconess, paved the exedra with mosaic.

92

Opposition to Teaching and Baptizing by Women

TERTULLIAN   late 2d or early 3d century C.E.

AUTHOR: Although many of his writings survive, surprisingly little is known about the details of the life of Quintus Septimius Florens Tertullian (ca. 160–225). A native of Carthage in Roman North Africa, he converted to Christianity sometime before 197 C.E. Although the chronology of his career as a Christian is disputed, it is known that at some point he joined the New Prophecy (also known as Montanism), a charismatic sect said to have been founded by two women prophets, Maximilla and Priscilla, and a male prophet, Montanus, from whom the name Montanism is derived. Some scholars believe that after some years, Tertullian separated from the community but the evidence is ambiguous at best.

A significant number of his extant works concern appropriate behavior for

Christian women: *On the Dress of Women; On the Veiling of Virgins; On Modesty; On Monogamy; On the Exhortation to Chastity*. Married himself, he nevertheless advocated celibacy and chastity as the ideal Christian life. He was also the author of numerous polemics against those he considered heretics, including Marcionites and Valentinians.

In a work dated around 203 C.E., Tertullian disparaged those who appealed to the story of Thecla [entry 105] on the grounds that some people used it inappropriately to legitimate baptism by women. This may suggest that attitudes toward the leadership roles of women were one of his points of contention with the New Prophecy.

Unfortunately, there is some uncertainty about what, exactly, Tertullian actually wrote. The entry below provides three possible readings, based on the one extant manuscript (Codex Trecensis), and the two sixteenth-century printed editions of a second manuscript which is no longer extant. In one reading, Tertullian knows a work called the *Acti Pauli*; in another he may only know "writings" about Paul that mention Thecla. In one reading, the audience of Tertullian's admonition is taken to be masculine, or perhaps of both genders, while in another, Tertullian explicitly addresses women. The key differences are in the first lines.

● 92A
On Baptism 17

TRANSLATION: RSK. See also the translation in Wilhelm Schneemelcher, in *NTA* 2:214.

TEXT: Borleffs, CCL 1.2, (Turnhout, 1954), 291f; CSEL 20, ed. A. Reifferscheid and G. Wissowa (1890), p. 215. For a critical edition of Mesnartius (1545): F. Oehler, *Quinti Septimii Florentis Tertulliani quae supersunt Omnia* (Lipsiae: T. O. Weigel, 1853); for a critical edition of the Codex Trecensis, see E. Evans, *Q. Septimii Florentis Tertulliani de baptismo liber. Tertullian's Homily on Baptism. The Text edited with an Introduction, Translation and commentary* (London, 1964).

BIBLIOGRAPHY: Willy Rordorf, "Tertullien et les Actes de Paul (à propos de *Bapt.* 17,5)" in *Hommage à René Braun: Textes Réunis par Grandarolo Jean; avec la collab. de Biraud Michèle* (Paris: Les Belles Lettres, 1990), vol. 2: 151–160; repr. in *Lex Orandi, Lex Credendi: Gesammelte Aufsätze zum 60. Geburtstag* (Freiburg Schweiz: Universitätsverlag, 1993), 475–484; A. Hilhorst, "Tertullian on the Acts of Paul," in Jan Bremmer, ed., *The Acts of Paul and Thecla*. Studies on the Apocryphal Acts of the Apostles 2 (Kampen: Kok Pharos, 1996), 150–163.

> *Mesnartius' 1545 edition of a manuscript no longer extant:*
>
> But if those writings which wrongly go under Paul's name adduce the example [or: writing] of Thecla as license for women to teach and to baptize, let them know that the presbyter who produced this text, as though adding something of his own reputation to Paul's, resigned his position, having been discovered, and having confessed that he did so out of love for Paul.

Gelenius's 1550 edition of the same manuscript:

But if those women who read the falsely named writings about Paul adduce the example [or: writing] of Thecla as license for women to teach and to baptize, let them [i.e. those women] know that the presbyter who produced this text, as though adding something of his own reputation to Paul's, resigned his position, having been discovered, and having confessed that he did so out of love for Paul.

Codex Trecensis:

But if certain Acts of Paul, which are falsely so named, adduce the example of Thecla as license for women to teach and to baptize, let them know that the presbyter who produced this text, as though adding something of his own reputation to Paul's, resigned his position, having been discovered, and having confessed that he did so out of love for Paul.

● 92B
On the Veiling of Virgins 9

TRANSLATION: ANF 4.33.

TEXT: SC 424 (E. Schulz-Flügel and P. Mattei, 1997).

It is not permitted to a woman to speak in the church [1 Cor. 14.33b]; but neither (is it permitted her) to teach, nor to baptize, nor to offer, nor to claim to herself a lot in any manly function, not to say (in any) sacerdotal office. Let us inquire whether any of these be lawful to a virgin. . . . nothing in the way of public honour is permitted to a virgin.

● 92C
On the Prescription against Heretics 41

TRANSLATION: ANF 3.263.

TEXT: SC 46 (R. F. Refoulé and P. de Labriolle, 1957).

The very women of these heretics, how wanton they are! For they are bold enough to teach, to dispute, to enact exorcisms, to undertake cures—it may be even to baptize.

● 93

A Montanist Visionary Who Submits Her Revelation to Careful Scrutiny

TERTULLIAN *On the Soul* 9 late 2d or early 3d century C.E.

AUTHOR: See entry 92.

TRANSLATION: *ANF* 3.181–235.

TEXT: See entry 92; also J. H. Waszink, *Tertullianus: "De Anima"* (Amsterdam: North-Holland Publishing Co., 1947).

BIBLIOGRAPHY: There is an extensive bibliography on Montanism (the New Prophecy): *Blessings*, 157–73; F. Forrester Church, "Sex and Salvation in Tertullian," *HTR* 68 (1975): 83–101; Nicola Denzey, "What Did the Montanists Read," *HTR* 94, no. 4 (2001): 427–49: Susanna Elm, "Montanist Oracles," in *Searching the Scriptures*, 2:131–38; Frederick C. Klawiter, "The Role of Martyrdom and Persecution in Developing the Priestly Authority of Women in Early Christianity: A Case Study of Montanism," *Church History* 49, no. 3 (1980): 251–61; John C. Poirier, "Montanist Pepuza-Jerusalem and the Dwelling Place of Wisdom," *JECS* 7, no. 4 (1999): 491–507; William Tabbernee, "Portals of the Montanist New Jerusalem: The Discovery of Pepouza and Tymion," *JECS* 11, no. 1 (2003): 87–94; Christine Trevett, *Montanism: Gender, Authority and the New Prophecy* (Cambridge: Cambridge University Press, 1996). Additional sources for Montanism are collected in Ronald Heine, *Montanist Oracles and Testimonia* (Macon, Ga.: Mercer University Press, 1989); and William Tabbernee, *Montanist Inscriptions and Testimonia: Epigraphic Sources Illustrating the History of Montanism*, North American Patristic Society Patristic Monograph Series 16 (Macon, Ga.: Mercer University Press, 1997).

> We have now amongst us a sister whose lot it has been to be favoured with gifts of revelation, which she experiences in the Spirit by ecstatic vision amidst the sacred rites of the Lord's Day in the church; she converses with angels, and sometimes even with the Lord; she both sees and hears mysterious communications; some men's hearts she discerns, and she obtains directions for healing for such as need them. Whether it be in the reading of the Scriptures, or in the chanting of psalms, or in the preaching of sermons, or in the offering up of prayers, in all these religious services matter and opportunity are afforded her of seeing visions. Perchance, while this sister of ours was *in the Spirit*, we had discoursed on some topic about the soul. After the people are dismissed at the conclusion of the sacred services, she is in the regular habit of reporting to us whatever things she may have seen in vision; for all her communications are examined with the most scrupulous care, in order that their truth may be probed. "Amongst other things," she says, "there was shown to me a soul in bodily shape, and a spirit appeared to me; not, however, a void and empty illusion, but such as would offer itself to be even grasped by the hand, clear and transparent and of an ethereal colour,

and in form resembling that of a human being in every respect." This was
her vision, and for her witness there was God; and the apostle is a fitting
surety that there were to be Spiritual gifts in the Church.

● 94

Hippolytus on the Montanist Prophets Maximilla and Priscilla

HIPPOLYTUS *Refutation of All Heresies* 8.12   2d or 3d century C.E.

AUTHOR: Little is known about the life of Hippolytus (ca. 170–236 C.E.), a Roman
presbyter, perhaps because he spent much of it opposing the leadership of the
Roman church, especially Callistas, bishop from 217 to 222. Hippolytus died in
Sardinia during the persecution of Emperor Maximinus. Portions of works attributed to him have survived, although their authorship has been debated. His principal work seems to have been the *Refutation of All Heresies*, which attempts to
demonstrate that all Christian heresies derive from Greek philosophical systems.
In Hippolytus, as in other antiheretical writers, women figure prominently in the
beliefs and practices opposed. He was also the author of a work called the *Apostolic
Tradition*.

TRANSLATION: ANF 5.9–153.

TEXT: GCS 26 (P. Wendland, 1916).

BIBLIOGRAPHY: See entry 93.

> But there are others who themselves are even more heretical in nature [than
> the foregoing], and are Phrygians by birth. These have been rendered victims
> of error from being previously captivated by [two] wretched women, called a
> certain Priscilla and Maximilla, whom they supposed [to be] prophetesses. And
> they assert that into these the Paraclete Spirit had departed; and antecedently
> to them, they in like manner consider Montanus as a prophet. And being in
> possession of an infinite number of their books, [the Phrygians] are overrun
> with delusion; and they do not judge whatever statements are made by them,
> according to [the criterion of] reason; nor do they give heed unto those who
> are competent to decide; but they are heedlessly swept onwards, by the reliance
> which they place on these [impostors]. And they allege that they have learned
> something more through these, than from law, and prophets, and the Gospels.
> But they magnify these wretched women above the Apostles and every gift of
> Grace, so that some of them presume to assert that there is in them a some-
> thing superior to Christ. These acknowledge God to be the Father of the uni-
> verse, and Creator of all things, similarly with the Church, and [receive] as
> many things as the Gospel testifies concerning Christ. They introduce, how-
> ever, the novelties of fasts, and feasts, and meals of parched food, and repasts
> of radishes, alleging that they have been instructed by women.

Women Bishops, Presbyters, and Prophets among the Followers of Quintilla and Priscilla

EPIPHANIUS *Medicine Box* 49   4th century C.E.

AUTHOR, TRANSLATION, TEXT, AND BIBLIOGRAPHY: See entry 38.

1 The Quintillians, who are also called Pepuzians, Artotyritai, and Priscillians, are all Cataphrygians and originate from them but differ somewhat among themselves. These Cataphrygians or Priscillians say that in Pepuza either Quintilla or Priscilla, I am not sure which, but one of them, was, as they said, sleeping in Pepuza when Christ came to her and lay beside her in the following fashion, as that deluded woman recounted. "In a vision," she said, "Christ came to me in the form of a woman in a bright garment, endowed me with wisdom, and revealed to me that this place is holy, and it is here that Jerusalem is to descend from heaven." Because of this they say that even to this day some women and men engage in incubation on the spot waiting to see Christ. Some women among them are called prophetesses, but I do not clearly know whether among them or among the Cataphrygians. They are alike and have the same way of thinking.

2 They use both the Old and New Testament and also speak in the same way of a resurrection of the dead. They consider Quintilla together with Priscilla as founder, the same as the Cataphrygians. They bring with them many useless testimonies, attributing a special grace to Eve because she first ate of the tree of knowledge. They acknowledge the sister of Moses as a prophetess as support for their practice of appointing women to the clergy. Also, they say, Philip had four daughters who prophesied. Often in their assembly seven virgins dressed in white enter carrying lamps, having come in to prophesy to the people. They deceive the people present by giving the appearance of ecstasy; they pretend to weep as if showing the grief of repentance by shedding tears and by their appearance lamenting human life. Women among them are bishops, presbyters, and the rest, as if there were no difference of nature. "For in Christ Jesus there is neither male nor female." These are the things we have learned. They are called Artotyritai because in their mysteries they use bread and cheese and in this fashion they perform their rites.

3 It is totally laughable among human beings to separate from the correct belief and turn to vanity and the variety of ecstasies and frenzies. Deranged minds follow those who do not hold fast to the anchor of truth and those who yield themselves to anyone who would lead them after any cause whatsoever. Even if women among them are ordained to the episcopacy and presbyterate because of Eve, they hear the Lord saying: "Your orientation will be toward your husband and he will rule over you." The apostolic saying es-

caped their notice, namely that: "I do not allow a woman to speak or have authority over a man." And again: "Man is not from woman but woman from man"; and "Adam was not deceived, but Eve was first deceived into transgression." Oh, the multifaceted error of this world!

Passing this judgment as on a toothless lizard full of madness, I will go on to the next things, beloved, calling upon God to help our inadequacy and to enable us to fulfill our promise [i.e., to write the book].

● 96

Fourth-Century Writers on the Montanist Prophets Maximilla and Priscilla

● 96A

Eusebius on Maximilla

EUSEBIUS *History of the Church* 5.16   4th century C.E.

AUTHOR, TRANSLATION, TEXT, AND BIBLIOGRAPHY: See entry 65.

7–10 In Phrygian Mysia there is said to be a village called Ardabav. There they say that a recent convert called Montanus, when Gratus was proconsul of Asia, in the unbounded lust of his soul for leadership gave access to himself to the adversary, became obsessed, and suddenly fell into frenzy and convulsions. He began to be ecstatic and to speak and to talk strangely, prophesying contrary to the custom which belongs to the tradition and succession of the church from the beginning. Of those who at that time heard these bastard utterances some were vexed, thinking that he was possessed by a devil and by a spirit of error, and was disturbing the populace; they rebuked him, and forbade him to speak, remembering the distinction made by the Lord, and his warning to keep watchful guard against the coming of the false prophets; but others, as though elevated by a holy spirit and a prophetic gift, and not a little conceited, forgot the Lord's distinction, and encouraged the mind-injuring and seducing and people-misleading spirit, being cheated and deceived by it so that he could not be kept silent. But by some art, or rather by such an evil scheme of artifice, the devil wrought destruction for the disobedient, and receiving unworthy honours from them stimulated and inflamed their understanding which was already dead to the true faith; so that he raised up two more women and filled them with the bastard spirit so that they spoke madly and improperly and strangely, like Montanus. The spirit gave blessings to those who rejoiced and were proud in him, and puffed them up by the greatness of its promises. Yet sometimes it flatly condemned them completely, wisely, and faithfully, that it might seem to be critical, though but few of the Phrygians were deceived. But when the arrogant spirit taught to blaspheme the whole Catholic church throughout the world, because the spirit of false prophecy received from it neither honour nor entrance, for the Christians of Asia after assembling for this purpose many times and in many parts of the province, tested the recent utterances, pronounced them profane, and rejected the heresy,—then at last the Montanists were driven out of the church and excommunicated.

17–19 ... and he writes thus: "And let not the spirit which speaks through Maximilla say, in the same work according to Asterius Orbanus, 'I am driven away like a wolf from the sheep. I am not a wolf, I am word and spirit and power.' But let him show clearly and prove the power in the spirit, and let him through the spirit force to recognize him those who were then present for the purpose of testing and conversing with the spirit as it spoke,—eminent men and bishops, Zoticus from the village Cumane, and Julian from Apamea, whose mouths the party of Themiso muzzled, and did not allow the false spirit which deceived the people to be refuted by them."

In the same book, again, after other refutations of the false prophecies of Maximilla, in a single passage he both indicates the time at which he wrote this, and quotes her predictions, in which she foretold future wars and revolutions, and he corrects the falsehood of them as follows: "Has it not been made obvious already that this is another lie? For it is more than thirteen years to-day since the woman died, and there has been in the world neither local nor universal war, but rather by the mercy of God continuing peace even for Christians."

● 96B

A Saying of Priscilla

EPIPHANIUS *Medicine Box* 49.1.3   4th century C.E.

AUTHOR, TEXT, AND BIBLIOGRAPHY: See entry 38.

TRANSLATION: RSK.

Appearing in the form of a woman, radiantly robed, Christ came to me and implanted wisdom within me and revealed to me that this place [Pepuza] is holy, and that Jerusalem is to come down from heaven.

● 96C

Sayings of Maximilla

EPIPHANIUS *Medicine Box* 48   4th century C.E.

AUTHOR, TEXT, AND BIBLIOGRAPHY: See entry 38.

TRANSLATION: RSK.

2.4 After me, there will be no prophet, but the completion.

12.4 Hear not me; rather, hear Christ [through me].

13.1. The Lord sent me to be partisan, informer, interpreter of this task and of the covenant and of the pronouncement; compelled, willingly or unwillingly, to learn the knowledge of God.

● 97
Epitaph of the Female Prophet Nanas

HASPELS *Highlands of Phrygia*, no. 107   mid–4th C.E.?

WORK: This Greek tomb inscription was found in Akoluk, a village in the region of Turkey known as the Phrygian highlands, an area with documented Jewish and Christian communities as early as the third century C.E. Scholars tend to classify the inscription as Christian, based on the title *prophetissa* and references to angelic visitations, fearing God, constant prayer, and so forth. Some consider it probably Montanist, given both Nanas's title and the considerable evidence for Montanism in this region from the second century on. Although it may be Montanist Christian, it might also be neither. The inscription contains no definitive Christian markings or any exclusively Christian language. Nanas might have been Jewish; she might also have been one of many persons in ancient Asia Minor whose piety drew heavily on ideas and images common to Judaism and Christianity, without being either.

TRANSLATION: RSK.

TRANSLATION, TEXT, AND BIBLIOGRAPHY: C. H. E. Haspels, *The Highlands of Phrygia: Sites and Monuments*, 2 vols. (Princeton: Princeton University Press, 1971), no. 107 (with partial translation); Ute Elsen, *Women Officeholders in Early Christianity: Epigraphical and Literary Studies*, trans. Linda M. Maloney (Collegeville, Minn.: Michael Glazier, Liturgical Press, 2000), 63–67, with a translation of lines 1–14; William Tabbernee, *Montanist Inscriptions and Testimonia: Epigraphic Sources Illustrating the History of Montanism*, North American Patristic Society Patristic Monographic Series 16 (Macon, Ga.: Mercer University Press, 1997), with a more complete translation.

For additional bibliography on Montanism, see entry 93.

The prophetess
Nanas, (daughter) of Hermogenes,
With prayers and supplications,
With hymns and adulations,
She beseeched the Lord who is worshipped,
The deathless One.
Praying all day and all night
She had from the first the fear of God.
She had angelic visitations and a strong voice.

Blessed Nanas,
whose "sleeping-place"
.... companion, much-beloved husband
went with....
into the all-(nourishing) earth....
s/he, in return, did....
those who grieve [for her] [hono]red [her] greatly....
for a memorial.

● 98
A Woman Philosopher(?), Probably Christian

NewDocs 4 (1987 [1979]): 257, no. 126   late imperial?

WORK: This burial inscription is from Nikaia, in Greece. The term *philosophissa*
is reminiscent of other late imperial terms formed by the addition of the feminine
ending *-issa*, such as *archisynagogis(s)a, diakonissa*, etc. Horsley argues that the
term identifies Attia as a consecrated virgin (a "nun" in his terminology), which
is reinforced by the phrase "garbing herself in virginity." The constellation of language as a whole should probably be taken as Christian.

TRANSLATION: RSK.

ADDITIONAL TEXT: M. Schede, *AM* 36 (1911): 103, no. 14.

Attia *philosophissa*,
garbing yourself in virginity you fled the evil of the world
exalting, through your faith(fulness) and love, the name of God.
Therefore, you and your soul have attained paradise,
wherein (are) holy Nous and the chorus of the saints with the prophets
      rejoicing.
Farewell, sweet child, farewell and have mercy on your parents....
[chil]d of God.

● 99
Regulations for Deaconesses

Constitutions of the Holy Apostles 2.26   4th century C.E.?

WORK: A lengthy work that purports to set down the regulations of the apostles
for appropriate Christian behavior, the *Constitutions of the Holy Apostles* (or *The
Apostolic Constitutions*), contains much material on women, although how reliably
it reflects the practices and thoughts of actual Christian women has been little
studied. In addition to including chapters on evil women and the subjugation of

wives to husbands, book 1 contains a passage on why women should not bathe with men. Book 3, concerning widows, is for the most part a commentary on 1 Timothy and other biblical texts on women. It also contains arguments against baptizing by women, on the grounds that Christ could have authorized women to baptize but did not, as well as arguments against teaching by women. Book 8 contains prayers for the ordination of deaconesses, including one that cites the spiritual replenishment of Miriam, Deborah, Anna, and Huldah.

TRANSLATION: Irah Chase, *The Work Claiming to Be the "Constitutions of the Holy Apostles," Including the Canons* (New York: D. Appleton, 1848).

TEXT: *SC* 320, 329 (Marcel Metzger, 1985–86); F. X. Funk, *Didascalia et Constitutiones Apostolorum* (Munich: Paderborn, 1905).

ADDITIONAL TRANSLATION: *ANF* 7.

BIBLIOGRAPHY: Francine Cardman, "Women, Ministry and Church Order in Early Christianity," in *Women and Christian Origins*, 300–329; Roger Gryson, *The Ministry of Women in the Early Church*, trans. Jean Laporte and Mary Louise Hall (Collegeville, Minn.: Liturgical Press, 1976); Aimé Georges Martimort, *Deaconesses: An Historical Study* (San Francisco: Ignatius Press, 1986); Carolyn Osiek, "The Widow as Altar: The Rise and Fall of a Symbol," *Second Century* 3 (1983): 159–69.

Let the Bishop, therefore, preside over you as one honored with the authority of God, which he is to exercise over the clergy, and by which he is to govern all the people. But let the deacon minister to him as Christ doth to his Father, and let him serve him unblamably in all things, as Christ doeth nothing of himself, but doeth always those things that please his Father. Let also the deaconess be honored by you in the place of the Holy Ghost, and not do nor say any thing without the deacon; as neither doth the Comforter say nor do any thing of himself, but giveth glory to Christ by waiting for his pleasure. And as we cannot believe on Christ without the teaching of the Spirit, so let not any woman address herself to the deacon or to the Bishop without the deaconess. Let the presbyters be esteemed by you to represent us the apostles, and let them be the teachers of divine knowledge; since our Lord, when he sent us, said, *Go ye, and make disciples of all nations, baptizing them in the name of the Father, and of the Son, and of the Holy Ghost; teaching them to observe all things whatsoever I have commanded you.* Let the widows and orphans be esteemed as representing the altar of burnt-offering; and let the virgins be honored as representing the altar of incense, and the incense itself.

100

Regulations for Christian Widows

Constitutions of the Holy Apostles 3.3–9, 13–15   4th century C.E.?

NOTE: See entry 99.

3. OF WHAT CHARACTER THE WIDOWS OUGHT TO BE, AND HOW THEY OUGHT TO BE SUPPORTED BY THE BISHOP

But the true widows are those who have had only one husband, having a good report among the generality for good works; *widows indeed*, sober, chaste, faithful, pious, who have brought up their children well, and have *entertained strangers* unblamably; who are to be supported, as devoted to God.

Besides, do thou, O Bishop, be mindful of the needy, both reaching out thy helping hand, and making provision for them, as the steward of God, distributing seasonably the oblations to every one of them, to the widows, the orphans, the friendless, and those who are tried with affliction.

4. THAT WE OUGHT TO BE CHARITABLE TO ALL SORTS OF PERSONS IN WANT

For what if some are neither widows nor widowers, but stand in need of assistance, either through poverty, or some disease, or the maintenance of a great number of children? It is thy duty to oversee all people, and to take care of them all. For they that bestow gifts do not immediately, and without the use of discretion, give them to the widows, but barely bring them in, calling them *free-will offerings*, that so thou, who knowest those that are in affliction, mayest, as a good steward, give them their portion of the gift. For God knoweth the giver, though thou distributest it to those in want, when he is absent. And he hath the reward of well-doing, but thou the blessedness of a just distribution of it. But do thou tell them who was the giver, that they may pray for him by name. For it is our duty to do good to all men, not fondly preferring one or another, whoever they may be. For the Lord saith, *Give to every one that asketh thee.* It is evident that it is meant of every one that is really in want, whether he be friend or foe, whether he be a kinsman or a stranger, whether he be single or married.

For in all the Scripture the Lord giveth us exhortations in respect to the needy, saying, first by Isaiah, *Deal thy bread to the hungry, and bring the poor who have no covering into thy house. If thou seest the naked, do thou cover him; and thou shalt not overlook those who are of thine own family and seed.* And then by Daniel he saith to the potentate, *Wherefore, O king, let my counsel please thee, and purge thy sins by acts of mercy, and thine iniquities by bowels of compassion to the needy.* And he saith by Solomon, *By acts of mercy and of faith, iniquities are purged.* And he saith again by David, *Blessed is he that hath regard to the poor and needy; the Lord shall deliver him in the evil day.*

And again, *He hath dispersed abroad; he hath given to the needy; his righteous-*
ness remaineth for ever. And Solomon saith, *He that hath mercy on the poor*
lendeth to the Lord; according to his gift it shall be paid him again. And afterwards, *He that stoppeth his ear, that he may not hear him that is in want, he*
also himself shall call, and there shall be none to hear him.

5. THAT THE WIDOWS ARE TO BE VERY CAREFUL OF THEIR DEPORTMENT

Let every widow be meek, quiet, gentle, sincere, free from anger; not talkative, not clamorous, not hasty of speech, not given to evil-speaking, not cap-
tious, not double-tongued, not a busy-body. If she see or hear any thing that
is not right, let her be as one that doth not see, and as one that doth not
hear; and let the widow mind nothing but to pray for those that give, and for
the whole church; and when she is asked any thing by any one, let her not
easily answer, except questions concerning faith, and righteousness, and hope
in God; remitting to the rulers those that desire to be instructed in the doctrines of godliness. Let her answer only so as may tend to subvert the error
of polytheism, and demonstrate the doctrine concerning the monarchy of
God. But of the remaining doctrines, let her not answer any thing rashly, lest,
by saying any thing unlearnedly, she should cause the Word to be blas-
phemed.

For the Lord hath taught us, that the Word is like *a grain of mustard seed,*
which is of a fiery nature; and, if any one useth it unskilfully, he will find it
bitter. For in the mystical points we ought not to be rash, but cautious. For
the Lord exhorteth us, saying, *Cast not your pearls before swine, lest they tram-*
ple them with their feet, and turn again and rend you. For unbelievers, when
they hear the doctrine concerning Christ not explained as it ought to be, but
defectively, and especially that concerning his incarnation or his passion, will
rather reject it with scorn, and laugh at it as false, than praise God for it.
And so the aged women will be guilty of rashness, and of causing blasphemy,
and will inherit a woe. For, saith he, *Woe to him by whom my name is blas-*
phemed among the Gentiles.

6. THAT WOMEN OUGHT NOT TO TEACH, BECAUSE IT IS UNSEEMLY; AND WHAT WOMEN FOLLOWED OUR LORD

We do not permit our *women to teach in the church*, but only to pray, and to
hear those that teach. For our Master and Lord, Jesus Christ himself, when
he sent us, the twelve, to make disciples of the people and of the nations, did
nowhere send out women to preach, although he did not want such; for
there were with us the mother of our Lord, and his sisters; also Mary Magdalen; and Mary, the mother of James; and Martha and Mary, the sisters of
Lazarus; Salome, and certain others. For, had it been necessary for women to
teach, he himself would have first commanded these also to instruct the peo-

ple with us. For, if *the head of the wife be the man*, it is not reasonable that the rest of the body should govern the head.

Let the widow, therefore, own herself to be the *altar of God*, and let her sit in her house, and not enter into the houses of the faithful, under any pretence, to receive any thing; for the altar of God never runneth about, but is fixed in one place. Let, therefore, the virgin and the widow be such as do not run about, or gad to the houses of those who are alien from the faith. For such as these are gadders and impudent; they do not make their feet to rest in one place, because they are not widows, but purses ready to receive, triflers, evil speakers, counsellors of strife, without shame, impudent; who, being such, are not worthy of him that called them. For they do not come to the common resting place of the congregation on the Lord's day, as those that are watchful. But they either slumber, or trifle, or allure men, or beg, or ensnare others, bringing them to the evil one; not suffering them to be watchful in the Lord; but taking care that they go out as vain as they came in, because they do not hear the Word of the Lord either taught or read. For of such as these the prophet Isaiah saith, *Hearing ye shall hear, and shall not understand; and seeing ye shall see, and not perceive; for the heart of this people is waxen gross.*

7. WHAT ARE THE CHARACTERS OF WIDOWS, FALSELY SO CALLED

In the same manner, therefore, the ears of the hearts of such widows as these are stopped, so that they will not sit within in their cottages to speak to the Lord, but will run about with the design of getting, and, by their foolish prattling, fulfil the desires of the adversary. Such widows, therefore, are not affixed to the altar of Christ.

For there are some widows who esteem gain their business; and, since they ask without shame, and receive without being satisfied, they render the generality more backward in giving. For when they ought to be content with their subsistence from the church, as having moderate desires; on the contrary, they run from the house of one of their neighbors to that of another, and disturb them, heaping up to themselves plenty of money, and lend at bitter usury; and are solicitous only about Mammon, whose bag is their god; who prefer eating and drinking before all virtue, saying, *Let us eat and drink, for to-morrow we die*; who esteem these things as if they were durable, and not transitory. For she that useth herself to nothing but talking of money, worshippeth Mammon instead of God; that is, she is a servant to gain, but cannot be pleasing to God, nor resigned to his worship; not being able to intercede with him, because her mind and disposition run after money; for *where the treasure is, there will the heart be also.* For she is thinking in her mind whither she may go to receive, or that a certain woman, her friend, hath forgotten her, and she hath somewhat to say to her. She that thinketh of such things as these will no longer attend to her prayers, but to that thought which offereth itself; so that, although sometimes she may wish to pray for some one, she will not be heard, because she doth not offer her petition to the Lord with the whole heart.

But she that will attend to God will sit within, and mind the things of the Lord, day and night, offering her sincere petition with a mouth ready to utter the same without ceasing. As, therefore, Judith, most famous for her wisdom, and of a good report for her modesty, *prayed to God night and day for Israel;* so also the widow who is like her, will offer her intercession, without ceasing, for the church of God; and he will hear her, because her mind is fixed on this thing alone, and is disposed to be neither insatiable nor expensive; when her eye is pure, and her hearing clean, and her hands undefiled, and her feet quiet, and her mouth prepared for neither gluttony nor trifling, but speaking the things that are fit, and partaking of only such things as are necessary for her maintenance. So being grave, and giving no disturbance, she will be pleasing to God; and, as soon as she asketh any thing, the gift will anticipate her; as he saith, *While thou art speaking, I will say, Behold I am here.* Let such a one also be free from the love of money, free from arrogance, not given to filthy lucre, not insatiable nor gluttonous; but continent, meek, giving nobody disturbance, pious, modest, sitting at home, singing, and praying, and reading, and watching, and fasting; speaking to God continually in songs and hymns. And let her take wool, and assist others, rather than herself be in need of any thing; being mindful of that widow who is honored with the Lord's testimony, who, coming into the temple, *cast into the treasury two mites, which make a farthing.* And Christ our Lord and Master, and Searcher of hearts, saw her, and said, *Verily I say unto you, that this widow hath cast into the treasury more than they all. For all they have cast in of their abundance; but this woman of her penury hath cast in all the living that she had.*

The widows, therefore, ought to be grave, obedient to their Bishops, and their Presbyters, and their Deacons, and besides these to the Deaconesses, with piety, reverence, and fear; not usurping authority, nor desiring to do any thing beyond the constitution, without the consent of the Deacon; as suppose the going to any one to eat or drink with him, or to receive any thing from any body; but, if without direction she do any one of these things, let her be punished with fasting, or else let her be separated on account of her rashness.

8. THAT A WIDOW OUGHT NOT TO ACCEPT OF ALMS FROM THE UNWORTHY; NOR OUGHT A BISHOP, NOR ANY OTHER OF THE FAITHFUL

For how doth such a one know of what character the person is from whom she receiveth; or from what sort of ministration he supplieth her with food,— whether it doth not arise from rapine, or some other ill course of life? while the widow is unmindful, that, if she receive in a way unworthy of God, she must give an account for every one of these things. For neither will the priests at any time receive a free-will offering from such a one, as suppose from a rapacious person, or from a harlot. For it is written, *Thou shalt not covet* those things that are *thy neighbor's;* and, *Thou shall not offer the hire of a harlot to the Lord God.* From such as these no offerings ought to be accepted, nor indeed from those that are separated from the church.

Let the widows also be ready to obey the commands given them by their superiors, and let them do according to the appointment of the Bishop, being obedient to him as to God. For he that receiveth from one so deserving of blame, or from one excommunicated, and prayeth for him while he purposeth to go on in a wicked course, and while he is not willing at any time to repent, holdeth communion with him in prayer, and grieveth Christ, who rejecteth the unrighteous; and he confirmeth them by means of the unworthy gift, and is defiled with them, not suffering them to come to repentance, so as to fall down before God with lamentation, and pray to him.

9. THAT WOMEN OUGHT NOT TO BAPTIZE; BECAUSE IT IS IMPIOUS, AND CONTRARY TO THE DOCTRINE OF CHRIST

Now as to women's baptizing, we let you know, that there is no small peril to those that undertake it. Therefore we do not advise you to do it; for it is dangerous, or, rather, wicked and impious. For if the *man* be *the head of the woman,* and he be originally ordained for the priesthood, it is not just to abrogate the order of the creation, and, leaving the ruler, to come to the subordinate body. For the woman is the body of the man, taken from his side, and subject to him, from whom also she was separated for the procreation of children. For the Scripture saith, *He shall rule over thee.* For the man is ruler of the woman, as being her head. But if in the foregoing *Constitutions* we have not permitted them to teach, how will any one allow them, contrary to nature, to perform the office of a priest? For this is one of the ignorant practices of the Gentile atheism, to ordain women priests to the female deities; not one of the constitutions of Christ.

But, if baptism were to be administered by women, certainly our Lord would have been baptized by his own mother, and not by John; or, when he sent us to baptize, he would have sent along with us women also for this purpose. But now he hath nowhere, either by constitution or by writing, delivered to us any such thing; as knowing the order of nature and the decency of the action; as being the Creator of nature, and the Legislator of the constitution.

13. HOW THE WIDOWS ARE TO PRAY FOR THOSE WHO SUPPLY THEIR NECESSITIES

Thou art blessed, O God, who hast refreshed my fellow-widow. Bless, O Lord, and glorify him who hath bestowed these things upon her; and let his good work ascend in truth to thee; and remember him for good in the day of his visitation. And as for my Bishop, who hath so well performed his duty to thee, and hath ordered such a reasonable alms to be bestowed on my fellow-widow, in need of clothing, do thou increase his glory, and give him a crown of rejoicing in the day when thy visitation shall be revealed.

In the same manner, let the widow who hath received the favor join with the other in praying for him who bestowed it.

14. THAT SHE WHO HATH BEEN KIND TO THE POOR OUGHT NOT TO BOAST, AND TELL ABROAD HER NAME, ACCORDING TO THE CONSTITUTION OF THE LORD

But if any woman hath done a kindness, let her, as a prudent person, conceal her own name, not sounding a trumpet before her, that her alms may be with God in secret, as the Lord saith, *When thou doest thine alms, let not thy left hand know what thy right hand doeth, that thine alms may be in secret.* And let the widow pray for him that gave her the alms, whosoever he be, as she is the holy altar of Christ; and the Father, who seeth in secret, will reward openly him that did good.

But those widows who will not live according to the command of God, are solicitous and inquisitive what Deaconess it is that hath administered the charity, and what widows have received it. And when such a one hath learned those things, she murmureth at the Deaconess who distributed the charity, saying, Dost not thou see that I am in more distress and in greater want of thy charity? Why, therefore, hast thou preferred her before me? She saith these things foolishly, not understanding that this doth not depend on the will of man, but on the appointment of God. For if she is herself a witness that she was nearer, and proved herself in greater want and more in need of clothing, than the other, she ought to understand who it is that made this constitution, and to hold her peace, and not to murmur at the Deaconess who distributed the charity, but to enter into her own house, and to cast herself prostrate on her face, to make supplication to God that her sin may be forgiven her. For God commanded her who did the kindness not to proclaim it; and this widow murmured, because proclamation was not made, so that she might know, and run to receive; nay, did not only murmur, but also cursed her, forgetting him that said, *He that blesseth thee is blessed, and he that curseth thee is cursed.* But the Lord saith, *When ye enter into a house, say, Peace be to this house; and if the son of peace be there, your peace shall rest upon it. But if it be not worthy, your peace shall return to you.*

15. THAT IT DOTH NOT BECOME US TO REVILE OUR NEIGHBORS, BECAUSE CURSING IS CONTRARY TO CHRISTIANITY

If, therefore, peace returneth upon those that sent it, nay, upon those that before had actually given it, because it did not find persons fit to receive it, much rather will a curse return upon the head of him that unjustly sent it, because he to whom it was sent was not worthy to receive it. For all those who abuse others without cause, curse themselves; as Solomon saith, *As birds and sparrows fly away, so the curse causeless shall not come upon any one.* And again he saith, *Those that bring reproaches are exceeding foolish.* But as the bee, a creature as to its strength feeble, if she stingeth any one, loseth her sting, and becometh a drone; in the same manner, ye also, whatsoever injustice ye do to others, will bring it upon yourselves. *He hath excavated and digged a pit; and he shall fall into the ditch that he hath made.* And again, *He that diggeth a pit for his neighbor shall fall into it.* Let him, therefore, who would avoid a curse, not curse another. For *what thou hatest should be done to thee, do not thou to another.*

Wherefore admonish the widows that are feeble-minded, strengthen those of them that are weak, and praise such of them as walk in holiness. Let them rather bless, and not calumniate. Let them make peace, and not stir up contention. Nor let a Bishop, nor a Presbyter, nor a Deacon, nor any one else of the sacerdotal catalogue, defile his tongue with calumny, lest he inherit a curse instead of a blessing. And let it also be the Bishop's business and care, that no lay person utter a curse. For he ought to take care of the Clergy, of the Virgins, of the Widows, of the Laity.

For which reason, O Bishop, do thou ordain thy fellow-workers, the laborers for life and for righteousness—such Deacons as are pleasing to God, such as thou provest to be worthy among all the people, and such as shall be ready for the necessities of their ministration. Ordain also a Deaconess, who is faithful and holy, for the ministrations to the women. For sometimes thou canst not send a Deacon, who is a man, to the women in certain houses, on account of the unbelievers. Thou shalt therefore send a woman, a Deaconess, on account of the imaginations of the bad.

And we stand in need of a woman, a Deaconess, for many occasions; and first in the baptism of women, the Deacon shall anoint their forehead with the holy oil, and after him the Deaconess shall anoint them. For there is no necessity that the women should be seen by the men; but only, in the laying on of hands, the Bishop shall anoint her head, as the priests and kings were formerly anointed, not because those who are now baptized are ordained priests, but as being Christians, or anointed, from Christ the Anointed; *a royal priesthood and a holy nation; the church of God, the pillar and ground of the present light;* who formerly were not a people, but now are beloved and chosen; upon whom is called his new name, as Isaiah the prophet testifieth, *And they shall call the people by his new name, which the Lord shall name for them.*

101

Regulations for Deaconesses, Virgins, Widows, and Other Christians during the Worship Service

Constitutions of the Holy Apostles 2.57   4th century C.E.?

NOTE: See entry 99.

Let the Porters stand at the entries of the men, and observe them. Let the Deaconesses also stand at those of the women, like ship-men. For the same description and pattern was both in the tabernacle of the testimony and in the temple of God. But if any one be found sitting out of his place, let him be rebuked by the Deacon, as a messenger of the fore-ship, and be removed into the place proper for him. For the church is not only like a ship, but also like a sheep-fold; for as the shepherds place all the irrational animals distinctly, I mean goats and sheep, according to their kind and age; and still every one runneth together, like to his like; so is it to be in the church. Let the young persons sit by themselves, if there be a place for them; if not, let them stand up. But let those who are already stricken in years sit in order. As to the children that stand, let their fathers and mothers take them to themselves. Let the younger women also sit by themselves, if there be a place for them; but, if there be not, let them stand behind the women. Let those women who are married, and have children, be placed by themselves. But let the virgins, and the widows, and the elder women, stand first of all, or sit; and let the Deacon be the disposer of the places, that every one of those that come in may go to his proper place, and may not sit at the entrance. In like manner let the Deacon oversee the people, that no one may whisper, nor slumber, nor laugh, nor nod. For in the church all ought to stand wisely, and soberly, and attentively, having their attention fixed upon the word of the Lord.

After this, let all rise up with one consent, and, looking towards the east, after the catechumens and the penitents are gone out, pray to God eastward, *who ascended up to the heaven of heavens to the east*; remembering also the ancient situation of paradise in the east, whence the first man, when he had yielded to the persuasion of the serpent, and disobeyed the command of God, was expelled.

As to the Deacons, after the prayer is over, let some of them attend upon the oblation of the Eucharist, ministering to the Lord's body. Let others of them watch the multitude, and keep them silent. But let that Deacon who is at the High Priest's hand, say to the people, *Let no one have any quarrel against another. Let no one come in hypocrisy.* Then let the men give the men, and the women give the women, the Lord's kiss. But let no one do it with deceit, as Judas betrayed the Lord with a kiss.

After this let the Deacon pray for the whole church, for the whole world, and the several parts of it, and the fruits of it; for the priests and the rulers, for the high priest and the king, and for universal peace. After this, let the High Priest pray for peace upon the people, and bless them in these words: *The Lord bless thee, and keep thee; the Lord make his face to shine upon thee, and give thee peace.* Let the Bishop pray for the people, and say, *Save thy people, O Lord, and bless thine inheritance, which thou hast obtained with the precious blood of thy Christ, and hast called a royal priesthood and a holy nation.*

Then let the sacrifice follow, all the people standing, and praying silently; and, when the oblation hath been made, let every rank by itself partake of the Lord's body and precious blood, in order, and approach with reverence and holy fear, as to the body of their King. Let the women approach with their heads covered, as is becoming the order of women. Moreover, let the door be watched, lest there come in any unbeliever, or one not yet initiated.

New Religious Affiliation and Conversion

One of the most interesting ways to study women's religions in Greco-Roman antiquity is to consider those religious activities women consciously chose. In the Greco-Roman period a profusion of religious alternatives was available. Many old devotions—the worship of Isis, Dionysos, Cybele, Mithras, and others—spread in expanded forms to the far reaches of the inhabited world. At least one new religion, Christianity, offered itself to the inquiring person. There is substantial evidence about individuals who both rejected older allegiances and practices and took on new ones.

Despite the plethora of evidence for religious change, how and why individuals made such choices in antiquity has received insufficient attention. Older generations of scholars often remarked on the prominence of women among those commonly classed as converts, whether to Judaism, Christianity, or other Greco-Roman religions. But they neither examined the accuracy of this apparent "prominence" nor offered much in the way of meaningful explanations beyond such vague generalizations as an assumed proclivity of women toward foreign cults and exotic religions. In retrospect, one might argue that many nineteenth- and twentieth-century male scholars (mis)took their own constructions of gender as convincing explanations for the behavior of ancient women.

The materials assembled in this section present a range of evidence for women's religious choices. Livy's account of the spread of Bacchic worship to Italy and Rome in the second century B.C.E. and Josephus's account of the conversion of Queen Helena of Adiabene and other members of her household might reflect actual historical situations. In the absence of other verification, however, it is difficult to assess the historicity of these narratives, and Livy's account, particularly, raises other problems that I will consider below.

Very different in some respects are the *Acts of Thecla* and the tale of *Aseneth* (conventionally titled *Joseph and Aseneth*). Both may be considered a form of "midrash"—that is, elaboration (and commentary) on a biblical text or earlier tradition. The conversion of Thecla of Iconium (the modern city of Konya in central Turkey) by the apostle Paul is nowhere mentioned in Christian Scripture, but the story seems like an expansion of Acts 14.1–7, which reports that Paul and his companion Barnabas, after successfully converting both Jews and Gentiles to belief in Christ, were expelled from Iconium by a coalition of offended Gentiles and Jews. Composed, like the *Acts of Thecla*, in Greek, *Aseneth* expands upon the terse report in Genesis (41.45, 50; 46.20) that Pharaoh rewarded Joseph's interpretations of Pharaoh's opaque dreams by making him second-in-command of all Egypt and by giving him Aseneth (As'nath in Hebrew), daughter of the priest of On, for a wife, with whom Joseph had two sons, Manasseh and Ephraim.

Although both stories are fictive, the Thecla story was clearly a paradigm of conversion for ancient Christian readers. Ancient Christian literature of the third and fourth centuries is replete with similar accounts of the conversion of various women by one or another apostle, such as the conversion of Maximilla by the apostle Andrew, the conversion of the Indian queen Mygdonia by the apostle Thomas, and the conversion of Drusiana by the apostle John, in the *Acts* of those male apostles, respectively. How many of these drew self-consciously on the Thecla narrative is uncertain, but the *Acts of Xanthippe and Polyxena*, perhaps dating to the fourth century, makes explicit reference to the figure of Thecla.

When I assembled the first edition of this sourcebook, I generally shared the thesis of many scholars that the tale of Aseneth was composed by a Jewish author around the first century C.E., and that it bore some useful relationship to the experiences and situations of actual newcomers to Judaism, probably in contemporaneous Egypt. In a study published in 1998, however, I argued in detail that these views are unsupported, that the text(s) probably date to the third or fourth century C.E., that the ethnic and/or religious identity of the author(s) cannot be determined, and that it is difficult to assess the relationship between the experiences of the character of Aseneth and that of actual persons when the text(s) were first composed. I further argued that the language of "conversion" may not be the most appropriate to describe Aseneth's transformation from an idolatrous daughter of an Egyptian priest to a devoted worshiper of Joseph's god, a point to which I will return momentarily.[1]

Apart from literary accounts of changes in religious affiliation and practice, we also possess some nonliterary evidence, especially in the Jewish burial inscriptions that refer to the deceased by the term "proselyte"; several are included in this section. In addition, a relatively small number of inscriptions refer to the deceased as one "who feared" (or perhaps "revered") God (usually *theosebes* in Greek; *metuens* or *metuentes* in Latin). It seems likely that these terms intend, at least in some cases, to convey that the deceased was a person of non-Jewish birth who had subsequently adopted some Jewish practices. There is considerable debate on the subject, and it seems clear, at least to me, that not every usage of the term,

[1] Ross S. Kraemer, *When Aseneth Met Joseph: A Late Antique Tale of the Biblical Patriarch and His Egyptian Wife, Reconsidered* (Oxford: Oxford University Press, 1998).

whether in literary sources or in inscriptions, carries this meaning.[2] Interestingly, the term *theosebes* is the preferred term in *Aseneth* not only for Joseph but also for Aseneth once she has renounced idolatry and become a devotee of Joseph's god. Two inscriptions containing the term *theosebes*, both the epitaphs of women, are included here.

My reasons for titling this section as I have (rather than simply using the label "conversion") has several justifications. The term "conversion," particularly as it has often been used with reference to the ancient world, frequently imposes on ancient narratives paradigms and values derived from Christian (and to a lesser extent, perhaps, Jewish) models. The now rarely read classic study by the late Arthur Darby Nock may be instructive.[3] Nock argued that it made sense to speak

---

[2] In particular, a long inscription found in Aphrodisias, in Turkey, has been construed by many scholars as proof that *theosebes* was used as a technical term for pagan adherents of or sympathizers with Judaism, although I am not altogether convinced this is the case, either at Aphrodisias or elsewhere (Joyce M. Reynolds and Robert Tannenbaum, *Jews and Godfearers at Aphrodisias: Greek Inscriptions with Commentary*, Cambridge Philological Society suppl. vol. 13 [Cambridge: Cambridge University Press, 1987]). Transcriptions of the Aphrodisias inscription circulated informally among scholars in advance of its actual publication by Reynolds and Tannenbaum, so that a few studies published prior to 1987 take that find into account, but most did not. The studies noted here for the most part take the evidence from Aphrodisias into account: Shaye J. D. Cohen, "Crossing the Boundary and Becoming a Jew," *HTR* 82 (1989): 13–33; Louis Feldman, "Proselytes and 'Sympathizers' in the Light of the New Inscriptions from Aphrodisias," *Revue des Études Juives* 148 (1989): 265–305; Martin Goodman, "Review of *Jews and Godfearers at Aphrodisias*, by Reynolds and Tannenbaum," *JRS* 78 (1988): 261–62; Jerome Murphy O'Connor, "Lots of God-fearers? *Theosebeis* in the Aphrodisias Inscription," *Revue Biblique* 99 (1992): 418–24; J. A. Overman, "The Godfearers: Some Neglected Features," *Journal for the Study of New Testament* 32 (1988): 17–26; R. Tannenbaum, "Jews and God fearers in the Holy City of Aphrodite," *Biblical Archaeology Review* 12, no. 5 (1986): 54–57+; Paul R. Trebilco, " 'God-worshippers' in Asia Minor," in his *Jewish Communities in Asia Minor*, Society for New Testament Studies Monograph Series 69 (Cambridge: Cambridge University Press, 1991), 147–66; Pieter W. van der Horst, "Jews and Christians in Aphrodisias in the Light of Their Relations in Other Cities of Asia Minor," *Nederlands Theologisch Tijdschrift* 43 (1989): 106–21, M. H. Williams," 'Θεοσε βὴς γὰρ ἦν'—The Jewish Tendencies of Poppaea Sabina," *JTS* 39 (1988): 97–111. For additional discussion and bibliography, see Kraemer, *When Aseneth Met Joseph*, 132–33, 272–73 (with detailed notes on 283–84).

[3] Arthur Darby Nock, *Conversion: The Old and the New in Religion from Alexander the Great to Augustine of Hippo* (Oxford: Clarendon Press, 1933), esp. 134–37. For newer treatments of conversion, see Martin Goodman, *Mission and Conversion: Proselytizing in the Religious History of the Roman Empire* (Oxford: Clarendon Press, 1994); Scot McKnight, *A Light Among the Nations: Jewish Missionary Activity in the Second Temple Period* (Minneapolis: Fortress Press, 1991); Shaye J. D. Cohen, "Crossing the Boundary and Becoming a Jew," *HTR* 82, no. 1 (1989): 13–33; Alan Segal, *Paul the Convert: The Apostolate and Apostasy of Saul the Pharisee* (New Haven: Yale University Press, 1990).

of conversion only with regard to Judaism and Christianity. For him, there was a crucial distinction between conversion to either of these religions, on the one hand, and adhesion to deities such as Isis or Mithras, a distinction that revolved around the possibilities of multiple allegiance. True conversion allowed only for singular allegiance and required not only revelation but also "dogma." Such a distinction seems now to be much more embedded in Nock's own Christian worldview and not terribly useful in analyzing ancient practice and self-understandings. Still, the term "conversion" is not without its utility, particularly if we take it to signify some radical changes of practice and perception.

Although narratives about women's intentional, deliberate adoption of the religious practices and worldviews of others may, in fact, tell us something about the actions and self-understandings of some ancient women, they, like many sources in this collection, are thornier evidence than they might initially seem to be. Many of them draw heavily on ancient understandings of hierarchically ordered gender difference. Consider, for instance, the speech Livy attributes to the Roman consul, where the consul notes that not only are a great many worshipers and instigators of this foreign cult women, but the men are "very like the women, debauched and debauchers." Participation in these rites endangers the appropriate masculine self-control and discipline necessary for Roman soldiers. "Do you think, citizens," asks the consul, "that youths initiated by this oath should be made soldiers? . . . Will men debased by their own debauchery and that of others fight to the death on behalf of the chastity of your wives and children?" So while there may be some historical truth to Livy's report that many participants in Bacchic rites in Italy in the early Roman period were women, it also seems clear that the characterization of such persons as women, or as men whose masculinity is jeopardized by their participation in these rites, is part of an intentional polemic to discredit foreign practices such as these. Like so many other ancient narratives of women's religious practices (and worldviews), narratives of women's conversion and/or transformation may tell us at least as much, if not more, about ancient anxieties about gender as about anything else.

This edition contains no new entries for this section, although in keeping with my revised assessment of *Aseneth*, I have retitled it and relocated it after the *Acts of Thecla*.

The Spread of the Bacchic Rites to Rome in 186 B.C.E., Attracting Women and Men to Their Frenzied Observance

LIVY *Annals of Rome* 39.8–18   1st century B.C.E.

AUTHOR: We know little about the life of Titus Livy, one of the most important ancient Roman historians, except the approximate dates of his life (1st century B.C.E.–1st century C.E.), the place of his birth (Patavium, modern Padua), and his work itself. His magnum opus was a 142-volume history of Rome written in annalistic fashion, according to which the official business of the state was set forth in a formal arrangement, year by year. In compiling his history, Livy relied heavily on other sources and has been criticized by modern scholars for his less-than-careful use of those sources.

Only about a quarter of the books of the *Ab urbe condita libri*, or *Annals of Rome*, have survived (1–10, 21–45). Concerned exclusively with a presentation of public history, Livy is an important source on the involvement of Roman women in public life, if a problematic one, as we see in the selection here on the importation of Bacchic rites into Rome and their subsequent banning.

TRANSLATION: LCL (B. O. Foster, F. G. Moore, E. T. Sage, A. C. Schlesinger, and R. M. Geer, 14 vols.).

TEXT: Budé (P. Bayet, 1940–54, 5 vols.; 1967–86, 33 vols.); OCT (R. S. Conway and C. F. Walters, 1914–65, 5 vols.).

BIBLIOGRAPHY: *Blessings*, 36–49; Marja-Leena Hänninen, "Conflicting Descriptions of Women's Religious Activity in Mid-Republican Rome: Augustan Narratives about the Arrival of Cybele and the Bacchanalia Scandal," in Lena Larsson Lovén and Agneta Strömberg, eds., *Aspects of Women in Antiquity: Proceedings of the First Nordic Symposium on Women's Lives in Antiquity, Göteborg 12–15 June 1997* (Jonsered: P. Åströms Förlag, 1998), 111–26; D. S. Levene, *Religion in Livy*, Mnemosyne, Bibliotheca Classica Batava Supplementum 127 (Leiden: E. J. Brill, 1993); S. A. Takacs, "Politics and Religion in the Bacchanalian Affair of 186 B.C.E.," *HSCP* 100 (2000): 301–10. See also the bibliography for entry 1.

> 8 . . . A nameless Greek came first to Etruria, possessed of none of those many arts which the Greek people, supreme as it is in learning, brought to us in numbers for the cultivation of mind and body, but a dabbler in sacrifices and a fortune-teller; nor was he one who, by frankly disclosing his creed and publicly proclaiming both his profession and his system, filled minds with error, but a priest of secret rites performed by night. There were initiatory rites which at first were imparted to a few, then began to be generally known among men and women. To the religious element in them were added the delights of wine and feasts, that the minds of a larger number might be attracted. When wine had inflamed their minds, and night and the mingling of

males with females, youth with age, had destroyed every sentiment of modesty, all varieties of corruption first began to be practised, since each one had at hand the pleasure answering to that to which his nature was more inclined. There was not one form of vice alone, the promiscuous matings of free men and women, but perjured witnesses, forged seals and wills and evidence, all issued from this same workshop: likewise poisonings and secret murders, so that at times not even the bodies were found for burial. Much was ventured by craft, more by violence. This violence was concealed because amid the howlings and the crash of drums and cymbals no cry of the sufferers could be heard as the debauchery and murders proceeded.

9 The destructive power of this evil spread from Etruria to Rome like the contagion of a pestilence. At first the size of the City, with abundant room and tolerance for such evils, concealed it: at length information came to the consul Postumius in about this manner. Publius Aebutius, whose father had performed his military service with a horse supplied by the state, was left a ward, and later, on the death of his guardians, was brought under the tutelage of his mother Duronia and his stepfather Titus Sempronius Rutilus. His mother was devoted to her husband, and his stepfather, who had so administered his guardianship that he could not render an accounting, desired that the ward should either be done away with or be made dependent upon them by some tie. The one method of corrupting him was through the Bacchanalia. The mother addressed the young man: while he was sick, she said, she had vowed for him that as soon as he had recovered she would initiate him into the Bacchic rites; being compelled, by the kindness of the gods, to pay her vow, she wished to fulfil it. For ten days, she continued, he must practise continence: on the tenth day she would conduct him to the banquet and then, after ritual purification, to the shrine. There was a well-known courtesan, a freedwoman named Hispala Faecenia, not worthy of the occupation to which, while still a mere slave, she had accustomed herself, and even after she had been manumitted she maintained herself in the same way. Between her and Aebutius, since they were neighbours, an intimacy developed, not at all damaging either to the young man's fortune or to his reputation; for he had been loved and sought out without any effort on his part, and, since his own relatives made provision for all his needs on a very small scale, he was maintained by the generosity of the courtesan. More than that, she had gone so far, under the influence of their intimacy, that, after the death of her patron, since she was under the legal control of no one, having petitioned the tribunes and the praetor for a guardian, when she made her will she had instituted Aebutius as her sole heir.

10 Since there were these bonds of affection between them, and neither had any secrets from the other, the young man jestingly told her not to be surprised if he were away from her for several nights: as a matter of religious

duty, he said, to free himself from a vow made for the sake of his health, he intended to be initiated in the Bacchic rites. When the woman heard this she exclaimed in great distress, "The gods forbid!" She said that it would be much better both for him and for her to die rather than do that; and she called down curses and vengeance upon the heads of those persons who had given him this counsel. Wondering both at her language and at her so manifest distress, the young man bade her spare her curses: it was his mother, he said, with the approval of his stepfather, who had ordered it. "Your stepfather, then," she replied, "is making haste—for perhaps it is not right to accuse your mother—to destroy in this way your virtue, your reputation and your life." As he marvelled the more and asked her what she meant, beseeching gods and goddesses for peace and forgiveness if, compelled by her love for him, she had declared what should be concealed, she told him that while she was a slave she had attended her mistress to that shrine, but that as a free woman she had never visited it. She knew, she said, that it was the factory of all sorts of corruptions; and it was known that for two years now no one had been initiated who had passed the age of twenty years. As each was introduced, he became a sort of victim for the priests. They, she continued, would lead him to a place which would ring with howls and the song of a choir and the beating of cymbals and drums, that the voice of the sufferer, when his virtue was violently attacked, might not be heard. Then she begged and besought him to put an end to this matter in any way he could and not to plunge into a situation where all disgraceful practices would have first to be endured and then performed. Nor would she let him go until the young man gave her his promise that he would have nothing to do with those mysteries.

11 When he came home and his mother began to tell him what he had to do that day and on the following days in connection with the rites, he informed her that he would do none of them and that it was not his intention to be initiated. His stepfather was present at the interview. Straightway the woman exclaimed that he could not do without his mistress Hispala for ten nights; infected with the enchantments and poisons of that vampire, he had no respect for his mother or his stepfather or yet the gods. Berating him thus, his mother on one side, his stepfather with four slaves on the other, drove him from the house. The young man thereupon went to his aunt Aebutia and explained to her the reason why his mother had driven him out, and on her recommendation the following day reported the affair to the consul Postumius with no witnesses present. The consul sent him away with instructions to return the third day; he himself asked his mother-in-law Sulpicia, a woman of high character, whether she was acquainted with an elderly woman, Aebutia, from the Aventine. When she replied that she knew that she was a virtuous woman of the old style, he said that he felt the need of an interview with her: Sulpicia should send her a message to come. Aebutia,

summoned by Sulpicia, came, and a little later the consul, as if he had come in by chance, brought in an allusion to Aebutius, the son of her brother. Tears flowed from the woman's eyes, and she began to bewail the fate of the young man who was robbed of his estate by those who should least of all have treated him thus, and who was then at her house, driven from home by his mother because the virtuous youth—might the gods be gracious—refused to be initiated into rites which, if reports were to be believed, were full of lewdness.

12 The consul, thinking that he had learned enough about Aebutius to trust his story, sent Aebutia away and asked his mother-in-law to summon to her Hispala, also from the Aventine, a freedwoman and no stranger in the neighbourhood: he wished to ask her also certain questions. Hispala, alarmed by her message, because without knowing the reason she was summoned to so important and respected a woman, when she saw the lictors in the vestibule and the consul's retinue and the consul himself, almost swooned. Conducting her into the inner part of the house, with his mother-in-law present, the consul told her that if she could bring herself to tell the truth she had no cause to feel alarmed; she would receive a pledge either from Sulpicia, a woman of such standing, or from himself; she should state to them what rites were usually performed in the nocturnal orgies at the Bacchanalia in the grove of Stimula. When she heard this, such fear and trembling seized the woman in all her limbs that for a long time she could not open her mouth. Being at length restored, she said that when quite young and a slave she had been initiated with her mistress; that for many years after her manumission she had known nothing of what went on there. Then the consul praised her on this ground, that she had not denied that she had been initiated; but she was to tell, under the same pledge, the rest as well. When she insisted that she knew nothing more, he told her that she would not receive the same forgiveness or consideration if she were convicted by the evidence of someone else as if she had confessed of her own accord; the man, he added, who had heard it from her had told him the whole story.

13 The woman, thinking without a doubt, as was indeed the fact, that Aebutius had revealed the secret, threw herself at the feet of Sulpicia, and at first began to plead with her not to try to turn the chatter of a freedwoman with her lover into something that was not merely serious but even fatal: she had spoken thus for the purpose of frightening him, not because she knew anything. At this point Postumius, inflamed with wrath, said that she believed even then that she was jesting with her lover Aebutius, and not speaking in the house of a most respectable matron and in the presence of a consul. Sulpicia too lifted up the terror-stricken woman, and at the same time encouraged her and mollified the anger of her son-in-law. At length regaining her self-control, and complaining much of the treachery of Aebutius, who had

returned such gratitude to one who deserved so well of him, she declared that she feared greatly the wrath of the gods whose hidden mysteries she was to reveal, but far more the wrath of the men who would, if she informed against them, with their own hands tear her limb from limb. Accordingly she begged Sulpicia and the consul that they would banish her somewhere outside Italy, where she could pass the rest of her life in safety. The consul bade her be of good cheer and assured her that it would be his responsibility to see that she could safely live in Rome. Then Hispala set forth the origin of the mysteries. At first, she said, it was a ritual for women, and it was the custom that no man should be admitted to it. There had been three days appointed each year on which they held initiations into the Bacchic rites by day; it was the rule to choose the matrons in turn as priestesses. Paculla Annia, a Campanian, she said, when priestess, had changed all this as if by the advice of the gods; for she had been the first to initiate men, her sons, Minius and Herennius Cerrinius; she had held the rites by night and not by day, and instead of a mere three days a year she had established five days of initiation in every month. From the time that the rites were performed in common, men mingling with women and the freedom of darkness added, no form of crime, no sort of wrongdoing, was left untried. There were more lustful practices among men with one another than among women. If any of them were disinclined to endure abuse or reluctant to commit crime, they were sacrificed as victims. To consider nothing wrong, she continued, was the highest form of religious devotion among them. Men, as if insane, with fanatical tossings of their bodies, would utter prophecies. Matrons in the dress of Bacchantes, with dishevelled hair and carrying blazing torches, would run down to the Tiber, and plunging their torches in the water (because they contained live sulphur mixed with calcium) would bring them out still burning. Men were alleged to have been carried off by the gods who had been bound to a machine and borne away out of sight to hidden caves: they were those who had refused either to conspire or to join in the crimes or to suffer abuse. Their number, she said, was very great, almost constituting a second state; among them were certain men and women of high rank. Within the last two years it had been ordained that no one beyond the age of twenty years should be initiated: boys of such age were sought for as admitted both vice and corruption.

14 Having finished her testimony, again falling at their feet, she repeated the same prayers that they should banish her. The consul asked his mother-in-law to vacate some part of the house into which Hispala might move. An apartment above the house was assigned to her, the stairs leading to the street being closed up and an approach to the house arranged. All the household goods of Faecenia were at once moved and her slaves summoned, and Aebutius was directed to move to the house of a client of the consul.

When both witnesses were thus available, Postumius laid the matter before the senate, everything being set forth in detail; first what had been reported, then what he had himself discovered. Great panic seized the Fathers, both on the public account, lest these conspiracies and gatherings by night might produce something of hidden treachery or danger, and privately, each for himself, lest anyone might be involved in the mischief. The senate, moreover, decreed that the consul should be thanked because he had investigated the affair both with great industry and without creating any confusion. Then the investigation of the Bacchanals and their nocturnal orgies they referred to the consuls, not as a part of their regular duties; they directed the consuls to see to it that the witnesses Aebutius and Faecenia did not suffer harm and to attract other informers by rewards; the priests of these rites, whether men or women, should be sought out, not only at Rome but through all the villages and communities, that they might be at the disposal of the consuls; that it should be proclaimed in addition in the city of Rome and that edicts should be sent through all Italy, that no one who had been initiated in the Bacchic rites should presume to assemble or come together for the purpose of celebrating those rites or to perform any such ritual. Before all, it was decreed that an inquiry should be conducted regarding those persons who had come together or conspired for the commission of any immorality or crime. Such was the decree of the senate. The consuls ordered the curule aediles to search out all the priests of this cult and to keep them under surveillance, in free custody for the investigation; the plebeian aediles were to see to it that no celebration of the rites should be held in secret. The task was entrusted to the *triumviri capitales* of placing guards through the City, of seeing that no night meetings were held, and of making provision against fire; as assistants to the *triumviri*, the *quinqueviri uls cis Tiberim* were to stand guard each over the buildings of his own district.

15 When the magistrates had been dispatched to these posts, the consuls mounted the Rostra and called an informal meeting of the people, and, when the consul had finished the regular formula of prayer which magistrates are accustomed to pronounce before they address the people, he thus began: "Never for any assembly, citizens, has this formal prayer to the gods been not only so suitable but even so necessary, a prayer which reminds us that these are the gods whom our forefathers had appointed to be worshipped, to be venerated, to receive our prayers, not those gods who would drive our enthralled minds with vile and alien rites, as by the scourges of the Furies, to every crime and every lust. For my part, I do not discover what I should refrain from telling or how far I should speak out. If you are left ignorant of anything, I fear that I shall leave room for carelessness; if I lay bare everything, that I shall scatter abroad an excess of terror. Whatever I shall have said, be sure that my words are less than the dreadfulness and the gravity of

the situation: to take sufficient precautions will be our task. As to the Bacchanalia, I am assured that you have learned that they have long been celebrated all over Italy and now even within the City in many places, and that you have learned this not only from rumour but also from their din and cries at night, which echo throughout the City, but I feel sure that you do not know what this thing is: some believe that it is a form of worship of the gods, others that it is an allowable play and pastime, and, whatever it is, that it concerns only a few. As regards their number, if I shall say that there are many thousands of them, it cannot but be that you are terrified, unless I shall at once add to that who and of what sort they are. First, then, a great part of them are women, and they are the source of this mischief; then there are men very like the women, debauched and debauchers, fanatical, with senses dulled by wakefulness, wine, noise and shouts at night. The conspiracy thus far has no strength, but it has an immense source of strength in that they grow more numerous day by day. Your ancestors did not wish that even you should assemble casually and without reason, except when the standard was displayed on the citadel and the army was assembled for an election, or the tribunes had announced a meeting of the plebeians, or some of the magistrates had called you to an informal gathering; and wherever there was a crowd collected they thought that there should also be a legal leader of the crowd. Of what sort do you think are, first, gatherings held by night, second, meetings of men and women in common? If you knew at what ages males were initiated, you would feel not only pity for them but also shame. Do you think, citizens, that youths initiated by this oath should be made soldiers? That arms should be entrusted to men mustered from this foul shrine? Will men debased by their own debauchery and that of others fight to the death on behalf of the chastity of your wives and children?

16 "Yet it would be less serious if their wrongdoing had merely made them effeminate—that was in great measure their personal dishonour—and if they had kept their hands from crime and their thoughts from evil designs: never has there been so much evil in the state nor affecting so many people in so many ways. Whatever villainy there has been in recent years due to lust, whatever to fraud, whatever to crime, I tell you, has arisen from this one cult. Not yet have they revealed all the crimes to which they have conspired. Their impious compact still limits itself to private crimes, since as yet it does not have strength enough to crush the state. Daily the evil grows and creeps abroad. It is already too great to be purely a private matter: its objective is the control of the state. Unless you are on guard betimes, citizens, as we hold this meeting in the day-time, summoned by a consul, in accordance with law, so there can be one held at night. Now, as single individuals, they stand in fear of you, gathered here all together in this assembly: presently, when you have scattered to your homes and farms, they will have come together and

they will take measures for their own safety and at the same time for your destruction: then you, as isolated individuals, will have to fear them as a united body. Therefore each one of you should hope that all your friends have been endowed with sound minds. If lust, if madness has carried off anyone into that whirlpool, let each consider that such a person belongs, not to himself, but to those with whom he has conspired to every wickedness and wrong. I am not free of anxiety lest some even of you, citizens, may go astray through error. Nothing is more deceptive in appearance than a false religion. When the authority of the gods is put forward as a defence for crime, there steals upon the mind a fear lest in punishing human misdeeds we may violate something of divine law which became mixed up with them. From this scruple innumerable edicts of the pontiffs, decrees of the senate, and finally responses of the *haruspices* free you. How often, in the times of our fathers and our grandfathers, has the task been assigned to the magistrates of forbidding the introduction of foreign cults, of excluding dabblers in sacrifices and fortune-tellers from the Forum, the Circus, and the City, of searching out and burning books of prophecies, and of annulling every system of sacrifice except that performed in the Roman way. For men wisest in all divine and human law used to judge that nothing was so potent in destroying religion as where sacrifices were performed, not by native, but by foreign, ritual. I have thought that this warning should be given you, that no religious fear may disturb your minds when you see us suppressing the Bacchanalia and breaking up these nightly meetings. All these things, if the gods are favourable and willing, we shall do; they, because they were indignant that their own divinity was being polluted by acts of crime and lust, have dragged these matters from darkness into the light, nor have they willed that they should be discovered in order that they might be unpunished, but that they might be coerced and suppressed. The senate has entrusted the investigation of this affair, by extraordinary assignment, to my colleague and myself. We shall zealously carry through what has to be done by ourselves; the responsibility of keeping watch through the City we have entrusted to the minor magistrates. For you too it is proper, whatever duties are assigned you, in whatever place each one is posted, to obey zealously and to see to it that no danger or confusion may arise from the treachery of criminals."

17 Then they ordered the decrees of the senate to be read and announced the reward to be paid the informer if anyone had brought any person before them or had reported the name of anyone who was absent. If anyone was named and had escaped, for him they would designate a fixed day, and, if he did not respond when summoned on that day, he would be condemned in his absence. If anyone was named of those who were at that time outside the land of Italy, they would fix a more elastic date if he wished to come to plead his cause. They next proclaimed that no one should venture to sell or buy

anything for the purpose of flight; that no one should harbour, conceal, or in any wise aid the fugitives.

When the meeting was dismissed there was great panic in the whole City, nor was this confined only to the walls or the boundaries of Rome; but gradually through all Italy, as letters were received from their friends concerning the decree of the senate, concerning the assembly and the edict of the consuls, the terror began to spread. Many during the night after the day when the revelation was made in the meeting were caught trying to escape and brought back by the guards whom the *triumviri* had posted at the gates: the names of many were reported. Certain of these, men and women, committed suicide. In the conspiracy, it was said, more than seven thousand men and women were involved. But the heads of the conspiracy, it was clear, were Marcus and Gaius Atinius of the Roman *plebs*, and the Faliscan Lucius Opicernius and the Campanian Minius Cerrinius: they were the source of all wickedness and wrongdoing, the story went, and they were the supreme priests and the founders of the cult. It was seen to that at the first opportunity they were arrested. They were brought before the consuls, confessed, and asked for no delay in standing trial.

18 But so numerous were the persons who had fled from the City that, since in many instances legal proceedings and causes were falling through, the praetors Titus Maenius and Marcus Licinius were compelled, through the intervention of the senate, to adjourn court for thirty days, until the investigations should be finished by the consuls. The same depopulation, because at Rome men whose names had been given in did not respond or were not found, compelled the consuls to make the rounds of the villages and there investigate and conduct trials. Those who had merely been initiated and had made their prayers in accordance with the ritual formula, the priest dictating the words, in which the wicked conspiracy to all vice and lust was contained, but had committed none of the acts to which they were bound by the oath against either themselves or others, they left in chains; upon those who had permitted themselves to be defiled by debauchery or murder, who had polluted themselves by false testimony, forged seals, substitution of wills or other frauds, they inflicted capital punishment. More were killed than were thrown into prison. There was a large number of men and women in both classes. Convicted women were turned over to their relatives or to those who had authority over them, that they might be punished in private: if there was no suitable person to exact it, the penalty was inflicted by the state. Then the task was entrusted to the consuls of destroying all forms of Bacchic worship, first at Rome and then throughout Italy, except in cases where an ancient altar or image had been consecrated. For the future it was then provided by decree of the senate that there should be no Bacchanalia in Rome or Italy. If any person considered such worship to be ordained by tradition or to be

necessary, and believed that he could not omit it without sin and atonement, he was to make a declaration before the city praetor, and the latter would consult the senate. If permission were granted to him, at a meeting where not fewer than one hundred were in attendance, he should offer the sacrifice, provided that not more than five people should take part in the rite, and that there should be no common purse or master of sacrifices or priest.

● 103

Helena, Queen of Adiabene, Converts to Judaism

JOSEPHUS *Antiquities of the Jews* 20.17–53, 92–96   late 1st century C.E.

AUTHOR, TRANSLATION, AND TEXT: See entry 15.

BIBLIOGRAPHY: Shelly Matthews, *First Converts: Rich Pagan Women and the Rhetoric of Mission in Early Judaism and Christianity* (Stanford, Calif.: Stanford University Press, 2001); see also the Introduction to this section.

17 At the same time Helena, queen of Adiabene, and her son Izates became converts to Judaism under the following circumstances. 18 Monobazus, surnamed Bazaeus, king of Adiabene, seized with a passion for his sister Helena, took her as his partner in marriage and got her pregnant. On one occasion as he was sleeping beside her, he rested his hand on his wife's belly after she had gone to sleep, whereupon he thought he heard a voice bidding him remove his hand from her womb so as not to cramp the babe within it, which by the providence of God had had a happy start and would also attain a fortunate end. 19 Disturbed by the voice, he at once awoke and told these things to his wife; and he called the son who was born to him Izates. 20 He had an elder son by Helena named Monobazus and other children by his other wives; but it was clear that all his favour was concentrated on Izates as if he were an only child. 21 In consequence of this, Izates' half-brothers by their common father grew envious of the child. Their envy grew into an ever-increasing hatred, for they were all vexed that their father preferred Izates to themselves. 22 Although their father clearly perceived this, he pardoned them, for he attributed their feeling not to any bad motive but rather to the desire that each of them had to win his father's favour for himself. Yet, as he was greatly alarmed for the young Izates, lest the hatred of his brothers should bring him to some harm, he gave him an abundance of presents and sent him off to Abennerigus the king of Charax Spasini, to whom he entrusted the safety of the boy. 23 Abennerigus welcomed the lad and viewed him with such goodwill that he gave him his daughter, named Symmacho, as a wife and conferred on him a territory that would insure him a large income.

24 Monobazus, being now old and seeing that he had not long to live, desired to lay eyes on his son before he died. He therefore sent for him, gave him the warmest of welcomes and presented him with a district called Carron. 25 The land there has excellent soil for the production of amomum in the greatest abundance; it also possesses the remains of the ark in which report has it that Noah was saved from the flood—remains which to this day are shown to those who are curious to see them. 26 Izates, accordingly, resided in this district until his father's death. On the day when Monobazus departed this life, Queen Helena sent for all the high nobles and satraps of the realm and those who were charged with military commands. 27 On their arrival she said to them: "I think that you are not unaware that my husband had set his heart on Izates succeeding to his kingdom and had deemed him worthy of this honour; nevertheless, I await your decision. For he is blessed who receives his realm from the hands not of one but of many who willingly give their consent." 28 She said this to test the disposition of those whom she had called together. They, on hearing her words, first of all, according to their custom, made obeisance to the queen, and thereupon replied that they gave their support to the king's decision, and would gladly obey Izates, who, as one and all had prayed in their hearts, had been justly preferred by his father to his brothers. 29 They added that they first wished to put his brothers and kinsmen to death in order that Izates might be seated on the throne with full security; for if they were destroyed, all fear arising from the hatred and envy that they bore towards Izates would be removed. 30 In reply Helena expressed her gratitude for their goodwill to herself and to Izates; but she nevertheless entreated them to defer their decision about putting the brothers to death until after Izates had arrived and given his approval.

31 Failing to persuade her to put the brothers to death as they advised, they, for their own safety, admonished her at least to keep them in custody until his arrival. They also advised her meanwhile to appoint as trustee of the realm someone in whom she had most confidence. 32 Helena agreed to this and set up Monobazus, her eldest son, as king. Putting the diadem upon his head and giving him his father's signet ring and what they call the *sampsera*, she exhorted him to administer the kingdom until his brother's arrival.

33 The latter, on hearing of his father's death, quickly arrived and succeeded his brother Monobazus, who made way for him.

34 Now during the time when Izates resided at Charax Spasini, a certain Jewish merchant named Ananias visited the king's wives and taught them to worship God after the manner of the Jewish tradition. 35 It was through their agency that he was brought to the notice of Izates, whom he similarly won over with the co-operation of the women. When Izates was summoned by his father to Adiabene, Ananias accompanied him in obedience to his urgent request. It so happened, moreover, that Helena had likewise been in-

structed by another Jew and had been brought over to their laws. 36 When Izates came to Adiabene to take over the kingdom and saw his brothers and his other kinsmen in chains, he was distressed at what had been done. 37 Regarding it as impious either to kill them or to keep them in chains, and yet thinking it hazardous to keep them with him if they were not imprisoned—cherishing resentment as they must—he sent some of them with their children to Claudius Caesar in Rome as hostages, and others to Artabanus the Parthian king with the same excuse.

38 When Izates had learned that his mother was very much pleased with the Jewish religion, he was zealous to convert to it himself; and since he considered that he would not be genuinely a Jew unless he was circumcised, he was ready to act accordingly. 39 When his mother learned of his intention, however, she tried to stop him by telling him that it was a dangerous move. For, she said, he was a king; and if his subjects should discover that he was devoted to rites that were strange and foreign to themselves, it would produce much disaffection and they would not tolerate the rule of a Jew over them. 40 Besides this advice she tried by every other means to hold him back. He, in turn, reported her arguments to Ananias. The latter expressed agreement with the king's mother and actually threatened that if he should be unable to persuade Izates, he would abandon him and leave the land. 41 For he said that he was afraid that if the matter became universally known, he would be punished, in all likelihood, as personally responsible because he had instructed the king in unseemly practices. The king could, he said, worship God even without being circumcised if indeed he had fully decided to be a devoted adherent of Judaism, for it was this that counted more than circumcision. 42 He told him, furthermore, that God Himself would pardon him if, constrained thus by necessity and by fear of his subjects, he failed to perform this rite. And so, for the time, the king was convinced by his arguments.

43 Afterwards, however, since he had not completely given up his desire, another Jew, named Eleazar, who came from Galilee and who had a reputation for being extremely strict when it came to the ancestral laws, urged him to carry out the rite. 44 For when he came to him to pay him his respects and found him reading the law of Moses, he said: "In your ignorance, O king, you are guilty of the greatest offence against the law and thereby against God. For you ought not merely to read the law but also, and even more, to do what is commanded in it. 45 How long will you continue to be uncircumcised? If you have not yet read the law concerning this matter, read it now, so that you may know what an impiety it is that you commit." 46 Upon hearing these words, the king postponed the deed no longer. Withdrawing into another room, he summoned his physician and had the prescribed act performed. Then he sent for both his mother and his teacher Ananias and notified them that he had performed the rite. 47 They were

immediately seized with consternation and fear beyond measure that, if it should be proved that he had performed the act, the king would risk losing his throne, since his subjects would not submit to government by a man who was a devotee of foreign practices, and that they themselves would be in jeopardy since the blame for his action would be attributed to them. 48 It was God who was to prevent their fears from being realized. For although Izates himself and his children were often threatened with destruction, God preserved them, opening a path to safety from desperate straits. God thus demonstrated that those who fix their eyes on Him and trust in Him alone do not lose the reward of their piety. But I shall report these events at a later time.

49 Helena, the mother of the king, saw that peace prevailed in the kingdom and that her son was prosperous and the object of admiration in all men's eyes, even those of foreigners, thanks to the prudence that God gave him. Now she had conceived a desire to go to the city of Jerusalem and to worship at the temple of God, which was famous throughout the world, and to make thank-offerings there. She consequently asked her son to give her leave. 50 Izates was most enthusiastic in granting his mother's request, made great preparations for her journey, and gave her a large sum of money. He even escorted her for a considerable distance, and she completed her journey to the city of Jerusalem. 51 Her arrival was very advantageous for the people of Jerusalem, for at that time the city was hard pressed by famine and many were perishing from want of money to purchase what they needed. Queen Helena sent some of her attendants to Alexandria to buy grain for large sums and others to Cyprus to bring back a cargo of dried figs. 52 Her attendants speedily returned with these provisions, which she thereupon distributed among the needy. She has thus left a very great name that will be famous forever among our whole people for her benefaction. 53 When her son Izates learned of the famine, he likewise sent a great sum of money to leaders of the Jerusalemites. The distribution of this fund to the needy delivered many from the extremely severe pressure of famine. But I shall leave to a later time the further tale of good deeds performed for our city by this royal pair.

92 Not long afterwards Izates passed away, having completed fifty-five years of his life and having been monarch for twenty-four; he left twenty-four sons and twenty-four daughters. 93 His orders were that his brother Monobazus should succeed to the throne. Thus Monobazus was rewarded for faithfully keeping the throne for his brother during the latter's absence from home after his father's death. 94 His mother Helena was sorely distressed by the news of her son's death, as was to be expected of a mother bereft of a son so very religious. She was, however, consoled on hearing that the succession had passed to her eldest son and hastened to join him. She arrived in Adiabene

but did not long survive her son Izates, for, weighed down with age and with the pain of her sorrow, she quickly breathed out her last. 95 Monobazus sent her bones and those of his brother to Jerusalem with instructions that they should be buried in the three pyramids that his mother had erected at a distance of three furlongs from the city of Jerusalem. 96 As for the acts of King Monobazus during his lifetime, I shall narrate them later.

● 104

The Jewish Proclivities of Some Non-Jewish Women

● 104A

Women of Damascus

JOSEPHUS *Jewish War* 2.559–61   late 1st century C.E.

AUTHOR, TRANSLATION, AND TEXT: See entry 15.

559 Meanwhile, the people of Damascus, learning of the disaster which had befallen the Romans, were fired with a determination to kill the Jews who resided among them. 560 As they had for a long time past kept them shut up in the gymnasium—a precaution prompted by suspicion—they considered that the execution of their plan would present no difficulty whatever, their only fear was of their own wives, who, with few exceptions, had all become converts to the Jewish religion, 561 and so their efforts were mainly directed to keeping the secret from them. In the end, they fell upon the Jews, cooped up as they were and unarmed, and within one hour slaughtered them all with impunity, to the number of ten thousand five hundred.

● 104B

Poppaea Sabina, wife of the Emperor Nero

JOSEPHUS *Antiquities of the Jews* 20.189–98   late 1st century C.E.

AUTHOR, TRANSLATION, AND TEXT: See entry 15.

BIBLIOGRAPHY: Shelly Matthews, "Ladies' Aid: Gentile Noblewomen as Saviors and Benefactors in the Antiquities," *HTR* 92 (1999): 199–218. Mary K. Smallwood, "The Alleged Jewish Tendencies of Poppaea Sabina," *JTS*, n.s., 10 (1959): 329–35; see also the Introduction to this section.

189 About this time King Agrippa built a chamber of unusual size in his palace at Jerusalem adjoining the colonnade. 190 The palace had been erected long before by the sons of Asamonaios and, being situated on a lofty site, afforded a most delightful view to any who chose to survey the city from

it. The king was enamoured of this view and used to gaze, as he reclined at
meals there, on everything that went on in the temple. 191 The eminent men
of Jerusalem, seeing this, were extremely angry; for it was contrary to tradition for proceedings in the temple—and in particular the sacrifices—to be
spied on. They therefore erected a high wall upon the arcade that was in the
inner temple facing west. 192 This when built blocked not only the view
from the royal dining room but also that from the western portico of the
outer temple, where the Romans used to post their guards at the festivals for
the sake of supervising the temple. 193 At this King Agrippa was indignant,
and still more Festus the procurator; the latter ordered them to pull it down.
But they entreated him for permission to send an embassy on this matter to
Nero; for, they said, they could not endure to live any longer if any portion
of the temple was demolished. 194 When Festus granted their request, they
sent to Nero the ten foremost of their number with Ishmael the high priest
and Helcias the keeper of the treasury. 195 Nero, after a full hearing, not
only condoned what they had done, but also consented to leave the building
as it was. In this he showed favour to his wife Poppaea, who was a worshipper of God [theosebēs] and who pleaded on behalf of the Jews. She then
bade the ten depart but detained Helcias and Ishmael in her house as hostages. 196 The king, on hearing this, gave the high priesthood to Joseph, who
was surnamed Kabi, son of the high priest Simon.

● 105
Thecla of Iconium, an Ascetic Christian and the Prototypical Convert

The Acts of Thecla   probably 2d century C.E.

WORK: Written before the beginning of the third century C.E., and possibly as
early as the mid–second century C.E., the work usually called *The Acts of Paul and
Thecla* is found within a larger composite work, *The Acts of Paul*, although it may
have circulated independently at first. It might more properly be called simply *The
Acts of Thecla*, since it is only tangentially concerned with Paul: the central theme
is the conversion and subsequent life of Thecla of Iconium. Originally written in
Greek, it exists in Latin, Syriac, and Ethiopic as well, testimony to its broad popularity.

The work engendered controversy early, in part because Thecla's self-baptism
was apparently used by some Christians to legitimate women's performance of the
rite of baptism on others. Tertullian denounced the work (or a similar text) around
203 C.E., arguing that it could not be used to give women the authority to baptize,
since it was a fraudulent work written by a presbyter in Asia Minor who had in
fact admitted the forgery (entry 92A). With the exception of D. MacDonald, Ter-

tullian's testimony has not been given much credence by modern scholarship, which still considers the author unknown. Some contemporary scholars have begun to pay serious attention to the possibility that the text was authored by a woman, but the evidence remains inconclusive at best (see Introduction to section two, note 2).

Several different endings for the life of Thecla exist. In the shortest version, Thecla "enlightens many with the word of God" and dies a peaceful death. In the longer versions, Thecla dies more of a martyr's death, hunted by opponents, and miraculously rescued from assaults on her chastity, which lead, however, to her death. In this edition of the sourcebook, I have included these longer endings as well; they probably date to about the fourth century C.E. and are fascinating evidence for issues posed by the story and cult of Thecla.

Was there ever a Thecla? Scholars have generally assumed that the story in its present form is untrue—that Paul did not convert a woman named Thecla of Iconium. Rather, they have tended to see the story as an enlargement on the few biblical hints of Paul's activity in that area, none of which would account for the development of the Thecla legend. Later Christians, however, were firmly convinced of her reality, and a cult developed around her figure (see entry 75). *The Acts of Thecla* are clearly the literary prototype for other similar stories such as *The Acts of Xanthippe and Polyxena* and are probably the prototype for similar stories about women converts in the Acts of other apostles. In any case, the text— many of whose characters, especially the more admirable ones, are women—is rich evidence for the kinds of stories told about ascetic Christian women.

TRANSLATION: RSK (7–43); Elliott, *ANT*, longer endings.

ADDITIONAL TRANSLATIONS: *NTA* 2:353–64; *ANT* 272–281; *ANF* 8:487–92.

TEXT: M. Bonnet and R. A. Lipsius, *Acta Apostolorum Apocrypha* (repr., Darmstadt: Wissenschaftliche Buchgesellschaft, 1959), 1:235–72.

BIBLIOGRAPHY: There is a particularly extensive bibliography on Thecla; recent (and/or major) works, all with additional bibliographic references, include *Blessings*, 128–56; Melissa Aubin, "Reversing Romance: The Acts of Thecla and the Ancient Novel," in Ronald F. Hock, J. Bradley Chance, and Judith Perkins, eds., *Ancient Fiction and Early Christian Narrative* (Atlanta: Scholars Press, 1998), 257–72; Jan N. Bremmer, ed., *The Apocryphal Acts of Paul and Thecla* (Kampen, the Netherlands: Kok Pharos, 1996); Kate Cooper, *The Virgin and the Bride: Idealized Womanhood in Late Antiquity* (Cambridge: Harvard University Press, 1996); Stephen J. Davis, *The Cult of Saint Thecla: A Tradition of Women's Piety in Late Antiquity* (Oxford: Oxford University Press, 2001); Andrew S. Jacobs, "A Family Affair: Marriage, Class and Ethics in the Apocryphal Acts of the Apostles," *JECS* 7 (spring 1999): 105–38; Jean Daniel Kaestli, "Les Actes apocryphes et la reconstitution de l'histoire des femmes dans le christianisme ancien," *Foi et Vie* 88 (1989): 71–79; Jean Daniel Kaestli, "Fiction litteraire et réalité sociale: Que peut-on savoir de la place des femmes dans le milieu du production des Actes apocryphes des apôtres?" *La fable apocryphe* 1 (1990): 279–302; David Konstan, "Acts of Love: A Narrative Pattern in the Apocryphal Acts," *JECS* 6 (spring 1998): 15–36; Dennis R. MacDonald, *The Legend and the Apostle: The Battle for Paul in Story and Canon* (Philadelphia: Westminster Press, 1983); Dennis R. MacDonald, "The Role of Women in the Production of the Apocryphal Acts of the Apostles," *Iliff Review* 41 (1984): 21–28; Sheila E. McGinn, "The Acts of Thecla," in *Searching the Scriptures*, 2: 800–828; Shelly Matthews, "Thinking of Thecla: Issues in Feminist Historiography," *JFSR* 17 no. 2 (2002): 39–55.

NOTE: The numbering here is taken from editions of the *Acts of Paul:* the Thecla story begins here.

7 And while Paul was speaking so in the middle of the assembly in the house of Onesiphorus, a certain virgin named Thecla (her mother was Theocleia), who was engaged to a man named Thamyris, sat at a nearby window in her house and listened night and day to what Paul said about the chaste life. And she did not turn away from the window but pressed on in the faith, rejoicing exceedingly. Moreover, when she saw many women and virgins going in to Paul she wished that she too be counted worthy to stand before Paul and hear the word of Christ, for she had not yet seen Paul in person but only heard him speak.

8 But since she did not move from the window, her mother sent to Thamyris. He came joyfully as if he were already taking her in marriage. So Thamyris said to Theocleia, "Where is my Thecla, that I may see her?" And Theocleia said, "I have something new to tell you, Thamyris. Indeed, for three days and three nights Thecla has not risen from the window either to eat or to drink, but gazing intently as if on some delightful sight, she so devotes herself to a strange man who teaches deceptive and ambiguous words that I wonder how one so modest in her virginity can be so severely troubled.

9 "Thamyris, this man is shaking up the city of the Iconians, and your Thecla too. For all the women and the young men go in to him and are taught by him that it is necessary, as he says, 'to fear one single God only and live a pure life.' And my daughter also, like a spider bound at the window by his words, is controlled by a new desire and a terrible passion. For the virgin concentrates on the things he says and is captivated. But you go and speak to her, for she is engaged to you."

10 And Thamyris went to her, loving her and yet fearing her distraction, and said, "Thecla, my fiancée, why do you sit like that? And what sort of passion holds you distracted? Turn to your Thamyris and be ashamed." And her mother also said the same thing: "Child, why do you sit like that, looking down and not answering, like one paralyzed?" And they wept bitterly, Thamyris for the loss of a wife, Theocleia for a daughter, the female servants for a mistress. So there was a great commingling of grief in the house. And while

that was going on Thecla did not turn away but was concentrating on Paul's word.

11 But Thamyris jumped up and went out into the street, and carefully observed those going in to Paul and coming out. And he saw two men in a bitter quarrel with each other and said to them, "Gentlemen, tell me, who are you? And who is this man who is inside with you, the beguiling one who deceives the souls of young men and virgins that they should not marry but remain as they are? I promise now to give you a lot of money if you will tell me about him, for I am the first man of this city."

12 So Demas and Hermogenes said to him, "Who this man is we do not know. But he deprives young men of wives and virgins of husbands, saying, 'Otherwise there is no resurrection for you, unless you remain chaste and do not defile the flesh but keep it pure.'"

13 Thamyris said to them, "Come to my house, gentlemen, and rest with me." And they went away to a fabulous banquet, with lots of wine, great riches, and a splendid table. And Thamyris gave them drinks, for he loved Thecla and wished to have her for his wife. And during the banquet Thamyris said, "Tell me, gentlemen, what his teaching is, that I also may know it, for I am very anxious about Thecla because she loves the stranger so and I am deprived of my wedding."

14 But Demas and Hermogenes said, "Bring him before the governor Castellius on the ground that he is seducing the crowds with the new doctrine of the Christians, and so he will destroy him and you will have your wife, Thecla. And we will teach you concerning the resurrection which he says is to come: that it has already taken place in the children whom we have and that we are risen again because we have full knowledge of the true God."

15 When Thamyris had heard this from them, he rose up early in the morning full of jealousy and wrath and went to the house of Onesiphorus, with rulers and officials and a great crowd, with clubs. He said to Paul, "You have corrupted the city of the Iconians, and my fiancée so that she does not want me. Let us go to governor Castellius!" And the whole crowd shouted, "Away with the *magus!* For he has corrupted all our women." And the crowds were persuaded.

16 And standing before the judgment seat Thamyris cried out, "Proconsul, this man—we don't know where he comes from—who does not allow virgins to marry, let him declare before you the reasons he teaches these things." And Demas and Hermogenes said to Thamyris, "Say that he is a Christian, and so you will destroy him." But the governor kept his wits and called Paul, saying to him, "Who are you and what do you teach? For they bring no light accusation against you."

17 Paul lifted up his voice and said, "If today I am interrogated as to what I teach, then listen, Proconsul. The living God, the God of vengeance, the jealous God, the God who has need of nothing has sent me since he longs for the salvation of humanity, that I may draw them away from corruption and impurity, and from all pleasure and death, that they may sin no more. Wherefore God sent his own child, the one whom I proclaim and teach that in him humanity has hope, he who alone had compassion upon a world gone astray, that humanity may no longer be under judgment but have faith, fear of God, knowledge of dignity, and love of truth. If then I teach the things revealed to me by God, what wrong do I do, Proconsul?" When the governor heard this, he commanded Paul to be bound and to be led off to prison until he could find a convenient time to give him a more careful hearing.

18 But during the night Thecla removed her bracelets and gave them to the doorkeeper, and when the door was opened for her she headed off to the prison. Upon giving a silver mirror to the jailer, she went in to Paul and sitting at his feet she heard about the mighty acts of God. And Paul feared nothing but continued to live with full confidence in God; and her faith also increased, as she kissed his fetters.

19 But when Thecla was sought by her own people and by Thamyris, they pursued her through the streets as if she were lost, and one of the doorkeeper's fellow slaves made it known that she had gone out during the night. And they questioned the doorkeeper, and he told them that she had gone to the stranger in prison. And they went just as he had told them and found her, so to speak, united with him in loving affection. And they left there, rallied the crowd about them, and relayed this to the governor.

20 He ordered Paul to be brought to the judgment seat. But Thecla rolled around in the place where Paul was teaching as he sat in the prison, so the governor commanded that she too be brought to the judgment seat. And she headed off joyfully exulting. But when Paul was brought forward again, the crowd shouted out even more, "He is a *magus!* Away with him!" But the governor gladly listened to Paul concerning the holy works of Christ. When he had taken counsel, he called Thecla, saying, "Why do you not marry Thamyris according to the law of the Iconians?" But she just stood there looking intently at Paul. And when she did not answer, Theocleia, her mother, cried out, saying, "Burn the lawless one! Burn her who is no bride in the midst of the theater in order that all the women who have been taught by this man may be afraid!"

21 And the governor was greatly moved. He had Paul whipped and threw him out of the city, but Thecla he sentenced to be burned. And immediately the governor arose and went off to the theater, and all the crowd went out to the inevitable spectacle. But Thecla, as a lamb in the wilderness looks around

for the shepherd, so she sought for Paul. And looking over the crowd, she saw the Lord sitting in the form of Paul and said, "As if I were not able to bear up, Paul has come to look after me." And she looked intently at him, but he took off into the heavens.

22 Now, the young men and the virgins brought wood and straw for burning Thecla. And as she was brought in naked, the governor wept and marveled at the power in her. The executioners spread out the wood and ordered her to mount the pyre, and making the sign of the cross she mounted up on the wood pile. They put the torch underneath the pile, and although a great fire blazed up, the flame did not touch her. For God in compassion produced a noise below the earth, and a cloud above full of water and hail overshadowed (the theater), and all its contents poured out, so that many were in danger and died. The fire was extinguished, and Thecla was saved.

23 Now, Paul was fasting with Onesiphorus and his wife and the children in an open tomb on the road by which they go from Iconium to Daphne. And after many days, as they were fasting the children said to Paul, "We're hungry." And they had no means to buy bread, for Onesiphorus had left behind worldly things and followed Paul with all his house. But Paul took off his coat and said, "Go child, (sell this,) buy several loaves, and bring them (back)." But while the boy was buying bread he saw his neighbor Thecla; he was astonished and said, "Thecla, where are you going?" And she said, "I am seeking Paul, for I was saved from the fire." And the boy said, "Come, I'll take you to him, for he has been mourning for you and praying and fasting six days already."

24 Now, when she came to the tomb, Paul was kneeling in prayer and saying, "Father of Christ, do not let the fire touch Thecla, but be present with her, for she is yours!" And standing behind him, she cried out, "Father, maker of heaven and earth, the Father of your beloved child Jesus Christ, I bless you because you saved me from the fire that I might see Paul." And rising up, Paul saw her and said, "God, the knower of hearts, Father of our Lord Jesus Christ, I bless you that you have so quickly (accomplished) what I asked, and have listened to me."

25 And inside the tomb there was much love, with Paul leaping for joy, and Onesiphorus, and everyone. They had five loaves and vegetables and water, and they were rejoicing over the holy works of Christ. And Thecla said to Paul, "I shall cut my hair short and follow you wherever you go." But he said, "The time is horrible, and you are beautiful. May no other temptation come upon you worse than the first and you not bear up but act with cowardice." And Thecla said, "Only give me the seal in Christ, and temptation will not touch me." And Paul said, "Have patience, Thecla, and you will receive the water."

26 And Paul sent away Onesiphorus with all his house to Iconium, and so taking Thecla he entered Antioch. But just as they came into town a Syrian by the name of Alexander, the first man of the Antiochenes, seeing Thecla, desired her and sought to win over Paul with money and gifts. But Paul said, "I don't know the woman of whom you speak, nor is she mine." But he, being a powerful man, embraced her on the open street; she, however, would not put up with it but sought Paul and cried out bitterly, saying, "Force not the stranger, force not the servant of God! I am the first woman of the Iconians, and because I did not wish to marry Thamyris I have been thrown out of the city." And grabbing Alexander, she ripped his cloak, took the crown off his head, and made him a laughingstock.

27 But he, partly out of love for her and partly out of shame for what had happened to him, brought her before the governor. When she confessed that she had done these things, he sentenced her to the beasts. But the women were horrified and cried out before the judgment seat, "An evil judgment! An impious judgment!" Thecla begged the governor that she might remain pure until her battle with the beasts. And a wealthy woman named Tryphaena, whose daughter had died, took her into custody and found comfort in her.

28 When the beasts were led in procession, they bound her to a fierce lioness, and the queen Tryphaena followed her. And as Thecla sat upon the lioness's back, the lioness licked her feet, and all the crowd was astounded. Now the charge on her inscription was Sacrilegious. But the women with their children cried out from above, saying, "O God, an impious judgment is come to pass in this city!" And after the procession, Tryphaena took her again, for her daughter Falconilla, who was dead, had spoken to her in a dream: "Mother, the desolate stranger Thecla you will have in my place in order that she may pray for me and I be translated to the place of the righteous."

29 So when Tryphaena received her back from the procession she was sorrowful because she was going to battle with the beasts on the following day, but at the same time she loved her dearly like her own daughter Falconilla and (she) said, "Thecla, my second child, come and pray for my child, that she may live forever; for this I saw in my dreams." And without hesitation she lifted up her voice and said, "My God, Son of the Most High, who is in heaven, give to her according to her wish, that her daughter Falconilla may live forever!" And when Thecla said this, Tryphaena grieved to think that such beauty was to be thrown to the beasts.

30 And when it was dawn, Alexander came to take her away—for he himself was arranging the hunt—and he said, "The governor has taken his seat, and the crowd is clamoring for us. Give me her who is to battle the beasts, that I may take her away." But Tryphaena cried out so that he fled, saying, "A second mourning for my Falconilla is come upon my house, and there is no

one to help; neither child, for she is dead, nor relative, for I am a widow. O God of Thecla my child, help Thecla."

31 And the governor sent soldiers in order that Thecla might be brought. Tryphaena, however, did not stand aside but, taking her hand, led her up herself, saying, "My daughter Falconilla I brought to the tomb, but you, Thecla, I bring to battle the beasts." And Thecla wept bitterly and groaned to the Lord, saying, "Lord God, in whom I believe, with whom I have taken refuge, who rescued me from the fire, reward Tryphaena, who had compassion upon your servant and because she kept me chaste."

32 Then there was a clamor, a roaring of the beasts, and a shouting of the people and of the women who sat together, some saying, "Bring in the sacrilegious one!" But the women were saying, "Let the city perish for this lawlessness! Slay us all, Proconsul! A bitter spectacle, an evil judgment!"

33 Now, when Thecla was taken out of Tryphaena's hands, she was stripped, given a girdle, and thrown into the stadium. And lions and bears were thrown at her, and a fierce lioness ran to her and reclined at her feet. Now, the crowd of women shouted loudly. And a bear ran up to her, but the lioness ran and met it, and ripped the bear to shreds. And again a lion trained against men, which belonged to Alexander, ran up to her, and the lioness wrestled with the lion and perished with it. So the women mourned all the more, since the lioness that helped her was dead.

34 Then they sent in many beasts while she stood and stretched out her hands and prayed. And when she had finished her prayer, she turned and saw a great ditch full of water and said, "Now is the time for me to wash." And she threw herself in, saying, "In the name of Jesus Christ, I baptize myself on the last day!" And when they saw it, the women and the whole crowd wept, saying, "Do not throw yourself into the water!"—so that even the governor wept that such a beauty was going to be eaten by seals. So then she threw herself into the water in the name of Jesus Christ, but the seals, seeing the light of a lightning flash, floated dead on the surface. About her there was a cloud of fire so that neither could the beasts touch her nor could she be seen naked.

35 Now, the women, as other more terrible beasts were thrown in, wailed, and some threw petals, others nard, others cassia, others amomum, so that there was an abundance of perfumes. And all the beasts, overcome as if by sleep, did not touch her. So Alexander said to the governor, "I have some very fearsome bulls. Let us tie her who battles the beasts to them." Although he was frowning, the governor gave his consent, saying, "Do what you want." And they bound her by the feet between the bulls and prodded them from underneath with red-hot irons at the appropriate spot, that being the more enraged they might kill her. The bulls indeed leaped forward, but the flame

that blazed around her burned through the ropes, and it was as if she were not bound.

36 But Tryphaena fainted as she stood beside the arena, so that her attendants said, "The queen Tryphaena is dead!" The governor observed this, and the whole city was alarmed. And Alexander, falling down at the governor's feet, said, "Have mercy upon me and the city, and set free her who battles the beasts, lest the city also perish with her. For if Caesar hears these things he will probably destroy both us and the city because his relative Tryphaena has died at the circus gates."

37 The governor summoned Thecla from among the beasts and said to her, "Who are you? And what have you about you that not one of the beasts touched you?" She answered, "I am a servant of the living God. As to what I have about me, I have believed in him in whom God is well pleased, his Son, on account of whom not one of the beasts touched me. For he alone is the goal of salvation and the foundation of immortal life. For to the storm-tossed he is a refuge, to the oppressed relief, to the despairing shelter; in a word, whoever does not believe in him shall not live but die forever."

38 When the governor heard this, he ordered clothing to be brought and said, "Put on the clothing." But she said, "The one who clothed me when I was naked among the beasts, this one shall clothe me with salvation in the day of judgment." And taking the clothing, she got dressed.

And the governor issued a decree immediately, saying, "I release to you Thecla, the God-fearing servant of God." So all the women cried out with a loud voice and as with one mouth gave praise to God, saying, "One is God who has saved Thecla!"—so that all the city was shaken by the sound.

39 And when Tryphaena was told the good news, she came to meet her with a crowd. She embraced Thecla and said, "Now I believe that the dead are raised up! Now I believe that my child lives! Come inside, and I will transfer everything that is mine to you." So Thecla went in with her and rested in her house for eight days, instructing her in the word of God, so that the majority of the female servants also believed. And there was great joy in the house.

40 Yet Thecla longed for Paul and sought him, sending all around in every direction. And it was made known to her that he was in Myra. So taking male and female servants, she got herself ready, sewed her *chiton* into a cloak like a man's, and headed off to Myra. She found Paul speaking the word of God and threw herself at him. But he was astonished when he saw her and the crowd that was with her, wondering whether another temptation was not upon her. So realizing this, she said to him, "I have taken the bath, Paul, for he who worked with you for the Gospel has also worked with me for my washing."

41 And taking her by the hand, Paul led her into the house of Hermias and heard everything from her, so that Paul marveled greatly and those who heard were strengthened and prayed on behalf of Tryphaena. And standing up, Thecla said to Paul, "I am going to Iconium." So Paul said, "Go and teach the word of God!" Now, Tryphaena sent her a lot of clothing and gold, so it could be left behind for Paul for the ministry of the poor.

42 So Thecla herself headed off to Iconium and entered the house of Onesiphorus and threw herself down on the floor where Paul had sat when he was teaching the oracles of God, and wept, saying, "My God, and God of this house where the light shone upon me, Christ Jesus, the Son of God, my help in prison, my help before the governor, my help in the flame, my help among the beasts, you are God, and to you be glory forever. Amen."

43 And she found Thamyris dead, but her mother alive. And calling her mother to her, she said to her, "Theocleia, my mother, are you able to believe that the Lord lives in the heavens? For whether you desire money, the Lord will give it to you through me, or your child, behold, I am standing beside you."

And when she had given this witness she headed off to Seleucia, and after enlightening many with the word of God, she slept with a fine sleep.

LONGER ENDINGS:

Some manuscripts contain, after "Seleucia," the following material:

and dwelt in a cave seventy-two years, living upon herbs and water. And she enlightened many by the word of God.

44 And certain men of the city, being Greeks by religion and physicians by profession, sent to her pompous young men to corrupt her. For they said, "She is a virgin and serves Artemis, and from this she has virtue in healing." And by the providence of God she entered into the rock alive and went under ground. And she departed to Rome to see Paul and found that he had fallen asleep. And after staying there a short time, she rested in a glorious sleep and she is buried about two or three stadia from the tomb of her master Paul.

45 She was cast into the fire when seventeen years old and among the wild beasts when eighteen. And she was an ascetic in the cave, as has been said, seventy-two years so that all the years of her life were ninety. And after accomplishing many cures she rests in the place of the saints, having fallen asleep on the twenty-fourth of the month of September in Christ Jesus our Lord to whom be glory and strength for ever and ever. Amen.

One manuscript contains the following additional material:

And a cloud of light guided her. And having come into Seleucia she went outside the city one stade. And she was afraid of them for they worshipped idols. And it guided her to the mountain called Calaman or Rhodeon, and having found there a cave she went into it. And she was there many years and underwent many and grievous trials by the devil and bore them nobly, being assisted by Christ. And some of the well-born women, having learned about the virgin Thecla, went to her and learned the miracles of God. And many of them bade farewell to the world and lived an ascetic life with her. And a good report was spread everywhere concerning her; and cures were done by her. All the city, therefore, and the country around, having learnt this, brought their sick to the mountain, and before they came near the door they were speedily released from whatever disease they were afflicted with; and the unclean spirits went out shrieking, and all received their own people in health, glorifying God who had given such grace to the virgin Thecla. The physicians of the city of Seleucia were thought nothing of, having lost their trade, and no one any longer had regard to them. Being filled with envy and hatred, they plotted against the servant of Christ to decide what they should do to her. The devil then suggested to them a wicked device. One day, having assembled, they took counsel and consulted with each other, saying, "This holy virgin has influence upon the great goddess Artemis and if she ask anything of her she hears her, being a virgin herself, and all the gods love her. Come, then, let us take unprincipled men and make them drunk with wine, and let us give them a great deal of money and say to them, 'If you can corrupt and defile her we shall give you even more money.' " The physicians said to themselves that if they should be able to defile her neither the gods nor Artemis would listen to her in the case of the sick. They therefore acted accordingly, and the wicked men went up to the mountain and rushed upon the cave like lions and knocked at the door. And the holy martyr Thecla opened it, emboldened by the God in whom she trusted, for she knew of their plot beforehand. And she said to them, "What do you want, my children?" And they said, "Is there someone here called Thecla?" And she said, "What do you want with her?" They said to her, "We want to sleep with her." The blessed Thecla said to them, "I am a poor old woman, a servant of my Lord Jesus Christ; and even though you want to do something unseemly to me you cannot." They said to her, "We must do to you what we want." And having said this, they laid fast hold of her and wished to insult her. But she said to them with mildness, "Wait, my children, that you may see the glory of the Lord." And when they took hold of her she looked up into heaven and said, "God, terrible and incomparable and glorious to your adversaries, who delivered me out of the fire, who did not give me up to Thamyris, who did not give me up to Alexander, who delivered me from the wild beasts, who saved me in the abyss, who has everywhere worked with me and glorified your name in me, now also deliver me from these lawless men and let them not insult my virginity which for your name's sake I have preserved till now because I love you and desire you and adore you, the Father, and the Son, and the Holy Ghost for ever. Amen." And there came a voice out of the heaven saying, "Fear not, Thecla, my true servant, for I am with you. Look and see where an opening has been made before you, for there shall be for you an everlasting house and there you shall obtain shelter." And looking around, the blessed Thecla saw the rock opened far enough to allow a person to enter, and in obedience to what had been said to her she courageously fled from the lawless men and entered into the rock; and the rock was immediately shut together so that not even a joint could be seen. And they, beholding the extraordinary wonder, became distracted, and they were not able to stop the servant of God but only caught hold of her dress and were able to tear off a certain part. All this happened by the permission of God for the faith of those seeing the venerable place and for a blessing in the generations afterwards to those who believe in our Lord Jesus Christ out of a pure heart.

Thus, then, suffered the first martyr of God and apostle and virgin, Thecla, who came from Iconium when eighteen years of age. With her journeying and travels and the retirement in the mountain she lived seventy-two years more. And when the Lord took her she was ninety years old. And thus is her consummation. And her holy commemoration is celebrated on the twenty-fourth of the month of September, to the glory of the Father and the Son and the Holy Ghost, now and ever and to ages of ages. Amen.

● 106

How the Egyptian Virgin Aseneth Becomes a Devotee of the God of Israel and Marries the Patriarch Joseph

Aseneth 1–21   date uncertain; perhaps 3d or 4th century C.E.

WORK: The tale that I now prefer to title *Aseneth* expands upon the brief note in Genesis 41.45 that among the rewards given by the Egyptian Pharaoh to the patriarch Joseph was a wife, the daughter of an Egyptian priest (As'nath in Hebrew; Aseneth in Greek). Composed in Greek, and surviving in both shorter and longer versions, it narrates her transformation from an unacceptable idolater and man-hating, disobedient daughter into a pious worshiper of the God of Israel, and a dutiful daughter and wife.

As noted in the Introduction to this section, in the previous edition of this sourcebook, I characterized this work as most twentieth-century scholars have done: as a Hellenistic Jewish romance that offered a veiled presentation of conversion to certain forms of Judaism, dating probably to the first century c.e. Since then, I have written a major study of *Aseneth*, concluding that it was more likely to have been composed in the third or fourth century c.e.; that we cannot tell the religious self-understanding of its author(s), who may have been Jewish but may also have been Christian or perhaps even, like Aseneth herself, a gentile worshiper of the God of Israel (sometimes called a "God-fearer"); and that it is unwise to read it as a veiled representation of rites and experiences associated with "conversion" to Judaism, particularly in the first century or so. I have also argued, against the prevailing scholarly consensus, that the so-called shorter version of Aseneth is likely to precede the extant longer versions, which I take to be intentional recastings of the shorter text. This is particularly important because some of the most interesting passages for the study of ideas about women and gender occur in the longer versions but not in the shorter.

Ancient manuscripts (all of them Christian) give the work a variety of titles, such as *The Prayer and Confession of Aseneth*. Modern scholarship has traditionally titled this work *Joseph and Aseneth*, based on the similarity of this title to other Hellenistic romances such as *Chareas and Callirhoe* or *Daphnis and Chloe*, which are usually called by the names of the hero and heroine. Since the manuscript traditions do not conclusively support any one name, I have taken the liberty of retitling the work. In the earlier edition of this sourcebook, I called it *The Conversion and Marriage of Aseneth*, a title I thought honored the ancient titles and reflected both the content of the work and the centrality of Aseneth's experience. Since I am now dubious that a paradigm of "conversion," as typically understood, underlies the text, I have this time chosen simply to call it *Aseneth*. However, I have continued to include it in this section, since it clearly describes a transformative process whereby the heroine goes from being a worshiper of the gods of Egypt to a devotee of the God of Israel.

TRANSLATION: RSK. In keeping with my view that the "shorter" version antedates the longer, I here translate that version, using the text of Philonenko cited below. I have, however, added occasional important material from the longer text reconstructed by Burchard, using his 1983 text (his 2003 edition having appeared too late for consideration). These "longer" readings are all set in boldface. The numbering of these is not identical to the "shorter" text: interested readers should consult Burchard's translation or text.

TEXT: M. Philonenko, *Joseph et Aseneth: Introduction, texte critique, traduction, et notes*, Studia Post Biblica (Leiden: E. J. Brill, 1968); Christoph Burchard, *Joseph und Aseneth: Jüdische Schriften aus hellenistich-römischer Zeit*, vol. 2 (Gütersloh: G. Mohn, 1983); also printed in Albert-Marie Denis, *Concordance grecque des pseudépigraphes d'ancien testament: Concordance, corpus des textes, indices*, (Louvain-la-Neuve: Université Catholique de Louvain, 1987), 852–59; Christoph Burchard, *Joseph und Aseneth*, Pseudepigraphica Veteris Testamenti Graece, vol. 5 (Leiden: E. J. Brill, 2003).

ADDITIONAL TRANSLATIONS: D. Cook, in *AOT* 465–503, using the text of Philonenko; C. Burchard in *OTP* 2:177–247, using his own text, with introduction and notes.

BIBLIOGRAPHY: Ross S. Kraemer, *When Aseneth Met Joseph: A Late Antique Tale of the Biblical Patriarch and His Egyptian Wife, Reconsidered* (Oxford: Oxford University Press, 1998); Ross S. Kraemer, "The Book of Aseneth," in *Searching the Scriptures*, 2:859–88; Gideon Bohak, *Joseph and Aseneth and the Jewish Temple in Heliopolis*, Early Judaism and its Literature 10 (Atlanta: Scholars Press, 1996); Randall Chesnutt, *From Death to Life: Conversion in "Joseph and Aseneth,"* Journal for the Study of the Pseudepigrapha Supplement Series 16 (Sheffield: Sheffield Academic Press, 1995); Edith Humphreys, *Joseph and Aseneth* (Sheffield, U.K.: Sheffield University Press, 2000); Angela Standhartinger, *Das Frauenbild im Judentum der hellenistischen Zeit: Ein Beitrag anhand von "Joseph und Aseneth"* (Leiden: E. J. Brill, 1995).

1.1 It happened that in the first year of the seven years of abundance, in the second month, on the fifth day, Pharaoh sent Joseph to travel around the entire land of Egypt. 1.2 And Joseph came, in the fourth month of the first year, on the eighteenth day of the month, to the region of Heliopolis. 1.3 And he was gathering together the grain of that area as the sands of the sea.

1.4 There was a man in that city, a satrap of Pharaoh, and he was the head of all Pharaoh's satraps and magnates. 1.5 And this man was exceedingly wealthy, and wise, and prudent; and was Pharaoh's councilor and the priest of Heliopolis.

1.6 And there was a virgin daughter of Pentephres, about eighteen years old, tall, in the bloom of youth, and gorgeous, surpassing in beauty any virgin in the land. 1.7 She in no way resembled the daughters of the Egyptians but in all things resembled the daughters of the Hebrews. 1.8 For she was tall like Sarah, and in the bloom of youth like Rebecca, and fair like Rachel; and the name of this virgin was Aseneth.

1.9 And the fame of her beauty spread through the whole land, even to its borders, and all the sons of the magnates and of the satraps and of the kings, all of them young men, sought to marry her. 1.10 And there was much rivalry among them because of her, and they began to fight with one another over Aseneth.

1.11 And the firstborn son of Pharaoh heard about her and persistently beseeched his father to give her to him as a wife. 1.12 And he said to him, "Give me Aseneth, the daughter of Pentephres, the priest of Heliopolis, as a wife." 1.13 And Pharaoh, his father, said to him, "Why do you seek a wife inferior to you? Are you not king of the whole inhabited world? No, but look, the daughter of King Joakim is promised to you, and the queen is very beautiful; take her as a wife for yourself."

2.1 And Aseneth was contemptuous and disdainful of all men, and no man had ever seen her, because Pentephres had a large and very high tower in his house.

2.2 And at the top of the tower there was an upper story with ten rooms. 2.3 And the first room was large and pretentiously beautiful, and paved with purple stones, and its walls were faced with precious stones of many colors. 2.4 And the ceiling of this room was gold, and in this room were affixed the gods of the Egyptians, who were without number, of gold and silver. 2.5 And Aseneth venerated all these and feared them and offered sacrifices to them.

2.6 And there was a second room, containing all of Aseneth's ornaments and chests. 2.7 And there was much gold and silver in it and garments of cloth woven with gold and many choice stones and fine linens. 2.8 And all the ornamentation of her virginity was there.

2.9 And there was a third room, containing all the good things of the earth; it was Aseneth's storehouse.

2.10 And seven virgins occupied the seven remaining rooms, one each. 2.11 And these were in servitude to Aseneth and were the same age, having been born in one night with Aseneth **and they loved her very much** and they were very beautiful, as the stars in heaven, and a man had never had contact with them, or [had] a male child.

2.12 And there were three windows to Aseneth's great room where her virginity was nurtured. 2.13 And there was one window looking out onto the courtyard toward (the) east and the second looking out toward (the) north onto the street and a third toward (the) south.

2.14 And a golden bed stood in the room looking out toward (the) east. 2.15 And the bed was covered with purple (cloth) of gold and linen, embroidered (the color of) hyacinth. 2.16 In this bed Aseneth slept alone, and neither man nor woman had ever sat on it except Aseneth alone.

2.17 And there was a great courtyard beside the house encircling it, and a very high wall beside the courtyard, encircling (it), constructed out of large rectangular stones. 2.18 And there were four gates to the courtyard, overlaid with iron, and eighteen strong young armed men guarded them. 2.19 And inside the courtyard, along the wall, there were all sorts of mature fruit-bearing trees planted, and all the fruit from them was ripe, for it was the harvest season. 2.20 And on the right side of the courtyard was an abundant spring of water, and underneath the spring a great trough received the water from this spring; from there, a river passed through the middle of the courtyard and watered all the trees of that courtyard.

3.1 And it happened that in the fourth month, on the eighteenth of the month, Joseph came to the region of Heliopolis. 3.2 And as he approached that city, Joseph sent ten men ahead of him to Pentephres the priest, saying,

3.3 "I will come and stay with you today, as it is noon, and the hour of the midday meal. The sun's heat burns greatly: I shall rest under your roof."

3.4 And Pentephres heard and rejoiced with great joy and said, "Blessed is the Lord God of Joseph." 3.5 And Pentephres called the man who managed his household and said to him, 3.6 "Hurry and make my house ready, and prepare a great meal, because Joseph, the Powerful One of God, comes to us today."

3.7 And Aseneth heard that her father and mother had come back from the family estate, and she rejoiced and said, 3.8 "I will go and see my father and my mother, for they have come back from the field of our inheritance."

3.9 And Aseneth hurried and put on a fine linen robe, the color of hyacinth (and) woven with gold, and girded herself with a gold girdle and put on bracelets around her hands and feet and threw on gold slippers(?) and an ornament around her neck. 3.10 And all around her, she had precious stones bearing the names of the gods of Egypt, everywhere on the bracelets and on the stones; and the faces of the idols were etched in relief on the stones. 3.11 And she placed a tiara on her head and bound a diadem around her temples and covered her head with a veil.

4.1 And she hurried down the steps outside her apartment and went to her father and mother and greeted them. 4.2 And Pentephres and his wife rejoiced in their daughter Aseneth with great gladness, for her parents beheld her adorned as a bride of God. 4.3 And they brought out all the good things they had brought from the family estate and gave them to their daughter. 4.4 And Aseneth rejoiced in these good things, in the fruits, and in the grapes and dates, in the doves, in the pomegranates and figs, because all these were in their prime.

4.5 And Pentephres said to his daughter, "Child." And she said, "Here I am, lord." And he said to her, "Sit down between us and I will tell you what I have to say." 4.6 And Aseneth sat down between her father and mother. 4.7 And her father, Pentephres, took her right hand in his right hand and said to her, "Child." And Aseneth said, "Let my lord and my father speak."

4.8 And Pentephres said to her, "Behold, Joseph, the Powerful One of God, comes to us today; and he is the ruler of all the land of Egypt, and Pharaoh has designated him ruler of our whole land: he is the grain distributor for the whole area and will save it from the coming famine. 4.9 For Joseph is a man who reveres God and is temperate and virgin, as you are today—a man strong in wisdom and knowledge—and the spirit of God is upon him, and the favor of God is with him. 4.10 Come, my child, and I will give you to him as a wife, and you will be a bride to him, and he will be your bridegroom for eternal time."

4.11 And as Aseneth heard the words of her father, a red sweat poured from her, and great anger overcame her, and she glanced sideways at her father with her eyes and said, 4.12 "Why does my lord and my father speak like this? Does he wish with such words to enslave me as a prisoner to a foreigner, to a fugitive who was sold into slavery? 4.13 Is he not the son of a shepherd from the land of Canaan, and was he not abandoned by his father? 4.14 Is he not the one who slept with the wife of his master? And didn't his master throw him into a gloomy prison, and didn't Pharaoh bring him out of the prison so that he could interpret Pharaoh's dream? 4.15 No, but I shall marry the firstborn son of the king, because he is king of the entire earth."

4.16 Hearing this, Pentephres was ashamed to speak further with his daughter about Joseph, because she had answered him with brashness and anger.

5.1 And behold, a young man broke in from Pentephres' retinue and said, "Behold, Joseph is before the doors of our court." 5.2 Then Aseneth fled from the presence of her father and mother and went up to her apartment and went into her room to the great window which faced east to see the one who came to her father's house.

5.3 And Pentephres went out to meet Joseph, with his wife and his whole family.

5.4 And the gates of the courtyard that faced east were opened, and Joseph entered, seated on the chariot of Pharaoh's second-in-command. 5.5 And four horses were yoked together, white like snow, with gold-studded bridles, and the chariot was covered in gold. 5.6 And Joseph was clothed in an unusual white tunic, and the robe wrapped around him was fine purple linen woven with gold. He had a gold crown on his head, and around the crown were twelve precious stones, and above the stones twelve gold rays, and a royal scepter in his right hand. 5.7 And he held an olive branch, and it had much fruit on it.

5.8 And Joseph entered the courtyard, and the gates were closed. 5.9 But foreigners, whether man or woman, remained outside, because the guards at the gates had closed the doors. 5.10 And Pentephres came, with his wife and his whole family, except their daughter Aseneth, and prostrated themselves before Joseph, with their faces upon the ground. 5.11 And Joseph descended from his chariot and gave them his right hand in greeting.

6.1 And Aseneth saw Joseph and her soul was pierced excruciatingly, and her insides dissolved and her knees became paralyzed, and her whole body trembled and she was overwhelmed with fright, and she groaned and said,

6.2 "Where will I go and where will I hide from before his face? How will Joseph, the son of God, regard me, since I have said evil things about him? 6.3 Where will I flee and hide myself, since he sees all that is concealed, and nothing hidden escapes him, on account of the great light that is in him?

6.4 And now, have mercy on me, O God of Joseph, because I have spoken evil words in ignorance.

6.5 "How will I regard myself now, miserable (as I am)? Did I not speak, saying, 'Joseph comes, the son of a shepherd from the land of Canaan'? And now, behold, the sun out of heaven comes toward us in his chariot and comes into our house today. 6.6 Foolish and presumptuous was I who took no account of him and spoke evil words concerning him and did not know that Joseph is God's son. 6.7 For who among humans will engender such beauty, and what womb will give birth to such light? Miserable and foolish am I, because I spoke evil words to my father. 6.8 And now, let my father give me to Joseph as a servant and a slave and I will serve him for eternal time."

7.1 And Joseph entered the house of Pentephres and sat down upon a chair and washed his feet and set himself up a table by itself, because he did not eat with the Egyptians, for such was an abomination to him.

7.2 And Joseph spoke to Pentephres and his whole family, saying, "Who is that woman standing by the window of the upper story? Let her go away from this house." 7.3 For Joseph feared that she also would attempt to seduce him, for all the wives [or "women"] and the daughters of the magnates and the satraps of all Egypt sought to sleep with him.

7.4 Many of the wives [or "women"] and daughters who saw Joseph suffered badly at the sight of his beauty and sent their envoys to him with gold and silver and valuable gifts. 7.5 Joseph sent them back with threats and insults, saying, "I will not sin before the God of Israel." 7.6 Joseph had before his eyes at all times the face of Jacob his father, and he remembered the commandments of his father, because Jacob said to Joseph and to his brothers, "Guard yourselves, children, absolutely from a foreign woman, from joining with her, for it is perdition and corruption." 7.7 That is why Joseph had said, "Let that woman go away from this house."

7.8 And Pentephres said to him, "Lord, she whom you saw in the upper story is not a foreigner but our daughter, a virgin who detests all men, and no other man has seen her except you only today. 7.9 And if you wish, she will come and meet with you, because our daughter is your sister." 7.10 And Joseph rejoiced with much gladness, because Pentephres had said that the virgin detested all men.

7.11 And Joseph spoke to Pentephres and his wife, saying, "If she is your daughter, let her come, for she is my sister, and I love her from this day as my sister."

8.1 And the mother of Aseneth went up to the upper rooms and led Aseneth to Joseph; and Pentephres said to his daughter, Aseneth, "Greet your brother, for he is a virgin as you are today and detests all foreign women as you detest all foreign men."

8.2 And Aseneth said to Joseph, "Welcome, lord, blessed of the Most High God." And Joseph said to her, "May the God who has made all living things bless you."

8.3 And Pentephres said to Aseneth, "Come forward and kiss your brother."

8.4 And as she came forward to kiss Joseph, he stretched out his right hand and placed it on her chest **between her two breasts, and her breasts were already standing up like ripe apples** and said, 8.5 "It is not appropriate for a man who reveres God, who blesses the living God with his mouth and eats the blessed bread of life and drinks the blessed cup of immortality and is anointed with the blessed ointment of incorruptibility, to kiss a foreign woman, one who blesses dead and deaf idols with her mouth and eats the bread of strangling from their table and drinks the cup of ambush from their libations and is anointed with the ointment of perdition. 8.6 But a man who reveres God kisses his mother; and his sister, who is of his own tribe and family; and his wife, who shares his bed; those women who with their mouths bless the living God. 8.7 Similarly, also, it is not appropriate for a woman who reveres God to kiss a strange man, because such is an abomination before God."

8.8 And as Aseneth heard the speech of Joseph, she grieved greatly and wailed aloud, and gazing intently at Joseph, her eyes filled with tears.

8.9 And Joseph saw her and pitied her greatly, for Joseph was gentle and merciful, and he feared the Lord. And he raised his right hand above her head and said,

8.10   "Lord, the God of my father Israel,
       The Most High, the powerful,
       Who gave life to all,
       And called them forth from the darkness into the light
       And from error into truth
       And from death into life,
       You, Lord, yourself, grant life to this virgin and bless her,
       And renew her by your spirit,
       And re-form her by your (unseen) hand,
       And revive her by your life,
       And may she eat the bread of your life,
       And may she drink the cup of your blessing,
         she whom you chose before she was conceived, **and number her among your people, that you have chosen before everything came into being**
       And may she enter into your rest,

which you have prepared for your chosen ones and live in your eternal life for eternal time."

9.1 And Aseneth rejoiced with great gladness at Joseph's blessing and hurried up to her upper rooms, where she collapsed exhausted upon her bed, feeling joy and grief and much fear. Ceaseless sweat clung to her once she heard these words from Joseph, which he spoke to her in the name of God the Most High. 9.2 And she wept copious, bitter tears and repented of her gods, whom she had revered, and awaited the onset of evening.

9.3 And Joseph ate and drank and said to his servants, "Yoke the horses to the chariot, for," he said, "I must depart and tour around the entire city and the land."

9.4 And Pentephres said to Joseph, "My lord, spend the night here today, and go on your way tomorrow."

9.5 And Joseph said, "No, but I must leave today, for it is the day in which the Lord began to do his work, and on the eighth day, I will return again to you and spend the night here."

10.1 Then Pentephres and his family went out to their estate.

10.2 And Aseneth remained alone with the virgins and was listless and cried until sunset; she did not eat bread nor drink water, but while everyone slept she alone remained awake. 10.3 And she opened (the door) and went down to the gate and found the gatekeeper sleeping with her children. 10.4 And Aseneth hurried and took down the leather curtain from the door and filled it with ashes and brought it up to her upper room and placed it on the floor. 10.5 And Aseneth closed the door securely and placed the iron bar across it sideways and sighed deeply and wept.

10.6 And the virgin whom Aseneth loved the most of all her virgins heard the sigh of her mistress. She woke the rest of the virgins and went and found the door closed. 10.7 She listened to the sighs and weeping of Aseneth and said, "Why are you sad, my lady, and what is it that grieves you? Open up for us and let us see you."

10.8 And Aseneth said to them from inside, (where she had) shut (herself) in, "I have a terrible headache and I am lying down on my bed and I do not have the strength to open up for you now, because I feel weak throughout my limbs, but each of you go to your chamber."

10.9 And Aseneth rose and opened the door gently and went into her second chamber, where her coffers filled with ornaments were, and opened her chest and took out a staid black *chiton*. 10.10 This was her mourning *chiton*, which she had worn when her firstborn brother died.

10.11 And Aseneth took off her royal robe and put on the black one and re-leased her golden girdle and tied a rope around herself and took her tiara off her head, and the diadem, and the bracelets from her hands.

10.12 And she took her favorite robe, all of it, and threw it out the window for the poor.

10.13 And she took all her gold and silver gods, which were innumerable, and broke them in pieces and threw them to the beggars and the needy.

10.14 And Aseneth took her royal dinner—the fatted meats and fish and dressed meat—and all the sacrifices to her gods and the vessels of wine for their libations and threw all of it out the window for the dogs to eat.

10.15 And after this, she took the ashes and spread them out on the floor. 10.16 And she took a sack and tied it about her hips and undid the braids from her head and covered herself with ashes. 10.17 And she beat her breast frequently with both hands and fell down into the ashes and cried bitterly, moaning all night until morning.

10.18 In the morning, Aseneth rose up and looked and, behold, the ashes underneath her were like mud, from her tears. 10.19 And Aseneth threw herself down again on her face in the ashes until the sun set. 10.20 And Aseneth did this for seven days, without tasting anything.

11 And on the eighth day, Aseneth lifted up her head from the floor on which she was lying, for her limbs were paralyzed from her great abasement.

> [and said] . . . But I have heard many saying
> that the God of the Hebrews is a true God,
> and a living God, and a merciful God,
> and compassionate and long-suffering and full of pity and gentle,
> and does not count the sin of a humble person,
> nor expose the lawless deeds of an afflicted person at the time of his
>   affliction.
> Therefore I will be daring, too, and turn to him,
> and take my refuge with him,
> and confess to him all my sins,
> and pour out my supplication before him.
> Who knows whether he will see my humiliation
> and have mercy on me.
> Perhaps he will see my desolation
> and have compassion on me;
> or see my orphanhood
> and protect me.

12.1 And she stretched out her hands toward the east and raised her eyes to heaven and said,

12.2   "Lord, God of the ages,
    Who gave to all the breath of life,
    Who brought into the light that which was unseen,
    Who made everything and made manifest that which was without
        manifestation,

12.3   "Who raised the heaven and established the earth upon the waters,
    Who fastened great stones on the abyss of the water,
        which shall not be immersed,
    But which, until the end, do your will.

12.4   "Lord, my God, to you I cry,
    Heed my prayer,
    And I will confess my sins to you,
    And I will reveal my lawlessness before you.

12.5   "I have sinned, Lord, I have sinned,
    I have been lawless and impious and have spoken evil before you.
    My mouth has been polluted by sacrifices to idols
        and by the table of the gods of the Egyptians.

12.6   "I have sinned, Lord, before you,
    I have sinned and have been impious, revering dead and mute idols,
    And I am not worthy to open my mouth before you,
    I, the wretched one.

12.7   "I have sinned, Lord, before you,
    I, the daughter of Pentephres the priest,
        insolent and arrogant.
    I bring my prayer before you, Lord,
        and cry unto you,
    Deliver me from my persecutors,
        for unto you I have fled for refuge,
        as a child to its father and mother.
    **and the father, stretching out his hands, grabs him up off the
        ground,**
    and hugs him around the chest,
    and the child clasps his hands around his father's neck,
    and catches his breath after his fright,
    and rests against his father's chest,
    while the father smiles at his childish agitation, likewise

12.8   "And you, Lord, stretch forth your hands to me,
        as a father who loves his child and is affectionate,
    And snatch me out of the hand of the enemy.

12.9   "For behold, the savage ancient lion pursues me,
And the gods of the Egyptians are his offspring,
Whom I cast away from myself and destroy them,
And their father, the devil, attempts to consume me.

12.10   "But you, Lord, deliver me from his hands,
And pull me out of his mouth,
Lest he snatch me up like a wolf and tear me apart,
And throw me into the abyss of fire,
And into the tempest of the sea,
And let not the great whale consume me.

12.11   "Save me, Lord, the desolate one,
Because my father and my mother disowned me, and said, "Aseneth
    is not our daughter,"
Because I destroyed and broke their gods, and have come to hate
    them,
And now I am desolate and orphaned,
And there is no hope for me, Lord, if not with you,
For you are the father of the orphans,
And the protector of the persecuted,
And the helper of the oppressed.
Have mercy upon me, Lord,
and guard me, a virgin abandoned and an orphan,
because you, Lord, are a sweet and good and gentle father.
What father is as sweet as you, Lord,
and who as quick in mercy as you, Lord,
and who as long-suffering toward our sins as you, Lord?

12.12 "For behold, all the worldly goods of my father, Pentephres, are transitory and without substance, but the dwelling places of your inheritance, Lord, are incorruptible and eternal.

13.1 "Consider my circumstance as an orphan, Lord, because I have sought refuge before you.

13.2 "Behold, I have stripped myself of the royal robe woven with gold and have put on a black chiton.

13.3 "Behold, I have released my golden girdle and have girded myself with a sack and rope.

13.4 "Behold, I have cast off the diadem from my head and covered myself with ashes.

13.5 "Behold, the floor of my chamber, which was paved with multicolored and purple stones and sprinkled with perfume, now is sprinkled with my tears and covered with dirt.

13.6 "Behold, Lord, from the ashes and my tears, there is as much mud in my chamber as on a broad street.

13.7 "Behold, Lord, my royal dinner and fatted meats I have given to the dogs.

13.8 "And behold, I have neither eaten bread nor drunk water for seven days and seven nights, and my mouth is parched like a drum, and my tongue is like a horn and my lips like bones; my face is wasted, and my eyes are failing from the inflammation of my tears.

13.9 "But pardon me, Lord, because I sinned against you in ignorance **being a virgin and erred unwittingly** and spoke blasphemy against my lord Joseph.

13.10 "For I did not know, wretched as I am, that he is your son, Lord, because people told me that Joseph is the son of a shepherd from the land of Canaan, and I believed them, and I erred, and I rejected your chosen one Joseph and spoke evil concerning him, not knowing that he is your son.

13.11 "For who among human beings could engender such beauty, and who else is wise and strong like Joseph? But, my Lord, I entrust him to you, for I love him more than my own soul.

13.12 "Guard him within the wisdom of your graciousness and deliver me to him as a servant and slave, that I will make his bed and may wash his feet and serve him and be a slave to him for all the rest of my life."

14.1 And as Aseneth finished confessing to the Lord, behold, the morning star rose in the heaven to the east, and Aseneth saw it and rejoiced and said, 14.2 "The Lord God has heard me indeed, for this star is a messenger, and the herald of the light of the great day." 14.3 And behold, the heaven split apart near the morning star, and an indescribable light appeared.

14.4 And Aseneth fell upon her face on the ashes and out of heaven a human figure came toward her. And he stood at her head and called her Aseneth.

14.5 And she said, "Who is it who calls me, since the door to my chamber is shut and the tower is high, and how is anyone able to come into my chamber?"

14.6 And the figure called to her a second time and said, "Aseneth, Aseneth." And she said, "Here I am, Lord, announce to me who you are."

14.7 And the figure said, "I am the commander of the house of the Lord and the commander of all the army of the Most High. Rise to your feet and I will speak with you."

14.8 And she raised her eyes and looked, and behold, a figure resembling Joseph in every way, with a robe and a crown and a royal scepter, 14.9 except that his face was like lightning and his eyes were like the light of the sun and the hair on his head was like a burning flame and his hands and his feet were like iron from the fire. 14.10 And Aseneth looked and threw herself on her face before his feet in great fear and trembling.

14.11 And the figure said to her, "Take courage, Aseneth, and do not fear, but rise to your feet and I will speak to you."

14.12 And Aseneth stood up, and the figure said to her, "Take off the *chiton* which you put on, the black one, and the sack around your hips, and shake off the ashes from your head and wash your face with living water. 14.13 And put on a brand-new robe and gird your hips with your brilliant girdle, the double one of your virginity. 14.14 And then come back to me and I will tell you the things I was sent to say to you."

14.15 And Aseneth went into her room where her treasure chests were and opened her chest and took out a new fine robe and took off the black robe and put on the new brilliant one, 14.16 and released the rope and the sack around her hips and girded herself with the brilliant double girdle of her virginity, one girdle around her hips and one around her breast. 14.17 And she shook the ashes out of her hair and washed her face with pure water and covered her head with a beautiful, fine veil.

15.1 And she went to the figure, and seeing her, he said to her, "Lift off the veil from your head, because today you are a holy virgin and your head is as a young man's." 15.2 And Aseneth removed it from her head. And the figure said to her, "Take courage, Aseneth, for behold, the Lord has heard the words of your confession and your prayer.

> Behold, I have seen both the humiliation and the affliction of the seven days of your deprivation.
> Behold, from your tears and these ashes, much mud has formed on your face.

15.3 "Take courage, Aseneth, holy virgin: behold, your name is inscribed in the Book of Life in the beginning of the book; your name was written first of all, by my finger and will never be erased in eternity.

15.4 "Behold, from this day you shall be made new and formed anew and revived, and you shall eat the blessed bread of life and drink the blessed cup of immortality and be anointed with the blessed ointment of incorruptibility.

15.5 "Take courage, Aseneth, holy virgin: behold, the Lord has given you to Joseph as a bride, and he will be your bridegroom.

15.6 "And no longer shall you be called Aseneth, but your name shall be City of Refuge, because in you many nations shall take refuge and under your wings many peoples shall take shelter and in your fortress those who devote themselves to God through repentance shall be protected.

15.7 "For Metanoia (Repentance) is in the heavens, an exceedingly beautiful and good daughter of the Most High, and she appeals to the Most High on your behalf every hour, and on behalf of all those who repent in the name of the Most High God, because he is the father of Metanoia and she is the guardian [replacing "mother"] of virgins, and loves you very much and at every hour she appeals to him for those who repent, for she has prepared a heavenly bridal chamber for those who love her, and she will serve them for eternal time. 15.8 And Metanoia is a very beautiful virgin, pure and laughing always and holy and gentle, and God the Most High loves her, and all the angels stand in awe of her. And I, too, love her exceedingly, because she is also my sister. And because she loves you virgins, I love you, too.

15.9 "And behold, I will go before Joseph and speak to him concerning you, and he will come before you today and will see you and will rejoice in you and will be your bridegroom.

15.10 "So listen to me, Aseneth, and put on a wedding robe, the ancient, first robe which is in your chamber, and wrap yourself in all your favorite jewelry and dress yourself as a bride and prepare to meet him.

15.11 "For behold, he comes to you today and will see you and rejoice."

15.12 And as the figure finished speaking to Aseneth, she was joyously happy and threw herself before his feet and prostrated herself face down to the ground before him and said to him,

15.13 "Blessed is the Lord God who sent you to me to deliver me from the darkness and to lead me into the light, and blessed is his name forever. What is your name, Lord; announce (it) to me so that I may praise and glorify you for eternal time. And the figure said to her: "Why do you seek this, my name, Aseneth? My name is in the heavens in the book of the Most High, written by the finger of God in the beginning of the book before all, because I am the ruler of the house of the Most High. And all names that are written in the book of the Most High are unspeakable, and it is not permitted for a person either to pronounce or to hear them in this world, because those names are exceedingly great and wonderful and praiseworthy.

15.14 "Let me speak now, lord, if I have found favor with you. Sit for a little while on the bed and I will prepare a table and bread, and you shall eat, and I will bring you good wine, whose perfume wafts unto heaven, and you shall drink and (then) depart on your way."

16.1 And the figure said to her, "Bring me a honeycomb also."

16.2 And Aseneth said, "I will send, lord, to the family estate, and I will bring you a honeycomb."

16.3 But the figure said to her, "Go into your chamber and you will find a honeycomb."

16.4 And Aseneth went into her chamber and found a honeycomb lying on the table, and the comb was as white as snow and full of honey, and its breath was like the scent of life. And Aseneth wondered and said in herself, Did then this comb come out of the man's mouth, because its breath is like the breath of this man's mouth?

16.5 And Aseneth took the comb and brought (it) to him, and the figure said to her, "Why did you say 'There is no honeycomb in my house,' and behold, you bring this to me?"

16.6 And Aseneth said, "I did not have, lord, any honeycomb in my house, but as you said, it has happened. Might it not have come from your mouth, since its breath is like the breath of your mouth [replacing 'perfume']?"

16.7 And the figure stretched forth his hand and took hold of her head and shook her head with his right hand. And Aseneth was afraid of the figure's hand, because sparks shot forth from his hand as from bubbling iron. And Aseneth looked, gazing intently with her eyes at the figure's hand. And the figure saw it and smiled and said, "Blessed are you, Aseneth, that the secrets of God have been revealed to you; and blessed are those who devote themselves to God in repentance, for they shall eat from this comb.

16.8 "For this honey the bees of the paradise of delight have made, from the dew of the roses of life that are in the paradise of God, and the angels of God eat of it, and all the chosen of God and all the sons of the Most High, because this is a comb of life and all who eat of it shall not die for eternity."

16.9 And the figure stretched out his right hand and broke off (a piece) from the comb and ate, and put (a piece of) the honey into Aseneth's mouth with his hand and said to her, "Eat." And she ate. And the figure said to Aseneth, "Behold, then, you have eaten bread of life and drunk a cup of immortality and have been anointed with ointment of incorruptibility. Behold, then, from today your flesh flourishes like living flowers from the earth of the Most High, and your bones will grow strong like the cedars of the paradise of delight of God, and powers that never tire will embrace you, and your youth will not see old age, and your beauty will not ever be eclipsed. And you shall be like a walled mother-city of all those who take refuge in the name of the Lord God, the king of the aeons." And the figure stretched out his right hand and touched the comb where he had broken off (a portion) and it was restored and filled up, and at once it became whole as it was in the beginning.

16.10 And the figure stretched forth his hand and put his finger on the edge of the comb facing east, and drew it over the edge facing west and the path of his finger became like blood.

16.11 And he stretched forth his hand a second time and put his finger on the edge of the comb facing north, and drew it over the edge facing south and the path of his finger became like blood.

16.12 And Aseneth stood to the left and observed everything the figure did.

New Religious Affiliation and Conversion

16.13 And the figure said to the comb, "Come." And bees came up out of the hive of the comb, and they were white as snow and their wings were purple and the color of hyacinth and as golden thread and there were gold diadems on their heads and sharp stingers and they would not injure anyone.

16.14 And all the bees entwined around Aseneth from (her) feet to (her) head, and other bees, as large as queen bees, attached themselves to Aseneth's lips and made upon her mouth . . . a comb similar to the comb which was lying before the figure. And all those bees ate of the comb which was on Aseneth's mouth.

16.15 And the figure said to the bees, "Go then away to your own place."

16.16 And they all left Aseneth, and all the bees rose and flew and went away into heaven. And those who wanted to injure Aseneth fell down to the ground and died.

16.17 And the figure stretched out his staff over the dead bees and said, "Arise and go back to your place." And the bees who had died rose up and went away, all of them, to the courtyard adjacent to Aseneth.

17.1 And the figure said to Aseneth, "Have you perceived what was said?" And she said, "Behold, lord, I have perceived all this."

17.2 And the figure said, "So shall be the words I have spoken to you."

17.3 And the man touched the comb, and fire rose up from the table and consumed the comb. The burning honeycomb exuded a sweet odor.

17.4 And Aseneth said to the figure, "There are, lord, seven virgins with me serving me, raised with me since my childhood, born on the same night with me, and I love them. Let me call them that you might bless them as you have blessed me."

17.5 And the figure said, "Call (them)." And Aseneth called them, and the figure blessed them and said, "God, the Most High, will bless you and you shall be seven pillars of the City of Refuge, and all the fellow inhabitants of the chosen of that city will rest upon you for eternal time."

17.6 And the figure said to Aseneth, "Remove this table." And Aseneth turned to move the table, and the figure disappeared from her sight, and Aseneth saw something like a fiery chariot being taken up into the heaven to the east.

17.7 And Aseneth said, "Senseless and audacious am I, because I have spoken with boldness and said that a figure came into my chamber from heaven; and I did not know that God (or: a god) came to me. And behold, now, he is returning again into heaven to his place. And she said to herself, "Be merciful, Lord, to your slave, because I spoke evil in ignorance before you."

18.1 And while this was taking place, behold, a servant from Joseph's retinue came, saying, "Behold, Joseph, the Powerful One of God, comes to you today." 18.2. And Aseneth called the steward of her house and said, "Prepare me a good dinner, for Joseph, the Powerful One of God, is coming to us."

18.3 And Aseneth went into her chamber and opened her chest and took out her first robe, which had the appearance of lightning, and put it on.
18.4 And she girded herself with a brilliant, royal girdle. This girdle was the one with precious stones. 18.5 And she put gold bracelets around her hands and gold trousers about her feet, and a precious ornament about her neck, and she placed a gold crown on her head; and on the front of this crown there were very expensive stones. 18.6 And she covered her head with a veil.

18.7 And she said to her young female attendant, "Bring me pure water from the spring and I will wash my face." And she brought her pure water from the spring and poured it into the basin. And Aseneth bent down to wash her face and saw her face into the water in the bowl on the conch shell. And her face was like the sun, and her eyes like the rising morning star and her cheeks like the fields of the Most High, and on her cheeks reddening like blood of a son of man, and her lips like a living rose coming out of its bud, and her teeth like warriors lined up for a war, and the hair of her head like a vine in the paradise of God flourishing in its fruits, and her neck like a varicolored cypress, and her breasts like the mountains of God the Most High.

19.1 And a little slave came and said to Aseneth, "Behold, Joseph [is] before the doors of our courtyard." And Aseneth went down with the seven virgins to meet him.

19.2 And when Joseph saw her, he was amazed at her beauty and said to her, "Who are you? Announce (it) to me quickly." And she said to him, "I am your servant, Aseneth, and all the idols I have thrown away from me and they were destroyed. And a figure came to me out of heaven today, and gave me bread of life, and I ate, and a cup of blessing, and I drank, and said to me 'I have given you as a bride to Joseph today, and he will be your bridegroom for eternal time.' And he said to me, 'No longer will your name be called Aseneth, but your name will be called City of Refuge and the Lord God will reign over many nations for ever, because in you many nations will take refuge with the Lord God, the Most High.' And the figure said to me, 'I will also go to Joseph and speak into his ears my words concerning you.' And now, you know, my lord, whether that figure has come to you and has spoken to you concerning me. And Joseph said to Aseneth, 'Blessed are you by the Most High God, and blessed (is) your name forever, because the Lord God founded your walls in the highest, and your walls (are) adamantine walls of life, because the sons of the living God will dwell in your City of Refuge and the Lord God will be king over them for ever and ever. For this man came to me today and spoke to me such words as these concerning you. And now, come here to me, holy virgin, because I have good news concerning you from heaven, which has told me everything about you."

19.3 And Joseph stretched out his hands and took Aseneth in his arms, and she him, and they embraced for a long time, and their spirits were rekindled. And Joseph kissed Aseneth and gave her spirit of life, and he kissed her the second time and gave her spirit of wisdom, and he kissed her the third time and gave her spirit of truth. And they embraced each other for a long time and intertwined their hands like chains.

20.1 And Aseneth said to him, "Come here, lord, come into my house." And she took his right hand and led him into her house.

20.2 And Joseph sat down upon the throne of Pentephres, her father, and she brought water to wash his feet. And Joseph said to her, "Let one of the virgins come and wash my feet."

20.3 And Aseneth said to him, "No, lord, for my hands are your hands, and your feet are my feet, and no other may wash your feet." And she constrained him and washed his feet.

20.4 And Joseph took her hand and kissed it (or "her"), and Aseneth kissed his head.

20.5 And the parents of Aseneth came from the family estate and saw Aseneth sitting with Joseph and wearing a wedding robe, and they rejoiced and glorified God and ate and drank.

20.6 And Pentephres said to Joseph, "Tomorrow I will call the magnates and straps of Egypt and make a wedding for you, and you shall take Aseneth as your wife."

20.7 And Joseph said, "First, I must report to Pharaoh concerning Aseneth, because he is my father, and he will give Aseneth to me as a wife."

20.8 And Joseph remained that day with Pentephres and did not go into Aseneth, because, he said, "It is not fitting for a man who reveres God to sleep with his wife before the wedding."

21.1 And Joseph rose up in the morning and went before Pharaoh and spoke to him concerning Aseneth.[1] 21.2. And Pharaoh sent and called for Pentephres and Aseneth. 21.3. And Pharaoh was amazed at her beauty and said, "The Lord, the God of Joseph, who has chosen you to be his bride, will bless you, because Joseph is the firstborn son of God and you will be called daughter of the Most High and Joseph will be your bridegroom for eternal time."

21.4 And Pharaoh took golden crowns and placed them upon their heads and said, "God the Most High will bless you and make you fruitful for eternal time."

---

[1] The Greek text of chapter 21 has been reconstructed from the Slavonic and from Greek fragments.

21.5 And Pharaoh turned them toward each other, and they kissed each other.

21.6 And Pharaoh made their wedding, with feasting and much drinking for seven days.

21.7 And he called all the rulers of Egypt and made a proclamation, saying, "Everyone who works during the seven days of the wedding celebration of Joseph and Aseneth will die a bitter death."

21.8 And when the wedding and feasting were finished, Joseph went into Aseneth and Aseneth conceived by Joseph. And she gave birth to Manasseh and Ephraim his brother, in the house of Joseph.

Chapters 22–29, which are not translated here, recount the events of the seven years of famine. When Joseph departs to distribute grain, Pharaoh's son attempts to abduct Aseneth with the aid of Joseph's brothers Dan and Gad. Their treachery is attributed to their being Jacob's sons by Bilhah and Zilpah, the servants of his wives Leah and Rachel. In good romantic form, the plot is foiled by the virtuous brothers of Joseph and the miraculous intervention of God, invoked by Aseneth. Since Pharaoh's son is killed in the action, Joseph becomes the heir to the throne of Egypt and rules for forty-eight years before returning the throne to Pharaoh's grandson. Presumably Joseph and Aseneth live happily ever after, more or less.

● 107
Two Roman Women Proselytes

● 107A
CIJ 462; *JIWE* 2.62   Rome, 3d to 4th centuries C.E.?

WORK: The following Latin burial inscription, now in the Pio Christiano section of the Vatican Museum, is originally from the Roman Jewish catacomb known as Monteverde. The text is difficult to decipher, although the letters are clear enough. It is possible, but not certain, that this inscription and the subsequent one demonstrate a practice of giving proselytes a new name.

TRANSLATION: RSK.

BIBLIOGRAPHY: *JIWE* 2.54–55.

Felicitas, a proselyte of six years. . . . (by the name of?) Peregrina, who lived 47 years. Her patron (m.) (erected this) to one most deserving.

● 107B
CIJ 523; *JIWE* 2.577   3d to 4th centuries C.E.?

WORK: The following sarcophagus inscription in Latin and transliterated Greek is no longer extant and is of uncertain origin and date. For a discussion of women officeholders in ancient synagogues, see also the Introduction to section 3.

ADDITIONAL TRANSLATION, TEXT, AND BIBLIOGRAPHY: Brooten, *Women Leaders*, 57–59; *JIWE* 2.54–55.

> Veturia Paulla. . . . consigned to her eternal home, who lived 86 years, 6 months, a proselyte of 16 years, by the name of Sarah, mother of the synagogues of Campus and Volumnius. In peace (be) her sleep.

● **108**

Two Women Called "God-Fearers"

NOTE: For a discussion of the meaning of the terminology of these inscriptions, see the Introduction to this section.

TRANSLATIONS: RSK.

● **108A**

CIJ 1².731e; *IG* 12.1, 593   Rhodes, date uncertain

> Euphrosyna, reverer of God [or, "God-fearer" or "pious"], worthy, farewell.

● **108B**

CIJ 642; *JIWE* 1.9   Pola, 3d to 5th centuries C.E.?

WORK: This Latin epitaph, now lost, was found in the church of Saint Vito. It is unclear whether the inscription identifies the deceased as a "fearer" of the Jewish religion (Noy) or as a "reverent" follower of the Jewish religion. I give here two possible translations.

BIBLIOGRAPHY: Ross S. Kraemer, "On the Meaning of the Term 'Jew' in Greco-Roman Inscriptions," *HTR* 82, no. 1 (1989): 35–53; reprinted in Andrew Overman and R. S. Maclennan, eds., *Diaspora Judaism: Essays in Honor of, and in Dialogue with, A. Thomas Kraabel,* South Florida Studies in Judaism (Atlanta: Scholars Press, 1992), 311–29; *JIWE* 1.16–17.

> Aurelius Soter and Aurelius Stephanus to Aurelia Soter, most devout [or "dutiful"] mother, of the Jewish religion, fearing (God) [or " 'fearer' of the Jewish religion"]. Her sons placed (this).

FIVE

Holy, Pious, and Exemplary Women

The excerpts in this section offer a sampling of women whose piety (in the contemporary sense of religious devotion—in antiquity, by contrast, piety often had much to do with loyalty and duty) might be considered exemplary in some fashion. To whom, for whom, and by whom their piety is commended are not issues easily resolved. Nor is it apparent just who thought these qualities laudatory, beyond the writers of the texts and inscriptions assembled here. Like much of the material in this anthology, these excerpts particularly exemplify the difficulty of disentangling the rhetoric of gender from actual historical and social experience, if such a disentangling is ever in fact possible.

The three fourth-century inscriptions in entry 117 are a case in point. All the three commemorate married women, one an elite Roman matron, one probably an elite Jewish matron, and the third demonstrably Christian. While there are differences, all three appear to draw heavily on ancient notions about gender difference and about expectations for elite, respectable women in this period that make it difficult to draw too much in the way of conclusions about the realities of these women's lives.

Also assembled here are various narratives of early Christian women martyrs. Here, too, problems of history and rhetoric loom large.[1] Accounts of the martyrdom of Blandina, and of the women among the Scillitan martyrs, are included in

---

[1] There is an extensive, relatively recent bibliography on the problem of rhetoric and early Christian women's history: see, e.g., Averil Cameron, *Christianity and the Rhetoric of Empire: The Development of Christian Discourse* (Berkeley: University of California Press, 1991); Averil Cameron, "Virginity as Metaphor: Women and the Rhetoric of Early Christianity," in Averil Cameron, ed., *History as Text: The Writing of Ancient History* (Chapel Hill: University of North Carolina Press, 1990), 181–205; Elizabeth A. Clark, "Ideology, History, and the Construction of 'Woman' in Late Ancient Christianity," *JECS* no. 2 (1994): 155–84; Elizabeth A. Clark, "The Lady Vanishes: Dilemma of a Feminist Historian after the 'Linguistic Turn,' " *Church History* 63 no. 1 (1998) 1–31.

documents that take the form of records of court proceedings against Christians. Romans did keep official written records of legal proceedings, but it is difficult to know whether the texts we now have are actually such records, especially since we owe their survival solely to Christian transmission.

Unquestionably, these stories, whether in the form of trial records or narratives such as that of the death of Potamiena and other women martyrs, contain the kinds of details that must reflect some degree of social reality. Equally unquestionably, they were composed and deployed by ancient Christians for a variety of ideological purposes. Martyrdom was a highly contested phenomenon among ancient Christians. Some actively promoted acceptance, if not active pursuit, of martyrdom, while others minimized or denigrated its value. Some actively fled from the threat of martyrdom, or recanted their Christianity when asked to do so by circuit courts (and sometimes subsequently retracted the recantation) or purchased forged documents that certified to the authorities that they had denied being Christians, and had performed some obligatory act of sacrifice as proof. One use of such stories was thus to support those who advocated the efficacy of martyrdom. But as Brent Shaw has so eloquently argued, both the act and the rhetoric of martyrdom were a particularly effective Christian attack on, and subversion of, imperial Roman power and cast Christians in general, and Christian martyrs in particular, as the truly powerful.[2]

Such claims were particularly aided by a rhetoric of gender, in which the passivity and suffering widely thought to be the condition of being female are both masculinized (as in the case, say, of Perpetua), and shown to be far more powerful than the seeming but ultimately false masculine power of the Roman authorities. Given such a rhetoric, stories of women martyrs were particularly valuable, for they began with the greatest example of weakness, a woman, and exalted her to the highest possible level, where, through God, she triumphs over the most powerful human male authorities. Such motifs are present also in 4 Maccabees, which is either an early instance of Jewish usage of such rhetoric, or, perhaps, a very early Christian example.

This section also includes several relatively late (fifth century C.E.) narratives of Christian women ascetics, including two lives of women who come to (or return to) their asceticism after having been prostitutes. Although martyrdom narratives were still composed in the Byzantine period, they were increasingly joined, if not supplanted, by narratives of renunciation, as the "new" martyrdom. This reflects, at least in part, the reality that the Christianization of the Roman Empire ended Roman imperial persecution of Christians (although it did not stop Christians from persecuting one another over their differences). Like the martyrdom ac-

---

[2] Brent Shaw, "Body/Power/Identity: The Passions of the Martyrs," *JECS* 4, no. 3 (1996): 269–312. See also Judith Perkins, *The Suffering Self: Pain and Narrative Representation in the Early Christian Era* (London and New York: Routledge, 1995).

counts, these tales of asceticism are heavily implicated in ancient constructions of gender, with particular Christian features.

New to this section in this edition are several selections. *The Martyrdom of Saints Perpetua and Felicitas* has been moved from its original location in section 2, consistent with my current view that it is unlikely to be the work of Perpetua herself, a point addressed in more detail in the Introduction to section 2 and in the notes to the entry itself. Also included here are several additional martyrdom accounts. Other new entries include the Christian epitaph mentioned above, two narratives of the gullibility of pious women (from the writings of Josephus), and several narratives of Syrian Christian women monastics.

Two new inclusions deserve further explanation. I have relocated the sayings of the desert mothers Sarah, Syncletica, and Theodora from their earlier location in section 2. Although there is no way to determine whether these, or other, women actually said these things, they are clearly representative of what exemplary ascetics are thought likely to have said and done. On balance, I prefer now to place them in this section, although some might find this skepticism excessive. I have also included a wholly new selection, a letter that purports to be written by an otherwise unknown woman, Mary of Cassabola, to the second-century Christian bishop Ignatius of Antioch. As my introduction to the letter indicates, the letter itself is clearly a forgery: whether it was authored by a woman or a man is simply unclear. It could have been included in several other sections of this anthology, but I have chosen to place it here because of what seems to me its transparent interest in ancient (probably fourth century) anxieties about the proper deference of women to male authority.

● 109

The Exemplary Self-Control and Piety of a Jewish/Judean Mother Forced to Watch the Martyrdom of Her Seven Sons

2 Macc. 7; 4 Macc. 14.11–18.24 dates disputed

WORKS: In the first half of the second century B.C.E., the Seleucid king Antiochus IV Epiphanes, desecrated the Jewish temple in Jerusalem, compelled some Judeans to perform acts they considered sacrilegious, and put to death some of those who resisted. Antiochus probably had the support of some Judeans, but a local uprising ultimately reclaimed the Temple and established a somewhat independent political state around 165 B.C.E. These events are chronicled in several ancient sources, including two works known as 1 and 2 Maccabees (Judah, known as the "Maccabee," or "hammer," was apparently a leader of some of the rebel forces) and Josephus's *Antiquities of the Jews* (which draws on the Maccabean books). Taken over by Christians as part of the "Old Testament," 1 and 2 Maccabees were part of ancient Jewish Scripture in Greek but were eventually excluded from the canon of the Hebrew Bible, although later rabbinic writers clearly seem to know some of the material in these works. The dates (and underlying sources) of both books are highly debated, but do not matter for the purposes of this entry.

2 Maccabees 7 briefly narrates Antiochus's sadistic martyring of a woman who is forced to watch her seven sons put to death before she also is butchered. In a subsequent anonymous work known as 4 Maccabees, the author greatly enlarges on this account, as part of a broader paean to the Maccabean martyrs. Traditionally thought to be the work of a Jewish author conversant in ancient philosophy, perhaps in the first century C.E., 4 Maccabees is now considered by some scholars to date somewhat later,—perhaps to the early to mid–second century C.E., and a few scholars have even proposed that it might be a Christian composition.

In any case, the author takes great pains to demonstrate the triumph of "religious" reason over emotion, exemplified in the courage and fortitude of martyrs, notably the unnamed mother, her seven tortured sons, and the priest Eleazar. For the author, it is precisely the fact that women, by virtue of being female, are generally unable to exercise the kind of self-discipline and endurance of pain that martyrdom requires that makes the mother so remarkable, and so praiseworthy. Here, too, ancient notions of masculinity as active, disciplined, and reasoned, and femininity as passive, undisciplined, and lacking the exercise of reason, loom large in the expanded narrative.

TRANSLATION: NRSV.

TEXT: A. Rahlfs, *Septuaginta* (Stuttgart: Deutsche Bibelgesellschaft, 1935), 1:1099–1139 (2 Macc.); 1:1157–84 (4 Macc.).

ADDITIONAL TRANSLATION: M. Hadas, *The Third and Fourth Books of Maccabees* (New York: Harper for Dropsie College, 1959, repr. New York: Ktav, 1976).

BIBLIOGRAPHY: Daniel Boyarin, *Dying for God: Martyrdom and the Making of Christianity and Judaism* (Stanford, Calif.: Stanford University Press, 1999); Stephen D. Moore and Janice Capel Anderson, "Taking It Like a Man: Masculinity in 4 Maccabees," *JBL* 117, no. 2 (1998): 249–73; Robin Darling Young, "The 'Woman with the Soul of Abraham': Traditions about the Mother of the Maccabean Martyrs," in Amy-Jill Levine, ed., *"Women Like This": New Perspectives on Jewish Women in the Greco-Roman Period* (Atlanta: Scholars Press, 1991), 67–81; Jan Willem van Henten, *The Maccabean Martyrs as Saviours of the Jewish People: A Study of 2 and 4 Maccabees*, Supplements to the Journal for the Study of Judaism 57 (Leiden: E. J. Brill, 1997).

2 MACCABEES

7 It happened also that seven brothers and their mother were arrested and were being compelled by the king, under torture with whips and thongs, to partake of unlawful swine's flesh. 2 One of them, acting as their spokesman, said, "What do you intend to ask and learn from us? For we are ready to die rather than transgress the laws of our ancestors."

3 The king fell into a rage, and gave orders to have pans and caldrons heated. 4 These were heated immediately, and he commanded that the tongue of their spokesman be cut out and that they scalp him and cut off his hands and feet, while the rest of the brothers and the mother looked on. 5 When he was utterly helpless, the king ordered them to take him to the fire, still breathing, and to fry him in a pan. The smoke from the pan spread widely, but the brothers and their mother encouraged one another to die nobly, saying, 6 "The Lord God is watching over us and in truth has compassion on us, as Moses declared in his song that bore witness against the people to their faces, when he said, 'And he will have compassion on his servants.' "

7 After the first brother had died in this way, they brought forward the second for their sport. They tore off the skin of his head with the hair, and asked him, "Will you eat rather than have your body punished limb by limb?" 8 He replied in the language of his ancestors and said to them, "No." Therefore he in turn underwent tortures as the first brother had done. 9 And when he was at his last breath, he said, "You accursed wretch, you dismiss us from this present life, but the King of the universe will raise us up to an everlasting renewal of life, because we have died for his laws."

10 After him, the third was the victim of their sport. When it was demanded, he quickly put out his tongue and courageously stretched forth his hands, 11 and said nobly, "I got these from Heaven, and because of his laws I disdain them, and from him I hope to get them back again." 12 As a result the king himself and those with him were astonished at the young man's spirit, for he regarded his sufferings as nothing.

13 After he too had died, they maltreated and tortured the fourth in the same way. 14 When he was near death, he said, "One cannot but choose to die at the hands of mortals and to cherish the hope God gives of being raised again by him. But for you there will be no resurrection to life!"

15 Next they brought forward the fifth and maltreated him. 16 But he looked at the king, and said, "Because you have authority among mortals, though you also are mortal, you do what you please. But do not think that God has forsaken our people. 17 Keep on, and see how his mighty power will torture you and your descendants!"

18 After him they brought forward the sixth. And when he was about to die, he said, "Do not deceive yourself in vain. For we are suffering these things on our own account, because of our sins against our own God. Therefore astounding things have happened. 19 But do not think that you will go unpunished for having tried to fight against God!"

20 The mother was especially admirable and worthy of honorable memory. Although she saw her seven sons perish within a single day, she bore it with good courage because of her hope in the Lord. 21 She encouraged each of them in the language of their ancestors. Filled with a noble spirit, she reinforced her woman's reasoning with a man's courage, and said to them, 22 "I do not know how you came into being in my womb. It was not I who gave you life and breath, nor I who set in order the elements within each of you. 23 Therefore the Creator of the world, who shaped the beginning of humankind and devised the origin of all things, will in his mercy give life and breath back to you again, since you now forget yourselves for the sake of his laws."

24 Antiochus felt that he was being treated with contempt, and he was suspicious of her reproachful tone. The youngest brother being still alive, Antiochus not only appealed to him in words, but promised with oaths that he would make him rich and enviable if he would turn from the ways of his ancestors, and that he would take him for his Friend and entrust him with public affairs. 25 Since the young man would not listen to him at all, the king called the mother to him and urged her to advise the youth to save himself. 26 After much urging on his part, she undertook to persuade her son. 27 But, leaning close to him, she spoke in their native language as follows, deriding the cruel tyrant: "My son, have pity on me. I carried you nine months in my womb, and nursed you for three years, and have reared you and brought you up to this point in your life, and have taken care of you. 28 I beg you, my child, to look at the heaven and the earth and see everything that is in them, and recognize that God did not make them out of things that existed. And in the same way the human race came into being. 29 Do not fear this butcher, but prove worthy of your brothers. Accept

death, so that in God's mercy I may get you back again along with your brothers."

30 While she was still speaking, the young man said, "What are you waiting for? I will not obey the king's command, but I obey the command of the law that was given to our ancestors through Moses. 31 But you, who have contrived all sorts of evil against the Hebrews, will certainly not escape the hands of God. 32 For we are suffering because of our own sins. 33 And if our living Lord is angry for a little while, to rebuke and discipline us, he will again be reconciled with his own servants. 34 But you unholy wretch, you most defiled of all mortals, do not be elated in vain and puffed up by uncertain hopes, when you raise your hand against the children of heaven. 35 You have not yet escaped the judgment of the almighty, all-seeing God. 36 For our brothers after enduring brief suffering have drunk of ever-flowing life, under God's covenant; but you by the judgment of God, will receive just punishment for your arrogance. 37 I, like my brothers, give up body and life for the laws of our ancestors, appealing to God to show mercy soon to our nation and by trials and plagues to make you confess that he alone is God, 38 and through me and my brothers to bring to an end the wrath of the Almighty that has justly fallen on our whole nation."

39 The king fell into a rage, and handled him worse than the others, being exasperated at his scorn. 40 So he died in his integrity, putting his whole trust in the Lord.

41 Last of all, the mother died, after her sons.

42 Let this be enough, then, about the eating of sacrifices and the extreme tortures.

4 MACCABEES

14 11 Do not consider it amazing that reason had full command over these men in their tortures, since the mind of woman despised even more diverse agonies, 12 for the mother of the seven young men bore up under the rackings of each one of her children.

13 Observe how complex is a mother's love for her children, which draws everything toward an emotion felt in her inmost parts. 14 Even unreasoning animals, as well as human beings, have a sympathy and parental love for their offspring. 15 For example, among birds, the ones that are tame protect their young by building on the housetops, 16 and the others, by building in precipitous chasms and in holes and tops of trees, hatch the nestlings and ward off the intruder. 17 If they are not able to keep the intruder away, they do what they can to help their young by flying in circles around them in the anguish of love, warning them with their own calls. 18 And why is it necessary to demonstrate sympathy for children by the example of unreasoning

animals, 19 since even bees at the time for making honeycombs defend themselves against intruders and, as though with an iron dart, sting those who approach their hive and defend it even to the death? 20 But sympathy for her children did not sway the mother of the young men; she was of the same mind as Abraham.

15 O reason of the children, tyrant over the emotions! O religion, more desirable to the mother than her children! 2 Two courses were open to this mother, that of religion, and that of preserving her seven sons for a time, as the tyrant had promised. 3 She loved religion more, the religion that preserves them for eternal life according to God's promise. 4 In what manner might I express the emotions of parents who love their children? We impress upon the character of a small child a wondrous likeness both of mind and of form. Especially is this true of mothers, who because of their birth pangs have a deeper sympathy toward their offspring than do the fathers. 5 Considering that mothers are the weaker sex and give birth to many, they are more devoted to their children. 6 The mother of the seven boys, more than any other mother, loved her children. In seven pregnancies she had implanted in herself tender love toward them, 7 and because of the many pains she suffered with each of them she had sympathy for them; 8 yet because of the fear of God she disdained the temporary safety of her children. 9 Not only so, but also because of the nobility of her sons and their ready obedience to the law, she felt a greater tenderness toward them. 10 For they were righteous and self-controlled and brave and magnanimous, and loved their brothers and their mother, so that they obeyed her even to death in keeping the ordinances.

11 Nevertheless, though so many factors influenced the mother to suffer with them out of love for her children, in the case of none of them were the various tortures strong enough to pervert her reason. 12 But each child separately and all of them together the mother urged on to death for religion's sake. 13 O sacred nature and affection of parental love, yearning of parents toward offspring, nurture and indomitable suffering by mothers! 14 This mother, who saw them tortured and burned one by one, because of religion did not change her attitude. 15 She watched the flesh of her children being consumed by fire, their toes and fingers scattered on the ground, and the flesh of the head to the chin exposed like masks.

16 O mother, tried now by more bitter pains than even the birth pangs you suffered for them! 17 O woman, who alone gave birth to such complete devotion! 18 When the firstborn breathed his last, it did not turn you aside, nor when the second in torments looked at you piteously nor when the third expired; 19 nor did you weep when you looked at the eyes of each one in his tortures gazing boldly at the same agonies, and saw in their nostrils the signs of the approach of death. 20 When you saw the flesh of children burned

upon the flesh of other children, severed hands upon hands, scalped heads upon heads, and corpses fallen on other corpses, and when you saw the place filled with many spectators of the torturings, you did not shed tears. 21 Neither the melodies of sirens nor the songs of swans attract the attention of their hearers as did the voices of the children in torture calling to their mother. 22 How great and how many torments the mother then suffered as her sons were tortured on the wheel and with the hot irons! 23 But devout reason, giving her heart a man's courage in the very midst of her emotions, strengthened her to disregard, for the time, her parental love.

24 Although she witnessed the destruction of seven children and the ingenious and various rackings, this noble mother disregarded all these because of faith in God. 25 For as in the council chamber of her own soul she saw mighty advocates—nature, family, parental love, and the rackings of her children— 26 this mother held two ballots, one bearing death and the other deliverance for her children. 27 She did not approve the deliverance that would preserve the seven sons for a short time, 28 but as the daughter of God-fearing Abraham she remembered his fortitude.

29 O mother of the nation, vindicator of the law and champion of religion, who carried away the prize of the contest in your heart! 30 O more noble than males in steadfastness, and more courageous than men in endurance! 31 Just as Noah's ark, carrying the world in the universal flood, stoutly endured the waves, 32 so you, O guardian of the law, overwhelmed from every side by the flood of your emotions and the violent winds, the torture of your sons, endured nobly and withstood the wintry storms that assail religion.

16 If, then, a woman, advanced in years and mother of seven sons, endured seeing her children tortured to death, it must be admitted that devout reason is sovereign over the emotions. 2 Thus I have demonstrated not only that men have ruled over the emotions, but also that a woman has despised the fiercest tortures. 3 The lions surrounding Daniel were not so savage, nor was the raging fiery furnace of Mishael so intensely hot, as was her innate parental love, inflamed as she saw her seven sons tortured in such varied ways. 4 But the mother quenched so many and such great emotions by devout reason.

5 Consider this also: If this woman, though a mother, had been fainthearted, she would have mourned over them and perhaps spoken as follows: 6 "O how wretched am I and many times unhappy! After bearing seven children, I am now the mother of none! 7 O seven childbirths all in vain, seven profitless pregnancies, fruitless nurturings and wretched nursings! 8 In vain, my sons, I endured many birth pangs for you, and the more grievous anxieties of your upbringing. 9 Alas for my children, some unmarried, others married and without offspring. I shall not see your children or have the happiness of being called grandmother. 10 Alas, I who had so many and beautiful children

am a widow and alone, with many sorrows. 11 And when I die, I shall have none of my sons to bury me."

12 Yet that holy and God-fearing mother did not wail with such a lament for any of them, nor did she dissuade any of them from dying, nor did she grieve as they were dying. 13 On the contrary, as though having a mind like adamant and giving rebirth for immortality to the whole number of her sons, she implored them and urged them on to death for the sake of religion. 14 O mother, soldier of God in the cause of religion, elder and woman! By steadfastness you have conquered even a tyrant, and in word and deed you have proved more powerful than a man. 15 For when you and your sons were arrested together, you stood and watched Eleazar being tortured, and said to your sons in the Hebrew language, 16 "My sons, noble is the contest to which you are called to bear witness for the nation. Fight zealously for our ancestral law. 17 For it would be shameful if, while an aged man endures such agonies for the sake of religion, you young men were to be terrified by tortures. 18 Remember that it is through God that you have had a share in the world and have enjoyed life, 19 and therefore you ought to endure any suffering for the sake of God. 20 For his sake also our father Abraham was zealous to sacrifice his son Isaac, the ancestor of our nation; and when Isaac saw his father's hand wielding a knife and descending upon him, he did not cower. 21 Daniel the righteous was thrown to the lions, and Hananiah, Azariah, and Mishael were hurled into the fiery furnace and endured it for the sake of God. 22 You too must have the same faith in God and not be grieved. 23 It is unreasonable for people who have religious knowledge not to withstand pain."

24 By these words the mother of the seven encouraged and persuaded each of her sons to die rather than violate God's commandment. 25 They knew also that those who die for the sake of God live to God, as do Abraham and Isaac and Jacob and all the patriarchs.

17 Some of the guards said that when she also was about to be seized and put to death she threw herself into the flames so that no one might touch her body.

2 O mother, who with your seven sons nullified the violence of the tyrant, frustrated his evil designs, and showed the courage of your faith! 3 Nobly set like a roof on the pillars of your sons, you held firm and unswerving against the earthquake of the tortures. 4 Take courage, therefore, O holy-minded mother, maintaining firm an enduring hope in God. 5 The moon in heaven, with the stars, does not stand so august as you, who, after lighting the way of your star-like seven sons to piety, stand in honor before God and are firmly set in heaven with them. 6 For your children were true descendants of father Abraham.

7 If it were possible for us to paint the history of your religion as an artist might, would not those who first beheld it have shuddered as they saw the mother of the seven children enduring their varied tortures to death for the sake of religion? 8 Indeed it would be proper to inscribe on their tomb these words as a reminder to the people of our nation:

9 "Here lie buried an aged priest and an aged woman and seven sons, because of the violence of the tyrant who wished to destroy the way of life of the Hebrews. 10 They vindicated their nation, looking to God and enduring torture even to death."

11 Truly the contest in which they were engaged was divine, 12 for on that day virtue gave the awards and tested them for their endurance. The prize was immortality in endless life. 13 Eleazar was the first contestant, the mother of the seven sons entered the competition, and the brothers contended. 14 The tyrant was the antagonist, and the world and the human race were the spectators. 15 Reverence for God was victor and gave the crown to its own athletes. 16 Who did not admire the athletes of the divine legislation? Who were not amazed?

17 The tyrant himself and all his council marveled at their endurance, 18 because of which they now stand before the divine throne and live the life of eternal blessedness. 19 For Moses says, "All who are consecrated are under your hands." 20 These, then, who have been consecrated for the sake of God, are honored, not only with this honor, but also by the fact that because of them our enemies did not rule over our nation, 21 the tyrant was punished, and the homeland purified—they having become, as it were, a ransom for the sin of our nation. 22 And through the blood of those devout ones and their death as an atoning sacrifice, divine Providence preserved Israel that previously had been mistreated.

23 For the tyrant Antiochus, when he saw the courage of their virtue and their endurance under the tortures, proclaimed them to his soldiers as an example for their own endurance, 24 and this made them brave and courageous for infantry battle and siege, and he ravaged and conquered all his enemies.

18 O Israelite children, offspring of the seed of Abraham, obey this law and exercise piety in every way, 2 knowing that devout reason is master of all emotions, not only of sufferings from within, but also of those from without.

3 Therefore those who gave over their bodies in suffering for the sake of religion were not only admired by mortals, but also were deemed worthy to share in a divine inheritance. 4 Because of them the nation gained peace, and by reviving observance of the law in the homeland they ravaged the enemy. 5 The tyrant Antiochus was both punished on earth and is being chas-

tised after his death. Since in no way whatever was he able to compel the Israelites to become pagans and to abandon their ancestral customs, he left Jerusalem and marched against the Persians.

6 The mother of seven sons expressed also these principles to her children: 7 "I was a pure virgin and did not go outside my father's house; but I guarded the rib from which woman was made. 8 No seducer corrupted me on a desert plain, nor did the destroyer, the deceitful serpent, defile the purity of my virginity. 9 In the time of my maturity I remained with my husband, and when these sons had grown up their father died. A happy man was he, who lived out his life with good children, and did not have the grief of bereavement. 10 While he was still with you, he taught you the law and the prophets. 11 He read to you about Abel slain by Cain, and Isaac who was offered as a burnt offering, and about Joseph in prison. 12 He told you of the zeal of Phinehas, and he taught you about Hananiah, Azariah, and Mishael in the fire. 13 He praised Daniel in the den of the lions and blessed him. 14 He reminded you of the scripture of Isaiah, which says, 'Even though you go through the fire, the flame shall not consume you.' 15 He sang to you songs of the psalmist David, who said, 'Many are the afflictions of the righteous.' 16 He recounted to you Solomon's proverb, 'There is a tree of life for those who do his will.' 17 He confirmed the query of Ezekiel, 'Shall these dry bones live?' 18 For he did not forget to teach you the song that Moses taught, which says, 19 'I kill and I make alive: this is your life and the length of your days.' "

20 O bitter was that day—and yet not bitter—when that bitter tyrant of the Greeks quenched fire with fire in his cruel caldrons, and in his burning rage brought those seven sons of the daughter of Abraham to the catapult and back again to more tortures, 21 pierced the pupils of their eyes and cut out their tongues, and put them to death with various tortures. 22 For these crimes divine justice pursued and will pursue the accursed tyrant. 23 But the sons of Abraham with their victorious mother are gathered together into the chorus of the fathers, and have received pure and immortal souls from God, 24 to whom be glory forever and ever. Amen.

● 110

The Spiritual Inheritance of the Daughters of Job

The Testament of Job 46–52   2d century C.E.?

WORK: Virtually nothing is known about the origins of *The Testament of Job*, an elaboration of the biblical story of Job, dating perhaps to the second century C.E. There are no clear references to it in ancient sources, and there is little scholarly consensus about authorship beyond the recognition that the author knew the canonical Book of Job in the Greek Jewish translation of the Hebrew Scriptures known as the Septuagint. Some scholars have argued for an Egyptian provenience, but no one really knows.

What is particularly compelling about the work is its attention to women, which is far in excess of anything found in the canonical Job. The wife of Job, who remains nameless and all but speechless in the canonical work, obtains a name, plays a significant part in the drama, and speaks frequently. Excerpted here is the account of Job's legacy to his three daughters, all of whom receive great spiritual powers. The account is a fascinating expansion on the biblical narrative and a significant aspect of the *Testament of Job* which until recently had gone unnoticed by scholars.

TRANSLATION AND TEXT: R. A. Kraft et al., "*The Testament of Job*": *Greek Text and English Translation*, SBLTT 5, Pseudepigrapha Series 4 (Missoula, Mont.: Scholars Press, 1974).

ADDITIONAL TRANSLATION: *AOT* 617–48; *OTP* 1:829–68.

ADDITIONAL TEXT: M. R. James, *Apocrypha Anecdota* (Cambridge, 1899), 2:lxxii–cii, 103–37; S. Brock, *Testamentum Iobi*, PVTG (1967), 1–60.

BIBLIOGRAPHY: P. van der Horst, "The Role of Women in the *Testament of Job*," *Nederlands Theologisch Tijdschrift* 40 (1986): 273–89; Susan R. Garrett, "The 'Weaker Sex' in the *Testament of Job*," *JBL* 112 (1993): 55–70.

46 And they brought forth the property for distribution to the seven males. And he did not present any of the goods to the females. And they were distressed and said to their father:

> Our father, sir, it can't be that we are (not) also your children, can it? Why did you not give us a portion of your property?

But Job said to the females:

> Do not be upset, my daughters, for I did not forget you. For I have already selected for you an inheritance better than that of your seven brothers.

And then when he had called his daughter named Hemera, he said to her:

> Take the signet ring, go to the chamber and bring me the three golden boxes so that I may give you the inheritance.

And she went away and brought them. And he opened them and brought forth (three bands), shimmering, so that no man could describe their form, since they are not from earth but are from heaven, flashing with bright sparks like rays of the sun. And he gave each of the daughters one band saying,

Place these around your breast so that it may go well with you all the days of your life.

47 And the other daughter, named Kassia, said to him:

Father, is this the inheritance which you said was better than that of our brothers? What then is so unusual about these bands? We won't be able to sustain our life from them, will we?

And the father said to them,

Not only will you sustain life from these, but these bands will also lead you into the better world, (to live) in the heavens. Are you ignorant, then, my children, of the value of these cords, of which the Lord considered me worthy on the day on which he wished to have mercy on me and remove from my body the diseases and the worms? When he called me he set before me these three bands and said to me:

Arise, gird your loins like a man!
I shall question you, and you answer me.

So I took them and girded myself, and immediately the worms disappeared from my body (and the plagues as well). And then, through the Lord, my body grew strong as if it had not suffered anything at all. But I could even forget the pains in my heart! And the Lord spoke to me by a powerful act, showing me things present and things to come. Now then, my children, since you have them you will not have the enemy opposing you at all, neither will you have anxieties about him in your mind, because it is a protective amulet of the Lord. Rise, then, gird them around you before I die in order that you may be able to see those who are coming for my departure, so that you may marvel at the creatures of God.

48 Thus, when the one of the three daughters (called) Hemera arose, she wrapped herself just as her father said. And she received another heart, so that she no longer thought about earthly things. And she chanted verses in the angelic language, and ascribed a hymn to God in accord with the hymnic style of the angels. And as she chanted the hymns, she permitted "the Spirit" to be inscribed on her garment.

49 And then Kassia girded herself and had her heart changed so that she was no longer anxious about worldly things. And her mouth received the dialect of the archons, (and glorified the creation of the exalted place). Wherefore if anyone wishes to know "the creation of the heavens," he will be able to find it in the "Hymns of Kassia."

50 And then the other one also, called Amaltheias-keras, girded herself and her mouth chanted verses in the dialect of those on high, since her heart also

was changed by withdrawing from worldly things. And she spoke in the dialect of (the) cherubim, glorifying the master of virtues by exhibiting their splendor. And the one who further wishes (to grasp the poetic rhythm of "the paternal splendor") will find it recorded in the "Prayers of Amaltheias-keras."

51 And after the three had stopped singing hymns, while the Lord was present as was I Nereos the brother of Job, while the holy angel was present, I was sitting near Job on the couch. And even I heard the magnificent compositions, as each [sister] noted things down for the other. And I wrote out the book (of notations for most of the hymns that issued from the three daughters of my brother,) so that these things would serve as a safeguard along with those, for these are the magnificent compositions of God.

52 And after three days, while Job was presumed to be sick on the couch, without suffering or pains since suffering could not touch him because of the omen of the sash with which he was girded—and after three days he saw those who had come for his soul. And rising immediately, he took a lyre and gave it to his daughter Hemera, and gave a censer to Kassia, and gave a kettledrum to Amaltheias-keras—so that they might praise those who had come for his soul. And when they had taken them, they praised (and glorified) God in the exalted dialect. (And) after these things, the one who sat in the great chariot came out and greeted Job, while the three daughters looked on, and their father himself looked on, but others did not see. And taking the soul, he flew up while embracing it, and made it mount the chariot, and set off for the east. But his body, wrapped for burial, was borne to the tomb as his three daughters led the way, girded about and singing hymns to God.

● 111

Two Juxtaposed Narratives of the Gullibility of Pious Women

JOSEPHUS *Antiquities of the Jews* 18.65–80, 81–84   late 1st century C.E.

AUTHOR, TRANSLATION, AND TEXT: See entry 15.

BIBLIOGRAPHY: Shelly Matthews, *First Converts: Rich Pagan Women and the Rhetoric of Mission in Early Judaism and Christianity* (Stanford, Calif.: Stanford University Press, 2001).

65 About this same time [ca. 19 C.E.] another outrage threw the Jews into an uproar; and simultaneously certain actions of a scandalous nature occurred in connexion with the temple of Isis at Rome. I shall first give an account of the daring deed of the followers of Isis and shall then come back to the fate of the Jews. 66 There was a lady Paulina, who because of her descent from noble Romans and because of her own practice of virtue was held in high

regard. She also enjoyed the prestige of wealth, had a comely appearance, and was at the age at which women are most exuberant, yet devoted her life to good conduct. She was married to Saturninus, who was fully a match for her in reputation. 67 Decius Mundus, who ranked high among the knights of his day, was in love with her. When he saw that her character was too strong to succumb to gifts, since, even when he sent them abundantly, she scorned them, his passion was inflamed all the more, so that he actually promised to give her 200,000 Attic drachmas if he could share her bed a single time. 68 When even this failed to shake her resolution, he, finding it intolerable not to win his suit, thought that it would be fitting to condemn himself to death by starvation and thus to put an end to the suffering that had overtaken him. And so he decided upon such a death and was actually proceeding to carry out his resolve. 69 Mundus, however, had a freedwoman named Ida, expert in every kind of mischief, whom his father had emancipated. She had no patience with the young man's resolve to die, for it was obvious what he intended. She went to him, used argument to rouse him, and by plausibly undertaking to find a way, held out hope that he might succeed in enjoying intimate relations with Paulina. 70 When he joyfully listened to her importunity, she informed him that she would require no more than 50,000 drachmas to secure the woman. These proposals encouraged the youth, and she received the sum for which she had asked. She did not, however, proceed by the same course as had previous agents, since she perceived that this woman would never succumb to bribes. But knowing that the lady was very much given to the worship of Isis, Ida devised the following stratagem. 71 She had an interview with some of the priests and promised them every assurance, above all, a sum of money amounting to 25,000 drachmas payable at once and as much more after the success of the plot. She then explained the young man's passionate desire for the woman and urged them to bend every effort to secure her for him. 72 The impact of the money was enough to sway them, and they agreed. The eldest of them hastened to Paulina's house and, on being admitted, requested a private talk with her. This being accorded, he said that he had been sent to her by the god Anubis; the god had fallen in love with her and bade her come to him. 73 The message was what she would most have wished. Not only did she pride herself among her lady friends on receiving such an invitation from Anubis, but she told her husband of her summons to dine with and share the bed of Anubis. Her husband concurred, since he had no doubt of his wife's chastity. 74 Go then she did to the temple. After supper, when it came time to sleep, the doors within the shrine were shut by the priest and the lamps were cleared away. Mundus, for he had been concealed there beforehand, was not rebuffed when he sought intercourse with her. Indeed it was a nightlong service that she performed for him, assuming that he was the god. 75 He departed before the priests, who had been informed of the scheme, had begun to stir. Paulina went early in the morning to her husband and described in detail the divine manifestation of Anubis, and before the ladies, her friends, she put on great airs in talking about him. 76 Those who heard, having regard to the substance of the matter, were incredulous; and yet, on the other hand, finding it impossible not to believe her when they took into consideration her chastity and position in society, they were reduced to marvelling. 77 Two days after the incident, Mundus put himself in her way and said: "Well, Paulina, you have indeed saved me 200,000 drachmas which you could have added to your estate, yet you have rendered to perfection the service I urged you to perform. As for your attempt to flout Mundus, I did not concern myself about names, though I did about the pleasure to be derived from the act, so I adopted the name of Anubis as my own." 78 With these words he departed. Then she, being now aware for the first time of his dastardly deed, rent her garment; and when she had disclosed to her husband the enormity of the scheme, she begged him not to neglect to obtain redress. He in turn brought the matter to the notice of the emperor. 79 When Tiberius had fully informed himself by examining the priests, he crucified both them and Ida, for the hellish thing was her doing and it was she who had contrived the whole plot against the lady's honour. Moreover, he razed the temple and ordered the statue of Isis to be cast into the Tiber River. 80 Mundus' sentence was exile, since Tiberius regarded the fact that his crime had been committed under the influence of passion as a bar to a more severe penalty. Such were the insolent acts of the priests in the temple of Isis. I shall now return to the story, which I promised to tell, of what happened at the same time to the Jews in Rome.

(81) There was a certain Jew, a complete scoundrel, who had fled his own country because he was accused of transgressing certain laws and feared punishment on this account. Just at this time he was resident in Rome and played the part of an interpreter of the Mosaic law and its wisdom. 82 He enlisted three confederates not a whit better in character than himself; and when Fulvia, a woman of high rank who had become a Jewish proselyte, began to meet with them regularly, they urged her to send purple and gold to the temple in Jerusalem. They, however, took the gifts and used them for their own personal expenses, for it was this that had been their intention in asking for gifts from the start. 83 Saturninus, the husband of Fulvia, at the instigation of his wife, duly reported this to Tiberius, whose friend he was, whereupon the latter ordered the whole Jewish community to leave Rome. 84 The consuls drafted four thousand of these Jews for military service and sent them to the island of Sardinia; but they penalized a good many of them, who refused to serve for fear of breaking the Jewish law. And so because of the wickedness of four men the Jews were banished from the city.

The Trial Account of Carthaginian Christian Women and Men

The Acts of the Martyrs of Scilli   July 17, 180 C.E.

WORK: The oldest dated Latin Christian document from North Africa (2d century C.E.), *The Acts of the Martyrs of Scilli* belongs to the genre of Acts that have traditionally been considered court records, as opposed to *passiones* or *martyria*, the reports of eyewitnesses or just legends about martyrs. As such, they have often been thought to be reliable accounts of the court proceedings against Christian martyrs. More recent scholarship, however, acknowledges that Christians apparently processed such accounts and even fabricated them from whole cloth, and Musurillo's introduction to these Acts points out some internal obstacles to their being considered verbatim court reports. Although the skepticism about the reliability of such documents seems well taken, the Acts offer important information to scholars studying Christian women since many of them report on the martyrdom of women as well as men.

These martyrdom accounts were, and are, typically read on the anniversary of the martyrdom, and they are collected in calendrical formats. The location of Scilli is unknown.

TRANSLATION: J. Stevenson, *A New Eusebius*, 2d ed. (London: SPCK, 1987), 44–45).

TEXT: Acta Sanctorum (Antwerp, 1643); Analecta Bollandiana (Brussels, 1882–).

ADDITIONAL TRANSLATION AND TEXT: H. Musurillo, *The Acts of the Christian Martyrs* (Oxford: Clarendon Press, 1972), 86–89; J. A. Robinson, "The Passion of Perpetua," with an Appendix on the Scillitan Martyrdom, CTS 1, 2 (1891).

BIBLIOGRAPHY: Stuart G. Hall, "Women among the Early Martyrs," in Diana Wood, ed., *Martyrs and Martyrologies*, Studies in Church History 30 (Oxford: Blackwell, 1993), 1–21; E. Glenn Hinson, "Women among the Martyrs," *Studia Patristica* 25 (Louvain: Peeters, 1993), 423–28; Judith Perkins, *The Suffering Self: Pain and Narrative Representation in the Early Christian Era* (London: Routledge, 1995); Brent Shaw, "Body/Power/Identity: The Passions of the Martyrs," *JECS* 4, no. 3 (1996): 269–312; see also bibliography for entry 114.

> In the consulship of Praesens, then consul for the second time, and Claudian, on the 17th of July, Speratus, Nartzalus and Cittinus, Donata, Secunda, Vestia were brought to trial at Carthage in the council-chamber. The proconsul Saturninus said to them: "You may merit the indulgence of our Lord the Emperor, if you return to a right mind."
>
> Speratus said: "We have never done harm to any, we have never lent ourselves to wickedness: we have never spoken ill of any, but have given thanks when ill-treated, because we hold our own Emperor in honours."

The proconsul Saturninus said: "We also are religious people, and our religion is simple, and we swear by the genius of our Lord the Emperor, and pray for his safety, as you also ought to do."

Speratus said: "If you will give me a quiet hearing, I will tell you the mystery of simplicity."

Saturninus said: "If you begin to speak evil of our sacred rites, I will give you no hearing; but swear rather by the genius of our Lord the Emperor."

Speratus said: "I do not recognize the empire of this world; but rather I serve that God, whom no man has seen nor can see. I have not stolen, but if I buy anything, I pay the tax, because I recognize my Lord, the King of kings and Emperor of all peoples."

The proconsul Saturninus said to the rest: "Cease to be of this persuasion."

Speratus said: "The persuasion that we should do murder, or bear false witness, that is evil."

The proconsul Saturninus said: "Have no part in this madness."

Cittinus said: "We have none other to fear save the Lord our God who is in heaven."

Donata said: "Give honour to Caesar as unto Caesar, but fear to God."

Vestia said: "I am a Christian."

Secunda said: "I wish to be none other than what I am."

The proconsul Saturninus said to Speratus: "Do you persist in remaining a Christian?"

Speratus said: "I am a Christian." And all were of one mind with him.

The proconsul Saturninus said: "Do you desire any space for consideration?"

Speratus said: "When the right is so clear, there is nothing to consider."

The proconsul Saturninus said: "What have you in your case?"

Speratus said: "The Books and the letters of a just man, one Paul."

The proconsul Saturninus said: "Take a reprieve of thirty days and think it over."

Speratus again said: "I am a Christian." And all were of one mind with him.

The proconsul Saturninus read out the sentence from his notebook:
"Whereas Speratus, Nartzalus, Cittinus, Donata, Vestia, Secunda, and the rest have confessed that they live in accordance with the religious rites of the Christians, and, when an opportunity was given them of returning to the usage of the Romans, persevered in their obstinacy, it is our pleasure that they should suffer by the sword."

Speratus said: "Thanks be to God."

Nartzalus said: "To-day we are martyrs in heaven: thanks be to God!"

The proconsul Saturninus commanded that proclamation be made by the herald: "I have commanded that Speratus, Nartzalus, Cittinus, Veturius, Felix, Aquilinus, Laetantius, Januaria, Generosa, Vestia, Donata, Secunda be led forth to execution."

They all said: "Thanks be to God!"

And so all were crowned with martyrdom together, and reign with the Father and Son and Holy Spirit for ever and ever. Amen.

● 113

The Martyrdom of the Christian Blandina and Three Male Companions in 177 C.E.

Letter of the Churches of Lyons and Vienne, in Eusebius
History of the Church 5.1.3–63   4th century C.E.

WORK: Our only evidence for this account of the martyrs of Lyons and Vienne in ancient Gaul comes from the fourth-century Eusebius, who presents it as a letter written from those communities to Christians in Asia Minor, from where many of the Christians at Lyons and Vienne had emigrated. It describes events of 177 C.E. There is some internal evidence that the text may have been reworked before Eusebius, and there are questions about the accuracy of the original writers.

TRANSLATION AND TEXT: H. Musurillo, *The Acts of the Christian Martyrs* (Oxford: Clarendon Press, 1972), 62–85.

ADDITIONAL TRANSLATION AND TEXT: See entry 96.

BIBLIOGRAPHY: See entries 112 and 114.

The servants of Christ who sojourn at Vienne and Lyons in Gaul to the brethren in Asia and Phrygia *who* have the same *faith* and hope *as we* of redemption: *peace and grace* and glory *from God* the Father, *and* Christ *Jesus our Lord.*

1.4 ... Indeed we are unable, and it is beyond the power of pen, to state with exactitude the greatness of the affliction here, the mighty rage of the heathen against the saints, and all that the blessed martyrs endured. For the adversary fell upon us with all his might, and gave us *already* a foretaste of what *his coming* in the future without restraint would be; he left nothing undone to train and exercise beforehand his own against the servants of God, insomuch that not only were we excluded from houses and baths and marketplace, but they even forbade any of us to be seen at all in any place whatsoever. Nevertheless the grace of God was our captain on the other side, rescued the weak, and ranged against the foe firm pillars, able by their endurance to draw upon themselves the whole attack of the evil one. And these joined battle, enduring every kind of reproach and punishment; yea, regarding their many trials as little, they hastened to Christ, truly showing *that the sufferings of this present time are not worthy to be compared with the glory which shall be revealed to us-ward.*

1.7 First of all they nobly endured the attacks which the whole mass of the people heaped upon them, clamours, blows, halings, plunderings, stonings and confinements, and all that an infuriated mob is wont to employ against foes and enemies. Then they were conducted to the market-place by the tribune and the authorities presiding over the city; and when they had been questioned before the whole multitude, and given their testimony, they were shut up in prison until the governor's arrival. But afterwards, when they were brought before the governor, who used all the usual savagery against us, Vettius Epagathus, one of the brethren, a man filled with the fulness of love towards God and his neighbour, came forward. His conduct had reached such a degree of perfection that, young though he was, his reputation equalled that of the elder Zacharias; for he had *walked in all the commandments and ordinances of the Lord blameless*; in every service to his neighbour he was untiring, *having* a great *zeal for God* and *fervent in spirit.* Such a man could not endure the passing of so groundless a judgement against us; but was exceeding angry, and requested that he himself might be heard in defence of the brethren, that there is nothing godless or impious among us. Those around the tribunal cried out against him (for he was indeed a man of note), and the governor would not listen to the just request he had thus put forward, but asked him this one question, if he too were a Christian. And having confessed in a very clear voice, he also attained to the inheritance of the martyrs, being called the advocate of Christians, but having the *Advocate in* himself, *the Spirit of Zacharias*; which Spirit he showed in the fulness of *his love,* in that he was *well pleased* to *lay down even* his *own life for* the defence of *the brethren.* For he was and is a true disciple of Christ, *following the Lamb whithersoever he goeth.*

1.11 Henceforward the rest were divided; some were manifestly ready for martyrdom, and fulfilled with all zeal the confession wherein they gave witness; but others were manifestly unready and untrained and still weak, unable to bear the strain of a mighty conflict: of which number some ten proved abortions. These last wrought in us great sorrow and immeasurable mourning, and hindered the zeal of the remainder who had not yet been seized, and who in spite of every terrible suffering nevertheless attended the martyrs and would not leave them. But then we were all greatly affrighted at the uncertainty of confession; not that we feared the punishments inflicted, but we looked to the issue and dreaded lest any should fall away. Nevertheless those who were worthy were seized day by day, thus filling up the number of the former class, so that from the two churches were gathered all the zealous members, by whose means our position here had been mainly established. And there were seized also certain of our heathen household servants, since the governor gave an official order that we should all be sought out. And they too, thanks to *the snares* of Satan, in their fear of the tortures which they saw the saints enduring, and at the instigation of the soldiers, falsely accused us of Thyestean banquets and Oedipodean intercourse, and things of which it is not right for us to speak or think, nay, not even to believe that the like was ever done by man. But these rumours spread, and all were infuriated at us, insomuch that those who had formerly acted with moderation, on the ground of friendship, were now greatly incensed and *cut to the heart* against us. Thus was fulfilled that which was said by the Lord: *The* time will *come,* when *whosoever killeth you shall think that he offereth service unto God.* From that time on the holy martyrs endured punishments beyond all description, Satan earnestly endeavouring to elicit from their lips also some of the slanders.

1.17 But the entire fury of the crowd, governor and soldiers fell upon Sanctus, the deacon from Vienne, and upon Maturus, a noble combatant though but lately baptized, and upon Attalus, a native of Pergamum, of which church he had been always *the pillar and ground*, and upon Blandina, through whom Christ showed that things which appear mean and unsightly and despicable in the eyes of men are accounted worthy of great glory in the sight of God, through love towards Him, a love which showed itself in power and did not boast itself in appearance. For when we were all afraid, and her mistress according to the flesh (who was herself also a combatant in the ranks of the martyrs) was in a state of agony, lest the weakness of her body should render her unable even to make a bold confession, Blandina was filled with such power that those who by turns kept torturing her in every way from dawn till evening were worn out and exhausted, and themselves confessed defeat from lack of aught else to do to her; they marvelled that the breath still remained in a body all mangled and covered with gaping wounds, and they testified that a single form of torture was sufficient to render life extinct, let alone such and so many. But the blessed woman, like a noble champion, in confession regained her strength; and for her, to say "I am a Christian, and with us no evil finds a place" was refreshment and rest and insensibility to her lot.

1.20 Now as for Sanctus, he also nobly endured with surpassing and superhuman courage all the torments that human hands could inflict, and though the wicked men hoped that the continuance and severity of the tortures would cause him to utter something that he ought not, he set the battle against them with such firmness that he would not state even his own name, or the people or city whence he came, or whether he were bond or free. But to every question he replied in Latin: "I am a Christian." This he confessed again and again, instead of name and city and race and all else, and no other word did the heathen hear from his lips. Hence there actually arose great contention on the part of the governor and the torturers against him, with the result that finally, when nothing else was left to inflict upon him, they applied red-hot brazen plates to the most tender parts of his body. And though these were burning, Sanctus himself remained unbending and unyielding, and firm in his confession; for he was bedewed and strengthened by the heavenly *fountain of the water of life* which issues from the bowels of Christ. But his poor body was a witness to what he had undergone—one whole wound and bruise, contracted, having lost the outward form of a man—in which body Christ suffered and accomplished mighty wonders, bringing the adversary to nought and *showing* for the *ensample* of those that remained that nothing is to be feared where the love of the Father is, nothing is painful where there is the *glory of Christ*. For the wicked men after certain days again tortured the martyr, thinking to overcome him when they applied the same instruments to limbs so swollen and enflamed that he could not bear even the hand to touch them; or that he would die under the tortures and so cause terror to the rest. Yet not only did nothing of the kind occur in this case, but, contrary to all human expectation, the poor body actually arose and became erect under the subsequent tortures, and regained its former shape and the use of its limbs. Thus by the grace of Christ the second torturing proved for him not punishment but healing. And Biblis too, one of those who had denied, *the devil* supposed that he had already *devoured*; but wishing to use her slander as a further ground of condemnation, he brought her to punishment, that he might compel an already fragile and craven woman to state impieties concerning us. She, however, regained her senses under the torture and awoke, so to speak, out of a deep sleep, when the passing retribution recalled to her mind the *eternal punishment* in hell; and she directly contradicted the slanderers, saying: "How could they eat their children, who may not eat blood even of creatures without reason?" And henceforth she confessed herself a Christian, and joined the inheritance of the martyrs.

1.27 Now when the tyrant's instruments of torture were brought to nought by Christ through the endurance of the blessed ones, the devil began to invent other devices: close confinement in prison, in darkness and its most noisome spot; stretching the feet in the stocks, and keeping them stretched five holes apart; and all those other torments which his servants when enraged—aye, and filled with their master—are wont to inflict upon prisoners. So that the more part were stifled in the prison, as many as the Lord willed thus to depart, that He might manifest *His glory*. For some, though tortured so cruelly that it seemed they could no longer live even with every attention, remained alive in the prison, destitute indeed of human care, but fortified afresh by *the Lord* and *strengthened* both in body and soul, cheering on and encouraging the rest. But others who were young and just recently apprehended, whose bodies had not been previously tortured, could not endure the rigour of their confinement, and died within its walls. Now the blessed Pothinus, to whom had been committed the ministry of the bishopric at Lyons, was above ninety years of age, and very weak in body. He was scarcely breathing because of the bodily *weakness* which was laid upon him, but the earnest desire for martyrdom filled him with that renewed strength which a *willing spirit* supplies. He too was haled to the tribunal, and though his body was weakened both by age and disease, his life was preserved within him, that through it Christ might *triumph*. He was conveyed to the tribunal by the soldiers, escorted by the city authorities and *the whole multitude*, who gave utterance to all sorts of cries, as if he were Christ Himself; and so he gave *the good* witness. Being examined by the governor as to who the God of the Christians was, he replied, "If thou art worthy, thou shalt know"; and thereupon he was haled without mercy, and received blows of every kind: those close by heaped on him all manner of insult with blows of hands and feet, regardless of his age, while those at a distance made him the object of whatever missile came to their hand; and all considered it a grievous fault and impiety to be behindhand in their wanton violence to him. For thus indeed they thought to avenge their gods. Scarcely breathing he was cast into prison, and after two days gave up the ghost.

1.32 Then in truth a mighty dispensation of God came to pass, and the measureless compassion of Jesus was displayed, in a manner rarely vouchsafed among the brethren, but not beyond the art of Christ. For they who had denied when the Christians were first arrested were also confined with [the others] and shared their sufferings; for on this occasion their denial had profited them nothing. On the contrary, those who confessed what they really were, were confined as Christians, no other charge being brought against them; while the others were detained thenceforward as murderers and scoundrels, and were punished twice as much as the rest. For the burden of the confessors was lightened by the joy of martyrdom, the hope of the promises, their love to Christ, and the Spirit of the Father; but the others were grievously tormented by their conscience, insomuch that their countenances could be clearly distinguished from all the rest as they passed by. For they went forth with joy, great glory and grace blended on their countenances, so that even their *chains* hung around them like a *goodly* ornament, as a bride adorned *with golden fringes of divers colours,* perfumed the while with the *sweet savour of Christ;* hence some supposed that they had been anointed with earthly ointment as well. But the others were dejected, downcast, unsightly and covered with every kind of confusion; reproached, moreover, by the heathen for baseness and cowardice; under the charge of murder, and having lost the one precious, glorious and life-giving Name. The rest beholding this were stablished, and those who were apprehended confessed without doubting, nor did they bestow even a thought upon the persuasion of the devil. . . . After this their martyrdoms henceforth embraced every different form of death. For having *woven* a single *crown* of divers colours and variegated flowers they offered it to the Father. And so it was fitting that the noble champions, after having endured a varied conflict and mightily conquered, should receive as their due the mighty *crown* of incorruptibility. Maturus, then, and Sanctus and Blandina and Attalus were led to contend with wild beasts to the amphitheatre, and to the public spectacle of heathen inhumanity, a day for contests with wild beasts being granted of set purpose for our benefit. And Maturus and Sanctus passed once more through every kind of torture in the amphitheatre, as if they had suffered absolutely nothing before, or rather as if they had already vanquished their antagonist in many rounds, and were now contending for the crown itself. Again they ran the gauntlet of scourges, as is the custom of the place; they were dragged by wild beasts; they endured all that the cries of a maddened populace ordered, now from this side, now from that; and last of all, the iron chair, which fried their bodies and choked them with smoke. Nor even at this point did the heathen stop, but were still further maddened, in their desire to conquer the Christians' endurance; nevertheless nothing escaped the lips of Sanctus save that word of confession which it had been his wont from the very first to utter. So then, these men, whose life had lasted long through a mighty conflict, were finally sacrificed, being *made* throughout that day *a spectacle unto the world* in place of all the varied show that single combats offered.

1.41 Now Blandina, suspended on a stake, was exposed as food to wild beasts which were let loose against her. Even to look on her, as she hung cross-wise in earnest prayer, wrought great eagerness in those who were contending, for in their conflict they beheld with their outward eyes in the form of their sister Him who was crucified for them, that He might persuade those who believe in Him that all who suffer for the glory of Christ have unbroken fellowship with the living God. And as none of the wild beasts then touched her, she was taken down from the stake and cast again into prison, being kept for another conflict, that she might conquer in still further contests, and so both render irrevocable the sentence passed on *the crooked serpent,* and encourage the brethren—she the small, the weak, the despised, who had *put on Christ* the great and invincible Champion, and who in many rounds vanquished the adversary and through conflict was crowned with the *crown* of incorruptibility.

1.43 As for Attalus, he too was loudly called for by the crowd (for he was well known), and entered the arena a ready combatant by reason of his good conscience, since he had been truly exercised in the Christian discipline, and always a *witness* among us of *truth*. He was conducted round the amphitheatre, preceded by a board, on which was written in Latin "This is Attalus the Christian," the people bursting with vehement indignation against him. But when the governor learnt that he was a Roman, he ordered him to be taken back to the prison, where also were the others concerning whom he wrote to Caesar and was awaiting his sentence.

1.45 But the intervening time proved *not idle nor unfruitful* in their case; nay, through their endurance the measureless compassion of Christ was displayed. For by the living the dead were quickened, and martyrs forgave those who were not martyrs, and the virgin mother rejoiced greatly to receive alive those whom her womb had brought forth dead. For by their means the more part of those who had denied were brought again to birth, were conceived again, were rekindled into life, and learnt to confess; full now of life and vigour they approached the tribunal, for their trial was made sweet by God, who *hath no pleasure in the death of the sinner,* but is kind towards *repentance;* that they might be again questioned by the governor. For Caesar had written that they should be tortured to death, but that any who denied should be set free. And as the national festival held in that place was then at its commencement—a festival largely attended by visitors from all the tribes—the governor had the blessed ones conducted to the tribunal, to make of them a spectacle, and to form a procession for the benefit of the crowds. Therefore he again examined them; and those who appeared to possess Roman citizenship he beheaded, but sent the others to the wild beasts. And Christ was mightily glorified in those who formerly denied Him, but then confessed, contrary to the expectation of the heathen. Indeed they were examined by themselves, presumably as a prelude to their release; but confessing, were added to the inheritance of the martyrs. And there remained outside those who had never even a trace of faith, or an idea of the marriage *garment,* or a thought for the fear of God, nay rather, *blaspheming the Way* by their manner of life—in fact, *the sons of perdition.* But all the rest *were added* to the Church.

1.49 While these were being examined, a certain Alexander, a Phrygian by race and a physician by profession, who had lived for many years in the Gauls, and was known almost to everyone for his love to God and *boldness* for *the word* (for he too was not destitute of the apostolic gift), stood by the tribunal and by signs encouraged them to confess. To the bystanders there he appeared to be, as it were, in travail. The crowd were enraged that those who had formerly denied should afterwards confess, and cried out against Alexander as the cause of this. Thereupon the governor summoned him and asked him who he was; and angry at his reply "A Christian," condemned him to the wild beasts. And on the following day he entered [the amphitheatre] in the company of Attalus as well; for indeed the governor, to please the crowd, had delivered Attalus too again to the wild beasts. These men experienced in turn every instrument that has been devised for torture in the amphitheatre, and, having endured a mighty conflict, at last were sacrificed like the rest. Alexander *neither groaned nor uttered* the slightest *cry*, but held converse with God in his heart. But Attalus, when he was placed in the iron chair and scorched, so that the fumes rose from his body, addressed the multitude in Latin: "Behold, this which ye do is devouring men; but we neither devour men nor practise any other wickedness." And on being asked the name of God, he replied, "God has not a name as a man has." And after all these, finally on the last day of the single combats Blandina was again brought in, in the company of Ponticus, a lad about fifteen years old. They had also been fetched in every day to view the tortures of the others. The heathen tried to force them to swear by their idols, and as they remained firm and set them at nought, the multitude was so infuriated at them that it had neither compassion for the youth of the boy nor respect for the sex of the woman. Nay, they exposed them to every cruelty and brought them through the entire round of tortures, again and again trying to force them to swear. But this they were unable to accomplish; for Ponticus, encouraged by his sister (so that the heathen themselves saw that it was she who was urging him on and strengthening him), having nobly endured every kind of torture *gave up his spirit.* But the blessed Blandina last of all, having, like a highborn mother, exhorted her children and sent them forth victorious to the King, travelled herself along the same path of conflicts as they did, and hastened to them, rejoicing and exulting at her departure, like one *bidden to* a marriage *supper*, rather than cast to the wild beasts. And after the scourging, after the wild beasts, after the frying-pan, she was at last thrown into a basket and presented to a bull. For a time the animal tossed her, but she had now lost all perception of what was happening, thanks to the hope she cherished, her grasp of the objects of her faith, and her intercourse with Christ. Then she too was sacrificed, and even the heathen themselves acknowledged that never in their experience had a woman endured so many terrible sufferings.

1.57 Nevertheless not even thus were their madness and cruelty towards the saints satisfied. For wild and barbarous tribes when incited by a wild beast were not easily checked; and their wanton violence found another distinct outlet with regard to the corpses. That they had been worsted did not put them out of countenance, since for them man's gift of reason did not exist; nay rather, in them as in a wild beast the fact inflamed anger, and the governor and people were at one in displaying an unjust hatred towards us, that the Scripture might be fulfilled: *He that is lawless, let him do lawlessness still; and he that is righteous, let him be accounted righteous still.* For indeed they cast those suffocated in prison to the dogs, and kept a careful guard by night and day lest any should receive funeral rites at our hands. And then they actually exposed what the wild beasts and the fire had left behind—mangled or charred, as the case might be—and the heads of the others together with their severed trunks, and guarded them likewise from burial, with a military watch, for many days. And some were moved with indignation and *gnashed on* them *with their teeth,* seeking to take still further vengeance upon them; while others laughed and jeered, at the same time exalting their own idols, to whom they attributed the punishment of the Christians; others again, of a more forbearing nature and seeming to extend to them a measure of fellow-feeling, uttered many reproaches, saying, "*Where is* their *god?* and what profit has their religion brought them, which they have preferred to their own life?" So varied, then, was their attitude; but as for us, we were plunged in great grief, in that we could not bury the bodies in the earth. For neither did night avail us for this purpose, nor did money persuade or prayers move them. But in every possible way they kept guard, as if the prevention of burial would bring them great gain.

1.62 ... The bodies, then, of the martyrs, which for six days were displayed and exposed to the elements in every way possible, the lawless men afterwards burnt and reduced to ashes. Then they swept them down into the river Rhone which flows close by, so that not even a trace of them might remain upon the earth. And this they did, thinking that they could conquer God and deprive them of *the regeneration,* "in order," as they themselves said, "that they may not even have hope of a resurrection, in faith of which they introduce into our midst a certain strange and new-fangled cult, and despise dread torments, and are ready to go to their death, and that too with joy. Now let us see if they will rise again, and if their *god can* help them, and *deliver them out of* our *hands.*"

● 114

A First-Person Account of a Christian Woman's Persecution

The Martyrdom of Saints Perpetua and Felicitas　　　　　early(?) 3d century c.e.

WORK: *The Martyrdom (or Passion) of Saints Perpetua and Felicitas* claims to contain a firsthand report of the detainment and visionary experiences of a young Roman matron martyred at Carthage, North Africa, for her recent adoption of Christianity in the very early third century (often said to be precisely in 203 c.e.). Everything we know about Vibia Perpetua, as well as a small group of other Christians martyred with her, comes from this text, which joins the first-person report to a third-person account of the death of Perpetua and her companions, woven together by a larger narrative framework. The author of the entire work remains unknown.

Were Perpetua to have composed the central portion of the *Martyrdom,* it would make this the earliest work known to have been authored by a Christian woman and would make Perpetua one of the few known women authors from the Roman period, Christian or otherwise. Many scholars have accepted this portion, often (although somewhat inaccurately) called a diary, as Perpetua's own composition, a position I shared for some time but no longer hold. My current views are set forth in an article jointly authored with Shira L. Lander, noted below. Consistent with our conclusion that Perpetua is unlikely to have authored any part of the *Martyrdom*, I have relocated it, in this edition, from section 2 to this section.

Whether or not Perpetua herself composed the central portion, there has been speculation that the author, at least of the larger narrative frame if not also Perpetua herself, was a member of the New Prophecy, also sometimes known as Montanism (see entries 93–96). Some of the language of the prologue of the text may support such an identification, and the New Prophecy was known to have adherents in North Africa in precisely this period, including the well-known Christian writer Tertullian (who has himself occasionally been proposed as the author of the *Martyrdom*).

TRANSLATION AND TEXT: H. Musurillo, *The Acts of the Christian Martyrs* (Oxford: Clarendon Press, 1972), 106–31.

ADDITIONAL TEXT: SC 417 (J. Amat, 1996); C. J. M. van Beek, *Passio Sanctarum Perpetuae et Felicitatis* (Nijmegen: Noviomagi, Deker and Van de Vegt, 1936; repr., 1956); J. A. Robinson, *"The Passion of Perpetua,"* with an Appendix on the Scillitan Martyrdom, CTS 1, 2 (1891).

ADDITIONAL TRANSLATION AND TEXT: W. H. Shewring, *"The Passion of Perpetua and Felicity": A New Edition and Translation of the Latin Text Together with the Sermons of Saint Augustine upon these Saints, now first translated into English* (London: Sheed and Ward, 1931).

ADDITIONAL TRANSLATIONS: Rosemary Rader, "Perpetua," in Patricia Wilson-Kastner, ed., *A Lost Tradition: Women Writers of the Early Church* (Washington, DC.: University Press of America, 1981), 1–32; *ANF*.

BIBLIOGRAPHY: There is an extensive bibliography on Perpetua. Recent (and/or important) studies include Ross S. Kraemer and Shira L. Lander, "Perpetua and Felicitas," in Philip Esler, ed., *The Early Christian World* (London: Routledge, 2000), 2:1048–68; Jan Bremmer, "Perpetua and Her Diary: Authenticity, Family and Visions," in Walter Ameling, eds., *Märtyrer und Märtyrerakten* (Stuttgart: Franz Steiner Verlag, 2002), 77–120; Susanna Elm, "Perpetua the Martyr—Perpetua the Saint: The Cultural Context of an Early Christian Phenomenon," in M. Behrman and F. Schiffauer, eds., *Martyrdom Religious/Political: The Rhetoric of Fundamentalism in the Age of Globalization* (Amsterdam: Amsterdam Institute for Religion and Society, forthcoming); Thomas Heffernan, "Philology and Authorship in the *Passio Sanctarum Perpetuae et Felicitatis*," *Traditio: Studies in Ancient and Medieval History, Thought, and Religion* 50 (1995): 315–25; Frederick C. Klawiter, "The Role of Martyrdom and Persecution in Developing the Priestly Authority of

Women in Early Christianity: A Case Study of Montanism," *Church History* 49, no. 3 (1980): 251–61; Judith Perkins, "Suffering and Power," in her *The Suffering Self: Pain and Narrative Representation in the Early Christian Era* (London and New York: Routledge, 1995), 104–23; Brent Shaw, *"The Passion of Perpetua,"* Past and Present 139 (1993): 3–45; Maureen Tilley, *"The Passion of Perpetua and Felicity," in Searching the Scriptures*, 2:829–58; Jane Snyder, *The Woman and the Lyre: Women Writers in Classical Greece and Rome* (Carbondale: Southern Illinois University Press, 1989); Andrezej Wypustek, "Magic, Montanism, Perpetua, and the Severan Persecution," *Vigiliae Christianae* 51 (1997): 276–97.

1 The deeds recounted about the faith in ancient times were a proof of God's favour and achieved the spiritual strengthening of men as well; and they were set forth in writing precisely that honour might be rendered to God and comfort to men by the recollection of the past through the written word. Should not then more recent examples be set down that contribute equally to both ends? For indeed these too will one day become ancient and needful for the ages to come, even though in our own day they may enjoy less prestige because of the prior claim of antiquity.

Let those then who would restrict the power of the one Spirit to times and seasons look to this: the more recent events should be considered the greater, being later than those of old, and this is a consequence of the extraordinary graces promised for the last stage of time. For *in the last days, God declares, I will pour out my Spirit upon all flesh and their sons and daughters shall prophesy and on my manservants and my maidservants I will pour my Spirit, and the young men shall see visions and the old men shall dream dreams.* So too we hold in honour and acknowledge not only new prophecies but new visions as well, according to the promise. And we consider all the other functions of the Holy Spirit as intended for the good of the Church; for the same Spirit has been sent to distribute all his gifts to all, as the Lord apportions to everyone. For this reason we deem it imperative to set them forth and to make them known through the word for the glory of God. Thus no one of weak or despairing faith may think that supernatural grace was present only among men of ancient times, either in the grace of martyrdom or of visions, for God always achieves what he promises, as a witness to the non-believer and a blessing to the faithful.

And so, my brethren and little children, *that which we have heard and have touched with our hands we proclaim also to you, so that* those of *you* that were witnesses may recall the glory of the Lord and those that now learn of it through hearing *may have fellowship* with the holy martyrs and, through them, *with* the Lord Christ Jesus, to whom belong splendour and honour for all ages. Amen.

2 A number of young catechumens were arrested, Revocatus and his fellow slave Felicitas, Saturninus and Secundulus, and with them Vibia Perpetua, a newly married woman of good family and upbringing. Her mother and father were still alive and one of her two brothers was a catechumen like herself. She was about twenty-two years old and had an infant son at the breast. (Now from this point on the entire account of her ordeal is her own, according to her own ideas and in the way that she herself wrote it down.)

3 While we were still under arrest (she said) my father out of love for me was trying to persuade me and shake my resolution. "Father," said I, "do you see this vase here, for example, or waterpot or whatever?"

"Yes, I do", said he.

And I told him: "Could it be called by any other name than what it is?"

And he said: "No."

"Well, so too I cannot be called anything other than what I am, a Christian."

At this my father was so angered by the word "Christian" that he moved towards me as though he would pluck my eyes out. But he left it at that and departed, vanquished along with his diabolical arguments.

For a few days afterwards I gave thanks to the Lord that I was separated from my father, and I was comforted by his absence. During these few days I was baptized, and I was inspired by the Spirit not to ask for any other favour after the water but simply the perseverance of the flesh. A few days later we were lodged in the prison; and I was terrified, as I had never before been in such a dark hole. What a difficult time it was! With the crowd the heat was stifling; then there was the extortion of the soldiers; and to crown all, I was tortured with worry for my baby there.

Then Tertius and Pomponius, those blessed deacons who tried to take care of us, bribed the soldiers to allow us to go to a better part of the prison to refresh ourselves for a few hours. Everyone then left that dungeon and shifted for himself. I nursed my baby, who was faint from hunger. In my anxiety I spoke to my mother about the child, I tried to comfort my brother, and I gave the child in their charge. I was in pain because I saw them suffering out of pity for me. These were the trials I had to endure for many days. Then I got permission for my baby to stay with me in prison. At once I recovered my health, relieved as I was of my worry and anxiety over the child. My prison had suddenly become a palace, so that I wanted to be there rather than anywhere else.

4 Then my brother said to me: "Dear sister, you are greatly privileged; surely you might ask for a vision to discover whether you are to be condemned or freed."

Faithfully I promised that I would, for I knew that I could speak with the Lord, whose great blessings I had come to experience. And so I said: "I shall tell you tomorrow." Then I made my request and this was the vision I had.

I saw a ladder of tremendous height made of bronze, reaching all the way to the heavens, but it was so narrow that only one person could climb up at a time. To the sides of the ladder were attached all sorts of metal weapons: there were swords, spears, hooks, daggers, and spikes; so that if anyone tried to climb up carelessly or without paying attention, he would be mangled and his flesh would adhere to the weapons.

At the foot of the ladder lay a dragon of enormous size, and it would attack those who tried to climb up and try to terrify them from doing so. And Saturus was the first to go up, he who was later to give himself up of his own accord. He had been the builder of our strength, although he was not present when we were arrested. And he arrived at the top of the staircase and he looked back and said to me: "Perpetua, I am waiting for you. But take care; do not let the dragon bite you."

"He will not harm me," I said, "in the name of Christ Jesus."

Slowly, as though he were afraid of me, the dragon stuck his head out from underneath the ladder. Then, using it as my first step, I trod on his head and went up.

Then I saw an immense garden, and in it a grey-haired man sat in shepherd's garb; tall he was, and milking sheep. And standing around him were many thousands of people clad in white garments. He raised his head, looked at me, and said: "I am glad you have come, my child."

He called me over to him and gave me, as it were, a mouthful of the milk he was drawing; and I took it into my cupped hands and consumed it. And all those who stood around said: "Amen!" At the sound of this word I came to, with the taste of something sweet still in my mouth. I at once told this to my brother, and we realized that we would have to suffer, and that from now on we would no longer have any hope in this life.

5 A few days later there was a rumour that we were going to be given a hearing. My father also arrived from the city, worn with worry, and he came to see me with the idea of persuading me.

"Daughter," he said, "have pity on my grey head—have pity on me your father, if I deserve to be called your father, if I have favoured you above all your brothers, if I have raised you to reach this prime of your life. Do not abandon me to be the reproach of men. Think of your brothers, think of your mother and your aunt, think of your child, who will not be able to live once you are gone. Give up your pride! You will destroy all of us! None of us will ever be able to speak freely again if anything happens to you."

This was the way my father spoke out of love for me, kissing my hands and throwing himself down before me. With tears in his eyes he no longer addressed me as his daughter but as a woman. I was sorry for my father's sake, because he alone of all my kin would be unhappy to see me suffer.

I tried to comfort him saying: "It will all happen in the prisoner's dock as God wills; for you may be sure that we are not left to ourselves but are all in his power."

And he left me in great sorrow.

6 One day while we were eating breakfast we were suddenly hurried off for a hearing. We arrived at the forum, and straight away the story went about the neighbourhood near the forum and a huge crowd gathered. We walked up to the prisoner's dock. All the others when questioned admitted their guilt. Then, when it came my turn, my father appeared with my son, dragged me from the step, and said: "Perform the sacrifice—have pity on your baby!"

Hilarianus the governor, who had received his judicial powers as the successor of the late proconsul Minucius Timinianus, said to me: "Have pity on your father's grey head; have pity on your infant son. Offer the sacrifice for the welfare of the emperors."

"I will not," I retorted.

"Are you a Christian?" said Hilarianus.

And I said: "Yes, I am."

When my father persisted in trying to dissuade me, Hilarianus ordered him to be thrown to the ground and beaten with a rod. I felt sorry for father, just as if I myself had been beaten. I felt sorry for his pathetic old age.

Then Hilarianus passed sentence on all of us: we were condemned to the beasts, and we returned to prison in high spirits. But my baby had got used to being nursed at the breast and to staying with me in prison. So I sent the deacon Pomponius straight away to my father to ask for the baby. But father refused to give him over. But as God willed, the baby had no further desire for the breast, nor did I suffer any inflammation; and so I was relieved of any anxiety for my child and of any discomfort in my breasts.

7 Some days later when we were all at prayer, suddenly while praying I spoke out and uttered the name Dinocrates. I was surprised; for the name had never entered my mind until that moment. And I was pained when I recalled what had happened to him. At once I realized that I was privileged to pray for him. I began to pray for him and to sigh deeply for him before the Lord. That very night I had the following vision. I saw Dinocrates coming out of a dark hole, where there were many others with him, very hot and thirsty, pale and dirty. On his face was the wound he had when he died.

Now Dinocrates had been my brother according to the flesh; but he had died horribly of cancer of the face when he was seven years old, and his death was a source of loathing to everyone. Thus it was for him that I made my prayer. There was a great abyss between us: neither could approach the other. Where Dinocrates stood there was a pool full of water; and its rim was higher than the child's height, so that Dinocrates had to stretch himself up to drink. I was sorry that, though the pool had water in it, Dinocrates could not drink because of the height of the rim. Then I woke up, realizing that my brother was suffering. But I was confident that I could help him in his trouble; and I prayed for him every day until we were transferred to the military prison. For we were supposed to fight with the beasts at the military games to be held on the occasion of the emperor Geta's birthday. And I prayed for my brother day and night with tears and sighs that this favour might be granted me.

8 On the day we were kept in chains, I had this vision shown to me. I saw the same spot that I had seen before, but there was Dinocrates all clean, well dressed, and refreshed. I saw a scar where the wound had been; and the pool that I had seen before now had its rim lowered to the level of the child's waist. And Dinocrates kept drinking water from it, and there above the rim was a golden bowl full of water. And Dinocrates drew close and began to drink from it, and yet the bowl remained full. And when he had drunk enough of the water, he began to play as children do. Then I awoke, and I realized that he had been delivered from his suffering.

9 Some days later, an adjutant named Pudens, who was in charge of the prison, began to show us great honour, realizing that we possessed some great power within us. And he began to allow many visitors to see us for our mutual comfort.

Now the day of the contest was approaching, and my father came to see me overwhelmed with sorrow. He started tearing the hairs from his beard and threw them on the ground; he then threw himself on the ground and began to curse his old age and to say such words as would move all creation. I felt sorry for his unhappy old age.

10 The day before we were to fight with the beasts I saw the following vision. Pomponius the deacon came to the prison gates and began to knock violently. I went out and opened the gate for him. He was dressed in an unbelted white tunic, wearing elaborate sandals. And he said to me: "Perpetua, come; we are waiting for you."

Then he took my hand and we began to walk through rough and broken country. At last we came to the amphitheatre out of breath, and he led me into the centre of the arena.

Then he told me: "Do not be afraid. I am here, struggling with you." Then he left.

I looked at the enormous crowd who watched in astonishment. I was surprised that no beasts were let loose on me; for I knew that I was condemned to die by the beasts. Then out came an Egyptian against me, of vicious appearance, together with his seconds, to fight with me. There also came up to me some handsome young men to be my seconds and assistants.

My clothes were stripped off, and suddenly I was a man. My seconds began to rub me down with oil (as they are wont to do before a contest). Then I saw the Egyptian on the other side rolling in the dust. Next there came forth a man of marvellous stature, such that he rose above the top of the amphitheatre. He was clad in a beltless purple tunic with two stripes (one on either side) running down the middle of his chest. He wore sandals that were wondrously made of gold and silver, and he carried a wand like an athletic trainer and a green branch on which there were golden apples.

And he asked for silence and said: "If this Egyptian defeats her he will slay her with the sword. But if she defeats him, she will receive this branch." Then he withdrew.

We drew close to one another and began to let our fists fly. My opponent tried to get hold of my feet, but I kept striking him in the face with the heels of my feet. Then I was raised up into the air and I began to pummel him without as it were touching the ground. Then when I noticed there was a lull, I put my two hands together linking the fingers of one hand with those of the other and thus I got hold of his head. He fell flat on his face and I stepped on his head.

The crowd began to shout and my assistants started to sing psalms. Then I walked up to the trainer and took the branch. He kissed me and said to me: "Peace be with you, my daughter!" I began to walk in triumph towards the Gate of Life. Then I awoke. I realized that it was not with wild animals that I would fight but with the Devil; but I knew that I would win the victory. So much for what I did up until the eve of the contest. About what happened at the contest itself, let him write of it who will.

11 But the blessed Saturus has also made known his own vision and he has written it out with his own hand. We had died, he said, and had put off the flesh, and we began to be carried towards the east by four angels who did not touch us with their hands. But we moved along not on our backs facing upwards but as though we were climbing up a gentle hill. And when we were free of the world, we first saw an intense light. And I said to Perpetua (for she was at my side): "This is what the Lord promised us. We have received his promise."

While we were being carried by these four angels, a great open space appeared, which seemed to be a garden, with rose bushes and all manner of flowers. The trees were as tall as cypresses, and their leaves were constantly falling. In the garden there were four other angels more splendid than the others. When they saw us they paid us homage and said to the other angels in admiration: "Why, they are here! They are here!"

Then the four angels that were carrying us grew fearful and set us down. Then we walked across to an open area by way of a broad road, and there we met Jucundus, Saturninus, and Artaxius, who were burnt alive in the same persecution, together with Quintus who had actually died as a martyr in prison. We asked them where they had been. And the other angels said to us: "First come and enter and greet the Lord."

12 Then we came to a place whose walls seemed to be constructed of light. And in front of the gate stood four angels, who entered in and put on white robes. We also entered and we heard the sound of voices in unison chanting endlessly: *"Holy, holy, holy!"* In the same place we seemed to see an aged man with white hair and a youthful face, though we did not see his feet. On his right and left were four elders, and behind them stood other aged men. Surprised, we entered and stood before a throne: four angels lifted us up and we kissed the aged man and he touched our faces with his hand. And the elders said to us: "Let us rise." And we rose and gave the kiss of peace. Then the elders said to us: "Go and play."

To Perpetua I said: "Your wish is granted."

She said to me: "Thanks be to God that I am happier here now than I was in the flesh."

13 Then we went out and before the gates we saw the bishop Optatus on the right and Aspasius the presbyter and teacher on the left, each of them far apart and in sorrow. They threw themselves at our feet and said: "Make peace between us. For you have gone away and left us thus."

And we said to them: "Are you not our bishop, and are you not our presbyter? How can you fall at our feet?"

We were very moved and embraced them. Perpetua then began to speak with them in Greek, and we drew them apart into the garden under a rose arbour.

While we were talking with them, the angels said to them: "Allow them to rest. Settle whatever quarrels you have among yourselves." And they were put to confusion.

Then they said to Optatus: "You must scold your flock. They approach you as though they had come from the games, quarrelling about the different teams."

And it seemed as though they wanted to close the gates. And there we began to recognize many of our brethren, martyrs among them. All of us were sustained by a most delicious odour that seemed to satisfy us. And then I woke up happy.

14 Such were the remarkable visions of these martyrs, Saturus and Perpetua, written by themselves. As for Secundulus, God called him from this world earlier than the others while he was still in prison, by a special grace that he might not have to face the animals. Yet his flesh, if not his spirit, knew the sword.

15 As for Felicitas, she too enjoyed the Lord's favour in this wise. She had been pregnant when she was arrested, and was now in her eighth month. As the day of the spectacle drew near she was very distressed that her martyrdom would be postponed because of her pregnancy; for it is against the law for women with child to be executed. Thus she might have to shed her holy, innocent blood afterwards along with others who were common criminals. Her comrades in martyrdom were also saddened; for they were afraid that they would have to leave behind so fine a companion to travel alone on the same road to hope. And so, two days before the contest, they poured forth a prayer to the Lord in one torrent of common grief. And immediately after their prayer the birth pains came upon her. She suffered a good deal in her labour because of the natural difficulty of an eight months' delivery.

Hence one of the assistants of the prison guards said to her: "You suffer so much now—what will you do when you are tossed to the beasts? Little did you think of them when you refused to sacrifice."

"What I am suffering now," she replied, "I suffer by myself. But then another will be inside me who will suffer for me, just as I shall be suffering for him."

And she gave birth to a girl; and one of the sisters brought her up as her own daughter.

16 Therefore, since the Holy Spirit has permitted the story of this contest to be written down and by so permitting has willed it, we shall carry out the command or, indeed, the commission of the most saintly Perpetua, however unworthy I might be to add anything to this glorious story. At the same time I shall add one example of her perseverance and nobility of soul.

The military tribune had treated them with extraordinary severity because on the information of certain very foolish people he became afraid that they would be spirited out of the prison by magical spells.

Perpetua spoke to him directly. "Why can you not even allow us to refresh ourselves properly? For we are the most distinguished of the condemned prisoners, seeing that we belong to the emperor; we are to fight on his very birthday. Would it not be to your credit if we were brought forth on the day in a healthier condition?"

The officer became disturbed and grew red. So it was that he gave the order that they were to be more humanely treated; and he allowed her brothers and other persons to visit, so that the prisoners could dine in their company. By this time the adjutant who was head of the gaol was himself a Christian.

17 On the day before, when they had their last meal, which is called the free banquet, they celebrated not a banquet but rather a love feast. They spoke to the mob with the same steadfastness, warned them of God's judgement, stressing the joy they would have in their suffering, and ridiculing the curiosity of those that came to see them. Saturus said: "Will not tomorrow be enough for you? Why are you so eager to see something that you dislike? Our friends today will be our enemies on the morrow. But take careful note of what we look like so that you will recognize us on the day." Thus everyone would depart from the prison in amazement, and many of them began to believe.

18 The day of their victory dawned, and they marched from the prison to the amphitheatre joyfully as though they were going to heaven, with calm faces, trembling, if at all, with joy rather than fear. Perpetua went along with shining countenance and calm step, as the beloved of God, as a wife of Christ, putting down everyone's stare by her own intense gaze. With them also was Felicitas, glad that she had safely given birth so that now she could fight the beasts, going from one blood bath to another, from the midwife to the gladiator, ready to wash after childbirth in a second baptism.

They were then led up to the gates and the men were forced to put on the robes of priests of Saturn, the women the dress of the priestesses of Ceres. But the noble Perpetua strenuously resisted this to the end.

"We came to this of our own free will, that our freedom should not be violated. We agreed to pledge our lives provided that we would do no such thing. You agreed with us to do this."

Even injustice recognized justice. The military tribune agreed. They were to be brought into the arena just as they were. Perpetua then began to sing a psalm: she was already treading on the head of the Egyptian. Revocatus, Saturninus, and Saturus began to warn the onlooking mob. Then when they came within sight of Hilarianus, they suggested by their motions and gestures: "You have condemned us, but God will condemn you" was what they were saying.

At this the crowds became enraged and demanded that they be scourged before a line of gladiators. And they rejoiced at this that they had obtained a share in the Lord's sufferings.

19 But he who said, *Ask and you shall receive*, answered their prayer by giving each one the death he had asked for. For whenever they would discuss among themselves their desire for martyrdom, Saturninus indeed insisted that he wanted to be exposed to all the different beasts, that his crown might be all the more glorious. And so at the outset of the contest he and Revocatus were matched with a leopard, and then while in the stocks they were attacked by a bear. As for Saturus, he dreaded nothing more than a bear, and he

counted on being killed by one bite of a leopard. Then he was matched with a wild boar; but the gladiator who had tied him to the animal was gored by the boar and died a few days after the contest, whereas Saturus was only dragged along. Then when he was bound in the stocks awaiting the bear, the animal refused to come out of the cages, so that Saturus was called back once more unhurt.

20 For the young women, however, the Devil had prepared a mad heifer. This was an unusual animal, but it was chosen that their sex might be matched with that of the beast. So they were stripped naked, placed in nets and thus brought out into the arena. Even the crowd was horrified when they saw that one was a delicate young girl and the other was a woman fresh from childbirth with the milk still dripping from her breasts. And so they were brought back again and dressed in unbelted tunics.

First the heifer tossed Perpetua and she fell on her back. Then sitting up she pulled down the tunic that was ripped along the side so that it covered her thighs, thinking more of her modesty than of her pain. Next she asked for a pin to fasten her untidy hair: for it was not right that a martyr should die with her hair in disorder, lest she might seem to be mourning in her hour of triumph.

Then she got up. And seeing that Felicitas had been crushed to the ground, she went over to her, gave her her hand, and lifted her up. Then the two stood side by side. But the cruelty of the mob was by now appeased, and so they were called back through the Gate of Life.

There Perpetua was held up by a man named Rusticus who was at the time a catechumen and kept close to her. She awoke from a kind of sleep (so absorbed had she been in ecstasy in the Spirit) and she began to look about her. Then to the amazement of all she said: "When are we going to be thrown to that heifer or whatever it is?"

When told that this had already happened, she refused to believe it until she noticed the marks of her rough experience on her person and her dress. Then she called for her brother and spoke to him together with the catechumens and said: "You must all *stand fast in the faith* and love one another, and do not be weakened by what we have gone through."

21 At another gate Saturus was earnestly addressing the soldier Pudens. "It is exactly," he said, "as I foretold and predicted. So far not one animal has touched me. So now you may believe me with all your heart: I am going in there and I shall be finished off with one bite of the leopard." And immediately as the contest was coming to a close a leopard was let loose, and after one bite Saturus was so drenched with blood that as he came away the mob roared in witness to his second baptism: "Well washed! Well washed!" For well washed indeed was one who had been bathed in this manner.

Then he said to the soldier Pudens: "Good-bye. Remember me, and remember the faith. These things should not disturb you but rather strengthen you."

And with this he asked Pudens for a ring from his finger, and dipping it into his wound he gave it back to him again as a pledge and as a record of his bloodshed.

Shortly after he was thrown unconscious with the rest in the usual spot to have his throat cut. But the mob asked that their bodies be brought out into the open that their eyes might be the guilty witnesses of the sword that pierced their flesh. And so the martyrs got up and went to the spot of their own accord as the people wanted them to, and kissing one another they sealed their martyrdom with the ritual kiss of peace. The others took the sword in silence and without moving, especially Saturus, who being the first to climb the stairway was the first to die. For once again he was waiting for Perpetua. Perpetua, however, had yet to taste more pain. She screamed as she was struck on the bone; then she took the trembling hand of the young gladiator and guided it to her throat. It was as though so great a woman, feared as she was by the unclean spirit, could not be dispatched unless she herself were willing.

Ah, most valiant and blessed martyrs! Truly are you called and chosen for the glory of Christ Jesus our Lord! And any man who exalts, honours, and worships his glory should read for the consolation of the Church these new deeds of heroism which are no less significant than the tales of old. For these new manifestations of virtue will bear witness to one and the same Spirit who still operates, and to God the Father almighty, to his Son Jesus Christ our Lord, to whom is splendour and immeasurable power for all the ages. Amen.

● 115

The Martyrdom of Potamiena in the Early Third Century C.E.

EUSEBIUS *History of the Church* 6.5.1–7   4th century C.E.

AUTHOR, TRANSLATIONS, AND TEXT: See entry 65.

BIBLIOGRAPHY: See entry 114.

5.1 Seventh among them must be numbered Basilides, who led away the famous Potamiaena. The praise of this woman is to this day still loudly sung by her fellow-countrymen, as of one who on behalf of the chastity and virginity of her body, in which she excelled, contended much with lovers (for assuredly her body, as well as her mind, was in the full bloom of its youthful beauty); as of one who endured much, and at the end, after tortures that were terrible and fearful to relate, was perfected by fire, along with her mother Marcella. 5.2 It is said, in fact, that the judge, whose name was Aquila, after inflicting severe tortures upon her entire body, at last threatened to hand her over to the gladiators for bodily insult, and that, when after a brief period of reflection she was asked what her decision was, she made a reply which involved from their point of view something profane. 5.3 No sooner had she spoken than she received the sentence, and Basilides, being one of those serving in the army, took her and led her away to death. And as the crowd tried to annoy her, and insult her with shameful words, he kept restraining them and driving away the insulters, displaying the greatest pity and kindness towards her. She on her part accepted his fellow-feeling for her and bade him be of good cheer, for that she would ask him from her Lord, when she departed, and before long would requite him for what he had done for her. 5.4 Thus speaking [it is said], she right nobly endured the end, boiling pitch being poured slowly and little by little over different parts of her body from head to toe. 5.5 Such was the contest waged by this maiden celebrated in song. And not long afterwards, when Basilides was asked by his fellow soldiers to swear for some reason or other, he stoutly affirmed that swearing was absolutely forbidden in his case, for that he was a Christian and acknowledged it openly. At first, indeed, for a time they thought he was jesting, but when he continued steadfastly to affirm it, they brought him to the judge. And when he admitted the constancy [of his profession] in his presence, he was committed to prison. 5.6 When his brethren in God came to him and inquired the reason of this sudden and incredible impulse, it is said that he stated that three days after her martyrdom Potamiaena appeared to him by night, wreathing his head with a crown and saying that she had called upon the Lord for him, and obtained what she requested, and that before long she would take him to herself. Thereupon the brethren imparted to him the seal in the Lord, and on the day afterwards he gave notable testimony for the Lord and was beheaded. 5.7 And it is related that many others of those at Alexandria came over all at once to the word of Christ in the time of the persons mentioned, because Potamiaena appeared to them in dreams and invited them. But this must suffice.

● 116

Women Martyred at Antioch under Diocletian in the Early Fourth Century C.E.

EUSEBIUS *History of the Church* 8.12.3–5   4th century C.E.

AUTHOR, TRANSLATIONS, AND TEXT: See entry 65.

BIBLIOGRAPHY: See entry 114.

12.3 And a certain holy person, admirable for strength of soul yet in body a woman, and famed as well by all that were at Antioch for wealth, birth and sound judgement, had brought up in the precepts of piety her two unmarried daughters, distinguished for the full bloom of their youthful beauty. Much envy was stirred up on their account, and busied itself in tracing in every manner possible where they lay concealed; and when it discovered that they were staying in a foreign country, of set purpose it recalled them to Antioch. Thus they fell into the soldiers' toils. When, therefore, the woman saw that herself and her daughters were in desperate straits, she placed before them in conversation the terrible things that awaited them from human hands, and the most intolerable thing of all these terrors—the threat of fornication. She exhorted both herself and her girls that they ought not to submit to listen to even the least whisper of such a thing, and said that to surrender their souls to the slavery of demons was worse than all kinds of death and every form of destruction. So she submitted that to flee to the Lord was the only way of escape from it all. 12.4 And when they had both agreed to her opinion, and had arranged their garments suitably around them, on coming to the middle of their journey they quietly requested the guards to allow them a little time for retirement, and threw themselves into the river that flowed by.

12.5 Thus were these their own executioners. But another pair of maidens, also at Antioch, godly in every respect and true sisters, famous by birth, distinguished for their manner of life, young in years, in the bloom of beauty, grave of soul, pious in their deportment, admirable in their zeal, the worshippers of demons commanded to be cast into the sea, as if the earth could not endure to bear such excellence.

● 117
Three Epitaphs from Fourth-Century Rome

WORKS: This entry juxtaposes three lengthy epitaphs for married women, two of which are dated to almost the same year (382 and 384 C.E.) and the third of which is probably also fourth century. All three come from the city of Rome. The first clearly represents traditional late Roman piety, the second is probably Jewish, and the third is explicitly Christian.

● 117A
Praises for the Traditional Roman Piety of Aconia Fabia Paulina

ILS 1259–61   384 C.E.

TRANSLATION: Lefkowitz and Fant, no. 264a, p. 279.

To the gods of the dead. Vettius Agorius Praetextatus, augur, priest of Vesta, priest of the Sun, quindecemvir, curialis of Hercules, initiate of Liber and the Eleusinian [mysteries], hierophant, neocorus, tauroboliatus, father of fathers.

In public office imperial quaestor, praetor of Rome, governor of Tuscia and Umbria, governor of Lusitania, proconsul of Achaia, praefect of Rome, senatorial legate on seven missions, prefect of the praetorian guard twice in Italy and Illyrica, consul ordinarius elect, and Aconia Fabia Paulina, initiate of Ceres and the Eleusinian [mysteries], initiate of Hecate at Aegina, taurobol-iata, hierophant. They lived together for forty years.

(On the right side of the tomb) Vettius Agorius Praetextatus to his wife Paulina. (In verse) Paulina, conscious of truth and chastity, devoted to the temples and friend of the divinities, who put her husband before herself, and Rome before her husband, proper, faithful, pure in mind and body, kindly to all, helpful to her family gods . . . (On the left side) Vettius Agorius Praetextatus to his wife Paulina. (In verse) Paulina, the partnership of our heart is the origin of your propriety; it is the bond of chastity and pure love and fidelity born in heaven. To this partnership I entrusted the hidden secrets of my mind; it was a gift of the gods, who bind our marriage couch with loving and chaste bonds. With a mother's devotion, with a wife's charm, with a sister's bond, with a daughter's modesty; with the great trust by which we are united with our friends, from the experience of our life together, by the alliance of our marriage, in pure, faithful, simple concord; you helped your husband, loved him, honoured him, cared for him.

(On the back of the monument. Paulina is speaking, in verse) My parents' distinction did nothing greater for me than that I even then seemed worthy of my husband. But all glory and honour is my husband's name, Agorius. You, descended from noble seed, have at the same time glorified your country, senate, and wife with your mind's judgment, your character and your industry, with which you have reached the highest pinnacle of excellence. For whatever has been produced in either language by the skill of the sages to whom the gate of heaven is open, whether songs that poets composed or writings in prose, these you make better than when you took them up to read. But these are small matters; you as pious initiate conceal in the secrecy of your mind what was revealed in the sacred mysteries, and you with knowledge worship the manifold divinity of the gods; you kindly include as colleague in the rites your wife, who is respectful of men and gods and is faithful to you. Why should I speak of your honours and powers and the joys sought in men's prayers? These you always judge transitory and insignificant, since your title to eminence depends on the insignia of your priesthood. My husband, by the gift of your learning you keep me pure and chaste from the fate of death; you take me into the temples and devote me as the servant of the gods. With you as my witness I am introduced to all the mysteries; you, my pious consort, honour me as priestess of Dindymene and Attis with sacrificial rites of the taurobolium; you instruct me as minister of Hecate in the triple secret and you make me worthy of the rites of Greek Ceres. On

account of you everyone praises me as pious and blessed, because you yourself have proclaimed me as good through the whole world; though unknown
I am known to all. For with you as husband how could I not be pleasing?
Roman mothers seek an example from me, and think their offspring handsome if they are like yours. Now men, now women want and approve the
insignia that you as teacher have given me. Now that all these have been
taken away I your wife waste away in sorrow; I would have been happy, if
the gods had given me a husband who had survived me, but still I am happy
because I am yours and have been yours and will now be yours after my
death.

(Another inscription) To Fabia Aconia Paulina, daughter of Aco Catullinus
formerly prefect and consul, wife of Vettius Praetextatus prefect and consul
elect, initiate at Eleusis to the god Iacchus, Ceres and Cora, initiate at Lerna
to the god Liber and Ceres and Cora, initiate at Aegina to the two goddesses,
tauroboliata, priestess of Isis, hierophant of the goddess Hecate, and initiate
in the rites of the Greek Ceres.

(Inscription on a statue base) In honour of Coelia Concordia, chief vestal virgin, Fabia Paulina arranged that a statue be made and set up first on account
of her distinguished chastity and celebrated holiness concerning the divine
cult, and chiefly because [Coelia Concordia] first had set up a statue to [Pau-
lina's] husband Vettius Agorius Praetextatus, who was a man in all ways exceptional and deserving of honour even by virgins and by priestesses of this
[high] rank.

● 117B

Epitaph of Regina, Extolled for her Piety and Observance of (Jewish) Law

CIJ 476; JIWE 2.103   3d to 4th centuries C.E.?

WORK: A Latin inscription from the Monteverde catacomb, now in the Pio Christiano section of the Vatican Museum. A notable Christian epigrapher thought that
Regina was Christian, but most scholars consider this a Jewish epitaph, particularly
in its expression of hope in an afterlife and its references to Regina's love for her
people and observance of the Law. Although the inscription may well be Jewish,
the next inscription in this entry may suggest that such language does not make
for easy classification.

TRANSLATION AND TEXT: Noy, *JIWE* 2, 85–88.

ADDITIONAL TEXT: *CIJ* 476.

BIBLIOGRAPHY: Harry J. Leon, *The Jews of Rome* (Philadelphia: Jewish Publication Society, 1960); Pieter W. van der Horst, *Ancient Jewish Epitaphs: An Introductory Survey of a Millennium of Jewish Funerary Epigraphy (300 BCE–700 CE)*
(Kampen, the Netherlands: Kok Pharos, 1991); Leonard V. Rutgers, *The Jews in*

Late Ancient Rome: Evidence of Cultural Interaction in the Roman Diaspora, RGRW 126 (Leiden: E. J. Brill, 1995).

> Here is buried Regina, covered by such a tomb, which her spouse set up in accordance to (his) love of her (?). After twice ten (years), she spent with him a year and a fourth month with eight days remaining. She will live again, return to the light again. For she can hope therefore that she may rise into the age promised for both the worthy and the pious, she, a true pledge, who deserved to have an abode in the venerable country. Your piety has achieved this for you, your chaste life, your love of your family (?) also, your observance of the law, the merit of your marriage, whose honour was your concern. From these deeds there is future hope for you, and your grieving spouse seeks his comfort in that.

● 117C

Epitaph of Theodora, Teacher of the Faith

ICUR 1.317; *ILCV* 1.316   382 C.E.

WORK: This explicitly Christian epitaph, found in the Basilica of Saint Agnes in Rome, commemorates a woman praised for being "the best keeper of the law" and "the best teacher of the faith." It bears interesting affinities with the previous epitaph (which most scholars take to be Jewish). Both are particularly interesting for their representation of beliefs about an afterlife.

TRANSLATION, BIBLIOGRAPHY, AND ADDITIONAL TEXT: Ute E. Eisen, *Women Officeholders in Early Christianity: Epigraphical and Literary Studies* (Collegeville, Minn.: Michael Glazier, Liturgical Press, 2001), 93–97. Eisen's translation, reproduced here, omits the top line of the inscription, which I have supplied.

> Theodora, who lived 21 years, 7 months, 23 days, lies in (this) double grave, in peace.
>
> While chaste Aphrodite lived a wonderful life,
> She prepared for herself a path to the stars,
>   and she now lives blissfully in the halls of Christ.
> She withstood the course of the world,
>   thinking only of heavenly things.
> She, the best keeper of the law and the best teacher of the faith,
>   devoted her superior spirit through all time to the Holy alone.
> Thus she lives now like a queen, in the sweet scents of Paradise,
>   where the herbs grow by the streams in an eternal spring,
> And she waits for God,
>   through whom she desires to be elevated to the uppermost airs.
> In this hill she has laid down her body, leaving what is mortal behind,
>   and her husband, Evacrius, has erected her tomb with devotion.

Charikleia, Condemned as a Poisoner, Rescued by Divine Intervention

HELIODORUS *An Ethiopian Story* 8.9   3d or 4th century C.E.?

AUTHOR, TRANSLATION, TEXT, AND BIBLIOGRAPHY: See entry 22.

The executioners built a gigantic bonfire and then lit it. As the flames took hold, Charikleia begged a moment's grace from the guards who held her, promising that she would mount the pyre without the use of force. She stretched her arms towards that quarter of the sky whence the sun was beaming, and prayed in a loud voice: "O Sun and Earth and you spirits above and beneath the earth who watch and punish the sins of men, bear me witness that I am innocent of the charges laid against me and that I gladly suffer death because of the unendurable agonies that fate inflicts on me. Receive me mercifully, but with all possible speed exact retribution from that she-devil, that evil adulteress—Arsake—who has contrived all this to rob me of my beloved."

At these words there was general uproar. While some of the crowd were still making up their minds to halt the execution for a second trial, others were already moving to do so, but, before they could act, Charikleia climbed onto the pyre and positioned herself at the very heart of the fire. There she stood for some time without taking any hurt. The flames flowed around her rather than licking against her; they caused her no harm but drew back wherever she moved towards them, serving merely to encircle her in splendor and present a vision of her standing in radiant beauty in a frame of light, like a bride in a chamber of flame.

Charikleia was astounded by this turn of events but was nonetheless eager for death. She leapt from one part of the blaze to another, but it was in vain, for the fire always drew back and seemed to retreat before her onset. The executioners did not let up but redoubled their efforts, encouraged by threatening signs from Arsake, hurling on logs and piling on reeds from the river, fueling the flames by whatever means they could, but all to no avail. The city was now in even greater uproar; this deliverance seemed to show the hand of god. "She is innocent," they yelled. "She has done nothing wrong!" The crowd surged forward and tried to drive the executioners away from the pyre. Their leader was Thyamis, who had joined them after being alerted to what was happening by the deafening tumult. He tried to embolden the people to go to Charikleia's assistance; but for all their eagerness to rescue her they did not have the courage to approach the fire, but instead urged the girl to leap out of the flames: anyone who could stand unscathed in the blaze had nothing to fear if she decided to come out.

Charikleia too had come to the conclusion that she owed her salvation to the gods, and when she saw what the people were doing and heard what they were calling to her, she decided not to show ingratitude to heaven by rebuffing its munificence. She leapt down from the pyre, whereupon, as with one voice, the city exclaimed in joyful awe and invoked the gods' majesty.

● 119

A Letter Written in the Name of a Woman to "Ignatius of Antioch"

PSEUDO-IGNATIUS *The Letter of Maria the Proselyte to Ignatius*   4th century C.E.?

WORK: Part of a corpus of letters written in the name of the second-century bishop Ignatius of Antioch, this letter attributed to Mary of Cassabola was clearly not written to the real Ignatius, nor was the historical bishop the author of its reply ("Ignatius" to Mary). Whether the true author was a man writing in the guise of a woman, or a woman writing in the guise of another woman, is unknown. Along with several other pseudonymous letters (including correspondence between "Ignatius" and the "Blessed Virgin Mary") this one is usually thought to date to sometime in the fourth century C.E. Nothing is known about a Mary of Cassabola who could have been a contemporary of the real Ignatius, and the location of Cassabola is uncertain. Particularly noteworthy is the author's apparent acknowledgment of the potential problems of a woman's counseling a man on ecclesiastical problems and scriptural interpretation.

TRANSLATION: RSK.

TEXT: PG 2, 5:873–80; Francis X. Funk, *Patres Apostolici*, vol. 2 (Tübingen: Henrik Laupp, 1913), 87.

ADDITIONAL TRANSLATION: *ANF* 1. 120–121.

BIBLIOGRAPHY: Ross S. Kraemer, "Women's Authorship of Jewish and Christian Literature in the Greco-Roman Period," in Amy-Jill Levine, ed., *"Women Like This": New Perspectives on Jewish Women in the Greco-Roman Period*, Early Judaism and Its Literature 1 (Atlanta: Scholar Press, 1991), 221–42.

Maria of Cassabola to Ignatius

Preface:

Maria, a proselyte of Jesus Christ, to Ignatius Theophoros, the most blessed bishop of the apostolic church in Antioch: greetings and love in God the father and Jesus the beloved. We pray always for you to have grace and health in him.

1.1 Since, miraculously, Christ has become known among us to be the son of the living God, and in latter times to have been made human through the virgin Mary from the seed of David and Abraham, in accordance with the announcements concerning him, previously made through him by the company of the prophets, on account of this, we think it appropriate that we call upon you to send, in accordance with your judgment, Marin our companion, bishop of our native Neapolis, which is near Zarbus, and Eulogios, presbyter of the Cassabolians, so that we not be deprived of those who preside over the divine word.

1.2 As Moses also says: Let the Lord God put in place as overseer a man who will lead this people, and the assembly of the Lord will not be as sheep for whom there is no shepherd [Num. 27.16–17, abridged].

2.1 Now, have no distress, blessed one, over the fact that those publicly proclaimed are young. For I wish you to know that they disdain the flesh and take no notice of its passions: newly ordained to the priesthood while youths, they are each in themselves brilliant with age. 2.2 Call up your reasoning through the spirit given to you by God through Christ, and you will know how Samuel, called "he who sees" and counted in the company of the prophets while he was (yet) a small child, rebuked the older Eli for transgression, because he had honored his deranged sons, who had made a mockery of the priesthood, acting brutally toward the people, more than God, the author of all, and had allowed them to go unpunished.

3.1 Furthermore, Daniel, wise while a young man, judged certain vigorous old men, showing them to be utterly pernicious, and not to be (true) elders, and that although they were Jews by birth, they were Canaanites in their way of life. 3.2 And when Jeremiah, on account of his youth, declined the prophetic office entrusted to him by God, he heard: "Do not say that 'I am a youth.' For to all those to whom I send you, you shall go; and you shall speak in accordance with everything that I command you, because I am with you." 3.3 Moreover, the wise Solomon, at twelve years of age, discerned the weighty question of the women's ignorance concerning their own children, so that the whole people were astonished at the wisdom of the child, and revered him not as a young boy but as a mature man. 3.4 And the riddles of the queen of the Ethiopians, which brought payment as though they were the streams of the Nile, he resolved in such a way that that wise woman was beside herself.

4.1 Josiah, moreover, the beloved of God, when he was barely able to speak articulately, reproached those possessed by an evil spirit as being speakers of falsehood and deceivers of the people, and reveals the deception of the demons, and exposes those who are no gods. He slaughters those who were priests for them with impunity, and overturns their altars and defiles the places for sacrificing dead remains: he demolishes the temple and cuts down the sacred groves, and smashes the pillars and breaks open the tombs of the impious, that that no sign be still left of the evil persons. In this way was he zealous for the sake of piety, and punishing the impious, while yet faltering in speech. 4.2 David, at once prophet and king, the root, according to the flesh, of the savior, is, while a young boy, anointed by Samuel to be king. For he himself says somewhere that "I was small among my brothers, and youngest in the house of my father." [LXX Ps. 151.1].

5.1 But time will fail me if I wish to trace out all those who were pleasing to God in their youth, entrusted by God with prophecy and priesthood and kingship. That which has been said is sufficient for remembrance. 5.2 But I implore you, lest to you I seem to be someone excessive or acting ostentatiously. For I have set forth these very words, not teaching you, but (merely) bringing them to the remembrance of my father in God. For I know the measure of (my) ability and I cannot compete with those who are as great as you. 5.3 I salute your holy clergy, and your Christ-loving people, who are shepherded under your care. All the faithful who are with us greet you. Pray, blessed shepherd, for me to be in good health before God.

⦿ 120

A Former Prostitute Becomes a Christian Ascetic, Taking on Male Disguise

The Life of Saint Pelagia the Harlot   5th century C.E.

WORK: Purportedly the work of Jacob, deacon to a bishop called Nonnos and the agent of Pelagia's conversion to Christianity, *The Life of Saint Pelagia the Harlot* recounts the repentance of a prostitute in Antioch, presumably in the late fourth century. It was one of the most popular hagiographies of antiquity and the Middle Ages and was translated into multiple languages. Shortly after her baptism, Pelagia disguises herself as a man. The motif of assuming male disguise or a male persona occurs in other Christian texts as well. While it may be part of a broader (Christian?) conceptualization of spiritual advancement as progressive masculinization, some scholars suggest that Pelagia, or women like her, may very well have adopted masculine dress and identity to live as monastics.

TRANSLATION: Sebastian Brock and Susan Ashbrook Harvey, *Holy Women of the Syrian Orient* (Berkeley: University of California Press, 1998), 40–62 (from the Syriac).

TEXT: J. Gildemeister, *Acta S. Pelagiae Syriace* (Bonn: A. Marcum, 1879); variants in Agnes Smith Lewis, *Select Narratives of Holy Women*, vol. 1, Studia Sinaitica 9 (London: C. J. Clay; New York: Macmillan, 1900), 306–35 (with translation in vol. 2).

ADDITIONAL TRANSLATION: Helen Waddell, *The Desert Fathers: Translation from the Latin with an Introduction* (London: Constable, 1936), 173–88 (from the Latin).

ADDITIONAL TEXT: Pierre Petitmengin et al., *Pélagie la Pénitente: Métamorphoses d'une légende, T. 1: Les textes et leur histoire, T. 2, La suivie dans la littératures européens* (Paris: Études Augustiniennes, 1981); see also *BHO* 919 (Latin).

BIBLIOGRAPHY: Elizabeth Castelli, " 'I Will Make Mary Male': Pieties of the Body and Gender Transformation of Christian Women in Late Antiquity," in J. Epstein and K. Straub, eds., *Body Guards: The Cultural Politics of Gender Ambiguity* (London and New York: Routledge, 1991), 29–49; Gillian Clark, *Women in Late Antiquity: Pagan and Christian Life-styles* (Oxford: Clarendon Press; New York: Oxford University Press, 1993); Gillian Cloke, *This Female Man of God: Women and Spiritual Power in the Patristic Age* (New York: Routledge, 1995), 350–450; Stephen J. Davis, "Crossed Texts, Crossed Sex: Intertextuality and Gender in Early Christian Legends of Holy Women Disguised as Men," *JECS* 10, no. 1 (2002): 1–36; Susannah Elm, *Virgins of God: The Making of Asceticism in Late Antiquity* (Oxford: Clarendon Press; New York: Oxford University Press, 1994); Susan Ashbrook Harvey, "Women in Early Byzantine Hagiography: Reversing the Story," in L. Coon, K. Haldane, and E. Sommer, eds., *"That Gentle Strength": Historical Perspectives on Women in Christianity* (Charlottesville: University Press of Virginia, 1990), 36–59.

1 Greetings from the sinful deacon Jacob to the spiritual believers in our Lord.

I wanted to write to you, my holy fathers and brethren, about the conversion of the prostitute Pelagia, in the hopes that you might find great benefit in hearing and learning of it, and accordingly give praise to our merciful Lord God who does not wish anyone to perish, but rather that all sinners should be saved and return to the knowledge of truth.

2 The beginning of this account is as follows: the bishop of Antioch, the capital of Syria, was obliged to summon his fellow bishops because of some pressing church business that concerned them. In accordance with his summons eight bishops assembled in the city. It is not necessary for me to record their names, with the exception of one: this was the holy bishop Nonnos, whose deacon I, the sinner Jacob, am in his own town. This glorious man excelled and was most perfect in his whole way of life; his religious upbringing was in Egypt, for he was from a famous well-populated monastery called "of Tabennesi," situated in the Thebaid.

Because of his chaste and perfect way of life this glorious man was held worthy of the rank of bishop through the will of God who chose him. 3 This holy bishop Nonnos, then, came to Antioch along with seven fellow bishops, and I, the miserable Jacob, his deacon, accompanied him.

When we had paid our respects to the archbishop of Antioch, he told us to lodge at the hostel of the shrine where the bones of the glorious martyr Julian are preserved. Accordingly we and the other bishops lodged there. Now it so happened there was a delay for some reason, and on one particular day all the bishops left their cells and met together, sitting by the outer gate of the shrine of the glorious martyr Julian, and they were conversing among themselves on various topics; 4 then they begged the holy Nonnos, my bishop, to speak the word of God with them as they sat, so as to benefit them with his wise teaching, for they knew that he used to speak in the Holy Spirit, and that he uplifted everyone who heard him with his divine teaching.

This God-loving and holy bishop Nonnos therefore spoke before his companions in an excellent way, and they, full of wonder at his teaching, rejoiced at his words. At that moment, as they were sitting—and I, his deacon Jacob, was near them, standing out of respect for him—all of a sudden a rich prostitute, the leader of the troupe of actors, happened to pass by us. It is her story that I, the wretched Jacob, have endeavored to write down and tell for the benefit of all those who are desirous of the truth and who love God.

This prostitute then appeared before our eyes, sitting prominently on a riding donkey adorned with little bells and caparisoned; in front of her was a great throng of her servants and she herself was decked out with gold ornaments, pearls, and all sorts of precious stones, resplendent in luxurious and expensive clothes. On her hands and feet she wore armbands, silks, and anklets decorated with all sorts of pearls, while around her neck were necklaces and strings of pendants and pearls. Her beauty stunned those who beheld her, captivating them in their desire for her. 5 Young boys and girls accompanied her in haughty fashion, holding her lascivious feet; they too were adorned with golden girdles and had jewelry strung round their necks. Some ran in front of her, while others escorted her with great pomp. Thus it was that her beauty and finery lured everyone who saw her to stare at her and at her appearance.

As this prostitute passed in front of us, the scent of perfumes and the reek of her cosmetics hit everyone in the vicinity. 6 The bishops as they sat there were amazed at her and her clothes, as well as the splendor of her cortege, and the fact that she went by with her head uncovered, with a scarf thrown round her shoulders in a shameless fashion, as though she were a man; indeed in her haughty impudence her garb was not very different from a man's, apart from her makeup, and the fact that her skin was as dazzling as snow. To put it briefly, her appearance incited everyone who set eyes on her to fall in love with her.

When the holy bishops saw her, they averted their eyes from her, as though she was some sinful object. 7 The holy bishop Nonnos, however, observed her carefully in his mind, filled with wonder. Once she had passed in front of them, he turned away his face, placed his head between his knees, and wept with great feeling, so much so that his lap was filled with tears.

Lamenting greatly for her, the holy bishop Nonnos sighed and said to his fellow bishops, "To be honest, fathers, did not the beauty of this prostitute who had passed in front of us astonish you?" They kept silent and did not answer a word. 8 But the holy Nonnos went on sighing bitterly, striking his chest, deeply moved and weeping so much that even his clothes—a hair shirt—got soaked with his tears. (He always wore a hair shirt next to his skin, hiding it with a soft woollen garment on top, so that it could not be seen; he spent his entire life in a harsh regime of strict asceticism.)

Having wept a great deal, he said to his fellow bishops, "I beg you, my brothers, tell me, did you lust in your minds after the beauty of that prostitute who passed in front of us? And did you suffer for her? I myself was greatly astonished at her beauty and I suffered because of her ornaments, which were a baited snare for all who beheld her, a stumbling block leading to perdition. In my weakness I beseech and supplicate God to turn her to a life of truth and to let her stand chastely before the awful throne of his majesty.

"Up to the present she has been a snare and a stumbling block for mankind; she has lived her life in the world in the vain pursuit of adorning herself, causing harm to many. 9 I imagine she must have spent many hours in her boudoir putting on her eye-black, making herself up and dressing in her finery; she will have looked at her face in the mirror with the greatest attention, making sure there is not the slightest speck of dirt on it, or anything that might not please those who behold her. And all this in order to lead astray and lure her lovers after her—lovers today, but gone tomorrow.

10 "In this prostitute we should reprove ourselves: we believe that we have a bridal chamber in heaven that will not pass away, in a place that will last for ever and ever; and we have a fiancé who will neither die nor become corrupted; we have in heaven an inheritance to which the entire world cannot be compared; a happiness whose joy and felicity cannot be described is ours; ours too is the fragrance that never fades away: 'eye has not seen, nor ear heard, nor has the mind of man imagined what God has prepared for those who love him.' What more need I say: we have vast promises in the supernal heights stored up with our hidden Lord who cannot be seen. It is he we should please, but we fail to do so; it is for him that we should adorn our bodies and souls, but we totally fail to do so. We should take pains over ourselves in order to scrub away the dirt of sins, to become clean from evil stains; but we have paid no attention to our souls in the attempt to adorn them with good habits so that Christ may desire to dwell in us. What a reproach to us, seeing that we have not taken pains to make ourselves pleasing to God nearly as much as this prostitute we saw passing in front of us has

taken pains to please men—in order to captivate them, leading them into perdition by her wanton beauty.

"Truly, my brothers, I am in a state of great amazement and wonder at my own soul and at her: we should have been trying to please our Lord in all things with even greater effort than she has expended on her embellishment and adornment. And maybe we should even go and become the pupils of this lascivious woman." 11 When the God-loving bishop Nonnos had uttered these words, his fellow bishops sighed with emotion at his wise words, so filled with feeling. Full of grief and compunction, they got up and went off to the places where they were staying.

The holy bishop Nonnos took me, his deacon Jacob, and we went off to where we were lodging. Once we had climbed up, he threw himself onto the ground (on which a sackcloth lay spread out) and, beating his hand against his face, said as he wept, "Lord God, have mercy on me a sinner: I am not worthy to stand before you seeing that I have never tried to embellish my soul for your presence. What that prostitute accomplished in a single day in beautifying herself surpasses everything I have ever achieved during all the years of my life. How can I have the face to look upon you, my God? I do not know what words to use in the attempt to justify myself in your presence, Lord. What excuse have I before you, seeing that all my hidden secrets are laid open before you? No, alas for me the sinner who, as I enter the threshold of your sacred temple and appear before your glorious altar, have failed to offer the beauty in my soul that you want.

12 "Instead, having failed to adorn myself as you would like, I stand before you who are so full of awe and are so mighty, despicably unworthy. You have allowed me to be a servant who shares in your mystery: I beseech you, Lord, do not remove me from your heavenly altar; let not the beautification of this prostitute bring about my condemnation in front of the fearful tribunal of your mighty and exalted throne. For she, a creature of dust and ashes, has employed the utmost zeal in trying to please Satan, 13 whereas I have neglected pleasing you the living and immortal one, seeing that I have given myself over to laxity. Indeed, through my neglect I have stripped off the fine robe of your holy commandments. That prostitute has given her promise to please lascivious men, and she has kept it by adorning herself like this; whereas I made a promise to you the compassionate God, undertaking a solemn pact to please you, but I have proved false to you, and here I am stripped of all the spiritual adornments on earth and in heaven. Consequently I have no hope of salvation resulting from my deeds; instead my wretched soul looks to your mercy, Lord, and to your hope, for it is only through the multitude of your mercies that I can hope to live. I, a sinner, Lord, beseech you, be pleased to choose me for your divine glory; for it is you who have adorned me in your heavenly beauty that does not pass away. I beg you, too,

to call this lost woman, so that she too may be found when you seek her: she has not neglected anything devised by sinful men in her ceaseless hunting after the lost. Change her in accordance with your will, Lord, as you consented to change the water into delicious wine that brings joy."

This is what the God-loving Nonnos said, groaning as he wept and confessed to God. He spent the whole of that day in prayer, fasting and praying. It was a Saturday, 14 and the next day was Sunday, the holy day. After we had said the night office, the holy Nonnos called to me, his deacon Jacob, and said, "My son, I saw a vision this night, and I am much perturbed when I ponder on it. In any case let God do whatever is beneficial, as he likes. What I saw in my dream just now was this: it was as though I was standing beside the horns of the altar, and all of a sudden a black dove, befouled with mud, flew above me. I was unable to endure the disgusting stench of the mud on this dove that I saw, but it fluttered above me until the prayer of the catechumens was ended. Then, as the deacon proclaimed, 'Depart, catechumens,' in my dream I saw the dove fly off at once, and it disappeared from my sight. 15 After the prayer of the faithful, when the oblation had been offered, and once the service had finished and I had left the sanctuary, I again saw the dove flying toward me, still befouled with a lot of mud, just as before. I stretched out my hands and grasped it, whereupon I immediately threw it into a basin of water that happened to be in the courtyard of the church. Once I had thrown the bird in, I saw in my dream that it left behind all its mud, washed off in the water, and the foul stench disappeared. I further saw the dove emerge from the water and fly off at once into the heights above until it had vanished from sight and was no longer visible. This is the dream I saw, my son, and I have been pondering much about it. I think that its explanation will come about in truth, if God wills."

16 This is what the holy bishop Nonnos told me, his deacon Jacob. He got up and took me with him to the great church, along with the seven other bishops who were with us. We approached together to greet the archbishop of the city of Antioch on the holy day of Sunday.

When it was time for the priests to enter the *thronos* of the church as was customary, the archbishop asked the eight bishops to come into the *naos* of the church for the holy office. Accordingly they went in and sat down on the *bema*, each sitting in his appropriate place in accordance with the honor of his see. After the completion of the office, and once the Scriptures and holy Gospel had been read, it was time for the homily, which follows the lections from the holy Scriptures. Everyone was waiting expectantly to see and hear who would give the homily. The archbishop decided to send the holy Gospel in the hands of his archdeacon to be given to the holy bishop Nonnos, with the permission that he should preach.

17 Thereupon the holy bishop Nonnos stood up and, opening his mouth, began to speak the word of God in glorious fashion. Fervent in the Holy Spirit, he gave his homily, not using ornate and pompous words employing human skill (for he had no secular education), but rather, being filled with the gift of the Holy Spirit, he uttered weighty and perfect words. He brought out clearly the meaning of the Gospel text, using wise words as he taught, with the result that the entire people were moved to contrition in their emotion as they listened. Now the subject of his sermon was the judgment in store for the wicked and the good hope stored up for the righteous. The whole congregation was reduced to weeping at his words, and the floor of the church became soaked with tears.

18 Through the merciful providence of God an excellent plan entered the head of the prostitute we have been talking about: her thoughts unsettled her so much that, against her custom, she came to church that day. She had joined the other women and gone into the church, where she had diverted her attention to the holy Scriptures, and she had even stayed on to listen to the homily.

As she heard the homily and the teaching of the God-loving bishop Nonnos, she was greatly moved and her conscience was pricked: tears poured down as she sobbed, and amid heavy sighs she recalled all her sins. She was groaning so much over her life as a prostitute that the congregation became aware of her emotion. Everyone recognized her as the city's famous playgirl, for as she groaned out aloud, people were telling each other, "It really is the sinful woman, and she's been converted by the teaching of the God-loving and holy bishop Nonnos. She, who had never paid the slightest attention to her sins, has all of a sudden come to penitence; she who never used to come to church, all of a sudden has had her mind turned to religion and to prayer as a result of the divine words she has heard from the mouth of the holy bishop Nonnos."

When she had wept a great deal, moved to compunction and ensnared for life by the holy Nonnos' sermon, it was then time for the oblation to be offered. She left at the start of the holy Mysteries with the catechumens and 19 called two of her household servants, telling them, "Wait here till church is finished, and when the disciple of Christ, the holy bishop Nonnos, whose sermon we have heard, comes out, make careful enquiries and find out where he is staying so that you can tell me."

Once the oblation had been offered and church was ended, we left to go to our lodgings, but the servants of the prostitute followed us as they had been instructed until they had found out where we were staying; then they returned at once to inform their mistress. She was extremely pleased to learn this, and she was praying that she might be allowed to see the holy and God-loving Nonnos and listen to his teaching. Her former haughtiness had been completely removed from her mind, and she was now full of compunction, shaking as she pondered the punishment that she had heard was due to sinners in the next world at the hand of God's justice. She was greatly afraid in her mind and sobbed with tears before God.

20 Stirred by contrition, Pelagia wrote down on a wax tablet a passionate and moving message with a plea concerning her salvation. This she sent to the holy bishop Nonnos by the hands of her servants. It read as follows: "To the holy bishop Nonnos, from the sinful woman Pelagia who is a disciple of Satan, many greetings. I supplicate your saintly feet, my lord, for I have now heard something about the God whom you love with all your heart: how he bent down his majesty toward us and descended from heaven to earth—and this was not for the sake of the righteous, but in order to save sinners in his mercy. This is what I gather the Christians say, that he, upon whom the cherubim and seraphim dare not look in heaven, has sat down and eaten and drunk with tax collectors and sinners, out of his love, during the time he appeared on earth and went around amongst us in human body, 21 as you yourself know, holy sir, even though you did not see him with the physical eye. He spoke with the Samaritan woman at the water well, with the Canaanite woman who cried out after him, with the woman who was smitten with illness, whom he healed, with Mary and Martha whose brother he raised. He did all this, as I have heard from Christians, and now, my lord, if you are the disciple of this God who has done all this, do not reject me or turn me away when I ask to appear before you and to see you in person, in case there is a possibility that I might be saved at your hands. You might thus take some pride in me the sinner if I were to become a disciple of your health-giving instruction."

22 The holy bishop Nonnos wrote the following reply to the prostitute: "God is well aware of what you are; he knows and sifts out your will, your intention, and your thoughts. This, however, is what I have to say to you: do not try to tempt me who am both insignificant and weak; for I am a sinful person and one who has never been righteous. If you want to see me, do so with the seven holy bishops: I cannot see you alone, lest the simple, who lack understanding, stumble and be offended."

23 Receiving this message, the prostitute got up at once and hurried to the shrine of the glorious martyr Julian. When she reached the shrine, she sent a note to us to inform us of her arrival. Now, previous to her arrival, the holy and God-loving bishop Nonnos had called his fellow bishops and made them sit with him. He then bade her approach for an audience with them. 24 As she drew near and saw them, she prostrated herself before them all together and ended by throwing herself down on the ground, clasping the feet of the holy Nonnos in a state of great emotion. She started to weep and groan, and the holy man's feet got soaked with the prostitute's tears. Without noticing

what was happening, she wiped onto herself the dirt from his feet. As she groveled before him, she was throwing dust from the ground onto her head, beseeching him amid loud groans, and saying, "I beg you, have pity on me a sinner. I am a prostitute, a disgusting stone upon which many people have tripped up and gone to perdition. I am Satan's evil snare: he set me and through me he has caught many people for destruction. I am a ravenous vulture, and many chicks of the heavenly Eagle have been caught by me. I am a sly she-wolf, and by my crafty wiles I have destroyed innocent lambs and sheep. I am a deep ditch of mire in which many have befouled themselves and got filthy: they had been clean, but I corrupted them. Have mercy on me, O pure and holy sir, I beg you; be like your leader Christ, who never averted his face from sinners, but instead out of his graciousness had compassion on them. Pour over me your kindness, imitating him, otherwise I shall perish and die in my sins. I am a destructive moth, and I have gnawed into many bodies that had previously been unscathed. Make me into a Christian this very day—for I am a sea of sins. Take me, sir, and make me holy by means of your pure instruction—for I am an abyss of evils. Take from me my sins and wickednesses today, and through your prayers cast them away from me in the cleansing bath of your God's baptism. Stand up, I beg you, my lord, and invoke over me the name of the holy Trinity; baptize me for the remission of my sins. Stand up, my lord, and strip off from me the dirty clothing of prostitution; clothe me with pure garments, the beautiful dress for the novel banquet to which I have come."

24 When they saw the prostitute's emotion and faith, the bishops and all the priests as well as everyone else who happened to be present, wept plentiful tears. Only with difficulty did the holy bishop Nonnos persuade her to get up from his feet; when she had done so, he addressed her: "My daughter, the canons of the church require that one should not baptize a prostitute without her having some sponsors, otherwise she may continue in her old ways."

26 On hearing these words, the prostitute at once threw herself down onto the ground again and clasped hold of the holy and God-loving Nonnos' feet. As she wept and groaned, she spoke as follows: "You will have to answer for me to God if you do not baptize me now: God will require my soul at your hands and he will inscribe all the bad things I have done against your name if you refuse to baptize me now; you will share in the wickedness of my ways. No, you must baptize me at once, and so make me a stranger to my evil deeds. You will become a stranger to your holy altar and deny your God if you don't make me a bride of Christ this very day, giving me rebirth by saving baptism and offering me up to your God—who will himself be a sponsor for me to you today. For I will not return to the ditch of mire from which you shall raise me to eternal life. My lord, have no fear of me; get up and receive me a sinner, just as your Lord received sinners."

27 The bishops and everyone with them gave praise to God when they saw how the mind of this sinful prostitute was set on fire and was burning with the love of God.

Now the holy bishop Nonnos summoned me, his deacon Jacob, and, giving me instructions, sent me off into the city to inform the archbishop of all that had taken place, in order that he might give permission to act in whatever way he wished with the prostitute. He also gave me strict orders, saying, "Let the archbishop send back with you one of the deaconesses if he gives you permission for us to baptize the prostitute."

28 So I, the wretched Jacob, went off to the archbishop and told him everything that the God-loving Nonnos, my bishop, had bidden me to say. I informed him about the prostitute's conversion and I described to him her emotion and her promise. I repeated everything, not omitting a word.

The archbishop was absolutely delighted, and he said to me, "Return to our brother, the holy bishop Nonnos, the blessed father and wise teacher, and tell him that I am most pleased with the message he has sent me, and that I had actually had it in my mind that this great and wonderful event might be in store for you, waiting to be fulfilled at your hands. For I know that you are like God's own mouth; for it was he who said, 'If you bring out something valuable from what is base, you shall be like my own mouth.' For the rest, be assured that I am very happy that you should carry out to the end what you have already commenced upon: it will please Christ, and it will edify the entire church, as well as bring salvation to the life of this prostitute. Baptize her, then, on the confession of her own mouth. So, we have now heard of the matter, and we are in agreement with your wise handling of it that will prove full of joy. It is right that you should baptize, just as you have converted her: simply let the lascivious woman become chaste, let the sinner be justified, and let our God be praised."

He then sent for the deaconess Romana from her house (she was the head deaconess). He told her to go with me and obey the holy bishop Nonnos, and do whatever he told her.

29 So I and the deaconess Romana returned to our holy father Nonnos to find the prostitute still sprawling on the ground, weeping at his feet. Then the deaconess Romana approached and begged her to get up, saying, "Rise up, my sister, collect yourself together. Recover your strength in preparation to receive what Grace has summoned you for. Get up, sister, and let us pray over you to remove all the power of the Adversary from you."

Only with difficulty was she persuaded to get up, but she still went on crying. Then the holy bishop Nonnos gave us instructions to get everything requisite ready for holy baptism. He addressed the prostitute and said, "Open your mouth and acknowledge God; renounce your sins before him."

Weeping, the prostitute said, "If I examine myself thoroughly, I cannot find a single good deed that I have done. I know that my sins are heavier and more numerous than all the grains of sand on the seashore; and all the sea's water is not sufficient to wash away my wicked and evil deeds. But I believe that God is merciful and will not look upon the multitude of my sins—just as he did not look upon the sin of that sinful woman in the Gospels, or that of the Canaanite woman or the one from Samaria: he did not shut his door in their faces but had pity and compassion upon them; he held them to be worthy of healing in their bodies and of forgiveness of their sins. I too have acknowledged and do acknowledge that I am wicked and bad, whereas my God is compassionate and merciful. And I beg you, my lord, a true priest and forgiving father who gives spiritual rebirth, be merciful to me; take me and wash me with fire and the Spirit."

30 Thereupon the holy Nonnos said to her, "Give me your name so that I can offer it up to God." The prostitute replied, "My actual parents called me Pelagia, but the entire city of Antioch, where I was born, called me Marganito, because of the quantities of jewelry I wore and prided myself on. You see, up to now I have been Satan's well-decked shop-front and home."

The holy Nonnos went on, "From birth your name was Pelagia?" "Yes, my lord," she replied. Having learnt her name, the bishop said the exorcism over her, marked her, and sealed her with the oil of anointing as she made the renunciation, saying, "I renounce you, Satan, and all your might." She went on to cry out, "I acknowledge you, Christ, and your Father and your living and holy Spirit. I acknowledge your church and your baptism; I acknowledge your kingdom on high, and the heavenly powers; I acknowledge your holy altar on earth, and your fearful mysteries in heaven, and your illustrious and pure priests who minister before you. I renounce the falsehood I have wrought, and the prostitute's profession I have been following up to now."

Then after this confession, the holy Nonnos baptized Pelagia, and her spiritual mother, Romana the deaconess, received her from the baptismal waters. She received the body and blood of Christ from the hands of the illustrious and holy Mar Nonnos.

The occasion brought great joy to God and his angels in heaven, and on earth to the entire church and its priests. Once Pelagia had been perfected as the bride of Christ, the deaconess Romana took her up to our lodgings after the bishops themselves had gone up there.

31 The holy Nonnos said to me, his deacon Jacob, "We should rejoice today, my son, and exult with the holy angels of God who today rejoice at the finding of Pelagia, Christ's lamb. Today, my son, let us eat our food with oil, and let us drink some wine, because of the new birth and mighty salvation of this glorious bride of Christ, Pelagia."

I got everything ready as he had instructed, and while we were eating, full of joy, all of a sudden Satan appeared to us, furious, in the form of a scowling man with tangled long sleeves and his hands on his head; he wailed out loudly, saying 32 "Fie on you, foolish old man who eats his own white hairs: the thirty thousand Arabs, whom you snatched from me, baptized, and donated to your God, should suffice for you. Weren't you satisfied with my city Heliopolis—Baalbek—where you converted a large number of women who worshipped and honored me? And now you've gone and captured from me this seductive lady and baptized her, removing her from my service and offering her to your God. Weren't you satisfied with the pagans you enticed away from me, converting them and donating them to your God? But now you have gone and cut off all my hopes today. Fie on you, ill-fated and luckless old man: I cannot endure your crafty tricks; cursed be the day that had the misfortune to see you born. The river full of tears you poured out has swept away the oaths and promises that large numbers of people had made with me. You have shattered my hopes today. What have I to do with you, you grave robber who has despoiled me as though I were a tomb, wickedly removing this woman alive from me, where she had been like a corpse confined by me in her error."

Such were Satan's words when he appeared to us and to all the bishops with us. Everyone present, including Pelagia and the deaconess Romana, who both had their eyes fixed on that Satan, heard him shouting and reviling the holy Nonnos. 33 Then Satan left the holy man and turned to address Pelagia; groaning, as though he was someone in tears, he cried out to her, "Is this my due, Pelagia? Didn't you belong to me, and I to you up to just now? How can you do this to me: you've made me a laughingstock to this old whitehead and to everyone who hears that you have jilted me. Wasn't it I who taught you how to make yourself up and become an object of lust for many? Didn't I bring you crowds of lovers to satisfy your prostitute's profession? Didn't I subject both the rich and the noble to you, so that they brought you expensive presents as a result of their lust-ridden passion? Why have you turned against me and tricked me like this? Why have you done this to me and jilted me, just because of a few misleading words from this ill-starred old man? All his life he has been annoying me with his tricks all over the place: he's like a nasty thorn to me wherever he goes. I'll bring about some calamity if you don't renounce him and acknowledge me—just as in the past you used to do what I wanted."

Then the holy Nonnos said to Pelagia, Christ's bride, "Rebuke this Satan, my daughter, rebuke him and don't be afraid of him, for he is weak and helpless before the Holy Spirit whom you have put on today."

Pelagia immediately crossed herself, plucked up courage, and rebuked the Satan who had turned up. In this way she quickly put him to flight and he vanished from our sight.

34 Two days later he came along quietly and manifested himself to Pelagia as she was asleep beside her spiritual mother, the deaconess Romana. Satan quietly awoke Pelagia and said to her gently, "Marganito, what wrong have I done you that you've turned against me? Didn't I deck you out with gold and pearls, piling up riches upon you? I beg you, tell me why have you deluded me and played me false? Please let me explain, and don't jilt me, otherwise everyone will laugh at me because of you."

35 Pelagia, however, bravely crossed herself and blew at Satan, whereupon he disappeared. She had shouted at him as follows: "May our Lord Jesus Christ Son of the living God rebuke you. It was he who seized me from you and made me a bride for his heavenly marriage chamber."

Then she woke up Romana the deaconess and said, "Mother, pray for me, because that wicked man came and troubled me." "Don't be disturbed by him, my beloved daughter," she replied, "for from now on he is afraid of you and will run away from your very shadow."

Thereupon the two of them, mother and daughter, signed themselves with the cross, rebuked Satan in the name of Christ, and he vanished and was not seen by them again.

36 The following day the holy Pelagia, like an eagle whose youthfulness had been renewed, having been weaned away from evil deeds, aroused her mind and summoned the head of her household who was in charge of all her belongings. She told him to go to her house, make an inventory of all she possessed—her gold, silver, and quantities of jewelry, together with her expensive wardrobe. He was to bring the list to her, because ever since this glorious lady had heard the words of the holy bishop Nonnos and had been converted, making a start on a life of penitence, she had not returned to her house at all or crossed its threshold; instead she had remained with us in penitence in the shrine of Christ until the completion of her baptism.

Her steward went off to her house as she had instructed and brought back an inventory listing all her wealth, not hiding anything. 37 Thereupon the glorious Pelagia sent by the deaconess Romana a request that the holy bishop Nonnos should come and pay her a visit. On his arrival at the place where she was staying, Pelagia asked him earnestly to accept her entire fortune. She handed over to him all that she desired with the words, "My lord, here is the wealth that Satan has bestowed upon me as a result of the sin of prostitution. From now on, my lord, it is entrusted to your care: do with it whatever you want. As far as I am concerned, from today on Christ's riches that were granted to me at your hands are sufficient for me; I have grown rich many times over through them."

38 Then she summoned all her servants and maids, freed them in accordance with the law, and gave each one of them an appropriate present. Whereupon she dismissed them, saying, "Up to now you have been my servants, living a life of sin and licentiousness, enslaved to sinful servitude to prostitution. Now I have freed you from this slavery of wickedness; it is up to you for your own part to free your souls from the slavery of sin. Henceforth you shall no longer work for me, and you will no longer have the reputation of belonging to a prostitute."

She then dismissed them, and they bade her farewell and left, astonished by the change that they beheld in their mistress Pelagia.

39 On receiving Pelagia's entire fortune, the holy Nonnos sent for the steward of the great church at Antioch, and in Pelagia's presence he handed over to him all that had belonged to her, telling him, "I adjure you by the exalted Trinity, let nothing out of all these belongings enter the church of God, or be given to any of the bishops; let none of it enter the house of any of the clergy, or even your own house: do not let anything be defiled by it, whether through your agency or through the agency of anyone else; for even though it might seem desirable and good, considering that there is so much of it, nevertheless this wealth has been amassed as the result of the sin of prostitution. So do not take any delight in these belongings. If this bride of Christ has renounced and rejected it as being nothing, for the sake of the spiritual possessions she has discovered, how much more should we consider it filthy; we must not exchange it for the heavenly riches stored up for us, which are pure, undefiled, and glorious. Take care, then, my son, in view of what I have bidden you under oath; if you transgress this oath, God's curse shall enter your house and you will be accounted as one of those who cried, 'Crucify him, crucify him.' No, you must use it only to provide for the orphans and widows, for the poor, the needy and the destitute, so that they can live off it. In this way, just as it was amassed in a wicked and wrong manner, so it shall now be administered in an upright and just fashion. What was sin's wealth shall henceforth be righteousness' treasury."

Accordingly he received this trust from the holy man as though it was from God's own apostle. The steward took it all and administered it, exactly following the instructions given by the saintly bishop Nonnos in the presence of the holy Pelagia: he did not go against or alter his orders in anything.

Everyone was astonished at all that Christ's bride, Pelagia, had done, how she had benefited many through this action of hers. All her licentious acquaintances, however, were extremely put out, and they were reduced to tears on seeing her abrupt new way of life. She kept herself away from her old friends, and they all felt puzzled and asked, "How is it that a famous prostitute can become a woman of renowned chastity overnight?" But many were uplifted by her example.

When Pelagia's fellow prostitutes and neighbors saw what she had done, they were themselves moved to compunction and started weeping over themselves. Many of them turned to chastity and abandoned their life of prostitution, going off to receive instruction about Christ; these came to the chaste Pelagia, and she exhorted and urged them to do what she had done. Numerous prostitutes listened to her advice and were converted by the chaste bride of Christ.

Many people thought highly of Pelagia for what she had done, and because of her, our Lord was glorified by everyone.

40 The handmaid of God kept herself apart from eating or drinking anything from her own house for the seven days following her baptism. During this time she did not use anything of her own; instead Romana the deaconess provided food and everything she required from her own pocket: in her faith and her love, like a fond mother, she considered Pelagia to be her own beloved daughter, and so looked after her. Now Pelagia had sworn not to touch anything ever again that had been bought out of the wealth she had amassed through sin. She kept to her oath and did not eat or drink anything derived from what had formerly been hers. She even refused to receive anything from her house, and she never again entered it. Nor did she ever again take anything that had belonged to her to give away, telling everyone, "Far be it from me that I should live off the wages of prostitution any longer, or think anything of them." Instead she held her fortune to be worse than blood and fouler than the smelly mud of the streets.

41 When the bridal days following Pelagia's baptism were at an end and the blessed eighth day, Sunday, had arrived, it was time for her to take off her holy baptismal robes in accordance with the canon of the church, and to put on ordinary everyday clothes. So, when Sunday was over, she got up during the night on which Monday dawned and went in to the holy bishop Nonnos; she prostrated herself before him and received his blessing, whereupon he gave her permission to take off her holy baptismal garments. But the holy Pelagia earnestly besought the priest of Christ that she might receive her clothing from some of his, rather than put on something else. The holy bishop Nonnos acceded to Pelagia's request and gave her some of his own clothing—a hair shirt and a woollen mantle. Straightaway she took off her baptismal robes and put on his clothes. Then she knelt down at his feet and received his blessing, having revealed to him all her plans.

That night she left dressed as a man and secretly went off without our being aware of it. She was no longer to be seen in the city. Now the holy bishop Nonnos, who knew her secret, did not tell anyone what had happened—not even me, Jacob, who served as his deacon.

When morning came, there was great consternation, for Pelagia was nowhere to be found: she was not with us, nor anywhere else in the entire city.

42 Stricken with grief, the deaconess Romana was in tears and kept inquiring after her all over the place. The holy bishop Nonnos, however, rejoiced greatly for only he knew of Pelagia's departure. He told the deaconess Romana, "Do not be despondent or weep for your daughter Pelagia. Rather, rejoice greatly over this, for she has chosen the good portion, just as did Mary, Lazarus' sister.

All this took place in the great city of Antioch. 43 A few days later the archbishop of Antioch dismissed all the foreign bishops who were there, and we and everyone else went back to our respective towns.

Three years later I, the deacon Jacob, felt the urge to go and pray in Jerusalem, the city of our Lord; I wanted to venerate his cross and receive a blessing from the site of his resurrection. I approached the holy Nonnos, my bishop, and sought his permission. He allowed me to go, giving me the following instructions: "When you reach the holy place of Jerusalem, remember me there in your prayer—in all those sacred sites that our Lord visited. And afterward be sure to make inquiries there about a certain monk Pelagios, a eunuch; when you have ascertained he is there, go and see him, for there is much that you can benefit from him. For truly he is a true and faithful servant of God, a monk who is perfect in his service."

Now he was speaking to me about Pelagia, the handmaid of God, but I did not grasp the meaning of his allusion, and he did not want to reveal the matter to me openly. So he sent me off with his blessing, and I set out in peace.

44 Eventually I arrived at the holy place, Jerusalem: I prayed and received a blessing from the tomb of our Lord and from all the places where he traveled, performing his glorious actions. The next day I, Jacob, went out to ask where the monk Pelagios lived. After a great deal of inquiry, I learnt that he dwelt on the Mount of Olives, where our Lord used to pray with his disciples. Accordingly I went up to the Mount of Olives and kept on asking until I discovered his cell. He was very well known in the area and held in high honor.

As I approached his cell, I saw it had no door to it; on close examination I espied a small window in the wall in front of me. I knocked, and Pelagia, the handmaid of God, opened it. She was dressed in the habit of a venerable man. 45 She came up and greeted me with great humility, clasping my hands and kissing them from within. She was overjoyed at my arrival, for the moment she saw me she recognized me. She was inside, and I outside, and I failed to recognize her because she had lost those good looks I used to know; her astounding beauty had all faded away, her laughing and bright face that I had known had become ugly, her pretty eyes had become hollow and cavernous as the result of much fasting and the keeping of vigils. The joints of her holy bones, all fleshless, were visible beneath her skin through emaciation brought on by ascetic practices. Indeed the whole complexion of her body was coarse and dark like sackcloth, as the result of her strenuous penance.

The whole of Jerusalem used to call her "the eunuch," and no one suspected anything else about her; nor did I notice anything about her that resembled the manner of a woman. I received a blessing from her as if from a male eunuch who was a renowned monk, a perfect and righteous disciple of Christ.

46 The holy Pelagia opened her mouth and spoke to me like a man. She said, "I think I have seen you somewhere, my brother, unless it was someone who looked just like you. By your life, do not conceal the truth from me, are you not the deacon of the holy bishop Nonnos who belongs to the archdiocese of Antioch? He was trained in Egypt."

I replied, "Yes, my lord, I am indeed the disciple of that servant of God, your admirer."

"Does he still live in the body?" she asked.

"Yes, he is still alive," I replied, "and he told me to make careful inquiry about your excellent life, and to come to see you and greet you who are so full of virtues." She then went on and said, "Blessed is our Lord who has preserved his life up to today. May he pray for me henceforth, for I know him to be an apostle of our Lord. And do you too, my brother, pray for me and greet the holy bishop Nonnos and all his companions."

This is all that the blessed Pelagia said to me. Since she was dressed as a man, I did not recognize her. She then closed her window at once and went in to her cell, without uttering a further word to me.

When she had gone in and I was still standing there full of wonder, she began to sing the office of the Third Hour. 47 I joined at once in prayer just by her lavra. I gave thanks and departed, moved by the virtuous way of life of this man of God—not realizing she was a woman, and unaware that she was Pelagia, our daughter in Christ.

I, Jacob, spent every day wandering around to see the holy monasteries; I received blessing from them and heard how they would relate stories of the virtuous deeds of the monk Pelagios who lived the life of a recluse on the Mount of Olives, performing miracles. 48 I was filled with amazement at him. Then along came some other people who announced that the monk Pelagios, the recluse on the Mount of Olives, had fallen asleep. As I heard this I rejoiced greatly, giving thanks to our Lord who had held me worthy to receive a blessing from him.

49 Then the monasteries around Jerusalem, and those of Jericho and Trans-jordan, and of the town of Nikopolis, all gathered on the Mount of Olives, a huge crowd of monks, to see the burial of Pelagios the recluse. Quantities of other people, men and women from the whole of Jerusalem, went up to join the funeral procession for the holy Pelagia who was known as a righteous man. The bishop and entire clergy of Jerusalem, together with the honorable abbots, approached and opened up the holy Pelagia's cell; they took out her body, laid it on a bier, whereupon the bishop and all the local holy men came close to anoint it decently with fragrant unguent. As they did so, they saw she was a woman. They gasped with astonishment in their hearts, then, raising their voices, they cried out to God, saying, "Praise to you, Lord; how many hidden saints you have on earth—and not just men, but women as well!"

50 They wanted to hide this astonishing fact from the people but were unable to do so. This was to fulfill what is written in the holy Gospel: "There is nothing hidden which shall not be revealed, and nothing concealed which shall not be made known." This wonder immediately became known to the entire people.

The whole crowd of men and women, carrying innumerable tapers and torches, then began to process for the blessed Pelagia, as for a righteous woman. They carried and escorted her holy body in true faith, and in this way they buried her amidst great honor and much splendor, giving praise to God. The Gospel words "Let your light shine before men that they may see your good works and praise your Father who is in heaven" were fulfilled with reference to her.

51 I, Jacob, sinner and deacon, have written down for you who love God these glorious deeds that concern a woman who previously had been a prostitute, but who later became a "perfect vessel." This is the panegyric we have received concerning her who was formerly an outcast, but who subsequently was chosen. Let us pray that our Lord will grant us mercy, along with her, at the judgment when the righteous receive reward, and sinners censure.

From all men and women who have repented or who shall repent, and from sinful me who saw and wrote this life, praise, thanksgiving, and honor be raised up to Father, Son, and Holy Spirit, now and always and to eternal ages, amen.

An Orphaned Prostitute Returns to the Christian Asceticism of Her Youth

The Life of Saint Mary the Harlot   5th century C.E.

WORK: Extracted from the *Life of Abraham*, which is about a fourth-century monk who was the uncle of our protagonist, *The Life of Saint Mary the Harlot* was extremely popular, circulating in Syriac, Greek, and Latin. Eventually, it was dramatized by the tenth-century nun Hroswitha, who also drew upon the Apocryphal Acts of the Apostles for her plays. As with all these texts, it is difficult to assess how much of women's experiences this *Life* reflects, and how much it owes to early Byzantine Christian conceptions of gender, the body, and so forth.

TRANSLATION: Sebastian Brock and Susan Ashbrook Harvey, *Holy Women of the Syrian Orient* (Berkeley: University of California Press, 1998), 27–39 (from the Syriac).

TEXT: T. J. Lamy, *Sancti Ephraem Syri Hymni et Sermones, vol. 4* (Mechliniae: H. Dessain, 1902), cols. 1–84.

ADDITIONAL TRANSLATION: Helen Waddell, *The Desert Fathers: Translations from the Latin with an Introduction* (London: Constable, 1936), 173–88 (from the Latin).

ADDITIONAL TEXT: See *BHO* 16–17 (Latin).

BIBLIOGRAPHY: See entry 120.

17 I want to tell you now of something amazing that Abraham did in his old age, a matter that my cultivated readers will find truly astonishing. The situation was as follows. The blessed Abraham had a brother with an only daughter. When the brother died leaving his daughter an orphan, his relatives took her to live with her uncle. She was seven years old at the time, and Abraham told her to live in the outer part of his home, while he lived as a recluse in the inner part. There was a small window that communicated between them, and it was through it that he gave the girl instruction in the Psalms and the Holy Scriptures. She used to keep vigil with him and minister to his needs. Just as he trained her soul in an excellent manner, so too she strove with a good will to attain to the perfection of his virtues. The blessed man would frequently supplicate God on her behalf, asking that she might apply her mind to a life of penitence and not get entangled by any of the world's attractions.

Now her father had left her ample money, but the blessed Abraham without any hesitation ordered that this should be given to the poor and orphans. She herself would daily beg her uncle and say, "Father, I beg of you, pray for me so that I may be delivered from bad thoughts and from all the effects of Satan's cunning snares." Willingly she trained herself in all the excellent ways of her blessed uncle, and he in turn delighted to see her fine intention, her tears and her humility, her quiet and gentle nature, and her love toward God. For twenty years did she emulate the blessed man's way of life: she was like a chaste lamb, like a spotless dove.

18 When these twenty years had elapsed, Satan took notice of her and tried to ensnare her; his intention was to cause the blessed Abraham grief and pain by these means, thus diverting his mind from God. Now there was a man who was nominally a monk, who used regularly to come and visit the blessed Abraham on the pretext of friendship. One day he happened to see the blessed girl through the window. He fell in love with her at the mere sight and wanted to get hold of her and sleep with her. He allowed his mad desire for her to burn like a flame of fire in his heart. For a whole year he treacherously lay in wait for her, until he succeeded in softening her firm resolve, and the girl eventually opened the door of the house where she lived as a recluse and came out to see him. He assaulted her with his blandishments, bespattering her with the mud of his lust.

Once this sinful episode had taken place, stupefaction seized hold of her mind: she tore off the garment she was wearing, beat her face and breasts in grief, and said to herself, "I am now as good as dead: I have lost all the days of my life; my ascetic labors, my abstinence, my tears are all wasted, for I have rebelled against God and slain my soul; and upon my holy uncle I have imposed bitter grief. I have wrapped myself in shame by becoming a laughingstock to the Enemy, Satan. Why should I continue to live, now that I have become so wretched? Alas, what will happen to me? Alas, what have I done! Alas, what will happen to me? Alas, how did I fall? How did my mind and senses become so darkened without my realizing it? How my downfall occurred, I was unaware; how I became corrupted, I do not know. A dark cloud overlaid my heart, preventing me from seeing what I was doing. How shall I hide myself? Where shall I go? Into what pit shall I cast myself? What has become of this saintly man's instruction, what has happened to the wise Ephrem's warnings? They told me to be careful of myself and preserve my virginity spotless for the immortal Bridegroom. 'Your Bridegroom is holy and jealous,' they said. No longer do I dare look up to heaven, for I have died to God and to men. I can no longer go near that window, for how can I, a sinner, full of horrid stains, speak with this saintly man? If I made bold to approach the window between us, then fire will issue forth and consume me. It would be better for me to depart to some other place where no one knows me, seeing that I have died once and for all, and no longer have any hope of salvation."

19 So straightaway she got up and left for another town. She changed the precious monastic garb she had been wearing and established herself in a low tavern.

After this had taken place, the blessed Abraham had a fearful vivid dream: he beheld a huge serpent, disgusting to look at and hissing in a fearsome way. On leaving its lair it came toward him; it found there a dove, swallowed it up, and went back to its lair. When the blessed man awoke, he was much troubled and started weeping. "Perhaps Satan is going to stir up persecution against Christ's church and alienate many from the faith," he said to himself. "Or maybe there will be schisms and divisions in the church of God." He then prayed to God with these words: "You know what is hidden, O lover of mankind; you alone know what this dream means."

Then once again, two days later, he saw the same serpent leave its lair and come toward his house, whereupon it placed its head beneath the blessed man's feet; the serpent's belly was then ripped open, and there, safe and sound in its belly was the dove that it had swallowed. The blessed man stretched out his hand and took the dove, which was still alive and unharmed.

On waking up he called to the blessed girl once and then a second time, saying, "My daughter, why are you so negligent: for two days you have not opened your mouth to praise God."

Seeing that she did not answer, and that for two days she had not ministered to his needs as was her wont, the blessed man realized that the dream he had seen referred to her. He groaned and wept plenteously, saying, "Alas for my lamb, the wolf has snatched her away; my daughter has been taken captive." He raised his voice in his tears, and said, "O Christ Savior of the world, return the lamb Mary to the fold of your flock; may I not go down to Sheol full of grief in my old age; do not turn aside my request, Lord; rather, send your aid at once and deliver her from the serpent's mouth."

Now the two days between the blessed man's two dreams represented the years during which his niece lived in the world. Continuously, night and day, did he supplicate God on her behalf.

20 After two years the blessed man discovered where she was living. He asked someone who knew her and sent him there to find out the truth about her and to ascertain where she was residing. The man duly found out about her and saw her, whereupon he returned and told Abraham of her situation and where she was living.

Convinced that this was she, the blessed man asked to have brought to him an outfit of soldier's clothing and a horse. When these arrived, he opened the door of his home and came out. He put on the military dress with a helmet on his head so that his face was covered, mounted the horse, and set off—

like a spy wanting to scout out some region or town, wearing the local dress to prevent detection: thus did the blessed man wear those clothes whereby he could overcome the Adversary.

My beloved, come and let us wonder at this second Abraham: the first Abraham went out to battle with kings; he vanquished them and brought back his nephew Lot; this second Abraham set out for battle with the Enemy, he conquered him and brought back his niece.

21 When he arrived at the spot where the tavern was situated, he spent a little while looking around in case he should see her. Failing to find her, he spoke to the tavern keeper with a smile on his lips, "My friend, I've heard you have a pretty lass here; I'd like to see her." Seeing Abraham's venerable white hair, the tavern keeper thought ill of him inwardly, but nevertheless said in reply, "Yes, there is; she is indeed pretty." The blessed girl, you should understand, was quite exceptionally beautiful.

Her uncle then said to the tavern keeper, "What is her name?" "Mary" was the reply. Then with radiant face, he said, "Summon her, so that we can enjoy ourselves together with her today. From what I've heard of her I am much attracted by her."

The tavern keeper called to her and she came. When Abraham caught sight of her dolled up and dressed like a prostitute, his whole body nearly began to run with tears, but he valiantly gripped hold of his emotions lest she notice and run away. As they sat drinking, this amazing old man began to chat with her, and she drew close to him, and started embracing him and kissing his neck. But as she caressed him, the smell of asceticism that issued from the blessed man's body hit her. Immediately she recalled the days of her own ascetic life, and choking with grief, she gasped, "Woe is me, me alone!" In astonishment the tavern keeper addressed her: "My lady Mary, you've been with us for two years to the day, and I've never heard you groan and say anything like that. What's the matter with you?" "Had I died three years ago, I would have received a great blessing," she replied. To prevent her realizing who he was, the blessed man said to her angrily, "Why do you have to recall your sins now that I've come?"

22 My beloved listeners, don't you suppose that she said in her heart, "How much the man resembles my uncle," or "Isn't his build like that of my father?" But God who alone is wise and loves mankind saw to it that she did not recognize him and so run away in panic. At that moment the blessed man brought out a daric and, handing it to the tavern keeper, said, "Take this, my friend, and prepare us a first-class meal so that we can enjoy ourselves today with this lass. I've come a long way to see her."

What wisdom of spirit, what true discernment in the company he kept! This man, who for fifty years had not even eaten any bread due to his ascetic way of life, now, for the sake of one soul, ate meat and drank wine, all in order to rescue a lost soul. The angel hosts stood in astonishment at the blessed man's discerning action, how with a good will and without any hesitation, he ate and drank, all in order to draw up a soul that had sunk into foul-smelling mire. How great is the wisdom of the truly wise, what perception do those who truly understand possess! Come and stand in awe at the "folly" of a man perfected in wisdom! Here is a man of sharp understanding who became a boorish fool in order to remove from the serpent's mouth the soul that had been swallowed up, who rescued and delivered from bonds and from the prison of darkness the soul that had been held captive, having strayed after vanity.

23 After they had chatted together, the girl said, "Please come into my bedroom so that we can sleep together." "Let's go in," he replied. On entering he espied a large bed made up, and of his own accord he sat down beside her. O perfect athlete of Christ, I know not what name I should give you, or what I should call you. Should I speak of you as a Nazirite, or someone who has compromised himself? Full of wisdom, or of folly? A man of discernment, or someone who has lost all sense of proportion? After fifty years of monastic life, sleeping on matting, how is it that you can sit down on such a bed? You did all this for the honor and glory of God: you made a long journey, you ate meat and drank wine, condescended to enter a tavern, all in order to save a lost soul. We hesitate to utter a single uplifting word to those present.

24 As he sat on the bed, the girl spoke to him: "Come, let me take off your shoes." "Shut the door first and then you can come and take them off." She objected and wanted to take off his shoes first, but he said no. So she shut the door and came back to him. "My lady Mary, draw close to me," he said. When she had done so, he grasped her firmly to prevent her escaping and, as though wanting to kiss her, he removed his helmet from his head and spoke to her with tears in his eyes: "My daughter Mary, don't you recognize me? Am I not your father Abraham? My beloved daughter, child of my dearest relations, don't you know who I am? Didn't I bring you up? What has happened to you, my daughter? Who has killed you this way—or so it seems? Where is that precious monastic habit you used to wear? Where is your ascetic way of life, where are the tears in your eyes? Where are your vigils, your bed on the ground? From what a height have you now sunk to such a pit as this! I brought you up as my daughter: why didn't you tell me when you committed the sin? I would have done penance for you along with my beloved Ephrem. Why have you acted like this? What was the reason for your leaving me, throwing upon me an unutterable sadness? Who is without sin, apart from God alone?"

As she listened to these words she became like a motionless stone in his hands, petrified with terror and fear.

"Won't you speak to me, my daughter?" the blessed man went on, in tears. "Wasn't it for your sake that I have come here? The sin shall be upon me, and I will answer on your behalf to God on the day of judgment. I will be the one who does penance for this sin."

He continued right up to midnight, begging her and admonishing her in tears. When she had plucked up enough courage, she said to him as she wept: "I cannot bring myself to look upon you, sir, seeing what a shameful thing I have done. How can I pray to God, now that I have befouled myself in this stench and mud?" The blessed man replied, "My daughter, I have taken upon myself your wrongdoing: God will require this sin at my hands. Just listen to me, and come back to our home. My beloved Ephrem is also full of grief because of you, and he makes supplication to God on your behalf: your soul is in his hands. Have pity on my old age, spare my white hairs, listen to your father's counsel, I beg of you."

He said this, having fallen on his knees trying to persuade her; whereupon she replied, "If you are certain that I *can* repent, and that God will receive me, then I come and fall at your feet, supplicating your venerable person; I kiss your holy feet because your compassion stirred you to come after me in order to raise me up from this foul abyss of mine."

Thus she spent the whole night in tears, saying, "How can I repay you, my father, for all that you have done for me?"

When morning came, he said, "My daughter, let's get up and get away from here." "There's a little gold and a lot of clothes that I've picked up in the course of my life of shame, what should I do with them?" she asked. "Leave them all here; they belong to the Evil One," he said.

25 So they got up and left without further ado. He sat her down on the horse, while he walked ahead, leading it. He traveled happy at heart, like a shepherd once he had found his sheep that had gone astray, carrying it home in joy on his shoulders. Such was the blessed man's joy of mind as he traveled home.

When they arrived, he enclosed her in the inner part of the house where he had previously lived, while he took up residence in the outer part, which had formerly been her place. Dressed in sackcloth and humility, she spent her time in tears and vigil, fasting and showing great diligence in her penitence as, without any hesitation, she called upon God who has pity on sinners. Her repentance was completely sincere.

This supplication and the reconciliation it effected astounded everyone. Who was so unfeeling that he did not open the eyes of his mind at her weeping? Who was so hard-hearted that he failed to praise God when he heard the sound of her lamenting her sins? Compared with hers, our repentance is a mere shadow; compared with hers, our supplications are just dreamlike.

Without any hesitation at all did she make supplication to God, asking him to forgive her what she had done. In order to provide a visible sign that God, the compassionate and the lover of mankind who receives the prayers of the penitent, accepted her back, a healing was effected through her prayer.

26 The blessed man lived for a further ten years. When he saw her excellent intention firm and unchanged, he praised and glorified God. He passed away at the age of seventy, having spent fifty years of his life in voluntary toil and great humility; he was unhesitating in his love, and he showed no respect for persons—contrary to what tends to happen with most people—who show preference to one person while they discriminate against another. For all these years he did not alter his rule of life, never faltering or losing heart. Instead he lived each day as though he was going to die during its course. 27 Such was the manner of the blessed Abraham's life. . . .

28 On the day when he died the entire town gathered; everyone was eager to follow the saint's body in the funeral cortege. People grabbed bits of his clothes to afford themselves salvation. Everyone who had some sickness applied to their bodies whatever part of his clothing had been removed, with the result that they received healing. The people of the town escorted his body amid psalms and spiritual songs, employing the hymns that the blessed Mar Ephrem had composed in his honor. They took him outside the town and laid him in a coffin in the cemetery, beneath the great church where the blessed Mar Ephrem was later to be laid, in the same coffin, after his death.

29 The lamb Mary lived on for five years after the death of the blessed Abraham. She lived a life of exceptional virtue as, night and day, she begged God in her tears to have pity on her and forgive her the sins she had committed. Very often those who passed that spot at night would stop and listen to the sound of her weeping, and would themselves weep with her and give praise to God.

At the time of her death everyone who saw her face gave praise to God for its radiance. In this way she completed her life. She left the world having made a good end, being reconciled with God.

LAMENT OF MARY, THE NIECE OF ABRAHAM OF QIDUN

ALAPH I will sit down and lament over my life;
    alas for me, for what has happened to me,
    how have I fallen!
    Fie on you, Evil One; what is it you have wrought in me?
Refrain Alas for me, my brethren, what has happened to me?
    Again alas for what the Evil One has wrought in me.

BETH With his blandishments he lured me,
    with his enticements he led me astray—alas is me!

How was it he captivated me, and caused me to sin?
Fie on you, Evil One, what is it you have wrought in me?

GOMAL He removed from my countenance
the honorable veil—alas is me!
He made me live, shamefaced, in a tavern.
Fie on you, Evil One; what is it you have wrought in me?

DALATH He thrust me from my position of honor,
he destroyed the opportunity for holy converse,
casting me into the mire of lusts and base deeds.
Fie on you, Evil One; what is it you have wrought in me?

HE I too became a cause for wickedness,
allowing it to be wrought in me—alas is me!
For in me was the Evil One's wish fulfilled.
Fie on you, Evil One; what is it you have wrought in me?

WAW Alas, how bitter is the trap
which the Evil One has laid for me—and caught me:
with his bait he chokes pure damsels.
Fie on you, Evil One; what is it you have wrought in me?

ZAYIN He made me a prostitute, skilled in shame's work;
alas, for I have fallen
from those who lead the life of the Spirit.
Fie on you, Evil One; what have you wrought in me?

ḤETH The ruler of the air saw me engaged in virtuous deeds
and became jealous of me;
using his guiles he stopped me from my excellent labor.
Fie on you, Evil one; what is it you have wrought in me?

ṬETH Great blessing would have been mine
had I died while still a virgin,
when the seal of virginity was preserved still sealed.
Fie on you, Evil One; what is it you have wrought in me?

YODH My weighty honor was turned into flightiness,
my modesty was changed into an object of contempt—alas is me!
For in me was the will of the Evil One fulfilled.
Fie on you, Evil One; what is it you have wrought in me?

KAPH That fair crown that was upon my head
has been snatched away by the Evil One—alas is me,
because I, of my own will, opened the door to him.
Fie on you, Evil One; what is it you have wrought in me?

LAMADH I have destroyed all my labors
through sin with the Devil—alas is me

who am stripped of the rank of virgins.
Fie on you, Evil One; what is it you have wrought in me?

MEM Merciful are you, Lord, kind and pitying all;
    have pity on me, the lost lamb who has returned.
    Heal all its ulcerous wounds,
    and may it find joy in you.

NUN May your mercies reach to me, Lord,
    and that salvation which you spoke of aid me,
    so that I may conquer and destroy the Enemy,
    and give thanks to your name, for you have had mercy on me.

SEMKATH Support my weak self with your arm
    raised up and mighty, O Lord,
    and may the Evil One be put to shame when he sees my firmness,
    may he collapse in confusion, destroyed forever in the pit.

ʿE The Evil One made me an object
    that was abominable and filled with stains.
    Answer me, my Savior, as you did that Sinful Woman;
    receive my tears as you did hers, O Lord.

PE Your door is open for penitents
    to enter before you, O Lord;
    you do not call their sins to mind,
    you are good, Lord, and have pity on all.

ṢADHE I have taken up your cross and followed after you, as you told us,
    Lord;
    make me worthy of the Kingdom and of salvation,
    along with the thief who gained salvation by your cross.
    Thus shall I confess your grace, Lord.

QOPH Receive the weeping and tears of my wretched state, Lord,
    wipe out the bill which I wrote through the Murderer's guile.
    May he be ashamed because your compassion has wiped it out
    so that it can never again be exacted.

RESH Great is your compassion,
    and your grace is poured out over sinners
    who take refuge in you,
    who come to your great and holy gate in penitence.

SHIN Receive the mite of my words, in your great mercy,
    just as you received the widow's mite,
    which she gave, Lord,
    to your great and holy name.

TAU Thanksgiving be to you from the just
   who have had faith in you, Lord,
   and from sinners as well, whom you have saved by your cross,
   and from all who have lived and are living be praise to you, Lord.

● **122**

The Endurance of Two Syrian Christian Monastic Women

Theodoret of Cyrrhus *A History of the Monks of Syria* 29   5th century C.E.

AUTHOR: Theodoret of Cyrrhus was a monastic who was consecrated as bishop of Cyrrhus in Syria against his will in 423 (when he was about thirty). He was deeply embroiled in the theological controversies of the fifth century, including those about the nature of Mary, the mother of Jesus.

TRANSLATION: R. M. Price, ed., *Theodoret, Bishop of Cyrrhus, "A History of the Monks of Syria"* (Kalamazoo, Mich.: Cistercian Publications, 1985).

TEXT: SC 234 and 257 (P. Canavet and A. Leroy-Molinghen, 1977–79).

After recording the way of life of the heroic men, I think it useful to treat also of women who have contended no less if not more; for they are worthy of still greater praise, when, despite having a weaker nature, they display the same zeal as the men and free their sex from its ancestral disgrace.

2 At this point I shall treat of Marana and Cyra who have defeated all the others in the contests of endurance. Their fatherland was Beroea, their stock the glory of their fatherland, and their upbringing appropriate for their stock. But despising all these, they acquired a small place in front of the town, and entering within it, walled up the door with clay and stones. For their maid-servants who were eager to share this life with them they built a small dwelling outside this enclosure, and in this they told them to live. Through a small window they keep a watch on what they are doing, and repeatedly rouse them to prayer and inflame them with divine love. They themselves, with neither house nor hut, embrace the open-air life.

3 In place of a door a small window has been constructed for them, through which they take in the food they need and talk with the women who come to see them. For this intercourse the season of Pentecost has been laid down; during the rest of the time they embrace the quiet life. And it is Marana alone who talks to visitors; no one has ever heard the other one speak.

4 They wear iron, and carry such a weight that Cyra, with her weaker body, is bent down to the ground and is quite unable to straighten her body. They wear mantles so big as to trail along behind and literally cover their feet and in front to fall down right to the belt, literally hiding at the same time face, neck, chest, and hands.

5 I have often been inside the door in order to see them; for out of respect for the episcopal office they have bidden me dig through the door. And so I have seen that weight of iron which even a well-built man could not carry. After long entreaty I succeeded in getting it off them for the nonce, but after our departure they again put it on their limbs—round the neck the collar, round the waist the belt, and on hands and feet the chains assigned to them.

6 In this mode of life they have completed not merely five or ten or fifteen years, but forty-two; and despite having contended for so long a time, they love their exertion as if they had only just entered on the contests. For contemplating the beauty of the Bridegroom, they bear the labor of the course with ease and facility, and press on to reach the goal of the contests, where they see the Beloved standing and pointing to the crown of victory. Because of this, in suffering the assaults of rain and snow and sun they feel neither pain nor distress but from apparent afflictions reap joy of heart.

7 Emulating the fast of the inspired Moses, they have three times spent the same length of time without food, for it was at the end of forty days that they took a little nourishment. Three times also have they emulated the abstinence from eating of the godly Daniel, completing three weeks and only then supplying nourishment to the body. On one occasion, out of a desire to behold the sacred places of the saving sufferings of Christ, they hastened to Aelia, enjoying no nutriment on the way. It was after reaching that city and accomplishing their worship that they took nourishment, and then returning back completed the journey without food—and there are not less than twenty stages. Conceiving a desire to behold as well the shrine of the triumphant Thecla in Isauria, in order from all sources to kindle the firebrand of their love for God, they journeyed both there and back without food—to such a degree has divine yearning driven them to frenzy, so much has divine love for the Bridegroom driven them mad. Since by such a way of life they have adorned the female sex, becoming as models for other women, they will be crowned by the Master with the wreaths of victory. I myself, having displayed the benefit therefrom and culled their blessing, shall pass on to another account.

● 123

A Syrian Monastic Woman Living in a Hut in Her Mother's Garden

THEODORET OF CYRRHUS *A History of the Monks of Syria*
30   5th century C.E.

AUTHOR, TRANSLATION, AND TEXT: See entry 122.

BIBLIOGRAPHY: Susan Ashbrook Harvey, "Sacred Bonding: Mothers and Daughters in Early Syriac Hagiography," *JECS* 4, no. 1 (1996): 27–56.

Emulating the life of the inspired Maron, whom we recalled above, the wonderful Domnina set up a small hut in the garden of her mother's house; her hut is made of millet stalks. Passing the whole day there, she wets with incessant tears not only her cheeks but also her garments of hair, for such is the clothing with which she covers her body. Going at cockcrow to the divine shrine nearby, she offers hymnody to the Master of the universe, together with the rest, both men and women. This she does not only at the beginning of the day but also at its close, thinking the place consecrated to God to be more venerable than every other spot and teaching others so. Judging it, for this reason, worthy of every attention, she has persuaded her mother and brothers to spend their fortune on it.

2 As food she has lentils soaked in water; and she endures all this labor with a body reduced to a skeleton and half-dead—for her skin is very thin, and covers her thin bones as if with a film, while her fat and flesh have been worn away by labors. Though exposed to all who wish to see her, both men and women, she neither sees a face nor shows her face to another, but is literally covered up by her cloak and bent down onto her knees, while she speaks extremely softly and indistinctly, always making her remarks with tears. She has often taken my hand, and after placing it on her eyes, released it so soaked that my very hand dripped tears. What discourse could give due praise to a woman who with such wealth of philosophy weeps and wails and sighs like those living in extreme poverty? For it is fervent love for God that begets these tears, firing the mind to divine contemplation, stinging it with pricks and urging it on to migrate from here.

3 Though spending in this way both the day and the night, nor does she neglect the other forms of virtue, but ministers, as far as she can, to the heroic contestants, both those we have mentioned and those we have omitted. She also ministers to those who come to see her, bidding them stay with the shepherd of the village and sending them all they need herself, for the property of her mother and brothers is available for her to spend, since it reaps a blessing through her. To myself too when I arrived at this place—it is to the south of our region—she sent rolls, fruit, and soaked lentils.

4 But how long can I expatiate in my eagerness to relate all her virtue, when I ought to bring into the open the life of the other women who have imitated both her and those we recalled above? For there are many others, of whom some have embraced the solitary life and others have preferred life with many companions—in such a way that communities of two hundred and fifty, or more, or less, share the same life, putting up with the same food, choosing to sleep on rush-mats alone, assigning their hands to card wool, and consecrating their tongues with hymns.

5 Myriad and defeating enumeration are the philosophic retreats of this kind not only in our region but throughout the East; full of them are Palestine,

Egypt, Asia, Pontus, and all Europe. From the time when Christ the Master honored virginity by being born of a virgin, nature has sprouted meadows of virginity and offered these fragrant and unfading flowers to the Creator, not separating virtue into male and female nor dividing philosophy into two categories. For the difference is one of bodies not of souls: "in Christ Jesus," according to the divine Apostle, "there is neither male nor female" [Gal. 3.28]. And a single faith has been given to men and women: "there is one Lord, one faith, one baptism, one God and Father of all, who is above all and through all and in us all" [Eph. 4.5–6]. And it is one kingdom of heaven which the Umpire has set before the victors, fixing this common prize for the contests.

6 As I have said, numerous are the pious wrestling-schools of men and women not only among us but also in all Syria, Palestine, Cilicia, and Mesopotamia. In Egypt, it is said, some retreats have five thousand men each, who work and in-between sing hymns to the Master, not only providing themselves with the necessary food out of their labor, but also supplying guests who come and are needy.

7 But to recount everything is impossible not only for me but for all writers. Even if it were possible, I consider it superfluous and an ambition without gain; for those who wish to cull some profit, what has been said is sufficient to provide what they desire. We have recalled different lives, and added accounts of women to those of men, for this reason: that men old and young, and women too, may have models of philosophy, and that each person, as he receives the impress of his favorite life, may have as a rule and regulator of his own life the one presented in our account. Just as painters look at their model when imitating eyes, nose, mouth, cheeks, ears, forehead, the very hairs of the head and beard, and in addition the sitting and standing postures, and the very expression of the eyes, whether genial or forbidding, so it is fitting that each of the readers of this work choose to imitate a particular life and order their own life in accordance with the one they choose. Just as joiners straighten their planks with a measuring-cord and remove what is excessive to the point where, applying the rule, they see the plank is equal, so too one who wishes to emulate a particular life must apply it to himself in place of a rule, and cut off the excesses of vice, while supplying what is lacking in virtue. It is for this reason that we have undertaken the labor of composition, offering to those who wish it a means of benefit. I ask my future readers, as they luxuriate effortlessly in the labors of others, to repay my labors with prayer.

8 I also beg those whose life I have written down not to leave me tarrying at a distance from their spiritual choir, but to draw me up, who am lying below, lead me up to the summit of virtue and join me to their own choir, so that I may not only praise the wealth of others, but also myself have some

cause to give praise—by deed, word, and thought glorifying the Saviour of the universe, with whom to the Father be the glory together with the Holy Spirit, now and always and for ever and ever. Amen.

● 124

Sayings Attributed to Ascetic Desert Monastic Women

Sayings of the Desert Fathers   5th century c.e.

WORK, TRANSLATION, AND TEXT: See entry 42. In the prior edition of this anthology, these sayings were included in section 2. Consistent with my greater skepticism about their authenticity, I have preferred here to include these as examples of pious and exemplary women, who may or may not have been responsible for these particular sayings.

BIBLIOGRAPHY: Averil Cameron, "Desert Mothers: Women Ascetics in Early Christian Egypt," in Elizabeth Puttick and Peter B. Clarke, eds., *Women as Teachers and Disciples in Traditional and New Religions*, Studies in Women and Religion 32 (Lewiston, N.Y.: Edwin Mellen Press, 1993), 11–24; Mary Forman, "Desert Ammas: Midwives of Wisdom," in Douglas Kries and Catherine Brown Tkacz, eds., *Nova Doctrina Vetusque: Essays on Early Christianity in Honor of Fredric W. Schlatter* (New York: Peter Lang, 1999), 187–201. See also the bibliography in entries 42 and 120.

● 124A

Sayings Attributed to Amma Sarah
                                                                  5th century c.e.

1 It was related of Amma Sarah that for thirteen years she waged warfare against the demon of fornication. She never prayed that the warfare should cease but she said, "O God, give me strength."

2 Once the same spirit of fornication attacked her more intently, reminding her of the vanities of the world. But she gave herself up to the fear of God and to asceticism and went up onto her little terrace to pray. Then the spirit of fornication appeared corporally to her and said, "Sarah, you have overcome me." But she said, "It is not I who have overcome you, but my master, Christ."

3 It was said concerning her that for sixty years she lived beside a river and never lifted her eyes to look at it.

4 Another time, two old men, great anchorites, came to the district of Pelusia to visit her. When they arrived one said to the other, "Let us humiliate this old woman." So they said to her, "Be careful not to become conceited thinking of yourself: 'Look how anchorites are coming to see me, a mere

woman.' " But Amma Sarah said to them, "According to nature I am a woman, but not according to my thoughts."

5 Amma Sarah said, "If I prayed God that all men should approve of my conduct, I should find myself a penitent at the door of each one, but I shall rather pray that my heart may be pure towards all."

6 She also said, "I put out my foot to ascend the ladder, and I place death before my eyes before going up it."

7 She also said, "It is good to give alms for men's sake. Even if it is only done to please men, through it one can begin to seek to please God."

8 Some monks of Scetis came one day to visit Amma Sarah. She offered them a small basket of fruit. They left the good fruit and ate the bad. So she said to them, "You are true monks of Scetis."

9 She also said to the brothers, "It is I who am a man, you who are women."

● 124B

Sayings Attributed to Amma Syncletica

5th century C.E.

1 Amma Syncletica said, "In the beginning there are a great many battles and a good deal of suffering for those who are advancing towards God and afterwards, ineffable joy. It is like those who wish to light a fire; at first they are choked by the smoke and cry, and by this means obtain what they seek (as it is said: 'Our God is a consuming fire' [Heb. 12.24]): so we also must kindle the divine fire in ourselves through tears and hard work."

2 She also said, "We who have chosen this way of life must obtain perfect temperance. It is true that among seculars, also, temperance has the freedom of the city, but intemperance cohabits with it, because they sin with all the other senses. Their gaze is shameless and they laugh immoderately."

3 She also said, "Just as the most bitter medicine drives out poisonous creatures so prayer joined to fasting drives evil thoughts away."

4 She also said, "Do not let yourself be seduced by the delights of the riches of the world, as though they contained something useful on account of vain pleasure. Worldly people esteem the culinary art, but you, through fasting and thanks to cheap food, go beyond their abundance of food. It is written: 'He who is sated loathes honey.' (Prov. 27.7) Do not fill yourself with bread and you will not desire wine."

5 Blessed Syncletica was asked if poverty is a perfect good. She said, "For those who are capable of it, it is a perfect good. Those who can sustain it receive suffering in the body but rest in the soul, for just as one washes coarse clothes by trampling them underfoot and turning them about in all

directions, even so the strong soul becomes much more stable thanks to voluntary poverty."

6 She also said, "If you find yourself in a monastery do not go to another place, for that will harm you a great deal. Just as the bird who abandons the eggs she was sitting on prevents them from hatching, so the monk or the nun grows cold and their faith dies, when they go from one place to another."

7 She also said, "Many are the wiles of the devil. If he is not able to disturb the soul by means of poverty, he suggests riches as an attraction. If he has not won the victory by insults and disgrace, he suggests praise and glory. Overcome by health, he makes the body ill. Not having been able to seduce it through pleasures, he tries to overthrow it by involuntary sufferings. He joins to this, very severe illness, to disturb the faint-hearted in their love of God. But he also destroys the body by very violent fevers and weighs it down with intolerable thirst. If, being a sinner, you undergo all these things, remind yourself of the punishment to come, the everlasting fire and the sufferings inflicted by justice, and do not be discouraged here and now. Rejoice that God visits you and keep this blessed saying on your lips: "The Lord has chastened me sorely but he has not given me over unto death.' (Ps. 118.18) You were iron, but fire has burnt the rust off you. If you are righteous and fall ill, you will go from strength to strength. Are you gold? You will pass through fire purged. Have you been given a thorn in the flesh? (2 Cor. 12.1) Exult, and see who else was treated like that; it is an honour to have the same sufferings as Paul. Are you being tried by fever? Are you being taught by cold? Indeed Scripture says: 'We went through fire and water; yet thou hast brought us forth to a spacious place.' (Ps. 66.12) You have drawn the first lot? Expect the second. By virtue offer holy words in a loud voice. For it is said: 'I am afflicted and in pain.' (Ps. 69.29) By this share of wretchedness you will be made perfect. For he said: 'The Lord hears when I call him.' (Ps. 4:3) So open your mouth wider to be taught by these exercises of the soul, seeing that we are under the eyes of our enemy."

8 She also said, "If illness weighs us down, let us not be sorrowful as though, because of the illness and the prostration of our bodies we could not sing, for all these things are for our good, for the purification of our desires. Truly fasting and sleeping on the ground are set before us because of our sensuality. If illness then weakens this sensuality the reason for these practices is superfluous. For this is the great asceticism: to control oneself in illness and to sing hymns of thanksgiving to God."

9 She also said, "When you have to fast, do not pretend illness. For those who do not fast often fall into real sicknesses. If you have begun to act well, do not turn back through constraint of the enemy, for through your endurance, the enemy is destroyed. Those who put out to sea at first sail with a

favourable wind; then the sails spread, but later the winds become adverse. Then the ship is tossed by the waves and is no longer controlled by the rudder. But when in a little while there is a calm, and the tempest dies down, then the ship sails on again. So it is with us, when we are driven by the spirits who are against us; we hold to the cross as our sail and so we can set a safe course."

10 She also said, "Those who have endured the labours and dangers of the sea and then amass material riches, even when they have gained much desire to gain yet more and they consider what they have at present as nothing and reach out for what they have not got. We, who have nothing of that which we desire, wish to acquire everything through the fear of God."

11 She also said, "Imitate the publican, and you will not be condemned with the Pharisee. Choose the meekness of Moses and you will find your heart which is a rock changed into a spring of water."

12 She also said, "It is dangerous for anyone to teach who has not first been trained in the 'practical' life. For if someone who owns a ruined house receives guests there, he does them harm because of the dilapidation of his dwelling. It is the same in the case of someone who has not first built an interior dwelling; he causes loss to those who come. By words one may convert them to salvation, but by evil behaviour, one injures them."

13 She also said, "It is good not to get angry, but if this should happen, the Apostle does not allow you a whole day for this passion, for he says: 'Let not the sun go down.' (Eph. 4.25) Will you wait till all your time is ended? Why hate the man who has grieved you? It is not he who has done the wrong, but the devil. Hate sickness but not the sick person."

14 She also said, "Those who are great athletes must contend against stronger enemies."

15 She also said, "There is an asceticism which is determined by the enemy and his disciples practice it. So how are we to distinguish between the divine and royal asceticism and the demonic tyranny? Clearly through its quality of balance. Always use a single rule of fasting. Do not fast four or five days and break it the following day with any amount of food. In truth lack of proportion always corrupts. While you are young and healthy, fast, for old age with its weakness will come. As long as you can, lay up treasure, so that when you cannot, you will be at peace."

16 She also said, "As long as we are in the monastery, obedience is preferable to asceticism. The one teaches pride, the other humility."

17 She also said, "We must direct our souls with discernment. As long as we are in the monastery, we must not seek our own will, nor follow our personal opinion, but obey our fathers in the faith."

18 She also said, "It is written, 'Be wise as serpents and innocent as doves.' (Matt. 10.16) Being like serpents means not ignoring attacks and wiles of the devil. Like is quickly known to like. The simplicity of the dove denotes purity of action."

19 Amma Syncletica said, "There are many who live in the mountains and behave as if they were in the town, and they are wasting their time. It is possible to be a solitary in one's mind while living in a crowd, and it is possible for one who is a solitary to live in the crowd of his own thoughts."

20 She also said, "In the world, if we commit an offence, even an involuntary one, we are thrown into prison; let us likewise cast ourselves into prison because of our sins, so that voluntary remembrance may anticipate the punishment that is to come."

21 She also said, "Just as a treasure that is exposed loses its value, so a virtue which is known vanishes, just as wax melts when it is near fire, so the soul is destroyed by praise and loses all the results of its labour."

22 She also said, "Just as it is impossible to be at the same moment both a plant and a seed, so it is impossible for us to be surrounded by worldly honour and at the same time to bear heavenly fruit."

23 She also said, "My children, we all want to be saved, but because of our habit of negligence, we swerve away from salvation."

24 She also said, "We must arm ourselves in every way against the demons. For they attack us from outside, and they also stir us up from within; and the soul is then like a ship when great waves break over it, and at the same time it sinks because the hold is too full. We are just like that: we lose as much by the exterior faults we commit as by the thoughts inside us. So we must watch for the attacks of men that come from outside us, and also repel the interior onslaughts of our thoughts."

25 She also said, "Here below we are not exempt from temptations. For Scripture says, 'Let him who thinks that he stands take heed lest he fall.' (1 Cor. 10.12) We sail on in darkness. The psalmist calls our life a sea and the sea is either full of rocks, or very rough, or else it is calm. We are like those who sail on a calm sea, and seculars are like those on a rough sea. We always set our course by the sun of justice, but it can often happen that the secular is saved in tempest and darkness, for he keeps watch as he ought, while we go to the bottom through negligence, although we are on a calm sea, because we have let go of the guidance of justice."

26 She also said, "Just as one cannot build a ship unless one has some nails, so it is impossible to be saved without humility."

27 She also said, "There is grief that is useful, and there is grief that is destructive. The first sort consists in weeping over one's own faults and weeping

over the weakness of one's neighbours, in order not to destroy one's purpose, and attach oneself to the perfect good. But there is also a grief that comes from the enemy, full of mockery, which some call *accidie*. This spirit must be cast out, mainly by prayer and psalmody."

⊛ 124C

Sayings Attributed to Amma Theodora

1 Amma Theodora asked Archbishop Theophilus about some words of the apostle saying, "What does this mean, 'Knowing how to profit by circumstances'?" (Col. 4, 5) He said to her, "This saying shows us how to profit at all times. For example, is it a time of excess for you? By humility and patience buy up the time of excess, and draw profit from it. Is it the time of shame? Buy it up by means of resignation and win it. So everything that goes against us can, if we wish, become profitable to us."

2 Amma Theodora said, "Let us strive to enter by the narrow gate. Just as the trees, if they have not stood before the winter's storms cannot bear fruit, so it is with us; this present age is a storm and it is only through many trials and temptations that we can obtain an inheritance in the kingdom of heaven."

3 She also said, "It is good to live in peace, for the wise man practises perpetual prayer. It is truly a great thing for a virgin or a monk to live in peace, especially for the younger ones. However, you should realize that as soon as you intend to live in peace, at once evil comes and weighs down your soul through *accidie*, faintheartedness, and evil thoughts. It also attacks your body through sickness, debility, weakening of the knees, and all the members. It dissipates the strength of soul and body, so that one believes one is ill and no longer able to pray. But if we are vigilant, all these temptations fall away. There was, in fact a monk who was seized by cold and fever every time he began to pray, and he suffered from headaches, too. In this condition, he said to himself, 'I am ill, and near to death; so now I will get up before I die and pray.' By reasoning in this way, he did violence to himself and prayed. When he had finished, the fever abated also. So, by reasoning in this way, the brother resisted, and prayed and was able to conquer his thoughts."

4 The same Amma Theodora said, "A devout man happened to be insulted by someone, and he said to him, 'I could say as much to you, but the commandment of God keeps my mouth shut.'" Again she said this, "A Christian discussing the body with a Manichean expressed himself in these words, 'Give the body discipline and you will see that the body is for him who made it.'"

5 The same amma said that a teacher ought to be a stranger to the desire for domination, vain-glory, and pride; one should not be able to fool him by

flattery, nor blind him by gifts, nor conquer him by the stomach, nor dominate him by anger; but he should be patient, gentle and humble as far as possible; he must be tested and without partisanship, full of concern, and a lover of souls.

6 She also said that neither asceticism, nor vigils nor any kind of suffering are able to save, only true humility can do that. There was an anchorite who was able to banish the demons; and he asked them, "What makes you go away? Is it fasting?" They replied, "We do not eat or drink." "Is it vigils?" They replied, "We do not sleep." "Is it separation from the world?" "We live in the deserts." "What power sends you away then?" They said, "Nothing can overcome us, but only humility." "Do you see how humility is victorious over the demons?"

7 Amma Theodora also said, "There was a monk, who, because of the great number of his temptations said, 'I will go away from here.' As he was putting on his sandals, he saw another man who was also putting on his sandals and this other monk said to him, 'Is it on my account that you are going away? Because I go before you wherever you are going.' "

8 The same amma was asked about the conversations one hears; "If one is habitually listening to secular speech, how can one yet live for God alone, as you suggest?" She said, "Just as when you are sitting at table and there are many courses, you take some but without pleasure, so when secular conversations come your way, have your heart turned towards God, and thanks to this disposition, you will hear them without pleasure, and they will not do you any harm."

9 Another monk suffered bodily irritation and was infested with vermin. Now originally he had been rich. So the demons said to him, "How can you bear to live like this, covered with vermin?" But this monk, because of the greatness of his soul, was victorious over them.

10 Another of the old men questioned Amma Theodora saying, "At the resurrection of the dead, how shall we rise?" She said, "As pledge, example, and as prototype we have him who died for us and is risen, Christ our God."

The Feminine Divine

In a collection of documents on women's religions this last section may be the most difficult to justify. It presents a sampling of representations of the divine as feminine, without being able to answer the question of how such representations correlate with the gender of those who produce and valorize them. The inclusion of these texts here is not intended to suggest that it is women who either exclusively or primarily envision divinity as feminine or worship female deities. We know, of course, that this is patently untrue: goddesses are not per se the object of women's devotion, nor do they by definition reflect women's perceptions of themselves and the universe in which they live. On the contrary, men regularly venerate goddesses and other feminine aspects of the divine. Further, at least some, if not all, such figures, may be vehicles for the expression and exploration of male constructions of femininity. This is particularly true in polytheist cultures who perceive the divine by default as manifest in multiple forms and both genders.

Nevertheless, the relative absence of worship of feminine divinity that we see clearly in the male monotheism of Judaism and Christianity is an issue that cannot be ignored and that the presentation of these texts endeavors to raise. Despite the claim of theologians over the centuries that God has no gender, the move to monotheism in Western religious tradition has in fact meant the promulgation of a divinity who, from ancient Israel on, is repeatedly and primarily referred to with masculine terminology.[1] Feminine aspects of the divine persist or recur in atten-

---

[1] Whether either Judaism or Christianity in antiquity was truly "monotheist" is a complex question. Many ancient Jews believed in the existence of a powerful second divine figure, sometimes known as the Name-Bearing Angel (meaning the angel who bears the name of God); see, e.g., Jarl E. Fossum, *The Name of God and the Angel of the Lord: Samaritan and Jewish Concepts of Intermediation and the Origin of Gnosticism* (Tübingen: Mohr Siebeck, 1985); Alan F. Segal, *Two Powers in Heaven: Early Rabbinic Reports about Christianity and Gnosticism* (Leiden: E. J. Brill, 1977); see also the discussion in Ross Shepard Kraemer, *When Aseneth Met Joseph: A Late Antique Tale of the Biblical Patriarch and His Egyptian Wife, Reconsidered* (Oxford: Oxford University Press, 1998), 110–54.

uated and often arcane forms in Jewish and Christian tradition, as in the personification of the Sabbath as bride, in the feminine presence, or Shekinah, of God, in the personification of Wisdom as female, in the figure of the male God's companion, the Matronit, in some Jewish mysticism, and in the form of female saints and even the Virgin Mary herself on the Christian side.[2] But as numerous feminist scholars of religion have observed, monotheism in Western religion has meant the suppression of Goddess.

Several of the texts here require us to pose the difficult question of why some religious communities in antiquity used texts with an abundance of feminine language for the divine, or for aspects of divinity, while others did not. Most of our evidence for this usage comes from Christian sources, although an interesting case is the figure of Metanoia (Repentance), the daughter of God, in the enigmatic tale of *Aseneth* (entry 106). If, as most scholars think, the story of Joseph and Aseneth is a Jewish composition, it is evidence for such imagery in a certain Jewish context by the end of the fourth century or so. As my introduction both to section 4 of this book and to the entry itself notes, this identification is not secure, and the very usage of such imagery might also factor into the problem of identifying the source of this material.

Can we draw any conclusions about the individuals who employed feminine imagery for the divine and/or the communities that read and disseminated such texts (assuming that these texts represent something more than the idiosyncratic views of single individuals or extremely small groups of persons—an assumption that does warrant more attention than it usually gets)?[3] Scholars of what is frequently, if imprecisely, called gnosticism initially suggested that gnostic use of feminine language for the divine reflected the more extensive roles women played in their communities both as leaders and as sources of revelation and authority.

Yet testing such a hypothesis has proved exceedingly frustrating. We know very little about who produced the writings conventionally labeled "gnostic" or the persons labeled "gnostic" by their opponents. Did such persons constitute separate communities, and if so, what might the social composition and gender arrangements of such communities have been like? The "orthodox" opponents of gnostics do sometimes say that women had prominent roles and exercised religious offices and authority among "gnostics." In several important texts, such as the *Dialogue of the Savior* and the *Gospel of Mary*, Mary (generally thought to be Magdalene)[4]

---

[2] For a discussion of the relatively few exceptions in ancient Jewish and Christian scripture, see the various entries in the third section of *Women in Scripture*.

[3] On the demographics of ancient Jewish and Christian groups and on the extremely small numbers of persons who would have been sufficiently literate to produce the entire corpus of ancient Jewish and Christian literature, see Rodney Stark, *The Rise of Christianity: A Sociologist Reconsiders History* (Princeton: Princeton University Press, 1996); and Seth L. Schwartz, *Imperialism and Jewish Society, 200 B.C.E.–640 C.E.* (Princeton: Princeton University Press, 2001).

[4] See F. Stanley Jones, ed., *Which Mary? The Marys of Early Christian Tradition*, SBLSS 19 (Atlanta: Society of Biblical Literature, 2002).

is a favored disciple of the Savior, to whom he gives special, secret revelations that she then shares with other, male, disciples. But in the absence of better evidence, it is extremely difficult to know whether the descriptions we have are reasonable reports of gnostic practices or whether inverted gender arrangements are a rhetorical device by which heresiologists demonstrate the perversity of their opponents. Of course, both might have been true: women may have held prominent positions of leadership and authority in some non-"orthodox" communities, and their opponents may have seen that as one manifestation of the heretical nature of such practices and their associated beliefs.

Yet those texts which come to be called "orthodox," whether canonical (within Scripture) or extracanonical but still acceptable, use predominantly male language not only for God but also for angels, demons, prophets, priests, messiahs, and virtually all the key players in the hyperhuman cosmos. Early Syriac Christian texts use feminine language for the Holy Spirit, and some feminine metaphors for Christ (see entries 127 and 128). Texts found near Nag Hammadi, and a relatively small number of others, in contrast, envision a cosmos populated by both male and female superhuman figures as well as male and female prophets and recipients of revelation, like Mary. If this is not to be explained by some difference in the social environment of the communities that wrote and used these texts, what alternative explanation accounts for the distinction? Or, to put it another way, in communities in which women did have publicly recognized religious authority and were seen as recipients and transmitters of revelation, what kind of gender language for the divine occurs? If women formulated, wrote, or transmitted such sources, did they use the overwhelmingly male metaphors that pervade most of Jewish and Christian tradition, or did they, at least on occasion, utilize different language and imagery? Certainly, in the modern period, Jewish and Christian women have been instrumental in the revision of religious language to be more gender inclusive. Whether, however, the agency of women accounts for the presence of female language in some ancient religious texts (and, if so, whether this indicates some self-conscious desire to counter masculine language) or whether the absence of that agency accounts for the absence of that language in the majority of other texts continues to elude contemporary historical inquiry. But if women are not the impetus for, nor the producers of, such female imagery, then it is the work of (some) men. Some recent scholarship has in fact proposed that this is more likely, not only for texts that image the divine as female but for tales of women in general. If that is the case, all such writings may be more useful for the light they shed on male thinking about gender than for anything they might say about women's practices and beliefs. In the absence of better evidence, the problem will continue to tantalize us.[5]

[5] I have explored some aspects of these issues in *Blessings*; for more recent treatment of the use of gender in ancient Christian polemic, see Virginia Burrus, "The Heretical Woman as Symbol in Alexander, Athanasius, Epiphanius, and Jerome," *HTR* 84 (1991): 229–48; see also Ross S. Kraemer, "The Other as Woman: Aspects of Polemic between Pagans, Jews, and Christians in Greco-Roman Antiquity," in Laurence J. Silberstein and Robert L. Cohn, eds.,

The Principal Version of the Myth of Demeter

The Homeric Hymn to Demeter   7th century B.C.E.

WORK: One of the only selections in this volume to antedate the fourth century B.C.E., the so-called *Homeric Hymn to Demeter* contains the classic legend of the seizure of Persephone by Hades, Demeter's subsequent revengeful famine, Zeus's eventual compromise solution of restoring Persephone to her mother for a portion of the year, and the establishment of the rites of Demeter and Persephone at Eleusis, outside Athens. Although Demeter was venerated by both women and men, her worship was of particular import for women, which feminist scholarship has fruitfully examined. While some work has emphasized the ways in which women's devotion to Demeter and Persephone addressed the particular needs and experiences of many Greek women, other work has pointed out some of the ways in which devotion to Demeter expressed and reinforced ancient Greek conceptions of femininity as subordinate, passive, and inferior.

TRANSLATION: David G. Rice and John E. Stambaugh, *Sources for the Study of Greek Religion*, SBLSBS 14 (Missoula, Mont.: Scholars Press, 1979), 171–83.

TEXT AND ADDITIONAL TRANSLATIONS: LCL (Hugh G. Evelyn-White, 1914); N. J. Richardson, *The Homeric Hymn to Demeter* (Oxford: Clarendon Press, 1974).

ADDITIONAL TRANSLATION: Helene P. Foley, ed., *The Homeric Hymn to Demeter: Translation, Commentary, and Interpretive Essays* (Princeton: Princeton University Press, 1994).

BIBLIOGRAPHY: There is an extensive bibliography on Demeter and Persephone, to which Foley's *Homeric Hymn to Demeter* provides entry; see also *Blessings*, 22–29.

> 1 I begin my song of the holy goddess, fair-haired Demeter, and of her slim-ankled daughter whom Aidoneus snatched away; and Zeus the loud-crashing, the wide-voiced one, granted it. She was playing with the deep-bosomed daughters of Ocean, away from Demeter of the golden weapon and glorious fruit, and she was gathering flowers throughout the luxuriant meadow—roses, saffron, violets, iris, hyacinth, and a narcissus which was a trap planted for the blossoming maiden by Earth in accord with Zeus's plans, a favor to Hades the receiver of many guests; it was radiantly wonderful, inspiring awe in all who saw it, whether immortal god or mortal man; a hundred stems grew from its root; and the whole wide heaven above, the whole earth, and the salt

---

The Other in Jewish Thought and History: Constructions of Jewish Culture and Identity (New York: New York University Press, 1994), 121–44. For the view that ancient Christian writers use stories about women to explore problems of masculine identity, see Kate Cooper, *The Virgin and the Bride: Idealized Womanhood in Late Antiquity* (Cambridge: Harvard University Press, 1996).

surge of the sea smiled for joy at its fragrance. The girl was charmed by it, and reached out both hands to pluck the pretty plaything—suddenly, the earth split open wide along the plain and from it the lord host of many, son of many names, darted out on his immortal horses. He grabbed her, resisting and screaming, and took her away in his golden chariot. She lifted her voice in a cry, calling upon father Zeus, the almighty and good. But no one, god or mortal, heard her voice, not even the glorious-fruited olive-trees, except the childish daughter of Perses, Hecate of the glistening veil, who—from her cave—heard, and so did Lord Helios the glorious son of Hyperion; as the maiden calling upon father Zeus, though he was sitting, removed from the other gods, in his much-besought temple, receiving fine sacrifices from mortal men.

30 Her, all unwilling, with the approval of Zeus, he took away on his immortal horses, Kronos' son of many names, brother of her father, designator of many, host of many. As long as the goddess could see the earth and the starry sky, the flowing, fish-filled sea and the rays of the sun, she still had hope that her holy mother and the race of the immortal gods would see her, and there was still much hope in her heart in spite of her distress. . . . The peaks of the mountains and the depths of the sea echoed back the immortal voice, and her blessed mother heard her. Then sharp grief seized the mother's heart; she tore the head-dress upon her ambrosial hair, and threw her dark veil down from both her shoulders; and like a bird she darted over land and sea, searching. None of the gods or of mortal men would give her a true report, nor would any of the birds come to her as a true messenger.

47 For nine days then lady Deo wandered the earth, holding blazing torches in her hands; in her grief she touched neither ambrosia nor the sweetness of nectar, nor did she bathe her body with water. But when the tenth day dawned Hecate, bearing light in her hands, encountered her and spoke to her this message: "Lady Demeter, bringer of seasons and glorious gifts, who of the gods of heaven or of mortal men has taken Persephone and pained your own heart? I heard her voice, but did not see who it was. I am telling you everything promptly, and accurately."

59 So spoke Hecate. The daughter of fair-haired Rheia did not answer a word, but she immediately darted off with her, holding blazing torches in her hands, and they came to Helios the viewer of gods and men. They stood before his horses and the divine goddess said, "Helios, as a god, respect me, as a goddess, if ever in word or deed, I have warmed your heart. The maiden whom I bore—sweetest blossom—beautiful—I heard her voice, sobbing, as if she were being raped, but I did not see her. But you survey from the bright heaven all the earth and the sea with your rays; tell me accurately whether you have seen who of gods or mortal men has forced her and taken her away, all unwillingly, in my absence."

74 So she spoke, and the son of Hyperion answered her: "Lady Demeter, daughter of fair-haired Rheia, you will know all: I have great respect for you

and pity you in your grief for your slim-ankled child: none of the immortals is responsible except Zeus the cloud-gatherer, who has granted to Hades his own brother that she be called his tender wife; and he has taken her, screaming a loud cry, away on his horses down into the misty darkness. So, goddess, stop your loud lament; you should not rashly hold on to this boundless anger; Aidoneus, the designator of many, is after all not an unsuitable son-in-law for you, since you have the same mother and father; and his honor he gained when at the beginning a division into three parts was made; and he dwells with those over whom the lot made him king." When he had said this he called to his horses, and at his command they bore the swift chariot like broad-winged birds.

90 Then grief still more horrible and oppressive came upon her heart, and in her anger at Zeus, shrouded in clouds, she deserted the gatherings of the gods and went far from Olympus to the cities and farms of men and for a long time disguised her appearance. No man, no woman who saw her recognized her, until she arrived at the home of clever Keleos, who was the king of fragrant Eleusis at the time. At the Spring Parthenion where the citizens draw water in the shade of a towering olive tree she sat by the side of the road in the guise of an old woman, one who is beyond the age of childbearing and the gifts of Aphrodite who bears the garland of love, one who might be a nurse of royal children or governess of important households. The daughters of Keleos of Eleusis saw her as they came to draw water and carry it in bronze vessels to their father's house. There were four of them, like goddesses in youthful bloom—Kallidike, Klesidike, lovely Demo and Kallirhoe, the eldest of them all. They did not recognize her, for gods are hard for mortals to see. They approached her and said, "Old woman, who are you? Why have you kept away from the city and not approached the settlement? There in the dusky houses there are women as old as you and younger, who would treat you kindly in word and deed."

118 So they spoke, and the goddess mistress said in answer, "Dear children, daughters of womanly mothers, be of good cheer, and I will tell you, for it is right to tell you the truth. The name my lady mother gave to me is Doso. I have just come across the sea from Crete, forced by pirate men who abducted me against my will. They brought their swift ship to shore at Thorikos, and a crowd of women came on board from the land and they all prepared their dinner by the ship's stern-cables. But my heart had no desire for a pleasant supper; instead I got up secretly and escaped those arrogant overlords across the dark countryside, so that they might not enjoy any profit from selling me. I wandered about until I arrived here; but I do not know what land it is nor which people dwell here. May all the gods who dwell on Olympus grant you vigorous husbands and all the progeny they want; but pity me, maidens; dear children, help me come propitiously to some home of a man and

woman where I may provide the services of an aged woman for them: I could hold their infant child in my arms and nurse it well, I could keep house, make the master's bed in the inmost chamber, and instruct the women in their tasks."

145 So said the goddess, and the maiden Kallidike, most beautiful of Keleos' daughters, answered her, "Mother, we humans endure the gifts of the gods, even under grievous compulsion, for they are much mightier. I will explain it all to you clearly, and tell you the men who hold the power of authority here, and who stand out in the government and direct the defense of the city with their counsels and decisions. There are Triptolemos the clever, Dioklos, Polyxeinos, Eumolpos the blameless, Dolichos, and our father the manly one. Their wives manage everything in their households, and not one of them would dishonor you at first sight by making you depart from their houses. They will receive you, for you are godlike. If you wish, wait here while we go to our father's house and tell Metaneira our deep-belted mother all these things, and see whether she bids you come to our house and not search for another's. A favorite son, born to her late, is being nursed in the strongly built palace; she prayed much for him, and rejoiced in him. If you would nurse him and he would reach adolescence, any woman would envy the sight of you, for she [Metaneira] would give you so great a reward for nursing him."

169 So she spoke, and she nodded her head, and then they filled their shining jugs with water and carried them proudly. Soon they reached their father's great house, and quickly told their mother what they had seen and heard. She told them to go quickly and bid her come, at a vast wage. As deer or heifers frolic across the meadow eating to their heart's content, so they darted along the road down the gulley, holding up the folds of their lovely gowns, and their hair streamed along their shoulders like saffron blossoms. They reached the spot near the road where they had left the glorious goddess, and they led her to their father's house. She, grieved at heart, walked behind them with her head veiled, and the dark robe trailed along around the slender feet of the goddess.

184 Soon they reached the house of Zeus-descended Keleos, and went through the portico to the place where their lady mother was sitting beside a column of the carefully made chamber, holding her new baby in her lap. The girls ran to her, but Demeter trod upon the threshold, and her head reached the roof-beam, and she filled the doorway with a divine radiance. At this awe, reverence and pale fear seized the woman. She rose from her chair and urged her to be seated, but Demeter the bringer of seasons and glorious gifts did not wish to be seated on the gleaming chair, but silently cast down her beautiful eyes and waited until Iambe understood and set a jointed stool out for her, and threw a shining white fleece upon it. She sat down, holding her

veil in front with her hands. For a long time she sat there on the stool sorrowfully, without speaking; and made no contact with anyone in word or gesture. Without smiling, without touching food or drink she sat, consumed with yearning for her daughter, until Iambe understood and made plenty of jokes and jests and made the holy Lady smile with kindly heart, and ever afterward she continues to delight her spirit. Then Metaneira filled a cup of sweet wine and offered it to her, but she refused it, for she said it was not right for her to drink red wine. Instead, she asked her to give her barley groats and water mixed with crusted pennyroyal to drink. She made the compound, the *kykeon*, as she commanded, and offered it to the goddess. Deo the greatly revered accepted it for the sake of the ceremony. . . . Fairbelted Metaneira began with these words, "Be of good cheer, woman; I do not expect that you are sprung from base stock, but from good; dignity and grace are manifest in your eyes, like those of kings, stewards of the right. But we humans endure the gifts of the gods, even under grievous compulsion, for a yoke lies upon our neck. But now that you have come here, all that is mine shall be yours. Nurse this child for me, whom the immortals have given me, late-born and unexpected, but much prayed for. If you would nurse him and he would reach adolescence, any woman would envy the sight of you, for I would give you so great a reward for nursing him."

224 Then Demeter of the fair crown said to her, "May you also be of good cheer, woman, and may the gods grant you all good things; I willingly accept the child, as you bid me. I will nurse him, and I do not expect that he will be injured by nurse's incompetence, supernatural attacks nor magical cuttings, for I know an antidote more mighty than the woodcutter, and I know a fine preventative against malignant attacks."

231 When she had said this she received him with her immortal hands in her fragrant lap, and the mother's heart rejoiced. So she nursed the glorious son of clever Keleos, Demophon, whom fair-belted Metaneira bore, and he grew like a god, eating no food, being suckled on no milk, for Demeter would [feed and] anoint him with *ambrosia*, like the progeny of a god, and she breathed sweetly on him and held him in her lap. At night she would hide him like a fire-brand within the might of the flame, without his parents' knowledge. It made them wonder greatly how he was so precocious, and why his appearance was like the gods'. She would have made him ageless and deathless, if it had not been that fair-belted Metaneira foolishly kept watch one night and watched her from her fragrant bed-chamber. She screamed and struck both her thighs in fear for her child and in a frenzy of mindlessness. Wailing, she said, "My child Demophon, the stranger woman is hiding you in the blazing fire, and is making grief and bitter sorrow for me."

250 So she spoke, lamenting, and the divine goddess heard her. Demeter of the beautiful crown was amazed at her; with her immortal hands she put

from her the dear child whom [Metaneira] had borne, all unexpected, in the palace, and threw him at her feet, drawing him out of the fire, terribly angry at heart, and at the same time she said to fair-belted Metaneira, "Humans are short-sighted, stupid, ignorant of the share of good or evil which is coming to them. You by your foolishness have hurt him beyond curing. Let my witness be the oath of the gods sworn by the intractable water of Styx, that I would have made your son deathless and ageless all his days, and given him imperishable honor. But now it is not possible to ward off death and destruction. Still he will have imperishable honor forever, since he stood on my knees and slept in my arms; in due season, as the years pass around, the children of the Eleusinians will conduct in his honor war (games) and the terrible battle-cry with each other for ever and ever. I am Demeter, the Venerable, ready as the greatest boon and joy for immortals and mortals. So now, let the whole people build me a great temple, and an altar beneath it, below the city and the towering wall, above Kallirhoe on the ridge which juts forth. I myself will establish rites so that henceforth you may celebrate them purely and propitiate my mind."

275 With these words the goddess altered size and form and sloughed off old age; beauty wafted about her. A lovely fresh smell radiated from her lovely gown and the radiance from the skin of the immortal goddess shone afar. Her blonde hair flowed down over her shoulders, and the sturdy house was filled with light like a flash of lightning. She went out through the palace. As for the other, her knees gave way, and for a long time she was speechless. She did not even remember the child, her favorite, to pick him up from the floor. His sisters heard his piteous crying, and they leapt down from their well-covered beds. Then one of them took the child in her hands and put him in her lap, one kindled a fire, and another hurried on gentle feet to rouse her mother out of the fragrant chamber. Crowding around they washed him, covering him with love as he squirmed; his heart was not comforted, however, for less skillful nurses and nurses maids were holding him now.

292 All night long the women, quaking with fear, propitiated the glorious goddess. As soon as dawn appeared they gave a full report to wide-ruling Keleos, as Demeter of the beautiful garlands commanded. He summoned the people from their many boundaries and ordered them to build an elaborate temple to fair-haired Demeter and an altar on the ridge which juts forth. They obeyed him straightway, and hearkened to him as he spoke, and started to build as he commanded. And it grew at the dispensation of the divinity. When they finished and ceased from their toil, each person went back to his home. Blonde Demeter stayed there, seated far from all the blessed gods, wasting with grief for her deep-belted daughter.

305 She made the most terrible, most oppressive year for men upon the nourishing land, and the earth sent up no seed, as fair-garlanded Demeter

hid it. Cattle drew the many curved plows in vain over the fields, and much white barley seed fell useless on the earth. By now she would have destroyed the entire race of men by grievous famine, and deprived those who dwell on Olympus of the glorious honor of offerings and sacrifices, if Zeus had not taken notice and taken counsel with his mind. First he roused gold-winged Iris to summon fair-haired Demeter, of the very desirable beauty. So he spoke, and she obeyed Zeus wrapped in clouds, the son of Kronos. She rushed down the middle and arrived at the citadel of fragrant Eleusis. In the temple she found Demeter dark-clad, and addressed her with winged words. "Demeter, father Zeus who understands imperishable things summons you to come among the race of the immortal gods. So come, and let my message from Zeus not be fruitless."

324 So she spoke in supplication, but her heart was not persuaded. Therefore the Father sent out the blessed, ever-living gods one after another, and they went in turn and implored her, and offered her many fine gifts and whatever honors she might choose among the immortal gods. None, however, was able to persuade the heart and mind of the angry goddess. She rejected their speeches firmly, and claimed that she would never set foot upon fragrant Olympus, nor allow any fruit to grow on the earth, until she saw with her eyes the beautiful face of her daughter.

334 When Zeus the loud-crashing, the wide-voiced one, heard this he sent Hermes the slayer of Argos with his golden wand to Erebos, to use smooth words on Hades and lead pure Persephone out of the misty darkness into the light to join the deities, in order that her mother might see her with her eyes and turn from her anger. Hermes obeyed, and eagerly rushed down under the recesses of the earth, leaving the seat of Olympus. He found the Lord inside his house, seated on couches with his modest and very unwilling wife, yearning for her mother. . . .

346 The mighty slayer of Argos came near and said, "Dark-haired Hades ruler of the departed, Father Zeus has ordered me to lead glorious Persephone out of Erebos to join them, in order that her mother might see her with her eyes and cease from her anger and terrible wrath, since she is contriving a tremendous deed, to destroy the fragile race of earth-born men, hiding the seed under the earth and obliterating the honors of the immortals. Her anger is terrible, she has no contact with the gods, but sits apart inside her fragrant temple, holding the rocky citadel of Eleusis."

357 So he spoke, and Aidoneus the lord of the underworld smiled with his brows, and did not disobey the injunctions of Zeus the king. Promptly he gave the command to diligent Persephone: "Go, Persephone, to your dark-clad mother, and keep gentle the strength and heart in your breast. Do not be despondent to excess beyond all others. I shall not be an inappropriate husband for you among the immortals; I am a brother of Father Zeus. Being

there, you will rule over all that lives and moves, enjoying the greatest honors among the immortals. And there shall be punishment forever on those who act unjustly and who do not propitiate your might with sacrifices, performing the pious acts and offering appropriate gifts."

370 So he spoke, and Persephone the discreet was glad, and swiftly leapt up for joy. But he gave her a honey-sweet pomegranate seed to eat, having secretly passed it around [himself?], so that she might not stay forever there by modest dark-clad Demeter, Aidoneus, designator of many, harnessed the immortal horses in front of the golden chariot, and she stepped on the chariot; beside her the mighty slayer of Argos took the reins and a whip in his hands and drove out of the palace. The pair of horses flew willingly. They finished the long journey quickly. Neither sea nor rivers nor grassy glens nor mountain peaks held back the rush of the immortal horses; they went above them, and cut through the high air. He drove them where Demeter of the fair crown waited in front of her fragrant temple, and he stopped them there. Seeing them, she darted up like a maenad in the woods on a thick-shaded mountain.

387 [Demeter asked Persephone if she had eaten anything in the underworld. If not,] "you will come up and dwell with me and Zeus of the dark clouds, and be honored by all the immortals. But if you have tasted anything, then you shall go back down and dwell there for the third part of the season, and for the other two, here with me and the other immortals. Whenever the earth blossoms with all the sweet-smelling flowers of spring, then you will come back up from the misty darkness, a great wonder to gods and to mortal men. But what trick did the powerful host of many use to deceive you?"

405 Persephone, the exceedingly beautiful, gave her this response: "I will tell you, Mother, everything accurately. When the swift slayer of Argos came to me from Father Zeus and the others in heaven with the message to come out of Erebos, so that seeing me with your eyes you might cease from your anger and terrible wrath, I leapt up for joy. But he secretly insinuated a pomegranate seed, honey-sweet food, and though I was unwilling, he compelled me by force to taste it. How he snatched me away through the clever plan of Zeus and carried me off, down into the recesses of the earth, I will tell you and I will go through it all as you ask. We were all there in the lovely meadow—Leukippe Phaino, Elektre, Ianthe, Melite, Iache, Rhodeia, Kallirhoe, Melobosis, Tyche, Okyrhoe of the flowering face, Chryseis, Ianeira, Akaste, Admete, Rhodope, Plouto, charming Kalypso, Styx, Ouranie, lovely Galaxaure, Pallas the inciter of battles, Artemis the shooter of arrows—playing and picking the lovely flowers, a profusion of gentle saffron blossoms, iris, hyacinth, rose birds and lilies, a marvel to see, and narcissus, which the broad land grew like saffron. Full of joy, I was picking them, but the earth under me moved, and the powerful Lord, the host of many, leapt out. And he took me

under the earth on his golden chariot, against my will, and I screamed loudly with my voice. Grieved though I am, I am telling you the whole truth."

434 Then with minds in concord they spent the whole day warming their hearts and minds, showering much love on each other, and her mind found respite from its griefs, as they gave and received joys from each other. And there came near them Hecate of the glistening veil, and she also showered much love on the daughter of holy Demeter, and ever since she has been her attendant and Lady-in-waiting.

441 Zeus the land-crashing, the wide-voiced one, sent fair-haired Rheia as a messenger to them, to bring dark-gowned Demeter among the race of the gods; he promised to give her whatever honors she might choose among the immortal gods. He granted that her daughter should spend the third portion of the year in its cycle down in the misty darkness, but the other two with her mother and the other immortals.

448 So he spoke, and the goddess obeyed the biddings of Zeus. Promptly she darted along the peaks of Olympus, and came to the Rarian plain, the life-bringing udder of plough-land formerly, but at that time not life-bringing at all, as it stood all barren and leafless. The white barley was concealed according to the plans of fair-ankled Demeter, but at this time it was about to grow shaggy with waves of grain as it became spring. In the field the rich furrows were to be loaded with the grain, and they were to be bound in sheaves. Here she first alighted from the boundless aether, and they saw each other gladly, and rejoiced in their hearts.

459 Rheia of the glistening veil said to her, "Come here, child. Zeus the loud-crashing, the wide-voiced one, summons you to come among the race of the immortal gods, and he has promised to give whatever honors you might choose among the immortal gods. He has granted that your daughter will spend the third portion of the year in its cycle down in the misty darkness, but the other two with you and the other immortals. So has he promised, and nodded his head in affirmation. Go, now, my child, and obey; do not be obdurately angry at Zeus of the dark clouds but give prompt increase to the fruit, bringer of life to men."

470 So she spoke, and Demeter of the fair crown obeyed. Promptly she sent up fruit on the rich-soiled fields, and the whole broad land was loaded with leaves and flowers. She went to the royal stewards of the right and to Tripto-lemos, Diokles the driver of horses, mighty Eumolpos and Keleos the leader of the people. She showed the tendance of the holy things and explicated the rites to them all, to Triptolemos, to Polyxeinos and to Diokles—sacred rites, which it is forbidden to transgress, to inquire into, or to speak about, for great reverence of the gods constrains their voice. Blessed of earth-bound men is he who has seen these things, but he who dies without fulfilling the

holy things, and he who is without a share of them, has no claim ever on such blessings, even when departed down to the moldy darkness.

483 When the divine goddess had ordained all this, she went to Olympus among the assembly of the other gods. And there they dwell, sacred and reverent, with Zeus who revels in thunder. Greatly blessed of earth-bound men is he whom they propitiously love: to him they promptly send to the hearth of his great house Ploutos [Wealth], who gives abundance to mortal men.

490 Now, ye that hold the people of fragrant Eleusis, and sea-girt Paros and rocky Antron, Lady mistress Deo, bringer of seasons and glorious gifts, thou thyself and Persephone, the exceedingly beautiful, do ye bestow a heartwarming livelihood in exchange for my song. Now I shall recall thee, and also another song.

● 126

Two Accounts of the Origins of the Worship of the Great Mother at Rome

NOTE: According to several ancient writers, a statue of the Phrygian goddess Cybele, often known as the Great Mother, arrived in Rome in 204 B.C.E., inaugurating her worship in that city.

● 126A

OVID *Fasti* 4.247–348   1st century B.C.E. or 1st century C.E.

AUTHOR, TRANSLATION, AND TEXT: See entry 11.

BIBLIOGRAPHY: Mary Beard, "The Roman and the Foreign: The Cult of the 'Great Mother' in Imperial Rome," in Nicholas Thomas and Caroline Humphrey, eds., *Shamanism, History, and the State* (Ann Arbor: University of Michigan Press, 1994), 164–90; Eugene N. Lane, ed., *Cybele, Attis, and Related Cults: Essays in Memory of M. J. Vermaseren* (Leiden: E. J. Brill, 1996); Ariadne Staples, *From Good Goddess to Vestal Virgins: Sex and Category in Roman Religion* (London and New York: Routledge, 1998).

"Tell me this, too, my work's guide, where she came from.
   Or has she always been in our city?"
"The Mother always loved Dindymus and Cybele,
   Ida's pleasant springs and Ilium's realm.   250
When Aeneas ferried Troy to Italy's fields,
   The goddess almost trailed his sacred ship,
But felt that fate did not demand her godhead yet
   For Latium, and kept her usual haunts.
Later, when mighty Rome had seen five centuries   255

And reared her head above a mastered world,
A priest inspects the Euboean song's fateful words.
    They say the inspection yielded this:
'Your mother is missing. Find your mother, Roman.
    Chaste hands must receive her when she comes.'   260
The dark oracle's riddles baffle the Fathers:
    What mother was missing? What place to search?
Paean is consulted. 'Fetch the Mother of Gods,'
    He says. 'She can be found on Ida's ridge.'
Leaders are sent. Attalus then held Phrygia's sceptre;   265
    He spurns the request of Ausonian men.
I'll sing of marvels. The earth shook and rumbled long,
    And the goddess uttered this from her shrine:
'I wanted this search. Do not delay; I want to go.
    Rome is a worthy place for any god.'   270
Her voice jerked Attalus with fear. 'Depart,' he said;
    'You will still be ours: Phrygian men formed Rome.'

"At once countless axes cut down the pine groves
    Used for the pious Phrygian's escape.
A thousand hands gather. A hollow ship painted   275
    With burnt colours holds the Mother of Gods.
She is freighted through her son's waters most safely,
    And nears the long strait of Phrixus' sister.
She passes wide Rhoeteum and Sigeum's beaches,
    Tenedos and Eëtion's old realm.   280
The Cyclades receive her, with Lesbos left behind,
    Then the waves breaking on Carystos' shoals.
She passed the Icarian sea, where Icarus lost
    His fallen wings and named the vast waters.
Then she leaves Crete to port, Pelops' waves to starboard,   285
    And heads for Venus' sacred Cythera.
Next the Trinacrian sea, where Brontes, Steropes
    And Acmonides dip the white iron.
She skirts Africa's seas and glimpses Sardinia's
    Realm to port and reaches Ausonia.   290

"She had arrived at the mouth where the Tiber
    Splits seaward and swims more unconfined.
All the knights, the grave senate, mingling with the *plebs*,
    Meet her at the mouth of the Tuscan stream.
With them parade mothers, daughters and wives, and those   295
    Whose virginity serves the sacred hearth.
The men tire their arms pulling heartily on the rope;

The foreign ship barely breaks the waves.
The earth had long been dry, drought and charred the grass;
   The loaded ship sat in muddy shoals. 300
All of those at the scene work more than their share
   And encourage the strong rope-men with shouts.
The ship sits like an island fixed in mid-ocean;
   Men stand dumbed by the portent, and quake.
Claudia Quinta traced her line to lofty Clausus, 305
   And her beauty equalled her noble birth.
She was chaste, but not believed. Malicious gossip
   Marred her, indicted on a false charge.
Culture and the display of differing hair-styles
   Told against her, and retorts to old prigs. 310
Her clear conscience mocked rumour's mendacity,
   But we are a mob prone to credit sin.
As she advances from the line of chaste mothers
   And her hands scoop the pure stream water,
She dabs her head thrice, thrice lifts her hands to heaven. 315
   (All those watching consider her witless.)
She kneels, fixes her gaze on the divine image,
   Undoes her hair and delivers these words:
'Gentle Mother, womb of the gods, accept the prayers
   Of your suppliant, on one condition. 320
I'm called unchaste. If you condemn me, I'll confess,
   And forfeit life on a goddess' verdict.
But if the charge is wrong, you will warrant my life
   By action and follow chaste my chaste hands.'
So she spoke and with little effort pulled the rope. 325
   I'll speak of marvels, but the stage attests them.
The goddess is moved and follows her leader, follows
   And lauds her. Sounds of joy rise starward.

"They reach the bend in the river (the ancients called it
   Tiber's Hall), where it veers toward the left. 330
Night came: they tether the rope to an oak tree's stump,
   Eat, and yield their bodies to weightless sleep.
Light came: they untie the rope from the oak tree's stump,
   But first made a hearth and offered incense,
First crowned the ship and sacrificed a flawless 335
   Heifer which knew no labour or sex.
There is a place where gliding Almo meets the Tiber,
   Losing its smaller name in the great river.
Here a silver-haired priest, robed in purple, bathed

> The Mistress and her emblems in Almo's stream.   340
> Her acolytes howl and the maddening flute blows,
>   And dainty hands pound the cowhide drums.
> Claudia advances in a crowd, beaming joy,
>   Finally thought chaste on a goddess' word.
> The goddess rode enthroned in a cart through the Porta   345
>   Capena, her ox-team strewn with fresh flowers.
> Nasica received her. Her shrine's founder is unknown:
>   Augustus now, before him Metellus."

● **126B**

LIVY *Annals of Rome* 29.14   1st century B.C.E. or first century C.E.

AUTHOR, TRANSLATION, AND TEXT: See entry 102.

Although Africa had not been openly assigned as a province, while the senators kept the matter dark, I believe, for fear the Carthaginians might know in advance, nevertheless the people were aroused to hope that the war would be waged that year in Africa, and that the end of the Punic war was at hand. That situation had filled men's minds with superstitious fears and they were inclined both to report and to believe portents. All the greater was the number of them in circulation: that two suns had been seen, and that at night there had been light for a time; and that at Setia a meteor had been seen shooting from east to west; that at Tarracina a city-gate had been struck by lightning, at Anagnia a gate and also the wall at many points; that in the temple of Juno Sospita at Lanuvium a noise was heard with a dreadful crash. To expiate these there was a single day of prayer, and on account of the shower of stones nine days of rites were observed. In addition they deliberated on the reception of the Idaean Mother, in regard to whom not only had Marcus Valerius, one of the ambassadors, arriving in advance, reported that she would be in Italy very soon, but also there was recent news that she was already at Tarracina. It was no unimportant decision that occupied the senate— the question who was the best man in the state. At any rate every man would have preferred a real victory in that contest to any high commands or magistracies, whether conferred by vote of the senators or of the people. Publius Scipio, son of the Gnaeus who had fallen in Spain, was the young man not yet of an age to be quaestor, whom they judged to be the best of good men among all the citizens. If writers who lived nearest in time to men who remembered those days had handed down by what virtues the senate was led to make that judgment, I should indeed gladly hand it on to posterity. But I shall not interject my own opinions, reached by conjecture in a matter buried by the lapse of time. Publius Cornelius was ordered to go to Ostia with all the matrons to meet the goddess, and himself to receive her from the ship, and carrying her to land to turn her over to the matrons to carry. After the ship had reached the mouth of the river Tiber, in compliance with the order he sailed out into open water on a ship, received the goddess from her priests and carried her to land. The foremost matrons in the state, among whom the name of one in particular, that of Claudia Quinta, is conspicuous, received her. Claudia's repute, previously not unquestioned, as tradition reports it, has made her purity the more celebrated among posterity by a service so devout. The matrons passed the goddess from hand to hand in an unbroken succession to each other, while the entire city poured out to meet her. Censers had been placed before the doors along the route of the bearers, and kindling their incense, people prayed that gracious and benignant she might enter the city of Rome. It was to the Temple of Victory, which is on the Palatine, that they carried the goddess on the day before the Ides of April, and that was a holy day. The people thronged to the Palatine bearing gifts for the goddess, and there was a banquet of the gods, and games also, called the Megalesia.

● 127
Imagery of Lactation and Childbearing in a Christian Ode

The Odes of Solomon 19   date uncertain

WORK: Little is known about the authorship or original language of *The Odes of Solomon*, which survive primarily in Syriac. In their present form, they are explicitly Christian and date to the fourth century C.E. or later, although they may have been composed significantly earlier. Of particular interest is their use of feminine imagery for the divine.

TRANSLATION: James H. Charlesworth, in *OTP* 2:725–71.

TEXT: James H. Charlesworth, *The Odes of Solomon* (Oxford: Clarendon Press, 1973).

ADDITIONAL TEXT: Marie-Joseph Pierre (avec la collaboration de Jean-Marie Martin), *Les odes de Solomon* (Turnhout, Belgium: Brepols, 1994).

BIBLIOGRAPHY: Edward Engelbrecht, "God's Milk: An Orthodox Confession of the Eucharist," *JECS* 7 (1999): 509–526; Majella Franzmann, *"The Odes of Solomon": An Analysis of the Poetical Structure and Form*, Novum Testamentum et Orbis Antiquus 20 (Freiburg: Universitätsverlag Göttingen: Vandenhoek and Ruprecht, 1991); Susan Ashbrook Harvey, "Women in Early Syrian Christianity," in Averil Cameron and Amelie Kuhrt, eds., *Images of Women in Antiquity* (Detroit: Wayne State University Press, 1983), 288–98; Susan Ashbrook Harvey, "Feminine Imagery for the Divine: The Holy Spirit, the *Odes of Solomon*, and Early Syriac Tradition," *St. Vladimir's Theological Quarterly* 37, nos. 2–3 (1993): 111–39; Susan Ashbrook Harvey, "*The Odes of Solomon*," in *Searching the Scriptures*, 2:86–98.

1   A cup of milk was offered to me,
and I drank it in the sweetness of the Lord's kindness.

2   The Son is the cup,
and the Father is he who was milked;
and the Holy Spirit is she who milked him;

3   Because his breasts were full,
and it was undesirable that his milk should be released without purpose.

4   The Holy Spirit opened her bosom,
and mixed the milk of the two breasts of the Father.

5   Then she gave the mixture to the generation without their knowing,
and those who have received (it) are in the perfection of the right hand.

6   The womb of the Virgin took (it),
and she received conception and gave birth.

7   So the Virgin became a mother with great mercies.

8   And she labored and bore the Son but without pain,
because it did not occur without purpose.

9   And she did not seek a midwife,
because he caused her to give life.

10   She bore as a strong man with desire,
and she bore according to the manifestation,
and possessed with great power.

11   And she loved with salvation,
and guarded with kindness,
and declared with greatness.

Hallelujah.

⊛ 128

The Female Spirit of the Lord

The Odes of Solomon 36   date uncertain

WORK, TRANSLATION, TEXT, AND BIBLIOGRAPHY: See entry 127.

1   I rested on the Spirit of the Lord,
and she raised me up to heaven;

2   And caused me to stand on my feet in the Lord's high place,
before his perfection and his glory,
where I continued praising (him) by the composition of his odes.

<table>
<tr><td>3</td><td>(The Spirit) brought me forth before the Lord's face,
and because I was the Son of Man,
I was named the Light, the Son of God;</td></tr>
<tr><td>4</td><td>Because I was most praised among the praised;
and the greatest among the great ones.</td></tr>
<tr><td>5</td><td>For according to the greatness of the Most High, so she made me;
and according to his newness he renewed me.</td></tr>
<tr><td>6</td><td>And he anointed me with his perfection;
and I became one of those who are near him.</td></tr>
<tr><td>7</td><td>And my mouth was opened like a cloud of dew,
and my heart gushed forth (like) a gusher of righteousness.</td></tr>
<tr><td>8</td><td>And my approach was in peace,
and I was established in the spirit of providence.</td></tr>
</table>

Hallelujah.

● 129

A Version of the Myth of Isis

PLUTARCH *On Isis and Osiris* 12–19 (*Moralia* 355–58)   1st or 2d century C.E.

NOTE: The Egyptian goddess Isis was worshiped extensively in the Greco-Roman period throughout the Mediterranean world and was frequently identified or associated with various other goddesses, especially Demeter. Women were prominent among her devotees and officiants.

AUTHOR AND TRANSLATION: See entry 16.

TEXT: Teubner (W. Nachstädt, W. Sieveking, J. B. Titchener, 1971, vol. 2, fasc. 3, pp. 1–80).

BIBLIOGRAPHY: *Blessings*, 71–79; F. Dunand, *Le culte d'Isis dans le bassin orientale de la Mediterranée*, 3 vols., EPRO 26 (Leiden: E. J. Brill, 1973); Sharon Kelly Heyob, *The Cult of Isis among Women in the Greco-Roman World*, EPRO 51 (Leiden: E. J. Brill, 1975); Petra Pakkanen, *Interpreting Early Hellenistic Religion: A Study Based on the Mystery Cult of Demeter and the Cult of Isis* (Helsinki: Suomen Ateenaninstituutin säätiö, 1996); Daniel S. Richter, "Plutarch on Isis and Osiris: Text, Cult and Cultural Appreciation," *Transactions of the American Philological Association* 131 (2001): 191–216; Sarolta A. Takacs, *Isis and Sarapis in the Roman World* (Leiden: E. J. Brill, 1995).

12 ... They say that the Sun, when he became aware of Rhea's intercourse with Cronus, invoked a curse upon her that she should not give birth to a child in any month or any year; but Hermes, being enamoured of the goddess, consorted with her. Later, playing at draughts with the moon, he won

from her the seventieth part of each of her periods of illumination, and from all the winnings he composed five days, and intercalated them as an addition to the three hundred and sixty days. The Egyptians even now call these five days intercalated and celebrate them as the birthdays of the gods. They relate that on the first of these days Osiris was born, and at the hour of his birth a voice issued forth saying, "The Lord of All advances to the light." But some relate that a certain Pamyles, while he was drawing water in Thebes, heard a voice issuing from the shrine of Zeus which bade him proclaim with a loud voice that a mighty and beneficent king, Osiris, had been born; and for this Cronus entrusted to him the child Osiris, which he brought up. It is in his honour that the festival of Pamylia is celebrated, a festival which resembles the phallic processions. On the second of these days Arueris was born whom they call Apollo, and some call him also the elder Horus. On the third day Typhon was born, but not in due season or manner, but with a blow he broke through his mother's side and leapt forth. On the fourth day Isis was born in the regions that are ever moist; and on the fifth Nephthys, to whom they give the name of Finality and the name of Aphroditè, and some also the name of Victory. There is also a tradition that Osiris and Arueris were sprung from the Sun, Isis from Hermes, and Typhon and Nephthys from Cronus. For this reason the kings considered the third of the intercalated days as inauspicious, and transacted no business on that day, nor did they give any attention to their bodies until nightfall. They relate, moreover, that Nephthys became the wife of Typhon; but Isis and Osiris were enamoured of each other and consorted together in the darkness of the womb before their birth. Some say that Arueris came from this union and was called the elder Horus by the Egyptians, but Apollo by the Greeks.

13 One of the first acts related of Osiris in his reign was to deliver the Egyptians from their destitute and brutish manner of living. This he did by showing them the fruits of cultivation, by giving them laws, and by teaching them to honour the gods. Later he travelled over the whole earth civilizing it without the slightest need of arms, but most of the peoples he won over to his way by the charm of his persuasive discourse combined with song and all manner of music. Hence the Greeks came to identify him with Dionysus.

During his absence the tradition is that Typhon attempted nothing revolutionary because Isis, who was in control, was vigilant and alert; but when he returned home Typhon contrived a treacherous plot against him and formed a group of conspirators seventy-two in number. He had also the co-operation of a queen from Ethiopia who was there at the time and whose name they report as Aso. Typhon, having secretly measured Osiris's body and having made ready a beautiful chest of corresponding size artistically ornamented, caused it to be brought into the room where the festivity was in progress. The company was much pleased at the sight of it and admired it greatly, whereupon Typhon jestingly promised to present it to the man who should find the chest to be exactly his length when he lay down in it. They all tried it in turn, but no one fitted it; then Osiris got into it and lay down, and those who were in the plot ran to it and slammed down the lid, which they fastened by nails from the outside and also by using molten lead. Then they carried the chest to the river and sent it on its way to the sea through the Tanitic Mouth. Wherefore the Egyptians even to this day name this mouth the hateful and execrable. Such is the tradition. They say also that the date on which this deed was done was the seventeenth day of Athyr, when the sun passes through Scorpion, and in the twenty-eighth year of the reign of Osiris; but some say that these are the years of his life and not of his reign.

14 The first to learn of the deed and to bring to men's knowledge an account of what had been done were the Pans and Satyrs who lived in the region around Chemmis, and so, even to this day, the sudden confusion and consternation of a crowd is called a panic. Isis, when the tidings reached her, at once cut off one of her tresses and put on a garment of mourning in a place where the city still bears the name of Kopto. Others think that the name means deprivation, for they also express "deprive" by means of "koptein." But Isis wandered everywhere at her wits' end; no one whom she approached did she fail to address, and even when she met some little children she asked them about the chest. As it happened, they had seen it, and they told her the mouth of the river through which the friends of Typhon had launched the coffin into the sea. Wherefore the Egyptians think that little children possess the power of prophecy, and they try to divine the future from the portents which they find in children's words, especially when children are playing about in holy places and crying out whatever chances to come into their minds.

They relate also that Isis, learning that Osiris in his love had consorted with her sister through ignorance, in the belief that she was Isis, and seeing the proof of this in the garland of melilote which he had left with Nephthys, sought to find the child; for the mother, immediately after its birth, had exposed it because of her fear of Typhon. And when the child had been found, after great toil and trouble, with the help of dogs which led Isis to it, it was brought up and became her guardian and attendant, receiving the name of Anubis, and it is said to protect the gods just as dogs protect men.

15 Thereafter Isis, as they relate, learned that the chest had been cast up by the sea near the land of Byblus and that the waves had gently set it down in the midst of a clump of heather. The heather in a short time ran up into a very beautiful and massive stock, and enfolded and embraced the chest with its growth and concealed it within its trunk. The king of the country admired the great size of the plant, and cut off the portion that enfolded the chest (which was now hidden from sight), and used it as a pillar to support the

roof of his house. These facts, they say, Isis ascertained by the divine inspiration of Rumour, and came to Byblus and sat down by a spring, all dejection
and tears; she exchanged no word with anybody, save only that she welcomed
the queen's maidservants and treated them with great amiability, plaiting their
hair for them and imparting to their persons a wondrous fragrance from her
own body. But when the queen observed her maidservants, a longing came
upon her for the unknown woman and for such hairdressing and for a body
fragrant with ambrosia. Thus it happened that Isis was sent for and became
so intimate with the queen that the queen made her the nurse of her baby.
They say that the king's name was Malcander; the queen's name some say
was Astartê, others Saosis, and still others Nemanûs, which the Greeks would
call Athenaïs.

16 They relate that Isis nursed the child by giving it her finger to suck instead of her breast, and in the night she would burn away the mortal portions of its body. She herself would turn into a swallow and flit about the
pillar with a wailing lament, until the queen who had been watching, when
she saw her babe on fire, gave forth a loud cry and thus deprived it of immortality. Then the goddess disclosed herself and asked for the pillar which
served to support the roof. She removed it with the greatest ease and cut
away the wood of the heather which surrounded the chest; then, when she
had wrapped up the wood in a linen cloth and had poured perfume upon it,
she entrusted it to the care of the kings; and even to this day the people of
Byblus venerate this wood which is preserved in the shrine of Isis. Then the
goddess threw herself down upon the coffin with such a dreadful wailing that
the younger of the king's sons expired on the spot. The elder son she kept
with her, and, having placed the coffin on board a boat, she put out from
land. Since the Phaedrus river toward the early morning fostered a rather
boisterous wind, the goddess grew angry and dried up its stream.

17 In the first place where she found seclusion, when she was quite by herself, they relate that she opened the chest and laid her face upon the face
within and caressed it and wept. The child came quietly up behind her and
saw what was there, and when the goddess became aware of his presence, she
turned about and gave him one awful look of anger. The child could not
endure the fright, and died. Others will not have it so, but assert that he fell
overboard into the sea from the boat that was mentioned above. He also is
the recipient of honours because of the goddess; for they say that the Maneros of whom the Egyptians sing at their convivial gatherings is this very child.
Some say, however, that his name was Palaestinus or Pelusius, and that the
city founded by the goddess was named in his honour. They also recount
that this Maneros who is the theme of their songs was the first to invent music. But some say that the word is not the name of any person, but an expression belonging to the vocabulary of drinking and feasting: "Good luck be

ours in things like this!", and that this is really the idea expressed by the ex-clamation "maneros" whenever the Egyptians use it. In the same way we may be sure that the likeness of a corpse which, as it is exhibited to them, is car-ried around in a chest, is not a reminder of what happened to Osiris, as some assume; but it is to urge them, as they contemplate it, to use and to enjoy the present, since all very soon must be what it is now and this is their pur-pose in introducing it into the midst of merry-making.

18 As they relate, Isis proceeded to her son Horus, who was being reared in Buto, and bestowed the chest in a place well out of the way; but Typhon, who was hunting by night in the light of the moon, happened upon it. Rec-ognizing the body he divided it into fourteen parts and scattered them, each in a different place. Isis learned of this and sought for them again, sailing through the swamps in a boat of papyrus. This is the reason why people sail-ing in such boats are not harmed by the crocodiles, since these creatures in their own way show either their fear or their reverence for the goddess.

The traditional result of Osiris's dismemberment is that there are many so-called tombs of Osiris in Egypt; for Isis held a funeral for each part when she had found it. Others deny this and assert that she caused effigies of him to be made and these she distributed among the several cities, pretending that she was giving them his body, in order that he might receive divine honours in a greater number of cities, and also that, if Typhon should succeed in over-powering Horus, he might despair of ever finding the true tomb when so many were pointed out to him, all of them called the tomb of Osiris.

Of the parts of Osiris's body the only one which Isis did not find was the male member, for the reason that this had been at once tossed into the river, and the lepidotus, the sea-bream, and the pike had fed upon it; and it is from these very fishes the Egyptians are most scrupulous in abstaining. But Isis made a replica of the member to take its place, and consecrated the phal-lus, in honour of which the Egyptians even at the present day celebrate a fes-tival.

19 Later, as they relate, Osiris came to Horus from the other world and exer-cised and trained him for the battle. After a time Osiris asked Horus what he held to be the most noble of all things. When Horus replied, "To avenge one's father and mother for evil done to them," Osiris then asked him what animal he considered the most useful for them who go forth to battle; and when Horus said, "A horse," Osiris was surprised and raised the question why it was that he had not rather said a lion than a horse. Horus answered that a lion was a useful thing for a man in need of assistance, but that a horse served best for cutting off the flight of an enemy and annihilating him. When Osiris heard this he was much pleased, since he felt that Horus had now an adequate preparation. It is said that, as many were continually trans-ferring their allegiance to Horus, Typhon's concubine, Thueris, also came over-

him; and a serpent which pursued her was cut to pieces by Horus's men, and now, in memory of this, the people throw down a rope in their midst and chop it up.

Now the battle, as they relate, lasted many days and Horus prevailed. Isis, however, to whom Typhon was delivered in chains, did not cause him to be put to death, but released him and let him go. Horus could not endure this with equanimity, but laid hands upon his mother and wrested the royal diadem from her head; but Hermes put upon her a helmet like unto the head of a cow.

Typhon formally accused Horus of being an illegitimate child, but with the help of Hermes to plead his cause it was decided by the gods that he also was legitimate. Typhon was then overcome in two other battles. Osiris consorted with Isis after his death, and she became the mother of Harpocrates, untimely born and weak in his lower limbs.

● 130
The Experiences of a Male Initiate of Isis

APULEIUS *Metamorphoses* bk. 11   2d century C.E.

AUTHOR, TRANSLATION, AND TEXT: See entry 19.

BIBLIOGRAPHY: See entries 19 and 129.

SALVATION, AND CONVERSION TO ISIS

1 A sudden fear aroused me at about the first watch of the night. At that moment I beheld the full moon rising from the sea-waves, and gleaming with special brightness. In my enjoyment of the hushed isolation of the shadowy night, I became aware that the supreme goddess wielded her power with exceeding majesty, that human affairs were controlled wholly by her providence, that the world of cattle and wild beasts and even things inanimate were lent vigour by the divine impulse of her light and power; that the bodies of earth, sea, and sky now increased at her waxing, and now diminished in deference to her waning. It seemed that Fate had now had her fill of my grievous misfortunes, and was offering hope of deliverance, however delayed. So I decided to address a prayer to the venerable image of the goddess appearing before my eyes. I hastily shook off my torpid drowsiness, and sprang up, exultant and eager. I was keen to purify myself at once, so I bathed myself in the sea-waters, plunging my head seven times beneath the waves, for Pythagoras of godlike fame proclaimed that number to be especially efficacious in sacred rites. Then with tears in my eyes I addressed this prayer to the supremely powerful goddess:

2 "Queen of heaven, at one time you appear in the guise of Ceres, bountiful and primeval bearer of crops. In your delight at recovering your daughter, you dispensed with the ancient, barbaric diet of acorns and schooled us in civilized fare; now you dwell in the fields of Eleusis. At another time you are heavenly Venus; in giving birth to Love when the world was first begun, you united the opposing sexes and multiplied the human race by producing ever abundant offspring; now you are venerated at the wave-lapped shrine of Paphos. At another time you are Phoebus' sister; by applying soothing remedies you relieve the pain of childbirth, and have brought teeming numbers to birth; now you are worshipped in the famed shrines of Ephesus. At another time you are Proserpina, whose howls at night inspire dread, and whose triple form restrains the emergence of ghosts as you keep the entrance to earth above firmly barred. You wander through diverse groves, and are appeased by varying rites. With this feminine light of yours you brighten every city and nourish the luxuriant seeds with your moist fire, bestowing your light intermittently according to the wandering paths of the sun. But by whatever name or rite or image it is right to invoke you, come to my aid at this time of extreme privation, lend stability to my disintegrating fortunes, grant respite and peace to the harsh afflictions which I have endured. Let this be the full measure of my toils and hazards; rid me of this grisly, four-footed form. Restore me to the sight of my kin; make me again the Lucius that I was. But if I have offended some deity who continues to oppress me with implacable savagery, at least allow me to die, since I cannot continue to live."

3 These were the prayers which I poured out, supporting them with cries of lamentation. But then sleep enveloped and overpowered my wasting spirit as I lay on that couch of sand. But scarcely had I closed my eyes when suddenly from the midst of the sea a divine figure arose, revealing features worthy of veneration even by the gods. Then gradually the gleaming form seemed to stand before me in full figure as she shook off the sea-water. I shall try to acquaint you too with the detail of her wondrous appearance, if only the poverty of human speech grants me powers of description, or the deity herself endows me with a rich feast of eloquent utterance.

To begin with, she had a full head of hair which hung down, gradually curling as it spread loosely and flowed gently over her divine neck. Her lofty head was encircled by a garland interwoven with diverse blossoms, at the centre of which above her brow was a flat disk resembling a mirror, or rather the orb of the moon, which emitted a glittering light. The crown was held in place by coils of rearing snakes on right and left, and it was adorned above with waving ears of corn. She wore a multicoloured dress woven from fine linen, one part of which shone radiantly white, a second glowed yellow with saffron blossom, and a third blazed rosy red. But what riveted my eyes above all else was her jet-black cloak, which gleamed with a dark sheen as it enveloped her. It ran beneath her right arm across to her left shoulder, its fringe partially descending in the form of a knot. The garment hung down in layers of successive folds, its lower edge gracefully undulating with tasselled fringes.

4 Stars glittered here and there along its woven border and on its flat surface, and in their midst a full moon exhaled fiery flames. Wherever the hem of that magnificent cloak billowed out, a garland composed of every flower and every fruit was inseparably attached to it. The goddess's appurtenances were extremely diverse. In her right hand she carried a bronze rattle; it consisted of a narrow metal strip curved like a belt, through the middle of which were passed a few rods; when she shook the rattle vigorously three times with her arm, the rods gave out a shrill sound. From her left hand dangled a boat-shaped vessel, on the handle of which was the figure of a serpent in relief, rearing high its head and swelling its broad neck. Her feet, divinely white, were shod in sandals fashioned from the leaves of the palm of victory. Such, then, was the appearance of the mighty goddess. She breathed forth the fertile fragrance of Arabia as she deigned to address me in words divine:

5 "Here I am, Lucius, roused by your prayers. I am the mother of the world of nature, mistress of all the elements first-born in this realm of time. I am the loftiest of deities, queen of departed spirits, foremost of heavenly dwellers, the single embodiment of all gods and goddesses. I order with my nod the luminous heights of heaven, the healthy sea-breezes, the sad silences of the infernal dwellers. The whole world worships this single godhead under a variety of shapes and liturgies and titles. In one land the Phrygians, first-born of men, hail me as the Pessinuntian mother of the gods; elsewhere the native dwellers of Attica call me Cecropian Minerva; in other climes the wave-tossed Cypriots name me Paphian Venus; the Cretan archers, Dictynna Diana; the trilingual Sicilians, Ortygian Proserpina; the Eleusinians, the ancient goddess Ceres; some call me Juno, others Bellona, others Hecate, and others still Rhamnusia. But the peoples on whom the rising sun-god shines with his first rays—eastern and western Ethiopians, and the Egyptians who flourish with their time-honoured learning—worship me with the liturgy that is my own, and call me by my true name, which is queen Isis.

"I am here out of pity for your misfortunes; I am here to lend you kindly support. End now your weeping, abandon your lamentation, set aside your grief, for through my providence your day of salvation is now dawning. So pay careful attention to my commands. The day to be born of this night has been dedicated to me in religious observance from time immemorial. Now that the storms of winter are stilled, and the tempestuous waves of the ocean are calmed, the sea is now safe for shipping, and my priests entrust to it a newly built vessel dedicated as the first fruits of our journeys by sea. You are to await this rite with an untroubled and reverent mind.

6 "As the procession forms up, a priest at my prompting will be carrying a garland of roses tied to the rattle in his right hand. So without hesitation part the crowd and join the procession, relying on my kindly care. Then, when you have drawn near, make as if you intend to kiss the priest's hand, and gently detach the roses; at once then shrug off the skin of this most hateful of animals, which has long been abominable in my sight. Do not be fearful and regard any of these commands of mine as difficult, for at this moment as I stand before you I am also appearing to my priest as he sleeps, and am instructing him what to do following this. At my command the close-packed crowds will give way before you. In the midst of the joyous ritual and the jolly sights, no one will recoil from your ugly shape, nor put a malicious complexion on your sudden metamorphosis, and lay spiteful charges against you.

"What you must carefully remember and keep ever locked deep in your heart is that the remaining course of your life until the moment of your last breath is pledged to me, for it is only right that all your future days should be devoted to the one whose kindness has restored you to the company of men. Your future life will be blessed, and under my protection will bring you fame; and when you have lived out your life's span and you journey to the realm of the dead, even there in the hemisphere beneath the earth you will constantly adore me, for I shall be gracious to you. You will dwell in the Elysian fields, while I, whom you now behold, shine brightly in the darkness of Acheron and reign in the inner Stygian depths. But if you deserve to win my divine approval by diligent service, you will come to know that I alone can prolong your life even here on earth beyond the years appointed by your destiny.

7 When she had reached the close of her sacred prophecy, that invincible deity retired to keep her own company. Without delay I was at once released from sleep. With mingled emotions of fear and joy I arose, bathed in sweat, utterly bemused by so vivid an epiphany of the powerful goddess. I sprinkled myself with sea-water, and as I meditated on her important commands, I reviewed the sequence of her instructions. At that moment the clouds of dark night were dispersed, and a golden sun arose. There and then groups of people filled the entire streets, darting here and there in quite exultant devotion. My personal sense of well-being seemed to be compounded by a general atmosphere of joy, which was so pervasive that I sensed that every kind of domestic beast, and entire households, and the very weather seemed to present a smiling face to the world. For a sunny, windless day had suddenly succeeded the previous day's frost, so that even the birds were enticed by the spring warmth to burst tunefully into sweet harmonies, as with their charming address they soothed the mother of the stars, the parent of the seasons, the mistress of the entire world. Why, even the trees, both those fertile with their produce of fruit, and the barren ones content with the provision of

mere shade, expanded under the southerly breezes, and smiled with the budding of their foliage; they whispered sweetly with the gentle motion of their branches. Now that the great din of the storms was stilled, and the waves' angry swell had subsided, the sea quietened and controlled its floods, while the sky dispersed the dark rain-clouds and shone with the cloudless and bright brilliance of its light.

8 And now the outrunners of the great procession formed up to lead the way, each most handsomely adorned in the garb of his choice. One had buckled on a belt, and was playing the soldier; a second had tucked up his cloak, and his high boots and spears identified him as a huntsman; a third was wearing gilded shoes, a silk gown, costly jewellery, and a wig, and was mincing along impersonating a woman; a fourth was conspicuous with greaves, shield, helmet, and sword; you would have thought that he was emerging from a school of gladiators. A fifth who made his appearance was guying a magistrate, with the rods of office and a purple toga; a sixth was pretending to be a philosopher with his cloak and staff, sandals, and a goatee beard. Two others were carrying different types of rod, the one playing the fowler with bird-lime, the other the angler with his hooks. I saw also a tame she-bear dressed up as a matron, being carried along in a chair, and a monkey in the woven cap and saffron garment that Phrygians wear, carrying a golden cup to ape the shepherd-boy Ganymede; and an ass with wings stuck to its shoulders ambling along beside a feeble old man, so that you might have labelled the one Pegasus and the other Bellerophon, and enjoyed a hearty laugh at both.

9 While the participants in these comic diversions for the townsfolk were prancing about here and there, the special procession in honour of the saviour goddess was being set in motion. Some women, sparkling in white dresses, delighting in their diverse adornments and garlanded with spring flowers, were strewing the ground with blossoms stored in their dresses along the route on which the sacred company was to pass. Others had gleaming mirrors attached to their backs to render homage to the goddess as she drew near them, and others with ivory combs gestured with their arms and twirled their fingers as if adorning and combing their queen's tresses. Others again sprinkled the streets with all manner of perfumes, including the pleasing balsam-scent which they shook out in drops. Besides these there was a numerous crowd of both sexes who sought the favor of the creator of the celestial stars by carrying lamps, torches, tapers and other kinds of artificial light. Behind them came musical instruments, pipes and flutes which sounded forth the sweetest melodies. There followed a delightful choir of specially chosen youths clad in expensive white tunics, who kept hymning a charming song composed to music by a talented poet with the aid of the Muses; the theme incorporated chants leading up to the greater votive prayers to follow. In the

procession too were flautists dedicated to the great god Sarapis; the pipes in their hands extended sideways to their right ears, and on them they repeatedly played the tune regularly associated with their temple and its god. There were also several officials loudly insisting that a path be cleared for the sacred procession.

10 Next, crowds of those initiated into the divine rites came surging along, men and women of every rank and age, gleaming with linen garments spotlessly white. The women had sprayed their hair with perfume, and covered it with diaphanous veils; the men had shaved their heads completely, so that their bald pates shone. With their rattles of bronze, silver, and even gold, they made a shrill, tinkling sound. Accompanying them were the stars of the great world-religion, the priests of the cult who were drawn from the ranks of famed nobility; they wore white linen garments which fitted tightly across their chests and extended to their feet, and they carried striking attributes of most powerful deities. Their leader held out a lamp gleaming with brilliant light; it did not much resemble those lanterns of ours which illumine our banquets at night, but it was a golden, boat-shaped vessel feeding quite a large flame from an opening at its centre. The second priest was similarly garbed; he carried in both hands the altar which they call the "altar of help," a name specifically bestowed on it by the providential help of the highest goddess. A third priest advanced, bearing a palm-branch, its leaves finely worked in gold; he carried also the staff of Mercury. A fourth priest exhibited a deformed left hand with palm outstretched, symbolizing justice; since it was impaired by nature and endowed with no guile or cunning, it was thought more suited to represent justice than the right hand. He also carried a small golden vessel rounded like a woman's breast, from which he poured libations of milk. A fifth priest bore a winnowing-fan of gold, fashioned from laurel-twigs, and a sixth carried an amphora.

11 Immediately behind marched gods who deigned to advance on human feet. Here was Anubis, the awesome go-between of gods above and subterranean dwellers; with face part-black, part-golden, tall and holding his dog's neck high, he carried a herald's staff in his left hand, and brandished a green palm-branch in his right. Hard on his heels followed a cow rearing upright, the fertile representation of the goddess who is mother of all; a member of the priesthood held it resting on his shoulders, and he bore it with a flourish and with proud gait. Another carried the box containing the mysteries and concealing deep within it the hidden objects of that august religion. Yet another priest bore in exultant arms the venerable image of the supreme deity. It was not in the shape of a farm-animal or bird or wild beast or the human form itself, but in its ingenious originality it inspired veneration by its very strangeness, for it expressed in a manner beyond description the higher religious faith which has to be cloaked in boundless silence. Fashioned from

gleaming gold, this was a small vase skillfully hollowed out on a perfectly rounded base, with remarkable Egyptian figures fashioned on its outer surface; it had not a high neck, but it projected into a long spout extending into a beak. On its other side a handle was set well back in a broad curve, and above it was an asp coiled in a knot, the striped swelling of its scaly neck rearing high.

12 Suddenly the blessings promised by that most supportive deity came near. A priest approached bearing with him my future fortune and my very salvation. Exactly in keeping with the divine promise, his right hand held an adorned rattle for the goddess and a crown of flowers for me; the crown was fittingly, God knows, a crown of victory, for after enduring countless exhausting toils and after surviving numerous hazards, I was now through the providence of the highest goddess overcoming Fortune, who had grappled with me so fiercely. But though seized with sudden joy, I did not bound forward at an uncontrolled gallop, for obviously I feared that the tranquil course of the ritual would be disturbed by the sudden charge of a four-footed beast. Hesitantly and with subdued steps such as a man might make, I gradually worked my body sideways, and crept slowly nearer as the crowd parted, doubtless at the command of the goddess.

13 What happened next made me realize that the priest recalled the divine message which he had received the previous night. He registered astonishment at how the task laid upon him had materialized; he halted abruptly, stretched out his right hand unprompted, and dangled the garland before my very face. Then in trembling haste (for my heart was beating wildly), I seized with greedy mouth the garland which gleamed with its texture of beautiful roses. I was eager to see the promise fulfilled, so with even greater eagerness I bolted it down. Nor was I cheated of that promise from heaven, for my ugly animal form at once deserted me. First my unsightly bristles disappeared, and then my thick skin thinned out; my fat belly contracted; the soles of my feet extended into toes where the hooves had been; my forefeet became hands equipped for two-footed tasks; my long neck shrank, my face and head became round, my projecting ears resumed their earlier modest shape; my rocklike teeth were restored to human size, and my tail, earlier the chief cause of my distress, totally disappeared.

The crowd stood amazed, and the devotees paid homage to the demonstrable power of the greatest deity and to this wonder-working which corresponded with the visions of the night; aloud and in unison as they raised their hands to heaven they acclaimed this notable kindness of the goddess.

14 As for me, total astonishment rendered me speechless. My mind was unable to contain so sudden and boundless a joy, and I dithered, wondering what it would be best for me to say first, and how I could make first use of my new-found voice; what words I should use to launch auspiciously my

tongue reborn, and how and at what length I should express my thanks to the great goddess. But the priest, who by some divine inspiration was aware of all my calamities from the start, took the initiative, though he too was deeply moved by the extraordinary miracle. With a nod he signalled an instruction to hand me a linen cloth to cover my nakedness, for as soon as the ass had stripped me of his accursed skin, I had jammed my thighs tightly together and placed my hands discreetly over them. So far as a naked man could, I had used nature's resources to cover myself decently. Thereupon one of the consecrated band quickly tore off his upper garment and hastily threw it over me. Then the priest, eyeing my appearance with astonishment, gazed on me indulgently with what I swear was a godlike look, and spoke these words.

15 "Lucius, the troubles which you have endured have been many and diverse. You have been driven before the heavy storms and the heaviest gales of Fortune, but you have finally reached the harbour of peace and the altar of mercy. Your high birth, and what is more, your rank and your accomplished learning have been of no avail to you whatever. In the green years of youth, you tumbled on the slippery slope into slavish pleasures, and gained the ill-omened reward of your unhappy curiosity. Yet somehow Fortune in her blind course, while torturing you with the most severe dangers, has in her random persecution guided you to this state of religious blessedness. So she can now head off and muster her most savage rage in search of some other victim for her cruelty, for hostile chance has no influence over those whose lives our majestic goddess has adopted into her service. Have brigands, or wild beasts, or slavery, or those winding, wholly crippling journeys to and fro, or the daily fear of death been of any avail to Fortune's malice? You have now been taken under the protection of Fortune with eyes, who with the brilliance of her light lends lustre even to the other gods. Show now a happier face in keeping with your white garment, and join the procession of the saviour goddess with triumphal step. Let unbelievers see you, and as they see you let them recognize the error of their ways; for behold, Lucius is delivered from his earlier privations, and as he rejoices in the providence of the great Isis, he triumphs over his Fortune. But to ensure your greater safety under closer protection, enroll in this sacred army to which you were invited to swear allegiance not long ago. Consecrate yourself from this moment to the obedience of our religion, and of your own accord submit to the yoke of service. Once you have begun to serve the goddess, you will then better appreciate the reward of your freedom."

16 This was how that remarkable priest phrased his prophecy. Then he fell silent, showing signs of weariness as he recovered his breath. I then took my place in the sacred procession and walked along, keeping close attendance on the sacred shrine. I was recognized, indeed I was the cynosure of all eyes; the

whole community singled me out with pointing fingers and nods, and gossiped about me: "Today the venerable power of the almighty goddess has restored him to the ranks of men. How happy, how blessed three times over he is! Doubtless through the purity and faith of his former life he has deserved such sovereign protection from heaven, and in consequence he had been in a manner reborn, and has at once pledged himself to the service of her cult."

Meanwhile amid the din of joyous prayers we edged our way slowly forward and drew near to the sea-shore, at that very place where as Lucius-turned-ass I had bivouacked the previous day. There the gods' statues were duly set in place, and the chief priest named and consecrated to the goddess a ship which had been built with splendid craftsmanship, and which was adorned on all its timbers with wonderful Egyptian pictures. Holding a flaming torch, he first pronounced most solemn prayers from his chaste lips, and then with an egg and sulphur he performed over it an elaborate ceremony of purification. The bright sail of this blessed craft carried upon it woven letters in gold, bearing those same petitions for trouble-free sailing on its first journeys. The mast was of rounded pine, gloriously tall and easily recognized with its striking masthead. The stern was curved in the shape of a goose, and gleamed with its covering of gold leaf. In fact the whole ship shone, polished as it was in clear citrus-wood.

Then the entire population, devotees and uninitiated alike, vied in piling the ship high with baskets laden with spices and similar offerings, and they poured on the waves libations of meal soaked in milk. Eventually the ship, filled with generous gifts and propitious offerings, was loosed from its anchor-ropes and launched on the sea before a friendly, specially appointed breeze. Once its progress had caused it to fade from our sight, the bearers of the sacred objects took up again those which each had brought, and they made their eager way back to the temple, following in tidy order the same detail of procession as before.

17 Once we reached the temple itself, the chief priest, those who carried the gods' images, and those previously initiated into the august inner sanctuary were admitted into the chamber of the goddess, where they duly set in place the living statues. Then one of the company, whom they all termed the scribe, stood before the entrance and summoned an assembly of the *pastophori*; this is the name of the sacred college. There from a high dais he first recited from a book formulaic prayers for the prosperity of the great emperor, the senate, the knights, and the entire Roman people; then for sea-travelers and for ships journeying within the bounds of our imperial world. Next he announced in the Greek language and according to Greek ritual the ceremony of the launching of the ships. The applause of the people that followed showed that this speech was well received by all. Then the folk, ecstatic with joy, brought up boughs, branches and garlands, and having kissed the feet

of the goddess (her statue, wrought from silver, was attached to the temple-steps), they departed to their homes. But my enthusiasm did not permit me to separate myself by more than a nail's breadth from that spot, and I gazed intently on the image of the goddess as I pondered my earlier misfortunes.

18 Meanwhile, however, swift Rumour had not been idle or slow in winging her way. She had been prompt in recounting throughout my native region that blessing of the provident goddess which was so worthy of veneration, as well as my own remarkable history. As a result, family friends, household slaves, and my closest blood-relatives dispelled the grief which had afflicted them at the false report of my death, and in raptures of sudden joy they all hastened with various gifts, wishing to set eyes on me at once as one re-turned from the dead to the light of day. I had despaired of ever seeing them again, so I was likewise restored by their presence. I accepted their kind offer-ings with gratitude, for my friends had considerately ensured that I had a generous allowance to cover clothes and living expenses.

19 So I dutifully spoke to each of them, and briefly recounted my earlier hard-ships and my present joys. But then I made my way back to feast my eyes on the goddess, for this gave me the greatest delight. I rented a dwelling within the temple-precinct, and made a temporary home for myself there, devoting myself to the goddess in service as yet unofficial, but associating closely with the priests and constantly worshipping that great deity. No single night, no siesta passed which was not haunted with the vision and advice of the god-dess. By numerous sacred commands she decreed that since I had been so inclined for some time, I should now at last undergo initiation. Though I was eager and willing, a kind of religious fear held me back, for I had carefully enquired about the difficulties of such religious service—the quite demanding abstinence prescribed by the rules of chastity, and the need to control with careful circumspection a life subject to many chance events. So through pon-dering these problems repeatedly I somehow kept postponing a decision, in spite of my enthusiasm.

20 One night the chief priest appeared to me in a dream, offering me an armful of gifts. When I asked the meaning of this, he replied that they had been sent to me as my belongings from Thessaly, and that there had also ar-rived from the same region a slave of mine by the name of Candidus. On awakening I pondered this vision long and repeatedly, wondering what it meant, especially as I was convinced that I had never had a slave of that name. But whatever the prophetic dream portended, I thought that in any case this offering of belongings gave promise of undoubted gain. So I was on tenterhooks, beguiled by this prospect of greater profit as I awaited the morning opening of the temple. The gleaming curtains were parted, and we addressed our prayers to the august image of the goddess. The priest made his rounds of the altars positioned there, performing the liturgy with the cus-

tomary prayers, and pouring from a sacred vessel the libation-water obtained from the sanctuary of the goddess. With the ceremony duly completed, the initiates greeted the dawning of the day, and loudly proclaimed the hour of Prime. Then suddenly the slaves whom I had left at Hypata, when Photis had involved me in those notorious wanderings, appeared on the scene. I suppose that they had heard the stories about me; they also brought back that horse of mine which had been sold to various owners, but which they had recovered after recognizing the mark on its back. This caused me to marvel more than anything else at the perspicacity of my dream, for quite apart from getting confirmation of its promise of profit, by its mention of a slave Candidus it had restored to me my white horse.

21 This event made me perform my diligent service of worship more conscientiously, for these present blessings offered a pledge of hope for the future. Every day my longing to be admitted to the mysteries grew more and more, and I repeatedly greeted the chief priest with the most ardent requests that he should at last initiate me into the secret rites of the sanctified night. But he was in general a sober character, well known for his adhesion to a strict religious routine, and he treated me in the same way as parents often restrain their children's untimely desires. In a gentle and kind way he postponed my pressing request, whilst at the same time calming my agitation with the comforting expectation of a rosier future. He explained that the day on which a person could be initiated was indicated by the will of the goddess, that the priest who was to perform the sacred ritual was chosen by the foresight of that same goddess, and in addition the expenses necessary for the ceremonies were indicated in the same instruction. His advice was that I, like the others, should observe all these rules with reverent patience. It was my duty to take stringent precautions against both over-enthusiasm and obstinacy, avoiding both faults so as not to hang back when summoned, nor to push forward unbidden. Not one individual in his community was so depraved in mind, or so enamoured of death as to undertake that ministry in a rash and sacrilegious spirit, without having received the call individually from his mistress; for that would incur a guilt that spelt death. Both the gates of hell and the guarantee of salvation lay in the control of the goddess. The act of initiation itself was performed as a rite of voluntary death and of salvation attained by prayer; indeed, it was the will of the goddess to select persons when their span of life was complete and they were poised on the very threshold of their final days. Such people could be safely entrusted with the profound mysteries of the sect. By her providence they were in some sense reborn, for she set them back on the course of renewed health. So I too was to submit to heaven's command, even though I had for long been named and designated for that blessed ministry by the notable and manifest favour of the great deity. Like the other worshippers, I should meanwhile abstain from profane and

unlawful foods, to allow myself worthier access to the hidden secrets of that most hallowed religion.

22 Once the priest had pronounced on the issue, I did not mar my allegiance by impatience, but in humble peace and praiseworthy silence I concentrated on performing the service of the sacred cult with diligence for several days. The saving kindness of the powerful goddess did not fail or torture me with lengthy delay, but in the darkness of the night by commands by no means dark she clearly warned me that the day I had always desired had arrived, on which she would bestow on me my greatest ambition. She also explained how much I needed to contribute to pay for the ceremonies; and she appointed Mithras himself, her own high priest, to carry out the ritual, since she said that he was joined to me by some divine conjunction of our stars.

I was invigorated by these and the other kindly commands of the supreme goddess. Before it was fully daylight, I abandoned my bed and hurried straight to the priest's lodging. I met him with a greeting just as he was leaving his chamber. I had decided that I would demand initiation into the sacred rites more insistently than usual because it was now apparently my due. But as soon as he set eyes on me, he anticipated me with the words: "Lucius, how lucky and blessed you are! The worshipful deity honours you so greatly with her kindly favour!" He added: "So why now stand idle there, the cause of your own delay? The day for which you longed in your constant prayers has dawned, when at the divine commands of the goddess with many names you are to be admitted through my agency to the most holy mysteries of our sacred rites." That most genial old man then put his hand in mine, and led me to the portals of that most splendid temple. He performed the task of opening the temple in accord with the solemn ritual, and performed the morning sacrifice. Then from a hidden recess in the shrine he extracted some books headed with unfamiliar characters. Some were in the shapes of every kind of animal, and served as summaries of formulaic phrases. Others were knotted and twisted into wheel-shapes, or intertwined like vine-tendrils at the top, to prevent their being read by inquisitive non-initiates. From these books the priest recited to me the preparations necessary for conducting the initiation.

23 At once I energetically made the necessary preparations regardless of expense. Some I purchased personally, and others through my friends. The priest now told me that the required moment had come, so he led me to the baths close by in company with a group of initiates. First I was ushered into the normal bath. Then the priest first asked for the gods' blessing, and cleansed me by sprinkling water all over me until I was wholly purified. I was then escorted back to the temple. Two-thirds of the day had now elapsed; the priest set me before the very feet of the goddess, and gave me certain secret instructions too sacred to divulge. Then he commanded me openly, for all to

witness, to discipline my pleasures in eating for the ensuing ten days, taking no animal flesh and drinking no wine.

I duly observed these commands with respectful self-discipline. The day now came which was appointed for my promise to the gods, and as the sun bent its course and ushered in the evening, suddenly crowds of initiates gathered from every side, and in accord with ancient custom they each paid me honour with a variety of gifts. Then all the non-initiates were removed to a distance. I was shrouded in a new linen garment, and the priest took my hand and led me into the heart of the sanctuary.

Perhaps the reader's interest is roused, and you are keen to enquire about the ensuing words and actions. I would tell you if it were permitted to reveal them; you would be told if you were allowed to hear. But both your ears and my tongue would incur equal guilt; my tongue for its impious garrulity, and your ears for their rash curiosity. I will not keep you long on tenterhooks, since your anxiety is perhaps motivated by religious longing. So listen, and be sure to believe that what you hear is true. I drew near to the confines of death and trod the threshold of Proserpina, and before returning I journeyed through all the elements. At dead of night I saw the sun gleaming with bright brilliance. I stood in the presence of the gods below and the gods above, and worshipped them from close at hand. Notice, then, that I have referred to things which you are not permitted to know, though you have heard about them. So I shall recount only what can be communicated without sacrilege to the understanding of non-initiates.

24 Morning came, and the rites were completed. I emerged sacramentally clothed in twelve garments. Though the clothing is quite germane to the ritual, there is no bar to my mentioning it, because at the time there were numerous persons present to see it. I took my stand as bidden on a wooden dais set before the statue of the goddess at the very heart of the sacred shrine. The linen garment that I wore made me conspicuous, for it was elaborately embroidered; the expensive cloak hung down my back from the shoulders to the heels, and from whatever angle you studied it, I was adorned all round with multicolored animals. On one side were Indian snakes, and on the other Arctic gryphons begotten by a world beyond this in the shape of winged birds. This garment the initiates call "Olympian." In my right hand I wielded a torch well alight; a garland of glinting palm-leaves projecting like the sun's rays encircled my head. When I was thus adorned to represent the sun and set there like a statue, the curtains were suddenly drawn back, and the people wandered in to gaze on me. Subsequently I celebrated a most happy birthday into the sacred mysteries; there was a pleasant banquet and a gathering of witty guests. There was also a third day of celebration with a similar programme of ceremonies, including a sacred breakfast and the official conclusion to the initiation.

For a few days I lingered on there, for I enjoyed the indescribable pleasure of gazing on the divine statue. I had pledged myself to Isis for the kindness which I could not repay. Finally, however, at the behest of the goddess I wound up my thanks, admittedly not expressed fully, but humbly and as far as my poor abilities allowed, and I prepared my long-delayed journey home. Even then the bonds of my most ardent yearning were hard to break. So finally I crouched before the image of the goddess, and for long rubbed her feet with my cheeks. With rising tears and frequent sobs I addressed her, choking on and swallowing my words.

25 "O holy, perennial saviour of the human race, you are ever generous in your care for mortals, and you bestow a mother's sweet affection upon wretched people in misfortune. No day, no period of sleep, no trivial moment hastens by which is not endowed with your kind deeds. You do not refrain from protecting mortals on sea and land, or from extending your saving hand to disperse the storms of life. With that hand you even wind back the threads of the Fates, however irretrievably twisted. You appease the storms raised by Fortune, and restrain the harmful courses of the stars. The gods above cultivate you, the spirits below court you. You rotate the world, lend the sun its light, govern the universe, crush Tartarus beneath your heel. The stars are accountable to you, the seasons return at your behest, the deities rejoice before you, the elements serve you. At your nod breezes blow, clouds nurture the earth, seeds sprout, and buds swell. The birds coursing through the sky, the beasts wandering on the mountains, the snakes lurking in the undergrowth, the monsters that swim in the deep all tremble at your majesty. But my talent is too puny to sing your praises, and my patrimony is too meagre to offer you sacrificial victims; I have neither the richness of speech, nor a thousand mouths and as many tongues, nor an endless and uninhibited flow of words to express my feelings about your majesty. Therefore I shall be sure to perform the one thing that a pious but poor person can do: I shall preserve your divine countenance and your most holy godhead in the recess of my heart, and there I shall for ever guard it and gaze on it with the eyes of the mind."

This was the sense of my prayer to the highest deity. I then embraced Mithras, the priest who was now my father. I clung to his neck and kissed him repeatedly; I begged him to pardon me for being unable to offer him worthy recompense for such great kindnesses.

26 After remaining for some time prolonging my words of thanks, I eventually parted from him. I hastened by the shortest route to set eyes once more after this long lapse of time on my ancestral home. A few days later the powerful goddess moved me to pack my bags in haste, and to board ship. I set out for Rome, and very quickly arrived safe and sound through the favour of a following wind at the harbour of Augustus. From there I speeded along by

carriage, and on the evening of 12 December I reached the sacred city. After that there was no task which I undertook with greater enthusiasm than my daily prayers addressed to the supreme godhead of queen Isis, who is appeased with the utmost reverence under the title of Campensis, which is adapted from the location of her temple. In short, I became a regular worshipper there, a stranger to the shrine but an adherent of the cult. By now the great sun had completed his year's course through the circle of the zodiac, when the watchful care of the beneficent deity again broke into my sleep to advise me a second time of the need for initiation and sacred ritual. I wondered what she was putting in hand, what coming event she was proclaiming. My surprise was natural, for I believed that my full initiation had been performed long ago.

27 As I debated this religious difficulty in my own mind, and further scrutinized it with the advice of initiates, I became aware of a new and surprising aspect: I had been initiated merely into the rites of the goddess, but had not as yet been enlightened by the sacred mysteries of that great god and highest father of the gods, the unconquered Osiris. The nature of this deity and his cult was closely aligned to, and in fact united with, hers, but there was the greatest difference in the mode of initiation. Hence I ought to consider that I was being asked to become the servant of this great god as well.

The issue did not for long remain undecided, for next night one of the initiates appeared in a dream before me clad in linen garments. He was bearing thyrsus-rods and ivy, and certain objects which must not be revealed. These he set before my household gods, and then settled himself on my chair, and gave notice of a sumptuous religious banquet. To allow me to recognize him by a clear identification-mark, he walked gingerly with hesitant step, for his left heel was slightly misshapen. In view of this clear intimation of the gods' will, the entire cloud of my uncertainty was dispelled. As soon as my early-morning respects to the goddess had been paid, I began to ask each and everyone with the greatest animation whether anyone had a walk as in my dream. Confirmation was forthcoming, for I at once set eyes on one of the *pastophori* who coincided exactly with the vision of the night, not only by the evidence of his foot, but also by the rest of his build and by his dress. I later discovered that he was called Asinius Marcellus, a name quite relevant to my transformation. I approached him there and then; he was well aware of what I was about to say, for he had been already similarly instructed to conduct the initiation. The previous night he had had a vision: while he was adorning the great god with garlands, he had heard from the statue's mouth (this is the means by which Osiris proclaims the future of individuals) that a man from Madauros who was quite poor was being sent to him, and that he must at once initiate him into his divine rites. By the god's providence this man would gain fame in his studies, and the priest himself would obtain a rich reward.

28 This was how I pledged myself to the rite of initiation, but my slender means with which to meet expenses delayed my aspiration. The expense of travel had reduced my modest capital, and the cost of living in Rome greatly exceeded my outgoings in the province. Harsh poverty was therefore the stumbling-block; as the old proverb has it, I was trapped and tortured "twixt axe and altar." None the less, the god continued to put repeated pressure on me. To my great embarrassment there were frequent attempts to cajole me, and finally came the command direct. So I scraped up just enough money by parting with my paltry wardrobe. This had been the specific instruction I received: "If you were embarking on some activity for pleasure, you would certainly not hesitate to part with your shabby clothes; so now that you are embarking on these noble rites, do you hesitate to resign yourself to a poverty which you can never regret?"

Therefore I made the detailed preparations; for a second time I happily confined myself to a meatless diet for ten days, and I also shaved my head. I gained enlightenment in the nocturnal mysteries of the highest god, and now with full assurance I regularly attended the divine services of this kindred religion. It brought the greatest consolation to me during my time abroad, and equally important, it furnished me with a more opulent standard of living. This was not surprising, for I made a little money in the courts by pleading in the Latin language, and was attended by the wind of favouring Success.

29 Only a short time elapsed when I was again confronted by unexpected and quite remarkable commands from the deities, compelling me to undergo yet a third initiation. At this point the concern that gripped me was not trivial; I was quite troubled in mind as with some anxiety I pondered these issues: what was the point of this strange, unprecedented instruction of the gods? I had now undergone initiation a second time, so what was lacking to make it complete? "I suppose," I reflected, "that the two priests performed the ceremony in my case incorrectly or incompletely." I swear that I even began to take a jaundiced view of their good faith. But while I tossed on the tide of such speculation, and was being driven to the point of madness, a kindly apparition of the god in a prophetic utterance at night explained the situation to me.

"You should not be apprehensive at this long series of initiations, or believe that some element has been previously omitted. On the contrary, you should be delighted and overjoyed at this continual favour of the deities. You should glory in the fact that on three occasions you will have a role scarcely granted once to any other mortal, and you can rightly believe that you will be ever blessed as a result of your three inductions. A further sacred initiation is necessary in your case, for as you must now reflect, the garb of the goddess which you donned in the province continues to rest in the temple there. The result is that here at Rome you cannot wear it for worship on feast days; when bidden you cannot appear in the radiance of those blessed vestments. So with joyful heart and at the prompting of the great gods you must be initiated once more, and I pray that this induction may be blessed and auspicious for you, and bring you saving help."

30 In this way the majestic persuasion of the god-sent dream declared what I must do. So without relegating or idly deferring the business, I at once reported the gist of my vision to my priest. Without delay I submitted to the abstemious and meatless diet, and by voluntary abstinence I exceeded the period of ten days laid down by the eternal law. I made generous provision for the initiation, providing all that was required with religious zeal rather than by calculation of my possessions. I swear that I had no regrets whatever about the hardship and expense; there was no reason for such regrets, since the bountiful provision of the gods had now made me comfortably off through the legal fees I was receiving.

Only a few days later Osiris, the god preferred before great gods, highest of the greater deities, greatest of the highest, ruler of the greatest, seemed to bid me welcome during the hours of sleep. He had not transformed himself into any other human shape, but deigned to address me in person with his own august words. He told me not to hesitate to continue as now with my celebrated advocacy in the lawcourts, and not to fear the aspersions of malignant men nettled by the expertise in my legal activities which was attained by strenuous application. So that I should not be one of the rank and file attending to his rites, he appointed me to the college of the *pastophori* and also one of the quinquennial administrators. So I had my head completely shaved once more, and gladly performed the duties of that most ancient college, founded as long ago as the days of Sulla. I did not cover or conceal my bald head, but sported it openly wherever I went.

● 131

The Titles of the Goddess Isis

● 131A

P. *Oxy.* 11.1380   early 2d century C.E.

TRANSLATION AND TEXT: B. P. Grenfels and A. S. Hunt, eds., *The Oxyrhynchus Papyri* (London: Egypt Exploration Fund, 1898–)

BIBLIOGRAPHY: See entry 129.

[I invoke thee, who at Aphrodito]polis [art called] One . . . ; in the House of Hephaestus . . . chmeunis; who at . . . ophis art called Bubastis . . . ; at Letopolis Magna, one . . . ; at Aphroditopolis in the Prosopite nome, fleet-commanding, many-shaped, Aphrodite; Delta, giver of favors; at Calamisis, gentle; at Carene, affectionate; at Niciu, immortal, giver; at Hierasus . . . athroichis; at Momemphis, ruler; at Psochemis, bringer to harbor; at Mylon, ruler . . . ; at Hermopolis, of beautiful form, sacred; at Naucratis, fatherless, joy, savior, almighty, most great; at Nithine in the Gynaecopolite nome, Aphrodite; at Pephremis, Isis, ruler, Hestia; lady of every country; . . . in Asia, worshiped at the three ways; at Petra, savior; at Hypsele, most great; at Rhinocolura, all-seeing; at Dora, friendship; at Stratonos Pyrgos Hellas, good; at Ascalon, mightiest; at Sinope, many-named; at Raphia, mistress; at Tripolis, supporter; at Gaza, abundant; at Delphi, best, fairest; at Bambyce, Arargatis; among the Thracians and in Delos, many-named; among the Amazons, warlike; among the Indians, Maia; among the Thessalians, moon; among the Persians, Latina; among the Magi, Kore, Thapscusis; at Susa, Nania; in Syrophoenicia, goddess; in Samothrace, bull-faced; at Pergamum, mistress; in Pontus, immaculate; in Italy, love of the gods; in Samos, sacred; at the Hellespont, mystic; at Myndus, divine; in Bithynia, Helen; in Tenedos, name of the sun; in Caria, Hecate; in the Troad and at Dindyma . . . , Palentra [?], unapproachable, Isis; at Berytus, Maia; at Sidon, Astarte, at Ptolemaïs, understanding; at Susa in the district by the Red Sea, Sarkounis; thou who expoundest by the fifteen commandments, first ruler of the world; guardian and guide of seas, and Lady of the mouths and rivers; skilled in writing and calculation, understanding; who also bringest back the Nile over every country, the beautiful animal [i.e., cow] of all the gods; the glad face in Lethe; the leader of the muses; the many-eyed; the comely goddess in Olympus; ornament of the female sex and affectionate; providing sweetness in assemblies; the lock of hair [? or bunch of grapes] in festivals; the prosperity of observers of lucky days; Harpocratis [i.e., the darling] of the gods; all-ruling in the processions of the gods, enmity-hating; true jewel of the wind and diadem of life; by whose command images and animals of all the gods, having . . . of thy name, are worshiped; O Lady Isis, greatest of the gods, first of names, Io Sothis; thou rulest over the mid-air and the immeasurable; thou devisest the weaving of . . . ; it is also thy will that women in health come to anchor with men; all the elders at E . . . ctus sacrifice; all the maidens who . . . at Heracleopolis turn[?] to thee and dedicated the country to thee; thou art seen by those who invoke thee faithfully; from whom . . . in virtue of the 365 combined days; gentle and placable is the favor of thy two ordinances; thou bringest the sun from rising unto setting, and all the gods are glad; at the risings of the stars the people of the country worship thee unceasingly and the other sacred animals in the sanctuary of Osiris; they become joyful when they name thee; the . . . daemons become thy subjects; . . . [the next few lines are very fragmentary] and thou bringest decay on what thou wilt and to the destroyed bringest increase, and thou purifiest all things; every day thou didst appoint for joy; thou ... having discovered all the ... of wine providedst it first in the festivals of the gods ...; thou becamest the discoverer of all things wet and dry and cold [and hot], of which all things are composed; thou broughtest back alone thy brother, piloting him safely and burying him fittingly; ... thou didst establish shrines of Isis in all cities for all time; and didst deliver to all men observances and a perfect year; ... thou didst establish thy son Horus Apollo everywhere, the youthful Lord of the whole world and ... for all time; thou didst make the power of women equal to that of men; ... thou hast dominion over winds and thunders and lightnings and snows; thou, the Lady of war and rule, easily destroyest tyrants by trusty counsels; thou madest great Osiris immortal, and deliveredst to every-country ... religious observances; likewise thou madest immortal Horus who showed himself a benefactor ... and good; thou art the Lady of light and flames. ...

● 131B

The Kyme Aretalogy recension, 2d or 3d century C.E.

WORK: Found in Kyme in Asia Minor, this second-century version of the virtues of Isis is probably a Hellenistic revision of an Egyptian hymn extolling the goddess. The first-person format is typical though by no means the only one used in aretalogies. Nothing is known about the person or person who composed the hymn in this form, which attributes to Isis characteristics of Greek deities such as Demeter in addition to her native Egyptian traits.

TRANSLATION: F. C. Grant, *Hellenistic Religions: The Age of Syncretism* (New York: Liberal Arts Press, 1953).

TEXT: W. Peek, *Der Isishymnus von Andros und verwandte Texte* (Berlin: Weidmann, 1930), 123–25.

BIBLIOGRAPHY: See entry 129.

[*Demetrius, son of Artemidorus, and Thraseas, the Magnesian from the Maeander, crave the blessing of Isis. The following was copied from the stele which is in Memphis, where it stands before the temple of Hephaestus:*]

I am Isis; the mistress of every land, and I was taught by Hermes, and with Hermes I devised letters, both the sacred [hieroglyphs] and the demotic, that all things might not be written with the same [letters].

I gave and ordained laws for men, which no one is able to change.
I am eldest daughter of Kronos.
I am wife and sister of King Osiris.
I am she who findeth fruit for men.
I am mother of King Horus.

I am she that riseth in the Dog Star.
I am she that is called goddess by women.
For me was the city of Bubastis built.
I divided the earth from the heaven.
I showed the paths of the stars.
I ordered the course of the sun and the moon.
I devised business in the sea.
I made strong the right.
I brought together woman and man.
I appointed to women to bring their infants to birth in the tenth month.
I ordained that parents should be loved by children.
I laid punishment upon those disposed without natural affection toward
    their parents.
I made with my brother Osiris an end to the eating of men.
I revealed mysteries unto men.
I taught [men] to honor images of the gods.
I consecrated the precincts of the gods.
I broke down the governments of tyrants.
I made an end to murders.
I compelled women to be loved by men.
I made the right to be stronger than gold and silver.
I ordained that the true should be thought good.
I devised marriage contracts.
I assigned to Greeks and barbarians their languages.
I made the beautiful and the shameful to be distinguished by nature.
I ordained that nothing should be more feared than an oath.
I have delivered the plotter of evil against other men into the hands of
    the one he plotted against.
I established penalties for those who practice injustice.
I decreed mercy to suppliants.
I protect [or honor] righteous guards.

With me the right prevails.
I am the Queen of rivers and winds and sea.
No one is held in honor without my knowing it.
I am the Queen of war.
I am the Queen of the thunderbolt.
I stir up the sea and I calm it.
I am in the rays of the sun.
I inspect the course of the sun.
Whatever I please, this too shall come to an end.
With me everything is reasonable.
I set free those in bonds.

The Feminine Divine

457

I am the Queen of seamanship.
I make the navigable unnavigable when it pleases me.
I created walls of cities.
I am called the Lawgiver [Thesmophoros, a classical epithet of Demeter].
I brought up islands out of the depths into the light.
I am Lord [note masculine form] of rainstorms.
I overcome Fate.
Fate harkens to me.
Hail, O Egypt, that nourished me!

● 132
Aspects of Female Divinity in Three Gnostic Texts

WORK: At the end of 1945, two Egyptian peasants from an area called Nag Hammadi stumbled upon an ancient jar containing thirteen Coptic codices that had been hidden for about fifteen hundred years. These codices, often called the Nag Hammadi Library, contain an assortment of works believed to have been read, if not also written, by gnostic Christians no later than the fifth century C.E. Together with the Dead Sea Scrolls found in Israel in 1947, these Coptic translations of Greek originals constitute the most exciting discoveries for the study of ancient religion in this century.

Of particular interest for the study of women's religion is the plethora of female aspects of the divine in these texts, as well as traditions about women as the sources of divine revelation and power. Unfortunately, very little is known about the individuals and communities that produced and transmitted the texts, making the precise correlations between religious language and social reality difficult to determine.

TRANSLATION (OF ALL): J. Robinson, ed., *The Nag Hammadi Library in English* (San Francisco: Harper and Row; Leiden: E. J. Brill, 1977).

ADDITIONAL TRANSLATION: Bentley Layton, *The Gnostic Scriptures: A New Translation with Annotations and Introductions* (Garden City, N.Y.: Doubleday, 1987).

BIBLIOGRAPHY: There is a particularly extensive bibliography on the subject of women and gender in texts usually designated as gnostic: Daniel L. Hoffman, *The Status of Women and Gnosticism in Irenaeus and Tertullian*, Studies in Women and Religion 36 (Lewiston, N.Y.: Edwin Mellen Press, 1995); Karen King, ed., *Images of the Feminine in Gnosticism*, Studies in Antiquity and Christianity (Philadelphia: Fortress Press, 1988); Karen King, *The Origins of Gnosticism* (Princeton: Princeton University Press, forthcoming); Anne McGuire, "Women, Gender, and Gnosis in Gnostic Texts and Traditions," in *Women and Christian Origins*, 257–99; Elaine Pagels, "God the Father/God the Mother," in *The Gnostic Gospels* (New York:

Random House, 1979), 57–83; Michael A. Williams, *Rethinking "Gnosticism": An Argument for Dismantling a Dubious Category* (Princeton: Princeton University Press, 1996); Michael A. Williams, "Uses of Gender Imagery in Ancient Gnostic Texts," in Caroline W. Bynum, Stevan Harrell, and Paula Richman, eds., *Gender and Religion: On the Complexity of Symbols* (Boston: Beacon Press, 1986), 196–227; Michael A. Williams, "Variety in Gnostic Perspectives on Gender," in King, *Images of the Feminine*, 2–22; Frederick Wisse, "Flee Femininity: Antifemininity in Gnostic Texts and the Question of Social Milieu," in King, *Images of the Feminine*, 297–307.

⊕ 132A

Thunder, Perfect Mind

TEXT: FENHC; NHS 11 (G. W. MacRose and D. M. Parrott, 1979).

ADDITIONAL BIBLIOGRAPHY: Anne McGuire, "Thunder, Perfect Mind," in *Searching the Scriptures*, 2:39–54.

> I was sent forth from [the] power,
>> and I have come to those who reflect upon me,
>> and I have been found among those who seek after me.
> Look upon me, you (pl.) who reflect upon me,
>> and you hearers, hear me.
>> You who are waiting for me, take me to yourselves.
> And do not banish me from your sight.
>> And do not make your voice hate me, nor your hearing.
>> Do not be ignorant of me anywhere or any time. Be on your guard!
>> Do not be ignorant of me.
> For I am the first and the last.
> I am the honored one and the scorned one.
> I am the whore and the holy one.
> I am the wife and the virgin.
> I am (the mother) and the daughter.
> I am the members of my mother.
> I am the barren one
>> and many are her sons.
> I am she whose wedding is great,
>> and I have not taken a husband.
> I am the midwife and she who does not bear.
> I am the solace of my labor pains.
> I am the bride and the bridegroom,
>> and it is my husband who begot me.
> I am the mother of my father

and the sister of my husband,
  and he is my offspring.
I am the slave of him who prepared me.
I am the ruler   14   of my offspring.
But he is the one who [begot me] before the time on a birthday.
  And he is my offspring [in] (due) time,
    and my power is from him.
I am the staff of his power in his youth,
  [and] he is the rod of my old age.
  And whatever he wills happens to me.
I am the silence that is incomprehensible
  and the idea whose remembrance is frequent.
I am the voice whose sound is manifold
  and the word whose appearance is multiple.
I am the utterance of my name.

Why, you who hate me, do you love me,
  and you hate those who love me?
You who deny me, confess me,
  and you who confess me, deny me.
You who tell the truth about me, lie about me,
  and you who have lied about me, tell the truth about me.
You who know me, be ignorant of me,
  and those who have not known me, let them know me.

For I am knowledge and ignorance.
I am shame and boldness.
I am shameless; I am ashamed.
I am strength and I am fear.
I am war and peace.
Give heed to me.
I am the one who is disgraced and the great one.

Give heed to my   15   poverty and my wealth.
Do not be arrogant to me when I am cast out upon the earth,
  [and] you will find me in [those that] are to come.
And do not look [upon] me on the dung-heap
  nor go and leave me cast out,
  and you will find me in the kingdoms.
And do not look upon me when I am cast out among those who
  are disgraced and in the least places,
    nor laugh at me.
And do not cast me out among those who are slain in violence.
But I, I am compassionate and I am cruel.
Be on your guard!

Do not hate my obedience
  and do not love my self-control.
In my weakness, do not forsake me,
  and do not be afraid of my power.
For why do you despise my fear
  and curse my pride?
But I am she who exists in all fears
  and strength in trembling.
I am she who is weak,
  and I am well in a pleasant place.
I am senseless and I am wise.

Why have you hated me in your counsels?
For I shall be silent among those who are silent,
  and I shall appear and speak.   16
Why then have you hated me, you Greeks?
  Because I am a barbarian among [the] barbarians?
For I am the wisdom [of the] Greeks
  and the knowledge of [the] barbarians.
I am the judgment of [the] Greeks and of the barbarians.
[I] am the one whose image is great in Egypt
  and the one who has no image among the barbarians.
I am the one who has been hated everywhere
  and who has been loved everywhere.
I am the one whom they call Life,
  and you have called Death.
I am the one whom they call Law,
  and you have called Lawlessness.
I am the one whom you have pursued,
  and I am the one whom you have seized.
I am the one whom you have scattered,
  and you have gathered me together.
I am the one before whom you have been ashamed,
  and you have been shameless to me.
I am she who does not keep festival,
  and I am she whose festivals are many.
I, I am godless,
  and I am the one whose God is great.
I am the one whom you have reflected upon,
  and you have scorned me.
I am unlearned,
  and they learn from me.
I am the one whom you have despised,

and you reflect upon me.
I am the one whom you have hidden from,
    and you appear to me. 17
    But whenever you hide yourselves,
        I myself will appear.
    For [whenever] you [appear],
        I myself [will hide] from you.
Those who have [. . .] to it [. . .] senselessly [. . .].

Take me [. . . understanding] from grief,
    and take me to yourselves from understanding [and] grief.
And take me to yourselves from places that are ugly and in ruin,
    and rob from those which are good even though in ugliness.
Out of shame, take me to yourselves shamelessly;
    and out of shamelessness and shame, upbraid my members in yourselves.
And come forward to me, you who know me and you who know my members,
    and establish the great ones among the small first creatures.
Come forward to childhood,
    and do not despise it because it is small and it is little.
And do not turn away greatnesses in some parts from the smallnesses,
    for the smallnesses are known from the greatnesses.

Why do you curse me and honor me?
You have wounded and you have had mercy.
Do not separate me from the first   18   ones whom you have [known].
[And] do not cast anyone [out nor] turn anyone away
    [. . .] turn you away and [. . . know] him not.
    [. . . him].
    What is mine [. . .].
I know the [first ones] and those after them [know] me.

But I am the mind of [. . .] and the rest of [. . .].
I am the knowledge of my inquiry,
    and the finding of those who seek after me,
    and the command of those who ask of me,
    and the power of the powers in my knowledge
        of the angels, who have been sent at my word,
        and of gods in their seasons by my counsel,
        and of spirits of every man who exists with me,
            and of women who dwell within me.
I am the one who is honored, and who is praised,
    and who is despised scornfully.
I am peace,
    and war has come because of me.

And I am an alien and a citizen.
I am the substance and the one who has no substance.

Those who are without association with me are ignorant of me,
  and those who are in my substance are the ones who know me.
Those who are close to me have been ignorant of me,
  and those who are far away from me are the ones who
    have known me.
On the day when I am close to   19   [you],
  [you] are far away [from me],
[and] on the day when I [am far away] from you,
  [I am close] to you.

[I am . . .] within.
[I am . . .] of the natures.
I am [. . .] of the creation of the [spirits].
[. . .] request of the souls.
[I am] control and the uncontrollable.
I am the union and the dissolution.
I am the abiding and I am the dissolving.
I am the one below,
  and they come up to me.
I am the judgment and the acquittal.
I, I am sinless,
  and the root of sin derives from me.
I am lust in (outward) appearance,
  and interior self control exists within me.
I am the hearing which is attainable to everyone
  and the speech which cannot be grasped.
I am a mute who does not speak,
  and great is my multitude of words.

Hear me in gentleness, and learn of me in roughness.
I am she who cries out,
  and I am cast forth upon the face of the earth.
I prepare the bread and my mind within.
I am the knowledge of my name.
I am the one who cries out,
  and I listen.   20
I appear and [. . .] walk in [. . .] seal of my [. . .].
I am [. . .] the defense [. . .].
I am the one who is called Truth,
  and iniquity [. . .].

You honor me [. . .] and you whisper against [me].
[. . .] victorious over them.

Judge them before they give judgment against you,
   because the judge and partiality exist in you.
If you are condemned by this one, who will acquit you?
   Or if you are acquitted by him, who will be able to detain you?
For what is inside of you is what is outside of you,
   and the one who fashions you on the outside
      is the one who shaped the inside of you.
   And what you see outside of you,
      you see inside of you;
      it is visible and it is your garment.
Hear me, you hearers,
   and learn of my words, you who know me.
I am the hearing that is attainable to everything;
   I am the speech that cannot be grasped.
I am the name of the sound
   and the sound of the name.
I am the sign of the letter
   and the designation of the division.
And I [. . .].
[. . .]   21   light [. . .].
[. . .] hearers [. . .] to you
[. . .] the great power.
And [. . .] will not move the name.
[. . .] to the one who created me.
   And I will speak his name.

Look then at his words
   and all the writings which have been completed.
Give heed then, you hearers
   and you also, the angels and those who have been sent,
   and you spirits who have arisen from the dead.
For I am the one who alone exists,
   and I have no one who will judge me.

For many are the pleasant forms which exist in
   numerous sins,
   and incontinencies,
   and disgraceful passions,
   and fleeting pleasures,
      which (men) embrace until they become sober
      and go up to their resting-place.
And they will find me there,
   and they will live,
   and they will not die again.

● 132B

The Thought of Norea

TEXT: FENHC; NHS 15 (S. Giverson and B. A. Pearson, 1981).

ADDITIONAL BIBLIOGRAPHY: Karen L. King, "The Book of Norea, Daughter of Eve," in *Searching the Scriptures*, 2:66–85; Reimund Leicht, "Gnostic Myth in Jewish Galb: Niriyah (Norea), Noah's Bride," *JJS* 51 (2000): 133–40.

> Father of the All, [Ennoia] of the Light, Nous [dwelling] in the heights above the (regions) below, Light dwelling [in the] heights,
>
>> Voice of Truth, upright Nous, untouchable Logos, and [ineffable] Voice, [incomprehensible] Father!
>
> It is Norea who [cries out] to them. They [heard], (and) they received her into her place forever. They gave it to her in the Father of Nous, Adamas, as well as the voice of the Holy Ones, 28 in order that she might rest in the ineffable Epinoia, in order that (she) might inherit the first mind which (she) had received, and that (she) might rest in the divine Autogenes, and that she (too) might generate herself, just as he himself [has] inherited the [living] Logos, and that she might be joined to all of the Imperishable Ones, and [speak] with the mind of the Father.
>
> And [again], speaking with words of [Life], (she) remained in the [presence] of the Exalted One, [possessing that] which she had received before the world came into being. [She has] the [great mind] of the Invisible One, [and she gives] glory to (her) Father, [and she] dwells within those who [. . .] within the Pleroma, [and] she beholds the Pleroma.
>
> There will be days when she will [behold] the Pleroma, and she will not be in deficiency, for she has the four holy helpers who intercede on her behalf with the Father of the All, Adamas, the one 29 who is within all of the Adams that possess the thought of Norea, who speaks concerning the two names which create a single name.

● 132C

The Hypostasis of the Archons; or, The Reality of the Rulers

TEXT: FENCH; NHS 20 (B. Layton, 1988); Roger Aubrey Bullard, *The Hypostasis of the Archons: The Coptic Text with Translation and Commentary* (Berlin: De Gruyter, 1970).

> On account of the reality (hypostasis) of the Authorities, (inspired) by the Spirit of the Father of Truth, the great apostle—referring to the "authorities of the darkness" (Colossians 1:13)—told us that "our contest is not against flesh and [blood]; rather, the authorities of the universe and the spirits of

wickedness" (Ephesians 6: 12). [I have] sent (you) this because you (sing.) inquire about the reality [of the] Authorities.

Their chief is blind; [because of his] Power and his ignorance [and his] arrogance he said, with his [Power], "It is I who am God; there is none [apart from me]."

When he said this, he sinned against [the Entirety]. And this speech got up 87 to Incorruptibility; then there was a voice that came forth from Incorruptibility, saying, "You are mistaken, Samael—which is, "god of the blind."

His thoughts became blind. And, having expelled his Power—that is, the blasphemy he had spoken—he pursued it down to Chaos and the Abyss, his mother, at the instigation of Ristis Sophia (Faith-Wisdom). And she established each of his offspring in conformity with its power—after the pattern of the realms that are above, for by starting from the invisible world the visible world was invented.

As Incorruptibility looked down into the region of the Waters, her Image appeared in the Waters; and the Authorities of the Darkness became enamored of her. But they could not lay hold of that Image, which had appeared to them in the Waters, because of their weakness—since beings that merely possess a soul cannot lay hold of those that possess a Spirit—; for they were from Below, while it was from Above.

This is the reason why "Incorruptibility looked down into the region (etc.)": so that, by the Father's will, she might bring the Entirety into union with the Light. The Rulers (Archons) laid plans and said, "Come, let us create a man that will be soil from the earth." They modelled their creature as one wholly of the earth.

Now the Rulers . . . body . . . they have . . . female . . . is . . . face(s) . . . are . . . bestial . . . They took some [soil] from the earth and modelled their [Man], after their body and [after the Image] of God that had appeared [to them] in the Waters.

They said, "[Come, let] us lay hold of it by means of the form that we have modelled, [so that] it may see its male counterpart [. . .], 88 and we may seize it with the form that we have modelled"—not understanding the force of God, because of their powerlessness. And he breathed into his face; and the Man came to have a soul (and remained) upon the ground many days. But they could not make him arise because of their powerlessness. Like storm winds they persisted (in blowing), that they might try to capture that image, which had appeared to them in the Waters. And they did not know the identity of its power.

Now all these (events) came to pass by the will of the Father of the Entirety. Afterwards, the Spirit saw the soul-endowed Man upon the ground. And the

Spirit came forth from the Adamantine Land; it descended and came to dwell within him, and that Man became a living soul.

It called his name Adam since he was found moving upon the ground. A voice came forth from Incorruptibility for the assistance of Adam; and the Rulers gathered together all the animals of the earth and all the birds of heaven and brought them in to Adam to see what Adam would call them, that he might give a name to each of the birds and all the beasts.

They took Adam [and] put him in the Garden, that he might cultivate [it] and keep watch over it. And the Rulers issued a command to him, saying, "From [every] tree in the Garden shall you (sing.) eat; yet—[from] the tree of recognizing good and evil do not eat, nor [touch] it; for the day you (pl.) eat [from] it, with death you (pl.) are going to die."

They [. . .] this. They do not understand what [they have said] to him; rather, by the Father's will, 89 they said this in such a way that he might (in fact) eat, and that Adam might (not) regard them as would a man of an exclusively material nature.

The Rulers took counsel with one another and said, "Come, let us cause a deep sleep to fall upon Adam." And he slept.—Now the deep sleep that they "caused to fall upon him, and he slept" is Ignorance.—They opened his side like a living Woman. And they built up his side with some flesh in place of her, and Adam came to be endowed only with soul.

And the spirit-endowed Woman came to him and spoke with him, saying "Arise, Adam." And when he saw her, he said, "It is you who have given me life; you will be called 'Mother of the Living.'—For it is she who is my mother. It is she who is the Physician, and the Woman, and She Who Has Given Birth."

Then the Authorities came up to their Adam. And when they saw his female counterpart speaking with him, they became agitated with great agitation; and they became enamored of her. They said to one another, "Come, let us sow our seed in her," and they pursued her. And she laughed at them for their witlessness and their blindness; and in their clutches, she became a tree, and left before them her shadowy reflection resembling herself; and they defiled [it] foully.—And they defiled the form that she had stamped in her likeness, so that by the form they had modelled, together with [their] (own) image, they made themselves liable to condemnation.

Then the Female Spiritual Principle came [in] the Snake, the Instructor; and it taught [them], saying, "What did he [say to] you (pl.)? Was it, 'From every tree in the Garden shall you (sing.) eat; yet—from [the tree] 90 of recognizing evil and good do not eat'?"

The carnal Woman said, "Not only did he say 'Do not eat,' but even 'Do not touch it; for the day you (pl.) eat from it, with death you (pl.) are going to die."

And the Snake, the Instructor, said, "With death you (pl.) shall not die; for it was out of jealousy that he said this to you (pl.). Rather your (pl.) eyes shall open and you (pl.) shall come to be like gods, recognizing evil and good." And the Female Instructing Principle was taken away from the Snake, and she left it behind merely a thing of the earth.

And the carnal Woman took from the tree and ate; and she gave to her husband as well as herself; and these beings that possessed only a soul, ate. And their imperfection became apparent in their lack of Acquaintance; and they recognized that they were naked of the Spiritual Element, and took fig leaves and bound them upon their loins.

Then the chief Ruler came; and he said, "Adam! Where are you?"—for he did not understand what had happened.

And Adam said, "I heard your voice and was afraid because I was naked; and I hid."

The Ruler said, "Why did you (sing.) hide, unless it is because you (sing.) have eaten from the tree from which alone I commanded you (sing.) not to eat? And you (sing.) have eaten!"

Adam said, "The Woman that you gave me, [she gave] to me and I ate." And the arrogant Ruler cursed the Woman.

The Woman said, "It was the Snake that led me astray and I ate." [They turned] to the Snake and cursed its shadowy reflection, [. . .] powerless, not comprehending [that] it was a form they themselves had modelled. From that day 91 the Snake came to be under the curse of the Authorities; until the All-powerful Man was to come that curse fell upon the Snake.

They turned to their Adam and took him and expelled him from the Garden along with his wife; for they have no blessing, since they too are beneath the curse.

Moreover they threw Mankind into great distraction and into a life of toil so that their Mankind might be occupied by worldly affairs, and might not have the opportunity of being devoted to the Holy Spirit.

Now afterwards, she bore Cain, their son; and Cain cultivated the land. Thereupon he knew his wife; again becoming pregnant, she bore Abel; and Abel was a herdsman of sheep. Now Cain brought in from the crops of his field, but Abel brought in an offering (from) among his lambs. God looked upon the votive offerings of Abel; but he did not accept the votive offerings of Cain. And carnal Cain pursued Abel his brother.

And God said to Cain, "Where is Abel your brother?"

He answered, saying, "Am I, then, my brother's keeper?"

God said to Cain, "Listen! The voice of your brother's blood is crying up to me! You have sinned with your mouth. It will return to you: anyone who kills Cain will let loose seven vengeances, and you will exist groaning and trembling upon the earth."

And Adam [knew] his female counterpart Eve, and she became pregnant, and bore [Seth] to Adam. And she said, "I have borne [another] man through God, in place [of Abel]."

Again Eve became pregnant, and she bore [Norea]. And she said, "He has begotten on [me a] virgin 92 as an assistance [for] many generations of mankind." She is the virgin whom the Forces did not defile.

Then Mankind began to multiply and improve.

The Rulers took counsel with one another and said, "Come, let us cause a deluge with our hands and obliterate all flesh, from man to beast."

But when the Ruler of the Forces came to know of their decision, he said to Noah, "Make yourself an ark from some wood that does not rot and hide in it—you and your children and the beasts and the birds of heaven from small to large—and set it upon Mount Sir."

Then Orea came to him wanting to board the ark. And when he would not let her, she blew upon the ark and caused it to be consumed by fire. Again he made the ark, for a second time.

The Rulers went to meet her intending to lead her astray. Their supreme chief said to her, "Your mother Eve came to us."

But Norea turned to them and said to them, "It is you who are the Rulers of the Darkness; you are accursed. And you did not know my mother; instead it was your female counterpart that you knew. For I am not your descendant; rather it is from the World Above that I am come."

The arrogant Ruler turned, with all his might, [and] his countenance came to be like (a) black [. . .]; he said to her presumptuously, "You must render service to us, [as did] also your mother Eve; for . . . [. . .]."

But Norea turned, with the might of [. . .]; and in a loud voice [she] cried out [up to] the Holy One, the God of the Entirety, 93 "Rescue me from the Rulers of Unrighteousness and save me from their clutches—forthwith!"

The (Great) Angel came down from the heavens and said to her, "Why are you crying up to God? Why do you act so boldly towards the Holy Spirit?"

Norea said, "Who are you?"

The Rulers of Unrighteousness had withdrawn from her. He said, "It is I who am Eleleth, Sagacity, the Great Angel, who stands in the presence of the Holy Spirit. I have been sent to speak with you and save you from the grasp of the Lawless. And I shall teach you about your Root."

—Now as for that angel, I cannot speak of his power: his appearance is like fine gold and his raiment is like snow. No, truly, my mouth cannot bear to speak of his power and the appearance of his face!

Eleleth, the Great Angel, spoke to me. "It is I," he said, "who am Understanding. I am one of the Four Light-givers, who stand in the presence of the Great Invisible Spirit. Do you think these Rulers have any power over you (sing.)? None of them can prevail against the Root of Truth; for on its account he appeared in the final ages (text corrupt); and these Authorities will be restrained. And these Authorities cannot defile you and that generation; for your (pl.) abode is in Incorruptibility, where the Virgin Spirit dwells, who is superior to the Authorities of Chaos and to their universe."

But I said, "Sir, teach me about the [faculty of] these Authorities—[how] did they come into being, and by what kind of genesis, [and] of 94 what material, and who created them and their force?"

And the Great Angel Eleleth, Understanding, spoke to me: "Within limitless realms dwells Incorruptibility. Sophia, who is called Pistis, wanted to create something, alone without her consort; and her product was a celestial thing.

"A veil exists between the World Above and the realms that are below; and Shadow came into being beneath the veil; and that Shadow became Matter; and that Shadow was projected apart. And what she had created became a product in the Matter, like an aborted fetus. And it assumed a plastic form molded out of Shadow, and became an arrogant beast resembling a lion." It was androgynous, as I have already said, because it was from Matter that it derived.

"Opening his eyes he saw a vast quantity of Matter without limit; and he became arrogant, saying, 'It is I who am God, and there is none other apart from me.'

"When he said this, he sinned against the Entirety. And a voice came forth from above the realm of absolute power, saying, 'You are mistaken, Samael—which is, 'god of the blind.'

"And he said, 'If any other thing exists before me, let it become visible to me!' And immediately Sophia stretched forth her finger and introduced Light into Matter; and she pursued it down to the region of Chaos. And she returned up [to] her light; once again Darkness [. . .] Matter.

"This Ruler, by being androgynous, made himself a vast realm, 95 an extent without limit. And he contemplated creating offspring for himself, and created for himself seven offspring, androgynous just like their parent.

"And he said to his offspring, 'It is I who am the god of the Entirety.'

"And Zoe (Life), the daughter of Pistis Sophia, cried out and said to him, 'You are mistaken, Sakla!'—for which the alternate name is Yaltabaoth. She breathed into his face, and her breath became a fiery angel for her; and that angel bound Yaldabaoth and cast him down into Tartaros below the Abyss.

"Now when his offspring Sabaoth saw the force of that angel, he repented and condemned his father and his mother Matter.

"He loathed her, but he sang songs of praise up to Sophia and her daughter Zoe. And Sophia and Zoe caught him up and gave him charge of the seventh heaven, below the veil between Above and Below. And he is called 'God of the Forces, Sabaoth,' since he is up above the Forces of Chaos, for Sophia established him.

"Now when these (events) had come to pass, he made himself a huge four-faced chariot of cherubim, and infinitely many angels to act as ministers, and also harps and lyres.

"And Sophia took her daughter Zoe and had her sit upon his right to teach him about the things that exist in the Eighth (Heaven); and the Angel [of] Wrath she placed upon his left. [Since] that day, [his right] has been called 96 Life; and the left has come to represent the unrighteousness of the realm of absolute power above. It was before your (sing.) time that they came into being (text corrupt?).

"Now when Yaldabaoth saw him in this great splendor and at this height, he envied him; and the envy became an androgynous product; and this was the origin of Envy. And Envy engendered Death; and Death engendered his off-spring and gave each of them charge of its heaven; and all the heavens of Chaos became full of their multitudes.

"But it was by the will of the Father of the Entirety that they all came into being—after the pattern of all the things Above—so that the sum of Chaos might be attained.

"There, I have taught you (sing.) about the pattern of the Rulers; and the Matter in which it was expressed; and their parent; and their universe."

But I said, "Sir, am I also from their Matter?"

—"You, together with your offspring, are from the Primeval Father; from Above, out of the imperishable Light, their souls are come. Thus the Authorities cannot approach them because of the Spirit of Truth present within them; and all who have become acquainted with this Way exist deathless in the midst of dying Mankind. Still that Sown Element will not become known now.

"Instead, after three generations it will come to be known, and free them from the bondage of the Authorities' error."

Then I said, "Sir, how much longer?"

He said to me, "Until the moment when the True Man, within a modelled form, reveals (?) the existence of [the Spirit of] Truth, which the Father has sent. 97

"Then he will teach them about every thing: And he will anoint them with the unction of Life eternal, given him from the undominated generation.

"Then they will be freed of blind thought: And they will trample under foot Death, which is of the Authorities: And they will ascend into the limitless Light, where this Sown Element belongs.

"Then the Authorities will relinquish their ages: And their angels will weep over their destruction: And their demons will lament their death.

"Then all the Children of the Light will be truly acquainted with the Truth and their Root, and the Father of the Entirety and the Holy Spirit: They will all say with a single voice, 'The Father's truth is just, and the Son presides over the Entirety': And from everyone unto the ages of ages, 'Holy—Holy—Holy! Amen!' "

The Reality
of the Rulers

⊛ 133

The Fall and Deliverance of the Soul, Which Is Feminine

The Exegesis on the Soul   3d century C.E.? (c.a. 200?)

WORK AND TRANSLATION: See entry 132.

TEXT: *FEHNC*; NHS 20, vol. 2 (B. Layton, 1989); J. M. Sevrin, *L'exégèse de l'âme*, Bibliothèque copte de Nag Hammadi (Quebec, 1983); Maddalena Scopello, *L'exégèse de l'âme: Nag Hammadi codex II, 6—introduction, traduction, et commentaire*, NHS 25 (1985).

Wise men of old gave the soul a feminine name. Indeed she is female in her nature as well. She even has her womb.

As long as she was alone with the Father, she was virgin and in form androgynous. But when she fell down into a body and came to this life, then she fell into the hands of many robbers. And the wanton creatures passed her from one to another and [. . .] her. Some made use of her [by force], while others did so by seducing her with a gift. In short, they defiled her, and she [. . .] 128 virginity.

And in her body she prostituted herself and gave herself to one and all, considering each one she was about to embrace to be her husband. When she had given herself to wanton, unfaithful adulterers, so that they might make use of her, then she sighed deeply and repented. But even when she turns her face from those adulterers, she runs to others and they compel her to live with them and render service to them upon their bed, as if they were her masters. Out of shame she no longer dares to leave them, whereas they deceive her for a long time, pretending to be faithful, true husbands, as if they greatly respected her. And after all this they abandon her and go.

She then becomes a poor desolate widow, without help; not even a measure of food was left her from the time of her affliction. For from them she gained nothing except the defilements they gave her while they had sexual intercourse with her. And her offspring by the adulterers are dumb, blind, and sickly. They are feeble-minded.

But when the Father who is above visits her and looks down upon her and sees her sighing—with her sufferings and disgrace—and repenting of the prostitution in which she engaged, and when she begins to call upon [his name] so that he might help her, [. . .] all her heart, saying, "Save me, my Father, for behold I will render an account [to thee, for I] abandoned my house and 129 fled from my maiden's quarters. Restore me to thyself again." When he sees her in such a state, then he will count her worthy of his mercy upon her, for many are the afflictions that have come upon her because she abandoned her house.

Now concerning the prostitution of the soul the Holy Spirit prophesies in many places. For he said in the prophet Jeremiah (3:1–4),

> If the husband divorces his wife and she goes and takes another man, can she return to him after that? Has not that woman utterly defiled herself? "And you (sing.) prostituted yourself to many shepherds and you returned to me!" said the Lord. "Take an honest look and see where you prostituted yourself. Were you not sitting in the streets defiling the land with your acts of prostitution and your vices? And you took many shepherds for a stumbling block for yourself. You became shameless with everyone. You did not call on me as kinsman or as father or author of your virginity."

Again it is written in the prophet Hosea (2:2–7),

> Come, go to law with your (pl.) mother, for she is not to be a wife to me nor I a husband to her. I shall remove her prostitution from my presence, and I shall remove her adultery from between her breasts. I shall make her naked as on the day she was born, and I [shall] make her desolate like a land without [water], and I shall make her [longingly] childless. [I] shall show her children no pity, for they are children of prostitution, since their mother prostituted herself and [put her children to shame]. 130 For she said, "I shall prostitute myself to my lovers. It was they who gave me my bread and my water and my garments and my clothes and my wine and my oil and everything I needed." Therefore behold I shall shut them up so that she shall not be able to run after her

adulterers. And when she seeks them and does not find them, she will say, "I shall return to my former husband, for in those days I was better off than now."

Again he said in Ezekiel (16:23–26),

It came to pass after much depravity, said the Lord, you built yourself a brothel and you made yourself a beautiful place in the streets. And you built yourself brothels on every lane, and you wasted your beauty, and you spread your legs in every alley, and you multiplied your acts of prostitution. You prostituted yourself to the sons of Egypt, those who are your neighbors, men great of flesh.

But what does "the sons of Egypt, men great of flesh" mean if not the domain of the flesh and the perceptible realm and the affairs of the earth, by which the soul has become defiled here, receiving bread from them, as well as wine, oil, clothing, and the other external nonsense surrounding the body—the things she thinks she needs.

But as to this prostitution the apostles of the Savior commanded (cf. Acts 15: 20, 29; 21:25; 1 Thessalonians 4:3; 1 Corinthians 6:18; 2 Corinthians 7:1),

Guard yourselves against it, purify yourselves from it,

speaking not just of the prostitution of the body but especially of that of the soul. For this [reason] the apostles [write to the churches] of God, that such [prostitution] might not occur among [us].

Yet the greatest [struggle] has to do with the prostitution 131 of the soul. From it arises the prostitution of the body as well. Therefore Paul, writing to the Corinthians (1 Corinthians 5:9), said,

I wrote you in the letter, "Do not associate with prostitutes," not at all (meaning) the prostitutes of this world or the greedy or the thieves or the idolators, since then you would have to go out from the world.

—here he is speaking spiritually—

For our struggle is not against flesh and blood—as he said (Ephesians 6: 12)—but against the world rulers of this darkness and the spirits of wickedness.

As long as the soul keeps running about everywhere copulating with whomever she meets and defiling herself, she exists suffering her just deserts. But when she perceives the straits she is in and weeps before the Father and repents, then the Father will have mercy on her and he will make her womb turn from the external domain and will turn it again inward, so that the soul will regain her proper character. For it is not so with a woman. For the womb of the body is inside the body like the other internal organs, but the womb of the soul is around the outside like the male genitalia, which are external.

So when the womb of the soul, by the will of the Father, turns itself inward, it is baptized and is immediately cleansed of the external pollution which was pressed upon it, just as [garments, when] dirty, are put into the [water and] turned about until their dirt is removed and they become clean. And so the cleansing of the soul is to regain the [newness] 132 of her former nature and to turn herself back again. That is her baptism.

Then she will begin to rage at herself like a woman in labor, who writhes and rages in the hour of delivery. But since she is female, by herself she is powerless to beget a child. From heaven the Father sent her her man, who is her brother, the first-born. Then the bridegroom came down to the bride. She gave up her former prostitution and cleansed herself of the pollutions of the adulterers, and she was renewed so as to be a bride. She cleansed herself in the bridal chamber; she filled it with perfume; she sat in it waiting for the true bridegroom. No longer does she run about the market place, copulating with whomever she desires, but she continued to wait for him—(saying) "When will he come?"—and to fear him, for she did not know what he looked like: she no longer remembers since the time she fell from her Father's house. But by the will of the Father (. . .). And she dreamed of him like a woman in love with a man.

But then the bridegroom, according to the Father's will, came down to her into the bridal chamber, which was prepared. And he decorated the bridal chamber.

For since that marriage is not like the carnal marriage, those who are to have intercourse with one another will be satisfied with that intercourse. And as if it were a burden they leave behind them the annoyance of physical desire and they do not [separate from] each other, but this marriage [. . .], but [once] they unite [with one another], they become a single life. 133 Wherefore the prophet said (Genesis 2:24) concerning the first man and the first woman,

They will become a single flesh.

For they were originally joined to one another when they were with the Father before the woman led astray the man, who is her brother. This marriage has brought them back together again and the soul has been joined to her true love, her real master, as it is written (cf. Genesis 3:16; 1 Corinthians 11:1, Ephesians 5:23),

For the master of the woman is her husband.

Then gradually she recognized him, and she rejoiced once more, weeping before him as she remembered the disgrace of her former widowhood. And she adorned herself still more so that he might be pleased to stay with her.

And the prophet said in the Psalms (45:10–11),

Hear, my daughter, and see and incline your ear and forget your people and your father's house, for the king has desired your beauty, for he is your lord.

For he requires her to turn her face from her people and the multitude of her adulterers, in whose midst she once was, to devote herself only to her king, her real lord, and to forget the house of the earthly father, with whom things went badly for her, but to remember her Father who is in the heavens. Thus also it was said (Genesis 12:1) to Abraham,

Come out from your country and your kinsfolk and from your father's house.

Thus when the soul [had adorned] herself again in her beauty [. . .] enjoyed her beloved, and [he also] loved her. And when she had intercourse with him, she got 134 from him the seed that is the life-giving Spirit, so that by him she bears good children and rears them. For this is the great, perfect marvel of birth. And so this marriage is made perfect by the will of the Father.

Now it is fitting that the soul regenerate herself and become again as she formerly was. The soul then moves of her own accord. And she received the divine nature from the Father for her rejuvenation, so that she might be restored to the place where originally she had been. This is the resurrection that is from the dead. This is the ransom from captivity. This is the upward journey of ascent to heaven. This is the way of ascent to the Father. Therefore the prophet said (Psalm 103:1–5),

Praise the Lord, O my soul, and, all that is within me, (praise) his holy name. My soul, praise God, who forgave all your sins, who healed all your sicknesses, who ransomed your life from death, who crowned you with mercy, who satisfies your longing with good things. Your youth will be renewed like an eagle's.

Then when she becomes young again she will ascend, praising the Father and her brother, by whom she was rescued. Thus it is by being born again that the soul will be saved. And this is due not to rote phrases or to professional skills or to book learning. Rather it [is] the grace of the [. . . , it is] the gift of the [. . .]. For such is this heavenly thing. Therefore the Savior cries out (John 6:44), 135

No one can come to me unless my Father draws him and brings him to me; and I myself will raise him up on the last day.

It is therefore fitting to pray to the Father and to call on him with all our soul—not externally with the lips but with the spirit, which is inward, which came forth from the depth—sighing; repenting for the life we lived; confessing our sins; perceiving the empty deception we were in, and the empty zeal;

weeping over how we were in darkness and in the wave; mourning for ourselves, that he might have pity on us; hating ourselves for how we are now. Again the Savior said (cf. Matthew 5:4, 6; Luke 6:21),

Blessed are those who mourn, for it is they who will be pitied; blessed, those who are hungry, for it is they who will be filled.

Again he said (cf. Luke 14:26),

If one does not hate his soul he cannot follow me.

For the beginning of salvation is repentance. Therefore (cf. Acts 13:24),

Before Christ's appearance came John, preaching the baptism of repentance.

And repentance takes place in distress and grief. But the Father is good and loves humanity, and he hears the soul that calls upon him and sends it the light of salvation. Therefore he said through the Spirit to the prophet (cf. 1 Clement 8:3),

Say to the children of my people, "[If your] sins extend [from earth to] heaven, and if they become [red] like scarlet and blacker than [sackcloth and if] 136 you return to me with all your soul and say to me, 'My Father,' I will heed you as a holy people."

Again another place (Isaiah 30:15),

Thus says the Lord, the Holy One of Israel: "If you (sing.) return and sigh, then you will be saved and will know where you were when you trusted in what is empty."

Again he said in another place (Isaiah 30:19–20),

Jerusalem wept much, saying, "Have pity on me." He will have pity on the sound of your (sing.) weeping. And when he saw he heeded you. And the Lord will give you (pl.) bread of affliction and water of oppression. From now on those who deceive will not approach you (sing.) again. Your eyes will see those who are deceiving you.

Therefore it is fitting to pray to God night and day, spreading out our hands towards him as do people sailing in the middle of the sea: they pray to God with all their heart without hypocrisy. For those who pray hypocritically deceive only themselves. Indeed it is in order that he might know who is worthy of salvation that God examines the inward parts and searches the bottom of the heart. For no one is worthy of salvation who still loves the place of deception. Therefore it is written in the poet (Homer, *Odyssey* I, 48–59),

Odysseus sat on the island weeping and grieving and turning his face from the words of Calypso and from her tricks, longing to see his village and smoke coming forth from it. And had he not [received] help from heaven, [he would] not [have been able to] return to his village.

Again [Helen] (. . .) saying (*Odyssey* IV, 260–261),

> [My heart] turned itself from me. 137 It is to my house that I want to return.

For she sighed, saying (*Odyssey* IV, 261–264),

> It is Aphrodite who deceived me and brought me out of my village. My only daughter I left behind me, and my good, understanding, handsome husband.

For when the soul leaves her perfect husband because of the treachery of Aphrodite, who exists here in the act of begetting, then she will suffer harm. But if she sighs and repents, she will be restored to her house.

Certainly Israel would not have been visited in the first place, to be brought out of the land of Egypt, out of the house of bondage, if it had not sighed to God and wept for the oppression of its labors. Again it is written in the Psalms (6:6–9),

> I was greatly troubled in my groaning. I will bathe my bed and my cover each night with my tears. I have become old in the midst of all my enemies. Depart from me, all you who work at lawlessness, for behold the Lord has heard the cry of my weeping and the Lord has heard my prayer.

If we repent, truly God will heed us, he who is long-suffering and abundantly merciful, to whom is the glory for ever and ever. Amen.

The Expository Treatise on the Soul

Index of Female Names

Abigail, 85
Admete, 425
Aebutia, 285–286
Agave, 13, 14, 15
Agele, 64
Agrippiane, 259
Agrippina, 251
Akaste, 425
Albina, 213
Alcmeonis, 21
Alexandra, 165
Alexandra (daughter of Phasael), 136
Alexandria, 162
Aline, 122
Althaea, 61
Amaltheias-keras, 342–343
Amasis, 132
Amata, 248
Ambrosia, 165
Amias, 162
Ammai, 162
Ammion, 256–257
Amphion, 40
Andromeda, 182
Anna, 269
Anna (daughter of Phanuel), 88
Anna (mother of Mary), 89
Anna (a prophetess), 213
Anthia, 58–62
Aphrodite, 13, 19, 55–57, 372, 434, 455, 478
Apollonia, 126
Appes, 162
Archidameia, 42

Archipe, 18
Arsake, 374
Arsinoe, 19, 122–123
Artemis, 17–18, 42, 57–58, 63, 306–307, 425
Artemisia, 114
Artimisie, 132
Aseneth, 243, 279–282, 308–317, 319–327, 416
Asopus, 15
Astarte, 436, 455
Athanasia, 258
Athena, 40–41, 57, 245
Athenais, 436
Attia, 268
Aurelia, 130
Aurelia Appes, 162
Aurelia Artemeis, 161
Aurelia Augusta, 160
Aurelia Domna, 162
Aurelia Flavia, 161
Aurelia Julia, 161
Aurelia Syncletica, 161
Aurelia Tation, 162
Aurelia Tryphaina, 160
Autonoe, 13
Auxanon, 162

Babatha, 120, 143, 145–147, 149, 152
Babathas, 152
Babtha, 148
Baubo, 22
Bellona, 44, 440
Berenice, 7, 19, 28, 136, 139–143, 249
Berenike, 123

Beroneikiane, 161
Beronike, 253
Biblis, 351
Blaesilla, 179–180
Blandina, 329, 350, 353, 355
Bubastis, 455

Cadmeis, 25
Callippe, 18
Callirhoe, 55–57, 309
Calypso, 477
Candida, 164
Canuleia, 245
Capitolina, 163
Carmenta, 24, 37, 38
Ceres, 175, 373, 439–440
Chaerippe, 18
Charikleia, 8, 52–53, 65, 374–375
Chloe, 64, 309
Chloris, 40
Chryseis, 425
Chrysis, 245
Claudia Quinta, 429, 430–431
Clea, 35
Coelia Concordia, 373
Colonis, 165
Cora, 373
Cosco, 22
Cybele, 175, 279, 427
Cypris, 19–20
Cypros, 136
Cyra, 404

Deborah, 269
Deianeira, 38
Demeter, 28, 39, 40–42, 65, 249, 251, 418–
     419, 421–426, 433, 456, 458
Demo, 420
Deo, 422, 427
Diana, 440
Dinah, 172
Dindymene, 373
Diogenis, 165
Dione, 19
Domitiana, 164
Domna, 162, 259
Domnina, 165, 406
Donata, 346–348
Dorcas, 182, 202

Dosarion, 129
Doso, 420
Drusiana, 280
Drusilla, 136
Duronia, 284

Egeria, 7, 236
Eileithyia, 41
Eirene, 121, 126
Elektre, 425
Elisanthia, 230–231, 233
Ennia Fructosa, 131
Epinoia, 465
Erotion (mother of Philiskos), 129
Esther, 176
Eucoline, 18
Eudoxia, 95
Eugenia, 162
Euippe, 58
Eulogia, 254
Euphemia, 237
Eupithis, 165
Eusebis, 162
Eustathis, 165
Eustochiane, 239
Eustochium, 167, 171, 176–181, 188, 190, 200–
     204
Euterpe, 129, 239
Eve, 87, 91–92, 106, 264, 465, 469
Eythycheianes, 162

Faccenia, 288
Falconilla, 303–304
Fate(s), 438, 451
Faustina, 254
Felicitas, 5, 6, 327, 331, 356, 359, 365–357
Flavia Sophe, 7, 238
Flavia Vibia Sabina, 250
Flavilla Domitilla, 181
Fortuna, 91
Fortuna Virilis, 26
Fortune, 444–445, 451
Fulvia, 345

Galaxaure, 425
Gaudentia, 255
Gegania, 245
Generosa, 348

Hannah, 169, 177
Hecate, 373, 419, 426, 440, 455
Hecuba, 20
Helen (mother of Sarapias), 132
Helen (of Troy), 19, 478
Helen (title of Isis), 455
Helena (Queen of Adiabene), 33, 182, 279, 292–293, 295
Hemera, 341–343
Hera, 40, 241, 249
Herais, 129, 132
Herakleia, 123–124
Hermiones, 162
Herodias, 133–137
Hestia, 455
Hippodameia, 40
Hispala Faecenia, 284–287
Homoia, 160
Horaia, 121
Huldah, 269

Iache, 425
Ianeira, 425
Ianthe, 425
Ida, 344–345
Idaean Mother, 430
Ino, 13, 23–25
Io, 455
Isis, 44–45, 59, 62, 175, 279, 282, 344–345, 373, 433–438, 440, 445, 452, 454–456

Januaria, 348
Johanna, 124
Jotape, 137
Judith, 273
Julia, 179
Juliana, 158
Juliane, 250
Juno, 23, 440

Kale, 256
Kallidike, 420–421
Kallirhoe, 420, 423, 425
Kalypso, 425
Kassia, 342–343
Klesidike, 420
Kore, 249, 455
Kyriakes, 162

Laeta, 169, 176, 200
Latina, 455
Leucothea, 24–25
Leukippe, 425
Lycia, 61

Maia, 455
Malthace, 18
Mannine, 254
Manto, 61
Marana, 404
Marcella, 169, 212–215, 217–220, 368
Marganito, 387, 389
Maria, 239, 255, 258
Mariamme, 136–137
Marin, 255
Marina, 232–233
Martha, 127
Martha (sister of Lazarus), 91, 186, 271, 384
Marthana (Deaconess), 236–237
Martia Papyria, 178
Martyria, 230–231
Mary (mother of James), 271
Mary (mother of Jesus), 9, 86–87, 89–93, 158, 170, 173, 176, 184, 188, 375–376, 404, 416, 432
Mary (sister of Aaron), 93
Mary (sister of Lazarus), 91, 186, 271, 384, 392
Mary (Maria) of Cassabola, 8, 331, 375
Mary the Harlot, 395, 397–399, 401
Mary Magdalen(e), 215, 271, 416–417
Marys (the Three), 215
Matrona, 7, 11, 80–85
Matronit, 416
Matuta, 23, 25
Maximilla, 86, 93–94, 259, 263, 265–266, 280
Mazauzala, 254
Medea, 49
Medullina, 43
Melite, 425
Melobosis, 425
Meroe, 47–49
Metaneira, 421–423
Metanoia, 243, 416
Minerva, 440
Miriam, 31, 269
Miriam (co-widow of Babatha), 152
Mneso, 18

Moundane, 161
Muses, 442
Mygdonia, 280

Naimia, 255
Nanas, 267
Nania, 455
Naomi, 203
Nasica, 430
Nausis, 18
Nephthys, 434–435
Nicostrate, 37
Niobe, 40
Norea, 465, 469
Nymphs, 64

Okyrhoe, 425
Olympias (benefactor of Chrysostom), 95, 220, 227–236
Olympias (mother of Alexander), 36
Olympias (mother of Mariamme), 137
Orea, 470
Ouranie, 425

Paculla Annia, 287
Palladia, 230–231
Pallantis, 25
Pallas, 425
Pamphile, 50
Panope, 24
Papais, 128
Paramone, 130
Paula, 167–171, 173, 176–179, 181–182, 184, 186–188, 190–191, 194–197, 199–204, 212, 215
Paulina, 180, 343–345
Paulina (Fabia Aconia), 372–373
Pelagia, 377–378, 384, 387–394
Peregrina, 327
Peristeria, 253
Perpetua (Vibia), 5–6, 118, 330–331, 356–357, 359–360, 362–368
Persephone, 418–419, 424–425, 427
Persis, 234
Phaino, 425
Pheidylla, 18
Phile, 18
Philous (mother of Seuthes), 129
Philumene, 18
Phoebe, 257
Photis, 448

Physcoa, 40–41
Pistis Sophia, 466, 470–471
Plangon, 56–57
Plouto, 425
Polyxena, 280, 298
Poppaea, 8, 297
Potamiaena, 8, 368–369
Praetextata, 171
Praxinoa, 19–20
Principia, 212, 220
Priscilla, 86, 93–94, 259, 263–266
Prosperina, 439, 450
Protous (daughter of Simon), 129
Ptollous (mother of Philous), 129
Pythias, 18

Queen of the Ethiopians, 376
Quintilla, 86, 264

Rachael, 29
Rachel, 183, 310
Rachelis, 122
Rebecca, 29, 310
Rebeka, 254
Regina, 371
Retibi, 80
Rhamnusia, 440
Rheia, 419, 426, 433
Rhode, 60–62
Rhodeia, 425
Rhodope, 425
Romana, 386–389, 391, 392
Rufina, 180–181, 251
Rumina, 37

Salampsio, 136
Salome, 91, 271
Salome Alexandra, 33
Salome Gropte, 153
Salome Komaise, 152–154
Salome (sister of Herod the Great), 136–137
Sambous, 129
Saosis, 436
Sara, 255
Sara Ura, 253
Sarah, 29, 185, 310, 328
Sarah (Amma), 118, 408–409
Sarapias, 132
Sarapis, 46
Saturnia, 24

Saufeia, 43
Secunda, 346–348
Selampious, 155
Semele, 13, 23–24
Shekinah, 416
Shelamzion, 150, 156
Shelamzious, 151
Sipylenes, 160
Sirens, 208
Sophia, 251
Sophia (the Deacon), 257–258
Sophron, 125–126
Sophronia, 215
Sosipolis, 41, 123
Stimula, 24
Sulpicia, 285–287
Symmacho, 292
Syncletica (Amma), 118, 331, 409, 412

Tachom, 166
Tacita, 26
Tamar (daughter of Thamous), 148
Tarpeia, 245
Tata, 241, 249
Tation, 163
Tegea, 24
Thapseusis, 455
Thases, 128
Thecla, 89, 228, 236–237, 242, 260–261, 279–
    280, 282, 297–308, 405

Themis, 37
Theocleia, 299, 301, 306
Theodora (Amma), 118, 331, 413–414
Theodora (of Minorca), 111–112
Theodora (teacher), 8
Theodosia, 227
Theodote, 125–126
Theopempte, 252
Thermoutharin, 132
Thettale, 22
Theudous, 129
Theuris, 437
Thyaene, 18
Trophimas, 162
Tryphaena (Queen), 303–306
Tryphaena, 234
Tryphaina, 129
Tryphosa, 234
Tyche, 125, 425
Urbana, 164

Venus, 26, 428, 439–440
Verenia, 245
Vesta, 247–248
Veturia Paulla, 328
Vestia, 346–348

Xanthippe, 280, 298

Zoe, 470–471

Index of Ancient Sources

NOTE: Literary works are listed alphabetically by author, or by title for works of unknown, or unattributed, authorship. Inscriptions and papyri are listed by source. (Some of the inscriptions listed under *CIJ* or *CPJ* are the same as those listed under *JIWE* or *JIGRE*. They are listed in both places to aid those who may know an inscription by either designation.)

Abbreviations used may be found in the list at the beginning of the book. As a convenience to students and general readers, works generally thought to be Jewish are marked by an asterisk (*). Works generally thought to be Christian are marked by a cross (†). Works generally considered "pagan" have no symbol. Works whose religious identity is uncertain or disputed are marked by a diamond (◇). Readers should consult the introductions for all texts for further discussion.

LITERARY WORKS

Achilles Tatius, *Leucippe and Clitophon* 7.13, **63**

◇ *Aseneth* 1–21, **308–27**

†*The Acts of the Martyrs of Scilli*, **346–48**

†*The Acts of Thecla* 7–43, **297–308**

†*The Acts of Thomas* 6, **67–72**

Apuleius, *Metamorphoses*
  Bk. 1.7–10, **47–49**
  Bk. 3.15–18, **49–51**
  Bk. 11, **438–54**
  Bk. 11.9–10, **45–47**

Aulus Gellius, *Attic Nights* 1.12, **247–48**

*Babylonian Talmud
  Kiddushin 29a–b, 34a–36a, **103–10**
  Sotah 22b, **78–80**
  Rosh Hashanah 32b, **100**
  Sukkah 28a–b, **100–102**

Cassius Dio, *Roman History* 66.15.3–5, **142**

Chariton, *Chareas and Callirhoe*
  2.2; 7.5; 8.8, **54–56**
  3.7–9, **56–57**

†*Constitutions of the Holy Apostles*
  2.26, **268–69**
  2.57, **277–78**
  3.3–9, 13–15, **270–76**

†*Debate between a Montanist and an Orthodox*, **93–94**

Demosthenes, *On the Crown* 259–60, **16**

Diodorus of Sicily, 4.3.2–5, **27–28**

†Dionysius of Alexandria, *Epistle to the Bishop Basilides*, canons 2, 4, **72–73**

Ecclesiastes Rabbah, 3.21.1, **85**

†Egeria, *Diary of a Pilgrimage* 22–23, **236–38**

†Epiphanius, *Medicine Box*
  48.2.4; 12.4; 13.1, **266–67**
  49, **264–65**
  49.1.3, **266**
  78.23, **85–86**
  79, **86–92**
Epitome of the Emperors 10.4–7, **142–43**
Euripides, *Bacchae*
  23–42, **12–13**
  677–768, **13–15**
†Eusebius, *History of the Church*
  5.1.3–63, **348–56**
  5.16.7–10; 17–19, **265–66**
  6.2.12–14, **158**
  6.5.1–7, **368–69**
  6.8.1–3, **157–58**
  6.17.1, **158**
  6.23.1–2, **159**
  8.12.3–5, **369–70**
The Exegesis on the Soul, **472–78**
Exodus Rabbah 3.12.2, **83–84**
Genesis Rabbah 4.6; 17.7; 25.1; 63.8; 68.4;
  84.21; 87.16, **81–83**
Heliodorus, *An Ethiopian Story*
  6.13–15, **51–54**
  5.15, **65**
  5.34, **65**
  8.9, **374–75**
†Hippolytus, *Refutation of All Heresies* 8.12,
  263
The Homeric Hymn to Demeter, **418–27**
◊ *The Hypostatis of the Archons*, or: *The
  Reality of the Rulers*, **465–72**
†Jerome, *Letters*
  107 (to Laeta), **167–77**
  108 (to Eustochium), **177–204**
  117 (to two unnamed women), **204–12**
  127 (to Principia), **212–20**
†John Chrysostom
  Against Judaizing Christians 2.3.3–6; 4.7.3,
  94–96
  Letter 9 (to Olympias), **220–27**
*Josephus
  Against Apion 2.102–104, **33–34**
  Antiquities of the Jews
    18.65–80, **343–45**
    18.81–84, **343–45**
    18.109–19, **133–36**
    18.130–42, **136–37**
    18.240–55, **133–36**

19.277, **138–40**
20.17–53, **292–96**
20.92–96, **292–96**
20.137–43, **137–38**
20.145–46, **138–40**
20.189–98, **296–97**
The Jewish War
  2.309–14, **138–40**
  2.559–61, **296**
  5.198–200, **33–34**
†Justin Martyr, *Second Apology* 2, **65–67**
Juvenal, *Satire* 6.314–41; 511–47, **43–45**
Leviticus Rabbah
  8.1, **83**
  28.6, **84**
†*The Life of Olympias*, **227–36**
†*The Life of Saint Mary the Harlot*, **395–404**
†*The Life of Saint Pelagia the Harlot*, 377–
  94
Livy, *Annals of Rome*
  29.14, **430–31**
  39.8–18, **283–92**
Longus, *Daphnis and Chloe* 2.2; 4.39, **64**
*2 Maccabees 7, **332–40**
◊ 4 Maccabees 14.11–18.24, **332–40**
†*The Martyrdom of Saints Perpetua and
  Felicitas*, **356–68**
*Mishnah *Niddah* 1.1–2.4, **74–78**
Numbers Rabbah 3.2, **84**
†*The Odes of Solomon*
  19, **431–32**
  36, **432–33**
Ovid, *Fasti*
  2.571–82, **26–27**
  4.133–62, **25–26**
  4.247–348, **427–30**
  6.473–568, **23–25**
†Palladius, *Lausiac History* 33, 52, 143, 98–
  99
Pausanias, *Description of Greece*
  2 (Corinth) 35.6–8, **39–40**
  4 (Messenia) 17, **42**
  5 (Elis 1) 16.2–8, **40–41**
  5 (Elis 1) 20.2–3, **41**
  7 (Achaia) 27.9–10, **41–42**
  7 (Achaia) 18.11–12, **42**
*Philo, *On the Contemplative Life* 2, 32–33,
  68–69, 83–88, **28–31**
  The Special Laws 3.169–75, **32–33**
Plutarch, *Life of Alexander* 2.1–5, **36**

Life of Numa Pompilius 10, 245–46
On the Bravery of Women 13 (Moralia
    249), 35–36
On Isis and Osiris 355–58 (Moralia 355–
    58), 433–38
Roman Questions
    56 (Moralia 278), 37
    57 (Moralia 278), 37
    60 (Moralia 278), 38
    96 (Moralia 286–87), 38
    100 (Moralia 287), 38–39
    104 (Moralia 288–89), 36
†Pseudo-Ignatius, The Letter of Mary the
    Proselyte to Ignatius, 375–77
†Sayings of the Desert Fathers 2.7, 96–97
†Sayings of the Desert Fathers
    Amma Sarah, 408–9
    Amma Syncletica, 409–13
    Amma Theodora, 413–14
†Severus of Minorca, Letter on the
    Conversion of the Jews, 110–16
Suetonius, The Divine Titus, 7.1–2, 141

†Shenoute, Letter to Tachom, 165–67
Tacitus, Histories 2.1.1; 2.1; 2.79; 2.81.1–3, 140–
    41
*The Testament of Job 46–52, 340–43
†Tertullian, On Baptism 17, 260–61
    On the Prescription Against Heretics 41,
        261
    On the Soul 9, 262–63
    On the Veiling of Virgins 9, 261
Theocritus, Idyll 15.95–149, 18–20
†Theodoret of Cyrrhus, A History of the
    Monks of Syria
    29, 404
    30, 405–8
◊ The Thought of Norea, 465
◊ Thunder, Perfect Mind, 459–64
Xenophon of Ephesos, Ephesian Tale of
    Anthia and Habrocomes
    1.2, 58–59
    4.3; 5.4, 59–60
    5.10–13, 60–62
    5.15, 63

INSCRIPTIONS AND PAPYRI

†Alt, Griechische Inschriften, no. 17, 257–58
◊ Antike Fluchtafeln, no. 5, 163–64
*CIG 2924, 163
*CIJ
    315, 255
    400, 253
    462, 327
    476, 372–73
    523, 327–28
    581, 253
    590, 254
    597, 254
    642, 328
    692, 254
    741, 251
    763, 162
    756, 252
    775, 160
    738, 163
    1007, 255
    I² 696b, 253
    I² 731c, 251–52
    I² 731e, 328

CIL 8.2756, 131
*CPJ
    19, 123–24
    133, 124
    144, 126
    146, 125–26
    148, 127
    421, 128–29
    473, 130
    483, 127–28
*CPJ/CIJ
    1508, 121
    1509, 121
    1510, 122
    1513, 122
    1514, 255
    1530, 122
†Ferrua, RAC 21 (1944/45), 185–93,
    238
†Gibson, Christians for Christians
    8; 12; 13, 162
    15, 162–63
    32, 161

†Guarducci, *Epigrafia*
    4:335, **257–58**
    4:373, **239**
    4:445, no. 4, **258**
    4:525, **239**
◊ Haspels, *Highlands*, no. 107, **267–68**
Henrichs, *HSCP* 82 (1978): 148, **21**
†*ICUR* 1.317, **373**
IG
    2² 1136, **245**
    2² 1514, **18**
    11, 8.389, **250**
    ◊ 12, 1.593, **328**
    12, 5.655, **249**
†*ILCV* 1.316, **373**
ILS 1259–61, **370–72**
I. Magn. 215a:24–40, **21–22**
I. Smyr. 232, **160**
**I. Syrie* 1322–27; 1329; 1332; 1335;
    1336, **165**
IvMag. 158, **250–51**
Jacopi, *Esplorazioni*, 33–36, **258**
*JIGRE
    31, **121**
    32, **121**
    33, **122**
    36, **122**
    38, **122**
    84, **254–55**
*JIWE
    1.9, **328**
    1.59, **253**
    1.62, **254**
    1.71, **254**
    2.11, **255**
    2.24, **253**
    2.62, **327**
    2.103, **372–73**
    2.577, **327–28**
†Körte, *Inscriptiones Bureschianae*, 31, no.
    55, **256–57**
*Kraemer, *HTR* 78 (1985): 431–38, **254**

The Kyme Aretalogy, **454–56**
*Lifshitz, *Donateurs*
    13, **163**
    30, **163**
    41–46; 48; 51; 54; 55, **165**
LSAM 48, **20–21**
LSCG Suppl. 115, **17**
MAMA
    6.231, **161**
    †7.471, **259**
    7.492b, **249**
NewDocs
    †2:193–94, no. 109, **258**
    †2:194, **259**
    ◊ 4:257, no. 126, **268**
PGM
    32.1–9, **131–32**
    40.1–18, **132**
P. Hibeh 54, **22**
P. Oxy.
    *1205, **130**
    11.1380, **454**
P. Se'elim* 13, **156–57
**P. Yadin*
    10, **144–45**
    14, **145–46**
    15, **146–47**
    16, **147–48**
    17, **149**
    18, **150–51**
    19, **151–52**
    26, **152**
    37, **154**
**P. Xhev/Se* gr
    64, **153–54**
    65, **154**
    69, **155**
†Petsas, *Arch. Delt.* 26 (1971): 161–63,
    259
†Piraino, *Iscrizioni*, 36–37, no. 13, **256**
*SEG 27 (1977), 1201, **254**
*TAM 3 (1941) 448, **161**

24884773R00277

Made in the USA
Lexington, KY
04 August 2013